Sara Pacchiarotti and Fernando Zúñiga (Eds.)
Applicative Morphology

Trends in Linguistics
Studies and Monographs

Editors
Chiara Gianollo
Daniël Van Olmen

Editorial Board
Walter Bisang
Tine Breban
Volker Gast
Hans Henrich Hock
Karen Lahousse
Natalia Levshina
Caterina Mauri
Heiko Narrog
Salvador Pons
Niina Ning Zhang
Amir Zeldes

Editor responsible for this volume
Chiara Gianollo

Volume 373

Applicative Morphology

Neglected Syntactic and Non-syntactic Functions

Edited by
Sara Pacchiarotti and Fernando Zúñiga

ISBN 978-3-11-163178-3
e-ISBN (PDF) 978-3-11-077794-9
e-ISBN (EPUB) 978-3-11-077802-1
ISSN 1861-4302

Library of Congress Control Number: 2022937520

Bibliographic information published by the Deutsche Nationalbibliothek
The Deutsche Nationalbibliothek lists this publication in the Deutsche Nationalbibliografie;
detailed bibliographic data are available on the internet at http://dnb.dnb.de.

© 2024 Walter de Gruyter GmbH, Berlin/Boston
This volume is text- and page-identical with the hardback published in 2022.
Typesetting: Integra Software Services Pvt. Ltd.

www.degruyter.com

Contents

Sara Pacchiarotti and Fernando Zúñiga
1   Introduction —— 1

Part I: **Americas**

Lilián Guerrero
2   Typical and atypical applicative constructions in Yaqui —— 21

Martin Kohlberger
3   The functions of applicative morphology in Shiwiar —— 51

Marianne Mithun
4   Applicatives and beyond: Barbareño Chumash —— 73

Sergio Ibáñez Cerda, Alejandra Itzel Ortiz Villegas, and Armando Mora-Bustos
5   Applicative periphrastic constructions in the Colombian Spanish from The Andes —— 97

An Van linden
6   Spatial prefixes as applicatives in Harakmbut —— 129

Part II: **Africa**

Hannah Gibson, Lutz Marten, Maarten Mous, and Kristina Riedel
7   Valency and saliency in Bantu applicatives: A diachronic reanalysis —— 163

Hilde Gunnink and Sara Pacchiarotti
8   Neglected functions of the Bantu applicative in relation to Locations: new insights from Fwe (K402) —— 189

Doris L. Payne
9   The applicative(-like) function of Nilotic directionals: Introducing THEMES —— 227

Part III: Asia (including the Middle East)

Shuan Osman Karim and Ali Salehi
10 An applicative analysis of Soranî "absolute prepositions" —— 263

Yankee Modi and Mark W. Post
11 Applicatives in Macro-Tani languages (Trans-Himalayan, Eastern Himalaya): Forms, functions and historical origins —— 299

Thomas E. Payne and Voltaire Q. Oyzon
12 Canonical and Non-canonical applicatives in Waray —— 329

Camille Simon
13 The sociative/benefactive applicative construction and the introduction of attitude holders in Tibetan —— 373

Christina L. Truong and Bradley McDonnell
14 Neglected functions of western Indonesian applicatives —— 405

Jozina Vander Klok and Bethwyn Evans
15 The evolution of non-syntactic functions of applicatives: -i suffixation in Javanese and neighboring languages —— 437

Subject index —— 475

Language index —— 477

Sara Pacchiarotti and Fernando Zúñiga
1 Introduction

Since at least the 16th century, applicative constructions have sparked the attention of linguists and missionaries describing languages of the Americas (De Olmos 1547; Del Rincón 1595) and Africa (Brugiotti da Vetralla 1659) and continue to do so to this day. Most narrow definitions of applicative morphology (see, e.g., Alsina and Mchombo 1993; Bresnan and Moshi 1993; Creissels 2016; Dixon and Aikhenvald 2000; Haspelmath and Müller-Bardey 2004; Kulikov 2011; Mithun 2002; Payne 1997; Payne 2002; Peterson 2007; Polinsky 2013) coincide in claiming that there are at least three fundamental attributes of applicativization. (For an influential study in the Chomskyan tradition that works with a definition that is narrow in some respects and broad in others, see Pylkkänen 2002, 2008). First, it is a productive verbal derivational process with syntactic consequences. Second, it introduces to the argument structure of the underived verb root/stem an internal argument we call the applied phrase (AppP) here, following Creissels (forthcoming) (in the literature, this is variously called the object argument, direct object, P/O, absolutive, O function, etc.) and thus often displays valence-increasing or transitivizing effects on the derived stem. Third, there are multiple, typically "peripheral" semantic roles that can be mapped onto the applied phrase (e.g. Beneficiary, Instrument, Location, etc.). Several definitions (Payne 1997; Dixon and Aikhenvald 2000; Peterson 2007) also assume that applicative morphemes are optional, that is, verb roots/stems without an applicative marker can appear in a construction with a syntactic oblique, and this very participant can alternatively be expressed as a core argument if the verb root/stem combines with an applicative. The features emerging from these rather narrow definitions have set a prototype or canon of applicative morphology, which can be summarized as follows (where AC stands for applicative construction and BC for base construction, typically thought of as simple verbal clauses):

- LEXICON: The AC is an optional variant of the BC to express a given state of affairs.
- MORPHOLOGY: The predicate of the AC is overtly derived from the predicate of the BC.

Sara Pacchiarotti, BantUGent – UGent Centre for Bantu Studies, Department of African languages and cultures, Ghent University, Blandijnberg 2, Ghent, Belgium,
e-mail: sara.pacchiarotti@ugent.be
Fernando Zúñiga, Institut für Sprachwissenschaft, Universität Bern, Länggasstrasse 49, Bern, Switzerland, e-mail: fernando.zuniga@unibe.ch

https://doi.org/10.1515/9783110777949-001

- SYNTAX: (i) The AC has a higher syntactic valence than the BC because the AppP is an object (or absolutive) in the AC and corresponds to an optional adjunct in the BC; and/or (ii) if the BC undergoing applicativization is transitive, the resulting AC might remain transitive: the object introduced by the applicative takes the place of the original object of the BC which is demoted to an adjunct (only some definitions acknowledge this possibility, e.g., Dixon and Aikhenvald 2000; Payne 1997). This second kind of applicativization has been variously called "redirective" (Kinkade 1980; Kiyosawa 2006), "redirecting" (Zúñiga and Creissels forthcoming), and "rearranging" (Comrie 1985).
- SEMANTICS: The AppP is a peripheral non-agentive participant (e.g., a Beneficiary, an Instrument, a Location).

Such canonical features apply to the following example:

(1) Ainu (unclassified, Japan; Shibatani 1996: 159)
    a. *poro   cise   ta   horari*
       big   house in   live
    b. *poro   cise   e-horari*
       big   house APPL-live
    Both: 'S/he lives in a big house.'

Nevertheless, more recent, broader definitions of applicativization (Creissels forthcoming; Zúñiga and Creissels forthcoming; Zúñiga and Kittilä 2019) encompass the possibility that (i) applicativization might be obligatory (see also Peterson 2007: 51, 160–162), that is, the sole morphological means to express a non-agentive semantic role in a given clause is by means of applicative derivation; and (ii) the AppP can be an object or P argument, but also an indirect object or dative, or even an oblique.

This volume is the outcome of the workshop "Neglected syntactic and non-syntactic functions of applicative morphology" held at the 2020 annual meeting of the *Societas Linguistica Europaea*. Its main goal is to show that syntactic, semantic, and pragmatic functions of applicative morphology not included in the applicative prototype appear to be recurrent and productive to various extents in a sample of geographically distant and genealogically unrelated languages. Besides speaking in favor of the attractiveness of broader characterizations of applicative constructions, this volume opens up a number of unexplored research questions about the diachronic and synchronic relations of syntactic and non-syntactic functions of applicative morphology. In order to include all non-syntactic functions of applicative(-like) morphology which emerged from the workshop presentations, we invited contributors to work with a definition of applicative even broader than the broad abovementioned definitions, namely "any derivational morphology occurring on a verb root/stem that has amongst its functions the introduction of a non-Actor semantic argument into a main clause. This non-Actor is usually mapped onto an applied phrase (AppP), that is, the morphosyntactic entity syntactically introduced and/or semantically/pragmatically manipulated by the applicative without any specifications about its syntactic category, argument status, and/or semantic role."

There are several ways in which this volume contributes to broadening our understanding of what applicative morphology can do. This introduction is divided into sections reporting on the main contributions.

1 Non-prototypical syntactic and semantic features

Several chapters show that obligatory applicative constructions are not uncommon. In the following example, for instance, there is no other way to express the Beneficiary introduced in (2b) vis-à-vis (2a) than to resort to applicativization; the language does not have case markers, adpositions, or multi-verb constructions that could accommodate that participant in the clause. This is common in other languages of the same family.

(2) Blackfoot (Algonquian, Canada/USA; Frantz 2009: 103)
    a. *k-otá's-iksi*   *nit-ii-yissksipist-aa-yi-aawa*
        2-mount-ANIM.PL   1-PST-tie.up-DIR-3PL-3PL
        'I tied up your horses.'
    b. *nit-ii-yissksipist-omo-aa-wa*   *n-itákkaa-wa*   *w-otá'-iksi*
        1-PST-tie.up-APPL-DIR-3SG.PROX   1-partner-PROX.SG   3-mount-ANIM.PL
        'I tied up his horse for my partner.'

By the same token, MODI & POST find that there are no fully semantically equivalent alternative ways of expression for the semantic roles introduced by the unusually large inventory of applicative affixes in Macro-Tani languages (Trans-Himalayan). Similarly, in Shiwiar (Chicham) applicative morphology is the only means to introduce all non-Actor participants except Instruments and Locations (KOHLBERGER). Obligatoriness can be lexically-determined or valence-dependent. As to the former, applicative morphology might be obligatory with certain verb roots to introduce specific semantic roles, such as Spatial Goal or Endpoint, General Location, and Substitutive in some Bantu languages (GUNNINK & PACCHIAROTTI), as well as superficially or invisibly affected Patients for a large class of verbs in Waray (Austronesian) (PAYNE T. & OYZON). As to the latter, applicativization introduces Beneficiaries and Recipients with one and two-place predicates (Tibetic languages, SIMON), Recipient and Themes of three-place predicates (Javanese, VANDER KLOK & EVANS) or Terrified Experiencers with one-place predicates (Macro-Tani, MODI & POST). Similarly, in languages where spatial and directional verbal morphology takes on applicative-like functions, this morphology is required to introduce moving Themes to verb roots with specific argument frames (PAYNE D.), as well as several Location-related semantic roles to transitive and intransitive roots with motion- or posture-related meanings (VAN LINDEN). The obligatory use of applicative morphology might be restricted to Beneficiaries and develop out of the high frequency with which applicative morphology is used to introduce these discourse-prominent/topical participants, as may be the case in Barbareño Chumash (MITHUN). Obligatory applicative constructions are also common in Niger-Congo (Creissels et al. 2008), Northwest Caucasian languages (Arkadiev and Lander 2020), Iroquoian (Mithun 2002), Algonquian (see, e.g., Drapeau 2014; 2015 for Innu) and other autochthonous languages of the Americas. This body of evidence calls into question why optionality and the intimately connected transformational concept of object promotion (see, e.g., Shibatani 1996) should be defining features of applicative constructions. In languages with optional applicative constructions, the peripheral semantic role introduced by the applicative can alternatively be expressed as an oblique in the construction of the verb root: this alternative is the structure on which the applicative "transformation" applies by promoting the erstwhile oblique to objecthood. GUERRERO shows that, in Yaqui (Uto-Aztecan), applicative constructions that are often employed in discourse to introduce a negatively affected participant involve a half-way promotion of the AppP, which has some, but not all, object properties of fully promoted AppPs.

Another aspect to which several chapters contribute new data is the syntactic nature of the AppP. The AppP can certainly be a core object argument, in which case applicativization increases the syntactic valence of the derived stem (in cases other than redirective applicative constructions). Nevertheless, the AppP can also be a non-core constituent. In the following example, for instance, the base verb *ret* 'go' takes a Goal argument, optionally marked by the semantically underspecified preposition *na* in (3a); the applicativized verb in (3b) takes a Source argument, but note that the latter is even less object-like than in the base clause, *na* being obligatory in (3b):

(3) Seereer (Atlantic, West Africa; Renaudier 2012: 183)
    a. *a-ret-a*   *(na)*   *marse*
       3SG.SBJ-go-COMPL   PREP   market
       'S/he went to the market.'
    b. *a-ret-it-a*   *na*   *marse*
       3SG.SBJ-go-APPL-COMPL   PREP   market
       'She left the market.' (lit: she went from the market)

In fact, an AppP can be an oblique case-marked genitive or ablative phrase (MODI & POST), a dative-marked phrase (IBÁÑEZ CERDA, ORTIZ VILLEGAS & MORA-BUSTOS, MODI & POST, SIMON), a zero anaphora (MODI & POST, SIMON), a prepositional phrase (IBÁÑEZ CERDA, ORTIZ VILLEGAS & MORA-BUSTOS, TRUONG & MCDONNELL), or a morphosyntactic entity in between an NP and a prepositional phrase (GIBSON, MARTEN, MOUS & RIEDEL, GUNNINK & PACCHIAROTTI). Elsewhere, dative AppPs are attested in Georgian where the applicative-like construction is called "version", see, e.g., Creissels (2006), Gurevich (2006), Harris (1981), and oblique AppPs in Atlantic (Creissels forthcoming) and Omaha (Siouan) (Marsault 2022), among others (see Creissels forthcoming for additional references). What is more, applicative morphology in some languages can also introduce different kinds of dependent clauses (see, e.g., Creissels 2004; Harford 1993 for Bantu; Jacques 2022 for the Rgyalrongic language Japhug; Marsault 2022 for Omaha). New conceptualizations such as the distinction between P-applicatives (adding a direct object), D-applicatives (adding a dative or indirect object), and X-applicatives (adding an oblique) (Creissels forthcoming; Zúñiga and Creissels forthcoming) appear to be especially useful to deal with variation in the syntactic status of the AppP. The varied syntactic nature of the AppP also corroborates that while applicative morphology might well increase syntactic valence, this need not be the case.

     Semantically, some chapters show that applicative morphology or morphology with applicative-like functions can introduce (moving) Themes and Experiencers (KOHLBERGER, MODI & POST, PAYNE D., TRUONG & MCDONNELL, VANDER KLOK & EVANS, PAYNE T. & OYZON). This situation is also attested elsewhere (e.g., Austin 2005; Mithun 2000; Onishi 2000), although not always labeled or analyzed as applicativization (e.g., "extraversion" in Lehmann and Verhoeven 2006), due to the violation of two features considered prototypical: (i) full productivity (the morphology introducing Themes, Patients, or Undergoers might be obligatory with certain verb classes but not others) and (ii) centrality of the semantic role of the introduced argument (applicative constructions "typically" introduce non-central participants such as Locations, Beneficiaries, Instruments, while Patients are central).

Finally, several chapters suggest that the specialization of individual applicative morphemes in terms of the semantic roles the AppP can bear follows a gradual cline. In some cases, many formally distinct applicative affixes can each express only one specific semantic role (KARIM & SALEHI), including cross-linguistically rare micro-roles corresponding to very precise subtypes of Experiencers, such as those introduced by the Territive (a participant shocked by the event described by the predicate) and the Eruditive derivations (a participant that is "educated" or "shown how" by means of the predicate) in Macro-Tani languages (MODI & POST). In others, the AppPs introduced by formally distinct applicative affixes can bear a semantic role from different sets, e.g., Theme, Instrument, and Beneficiary vs. Location, Goal, and Recipient (PAYNE T. & OYZON, TRUONG & MCDONNELL, VANDER KLOK & EVANS). In yet other cases, the argument introduced by one single form (and its allomorphs) can bear virtually any semantic role (with language-specific restrictions) depending on the lexical meaning of the root, the communicative context, and the intention of the speaker (GUNNINK & PACCHIAROTTI, KOHLBERGER, GIBSON, MARTEN, MOUS & RIEDEL).

2 Derivational and syntactic functions other than applicativization

An extremely common feature of applicative morphology is its tendency to be isomorphic with causative morphology (Bahrt 2021; Franco 2019; Zúñiga and Kittilä 2019: ch. 8.2.1 for a list of references). Several chapters in this volume (MODI & POST, TRUONG & MCDONNELL, VANDER KLOK & EVANS) corroborate this common trend and show that morphemes formally identical to applicative markers can be used to derive causative stems. Moving on to less known derivational and syntactic functions, several contributions show that applicative morphology can function as a denominal/deadjectival verbalizer (KOHLBERGER, PAYNE T. & OYZON, TRUONG & MCDONNELL, VANDER KLOK & EVANS), and as a nominalizer (MITHUN). The verbalizing ability of the applicative appears to be common elsewhere, see, e.g., Bantu (Trithart 1983), Germanic (Michaelis and Ruppenhofer 2001), but other verbal derivational morphology can also serve as a verbalizer (see, e.g., Pacchiarotti and Kulikov 2022 on the verbalizing function a middle voice suffix in Bribri, Chibchan). There appears to be even a diachronic link between word-formation and applicativization: Jacques (2014) posits that in Japhug (Rgyalrongic) applicative morphology originates in denominal affixes. Beside word-formation, applicative morphology can be recruited at the syntactic level, e.g., in the formation of headless and headed relative clauses (MITHUN).

3 Semantic and lexical aspectual functions

An apparently very common non-syntactic function of applicative morphology is to convey semantic and/or aspectual nuances such as intensity, forcefulness, thoroughness, iterativity, habituality, and pluractionality (multiple events, times, or participants). Preverbation in Indo-European languages, by some considered akin to applicativization (Haspelmath and Müller-Bardey 2004; Kulikov 2012; Michaelis and Ruppenhofer 2000), can also convey similar aspectual nuances to the derived stem (see Kozhanov 2016 and references therein). Depending on the language, this function might not be fully productive, but available only with a lexically restricted set of verbs.

It is a well-known fact from the literature on German, for instance, that *be*-prefixation is a considerably heterogeneous phenomenon, both syntactically and semantically (see Michaelis & Ruppenhofer 2000 and references therein). On the one hand, verbs like *sprühen X (auf/über Y)* 'spray X (on Y)' and *besprühen Y (mit X)* 'spray Y (with X)' participate in locative-alternation-like oppositions that exemplify a familiar brand of canonical applicativization. On the other hand, verbs like *fragen* 'ask' and *befragen* 'question, interrogate' show quite a different picture, as illustrated in (4). Here, *be*-prefixation causes neither the promotion of an oblique nor the rearranging of a direct and an oblique object; it alters the kind and/or degree of affectedness of the direct object:

(4) German (Germanic, Central Europe; p.k.)
    a. *Sie frag-te ihn nach seiner Meinung*
        she ask-PST[3SG] him after his.DAT.SG opinion
        'She asked him about his opinion.'
    b. *Sie be-frag-te ihn nach seiner Meinung*
        she BE-ask-PST[3SG] him after his.DAT.SG opinion
        'She questioned/interrogated/interviewed him about his opinion.'

In some families, only some specific applicative affixes might have such functions. These semantic features might either apply to the applicative stem alone (GUNNINK & PACCHIAROTTI) or extend also to the participants of the event (TRUONG & MCDONNELL, VANDER KLOK & EVANS). As argued by TRUONG & MCDONNELL, the intensity function also accounts for why applicative morphology is involved in the formation of comparative degree constructions (e.g., 'sad-APPL' = 'sadder') in Western Indonesian languages. Less-known semantic effects of applicative derivation uncovered in this volume, all found in contexts where applicatives are optional, include greater affectedness of the AppP (TRUONG & MCDONNELL, VANDER KLOK & EVANS, PAYNE T. & OYZON), and definiteness or specificity of the AppP (TRUONG &

McDonnell, Vander Klok & Evans). As it happens with the word-formation function (§2), the expression of meanings such as intensity, repetitiveness, and thoroughness is not a function unique to applicative morphology (see Kiessling 2004: 171 on causative suffixes developing intensifying and frequentative meanings in Grassfield languages). Perhaps due to the frequently erratic nature of some kinds of semantic change, applicative morphology can also convey meanings of attenuation or mitigation. Payne T. & Oyzon report that in Waray (Austronesian) applicative morphology can indicate that the AppP is a partitive absolutive, i.e., a less than completely affected participant. In some Bantu languages, besides the widely reported functions of expressing intensity, iterativity, completeness, thoroughness, etc. (Trithart 1983: 188–189), a suffix formally identical to the applicative can apparently convey meanings such as "less of the action of the verb" (Sharman 1963: 68) which is conceptually similar to what is reported by Payne T. & Oyzon.

4 Discourse functions

One of the functional explanations for the existence of applicative constructions in languages where they are optional is to signal that the AppP is a topic or discourse salient participant (Donohue 2001; Givón 1984; Peterson 2007: 83; Rude 1986), see also Trithart (1983: 181–183), Kisseberth and Abasheikh (1977) and Rapold (1997) for similar claims in Bantu languages, Kiyosawa and Gerdts (2011: 299–327) for Salish languages, and Guerrero for Yaqui (Uto-Aztecan).

At the same time, across languages, including those where it can function as a topic-continuity device, applicative morphology can also serve as a focalizer, e.g. in Niger-Congo groups such as Bantu (Creissels 2004; De Kind and Bostoen 2012; Harford 1993; Trithart 1983) and Atlantic (see Nouguier-Voisin 2002 for Wolof), Mojeño Trinitario (Arawak, Rose 2019), Acazulco Otomí (Otomanguean, Hernández-Green 2016), and in Eastern Mayan and Mixean languages (Mora-Marín 2003). In the following example from K'iche' the Instrument prepositional phrase *chi ch'iich'* 'with a machete' in (5a) becomes a primary object fronted to clause-initial focus position when the root 'cut' combines with the applicative in (5b). Constructions like (5b) are used in K'iche' and throughout Eastern Mayan languages to focalize instruments, locatives and addressees (Mora-Marín 2003: 202–210).

(5) K'iche' (Eastern Mayan, Guatemala; Kaufman 1990: 78 cited in Mora-Marín 2003: 202)
    a. *k-Ø-in-rami-j*   *lee*   *chee'* *chi*   *ch'iich'*
        INC-3SG.ABS-1SG.ERG-cut-TRZ DET wood PREP machete
        'I cut (habitually) the wood with a machete.'
    b. *ch'iich'*   *k-Ø-in-rami-b'e-j*   *lee*   *chee'*
        machete INC-3SG.ABS-1SG.ERG-cut-APPL-TRZ DET wood
        'A machete is what I cut the wood with.'

Data from several chapters in this volume (GIBSON, MARTEN, MOUS & RIEDEL, MODI & POST, GUNNINK & PACCHIAROTTI) add to this list and offer novel insights on the focalizing function. One of the generalizations emerging from these chapters is that applicative(-like) morphology usually expresses different types of narrow-focus on individual clause constituents (e.g., in answers to content questions, in constructions of the type *it is X and not Y*, etc.). In Bantu languages, this function is available only for AppPs with a specific semantic role, such as Location and/or Instrument, whenever the root does *not* require applicative morphology to introduce AppPs with these semantic roles. Bantu applicatives can also combine with other focus-marking strategies, such as cleft constructions, to convey certain types of narrow focus (GUNNINK & PACCHIAROTTI); they can even co-occur with prepositional phrases to place these constituents under narrow focus (GIBSON, MARTEN, MOUS & RIEDEL). For Macro-Tani languages, MODI & POST show that the focalizing function of certain applicative affixes requires specific case assignments to the AppP depending on which constituent is under focus.

KOHLBERGER demonstrates that an extremely frequent discourse function of applicative morphology in Shiwiar is to shift the attention of the listener towards a notional, but often not overtly expressed, Location. Although we discuss his chapter in this section, the author actually refrains from labelling this discourse function as focalization and prefers the term "location highlighting." This is because while applicative morphology can introduce a Location AppP as new information, in most instances of this usage the Location AppP in Shiwiar is actually left unexpressed.

Finally, IBÁÑEZ CERDA, ORTIZ VILLEGAS & MORA-BUSTOS and SIMON uncover a novel pragmatic function: the use of applicative constructions as a mitigation or politeness strategy in face-threatening speech acts such as commands, requests, and complaints.

5 Diachrony of sources

Several chapters in this volume deal with diachronic sources of applicative morphology. MODI & POST reconstruct the origin of Macro-Tani applicative constructions in the morphologization of an earlier serial verb construction. SIMON shows that the morphology found in the benefactive/sociative applicative construction in Tibetic languages originates in a compound noun featuring a lexical verb followed by a bound root with meanings of association or help. The resulting compound noun is then re-verbalized by a light verb. Although he does not explore the topic in detail, KOHLBERGER hints at the possibility that there might be a historical connection between two applicative allomorphs formally identical to two first person object indexes in Shiwiar (Chicham). KARIM & SALEHI argue that so-called "absolute" prepositions in Soranî (Indo-Iranian) function synchronically as obligatory applicative affixes introducing exclusively anaphoric, pronominal AppPs. The absolute prepositions are the historical result of the phonological reduction and fusion of a preposition followed by a third-person-singular pronoun in the oblique case. KARIM & SALEHI demonstrate that the reanalysis of absolute prepositions as applicative affixes was made possible due to an ambiguity in the Soranî past tense paradigm, where third-person-singular objects are zero-marked. KARIM & SALEHI posit multiple, synchronically identifiable, layers of applicative recruitment in Soranî, ranging from older preverbs (originally applicative in function but no longer productive) to synchronically productive applicatives originating in "absolute" and complex prepositions.

Two chapters show that spatial-related morphology can develop applicative-like functions over time. Along with the denominal affixes (Jacques 2014) and nominal classifiers (Rose 2019), this is a newly discovered source for applicative morphology found in languages with dedicated and productive applicative morphology, such as Nilotic (PAYNE D.) and Harakmbut, an isolate from Peru (VAN LINDEN). PAYNE D. shows that in some Nilotic languages, itive and ventive directionals can combine with transitive roots with an argument frame <Actor Goal/Source> to derive an <Actor Theme> argument frame (where Theme is a moving entity). PAYNE D. treats these as instances of redirective applicatives (see §1), because the Goal/Source of the root construction can only appear as an oblique in the derived <Actor Theme> frame. She suggests that Nilotic directionals might have developed applicative(-like) functions due to the associated motion function of a participant (Theme) moving through space. VAN LINDEN describes the applicative uses of three spatial prefixes in Harakmbut, whose main function is to specify the spatial configuration of S and P arguments in the language. These prefixes are also the only morphological means to add a Goal, Source or Endpoint object AppP to intransitive and transitive verb roots with self-motion or posture meanings. In this applicative function, they still specify the location of the base S or P argument with respect to the AppP. Two of these morphemes later grammaticalized even further and developed a purely applicative (i.e., valence-increasing) function devoid of any spatial meaning, such as introducing Beneficiary, Maleficiary, and Human Goal AppPs.

6 Diachrony of functions

Several chapters deal with the diachronic relationship of syntactic and non-syntactic functions of applicative morphology. Three chapters posit either SYNTAX > SEMANTICS or SYNTAX > DISCOURSE/PRAGMATICS pathways. VANDER KLOK & EVANS argue that the Javanese locative applicative -*i* developed semantic and lexical aspect meanings, such as intensity and iteration (see §3), due to the semantic features associated with highly transitive events morphologically expressed through applicative morphology (more effective transfer of the action to an object, greater affectedness of the object, etc.). This direction of change is corroborated by the fact that only the syntactic function of -*i* is attested in Old Javanese. Similarly, Hyman (2014, 2018) argues valence-related extensions in several Benue-Congo languages tend to develop aspectual-like functions which might entirely replace the original valence-related function. Although they do not explore different historical scenarios, PAYNE T. & OYZON argue that the canonical syntactic uses of applicatives in Waray and their extended non-canonical uses (e.g., conveying the idea that an absolutive is only partially affected by the action of the verb) can all be captured under the unifying concept of "mitigated transitivity" (e.g., indirect or partial affect on the endpoint, distributed control on the starting point, etc.).

GIBSON, MARTEN, MOUS & RIEDEL posit an original syntactic function for the applicative construction in Proto-Bantu and argue, alongside existing proposals, that it introduced participants with locative marking (e.g. a locative noun class prefix) and locative semantics not subcategorized for by the verb root. The presence of both the applicative and locative marking on the AppPs in this initial stage is interpreted by GIBSON, MARTEN, MOUS & RIEDEL as a case of double marking with focus-like effects. Eventually, the applicative was reanalyzed as a saliency marker while the AppP with locative semantics is licensed exclusively by the locative marking, without the need of an applicative form of the verb.

After having established its applicative nature, SIMON argues for the pragmaticization of an original sociative/benefactive applicative construction in several Tibetic languages, where it is often used as a politeness strategy in commands and complaints. In this illocutionary use, the AppP cannot be overtly expressed and is co-referential with the speaker who utters the command. SIMON posits that the dative-marked Beneficiary AppP usually introduced by the applicative construction developed into the pragmatic role of Attitude Holder, a participant pragmatically related to the event via a specific attitude, through an intermediate stage of Affected Experiencer. This pragmaticization appears to be old: it can be traced back to Classical Tibetan.

IBÁÑEZ CERDA, ORTIZ VILLEGAS & MORA-BUSTOS, on the other hand, posit a PRAGMATICS > SYNTAX direction of change to account for some unusual inherent semantic features of a periphrastic applicative construction in Colombian Andean Spanish. This construction is frequently used as an attenuation strategy in commands and request speech acts, but also as a means to introduce primarily Deputative-Beneficiary AppPs in declarative clauses. In this locutionary use, the periphrastic applicative construction obligatorily implies the sudden involvement of the Agent in the action described by the verb as a favor to the speaker, the addressee, or another referent. IBÁÑEZ CERDA, ORTIZ VILLEGAS & MORA-BUSTOS propose that this semantic feature originates in the primary pragmatic use of the construction in commands and requests and was carried over to the newer declarative function.

7 Mysteries and miscellanea

This final section combines language/family-specific functions of applicative morphology not found in other chapters, as well as recurrent constructions involving the co-occurrence of applicative morphology and a non-promoted oblique for which no clear function has been identified.

As for functions that appear to be less widespread than others, GUNNINK & PACCHIAROTTI report that applicative morphology in the eastern Bantu language Fwe can broaden the scope of a Location AppP to include the speaker who utters the sentence (e.g., 'they are playing-APPL outside' implies that the speaker is also outside). While the applicative in Bantu can broaden the scope of a Location AppP to include the subject of the clause (e.g., 'John saw-APPL Mary on the boat' implies that John is also on the boat), the inclusion of the speaker in the scope of the Location AppP has not been observed before. TRUONG & McDONNELL report that in two western Indonesian languages, ditransitive verb roots become monotransitive when they combine with applicative-like morphology. The Recipient of these ditransitive verb roots can be expressed either as a core object argument in the construction of the underived verb root or as an oblique introduced by a locative preposition in the construction of the applicativized stem. PAYNE T. & OYZON describe two constructions in the Philippine language Waray (Austronesian) that do not have a parallel in other chapters. In what they call "evaluative applicative constructions," the Waray applicative suffix -*an* verbalizes a root describing an attribute (see §2) and occurs in a construction with two participants: an evaluator in the absolutive case and an evaluee (the participant of which the attribute is predicated) in the locative or genitive case. The presence of applicative-like morphology in evaluative or estimative constructions is apparently found also outside of Austronesian (Guillaume Jacques, p.c.). In what they call "registration applicatives," the Waray applicative prefix *i-* co-occurs with a peripheral participant (Beneficiary, Associate, or External Force), which is usually not overtly expressed but optionally expressible in an oblique role. According to PAYNE T. & OYZON, the function of this construction is to present the situation as being under the shared control of an ergative-marked Agent and another participant or force.

The co-occurrence of applicative morphology and a non-promoted oblique without a clear function is reported by TRUONG & MCDONNELL for Western Indonesian languages where applicative constructions are an alternative way to express certain semantic roles. In some of these languages, an applicativized stem can co-occur in a main clause with the oblique constituent which should have been promoted to objecthood by the applicative. The optional presence of applicative morphology is described as not causing any clear semantic or syntactic effects. The extent to which discourse/pragmatic effects could be brought about by the applicative is unknown at present. The co-occurrence of a non-promoted, oblique(-like) AppP and applicative morphology has also been reported in Australian aboriginal languages (Austin 2005), Abaza (Northwest Caucasian, O'Herin 2001), Acazulco Otomí (Otomanguean, Hernández-Green 2016), and Omaha (Siouan, Marsault 2022). In the Otomanguean tradition, they are called "registration applicatives" and are used to focus an extra-thematic participant that is indexed (or registered) in the verbal morphology. Investigating whether these constructions might have discourse functions in other languages seems a promising research endeavor.

In sum, this volume shows that the time is ripe to broaden the received wisdom view on applicativization. The body of evidence found in the contributions adds to the already attested cases of "non-canonical" syntactic behavior and seldom-described non-syntactic functions of applicative morphology. Because some of these features and functions are found recurrently in geographically distant and genetically unrelated languages, their co-occurrence is unlikely to be due to chance. Rather, one wonders whether there is a unified concept to account for at least some of the syntactic and non-syntactic functions and what might be the diachronic driving forces behind this synchronic polyfunctionality.

Abbreviations

1	first person
2	second person
3	third person
ABS	absolutive
ANIM	animate
APPL	applicative
COMPL	completive
DAT	dative
DET	determiner
DIR	direct
ERG	ergative
INC	incompletive
PL	plural
PREP	preposition
PROX	proximate
PST	past
SBJ	subject
SG	singular
TRZ	transitivizer

References

Alsina, Alex & Sam A. Mchombo. 1993. Object Asymmetries and the Chichewa Applicative Construction. In Sam A. Mchombo (ed.), *Theoretical Aspects of Bantu Grammar*, 17–45. Stanford: CSLI.

Arkadiev, Peter & Yury Lander. 2020. The Northwest Caucasian languages. In Maria Polinsky (ed.), *The Oxford handbook of the languages of the Caucasus*, 369–446. Oxford: Oxford University Press.

Austin, Peter K. 2005. Causative and applicative constructions in Australian Aboriginal Languages. In Kazuto Matsumura & Tooru Hayasi (eds.), *The dative and related phenomena*, 165–225. Tokyo: Hitsuji Shobo.

Bahrt, Nicklas. 2021. *Voice syncretism*. Berlin: Language Science Press.

Bresnan, Joan & Lioba Moshi. 1993. Object asymmetries in comparative Bantu syntax. In Sam A. Mchombo (ed.), *Theoretical aspects of Bantu grammar*, 47–91. Stanford: CSLI Publications.

Brugiotti da Vetralla, Giacinto. 1659. *Regulae quaedam pro difficillimi Congensium idiomatis faciliori captu, ad grammaticae normam redactae, a F. Hyacintho Brusciotto, a Vetralla* [Some rules for the more easy understanding of the most difficult idiom of the people of the Congo, brought into the form of grammar by Fr. Hyacinth Brusciotto from Vetralla]. Rome: Tipografia della Congregazione di Propaganda Fide.

Comrie, Bernard. 1985. Causative verb formation and other verb-deriving morphology. In Timothy Shopen (ed.), *Language typology and syntactic description, Vol. III: Grammatical categories and the lexicon*, 309–348. Cambridge: Cambridge University Press.

Creissels, Denis. 2004. Non-canonical applicatives and focalization in Tswana. Paper presented at the Syntax of the World's Languages, Leipzig, Available at http://email.eva.mpg.de/~cschmidt/SWL1/handouts/Creissels.pdf.

Creissels, Denis. 2006. *Syntaxe générale, une introduction typologique. 2. La phrase*. Paris: Lavoisier.

Creissels, Denis. 2016. Transitivity, valency and voice. Paper presented at the Course given at the European Summer School in Linguistic Typology, Porquerolles, September 2016, Porquerolles.

Creissels, Denis. forthcoming. *Transitivity, Valency, and Voice*. Oxford: Oxford University Press.

Creissels, Denis , Gerrit J. Dimmendaal, Zygmunt Frajzyngier & Christa König. 2008. Africa as a morphosyntactic area. In Bernd Heine & Derek Nurse (eds.), *A linguistic geography of Africa*, 86–150. (Cambridge Approaches to Language Contact). Cambridge: Cambridge University Press.

De Kind, Jasper & Koen Bostoen. 2012. The Applicative in Cilubà Grammar and Discourse: A Semantic Goal Analysis. *Southern African linguistics and applied language studies* 30(1). 101–124.

De Olmos, André. 1547. *Grammaire de la langue Nahuatl ou mexicaine, composée en 1547, par le Franciscain André de Olmos et publié avec notes, éclaircissements, etc. par Rémi Siméon*. Paris: Imprimerie nationale.

Del Rincón, Antonio. 1595. *Arte mexicana compuesta por el padre Antonio del Rincón de la Compania de Jesus dirigido al illustrissimo y reverendissimo S. Don Diego Romano Obispo de Tlaxcallan, y del consejo de Su Magestad, &c. en Mexico en casa de Pedro, Balli. 1595: Se reimprime en 1885 bajo el cuidado del Antonio Peñafiel. [Auf. d. Umsell.]: Gramática y vocabulario mexicanos por el padre Antonio del Rincon*. México: Oficina tipográfica de la Secretaría de Fomento.

Dixon, Robert M. W. & Alexandra I. U. Aikhenvald. 2000. Introduction. In Robert M. W. Dixon & Alexandra I. U. Aikhenvald (eds.), *Changing valency: case studies in transitivity*, 1–29. Cambridge: Cambridge University Press.

Donohue, Mark. 2001. Coding choices in argument structure: Austronesian applicatives in texts. *Studies in Language* 25(2). 217–254.

Drapeau, Lynn. 2014. *Grammaire de la langue innue*. Quebec: Presses de l'Université du Québec.

Drapeau, Lynn. 2015. A generalized applicative in Innu. In Monica Macaulay (ed.), *Papers of the Forty-Third Algonquian Conference*, 58–71. Buffalo: SUNY Press.

Franco, Ludovico. 2019. A syntactic interpretation of the applicative-causative syncretism. *Quaderni di Linguistica e Studi Orientali* 5. 107–134.

Frantz, Donald. 2009. *Blackfoot grammar*. 2nd edn. Toronto: University of Toronto Press.

Givón, Talmy. 1984. Direct object and dative shifting: Semantic and pragmatic case. In Frans Plank (ed.), *Objects: Towards a theory of grammatical relations*, 151–182. London: Academic Press.

Gurevich, Olga I. 2006. *Constructional morphology: The Georgian version*. Berkeley: University of California at Berkeley.

Harford, Carolyn. 1993. The applicative in Chishona and lexical mapping theory. In Sam A. Mchombo (ed.), *Theoretical aspects of Bantu grammar*, 93–112. Stanford: CSLI Publications.

Harris, Alice C. 1981. *Georgian syntax: A study in relational grammar*. Cambridge: Cambridge University Press.

Haspelmath, Martin & Thomas Müller-Bardey. 2004. Valency change. In Gert Booij, Christian Lehmann & Joachim Mugdan (eds.), *Morphology: A handbook on inflection and word formation. Vol. 2,* 1130–1145. (Handbücher zur Sprach und Kommunikationswissenschaft, HSK 17.2). Berlin/New York: De Gruyter.

Hernández-Green, Néstor. 2016. Registration versus applicative constructions in Acazulco Otomí. *International Journal of American Linguistics* 82(3). 353–383.

Hyman, Larry M. 2014. Reconstructing the Niger-Congo verb extension paradigm: What's cognate, copied or renewed? In Martine Robbeets & Walter Bisang (eds.), *Paradigm change: In the Transeurasian languages and beyond*, 103–125. Amsterdam: John Benjamins.

Hyman, Larry M. 2018. Common Bantoid verb extensions. In John R. Watters (ed.), *East Benue-Congo: Nouns, Pronouns, and Verbs*, 173–198. Berlin: Language Science Press.

Jacques, Guillaume. 2014. Denominal affixes as sources of antipassive markers in Japhug Rgyalrong. *Lingua* 138. 1–22.

Jacques, Guillaume. 2022. Applicatif et complétives en japhug. Paper presented at the Journée de la Société Linguistique de Paris "L'applicatif dans les langues: Regard typologique", École Normale Supérieure Paris.

Kaufman, Terrence. 1990. Algunos rasgos estructurales de los idiomas Mayances. In Nora C. England & Stephen R. Elliot (eds.), *Lecturas sobre la lingüística maya*, 59–114. Antigua: CIRMA.

Kiessling, Roland. 2004. Kausation, Wille und Wiederholung in der verbalen Derivation der westlichen Ring-Sprachen (Weh, Isu). In Raimund Kastenholz & Anne Storch (eds.), *Sprache und Wissen in Afrika: Beiträge zum 15. Afrikanistentag, Frankfurt am Main und Mainz: 30. September – 2. Oktober 2002*, 159–181. Cologne: Rüdiger Köppe Verlag.

Kinkade, M. Dale 1980. Columbian Salish -xí, -ɬ, -túɬ. *International Journal of American Linguistics* 46(1). 33–36.

Kisseberth, Charles W. & Mohammad Imam Abasheikh. 1977. The object relation in Chi-Mwi:ni, a Bantu language. In Peter Cole & Jerrold M. Sadock (eds.), *Syntax and semantics 8: Grammatical relations*, 179–218. New York: Academic Press.

Kiyosawa, Kaoru. 2006. *Applicatives in Salish languages*. Vancouver, BC: Simon Fraser University doctoral dissertation.

Kiyosawa, Kaoru & Donna Gerdts. 2011. *Salish applicatives*. Leiden: Brill.

Kozhanov, Kirill. 2016. Verbal prefixation and argument structure in Lithuanian. In Axel Holvoet & Nicole Nau (eds.), *Argument realization in Baltic*, 363–402. Amsterdam: John Benjamins.

Kulikov, Leonid. 2011. Voice Typology. In Jae Jung Song (ed.), *The Oxford Handbook of Linguistic Typology*, 368–398. Oxford: Oxford University Press.

Kulikov, Leonid. 2012. Vedic preverbs as markers of valency-changing derivations: Transitivity and objecthood in Indo-European (evidence from Old Indo-Aryan). *Studies in Language* 36(4). 721–746.

Lehmann, Christian & Elizabeth Verhoeven. 2006. Extraversive transitivization in Yucatec Maya and the nature of the applicative. In Leonid Kulikov, Andrej Malchukov & Peter de Swart (eds.), *Case, valency, and transitivity*, 465–493. Amsterdam: John Benjamins.

Marsault, Julie. 2022. Constituants syntaxiques introduits par les préfixes applicatifs Omaha. Paper presented at the Journée Annuelle de la Société Linguistique de Paris "L'applicatif dans les langues: Regard typologique", École Normale Supérieure Paris.

Michaelis, Laura A. & Josef Ruppenhofer. 2000. Valence creation and the German applicative: The inherent semantics of linking patterns. *Journal of Semantics* 17(4). 335–395.

Michaelis, Laura & Josef Ruppenhofer. 2001. *Beyond alternations: A constructional model of the German applicative*. Stanford: CSLI Publications.

Mithun, Marianne. 2000. Valency-changing derivation in Central Alaskan Yup'ik. In Robert M. W. Dixon & Alexandra Y. Aikhenvald (eds.), *Changing valency: Case studies in transitivity*, 84–114. Cambridge: Cambridge University Press.

Mithun, Marianne. 2002. Understanding and explaining applicatives. In Mary Andronis, Cristopher Ball, Heidi Elston & Sylvain Neuvel (eds.), *Proceedings of the 37th Meeting of the Chicago Linguistic Society: Functionalism and formalism in Linguistic Theory*, 73–98. Chicago: Chicago Linguistic Society.

Mora-Marín, David F. 2003. Historical reconstruction of Mayan applicative and antidative constructions. *International Journal of American Linguistics* 69(2). 186–228.

Nouguier-Voisin, Sylvie. 2002. *Relations entre fonctions sémantiques et fonctions syntaxiques en wolof*. Lyon: Université Lumière Lyon 2 doctoral dissertation.

O'Herin, Brian. 2001. Abaza applicatives. *Language* 77(3). 477–493.

Onishi, Masayuki. 2000. Transitivity and valency-changing derivations in Motuna. In Robert M. W. Dixon & Alexandra Y. Aikhenvald (eds.), *Changing valency: Case studies in transitivity*, 115–144. Cambridge: Cambridge University Press.

Pacchiarotti, Sara & Leonid Kulikov. 2022. Bribri media tantum verbs and the rise of labile syntax. *Linguistics* 60(2). 617–657.

Payne, Thomas E. 1997. *Describing morphosyntax: A guide for field linguists*. Cambridge: Cambridge University Press.

Payne, Thomas E. 2002. Towards a substantive typology of applicative constructions. Paper presented at the Third Winter Typological School, Moscow.

Peterson, David A. 2007. *Applicative constructions*. Oxford/New York: Oxford University Press.

Polinsky, Maria. 2013. Applicative constructions. In Martin Haspelmath, Matthew S. Dryer, David Gil & Bernard Comrie (eds.), *The World Atlas of Language Structures Online*. Munich: Max Planck Digital Library, chapter 109. Available online at http://wals.info/feature/109.

Pylkkänen, Liina. 2002. Introducing arguments. Cambridge, MA: MIT Doctoral dissertation.

Pylkkänen, Liina. 2008. *Introducing arguments*. Cambridge, MA: MIT Press.

Rapold, Christian. 1997. *The applicative construction in Lingala*. Leiden: Universiteit Leiden M.A. thesis.

Renaudier, Marie. 2012. *Dérivation et valence en Seereer*. Lyon: Lumière University Lyon 2 dissertation.

Rose, Françoise. 2019. From classifiers to applicatives in Mojeño Trinitario: A new source for applicative markers. *Linguistic Typology* 23(3). 435–466.

Rude, Noel. 1986. Topicality, transitivity, and the direct object in Nez Perce. *Journal of American Linguistics* 52(2). 124–153.

Sharman, John Campton. 1963. *Morphology, morphophonology and meaning in the single-word verb-forms in Bemba*. Pretoria: University of South Africa dissertation.

Shibatani, Masayoshi. 1996. Applicatives and benefactives: A cognitive account. In Masayoshi Shibatani & Sandra A. Thompson (eds.), *Grammatical constructions: Their form and meaning*, 157–194. Oxford: Clarendon Press.

Trithart, Mary Lee. 1983. *The applied suffix and transitivity: A historical study in Bantu*. Los Angeles: UCLA dissertation.

Zúñiga, Fernando & Denis Creissels. forthcoming. Applicative constructions: An introductory overview. In Fernando Zúñiga & Denis Creissels (eds.), *Applicative Constructions in the World's Languages*. (Comparative Handbooks of Linguistics, CHL7). Berlin/Boston: Mouton de Gruyter.

Zúñiga, Fernando & Seppo Kittilä. 2019. *Grammatical Voice*. Cambridge: Cambridge University Press.

Part I: **Americas**

Lilián Guerrero
2 Typical and atypical applicative constructions in Yaqui

Abstract: In Yaqui, the applicative -*ria* is an optional morpheme that adds a new non-Actor argument to the argument structure of the base verb. Semantically, this applied argument is a Beneficiary; syntactically, it serves as a core argument of the derived applicative clause. Based on the morphosyntactic properties of the applied argument. I propose that Yaqui has two types of applicative clauses, typical and atypical. In typical applicative clauses, the applied argument is promoted to primary object and acts as the privileged syntactic argument in passive clauses; these clauses usually express recipient-benefactive readings. In atypical applicative clauses, the applied argument is *half-way* promoted: it shows object properties but cannot serve as the passive subject; such applicative clauses convey self-benefactive and possessor-benefactive readings. A closer examination of applicative clauses in oral texts reveals a tendency in some discourse genres to use atypical applicative clauses for introducing a discourse salient participant who is negatively affected. This means that atypical applicative clauses are often employed in Yaqui discourse even though they are syntactically non-promotional.

1 Introduction

In this chapter, I discuss applicative constructions in Yaqui. Yaqui (ISO cod: yaq) is a Uto-Aztecan language spoken in Sonora (Mexico) and Arizona (United States); this study is based on the Sonoran variety.[1] According to previous studies on the language (Rude 1996; Dedrick and Casad 1999; Guerrero and Van Valin 2004; Gue-

---

[1] Most data analyzed here come from my fieldwork (uncited); the original orthography for data quoted from other materials has been preserved. I gratefully acknowledge my Yaqui language consultants: the Flores Buitimea family, Aurelia Mendoza, Angélica Valenzuela, and Maria Luisa Buitimea García. Many thanks also to the editors and two anonymous reviewers for their valuable comments and suggestions on preliminary versions of this paper. Any views or errors represented here are my own. This study was partially supported by the UNAM-DGAPA-PAPIIT (IN400919) and Conacyt-Ciencia Básica (A1-S-24378) grants.

Lilián Guerrero, Universidad Nacional Autónoma de México (UNAM), Instituto de Investigaciones Filológicas-Seminario de Lenguas Indígenas, Circuito Mario de la Cueva, Ciudad de México, México, e-mail: lilianguerrero@yahoo.com

rrero 2007), the applicative *-ria* is a verbal suffix with syntactic consequences: it introduces a peripheral animate participant as a direct core argument with the semantic role of Beneficiary.² The two clauses in (1) express a benefactive situation in which one participant benefits from the event; in this case, 'Mary' is the recipient of 'a house'. In the base clause (BC) in (1a), the Beneficiary is coded as an adjunct marked by the postposition *betchi'ibo* 'for'; in the applicative clause (AC) in (1b), the same participant takes accusative case, i.e., applied argument or phrase (AppP).

(1) a. *kari-ta=ne   ya'a-k   Maria-ta-betchi'ibo.*
       house-ACC=1SG.NOM make-PFV   Mary-ACC-for
       'I made a house for Mary.'

  b. *kari-ta=ne   Maria-ta   ya'a-ria-k.*
       house-ACC=1SG.NOM Mary-ACC   make-APPL-PFV
       'I made Mary a house.'

The AC in (1b) satisfies the expected attributes of typical applicative constructions (Shibatani 1996; Peterson 2007; Zúñiga and Kittilä 2019; Creissels 2016). Namely, the AC is an optional variant of the BC in terms of introducing the Beneficiary, the verb of the AC is overtly derived from the verb of the BC, and the suffix *-ria* has a valency-increasing function since the derived clause shows a new participant coded as a direct core argument. I will show that the AppP 'Mary' also corresponds to the primary object

---

2 Following Van Valin (2005: 57), in the present analysis I distinguished between semantic valency and syntactic valency. Semantic valency is understood to be the number and semantic roles of participants that a verb requires, i.e., one-, two-, or three-place predicates refer to the number of semantic core arguments. Based on their marking, semantic core arguments can be direct or oblique; direct core arguments are unmarked or marked by direct case (e.g., NOM, ACC, ABS, ERG, DAT), while oblique core arguments are marked by oblique case (OBL) or adpositions. Only direct core arguments count for syntactic valency, i.e., intransitive, transitive, ditransitive refer to the number of direct core arguments within the clause. Oblique core arguments are syntactic arguments too, but they show fewer morphosyntactic properties as compared to direct core arguments. Unlike oblique core arguments, adjuncts do not have object properties, they are optional, and their semantic role is not determined by the lexical meaning of the verb. For instance, *-betchi'ibo* marks adjuncts with the semantic roles of Beneficiary, Recipient, Destination, Purpose, and Cause. Valency-changing morphemes can add or remove a new participant and/or a new syntactic argument. For example, the passive clause *The dog was killed by the man* involves a two-place predicate 'kill' taking an Actor and a Theme, but only one direct core argument, 'the dog'. The Actor 'the man' is a semantic argument, but is coded as an adjunct. See Guerrero (2019a, b, in press a, in press b) for a detailed discussion of Yaqui direct and oblique core arguments, and the use of postpositions as oblique markers.

of the derived AC. For instance, the passive version of (1a) would be 'the house was made for Mary', with the Theme functioning as the passive subject, whereas the passive version of (1b) would be 'Mary was made the house', with the Beneficiary serving as the passive subject. Consequently, the applicative -*ria* not only promotes the optional Beneficiary expressed by a postpositional phrase to a direct core argument, but the AppP serves as the grammatical subject in passive clauses, i.e., it is a passive subject.

Some AppPs may have a malefactive reading. For example, in (2a) 'John' is negatively affected because 'Peter' ate his tortillas. Moreover, with some three-place predicates, -*ria* does not add a new semantic participant, but rather reallocates the morphological coding of the core arguments. Compare (2b) and (2c). In the BC, the Recipient is marked by the directional postposition -*u* 'to' (oblique core argument); in the AC, the same participant takes accusative case (direct core argument). The passive version of (2a) would have the AppP as the passive subject and could be literally translated as '[to] John was eaten the tortillas'; the passive version of (2c) would be equivalent to 'Joseph was sold the pot'. Since the AppPs serve as the passive subject, (2a) and (2c) correspond to typical ACs in Yaqui.

(2) a. *Peo-Ø   tajkaim   Joan-ta   bwa'e-ria-k.*
       Peter-NOM   tortilla.PL   John-ACC   eat-APPL-PFV
       'Peter ate John's tortillas.'

   b. *Malena-Ø   Jose-ta-u   soto'i-ta   nenka-k.*
       Malena-NOM   Joseph-ACC-DIR   pot-ACC   sell-PFV
       'Malena sold the pot to Joseph.'

   c. *Malena-Ø   Jose-ta   soto'i-ta   nenka-ria-k.*
       Malena-NOM   Joseph-ACC   pot-ACC   sell-APPL-PFV
       'Malena sold Joseph the pot.'

Nevertheless, new data have revealed the existence of atypical ACs based on the properties of the AppP. First, -*ria* may occur in clauses in which the Actor and the Beneficiary refer to the same participant. In this context, the AppP is not an accusative NP, but a reflexive pronoun (3a). Second, the AppP may be inanimate when there is an inherent possessive relationship. For example, in the AC in (3b) -*ria* allows the Possessor of 'the car' to be coded as an independent direct core argument. And third, although the AppPs in (3) satisfy the syntactic valency of the applied verb, they cannot function as the passive subject, i.e., *'myself was bought a house', *'the car was fixed the brakes' are ruled out as passive versions with the same meanings of (3a) and (3b), respectively.

(3) a. kari-ta=ne　　　　　ino　　　jinu-ria-k.
　　　house-ACC=1SG.NOM　1SG.REFL　buy-APPL-PFV
　　　'I bought a house for myself.'

　　b. karo-ta=te　　　　　maniam　　tu'ute-ria-k.
　　　car-ACC=1PL.NOM　　brake.PL　fix-APPL-PFV
　　　'We fixed the car's brakes.' (lit. fixed the car the brakes)

Previous studies on the language have briefly mentioned that certain usages of *-ria* can have reflexive (Dedrick and Casad 1999: 290) or possessive readings (Guerrero 2007: 193). However, atypical ACs have not been studied in depth in Yaqui grammar. Based on this gap in the literature, my aim in this study is twofold. First, I seek to investigate the semantic and syntactic features of typical and atypical ACs in Yaqui, focusing on the applied argument, and second, I offer a preliminary exploration of the ACs used in Yaqui oral narratives. On the semantic side, I show that the semantic role of the AppP varies in two senses. First, the applied argument can be positively (benefactive) or negatively (malefactive) affected by the event (Kittilä and Zúñiga 2010: 5). Second, it denotes several semantic roles including Beneficiary, Recipient, Addressee, Source, Goal, Possessor, as well as a 'self' Actor. There are other morphosyntactic ways to introduce these semantic roles; for instance, the Beneficiary can be expressed as a an adjunct marked by *-betchi'ibo* 'for' in basic clauses. I also show that typical ACs mainly express recipient-benefactive readings, while atypical ACs express self-benefactive and possessor-benefactive readings. On the syntactic side, I argue that the syntactic behavior of the AppP is not uniform: while the AppP in typical ACs is promoted to primary object and functions as a passive subject, the AppP in atypical ACs is half-way promoted. On the discourse-functional side, recipient-benefactives are quite common in Yaqui oral narratives. However, there is a tendency in life story texts to express possessor-benefactive ACs in which a discourse salient animate participant is negatively affected by the ongoing situations in the narrative.

This chapter begins by presenting some morphosyntactic features of Yaqui, including valency-changing mechanisms, immediately relevant to the discussion at hand (§2.1). It then moves on to the analysis of typical ACs with one-, two- and three-place predicates (§3.1–§3.3), and the status of the AppP (§3.4). Atypical ACs are then discussed, beginning with the properties of self-benefactives (§4.1) and then possessor-benefactives (§4.2); the proposal of half-way promoted AppPs is introduced in §4.3. In §5 the use of ACs in oral texts is explored. §6 offers some final comments.

2 The Yaqui language

2.1 Basic grammatical features

Yaqui is an agglutinating, accusative, dependent-marking, primary-object, head-final language (Lindenfeld 1973; Dedrick and Casad 1999; Guerrero 2006). Verbs do not inflect for person or number, though there is a set of suppletive verbs that show number agreement (4a). Direct core arguments take nominative case (unmarked -Ø) and accusative case marked by -*ta* (4a–b). Oblique core arguments are marked by postpositions such as the directional -*u* 'to' (4c). Adjuncts are also marked by postpositions. Unlike core arguments, adjuncts freely occur before or after the verb; in (4b), the locative adverb *junama* 'there' occurs at the beginning of the clause, and the phrase *bo'ochi* 'on the road' at the end.

(4) a. *u-Ø   chu'u-Ø   kaatama-u   yeu=siika.*
       DET-NOM dog-NOM   patio-DIR   out=go.SG-PFV
       'The dog went out on the patio.'

   b. *junama='e   u-ka   chu'u-ta   bicha-k   bo'o-chi.*
       there=2SG.NOM   DET-ACC   dog-ACC   see-PFV   road-LOC
       'You saw the dog there on the road.'

   c. *inepo   u-e   jamut-ta-u   waate-Ø.*
       1SG.NOM   DET-OBL   woman-ACC-DIR   miss-PRS
       'I miss the woman.'

   d. *u-me   o'ou-im   u-me   chu'u-im   bicha-k.*
       DET-PL   man-PL   DET-PL   dog-PL   see-PFV
       'The men saw the dogs.'

There are some characteristics of Yaqui case marking that warrant clarification. First, nominative and accusative cases occur with singular NPs; plural NPs in Yaqui simply take the plural suffix –*(i)m*.[3] The fixed SOV word order in (4d) helps to distinguish the syntactic functions of the plural core arguments. Second, the accusative -*ta* appears on several constituents including the possessed noun in genitive phrases, the dependent subjects in subordinate clauses, and the nominal

---

[3] There is also a set of nouns that are always plural (*pluralia tantum*; Guerrero 2014), e.g., *tajkaim* 'tortilla(s)' (2a), *maniam* 'break(s)' (3b), and *ba'am* (8). For these nouns, the plural suffix is not morphologically segmented.

complement of some postpositions (Guerrero 2019a, in press b). This explains the occurrence of -*ta* in the adjunct Beneficiary *Maria-ta-betchi'ibo* 'for Mary' in (1a), as well as in the oblique core argument *u-e jamut-ta-u* 'to the woman' in (4c). Third, when determiners are present, they reflect the case marking of the head noun. Thus, they are unmarked when modifying a nominative NP (4a), take -*ka* when modifying an accusative NP (4b), take -*e* when modifying an oblique NP, and -*me* when modifying a plural NP (4d). The absence of a determiner favors an indefinite reading of the NP.

The Yaqui pronominal system formally distinguishes syntactic functions (Table 1). Pronominal elements range in status from fully independent forms to clitics and affixes. Full pronouns, such as *inepo* 'I' in (4c), behave like lexical elements in terms of their distribution; reduced nominative pronouns can behave like second position clitics, see =*e*' (4b), while reduced accusatives (available only for third person) tend to cliticize to the verb, as in (5b) below.

Table 1: Yaqui pronominal system.

	Nominative	Accusative	Oblique	Possessive	Reflexive
1 SG	inepo, ne	nee, ne	ne-	in, nim	ino, emo,omo
2 SG	empo, 'e	enchi	e-	em	emo,omo
3 SG	aapo, Ø	aapo'ik, a'a, a	a-	aapo'ik, a, -wa	au, emo,omo
1 PL	itepo, te	itom	ito-	itom	ito, emo,omo
2 PL	eme'e, 'em	enchim	emo-, eme-	em, enchim	emo,omo
3 PL	bempo, Ø	bempo'im, am	ame-	bem, bempo'im	emo,omo

In Yaqui, there are a few syntactically intransitive/transitive verb pairs coded by suppletion, e.g., *uba/ubba* 'take a bath/bathe someone', and many verb pairs that morphologically mark transitivity: -*e*, -*te*, -*ke* for intransitives, and -*a*, -*ta*, or -*cha* for transitives (Dedrick and Casad 1999; Guerrero 2006, in press b). See the verb pair *jamte/jamta* 'break' in (5). There are, however, several verbs ending in -*e* that do not have a transitive counterpart or are themselves transitive; similarly, there are verbs ending in -*a* that do not have an intransitive version or are themselves intransitive.

(5) a. u-Ø   limeete-Ø   jamte-k.
      DET-NOM   glass-NOM   break.INTR-PFV
      'The glass broke.'

    b. empo   a=jamta-k.
       2SG.NOM   3SG.ACC=break.TR-PFV
       'You broke it.'

2.2 Valency-changing mechanisms

Previous studies have established that Yaqui has two morphological mechanisms for increasing the valency of a verb: the causative *-tua* and the applicative *-ria* (Guerrero 2007, 2008; Álvarez 2007; Estrada et al. 2015; Tubino 2017). The causative suffix *-tua* adds a new Agent or Cause (Actor). To illustrate, (6a) is the causative counterpart of (5a), and (6c) is the causative version of (6b).[4] Note that the new Actor takes nominative case and the Patient or Causee (Undergoer) takes accusative case. The causative *-tua* can also be added to several adjectives and nouns to derive causative/transitive verbs, such as *maatu* 'charcoal' and *maatu-tua* 'to blacken'.

(6) a. *empo   limeete-ta   jamti-tua-k.*
       2SG.NOM   glass-ACC   break.INTR-CAUS-PFV
       'You made the glass break.'

   b. *empo   bwite-k.*
       2SG.NOM   run.SG-PFV
       'You ran.'

   c. *Peo-Ø   enchi   bwite-tua-k.*
       Peter-NOM 2SG.ACC   run.SG-CAUS-PFV
       'Peter made you run.'

There is a small set of Yaqui adjectives, nouns, and adverbs that derive a transitive verb by adding the applicative suffix, e.g., *bali-ria* '(cold-) cool, freeze', *awi-ria* '(fat-) fatten'. In this context, *-ria* adds a new Actor. For some of these derived verbs, there is also an intransitive counterpart. Take for example 'make hot/heat'. In (7a) the adjective *suka* 'hot' describes the actual state of the single participant; in (7b) *suka-e* denotes the change of state, and in (7c) *suka-ria* expresses a caused change of state.

(7) a. *ba'am   suka.*
       water.PL   hot
       'The water is hot.'

   b. *ba'am   suka-e-Ø.*
       water.PL   hot-INTR-PRS
       'The water is getting hot.'

---

4 Some verbal suffixes cause phonological changes to the verb root; for instance, the vowel *-e* in *jamte* changes to *-i* when *-tua* is added to the underived verb. A similar process is observed with *-ria* in (9a) below.

c. *nepo   ba'am   suka-ria-Ø.*
   1SG.NOM   water.PL   hot-APPL-PRS
   'I heat the water.'

With respect to valency-decreasing mechanisms, the passive voice distinguishes between core arguments in Yaqui: only direct core arguments can serve as the passive subject. The verbal suffix -*wa* derives impersonal and passive clauses. For example, (8a) is the impersonal version of the underived transitive clause in (4b) above; note that the accusative (Theme) core argument 'the dog' of (4b) is still marked as accusative in (8a). In the passive version in (8b), 'the dog' serves as the passive subject; as such, it takes nominative case. (8c) is the impersonal counterpart of (4c); since the unique core argument is marked by oblique case, it is ruled out as the passive subject (8d). Therefore, in -*wa* clauses, the Actor must be omitted, but there is no promotion to subjecthood in impersonal *wa*-clauses. For clarity, in this paper -*wa* is glossed IMPRS in clauses without a passive subject (8a, 8c), but PASS in classes with a passive subject (8b, 8d).

(8) a. *u-ka   chu'u-ta   bicha-wa-k.*
       DET-ACC   dog-ACC   see-IMPRS-PFV
       '(Someone) saw the dog.'

   b. *u-Ø   chu'u-Ø   bicha-wa-k.*
      DET-NOM   dog-NOM   see-PASS-PFV
      'The dog was seen.'

   c. *u-e   jamut-ta-u   waate-wa-Ø.*
      DET-OBL woman-ACC-DIR   miss-IMPRS-PRS
      '(Someone) misses the woman.'

   d.* *u-Ø   jamut-Ø   waate-wa-Ø.*
       DET-NOM   woman-NOM   miss-PASS-PRS
       'The woman was missed.'

The examples in this section show that, although direct and oblique core arguments are syntactic arguments of the clause, only the accusative direct core argument has all the morphosyntactic features of objecthood. When there are two or more accusative direct core arguments in the clause, the use of passive voice is crucial in distinguishing the syntactic status of each non-Actor core argument.

3 Typical applicative constructions

There are no known historical documents on Yaqui that allow us to diachronically examine the evolution of the applicative suffix. However, there is a grammatical sketch of Cahita, a linguistic ancestor of Yaqui, that documents -*ria* ~ -*ia* with the meaning "hacer para otros lo significado del verbo radical [to make/do for others the underived verb meaning]" (Buelna 1890: 25).[5] Synchronically, the applicative morpheme -*ria* in Yaqui has been characterized as follows: (i) it is the language's only applicative suffix;[6] (ii) it adds a new non-Actor direct core argument to the verb; (iii) the new argument must be animate and it mostly refers to a Beneficiary; (iv) it is an optional marker since the same participant can be coded as an adjunct marked by -*betchi'ibo* 'for' in (underived) base clauses (BCs); and (v) the applied argument or phrase (AppP) displaces the basic object (Theme) for some syntactic functions, i.e., primary object (Rude 1996; Dedrick and Casad 1999; Guerrero 2007). In this section, I examine the typical uses of -*ria* (§3.1–§3.3) and then discuss the semantic and syntactic status of the AppP (§3.4).[7]

3.1 Applicative clauses with one-place predicates

Applicative morphemes are usually described as transitivizing; if there is an intransitive verb, the derived verb forms a transitive clause with a direct object (Peterson 2007: 2). When -*ria* combine with one-place predicates, the resulting AC has two direct core arguments, the nominative Actor and the accusative applied argument. According to Harley et al. (2009, 2017), some unergative (active) intransitive verbs whose subjects are intentional and agentive can undergo applicative derivation. In the Arizona variant of Yaqui, -*ria* can combine with 'dance' (9a), but not with 'run', 'go', 'wander', 'enter', or other intransitive verbs. In my corpus, -*ria* can combine with several active intransitive verbs, including *ye'e* 'dance' and *bwika* 'sing'. In the BC in (9b), there is an

---

[5] Langacker (1977: 146) proposes the applicative suffix *-wi-(ya) for Proto-Uto-Aztecan and its allomorph *-li-ya for the Proto-Southern Uto-Aztecan branch. Cahita and Yaqui -*ria* are reflexes of this suffix.
[6] Yaqui, Mayo, Guarijío, and Tarahumara form together the Taracahita subgroup of Southern Uto-Aztecan languages. Guarijío and Tarahumara have more than one applicative morpheme.
[7] A preliminary study on (typical) applicative clauses published in Spanish (Guerrero 2007) explores the alternative coding of the beneficiary either as an adjunct or as a primary object. The following section is partially based on that study.

adjunct Beneficiary and the clause is syntactically intransitive; in the AC in (9c), there is a Beneficiary coded as direct core argument, and the clause is therefore syntactically transitive.

(9) a. *u'u-Ø*   *maso-Ø*   *uusi-m*   *yi'i-ria-k.*
    DET-NOM   deer_dancer-NOM   child-PL   dance-APPL-PFV
    'The deer dancer dances for the children.'
    (Harley et al. 2009: 43)

   b. *aapo*   *bwika-k*   *e-betchi'ibo.*
      3SG.NOM   sing-PFV   2SG.OBL-for
      'He/she sang for/on behalf of/instead of you.'

   c. *aapo*   *enchi*   *bwika-ria-k.*
      3SG.NOM   2SG.ACC   sing-APPL-PFV
      'He/she sang for you.'

In the Sonoran variant, *-ria* can also combine with motion verbs like *bwite* 'run', *gojana* 'run away', and *siime* 'go'. Compare the intransitive BCs in (10a) and (10c) and the transitive ACs in (10b) and (10d). In (10d) *siim-ria* seems to have developed an extended meaning similar to 'to leave for good/abandon someone'; in the example, 'Peter' is affected by 'Lupe' abandoning him.

(10) a. *Luis-Ø*   *bwite-k*   *polobem-betchi'ibo.*
        Luis-NOM   run.SG-PFV   poor_people.PL-for
        'Luis ran on behalf/instead of the poor.'

    b. *Luis-Ø*   *polobem*   *bwiti-ria-k.*
       Luis-NOM   poor_people.PL   run.SG-APPL-PFV
       'Luis ran on behalf of the poor.'

    c. *Lupe-Ø*   *Potam-meu*   *siika*
       Lupe-NOM   Potam.PL-.PL.DIR   go.SG.PFV
       'Lupe went to Potam on behalf of/instead of Peter.'

    d. *Lupe-Ø*   *Peo-ta*   *siim-ria-k.*
       Lupe-NOM   Peter-ACC   go.SG-APPL-PFV
       'Lupe abandoned Peter.'

Although it is uncommon, *-ria* can also combine with stative (unaccusative) verbs like *muuku* 'die' and *alle'a* 'be happy'. The BC in (11a) is understood to mean that

'Jesus' died on behalf of 'the people,' but the AC in (11b) has a malefactive reading: it is understood to mean that 'the people' died to the detriment of 'Jesus.'[8]

(11) a. *Jesus-Ø   muuku-k   yoemmia-ta-betchi'ibo.*
       Jesus-NOM   die.SG-PFV   people-ACC-for
       'Jesus died for/on behalf of the people.'

   b. *Jesus-Ø   yoemmia-ta   muuk-ria-k.*
       Jesus-NOM   people-ACC   die.SG-APPL-PFV
       'Jesus's people up and died on him.'
       (Guerrero 2007: 186)

In addition to these benefactive and malefactive readings, whose interpretation depends on the semantics of the verb and/or the context, there are different semantic subtypes of benefactive constructions. While the Beneficiary AppP with one-place predicates only allow plain-benefactive readings, i.e. the Actor's actions provide the Beneficiary with amusement, enjoyment, or some other kind of benefit, the Beneficiary adjunct introduced by *-betchi'ibo* allow deputative-benefactive readings, i.e. the Actor performs the action in place of the Beneficiary (Van Valin and LaPolla 1997; Kittilä 2005).

3.2 Applicative clauses with two-place predicates

Most two-place predicates in Yaqui form transitive clauses with two direct core arguments, the nominative Actor and the accusative Theme; when these verbs combine with *-ria*, the AC has an additional accusative direct core argument, i.e., it is a double-accusative clause. In the examples in (12), the Actor did something to benefit someone else. In the BC in (12a), the Beneficiary is expressed as an adjunct; in the ACs in (12b) and (12c), the Beneficiary is coded as an accusative AppP. Whereas (12a) allows both recipient- and deputative-benefactive readings, (12b) means that the participant will receive (and eat) what 'Lupe' is cooking, and (12c) that they will receive and live in the new house, i.e., these are recipient-benefactive constructions.

(12) a. *Lupe-Ø   u-ka   bwa'am-ta   joa-k   Maria-ta-betchi'ibo.*
       Lupe-NOM   DET-ACC   food-ACC   cook-PFV   Mary-ACC-for
       'Lupe cooked the food on behalf of/instead of Mary.'

---

[8] It is hard to capture the meaning of this AC in English. My consultants translated it into Spanish as '*A Jesús se le murió la gente*' with a dative phrase interpreted as the maleficiary.

b. *Lupe-Ø   Maria-ta   u-ka   bwa'am-ta   joa-ria-k.*
   Lupe-NOM Mary-ACC   DET-ACC   food-ACC   cook-APPL-PFV
   'Lupe cooked Mary the food.'

c. *aman=te   kari-ta   am=ya'a-ria-k.*
   there=1PL.NOM house-ACC   3PL.ACC=make-APPL- PFV
   'There we built them a house.'
   (Silva 2004; HVH:13)

The adversely-affected reading of *-ria* is also present with certain active transitive verbs referring to cognate objects like 'eat' and 'drink', as depicted in (13a). In (13b) *etbwaria* 'steal for', 'the people' do not receive the money, but they are deprived of it.

(13) a. *Goyo-Ø   serbesa-ta   Fermin-ta   ji'i-ria-k.*
        Goyo-NOM beer-ACC   Fermin-ACC   drink-APPL-PFV
        'Goyo drank Fermin's beer.' (intended: he drank the beer on behalf of Fermin)

   b. *bato'o-ta=ne   tomi-etbwa-ria-k.*
      people-ACC=1SG.NOM money-steal-APPL-PFV
      'I stole money [from] the people.'
      (Buitimea 2007; chapayeka: 81)

3.3 Applicative clauses with three-place predicates

Three-place predicates require three semantic core arguments: the Actor, the Theme, and a third participant that may refer to the Recipient, Addressee, Goal, Source, or Location. Yaqui has, at least, three types of three-place predicates depending on the morphological coding of the third participant (Guerrero and Van Valin 2004; Guerrero 2019a). Each of these predicates behaves differently when deriving an AC.

Members of the first class mark the third participant as an accusative direct core argument. For example, *miika* 'give' takes an accusative Theme and an accusative Beneficiary in (14a), and *u'ura* 'take away' takes an accusative Theme and an accusative Source in (14c). The verb *miika* cannot combine with *-ria* (14b). One may think that this limitation is due to the presence of three accusative NPs within the AC. However, *u'ura* does combine with *-ria*, resulting in an AC with three accusative NPs: the AppP *Joana*, the Source *Lupe*, and the Theme *tomi* 'money'. This means that there is not a syntactic, but rather a semantic-pragmatic restriction: -ria is avoided when the derived AC can have two participants that compete with each other to benefit from the Actor's action because of their animacy status.

(14) a. *Joana-Ø   Lupe-ta   soto'i-ta   miika-k.*
       Juana-NOM   Lupe-ACC pot-ACC   give-PFV
       'Juana gave Lupe the pot.'

   b.* *Joana-Ø   Maria-ta   soto'i-ta   Lupe-ta   miik-ria-k.*
        Juana-NOM   Mary-ACC   pot-ACC   Lupe-ACC give-APPL-PFV
        (intended meaning: 'Juana gave Lupe the pot for Mary.')

   c. *Carmen-Ø   Lupe-ta   tomi-ta   u'ura-k.*
       Carmen-NOM Lupe-ACC money-ACC   take-PFV
       'Carmen took the money (from) Lupe.'

   d. *Carmen-Ø   Joana-ta   Lupe-ta   tomi-ta   u'ura-ria-k.*
       Carmen-NOM Juana-ACC Lupe-ACC money-ACC   take-APPL-PFV
       'Carmen took the money (for) Juana (from) Lupe.'

Members of the second class mark the third argument with locative postpositions including the directional -*u* 'to', i.e., oblique core argument. The verb *nenka* 'sell' semantically requires three participants in Yaqui: the seller, the buyer, and the thing bought; in (15a), the Recipient is marked by -*u*. The verb *teuwa* 'tell' requires the speaker, the addressee, and the message; in (15c), the Addressee is also marked by -*u*. When combined with these verbs, -*ria* does not necessarily add a new semantic participant, but it does rearrange the morphological coding of the two non-Actor core arguments. Instead of the oblique marking, the Recipient of *nenka* in (15b) and the Addressee of *teuwa* in (15d) take accusative case. Thus, the derived ACs show two accusative direct core arguments.

(15) a. *bempo   kowi-ta   u-e   jamut-ta-u   nenki-ne.*
       3PL.NOM   pig-ACC   DET-OBL   woman-ACC-DIR sell-POT
       'They will sell the pig to the woman.'

   b. *bempo   kowi-ta   u-ka   jamut-ta   nenka-ria-ne.*
       3PL.NOM   pig-ACC   DET-ACC   woman-ACC   sell-APPL-POT
       'They will sell the woman the pig.'

   c. *Maria-Ø   Luisa-ta-u   lutu'uria-ta   teuwa-k.*
       Mary-NOM Luisa-ACC-DIR truth-ACC   tell-PFV
       'Mary told the truth to Luisa.'

d. *Maria-Ø   Luisa-ta   lutu'uria-ta   teuwa-ria-k.*
   Mary-NOM Luisa-ACC   truth-ACC   tell-APPL-PFV
   'Mary told Luisa the truth.'

In (14d), (15b) and (15d) the AppP is positively affected by the event: *Joana* receives 'the money', 'the woman' will own 'the pig', and 'Luisa' knows 'the truth', respectively. In (16b), the AppP is understood to be negatively affected. In the BC in (16a), the human Goal of *jima* 'throw' is 'the boy' and the clause is understood to mean that 'Peter' and 'the child' are playing ball together. The AC in (16b) is understood to mean that 'Peter' threw 'the ball' at 'the child' in order to hurt him or hit him. It means that, besides modifying the case marking of one of the two non-Actor core arguments, *-ria* can also add semantic nuances to the meaning of the clause. The remapping function of *-ria* is not limited to oblique core arguments marked by *-u*. *Mabeta* 'receive' also requires three participants: the Recipient, the Theme, and the Source; in the BC (16c), the human Source is marked by *-betana* 'from'; in the AC version (16d), the human Source is coded as the AppP.

(16) a. *Peo-Ø   ili   usi-ta-u   pelotam   jima-k.*
        Peter-NOM little   child-ACC-DIR   ball.PL   throw-PFV
        'Peter threw a ball to the boy.' (=benefactive reading)

   b. *Peo-Ø   ili   usi-ta   pelotam   jima-ria-k.*
      Peter-NOM little   child-ACC   ball.PL   throw-APPL-PFV
      'Peter threw a ball (at) the boy.' (=malefactive reading)

   c. *inepo   u-ka   bwa'am-ta   mabeta-k   kobanao-ta-betana.*
      1SG.NOM   DET-ACC   food-ACC   receive-PFV   governor-ACC-from
      'I received the food from the governor.'

   d. *u-Ø   kobanao-Ø   tomi-ta   kaa   ne*
      DET-NOM   governor-NOM   money-ACC   NEG   1SG.ACC
      mabeti-ria-k.
      receive-APPL-PFV
      'The governor didn't receive the money [from] me.'

The verb *jinu* 'buy' also belongs to the second class and shows an interesting pattern.[9] *Jinu* semantically requires three participants: the buyer, the thing sold,

---

9 I'd like to express my thanks to one of the anonymous reviewers for pointing out the peculiarity of *jinu* 'buy'. This reviewer asked if *jinu* and the other members of the class were inherently trivalent since they can also be used transitively in Yaqui "by just dropping the third

and the seller; in (17a), the seller or human Source 'Lupe' is marked by -*u*. There are two ways to introduce a Beneficiary with *jinu*: as an adjunct (17b) or as an AppP (17c). Unlike the BC in (17b), there is not an additional semantic participant in the applicative clause in (17c), but the third argument changes its semantic role from Source to Recipient. In (17c), 'Lupe' does not sell the skirt, but she receives it. The clause (17d) confirms the semantic manipulation of -*ria*: an additional Beneficiary is accepted if the third argument introduces the Source of the event (17b), but it is ruled out if there is a Beneficiary/Recipient coded as the AppP (17d).

(17) a. *Aurelia-Ø   koarim   Lupe-ta-u   jinu-k.*
       Aurelia-NOM skirt.PL Lupe-ACC-DIR   buy-PFV
       'Aurelia bought the skirt from Lupe.'

   b. *Aurelia-Ø   koarim   Lupe-ta-u   jinu-k   e-betchi'ibo.*
       Aurelia-NOM skirt.PL Lupe-ACC-DIR   buy-PFV   2SG.OBL-for
       'Aurelia bought the skirt from Lupe for you.'

   c. *Aurelia-Ø   koarim   Lupe-ta   jinu-ria-k.*
       Aurelia-NOM skirt.PL Lupe-ACC   buy-APPL-PFV
       'Aurelia bought the skirt for Lupe.'

   d. * *Aurelia-Ø   koarim   Lupe-ta   jinu-ria-k   e-betchi'ibo.*
       Aurelia-NOM skirt.PL Lupe-ACC   buy-APPL-PFV   2SG.OBL-for
       'Aurelia bought the skirt for Lupe for you.'

The third verb class semantically requires three participants: the Actor, the Theme, and the Location. The third participant is marked by the postpositions -*po* 'in, on' or -*t* 'at'; see the example of *jo'a* 'put/lay' in (18a). The derived AC version of *jo'a* in (18b) has a new Beneficiary.

---

participant." Direct core arguments as well as oblique core arguments can be omitted in the right discourse-pragmatic context, thus this possibility does not contradict the fact that these participants are required by the semantic valency of the verb (a couple of Dedrick and Casad's (1999: 290–291) examples of -*ria* have implicit AppPs). The same reviewer suggested adopting the categories S, A, P, T and R in the analysis. Although these categories are useful in typological studies, they don't necessarily capture the morphosyntactic patterns of individual languages. For example, since R is defined as the third syntactic argument of 'GIVE' verbs (the smallest class in Yaqui), another term would be needed for the indirect/oblique object of the other three verb classes (the most productive classes), as these arguments have many of the same properties as objects (and are not adjuncts).

(18) a. *u-Ø   jamut-Ø   tomi-ta   mesa-po   jo'a-k.*
DET-NOM woman-NOM money-ACC table-LOC lay.PL-PFV
'The woman put the money on the table.'

b. *u-Ø   jamut-Ø   Jose-ta   tomi-ta   mesa-po*
DET-NOM woman-NOM Joseph-ACC money-ACC table-LOC
jo'a-ria-k.
lay.PL-APPL-PFV
'The woman put the money on the table (for) Joseph.'

In sum, *-ria* behaves differently when combined with three-place predicates. With the first and third classes, *-ria* increases the semantic and syntactic valency of the underived verb by adding the Beneficiary that receives the Theme and an accusative direct core argument to the clause. However, *-ria* is avoided if the base verb already profiles/"subcategorizes" for a Beneficiary (e.g., 'give'). With members of the second class such as *nenka* 'sell', *teuwa* 'tell', *mabeta* 'receive' and *jinu* 'buy', *-ria* behaves unexpectedly: it does not introduce an extra-thematic Beneficiary participant, but it changes the case marking of one of the non-Actor core arguments: the AppP is the Recipient, the Addressee, the Source or the Goal. Because there is a transfer of the Theme between two other participants, they are all interpreted as recipient-benefactives. As I will show in the next section, I consider these derived ACs to be typical because of the behavior of the AppP.

3.4 The status of typical AppP

It is clear that *-ria* is an applicative morpheme that marks a participant usually encoded as an adjunct or with oblique case, to be coded as a direct core argument. Semantically, the AppP denotes a human or animate participant with different semantic roles (amused Beneficiary, Recipient, Goal, Addressee, or Source) which is affected by the denoted event. Animate Comitatives, inanimate Goals/Recipients, Sources, Locations, and Instruments cannot be expressed as AppPs, but only as adjuncts; compare (19a) and (19b).

(19) a.* *inepo   bwa'a-ta   ota-ta   toi-ria-k.*
1SG.NOM soup-ACC bone-ACC bring-APPL-PFV
'I brought a bone (for) the soup.'

b. *inepo   ota-ta   toja-k   bwa'a-ta-betchi'ibo.*
1SG.NOM bone-ACC bring-PFV soup-ACC-for
'I brought a bone for the soup.'

Therefore, typical ACs in Yaqui correspond to benefactive constructions since the applicative most often occurs on two- and three-place predicates (and not on one-place predicate), and the AppP refers to an animate participant which is advantageously affected by the denoted event (Kittilä and Zúñiga 2010). When the underived verb is a one-place predicate, there is a plain-benefactive reading; otherwise, the AC expresses a recipient-benefactive situation.

Syntactically, the AppP is a direct core argument marked by accusative case and occupies the object position (i.e., it appears pre-verbally). Consequently, syntactically intransitive-based ACs have one accusative direct core argument (AppP), transitive-based ACs have two accusative direct arguments (Theme and AppP), and ditransitive-based ACs have two accusative direct core arguments (Theme and AppP) plus an oblique core argument; a few ditransitive verbs may have three accusative direct core arguments (e.g., the Theme, the Beneficiary, and the Source in (14d)). When a clause shows more than one accusative direct core argument, one may wonder if the arguments behave similarly. In order to determine the syntactic status of double-object constructions in Yaqui, Rude (1996) and Guerrero and Van Valin (2004) examined passivization, cliticization, right-dislocation, reflexivization, relativization, and adjective-marking processes. The two objects have equal access to all these syntactic functions except passive voice. I begin the discussion with the passive versions of non-applicativized three-place predicates in (14) to (18). The passive version of *miika* 'give' in (20a) involves the beneficiary as the passive subject (primary object pattern). By contrast, the passive versions of *nenka* 'sell' (20b), and *jo'a* 'put/lay' (20c) must take the Theme as the passive subject since oblique core arguments cannot satisfy this syntactic function (secondary object pattern).

(20) a. Lupe-Ø   soto'i-ta   miika-wa-k.   (=(14a))
        Lupe-NOM pot-ACC   give-PASS-PFV
        'Lupe was given a pot.'

   b. u-Ø   kowi-Ø   u-e   jamut-ta-u   nenka-wa-k. (=(15a))
       DET-NOM   pig-NOM DET-OBL   woman-ACC-DIR   sell-PASS-PFV
       'The pig was sold to the woman.'

   c. u-Ø   tomi-Ø   mesa-po   jo'a-wa-k.   (=(18a))
       DET-NOM   money-NOM   table-LOC   lay.PL-PASS-PFV
       'The money was put on the table.'

Because the AppP introduced by *-ria* in Yaqui is an animate participant marked with accusative case, it is also expected to act as the passive subject (primary object pattern). My consultants avoid the impersonal/passive versions of applicative clauses based on one-place predicates, as shown in (21a) and (21b). The AppP of applicative clauses derived from two- and three-place predicates does serve as the passive subject, as can be seen in (21c) to (21g). No other syntactic constituent in (21c)–(21g) could function as the subject of the passive clause.

(21) a. ?? *enchi   bwika-ria-wa-k.*   (=(9c))
       2SG.ACC   sing-APPL-IMPRS-PFV
       '(someone) was sung for you.'

   b. ?? *Peo-Ø   siim-ria-wa-k.*   (=(10d))
       Peter-NOM   go.SG-APPL-PASS-PFV
       'Peter was abandoned.'

   c. *Maria-Ø   u-ka   bwa'am-ta   joa-ria-wa-k.*   (=(12b))
       Mary-NOM   DET-ACC   food-ACC   cook-APPL-PASS-PFV
       'Mary was cooked the food.'

   d. *Joana-Ø   Lupe-ta   tomi-ta   u'ura-ria-k.*   (=(14d))
       Juana-NOM Lupe-ACC   money-ACC take-APPL-PFV
       'Juana was taken the money from Lupe (for).'

   e. *u-Ø   jamut-Ø   kowi'i-ta   nenka-ria-wa-ne.*   (=(15b))
       DET-NOM   woman-NOM   pig-ACC   sell-APPL-PASS-POT
       'The woman will be sold the pig.'

   f. *Jose-Ø   tomi-ta   mesa-po   jo'a-ria-wa-k.*   (=(18b))
       Joseph-NOM money-ACC   table-LOC lay.PL-APPL-PFV
       'Joseph was put the money on the table (for).'

4 Atypical applicative constructions

Not all AppPs show the semantic and syntactic properties typical of ACs. At least two unusual applicative constructions have been identified so far in Yaqui: those involving Actor-Beneficiary coreference (§4.1) and those denoting a Possessor as the Beneficiary (§4.2). The status of the AppP in atypical ACs is discussed in §4.3.

4.1 Self-benefactive Acs

While some languages simply ban Agent-Beneficiary coreference, other languages use a specialized construction in this context, e.g., a self-benefactive or auto-benefactive construction (Kittilä and Zúñiga 2010: 4). Direct reflexive constructions in Yaqui involve two-place predicates in which the Actor serves as the antecedent and the Patient is coded by an anaphoric pronoun; compare (22a) and (22b). In (22a), *bicha* 'see' takes a non-coreferential Actor and Patient; hence there is an accusative NP. In the reflexive construction in (22b), the two participants are coreferential and there is a reflexive pronoun. The reflexive pronoun counts as a syntactic argument since it must occur with the syntactically transitive verb form *omta* (22c) rather than *omte* 'hate/get mad' (22d).

(22) a. *Pati-Ø   Leo-ta   bicha-k.*
       Paty-NOM Leo-ACC   see-PFV
       'Paty saw Leo.'

   b. *Pati-Ø   ejpeeko-po   emo   bicha-k.*
       Paty-NOM mirror-LOC   REFL   see-PFV
       'Paty saw herself in the mirror.'

   c. *inepo   ino   omta-Ø.*
       1SG.NOM   1SG.REFL   angry.TR-PRS
       'I hate myself.'

   d.* *inepo   ino   omte-Ø*
        1SG.NOM   1SG.REFL   angry.INTR-PRS
        'I hate myself.'

Within indirect reflexive constructions, the Actor is coreferential with a Goal, Recipient, or Beneficiary participant. Dedrick and Casad (1999: 290) were the first to comment that the "applicative activity can be reflexive, i.e., one can do something on his/her own behalf." In the BC in (23a), the Actor and the adjunct Beneficiary are coreferential; in the AC in (23b), the Actor and the Beneficiary AppP also refer to the same participant. Note that the pronominal coding of the AppP differs. In the BC, the Beneficiary is expressed by an oblique pronoun since Yaqui reflexive pronouns are not compatible with postpositions (Guerrero, in press a). In the AC, the AppP is coded by a reflexive pronoun (23b).

(23) a. *inepo   kari-ta   ya'a-k   ne-betchi'ibo.*
       1SG.NOM   house-ACC   make-PFV   1SG.OBL-for
       'I made a house for myself.'

b. *inepo   kari-ta   ino   ya'a-ria-k.*
   1SG.NOM house-ACC 1SG.REFL   make-APPL-PFV
   'I made a house for myself.'

Yaqui is thus a good example of a language that makes use of self-benefactive applicative clauses. Nevertheless, this construction has some limitations when compared to typical ACs. For instance, it cannot serve as the passive subject. In fact, self-benefactive ACs avoid *wa*-clauses. (24a) was intended as an impersonal clause, and (24b), (24c) and (24d) as passive clauses. They were all rejected by my consultants.

(24) a.* *kari-ta   ino   jinu-ria-wa-k.*
         house-ACC   1SG.REFL   buy-APPL-IMPRS-PFV
         '(Someone) bought a house (for) me/myself.'

   b.* *kari-Ø   ino   jinu-ria-wa-k.*
       house-NOM   1SG.REFL   buy-APPL-PASS-PFV
       'A house was bought (for) me/myself.'

   c.* *ino   kari-ta   jinu-ria-wa-k.*
       1SG.REFL   house-ACC   buy-APPL-IMPRS-PFV
       'Myself was bought a house.'

   d.* *inepo   kari-ta   ino   jinu-ria-wa-k.*
       1SG.NOM   house-ACC   1SG.REFL   buy-APPL-PASS-PFV
       'I was bought a house (for) myself.'

Whereas the ungrammaticality of (24c) can be explained by the fact that reflexive pronouns are banned from subject position, this restriction does not explain the ungrammaticality of the impersonal clause in (24a) with the Theme maintaining its coding as accusative direct core argument, the passive clause in (24b) with the Theme serving as the passive subject, or the passive clause in (24d) with the Beneficiary functioning as the subject.[10] The fact that *wa*-clauses were deemed ungrammatical lends weight to the claim that the AppP in self-benefactive ACs behaves atypically.

---

[10] The clause *inepo kari-ta jinu-ria-wa-k* 'I was bought a house' is grammatical in Yaqui, but it is not the passive counterpart of (23b). This clause is understood to mean that someone else bought me a house.

4.2 Possessor-benefactive ACs

As many other languages, Yaqui has several types of possessive constructions, including some subtypes of external possession (Guerrero 2020). In (25a), *baksia* 'wash' takes two direct core arguments: a nominative NP as the Actor, and an internal possessive phrase as the Patient/Theme. In (25b), *-ria* allows the coding of three core arguments: the Actor, the Theme, and the Possessor of the Theme. The derived AC is an instance of external possession since the Possessed entity 'mouth' and the Possessor 'you' are two independent constituents that receive accusative case.

(25) a. Ma'e-Ø   em   tem-ta   baksia-k.
        mother-NOM   2SG.POSS   mouth-ACC   wash-PFV
        'Mother washed your mouth.'

   b. Ma'e-Ø   tem-ta   enchi   baksia-ria-k.
        mother-NOM   mouth-ACC   2SG.ACC   wash-APPL-PFV
        'Mother washed your mouth.' (lit. washed you the mouth)

Possessor-benefactive ACs in Yaqui commonly involve body parts, as seen in (25b), as well as some part-whole relations, as in (26a) and (26b), and the ownership of garments or other unique objects such as water, domestic animals, or kitchen artefacts, as in (26c) and (26d). Note that the AppPs in the first two clauses correspond to an inanimate Possessor, a possibility that is banned in typical ACs.

(26) a. kandaom=te   pueta-ta   jinu-ria-bae.
        padlock.PL=1PL.NOM   door-ACC   buy-APPL-want
        'We want to buy a padlock (for) the door.' (lit: the padlock the door)

   b. karo-ta=te   maniam   tu'ute-ria-k.
        car-ACC=1PL.NOM   brake.PL   fix-APPL-PFV
        'We fixed the car's brakes.' (lit: the brakes the car)

   c. u-ka   kaba'i-ta   bato'im   nee   a=bwa'a-su-ria-k.
        DET-ACC   horse-ACC   people.PL   1SG.ACC   3SG.ACC=eat-CMPL-APPL-PFV
        'With respect to the horse, the people eat it.' (lit. eat me the horse)
        (Buitimea 2007: pueplou 59)

   d. soto'i-ta=ne   jamut-ta   jamta-ria-k.
        pot-ACC=1SG.NOM   woman-ACC   break.TR-APPL-PFV
        'I broke the woman's pot.' (lit. broke the pot the woman)

According to Kittilä and Zúñiga (2010: 20), the motivation behind the overlapping of benefaction and possession is that "actions targeted at entities in my possession affect me in a more direct fashion, and usually in more ways, than actions that are only carried out instead of me. This is especially evident in the case of external possession, where the effect is often beneficial." In Yaqui, the Possessor AppP can be interpreted as being positively affected, as in (25b), (26a) and (26b), or negatively affected, as in (26c) and (26d). Since there are two accusative direct arguments in these ACs, the expected pattern would be for the applied Possessor to act as the passive subject. However, impersonal clauses are preferred in this context. The grammatical impersonal *wa*-clause for 'Mother washed your mouth' is shown in (27a); the passive *wa*-clauses in (27a')–(27a") are ruled out. For 'I broke the woman's pot', two consultants offered the impersonal clause in (27b); the passive version in (27b') with the possessed Theme as the passive subject was provided by one consultant and rejected by two others.[11] Again, the behavior of the AppP in possessor-benefactive constructions is unexpected because it cannot serve as the passive subject.

(27) a.   *tem-ta*   *enchi*   *baksia-ria-wa-k.*
       mouth-ACC   2SG.ACC   wash-APPL-IMPRS-PFV
       '(Someone) washed your mouth.'

---

11 One reviewer argued that the passive version of (27d) is possible and corresponds to (i). I agree that (i) is grammatical but it was not offered by any of my consultants as the passive counterpart of (26d). In the context of 'the woman' owning 'the pot', they considered (i) nonsensical because "either the woman broke the pot on behalf of someone else or the woman isn't the owner of the pot and, in that case, why bother mentioning it". My consultants provided the clause with a benefactive adjunct in (ii) as well as the impersonal and passive examples in (27b–b') as passive counterparts of (26d). Note that (ii) can be read as a deputative-benefactive ('someone else broke the pot in place of the woman') or plain-benefactive ('the woman was benefitted in some way by the pot's breaking'). In both scenarios, the woman was not the pot's owner. I agree with the reviewer that Yaqui passivization needs to be researched further.

(i)   *jamut-Ø*   *soto'i-ta*   *jamta-ria-wa-k.*
      woman-NOM   pot-ACC   break.TR-APPL-PASS-PFV
      'The woman was broken the pot.'

(ii)   *soto'i-Ø*   *jamta-wa-k*   *jamut-ta-betchi'ibo.*
      pot-NOM   break.TR-PASS-PFV   woman-ACC-for
      'The pot was broken on behalf/instead of the woman.'

a'.* *empo*   *tem-ta*   *baksia-ria-wa-k.*
      2SG.NOM   mouth-ACC   wash-APPL-PASS-PFV
      Intended: The mouth was washed (for) you.

a''.* *tem-Ø*   *enchi*   *baksia-ria-wa-k.*
      mouth-NOM 2SG.ACC   wash-APPL-PASS-PFV
      Intended: The mouth was washed (for) you.

b.   *soto'i-ta*   *jamut-ta*   *jamta-ria-wa-k.*
      pot-ACC   woman-ACC   break.TR-APPL-IMPRS-PFV
      '(Someone) broke the woman's pot.'

b'.#* *soto'i-Ø*   *jamut-ta*   *jamta-ria-wa-k.*
      pot-NOM   woman-ACC   break.TR-APPL-PASS-PFV
      'The woman's pot was broken.'

4.3 The status of atypical AppPs

Semantically, the AppP in self- and possessor-benefactive ACs can refer to the Actor or the Theme's Possessor and can be inanimate if there is an inherent possessive relationship with the theme. Syntactically, the AppP is coded as a direct core argument, but it has fewer morphosyntactic properties if compared to typical AppP. In accordance with these data, I argue that the AppP in self- and possessor-benefactive ACs is a half-way promoted argument: it functions as a direct core argument, but it cannot function as the passive subject.

5 The discourse-functional use of applicative constructions

According to Peterson (2007: 83), the function of applicative constructions in the world's languages is to indicate that "the [AppP] entity the construction refers to has a greater discourse salience or topic continuity than would otherwise be expected of it." Consequently, there is a tendency for ACs in discourse to give attenuated (pronominal or zero) expression to the AppP, especially when they refer to animate entities, since animate participants such as beneficiaries show a higher degree of topic continuity and topic worthiness than patient and (most) oblique objects (Peterson 2007: 232–234). Yaqui closely follows these discourse patterns. As expected, recipient-benefactives like those illustrated in (28a–c) are very common in Yaqui oral texts. An example of self-benefactive

ACs is offered in (28d). With few exceptions, see, e.g., (28a), the AppP is realized as an anaphoric pronominal element. In the following examples from oral texts, the AppP is in bold.

(28) a. *'abue_'achai 'itepo tua 'i-ka'a 'ili 'uusi Chirindo-ta*
grandfather 1PL.NOM INT DEM-ACC little child Chirindo-ACC
tekil-ta jariu-ria-Ø.
work-ACC look-APPL-PRS
'Grandfather, we're looking for work for this little Chirindo.'
(Johnson 1962; Chirindo: 203)

b. *si'ime-ta a=etejo-ria-k.*
everything-ACC 3SG.ACC-tell-APPL-PFV
'And she told him everything.'
(Silva et al. 1998; gato_salvaje: 23)

c. *ne-u yepsa-ka inen te'eka:*
1SG.OBL-DIR arrive.SG-CLM DEM say
*ili ujbwan-ta **nee** ya'a-ria-ne.*
little favor-ACC 1SG.ACC do-APPL-POT
'He came to me and said this: Do me a small favor!'
(Buitimea 2007; maejto: 91)

d. *junama'a **emo** ji'i-bwa-jariu-ria-ne, ju'u-Ø mochik-Ø.*
there REFL thing-eat-look-APPL-POT DET-NOM turtle-NOM
'With respect to the turtle, she will look for something to eat around there.'
(Silva et al. 1998; tortuga: 5)

I have observed that possessor-benefactive ACs are more common in life stories than other narrative texts such as folk stories and conversations. In life stories, the speaker talks about personal things and experiences that have happened to them or someone close to them. Although recipient-benefactives are present in these texts, possessor-benefactive/malefactive readings are much more common. Take for example Hilario's life story. Hilario was a child when the Mexican Revolution began. In the story referenced here, he told of how many Yaqui fled from the mountain to avoid being captured by soldiers, and how he and some of his family members were captured. In the excerpt in (29) he tells of the moment in which he arrived at the military camp, and how he and the others were bathed and had their heads and mustaches shaved off. The event of forced shaving in (29c) provides an example of an AppP that has been negatively affected. The excerpt in (30) describes the moment in which Hilario requested that he be dismissed from the army; since he could not read or write, someone else prepared and signed the request form for him. The two ACs here are positively affected. Finally, after leaving the army, Hilario got a job watering the fields; in (31) he tells of how two non-Yaqui Mexicans cut off the water so he couldn't water the fields and kept him from doing his work. This is yet another example of a negatively-affected AppP.

(29) a. *yokoria-po   pelukeo-Ø   ito-u   toji-wa-k,*
       next_day-LOC   barber-NOM   1PL.OBL-DIR   bring-PASS-PFV

   b. *si   lo-lobo-la   sika'a-wa-k,*
      INT   RED-bald-ADJV   cut_hair-PASS-PFV

   c. *ju-me'e jimse-ka-me   into   **am**=bekta-ria-wa-k.*
      DET-PL   mustache-PFV-NMLZ   and   3PL.ACC=shave-APPL-PASS-PFV
      'The next day a barber was brought to us, we were shaved bald, and those with mustaches had them shaved off.'
      (Silva 2004; HVH: 87–89)

(30) a. *junak=bea   **n**=a   ya'a-ria-wa-k   ju-ka'a*
       then=DM   1SG.NOM=3SG.ACC   make-APPL-PASS-PFV   DET-ACC
       solisitu-ta,
       request-ACC

   b. *junak=bea   **n**=a   firmaroa-ria-wa-k.*
      then=DM   1SG.NOM=3SG.ACC   sign-APPL-PASS-PFV
      'Then they completed the form for me and signed it.'
      (Silva 2004; HVH: 308–309)

(31) *sejtul ta'a-po   into   waate   yoeme-m   **nee**   ba'a-ta*
     one   day-LOC   DM   DEM   people-PL   1SG.ACC   water-ACC
     patta-ria-k.
     stop-APPL-PFV
     'And one day, some people deprived me of the water.'
     (Silva 2004; HVH: 337)

In Lalo's life story, quoted below, Lalo's mother tells of the adventures, mishaps, and multiple accidents her son had experienced in his short life. At the moment the text was collected, Lalo was ten years old and had had an accident and had been taken to the hospital just the day before. In the ACs below, the AppP is coded pronominally and expresses an extra-thematic salient participant that has been negatively affected in the extreme: in (32b) and (33a–b) this participant is Lalo's mother, while in (34b) and (35) it is Lalo himself.

(32) a. ne   nuen   jiba   ne   eme-u   jia-n   kee
1SG.NOM like.this always 1SG.NOM 2PL.OBL-DIR say-IPFV that

b. inen   jiba   **nee**   a=joo-ria-n,   u-ka   ili
DEM always 1SG.ACC 3SG.ACC=hurt-APPL-IPFV DET-ACC little
usi-ta=ti
child-ACC=CLM

c. ne   a-u   jia,   u-e   maejtra-ta-wi.
1SG.NOM 2SG.OBL-DIR say DET-OBL teacher-ACC-DIR
'I told them that my little boy was always getting mistreated, so I told the teacher.' (Guerrero; HVL: 19–20)

(33) a. porque   tua   jiba   **nee**   nuen   a=joo-ria-Ø
because INT always 1SG.ACC like.this 3SG.ACC=hurt-APPL-PRS
untuchi
also

b. naa=bea   untuchi   inen   **nee**   a=bek-ria-Ø.
again=DM also like.this 1SG.ACC 3SG.ACC=hit-APPL-PRS
'Because they always hurt him [my boy], again and again they beat him.'
(Guerrero; HVL: 41–42)

(34) a. naa=bea   ama-u   bicha   u-ka   ili   usi-ta   yoria-ka
DM=DM there-DIR toward DET-ACC little child-ACC swing-CLM

b. junak=bea   mamam   ama-u   bichaa   **a=totta-ria-k**
then=DM harm.PL there-DIR toward 3SG.ACC=hit-APPL-PFV
a=jamta-ria-k.
3SG.ACC=break-APPL-PFV
'So when he was swinging (my) boy back, he bent his hand back, he broke it (to) him.'
(Guerrero; HVL: 150–151)

(35) a. doctor-Ø   into   inen   ori   nau   bichaa   **ime'e**
doctor-NOM and like.this DM together toward DEM.PL
ore-ria-k
put-APPL-PFV

b. *naa=bea   tosisisi-ta   aman   a=ore-ria-k,*
   DM=DM   crack-ACC   there   3SG.ACC=put-APPL-PFV
   u-Ø   *doctor-Ø*   *ousi*   *jia;*
   DET-NOM   doctor-NOM   a.lot   noise
   chukula *aman*   *am*   ***a**=ore-ria-su-wa-k.*
   later   there   3PL.ACC 3SG.ACC=put-CMPL-APPL-IMPRS-PFV

'So then the doctor set it [the arm] like this, facing outward; then the doctor cracked it [the arm] (to) him, it made a lot of noise; then a bit later they finished setting it (to) him.'
(Guerrero; HVL: 316–319)

6 Final comments

The data analyzed in this chapter show that applicative *-ria* in Yaqui optionally introduces a participant which can be coded as a benefactive adjunct or an oblique core argument in the construction of the root. The AppP introduced by *-ria* is a human or animate participant that is positively or negatively affected in some way by the denoted event. Still, the AppP may be inanimate when it is in a part-whole possessive relationship with a Theme in an external possession construction. By contrast, the AppP shows variable syntactic behavior. Within the most common and typical construction type, recipient-benefactive ACs, not only is the AppP a direct core argument, but it also displaces the Theme as the passive subject. Within the atypical constructions expressing self-benefactive and possessor-benefactive meanings, the AppP is partially promoted: it is coded as a direct core argument, but it cannot serve as the passive subject. The feature that self-benefactive and possessor-benefactive ACs seem to share is that the AppP is not maximally distinguished from the Actor or the Theme. In self-benefactive ACs, the Actor and the reflexive AppP refer to the same person; in possessor-benefactives, the Theme and the Possessor AppP also refer to the same person (or the person and one of their body parts or belongings). Based on Kemmer's (1993) notion of a "relative elaboration event", Næss (2007: 22) proposes that a central factor influencing the elaboration of a transitive event is the distinguishability of the participants, i.e., we expect the Actor and the Patient/Theme to be physically and conceptually distinct from each other. As such, the AppP in Yaqui applicative constructions must be conceptually distinct from other direct core arguments to show all the morphosyntactic privileges.

I have also provided evidence that applicative constructions are common in Yaqui narratives. Some discourse genres seem to favor atypical ACs. In particular, life stories show a preference for possessor-benefactives. Despite the fact that the AppP within atypical ACs is only partially promoted, its semantic and discourse functions are the same as those of typical ACs: they highlight a discourse salient participant who is affected by the ongoing situations in the narrative.

Finally, this study has highlighted several promising research topics that are beyond the scope of the current chapter (but which I am currently exploring using Yaqui data). These include the causative-applicative syncretism found with some derived verbs, the malefactive readings of the AppP, the subtypes of benefactive situations, and the semantic/pragmatic restrictions found in impersonal and passive *wa*-clauses.

Abbreviations

1	first person
2	second person
3	third person
ABS	absolutive
ACC	accusative
ADJV	adjectival
AGTV	agentivizer
APPL	applicative
CAUS	cause
CLM	clause linkage marker
COMPL	completive
DAT	dative
DEM	demonstrative
DET	determiner
DIR	directional
DM	discourse marker
EMPH	emphatic
ERG	ergative
IMPRS	impersonal
IPFV	imperfective
INT	intensifier
INS	instrument
INTR	intransitive
LOC	locative
NEG	negation
NOM	nominative
OBL	oblique
PASS	passive
PFV	perfective

PL	plural
POSS	possessive
POT	potential
PRS	present
RED	reduplication
REFL	reflexive
SG	singular
TR	transitive
VBLZ	verbalizer.

References

Álvarez, Albert. 2007. Eventos no-agentivos, alternancia causativo/incoativo y gramaticalización en lengua yaqui. *Lingüística Mexicana* IV (1). 5–29.

Buitimea, Crescencio. 2007. *Peesio Betana Nottiwame. Regreso de Hermosillo*. Hermosillo: Uson.

Buelna, Eustaquio. 1890. *El arte de la lengua cahita*. México: Siglo XXI.

Creissels, Denis. 2016. Transitivity, valency and voice. Course given at the European Summer School in Linguistic Typology, Porquerolles. http://www.deniscreissels.fr/public/Creissels-ESSLT.pdf (accessed 22 January 2021).

Dedrick, John & Eugene Casad. 1999. *Sonora Yaqui language structures*. Tucson: University of Arizona Press.

Estrada, Zarina, Mercedes Tubino & Jesús Villalpando. 2015. Valency classes in Yaqui. In Andrej Malchukov & Bernard Comrie (eds.), *Valency classes in the world's languages*, 1359–1390. Berlin: Mouton de Gruyter.

Guerrero, Lilián. n.d. HVL (oral text).

Guerrero, Lilián. 2006. *The structure and function of Yaqui complementation*. Munich: Lincom.

Guerrero, Lilián. 2007. Estructuras argumentales alternativas: las cláusulas aplicativas en yaqui. In Zarina Estrada, Albert Álvarez, Lilián Guerrero, & María Belén Carpio (eds.), *Mecanismos de voz y formación de palabra*, 177–204. México/Hermosillo: Plaza y Valdés/Universidad de Sonora.

Guerrero, Lilián. 2008. Yaqui causation, its form-function interface. In Zarina Estrada, Søren Wichmann, Claudine Chamoreau & Albert Álvarez (eds.), *Studies in voice and transitivity*, 201–221. Munich: Lincom.

Guerrero, Lilián. 2014. ¿Sustantivos plurales, *pluralia tantum* o clases de sustantivos? La codificación de plural en lenguas yutoaztecas. In Rebeca Barriga & Esther Herrera Zendejas (eds.), *Lenguas, estructuras y hablantes. Estudios en homenaje a Thomas C. Smith Stark*. Vol. 2, 619–642. México: Colmex.

Guerrero, Lilián. 2019. Grammatical relations in Yaqui. In Alena Witzlack-Makarevich & Balthasar Bickel (eds.), *Argument selectors: A new perspective on grammatical relations*, 433–467. Amsterdam: John Benjamins.

Guerrero, Lilián. 2020. Yaqui possessive constructions: evidence for external possession. *Amerindia* 42. 75–101.

Guerrero, Lilián. In press (a). Reflexive constructions in Yaqui. In Katarzyna Janic, Nicoletta Puddu & Martin Haspelmath (eds.), *Reflexive constructions in the world's languages*. Berlin: Language Science Press.

Guerrero, Lilián. In press (b). Transitivity and split argument coding in Yaqui. *International Journal of American Linguistics* 88: 4.

Guerrero, Lilián & Robert Van Valin. 2004. Yaqui and the analysis of primary object language. *International Journal of American Linguistics* 70(3). 290–319.

Harley, Heidi, Mercedes Tubino & Jason Haugen. 2009. Applicative constructions and suppletive verbs in Hiaki (Yaqui). *Rice Working Papers in Linguistics* 1. 42–51.

Harley, Heidi, Mercedes Tubino & Jason Haugen. 2017. Locality conditions on suppletive verbs in Hiaki. In Vera Gribanova & Stephanie S. Shih (eds.), *The morphosyntax-phonology connection*, 91–112. Oxford: Oxford University Press.

Johnson, Jean B. 1962. *El idioma yaqui*. México: Instituto Nacional de Antropología e Historia.

Kemmer, Suzanne. 1993. *The middle voice*. Amsterdam: John Benjamins.

Kittilä, Seppo. 2005. Recipient prominence vs. beneficiary prominence. *Linguistic Typology* 9(2). 269–297.

Kittilä, Seppo & Fernando Zúñiga. 2010. Introduction: Benefaction and malefaction from a cross-linguistic perspective. In Fernando Zúñiga & Seppo Kittilä (eds.), *Benefactives and malefactives: Typological perspectives and case studies*, 1–28. Amsterdam: John Benjamins.

Langacker, Roland W. 1977. *An overview of Uto-Aztecan grammar: Studies in Uto-Aztecan grammar, Vo1. 1*. Dallas: Summer Institute of Linguistics/University of Texas at Arlington.

Lindenfeld, Jacqueline. 1973. *Yaqui syntax*. Berkeley: University of California.

Næss, Åshild. 2007. *Prototypical transitivity*. Amsterdam: John Benjamins.

Peterson, David A. 2007. *Applicative constructions*. Oxford: Oxford University Press.

Rincón, Antonio del. 1595. *Arte mexicana compuesta por el padre Antonio del Rincón de la Compañía de Jesús*. México: Oficina Tipográfica de la Secretaría de Fomento.

Rude, Noel. 1996. Objetos dobles y relaciones gramaticales: el caso del yaqui, in Zarina Estrada, Max Figueroa & Gerardo López (eds.), *Memorias del III Encuentro de Lingüística en el Noroeste*, 491–522. México: Uson.

Shibatani, Masayoshi. 1996. Applicatives and benefactives: a cognitive account. In Masayoshi Shibatani & Sandra Thompson (eds.), *Grammatical constructions: Their form and meaning*, 157–194. Oxford: Oxford University Press.

Silva, Carlos. 2004. *La secuencia temporal en el discurso narrativo en lengua yaqui*. Hermosillo: Universidad de Sonora M.A. thesis. (Annex: HVH oral text).

Silva, Carlos, Pablo Álvarez, & Cresencio Buitimea. 1998. *Jiak nokpo etejoim, Pláticas en lengua yaqui*. Hermosillo: Uson.

Tubino Blanco, Mercedes. 2017. Sufijos de transitividad en lengua yaqui y su impacto en la sintaxis. *Cuadernos de Lingüística* 4(2). 1–41.

Van Valin, Robert. 2005. *Exploring the syntax-semantics interface*. Cambridge: Cambridge University Press.

Van Valin, Robert & Randy LaPolla. 1997. *Syntax: Structure, meaning, and function*. Cambridge: Cambridge University Press.

Zúñiga, Fernando & Seppo Kittilä. 2019. *Grammatical voice*. Cambridge: Cambridge University Press.

Martin Kohlberger
3 The functions of applicative morphology in Shiwiar

Abstract: Shiwiar is a Chicham language spoken by about 1,200 people in eastern Ecuador and northern Peru. Like many other languages of the region, Shiwiar exhibits an array of valency-changing morphology, including an applicative morpheme. In this chapter, the grammatical role of the Shiwiar applicative will be discussed based on data from a 30-hour audiovisual documentary corpus of natural speech collected between 2011 and 2016 in Ecuador. The Shiwiar applicative can raise the valency of a verb by introducing a novel object argument, typically one that has the semantics of a beneficiary or an experiencer. However, the same morpheme can also appear without triggering a change in valency, for example when it is used in discourse to highlight a notional location or when it is used to verbalise a noun.

1 Introduction

An applicative construction is typically defined in morphological and syntactic terms as a derivational process (usually involving a bound morpheme) that increases the syntactic valency of a verb by introducing a non-agentive participant as an additional core argument of a predicate (Kulikov 2011; Mithun 2001; Peterson 2007; *inter alia*). Constructions that fit this description are widespread in northwestern Amazonian languages (Crevels & van der Voort 2020; Valenzuela 2010; Valenzuela 2016; Vallejos 2014; Wise 2002). However, in many languages of the region, applicative constructions also have further discourse-oriented and derivational functions which do not fall under the canonical definition, namely location highlighting and denominal verbalisation. This chapter will exemplify these functions by describing the use of applicative morphology in Shiwiar, a language of Ecuador and Peru.[1]

---

[1] I am indebted to all my Shiwiar collaborators, in particular Verónica Suquilanda and Francisco Timias who were central in the collection and analysis of the data presented in this chapter.

Martin Kohlberger, University of Saskatchewan, Department of Linguistics, 9 Campus Drive, Saskatoon, SK, Canada, e-mail: martin.kohlberger@usask.ca

In section 2, the Shiwiar people and language are introduced along with a description of the sources and the layout of the examples in this work. Section 3 summarises how grammatical relations are expressed in Shiwiar. Section 4 provides a description of the syntactic functions of the Shiwiar applicative morpheme as well as a thorough account of the allomorphy it exhibits.[2] The two non-canonical functions of the Shiwiar applicative are laid out in section 5, namely the use of applicative morphology to highlight notional locations and their function as deverbal nominalisers. Finally, section 6 concludes this chapter by summarising the insights from Shiwiar applicatives and by offering methodological recommendations for future studies.

2 Shiwiar people and their language

The Shiwiar Nation is one of the fifteen officially recognised Indigenous nations in Ecuador (CODENPE 2015). According to census data, 1,198 people identify as Shiwiar (INEC 2010). The Shiwiar language – referred to locally as *shiwiar chicham* – is a member of the Chicham[3] family and it is spoken by the vast majority of Shiwiar people. Although Shiwiar is the primary language of the Shiwiar Nation, most Shiwiar people also speak Northern Pastaza Kichwa (an unrelated Quechuan language) and Spanish. The Shiwiar Nation is located at the heart of a particularly linguistically diverse corner of northwestern Amazonia, so Shiwiar people have long been in close proximity to speakers of many different language families (including Quechuan, Zaparoan and Kawapanan) and isolates (including Kandozi-Chapra, Taushiro and Wao). A comprehensive description of the language and its historical and socio-cultural context can be found in Kohlberger (2020).

The data discussed in this paper are taken from a 30-hour corpus of natural speech. The corpus was recorded and transcribed between 2011 and 2016 as a collaborative effort involving 30 Shiwiar people and the author. It consists of over

---

I am very grateful to Sara Pacchiarotti, Fernando Zúñiga and two anonymous reviewers for their thorough and insightful comments on earlier versions of this work, as well as for their patience and encouragement. All shortcomings of this chapter are mine.
2 A brief discussion of Shiwiar applicative morphology can be found in section 8.2.2 of the author's doctoral dissertation (Kohlberger 2020: 297–301). Although based on that description, this paper has been expanded to include broader considerations.
3 The Chicham language family was formerly referred to as the Jivaroan language family. The latter term is deemed offensive by many speakers of Chicham languages, so at the request of Chicham scholars the name of the language family has been changed (Deshoulliere & Utitiaj Paati 2020; Katan Jua 2011; Overall & Kohlberger *forthcoming*).

100 recordings, spanning a range of genres that include day-to-day conversations, anecdotes, political speeches, radio interviews, autobiographical accounts and traditional narratives.

The fact that the data are drawn from a corpus of natural speech is particularly significant for the analysis in this chapter given that the full breadth of uses of applicative morphology would have been difficult or impossible to gather using elicitation. As will be argued further in 5.1, the frequent use of Shiwiar applicative morphology to express notional locations is only made apparent through the lens of richly contextualised discourse.

Examples in this text are presented in 6 lines. The first line is a broad phonetic transcription of the utterance in IPA. The second line is an italicised and morphologically-parsed phonological abstraction, following the conventions established in Kohlberger (2020).[4] Loanwords are identified in this line by subscripted square brackets with an abbreviation of the source language, e.g. *pero*$_{[Sp]}$ indicates that the word *pero* is a loanword from Spanish. The third line contains the English glosses that correspond to the morphemes in line 2. A full list of glosses used can be found at the end of this chapter. If the text in a particular example is too long for a single line 2 and line 3, these two are continued below in indented lines. The fourth and fifth lines are free translations into English and Spanish respectively. Note that the Spanish translations in line 5 are part of the original documentation and were produced by bilingual Shiwiar-Spanish speakers (and thus are written in local Ecuadorean Spanish), whereas the English translations in line 4 were added by the author. Finally, the sixth line contains the name of the recording and the time stamp of the utterance. More detailed information about the compilation and curation of the corpus (including a description of the method used for naming recordings) can be found in Kohlberger (2020: 73–81).

3 Grammatical relations in Shiwiar

Shiwiar has strict nominative-accusative alignment, and grammatical relations in the language primarily revolve around the distinction between subject and object.[5]

---

4 These conventions include representing allophones by a single abstract phoneme (e.g. [w] and [ʊ] as /w/; [k] and [g] as /k/, [p] and [b] as /p/, etc.), the removal of epenthetic segments (e.g. [mbr] as /mr/) and the representation of the underlying nasality of a morpheme by means of a superscript N (e.g. /ta^N/).

5 For a more in-depth discussion of grammatical relations in Shiwiar, as well as a general overview of Shiwiar phonetics, phonology and morphology, see Kohlberger (2020).

This distinction is morphologically marked on both the predicate and its arguments: verbs have pronominal indexation and nominals are flagged by case. A subject in Shiwiar is the sole argument of an intransitive clause or the more agent-like argument of a transitive clause, such as the man in (1).

(1) túɾa **nú aʃmaŋga** wakɨɾumiaji nũwĩ́nga
    túɾa **nú** **aʃmaŋ=ka**
    and **ANA** **man=TOP**
    wakɨɾu-mia-ji   nũwĩ́=n=ka
    love-DIST.PST-3.S.DECL   wife.1PL/2PL/3.P=OBJ=TOP
    'And **that man** loved his wife.'
    'Y **ese hombre** quería a su mujer.'
    (T01-S03-01.wav; 00:52-00:55)

An object in Shiwiar is any of the following types of semantic arguments: the more patient-like argument of a transitive clause, such as the enemy in (2); the patient/theme-like argument of a ditransitive clause, such as the monkey's head in (3); and the goal/recipient/beneficiary-like argument of a ditransitive clause, such as the wife in (3). Crucially, all objects are treated equally in Shiwiar grammar. This results in the following generalisations: every clause in Shiwiar has one subject and some clauses additionally have one or more objects.

(2) **nípa nimasínak** t͡saŋgúɾaɾ nujáŋga
    ní=nʲa   **nimasí=na=k**
    3=OBJ(P)   **enemy.1PL/2PL/3.P=OBJ=RESTR**
    t͡saŋkú-ɾa-ɾ   nujáŋka
    forgive-APPL.PFV-3PL.SS   then
    'They then forgave **only their enemy**.'
    'Después perdonaron **solo a su enemigo**.'
    (T01-S02-03.wav; 03:38-03:42)

(3) t͡ʃuú muukĩ́n nu nũwĩ́n susáɾi
    t͡ʃuú   muukĩ́=n
    monkey.GEN   head.1PL/2PL/3.P=OBJ
    nu   nũwĩ́=n   su-sá-ɾ-i
    ANA   wife.PL/2PL/3.P=OBJ   give-PFV-PL-3.S+DECL
    'They gave **his wife the head of the monkey**.'
    'Le dieron **a su mujer la cabeza del mono**.'
    (T03-S01-07.wav; 27:48-27:51)

Shiwiar verbs have pronominal indexes for both subjects and objects. These indexes express both person (first, second or third) and number (singular or plural). Subject marking is completely ubiquitous in verbs, but object indexing depends on the person. First and second person objects exhibit overt marking, as in (4), which shows the first person singular object marker -r. Third person objects are never indexed on the verb, but they can be inferred despite the lack of marking because the valency of every underived verb is lexically specified. In example (5), there is no explicit object indexing on the verb and there is no overt nominal object argument. Nevertheless, it is clear that that there must be a notional third person object because the verb *at͡ʃi-* 'to grab' is transitive.

(4) *und͡zúɾwai*
 unt͡sú-r-wa-i
 call-**1SG.O**-3.S-DECL
 'He's calling **me**.'
 '**Me** está llamando.'
 (T01-S02-02.wav; 09:12-09:13)

(5) *at͡ʃiktái*
 at͡ʃi-k-tái
 grab-PFV-1PL.S.IMP
 'Let's grab **him**.'
 'Cojámos**lo**.'
 (T01-S02-03.wav; 04:38-04:38)

Most ditransitive predicates in the Shiwiar corpus have two third person objects, as in (3). In these cases, no object is indexed on the verb, as expected. Some ditransitive predicates in the corpus have one speech act participant object which is indexed on the verb as shown in (6). In this example, the object is indexed through the portmanteau suffix *-hamɨ* which marks both a first person singular subject and a second person singular object. There are no examples in the Shiwiar corpus of a ditransitive verb with two speech act participant objects, so it is unclear whether first or second person objects would get marked preferentially in that situation. Other researchers have made similar observations about this in other Chicham languages (Overall 2017: 242), so it seems that scenarios with two speech-act participant objects are avoided across the language family.

(6) kuiʃmɨ́ɲ hapirkítʲa**thami**
    kuiʃ-mí=nʲ   hapi-r-kí-tʲat-**hami**
    ear-2SG.P=OBJ   pull-APPL-PFV-FUT-**1SG.S>2SG.O.DECL**
    'I will pull your ear **for you** (i.e. to your detriment).'
    '**Te** voy a jalar la oreja.'
    (T01-S01-01.wav; 08:04-08:05)

Grammatical relations are also flagged on nominal arguments by means of case (except for subject arguments which are not case-marked). Speech act participant (first and second person) objects appear with the object case enclitic =n(ʲa), as in (7) and (8).[6]

(7) *vɨ́**ɲa** hirɨ́ɲak*
    wí=**nʲa**   hi-r-íɲʲa-k
    1SG=**OBJ**   look.at-1SG.O-IPFV.PL-3.S.SIM
    'They were looking at me...'
    'Me estaban viendo...'
    (T01-S03-04.wav; 02:40-02:42)

(8) *vɨ́i nikásnaka amɨ́ɲga hukítʲhʲami*
    wíi   nikás-na=ka   amí=**n**=ka   hu-kí-tʲ-hʲami
    1SG   truly-1SG.A=TOP 2SG=**OBJ**=TOP take-PFV-IFUT-1SG.S>2SG.O.DECL
    'I will truly take you.'
    'Yo te voy a llevar de verdad.'
    (T01-S05-01.wav; 01:18-01:21)

Finally, Shiwiar exhibits a typologically unusual type of differential object marking when it comes to third person objects. These objects are only marked by object case morphology if the subject of the clause is first person singular or third person (singular or plural), as in (9) and (10). If the subject of the clause is first person plural or second person (singular or plural), the object remains unmarked. In (11), the distal pronoun *áu* is the object of the verb and yet it remains unmarked by an object case enclitic because the subject is a first person plural. Similarly, in (12), the topicalised noun *namáŋ* 'game (animals)' is the object of the verb, but it is not marked by an object case enclitic because the subject is a second person plural.

---

6 The object case in Shiwiar is comparable to what is often labelled accusative case in other languages. The choice of the label 'object case' follows a convention used for other northwestern Amazonian languages, like in Epps (2008:166–181) and Bolaños (2016:188–191), and it is motivated by the fact that Shiwiar grammar treats all types of objects identically.

This type of pattern is referred to in the typological literature as a global or scenario-conditioned split (Silverstein 1976: 178; Witzlack-Makarevich & Seržant 2018: 12) because it is conditioned by characteristics of both the subject and the object.

(9) jamáikʲa aɨndzun waingʲáhai nukuá
    jamái=kʲa   aɨntsu=**n**   wain-kʲá-ha-i   nuku=á
    now=TOP   person=**OBJ** find-PFV-1SG.S-DECL   mother=VOC
    'I just found a person now, aunt.'
    'Acabo de encontrar a una persona, tía.'
    (T01-S05-01.wav; 02:38-02:41)

(10) nujá numíɲmaʃ tikiʃín ahiármiaji
     nujá^N   numí=nʲmaⁿ=ʃ   tikiʃí=**n**   ahi-á-r-mia-ji
     then   branch=LOC=FOC   shin=**OBJ**   hit-PFV-PL-DIST.PST-3.S.DECL
     'Then they kept hitting their shins on (fallen) branches.'
     'Después se golpeaban sus canillas en ramas (caídas).'
     (T01-S02-03.wav; 01:44-01:47)

(11) máikʲa áu atʃiktái
     mái=kʲa   áu   atʃi-k-tái
     now=TOP   DIST   grab-PFV-1PL.S.IMP
     'Let's grab that one now.'
     'Cojámoslo ahora.'
     (T01-S02-03.wav; 04:27-04:29)

(12) aa pero namáŋga wáindrumi
     aa_[Sp]   pero_[Sp]   namáŋ=ka   waín-t-rumi
     oh   but   game=TOP   find-APPL-2PL.S.DECL
     'Oh, but you find game animals.'
     'Ah, pero encuentran animales.'
     (T03-S03S14-02.wav; 04:43-04:45)

4 Applicative morphology in Shiwiar

4.1 Basic syntactic function

There is only one applicative morpheme in the Shiwiar language. It is a verbal suffix which can appear as one of two allomorphs: -r(u) or -t⁽ʲ⁾(u). The form and distribution of the allomorphs will be described in further detail below. The applicative morpheme can raise the valency of a verb by introducing a new object. For example, the verb t͡ʃit͡ʃ(a)- 'to speak' is syntactically intransitive in its underived form, as shown in (13a). However, when that same verb occurs with an applicative suffix it becomes transitive and is better translated as 'to speak to someone'. This can be seen in (13b), where núwa wahɨ́ puháu 'the woman who lived as a widow' is the object introduced by the applicative.

(13) a. *kit͡ʃ t͡ʃit͡ʃák*
kit͡ʃ   t͡ʃit͡ʃ-á-k
another **speak**-IPFV-3.S.SIM
'Another person was speaking...'
'Otro hablaba...'
(T01-S02-10.wav; 00:26-00:29)

b. *amasáŋ t͡ʃit͡ʃárak núwa wahɨ́ puháun*
amasáŋ   t͡ʃit͡ʃá-**r**-a-k
Amasank   **speak-APPL**-IPFV-3.S.SIM
núwa   wahɨ́   puh-á-u=n
woman   widowed   live-IPFV-S.NMLZ=OBJ
'Amasank spoke to the woman who lived as a widow...'
'Amasank le habló a la mujer viuda...'
(T01-S02-04.wav; 01:32-01:34)

This applicative suffix is the only way to introduce a novel non-agentive participant argument in Shiwiar and is therefore obligatory in these contexts. The introduced argument (i.e. the applied phrase) is treated as a syntactic object and flagged by object case morphology in the same way as any other object in the language. In (14), the speaker is talking about a group of people who went away, leaving behind some burning fire pits. The applied phrase, *máʃ hí͡i* 'all the fire', appears with the object case enclitic =n.

(14) *máʃ hí͡in ukursár*
máʃ   hí͡i=**n**   uku-r-sá-r
all   fire=**OBJ** leave-APPL-PFV-3PL.SS
'They left all the fire.'
'Dejaron toda la candela.'
(T01-S02-04.wav; 04:47-04:48)

The applicative morpheme in Shiwiar is semantically underspecified given that the semantic role of the introduced object varies widely. In some cases it is simply a patient-like argument, as in (14). More frequently however, the applied phrase has the role of a beneficiary, as can be seen with the first person object in (15). The applied phrase can also have the role of an experiencer, as is the case of the first person object in (16). If the beneficiary/experiencer also happens to be the subject of the verb, the applicative suffix appears together with the reflexive suffix -m(a), as in (17) and (18). Importantly, however, the Shiwiar applicative does not introduce locations or instruments.

(15) papárka hĩã́n nahat**ru**ámiaji
papá-r=ka   hĩã́=n   naha-t-**ru**-á-mia-ji
father[Sp]-1SG.P=TOP   house=OBJ   make-APPL-**1SG.O**-PFV-DIST.PST-3.S.DECL
'My father made **me** a house.'
'Mi papá **me** hizo una casa.'
(T01-S03-03.wav; 03:29-03:31)

(16) vĩɲa muukúɾ nahambɾútawai
wĩ=nʲa   muuk-úɾ   naham-rú-t-a-wa-i
1SG=OBJ   head-1SG.P   hurt-APPL-**1SG.O**-IPFV-3.S-DECL
'My head hurts **me**.'
'**Me** duele la cabeza (**a mí**).'
(T01-S01-01.wav; 11:09-11:11)

(17) ʃaukán sumáɾmakhai
ʃauká=n   sumá-**r-ma**-k-ha-i
wristband=OBJ   buy-**APPL-REFL**-PFV-1SG.S-DECL
'I just bought **myself** a wristband.'
'**Me** acabo de comprar una pulsera.'
(T01-S03S05-01.wav; 03:32-03:33)

(18) máikʲa viʃá hiamɾúmhai
mái=kʲa   wi=ʃá   hiam-**rú-m**-ha-i
now=TOP   1SG=FOC   build.house-**APPL-REFL**-1SG.S-DECL
'I'm building **myself** a house.'
'**Me** estoy construyendo una casa.'
(T03-S11-01.wav; 00:56-00:58)

4.2 Form of the applicative suffix

The applicative suffix in Shiwiar has two allomorphs: -*r(u)* and -*t*$^{(j)}$*(u)*. They are in complementary, lexically-determined distribution: every verb in the corpus only ever appears with one of the two allomorphs. Both allomorphs occur with similar frequency in the lexicon, so that roughly half of the verbs in the corpus occur with each of the allomorphs. Although the distribution of the allomorphs presumably had phonological or semantic motivations at one point in history, these are no longer apparent synchronically in the language. The same allomorphy is found for applicative suffixes in other Chicham languages, but there are also no insights from related languages to explain the distribution of the two forms (Overall 2017: 248–250, 302–305; Peña 2015: 584–592; Saad 2014: 99–100). Examples of the two allomorphs can be seen in (19) to (22). The vowel in both of the allomorphs is present or absent depending on the metrical position of the suffix in the word; see Kohlberger (2020: 129–131) for an overview of vowel elision rules in the language. Note that -*r(u)* never palatalises, but in the case of -*t*$^{(j)}$*(u)* the initial dental stop /t/ becomes palatalised when it follows the high front vowel /i/, as in (23).

(19) *ajamrútmaktatrumi*
ajam-**rú**-tma-k-tat-rumi
protect-**APPL**-1PL/2.O-PFV-FUT-2PL.O.DECL
'He will protect you.'
'Él les va a proteger.'
(T03-S01-05.wav; 07:11-07:12)

(20) *tsaŋgurtúrta*
tsaŋku-**r**-tú-r-ta
forgive-**APPL**-1SG.O-PFV-2SG.S.IMP
'Forgive me.'
'Perdóname.'
(T01-S03-06.wav; 14:14-14:16)

(21) *túra núna inindimdur puhús*
túra nú=na   inintím-**tu**-r   puhú-s
and   ANA=OBJ   think-**APPL**-PFV   live-PFV
'And having thought about it. . .'
'Y después de pensar en eso. . .'
(T01-S02-03.wav; 01:05-01:07)

(22) íiʃa ʃivʲártiʃa písta nahátmauaɾmi
  íi=ʃa   ʃiwʲár-ti=ʃa   písta₍ₛₚ₎
  1PL=FOC   Shiwiar-1PL.SAP=FOC   runway
  nahá-**t**-m-au-ar-mi
  make-**APPL**-REFL-PFV-PL-1PL.S.IMP
  'We, the Shiwiar, let's build ourselves a runway.'
  'Nosotros, los shíwiar, construyámonos una pista.'
  (T01-S02-07.wav; 00:34-00:36)

(23) viʃá pístan nahátmathai; turán víʃa víɲa utʃírun unuítʰumbɾathai
  wi=ʃá   písta₍ₛₚ₎=n   nahá-t-m-a-t-ha-i
  1SG=FOC   runway=OBJ   make-APPL-REFL-IFUT-1SG.S-DECL
  turá-n   wí=ʃa   wí=nʲa   utʃí-ru=n
  and-1SG.SS   1SG=FOC   1SG=OBJ(P)   child-1SG.P=OBJ
  unuí-**tʰu**-m-ra-t-ha-i
  teach-**APPL**-REFL-PFV-IFUT-1SG.S-DECL
  'I will build a runway and I will teach my children.'
  'Voy a construir una pista y voy a enseñarles a mis hijos.'
  (T01-S02-07.wav; 01:17-01:21)

4.3 Interaction with pronominal object markers

The way that first person objects are indexed on Shiwiar verbs is by means of a pronominal suffix that can appear in one of two forms: -r(u) and -t⁽ʲ⁾(u). Not only are these two object suffixes identical in form to the two applicative suffixes, but they also have an identical distribution. That is, verbs that appear with the -r(u) applicative also mark first person object with -r(u), and verbs that appear with the -t⁽ʲ⁾(u) applicative also mark first person object with -t⁽ʲ⁾(u). This can be seen in the examples below, where the transitive verb root hu- 'to take' appears with the suffix -r(u) regardless of whether that suffix expresses an applicative, as in (24), or a first person object, as in (25). However, when an applicative suffix and a first person object suffix co-occur in a single verb, as in (26), a dissimilation process takes place: the applicative suffix appears in the form of the allomorph that is expected for that particular verb (namely -r(u) in the case of the verb hu- 'to take'), but the first person object suffix follows it in the form of the *other* suffix, namely -t⁽ʲ⁾(u). This morphological dissimilation process is reminiscent of phonological phenomena that have been explained by the so-called "obligatory contour principle", whereby identical tones are prohibited from following each other and they therefore dissimilate when they do (Goldsmith 1976; Leben 1973). However, it is noteworthy because it is the only morphological dissimilation process of this kind found in Shiwiar.

(24) wíi huɾumgítʲhʲai
      wíi   hu-**ɾu**-m-kí-tʲ-hʲa-i
      1SG   take-**APPL**-REFL-PFV-IFUT-1SG.S-DECL
      'I will take her for myself.'
      'Me la llevaré.'
      (T01-S02-04.wav; 07:21-07:22)

(25) wiákmika; huɾuktʲá
      wi-á-k-mi=ka;   hu-**ɾu**-k-tʲá
      go-IPFV-SIM-2SG.SS=TOP   take-**1SG.O**-PFV-2SG.S.IMP
      'If you go, take me.'
      'Si te vas, llévame.'
      (T01-S03-01.wav; 04:10-04:11)

(26) taɾát͡ʃuɾ huɾutkítʲa
      taɾát͡ʃ-uɾ   hu-**ɾu**-t-kí-tʲa
      clothes-1SG.P   take-**APPL**-**1SG.O**-PFV-2SG.S.IMP
      'Take my clothes for me.'
      'Llévame mi ropa.'
      (T03-S08-02.wav; 06:28-06:29)

The similarity in form between applicative suffixes and object suffixes, as well as their interaction, suggest that the two are likely historically related.[7] Although a more detailed analysis of the diachronic relationship of applicative and object markers in Shiwiar is beyond the scope of the current paper, it is important for the reader to be aware of the interactions between these two verbal suffixes in order to understand the argumentation presented in 4.2.

5 Non-syntactic uses of the applicative

The functions of applicative morphology in Shiwiar described so far are well within the realm of what would be expected cross-linguistically. However, even

---

[7] See Kohlberger (2020: 336–338) for further discussion about the interaction between the applicative morpheme and object suffixes in Shiwiar.

a cursory glance at the data from the Shiwiar corpus reveals a surprising observation. In natural discourse, Shiwiar speakers frequently make use of applicative morphology even in cases where there does not seem to be an introduction of a novel non-agentive argument. In fact, in these cases it is even questionable whether the Shiwiar applicative has a syntactic function at all. The two non-syntactic functions of the applicative are discussed below.

5.1 Location highlighting

A very frequent discourse function of the Shiwiar applicative is to shift the attention within a predicate towards a notional (but not necessarily overtly expressed) location. Compare examples (27a) and (27b), which both feature the verb 'to leave'. The sentence in (27a) is uttered in the context of a breakup between a former husband and wife. The husband announces dramatically to his wife that he is leaving her and going away. The emphasis of this utterance is on the action of leaving. On the other hand, (27b) was uttered in the context of a search party looking for a woman, and the speaker explains that the missing woman was left behind by a group of people in a particular location, and the emphasis of the utterance is on that location rather than on the action itself.

(27) a. *ukuáhmĩ*
 uku-á-hmĩ
 leave-IPFV-1SG.S>2SG.O.DECL
 'I'm leaving you.'
 'Te estoy dejando.'
 (T01-S03-01.wav; 03:51-03:52)

 b. *ukúɾkiáɾmiaji*
 ukú-r-ki-áɾ-mia-ji
 leave-**APPL**-PFV-PL-DIST.PST-3.S.DECL
 'They left her **there**.'
 'La dejaron **ahí**.'
 (T01-S02-03.wav; 02:05-02:06)

A similar contrast is shown in (28a) and (28b) with the verb 'to stay'. In (28a), the speaker has just been abandoned and she is lamenting that she is staying behind, all alone. The emphasis of the utterance is on being alone and on her solitude (expressed by the restrictive enclitic). Meanwhile, in example (28b), the speaker is giving the interlocutor an order to stay put and not leave the spot, emphasising the location where they currently are.

(28) a. *wíkʲa jamáikʲa wikí huwákhai*
wí=kʲa   jamái=kʲa   wi=kí   huwá-k-ha-i
1SG=TOP   now=TOP   1SG=RESTR   stay-PFV-1SG.S-DECL
'I stayed all alone now.'
'Ahora me quedé sola.'
(T01-S02-02.wav; 12:30-12:31)

b. *ámɨ huwáɾkata jamáikʲa*
ámɨ   huwá-**r**-ka-ta   jamái=kʲa
1PL   stay-**APPL**-PFV-2SG.S.IMP   now=TOP
'You stay **here** now.'
'Tú quédate **aquí** ahora.'
(T01-S02-03.wav; 01:54-01:56)

Although this function of the applicative has some properties that are reminiscent of focusing constructions, for example the fact that it can introduce new information like a novel location that was not previously mentioned in the discourse, I have intentionally chosen to label this function with the vaguer term "highlighting" for one main reason. As can be seen in (27b) and (28b), the notional location does not need to be expressed by an overt noun phrase. In fact, in most cases when the applicative is used this way, the location remains unexpressed. In other words, this use of the applicative only signals to the listener that the speaker has a location in mind, but that location does not need to be further specified. Therefore, this use of the applicative does not necessarily provide the listener with concrete new information to focus on beyond the fact that it shifts the emphasis of the clause away from the action itself and towards a vague notional location.

A striking characteristic of this particular usage of the Shiwiar applicative is that it does not seem to raise the valency of the verb root. In (27a) and (27b), the verb 'to leave' is transitive regardless of whether the applicative is used. Similarly in both (28a) and (28b), the verb 'to stay' is intransitive. There is no novel argument introduced in either of these examples. Nevertheless, the semantic contribution of the applicative is unequivocable: Shiwiar speakers systematically translate sentences such as (27b) and (28b) using a location adverb in Spanish, even though no equivalent location adverb is used in the Shiwiar clause.

Beyond the clues in the translation, the discourse context shows further evidence that speakers have a location in mind when they use the applicative in this way. In (29), a notional location is introduced by an applicative, and then referred to again by a location adverb in a subsequent clause.

(29) nujáŋga hiaɾkáɾ; **wahí** puhúmhi
      nujáŋka   hia-**r**-ká-r
      then   return-**APPL**-PFV-1PL.SS
      wahí puhú-m-hi
      here live-REC.PST-1PL.S.DECL
      'After returning **here**, we lived **here**.'
      'Después de volver **aquí**, vivimos **aquí**.'
      (T01-S02-04.wav; 03:53-03:55)

In example (30), the speaker explains that, as a disaster unfolded in a village, a mother was *just in the right place* to wake her child up in time to flee. This notional location is expressed by the applicative, which shifts the semantics of the verb 'to live' to a slightly different interpretation: 'to be located there/here'.

(30) nii utʃirin iʃindʲáɾtas puhúɾmiaji
      nii   utʃi-ri^N=n   i-ʃintʲá-r-tas
      3   child-1PL/2PL/3.P=OBJ CAUS-wake-PFV-INTENT
      puhú-**r**-mia-ji
      live-**APPL**-DIST.PST-3.S.DECL
      'She was **there** to wake her child up.'
      'Estaba **ahí** para despertar a su hijo.'
      (T01-S02-04.wav; 03:53-03:55)

The non-syntactic nature of the location-highlighting use of the applicative is confirmed in (31). In this excerpt, the speaker is telling a traditional story about flesh-eating demons that are terrorising a village. This utterance describes the moment when the demons return *to the place where those people lived*. Unlike in other instances we have considered thus far, the location introduced by the applicative is expressed as a noun phrase: *nu aintś puhámau* 'the place where those people lived'.[8] Crucially, this noun phrase does not appear with the object case enclitic, as one might expect if it had been introduced by the applicative as a novel syntactic object. Instead, it is marked as an oblique argument in locative case. In other words, the valency of the

---

[8] The non-subject nominalizer *-mau* can productively derive a nominal location from a verb. It turns a verb 'X' into a noun meaning 'the place where X happens'.

verb 'to return' remains unchanged: it continues to be intransitive even though the applicative was used to shift the attention to an overtly expressed location.

(31) huríhurik̃ʲa ma hiarkármiaji **nu aintś puhámaunmaŋga**
 huríhuri=kʲa ma hia-r-ká-r-mia-ji
 demons=TOP but return-APPL-PFV-PL-DIST.PST-3.S.DECL
 nu aintś puh-á-mau=nma^N=ka
 ANA person live-IPFV-NS.NMLZ=LOC=TOP
 'The demons returned to **the place where those people lived**.'
 'Los demonios volvieron **adonde vivía esa gente**.'
 (T01-S02-04.wav; 04:28-04:32)

In discussing these examples with Shiwiar speakers and collaborators, a salient observation was that this pragmatic use of the applicative is very difficult to elicit in a translation-based framework. In the other languages spoken widely by the Shiwiar community, Spanish and Northern Pastaza Kichwa, the primary way to highlight a location is by using an adverb. Therefore, when Shiwiar speakers translated Spanish and Northern Pastaza Kichwa utterances that involved specifying a location into Shiwiar, the resulting Shiwiar utterance also had an explicit location adverb. In contrast, in Shiwiar natural discourse, locations are often highlighted solely by the presence of the applicative.

Even though I have called this function of the applicative location highlighting, it is very similar in nature to the focalizing function of applicative morphology which has been reported for other languages of the Americas such as Eastern Mayan and Mixean languages (see Hernández-Green 2016 and Mora-Marín 2003) as well as Mojeño Trinitario (Arawakan) (Rose 2019), but also outside of the Americas, see, e.g., this volume, chapters 8 and 11.

5.2 Denominal verbalisation

Another seldom reported use of the applicative in Shiwiar is as a denominal verbaliser. This verbalisation strategy seems to be no longer productive but is pervasive in the lexicon, particularly in the domain of meteorological and environmental verbs.[9] Examples (32) to (34) show how the suffixes -r(u) and -t^{(j)}(u) can both be used

---

9 There are two other verbalising suffixes in Shiwiar, -m(a) and -ni, but they are much less widespread than the applicative suffixes discussed in this chapter. None of the verbalisers in the language are productive. For more examples of the -m(a) and -ni verbalisers, see Kohlberger (2020): 275–277).

derivationally. Exactly as with the applicative allomorphy in the verbal domain, it is not clear what motivates the use of either allomorph when they appear with nouns. As with verbs, the use of one particular allomorph in connection with a particular nominal root is lexically determined.

(32) nuhángruaji
      nuhán-**ru**-a-ji
      flood-**APPL**-PFV-3.S.DECL
      'The river has swollen.'
      'El río creció.'
      (T01-S01-02.wav; 31:22-31:23)

(33) sáurwai
      sáu-**r**-wa-i
      bubble-**APPL**-3.S-DECL
      'It's bubbling.'
      'Está burbujeando.'
      (T01-S01-02.wav; 52:11-52:12)

(34) nasĩnduwai
      nasĩ-**tu**-wa-i
      wind-**APPL**-3.S-DECL
      'It's windy.'
      'Hace viento.'
      (T01-S01-02.wav; 25:15-25:16)

Given that these two verbalisers, -r(u) and -$t^{(j)}(u)$, are not productive and appear with nouns rather than verbs, one might be tempted to argue that these are not related to the applicative suffixes and that their formal similarity is simply due to chance. There is, however, evidence that connects these suffixes to the Shiwiar applicative. In section 4.3, it was shown that when first person object markers co-occur with an applicative marker, they dissimilate. This dissimilation process occurs when the verbalizers -r(u) and -$t^{(j)}(u)$ are followed by an object marker. In (35), the noun 'woman' is verbalised by the applicative -$t^{(j)}(u)$, resulting in a verb meaning 'to marry'. As shown in 4.3, the object marker that follows the applicative in (35) appears in the opposite form, namely -r(u). This suggests that these verbalisers are indeed instantiations of the Shiwiar applicative suffix, because the suffix shows identical morphophonological behavior in both functions.

(35) *víɲa nuwátrukaɾka apáɾmaunak awikáɾtiɲuitʲai*
 wí=nʲa nuwa-**t-ru**-ka-r=ka
 1SG=OBJ woman-**APPL-1SG.O**-PFV-3PL.SS=COND
 aparmau=na=k awikár-tinʲu=itʲ-a-i
 sewn=OBJ=RESTR wear-AS.NMLZ=COP-3.S-DECL
 'If you marry **me**, you will have to wear only sewn [clothes].'
 'Si se casan **conmigo**, tienen que ponerse solo [ropa] cosida.'
 (T03-S08S09-02.wav; 10:44-10:47)

The derivational use of applicative morphology appears to be common in other language families, see, e.g., this volume, chapter 12 and chapter 14 for a parallel use of applicative morphology in Waray and western Indonesian languages respectively.

6 Conclusion

The applicative in Shiwiar has two basic types of functions. On the one hand, it can be used to increase the valency of a verb by introducing a novel non-agentive participant. This new argument is morphologically coded as an object and most often has the semantic role of a beneficiary or experiencer. In this sense, the Shiwiar applicative behaves as a syntactic operator in ways that are reported widely cross-linguistically.

On the other hand, the Shiwiar applicative displays functions which are not valence-increasing. First, in natural discourse, the applicative is often used to highlight a notional location that usually remains unexpressed. Although using the applicative in this way results in a clear pragmatic and discourse-oriented effect, the valency of the verb remains unchanged. Second, the applicative can be used morphologically as a denominal verbaliser. This use of the applicative does not seem to be productive anymore, but suffixes that are identical to the synchronic Shiwiar applicative allomorphs can be found in a number of denominal verbs. Evidence from their distribution and morphological behaviour suggests that the verbalising suffixes are indeed related to the applicative.

An important methodological consideration is that the discourse use of applicative morphology in Shiwiar is only prevalent in natural discourse data and is difficult to come by in elicitation. A richly contextualised source, such as a corpus of interactive conversation, is therefore central in analysing the full breadth of functions that applicative morphology may have in languages of the world. Only then can more nuanced semantic and pragmatic uses of what are primarily thought of as syntactic devices be identified.

Abbreviations

1	first person
2	second person
3	third person,
A	adverbial pronominal suffix,
O	object pronominal suffix
P	possessive pronominal suffix
S	subject pronominal suffix
SS	same-subject pronominal suffix
ANA	anaphoric pronoun
APPL	applicative
AS.NMLZ	action/state nominaliser
CAUS	causative
COM	comitative case
COORD	coordinator
DECL	declarative
DIST	distal pronoun
DIST.PST	distant past tense
FOC	focus
FUT	future tense
GEN	genitive case
IDEO	ideophone
IFUT	immediate future tense
IMP	imperative
INTENT	intentional
INTERJ	interjection
IPFV	imperfective aspect
LOC	locative case
NS.NMLZ	non-subject nominaliser
NEG	negation
NMLZ	nominaliser
NSBJ	non-subject
OBJ	object case
OBJ(P)	object case as used in possessive constructions
PFV	perfective aspect
PL	plural number
PROH	prohibitive
PROX	proximal pronoun
PST	past tense
RECIP	reciprocal
REC.PST	recent past
REFL	reflexive
RESTR	restrictive
S.NMLZ	subject nominaliser
SAP	speech act participant marker
SBD	subordinator

SG	singular number
SIM	simultaneous
SS	same-subject
TOP	topic
VBLZ	verbaliser
VOC	vocative.

References

CODENPE. 2015. ¿Qué es Codenpe? *Consejo de Desarrollo de las Nacionalidades y Pueblos del Ecuador*. http://www.codenpe.gob.ec/index.php?option=com_content&view=article&id=161&Itemid=465 (14 April, 2015).

Crevels, Mily & Hein van der Voort. 2020. Areal diffusion of applicatives in the Amazon. In Norval Smith, Tonjes Veenstra & Enoch O. Aboh (eds.), *Advances in Contact Linguistics: In honour of Pieter Muysken*, 180–216. (Contact Language Library 57). Amsterdam: John Benjamins.

Deshoulliere, Gregory & Santiago Utitiaj Paati. 2020. Acerca de la Declaración sobre el cambio de nombre del conjunto Jívaro. *Journal de la Société des Américanistes* 105(2). 167–179.

Goldsmith, John. 1976. *Autosegmental phonology*. Cambridge: Massachusetts Institute of Technology PhD thesis.

INEC. 2010. VII Censo de Población y VI de Vivienda. *Instituto Nacional de Estadísticas y Censos*. http://redatam.inec.gob.ec/cgibin/RpWebEngine.exe/PortalAction? (18 February, 2013).

Hernández-Green, Néstor. 2016. Registration versus applicative constructions in Acazulco Otomí. *International Journal of American Linguistics* 82(3). 353–83.

Katan Jua, Tuntiak. 2011. Ii chichame unuimiamu / Investigando nuestra lengua / Investigating our language: Shuar Chicham. In Marleen Haboud & Nicholas Ostler (eds.), *Endangered languages: voices and images. Proceedings of the FEL XV Annual Conference*, 103–105. Bath: Foundation for Endangered Languages.

Kohlberger, Martin. 2020. *A grammatical description of Shiwiar*. Leiden: Leiden University dissertation.

Kulikov, Leonid. 2011. Voice typology. In Jae Jung Song (ed.), *The Oxford Handbook of Linguistic Typology*, 368–398. Oxford: Oxford University Press.

Leben, William. 1973. *Suprasegmental phonology*. Cambridge: Massachusetts Institute of Technology dissertation.

Mithun, Marianne. 2001. Understanding and explaining applicatives. In Mary Andronis, Christopher Ball, Heidi Elston & Sylvain Neuvel (eds.), *CLS 37, The panels 2001: Proceedings from the parasessions of the thirty-seventh meeting of the Chicago Linguistic Society*, 73–97. Chicago: Chicago Linguistics Society.

Mora-Marín, David F. 2003. Historical reconstruction of Mayan applicative and antidative constructions. *International Journal of American Linguistics* 69(2). 186–228.

Overall, Simon E. 2017. *A grammar of Aguaruna (Iiniá Chicham)*. (Mouton Grammar Library 68). Berlin/Boston: De Gruyter Mouton.

Overall, Simon E. & Martin Kohlberger. forthcoming. The Chicham languages. In Patience Epps & Lev Michael (eds.), *Amazonian languages: An international handbook, Vol. 3*. (Handbooks of Linguistics and Communication Science 44). Berlin/Boston: De Gruyter Mouton.
Peña, Jaime Germán. 2015. *A grammar of Wampis*. Eugene: University of Oregon dissertation.
Peterson, David A. 2007. *Applicative constructions* (Oxford Studies in Typology and Linguistic Theory). Oxford: Oxford University Press.
Rose, Françoise. 2019. From classifiers to applicatives in Mojeño Trinitario: A new source for applicative markers. *Linguistic Typology* 23(3). 435–466.
Saad, George Michael. 2014. *A grammar sketch of Shuar: With a focus on the verb phrase*. Nijmegen: Radboud University Nijmegen M.A. thesis.
Silverstein, Michael. 1976. Hierarchy of features and ergativity. In R. M. W. Dixon (ed.), *Grammatical categories in Australian languages*, 112–171. New Jersey: Humanities Press.
Truong, Christina & Bradley McDonnell. this volume. Neglected functions of western Indonesian applicatives. In Sara Pacchiarotti & Fernando Zúñiga (eds.), *Applicative morphology: neglected syntactic and non-syntactic functions*, XX-XX. (Trends in Linguistics 373). Berlin/Boston: De Gruyter Mouton.
Valenzuela, Pilar M. 2010. Applicative constructions in Shipibo-Konibo (Panoan). *International Journal of American Linguistics* 76(1). 101–144.
Valenzuela, Pilar M. 2016. "Simple" and "double" applicatives in Shiwilu (Kawapanan). *Studies in Language* 40(3). 513–550.
Vallejos, Rosa. 2014. Cambio de valencia en kukama. In Francesc Queixalós, Stella Telles & Ana Carla Bruno (eds.), *Incremento de valencia en las lenguas amazónicas*, 261–282. Bogotá: Instituto Caro y Cuervo.
Wise, Mary Ruth. 2002. Applicative affixes in Peruvian Amazonian languages. In Mily Crevels, Simon van de Kerke, Sérgio Meira & Hein van der Voort (eds.), *Current studies on South American languages*, 329–344. (Indigenous Languages of Latin America (ILLA) 3). Leiden: Research School of Asian, African, and Amerindian Studies (CNWS).
Witzlack-Makarevich, Alena & Ilja A. Seržant. 2018. Differential argument marking: Patterns of variation. In Ilja A. Seržant & Alena Witzlack-Makarevich (eds.), *Diachrony of differential argument marking*, 140. (Studies in Diversity Linguistics 19). Berlin: Language Science Press.

Marianne Mithun
4 Applicatives and beyond: Barbareño Chumash

Abstract: Prototypical applicative constructions add a non-agentive participant to the set of core arguments of the clause. The added argument usually takes on the grammatical role of a transitive object, absolutive, or grammatical patient. Though applicatives are basically word-formation devices, their functions are not necessarily limited to the lexicon; they typically extend into higher levels of structure. Their role in allowing speakers to code more topical and significant participants as core arguments is now generally recognized. Such functions may set the stage for further grammatical developments. One such trajectory is illustrated here with examples from Barbareño Chumash, a language indigenous to California. Section 1 provides a brief overview of the structure of the language. Section 2 describes the four Barbareño applicatives, an Instrumental, a Locative, a Directional, and a Benefactive. Section 3 shows how the first three are used by speakers to shape the flow of information in discourse. Section 4 describes how the fourth has become crystallized in the grammar, so it is the only option for mentioning third person beneficiaries. And Section 5 traces how the discourse uses of all of them have been exploited in pervasive syntactic constructions: nominalization and the formation of headless and headed relative clauses.

1 Barbareño Chumash

Barbareño Chumash, sometimes referred to as Šmuwič, is one of six languages of the Chumashan family traditionally spoken along the south-central coast of California. There are no longer any first-language speakers, but we are fortunate to have extensive documentation of the language from three generations of skilled speakers, recorded by John Peabody Harrington over a period from 1913 to 1961, and by Madison Beeler from 1954 to 1963. All examples of connected speech

---

Marianne Mithun, University of California, Santa Barbara, Department of Linguistics, UCSB, Santa Barbara, California, USA, e-mail: mithun@linguistics.ucsb.edu

https://doi.org/10.1515/9783110777949-004

are drawn from texts dictated by Mary Yee,[1] in the Harrington and Beeler field notes (Harrington 1907–1957; Beeler 1954–1963, 1954–1963ms.). Additional discussion of the language can be found in Beeler 1970ms, 1975, 1979; Whistler 1980ms; Beeler & Whistler 1980; Ono 1996; Wash 1999ms, 2001; Mithun 2002, 2021; and especially Applegate 2015ms, 2017ms.

The language is prototypically polysynthetic. Words can contain large numbers of morphemes, and verbs contain pronominal reference to their core arguments. They can accordingly serve as complete clauses on their own. A typical verb is in (1).

(1) Basic sentence[2]
Siysa'taksuwe'nin.
s-iy-sa'-tak-su-we'n-**in**
3SBJ-PL-FUT-by.hand-CAUS-sleep-**2SG.OBJ**
'**They**'ll rock **you** to sleep.'

Subject prefixes distinguish first, second, and third persons, and singular, dual, and plural numbers, as well as indefinites. Object suffixes distinguish first, second, and third persons, and singular and duo-plural numbers, though there is just one form for first and second person object plurals, and third person singular objects are unmarked. The pronominal affixes are displayed in Tables 1 and 2.

Table 1: Pronominal Subject Prefixes.

1SG	*k-*
2SG	*p-*
3SG	*s-*
3INDEFINITE	*s-am-*
1DU	*k-iš-*
2DU	*p-iš-*
3DU	*s-iš-*
1PL	*k-iy-*
2PL	*p-iy-*
3PL	*s-iy-*

---

1 Work with the Harrington field notes was funded by NSF grant BNS-9011018. Special thanks to Suzanne Wash for her fastidious work on the Chumash Language Project. Special thanks to anonymous reviewers for their careful reading and helpful suggestions.
2 Symbols generally match their Americanist values: <š> = IPA [ʃ], <č> = IPA [tʃ], <y> = IPA [j], and apostrophe <'> = IPA [ʔ]. Codes at the ends of lines, like JPH 59.67, refer to the microfilm reel and frame numbers of the Harrington notes.

Table 2: Pronominal Object Suffixes.

1SG	-it
2SG	-in
3SG	--
1,2DU/PL	-iyuw
3DU/PL	-wun

Basic clauses are predicate-initial. There is no noun case. All dependents are marked with a loosely attached proclitic *hi* whatever their syntactic or semantic role.[3] In (2), the proclitic marks the dependency within the clause of the object 'cowhide', and of the location 'wagon floor'. It also marks the dependency of elements within dependents, here of 'cattle' within 'the hide of a cow', and of 'wagon' within 'the floor of the wagon'.

(2) Larger sentence
    S-am -su-mexkeken **hi** *s-pax* **hi** *l=les*
    3-INDF-CAUS-extend **DEP** 3POSS-skin **DEP** ART=cattle
    'They would spread the hide of a cow'
    hi *mišup* **hi** *ho'=l=kaleta.*
    DEP floor **DEP** DISTAL=ART=wagon
    'on the floor of the wagon.' JPH59.67

The only distinction between core and oblique arguments is thus reference within the verb, in a pronominal subject prefix or pronominal object suffix. Obliques are never referenced pronominally within the verb. Third person singular objects are unmarked, but all other objects, first and second persons, and third person plurals, are represented.

New topics are typically introduced before the nuclear clause, which is then preceded by a proclitic *'i=*.

---

[3] The proclitic *hi=* is written as a separate word here, because it was apparently much more loosely attached to its host than other proclitics. When Mrs. Yee read her notebooks, she would pause after it on occasion.

(3) New topic
He'=k-iy-'aqliw'
PROX=1POSS-PL-language
'Our language'
'i=siwawil hi ka='al-čʰo hi he'=s-iy-'aqli'w
TOP=sometimes DEP COP=ST-be.good DEP PROX=3SBJ-PL-language
'is sometimes a better language'
hi he'=l='is'ispanyol k'el 'in'inilés.
DEP PROX=ART=RDP.Spanish or RDP.English
'than Spanish or English.' (JPH59.257)

2 Applicatives

There are four applicative suffixes: an Instrumental, a Locative, a Directional, and a Benefactive.

(4) Barbareño applicatives

Instrumental	-(')in	-ta'luliš	'pinch'
		-ta'luliš-**in**	'pinch **with**'
Locative	-**pi(y)**	-eleyep	'travel'
		-eleyep-**pi**	'travel **on**'
Directional	-**li('l)**	-tap	'enter'
		-tap-**li'l**	'go **into**'
Benefactive	-**us**	-eqwel	'make'
		-eqwel-**us**	'make **for**'

The form of the Directional suffix is lexically conditioned; those of the Instrumental and Locative suffixes are phonologically conditioned.

All add a participant to the set of core arguments as a grammatical object. They are added to both intransitive and transitive roots. All are derivational, used to form new lexical items. As would be expected, the meanings of the stems they form are not always perfectly compositional semantically.

(5) Locative applicative
*aq-kum-**pi***
quickly-arrive-**LOC.APPL**
'blame'

(6) Benefactive applicative
 ixip-**us**
 finish-BEN.APPL
 'beat' (in a competition)

The original roots of the derived stems may no longer exist on their own. The stem *mon-us* means 'smear on', for example, but there is no attested root *mon-* in Barbareño, though a cognate survives in the closely-related Samala language (Ineseño Chumash).

(7) Benefactive applicative
 *S-am-mon-**us***
 3SBJ-INDF-smear-BEN.APPL
 'They smear it **on**'
 hi l='is'axpinaš hi l='e-sili-xalas.
 DEP ART=sore   DEP ART=NEG-DES-heal
 'a sore that does not want to heal.' (JPH59.656L)

There may be layers of derivation: an applicative suffix may be added to a verb stem that already contains an applicative suffix. Example (8) was part of a description of baby baskets. The speaker had just mentioned that a piece was attached near the top of the basket to serve as a sort of awning. Her next sentence was based on a verb root 'stick' with Benefactive applicative suffix, which yielded a new transitive verb stem 'stick.to' = 'decorate'. This stem served in turn as a base for the addition of an Instrumental applicative, yielding a new stem 'decorate with'.

(8) Layered applicatives
 *K'e s-am-**huqpeyun-us-'in***
 and 3SBJ-INDF-stick-BEN-INS.APPL
 'And they decorated it (**stuck on** it) **with**'
 hi   l='iy-waywayan
 DEP ART=PL-RDP.hang
 'dangling'
 hi   s-tuhtuhiwaš'   hi   l='uš'ušq'oyič^{h}aš'.
 DEP 3POSS-RDP.shell DEP ART=RDP.shellfish
 'shells of shellfish.' (JPH59.552L)

(It is not possible to determine the syntactic status of the unmentioned awning here, since third person singular objects are unmarked in the verb morphology.)

The ranges of meaning contributed by the four applicative suffixes are not fully predictable, but for the most part they are not entirely unexpected. Applegate provides some useful lists of examples (2015ms, 2017ms).

The Instrumental applicative *-in* generally adds an instrument or source to the core arguments of the verb. In (9), nouns in parentheses indicate the instruments that appear with the derived verbs in the field notes.

(9) Instrumental applicatives *-in*

salaqwa'y	'fasten'	*salaqwa'y-**in***	'fasten **with**' (a cord)
niloq	'pierce'	*niloq-**in***	'pierce **with**' (a needle)
sulo'm	'soften'	*sulo'm-**in***	'soften **with**' (lime)
siniwe'	'kill'	*siniwe'-**lin***	'kill **with**' (arrows)
iqmay	'cover'	*iqmay-**in***	'cover **with**' (hands)
sutip	'salt (food)'	*sutip-**in***	'salt **with**' (ashes)
salaqwa'y	'fasten'	*salaqwa'y-**in***	'fasten **with**'
ta'luliš	'pinch'	*ta'luliš-**in***	'pinch **with**'
ušlawilpi	'rub'	*ušlawilpi'-**yin***	'rub **with**'
eqwe'l	'make'	*eqwe'l-**in***	'make **out of**' (wood)

The Locative applicative *-pi* adds a location or, in some formations, a goal.

(10) Locative applicatives *-pi*

wil	'be, exist'	*wil-**pi***	'be located **at**'
wayan	'hang'	*wayan-**pi***	'hang **on/in**'
eleyep	'travel'	*eleyep-ʰ**i***	'travel **along**' (a trail)
oqmol	'spit'	*oqmol-**pi***	'spit **on**'
'anuč	'bleed'	*'anuč-**pi***	'bleed **on**' (a shirt)
oxšol	'pee'	*oxšol-**pi***	'pee **on**'
šušonowon	'splash water'	*šunowon-**pi***	'water to splash **on**'
pux	'string'	*pux-**pi***	'string **on**' (fish on a stick)
qalawil	'tie'	*qalawil-**pi***	'tie **to**'

The location or goal is usually an inanimate place, but with some stems it is animate.

(11) Locative applicatives *-pi*

xal	'assault'	*xal-**pi***	'jump, run after (someone)'
axšik'in	'be envious, resentful'	*axšikin-**pi***	'envy (someone)'

Directional applicatives are rarer, but their functions are similar. They add a goal to verbs of directed motion, usually a physical location.

(12) Directional applicatives *-li'l ~ -li*
tap	'go in'	*tap-li'l*	'enter' (a place)
nukum	'take'	*nukum-li*	'take to' (a place)
kum	'arrive'	*kumu-'li*	'reach' (a place)
axkuy	'hold'	*axku'y-li*	'depart for, head for'

Benefactive applicatives are ubiquitous, appearing with a large number of verbs and occurring pervasively in texts. They bring an indirectly affected participant, usually a person or animal, into the set of core arguments. This might be a recipient, a beneficiary, a goal, occasionally a source, or more.

(13) Benefactive applicatives *-us*
asʰunan	'send'	*asʰunan-us*	'send **to**'
alaqut'ay	'be kind'	*alaqut'ay-us*	'be kind **to**'
alikum	'arrive'	*alikum-us*	'be near **to**'
aqʰina'	'be grateful'	*aqʰinal-us*	'be grateful **to**'
'ip	'talk, say, think'	*'ip-us*	'tell'
išpi'weč	'sell'	*išpi'weč-us*	'sell **to**'
itaq	'hear'	*itaq-us*	'listen **to**'
saqʰala'lan	'holler, shout'	*saqʰala'lan-us*	'holler **at**'
ašyán	'buy'	*ašyan-us*	'buy **for**'
eqwel	'make'	*eqwel-us*	'make **for**'
si'nay	'place/put'	*si'nay-us*	'set (it) out **for**'
ušqʰal	'be open'	*ušqʰal-us*	'open **for**'
xonon	'steal'	*xonon-us*	'steal **from**'
seqen	'remove'	*seqen-us*	'take away **from**'
qunumak	'hide'	*qunumak-us*	'hide **from**'
uxnik'	'escape'	*uxnik-us*	'flee **from**'
qon	'laugh'	*qon-us*	'laugh **at**' (someone)
tuhuy	'to rain'	*tuhuy-us*	'to rain **on**'
tap	'enter'	*tap-us*	'visit' (enter **for** someone)

The applied objects generally behave like base objects syntactically. As seen in (2), 'They spread the hide of a cow on the floor of the wagon', objects generally immediately follow the predicate. Applied objects follow this pattern as well, taking precedence over other constituents. In (14) the Instrumental applied object, the California poppy, was mentioned before the poison.

(14) Constituent order
He'=l='iy-'alapmilimol
PROX=ART=PL-Tulareño
*'i=s-iy-qili-eqwe'l-**in**   hi   l=qupe*
TOP=3SBJ-HAB-make-INS.APPL   DEP   ART=California.poppy
hi   l='ušk'al'   hi   l='atišwiči's.
DEP   ART=be.strong   DEP   ART=poison
'The Tulareños used to make a strong poison out of the California poppy.'
(JPH59.658R)

The base object, here the strong poison, is not differentiated from other non-arguments. All dependents are set off with the same dependency marker *hi*.

It is no longer possible to determine the origin of any of the applicative suffixes. Their counterparts in all of the related languages are suffixes as well, and there are no adpositions or noun or verb roots that would be likely candidates for their sources.

3 Functions beyond the lexicon

There is now substantial work on the discourse functions of applicatives. Donohue examined a corpus of Tukang Besi, an Austronesian language of Indonesia, and concluded that "the prime reasons for the choice of an applicative rather than an oblique coding strategy are to do with pragmatic prominence" (2001: 218–219). He found correlations with animacy, noting that animate participants tend to be more topical in any case. He also found correlations with position in a hierarchy of semantic roles:

agent > beneficiary > instrument > local goal > location source

"When an argument appears in a higher-than-canonical position, the reasons are discourse-driven . . . Especially for goals, the appearance in an applicative construction is associated with a higher degree of topicality and prominence in the narrative" (2001: 250). Similar discourse motivations can be seen in speaker choices of Barbareño Instrumental, Locative, and Directional applicatives: the applicatives allow speakers to code topical or otherwise important participants as core arguments, similar to those observed in Tukang Besi and other languages.

A Barbareño Instrumental applicative can be seen in (15). Mrs. Yee had been explaining how tule mats were made: 'When they wove a mat, they would first semi-dry **the round tule**, and then weave with (it)'. The applicative 'weave with' in the following sentence allowed her to carry the topical tule, the most important point of the sentence, along as a core argument.

(15) Instrumental applicative
k'ayke   na   s-am-**'es-'in**
because if   3SBJ-INDF-**weave-INS.APPL**
'because if they **wove** (it) **with**'
hi   l='meka   s-am-ini-t'inoqš-waš   hi   stapan,
DEP ART=soon 3-INDF-RECENTLY-CUT-PAST DEP round.tule
'**freshly cut tule**,'
'i=mal'i   s-axwiwik   hi-   ho'=l='ešeš
TOP=as   3SBJ-dry   DEP   DISTAL=ART=weaving
'then as it dries the weaving'
'i=non'o'   s-sa'-šalwililin.
TOP=very   3SBJ-FUT-get.loose
'will get really loose.' (JPH 59.614R)

Instruments need not be packaged as core arguments of course. Mention of an instrument as an oblique can be seen in (16). Mrs. Yee had encountered some Japanese wood cutters. Noting that one of them had covered her face with a white cloth, she used a base transitive verb *iqmay* 'cover', rather than the Instrumental applicative verb *iqmay-in* 'cover **with**', which does exist. The sentence which followed made it clear that the face was more central to her message than the cloth.

(16) Oblique instrument
S-iqmay-waš
3SBJ-cover-PAST
'She covered'
hi   ho'=s-tiq'   hi   l='ow'ow   hi   l=maxakiš,
DEP DISTAL=3POSS-face DEP ART=white   DEP ART=cloth
'her face with a white cloth,'
k'e=ka=s-'ip-waš:
and=so=3SBJ-say-PAST
'saying,'
"'alkanu   k-e-sa'-ap'iyulun-us."
  so.that   1SBJ-NEG-FUT-be.tanned-RES
'"It is so I don't get tanned."' (JPH59.467L)

The object 'face' immediately follows the predicate 'cover', appearing before the oblique instrument 'white cloth'.

The second applicative, the Locative, can be seen in (17). Explaining how to cook crayfish, Mrs. Yee began, 'You first get the water boiling.' She then carried the reference to the boiling water into the next sentence as a core argument with the locative applicative 'throw into **it**'.

(17) Locative applicative *-pi*
 Hi 'meka p-su-pintap-**pi**
 DEP so 2SBJ-CAUS-through.air-enter-**LOC.APPL**
 'And then you **throw in**[to it]'
 ho'=l=wulu'wul
 DISTAL=ART=crayfish
 'the crayfish.' (JPH 59.180L)

This contrasts with the oblique location in (18). The floor was incidental to the discussion.

(18) Oblique location
 Na=p-su-pili-qlaw
 if=2SBJ-CAUS-through.air-descend
 'If you drop'
 hi l=pʰlegalól hi ho'=l=pisu,
 DEP ART=dishrag DEP DISTAL=ART=floor
 'a dish-rag **on the floor**,'
 ['it is a sign that someone will arrive that has not been seen for a long time.']
 (JH59.212L)

The third applicative, the Directional, can be seen in (19). Mrs. Yee had just brought up the topic of traditional sweathouses: 'All of the villages had one or two sweathouses depending on how many people were there.' She then carried reference to the sweathouses into the following sentence as a core argument with the Directional applicative.

(19) Directional applicative *-li'l*
 S-iy-**tap-li'l**
 3SBJ-PL-**enter-DIR.APPL**
 hi l='ihihiy k'e l='en'eneq.
 DEP ART=RDP.man and ART=RDP.woman
 'Men and women would **go in**[to it].' (JPH59.673R)

Not surprisingly, directions are more often expressed as obliques than as core arguments, as predicted by Donohue. Describing earlier times, Mrs. Yee explained that 'The road that ran between the missions the Spanish called The King's Highway. The Spanish were in this country only about two generations.' In the next sentence, she again mentioned this country, but with just the demonstrative 'here'. The country was not a main topic of discussion or a significant part of the message and remained oblique.

(20) Oblique direction
Kim ka s-iy-tap **hi** *'it'i*
and then 3SBJ-PL-enter **DEP** here
hi he'=l='am'amelikanu'
DEP PROX=ART=RDP.American
'And then the Americans came in **here**.' (JPH59.533L)

The fourth applicative, the Benefactive -*us*, can be seen in (21).

(21) Benefactive applicatives
*'akimpi hu=**k-talawaxan-us**-wun* hi l=us'ustliyaku'
during REM=1SBJ-**work-BEN.APPL**-3PL.OBJ DEP ART=RDP.Austrian
'When I **work**ed **for** the Austrians'
*s-am-qili-**itaq-us**-wun*
3SBJ-INDF-HAB-**hear-BEN.APPL**-3PL.OBJ
'you could **hear** them'
hi ma'li s-iy-axlaxlulun hi ho'=s-iy-kaltu.
DEP when 3SBJ-PL-RDP.sip DEP DISTAL=3POSS-PL-soup
'sipping their soup.' (JPH59.643L)

The third person plural object suffix -*wun* on the verbs 'work for' and 'hear' confirms that the Austrians are indeed the objects of those clauses.

Barbareño Benefactive applied objects are most often human or at least animate, but not always, as in (22), part of a description of cheese making.

(22) Dative/Benefactive applicatives
Ču =ho'=l=čtin'čtin'
and=DISTAL=ART=RDP.dog
'And the dogs'
*'i'=ka=s-iy-ali-**kuyam-us*** hi ho'=l=swelu.
TOP=then=3SBJ-PL-DUR-**wait-BEN.APPL** DEP DISTAL=ART=whey
'are **waiting for** the **whey**.' (JPH59.459.490L)

The propensity for Benefactive applicatives to involve humans or at least animates has had consequences for their development.

4 Crystallization: Benefactives

It might be expected that where there are multiple applicatives in a language they would behave in parallel ways. All of the Barbareño applicative markers are verb suffixes, and all bring a referent into the core as an object. The Benefactive applicative -*us* 'to, for, from', etc., however, has developed further than the Instrumental, Locative, and Directional applicatives. Speakers no longer make choices in how they code recipients, beneficiaries, and these goals: all are routinely cast as core arguments for discourse purposes. (Benefactives are discussed further in Section 5.4.)

It is not difficult to imagine the factors which could lead to this development. High frequencies of expression can lead to routinization, which can, in turn, ultimately result in obligatoriness. As is well known, humans (and personified animals) are generally more topical than inanimates, and the effects of situations on humans are more often recognized by speakers than their effects on instruments, locations, or directions. Just this point is made by Peterson in his survey of applicatives.

> It appears almost never to be the case that benefactive applicative constructions are truly optional. Other applicative types tend to have alternative expressions and applicative objects which do not display all object properties, and which may have base objects which also display object properties . . . It seems likely that these tendencies ultimately have to do with the relative animacy of the applicative objects in question, but it is clear that such tendencies may be violated. (Peterson 2007: 60)

Peterson cites Gerdts' description of Halkomelem, a Salishan language indigenous to western Canada.

> In Halkomelem (Gerdts 1988), whether an applicative construction is used or not depends primarily on the animacy of the potentially applicative object: if the object in question is animate, the applicative construction must be used. Thus, since beneficiaries are always animate, beneficiaries are found only in applicative constructions. (Peterson 2007: 48)

The Barbareño crystallization of the Benefactive constructions has left a mark on the inflectional system. Cross-linguistically, two patterns of object alignment are often recognized, termed indirective (in which direct objects are distinguished from indirect objects) and secundative (in which primary objects are distinguished from secondary objects) (Haspelmath 2005). The two differ essentially in whether recipients, beneficiaries, etc. are grouped with themes or not.

(23) Object alignment patterns
Indirective
    Direct objects   *She teased **her brother**.*
                                *She gave **a card** to her brother.*
                                *She baked **a cake**.*
                                *She baked **a cake** for her mother.*
    Indirect objects *She gave a card **to her brother**.*
                                *She baked a cake **for her mother**.*
Secundative
    Primary objects   *She teased **her brother**.*
                                *She gave **her brother** a card.*
                                *She baked **a cake**.*
                                *She baked **her mother** a cake.*
    Secondary objects *She gave her brother **a card**.*
                                *She baked her mother **a cake**.*

In Barbareño, first and second person objects show clear secundative patterning. The same object suffixes are used for themes, recipients, and beneficiaries.

(24) Barbareño first and second person objects
    a. *s-kutiy-**it***   's/he sees **me**'
          *s-ikš-**it***   's/he gives (it) **to me**'
    b. *s-kutiy-**in***   's/he sees **you**'
          *s-ikš-**in***   's/he gives (it) **to you**'

Third person objects show an interesting difference in detail. If the third person object is a recipient/beneficiary/goal etc., the Benefactive applicative suffix *-us* must be present. (Recall that third person singular objects are unmarked.)

(25) Barbareño third persons
    a. *s-kuti*   's/he sees (him/her/it)'
          *s-ikš-**us***   's/he gives (it) **to** (him/her)'
    b. *s-kuti-**wun***   'she sees **them**'
          *s-ikš-**us**-**wun*** 's/he gives (it) **to them**'

The third person object suffixes could still be said to show secundative patterning, but the distinction between what would be direct and indirect objects in indirective systems is expressed in the verb stem.

5 Further crystallization: Nominalization

The discourse function of applicatives, ensuring that topical participants are packaged as core arguments, has been exploited in a pervasive syntactic construction in Barbareño Chumash.

5.1 Participant nominalization

In Chumash languages, verbs can be nominalized in several ways. The most common is simply the addition of the article *l=* (with a glottal stop before a following vowel). The third person subject prefix is omitted, though the subject number is not. The resulting nominalized verb can be used to refer to any core argument. The nominalized verb in (26) refers to an intransitive subject.

(26) Intransitive subject
   a. *s-iy-akt-eqen*
      3SBJ-PL-coming-be.gone
      'they pass by'
   b. *l='iy-akt-eqen*
      ART-PL-coming-be.gone
      '**those who** pass by' = 'passers-by'

That in (27) refers to a transitive subject.

(27) Transitive subject
   l=sa'-uti-kuy-us-wun
   ART=FUT-start-grasp-BEN.APPL-3PL.OBJ
   '**what** would happen to them'

That in (28) refers to a base object.

(28) Object
   l='am-kut-iwaš
   ART=INDF.SBJ-see-NOM.PAST
   '**the one** they saw'

That in (29) refers to an applied object.

(29) Applied object
*l=wayi-tap-**pi***
ART=walking-enter-**LOC.APPL**
'entrance'

5.2 Larger nominalizations

Multi-word clauses can be nominalized in the same way to produce headless relatives, with the addition of the article *l=* on the verb. The referent may again be any core argument of the clause, specified just in a pronominal prefix or suffix, including unmarked third person singular objects. The referent of the nominalized clause in (30) is the base object of 'find'.

(30) Referent = Base object
Liya ho'=s-ʰasʰa'   'i=mok'e   s-iy-axiqen-waš
all   DIS=3POSS-RDP.tooth   TOP=already   3SBJ-PL-wear.down-PAST
'His teeth were all of them worn down,'
*ka'neč   hu=l='am-išti-**wun***
like   REM=**ART**=INDF.SBJ-find-**3PL.OBJ**
'like **those one finds**'
hu=l=molmoloq-iwaš
REM=ART=RDP.long.ago-NOM.PAST
'**in ancient**'
hi   s-noqnoqš-iwaš'   hi   l='iy-'al-aqšan.
DEP   3SBJ-RDP.head-NOM.PAST   DEP   ART=PL-NMLZ-die
'**skulls**.' (JPH59.475R)

The referent may be an applied object. In (31) it is a location.

(31) Referent = Locative applied object
Hi   l=čʰo-waš   hi   s-iy-ašnipit-waš   he'=l=kuhku'
DEP   ART=be.good-PAST   DEP   3SBJ-PL-step.on-PAST   PROX=ART=RDP.person
'The best place for a person to stand'

In (34) it is a transitive subject.

(34) Coreferential transitive subject
S-wil   [hi   l=kul
3SBJ-be DEP   ART=person
'There are **people**'
[hi   l='iy-axtap-wun]].
DEP   ART=PL-eat.raw-3PL.OBJ
'**[who eat them raw]**.' (JPH59.485L)

In (35) it is a base direct object.

(35) Coreferential object
S-iy-qili-xinxinči'   [hi   l='aq'aqli'w
3-PL-HAB-RDP.be.bad   DEP   ART=RDP.word
'The **words** were bad'
[hi   l='iy-hik'en-wun]].
DEP   ART=PL-use-3PL.OBJ
'**[that they used]**.'
= 'They sure talk mean and use a lot of cuss-words.' (JPH59.21R)

The referent of the associated nominalized clause may also be an applied object. In (36) it is an Instrumental applied object.

(36) Coreferential Instrumental applied object
Wa   'al'al-sax'anpinč-waš   hi   ho'=l='al-aqšan
if   AGT.NMLZ-to.fish-PAST   DEP   DIS=ART=NMLZ-die
'If the one that died was a fisherman'
'i= s-am-si'nay-us   [hi   s-is-hahsʰa'
TOP=3SBJ-INDF-put.into-BEN.APPL   DEP   3POSS-AL-RDP.fishhook
'then they put in **his fishhooks**,'
[hi   l=sa'-sax'anpi-n-š-'in]].
DEP   ART=FUT-fish-IPFV-ANTIP-**INS.APPL**
'**[the ones he would have fished with]**.' (JPH59.672L)

'i=hu=l='uš-napay-**piy**-waš
TOP=REM=**ART**=by.hand-ascend-**LOC.APPL**-PAST
hi   l=šupšup'   hi   l='oxwon'.
DEP   ART=RDP.dirt DEP   ART=gopher
'was **where a gopher had thrown out dirt**.' (JPH59.502R)

The sentence in (32) contains two nominalizations, one referring to an intransitive subject ('the survivors'), the other to a Benefactive applied object ('those it came to' = 'those who inherited it').

(32)   Referent = Benefactive applied object
       ['If a canoe was owned by two or three persons and one died']
       'i=ho'=**l**='iy-uni-'lek'en
       TOP=DISTAL=**ART**=PL-remaining-be.alive
       '**then the ones left alive**'
       ka=**l**-utikuyupiy-**us**-wun   hi   ho'=l=tomol.
       COP=ART-turn.pass.to-**BEN.APPL**-3PL.OBJ   DEP   DISTAL=ART=canoe
       'just continued to own it.' (JPH59.671R)

The discourse function of applicatives as devices for casting topical referents as core arguments has been exploited for the regular formation of headless relatives, ensuring that the referent is a core argument of the clause.

5.3 Headed relatives

Nominalized clauses may be combined with a coreferential nominal to form headed relative clauses. Again the referent may be any core argument of the nominalized clause. The full relative construction is set off by the dependency marker *hi*, and within this, the relative clause is set off by the same dependency marker.

In (33) the sore is coreferential with the intransitive subject of the associated clause.

(33)   Coreferential intransitive subject
       S-am-mon-us
       3SBJ-INDF-smear-BEN.APPL
       'They smear it on'
       [hi   l='is'axpinaš   [hi   l='e-sili-xalas]].
       DEP   ART=sore   DEP   **ART**=NEG-DES-heal
       '**a sore [that does not want to heal]**.' (JPH59.656L)

In (37) it is a Locative applied object.

(37) Coreferential Locative applied object
'al-wilwil'   [hi   l=nuknuk'a'
ST-RDP.be   DEP   ART=RDP.place
'There are certain **places**'
[hi   l='iy-lek'en-**pi**   hi   he'=l=tiš'il'il].
DEP   **ART**=PL-live-**LOC.APPL**   DEP   PROX=ART=RED.ant.species
'[**where** red ants live]'. (JH59.563R)

In (38) it is a Benefactive applied object.

(38) Coreferential Benefactive applied object
Walelyu   'i='me   ma'liwaš   hi   l=pak'a-waš,
NAME   TOP=just   only-PAST   DEP   ART=one-PAST
'Valerio had only one person,'
[hi   l='ihi'y   hi   l=tupmekč
DEP   ART=male   DEP   ART=child
'a little boy'
[hi   l=saxkuy-**us**-waš]].
DEP   **ART**=trust-**BEN.APPL**-PAST
'[**whom** he could trust].' (Beeler 15.49)

The nominal often precedes the nominalized clause, but on occasion it follows, as in (39).

(39) Clause – noun
Na   he'=l=tiptip'   hi   p-ton'   hu=sulkuw
when PROX=ART=RDP.brush DEP   2-EMPH   REM=night
'When you are lying down at night out in the woods'
'i=p-kutiy-wun   hi   l='iy-ali-uquštay   hi   l=tiqtiq'
TOP=2SBJ-see-3PL.OBJ   DEP   **ART**=PL-DUR-shine   DEP   ART=RDP.eye
'you see the shining eyes.' (JPH59.300L)

5.4 Beneficiaries redux

It was seen in Section 4 that cross-linguistically, Benefactive applicatives can be more frequent in speech than other applicatives, because the participants they promote to core status tend to be human and accordingly highly topical. High frequency can lead to obligatoriness, as it has in Barbareño discourse. They are not obligatory, however, in the syntactic constructions which exploit their functions.

The Benefactive applicative has developed a function not shared by the other applicatives, which involves causatives. A causative prefix *su-/sus-/si-* adds a causer to the set of core arguments as a subject. If the base verb was intransitive, the causee is the object of the causative construction, as in (40)–(42).

(40) Causative of intransitive
    a. ***p*-'ololtuš**
       2SBJ-be.numb
       '**you** are numb' (JPH59.288R)

    b. *s-**su**-'olotuš-**in***
       3SBJ-**CAUS**-be.numb-**2OBJ**
       'it strikes **you** numb' (JPH59.287L)

(41) Causative of intransitive
    a. *s-ušk'al*
       3SBJ-be.strong
       '**s/he** is strong' (JPH 59.554L)

    b. *s-ʰu-'ušk'al*
       3SBJ-**CAUS**-be.strong
       'it made **him** strong' (JPH 59.287L)

(42) Causative of intransitive
    a. ***s**-yinc'i*
       3SBJ-be.hot
       'it is hot' (JPH59.466R)

    b. *s-iy-**si**-yinc'i-**wun***
       3SBJ-PL-**CAUS**-be.hot-**3PL.OBJ**
       'they heat **them**' (JPH59.535L)

If the base verb was transitive, now the causee or secondary agent is coded as an object. A base verb 'bite' can be seen in (43). Mrs. Yee was describing the two medicinal uses of red ants. To cure rheumatism, people applied the ants to the affected body part. The sentence that followed was based on the base transitive verb 'bite'.

(43) Base transitive
*Na=s-iy-**'uw**-in*   *'i=ka=no'no'*   hi   *s-popoč.*
when=3SBJ-PL-**bite**-2OBJ   TOP=that=very   DEP   3SBJ-hurt
'When they bite you, it stings a lot.' (JPH59.569L)

To cure consumption, people had the patient swallow the ants. The verb used here was a causative of the transitive verb 'bite': *sus-'uw-* 'make bite'. The causee, the ants, were coded as an applied object by means of the Benefactive suffix. The ants were not mentioned again with a full nominal, but their status is clear from the third person plural object suffix *-wun*.

(44) Causative of transitive
*S-am-**sus**-**'uw**-**us**-wun*   hi   *l=ku.*
3SBJ-INDF-**CAUS-bite-BEN.APPL**-3PL.OBJ   DEP   ART=person
'They **make them** [red ants] **bite** people.' (JPH59.564R)

It should be noted that in the corpus, causatives of transitives do not always contain the Benefactive applicative suffix. The sentence immediately before (43) contained a causative prefix *-sus-*. The plural object suffix *-wun* apparently referred to the ants, but there was no Benefactive applicative suffix *-us*.

(45) Causative of transitive
Mal'i   *s-iy-**sus**-'uw-**wun***
when   3SBJ-PL-**CAUS**-bite-**3PL**
'When they **make them** bite'
hi   *l=ku*   hi   *mitipin*   hi   *he'=s-'a'min*
DEP   ART=person   DEP   outside   DEP   PROX=3POSS-body
'a person on the outside of his body'
'i='al=ka=s-'axiyep   hi   *l=maxcuč'eq*
TOP=ST=COP=3SBJ-cure   DEP   ART=rheumatism
'it is as a remedy for rheumatism.' (JPH59.569R)

It is difficult to know how widespread this omission of the applicative was. It can only be detected when the base or applied object of a causative of a transitive is third person plural.

There is however, another situation in which Benefactive applicatives are not obligatory. In participant nominalizations, including headless and headed relativizations, the syntactic requirement that the referent of the nominalization be a core argument takes precedence over discourse topicality. In the description of the red ant cures, Mrs. Yee explained that to cure consumption, people had the patient lie on his back and open his mouth. In the sentence that followed, 'It was always eight red ants that they made him swallow', the causee was the invalid, the one made to swallow, but the referent of the relative clause 'that they made him swallow' was the base object of the clause, coreferential with 'the red ants'.

(46) Causative relative clause
 M'eči 'al-malawa-waš hi l=tiš'il'il
 always ST-eight-PAST DEP ART=red.ant.species
 'It was always eight red ants'
 [hi l='am-su-aqliwin].
 DEP ART=INDF-CAUS-swallow
 '[that they made him swallow].' (JPH 59.570R)

6 Conclusion: Beyond word formation

The Barbareño applicatives pattern much like those described for other languages. The applicative suffixes are derivational morphemes which create new lexical items, but their effects extend beyond the domain of word formation into the realms of syntax and discourse. They have syntactic effects which are used for shaping the flow of discourse. These effects have, furthermore, entered into the development of widespread syntactic constructions: in particular relative clauses.

The language contains four applicatives: Instrumental, Locative, Directional, and Benefactive. They match the standard definition proposed in this volume: they are derivational verb suffixes that function to introduce a non-Actor semantic argument into the clause. They ensure that instruments, locations, directions, and recipients/beneficiaries, etc. are cast as syntactic objects. Like other derivational morphology, they form lexical items, sometimes with unexpected meanings. They may be recursive, applied to verb bases that already contain applicative suffixes. The suffixes are so old that their lexical sources are no longer recoverable, but their development has not come to a halt. And they have not developed in lockstep.

The first three, the Instrumental, Locative, and Directional applicatives have retained their discourse function: instruments, locations, and directions may be expressed either as obliques or as applied objects, depending on their place in the discourse at that point. More topical referents, of significance to the message, can be coded as applied objects, while more peripheral, incidental participants are coded as obliques. Recipients and beneficiaries, by contrast, *must* be expressed as applied objects. There are no oblique alternatives. This differential development may be explicable in terms of frequency. As is well known, humans (and some animals) tend to be more topical than tools and places. Recipients and beneficiaries are more often human than are instruments, locations, and directions. It is not surprising that Benefactive applicatives would be used much more often than the other applicatives. And high frequency is usually a precursor to obligatoriness.

The preference for coding humans as core arguments, particularly interlocutors, is reflected in the secundative patterning of first and second person objects in Barbareño. First and second person recipients and beneficiaries, always humans, are given preference for object status. Third person objects reflect a similar preference, but with an additional detail. When they are recipients or beneficiaries, this fact is marked by an obligatory Benefactive applicative suffix in the verb stem.

The role of applicative constructions in ensuring that topical referents are coded as core arguments has crystallized in another major syntactic construction. Participant nominalization is highly productive in Barbareño, Used to form not just lexical items, but also headless and headed relatives. But the referent of the nominalized clause must be a core argument. Applicatives are regularly exploited to ensure that the target is part of the core, even if it is an instrument, location, direction, or recipient/beneficiary etc. The requirement of core argument status for the referents of nominalized clauses takes precedence over the obligatory coding of beneficiaries as core when they are present.

The Barbareño applicatives illustrate the fact that applicative constructions are not necessarily static. Like other constructions they can undergo further development, not necessarily all at the same rate or in the same direction. Though the Barbareño applicatives are basically word formation devices, their discourse functions set the stage for further syntactic developments.

Abbreviations

AL	alienable.possession
ANTIP	antipassive
APPL	applicative
ART	article
BEN	benefactive
CAUS	causative
COP	copula
DEP	dependent
DES	desiderative
DIR	directional
DUR	durative

FUT	future
HAB	habitual
INDF	indefinite
INS	instrumental
IPFV	imperfective
LOC	locative
NEG	negative
NMLZ	nominalizer
NOM.PAST	nominal past
OBJ	object
PL	plural
POSS	possessive
PROX	proximal
RDP	reduplicand
REM	remote
RES	resultative
SBJ	subject
ST	stative
TOP	topicalizer

References

Applegate, Richard. 2015ms. Integrated dictionary of Shmuwich: Barbareño Chumash.

Applegate, Richard. 2017ms. Topics in Shmuwich grammar: An interim grammar of Barbareño Chumash.

Beeler, Madison. 1954–1963. The Madison Beeler collection of Chumash sound recordings. Survey of California and other Indian Languages – California language Archive. https://cla.berkeley.edu/list.php?collid=10010. 1954–1963. Yee, Mary J., Barbareño Texts, transcribed by Madison Beeler, Beeler Papers, Department of Anthropology, Santa Barbara Museum of Natural History.

Beeler, Madison. 1954–1963ms. Santa Barbara Museum of Natural History.

Beeler, Madison. 1970ms. Topics in Barbareño Chumash grammar.

Beeler, Madison. 1975. Barbareño Chumash grammar: A farrago. In Margaret Langdon & Shirley Silver (eds.), *Papers from the First Conference on Hokan Languages, April 23–25, 1970*. 251–269. The Hague: Mouton Publishers.

Beeler, Madison. 1979 Barbareño Chumash text and lexicon. In Mohammad Ali Jazayery, Edgar Polome, & Werner Winter (eds.), *Linguistic and literary studies in honor of Archibald A. Hill, Vol. 2*, 171–193. Lisse: Peter de Ridder.

Beeler, Madison & Kenneth Whistler. 1980. Coyote, Hawk, Raven and Skunk (Barbareño Chumash). In Martha Kendall (ed.), *Coyote stories II*, 88–96. (Native American Text Series 6). Ann Arbor: University Microfilms.

Donohue, Mark. 2001. Coding choices in argument structure: Austronesian applicatives in texts. *Studies in Language* 25(2). 217–254.

Gerdts, Donna. 1988. *Object and absolutive in Halkomelem*. New York: Garland.
Harrington, John Peabody. 1907–1957. Boxes 410–485, 491–506, especially 491–496, microfilm reels 59–66. Papers of J. P. Harrington, National Anthropological Archives, Smithsonian Institution. Detailed in Mills & Brickfield (eds.) 1986 and online: https://anthropology.si.edu/naa/harrington/pdf/box_lists/pdf/harrington_v3_boxlist_SC_cal_basin.pdf
Haspelmath, Martin. 2005. Argument marking in ditransitive alignment types. *Linguistic Discovery* 3(1). 1–21.
Mills, Elaine L. & Ann J. Brickfield (eds). 1986. *The Papers of John Peabody Harrington in the Smithsonian Institution 1907–1957, Vol 3: Native American History, Language and Culture of Southern California/Basin*. Millwood, NY: Kraus International
Mithun, Marianne. 2002. Rhetorical nominalization in Barbareño Chumash. Report #12. In Lisa Conathan & Teresa McFarland (eds.), *Proceedings of the 50th Anniversary Conference of the Survey of California and Other Indian Langauges*, 55–63. Berkeley: University of California.
Mithun, Marianne. 2021. In celebration of the differences: Distributing meanings over structures. *Language* 97(4). 732–751.
Peterson, David A. 2007. *Applicative constructions*. Oxford: Oxford University Press.
Ono, Tsuyoshi. 1996. *Information flow and grammaticalization in Barbareño Chumash*. Santa Barbara: University of California dissertation.
Wash, Suzanne 1999ms. On the structure and function of relative clauses in Barbareño Chumash.
Wash, Suzanne. 2001. *Adverbial clauses in Barbareño Chumash narrative discourse*. Santa Barbara: University of California dissertation.
Whistler, Kenneth. 1980ms. An interim Barbareño Chumash dictionary.

Sergio Ibáñez Cerda, Alejandra Itzel Ortiz Villegas, and Armando Mora-Bustos

5 Applicative periphrastic constructions in the Colombian Spanish from The Andes

Abstract: This paper focuses on an applicative construction in Colombian Andean Spanish, specifically the variant spoken in Ipiales-Nariño, a city in southwestern Colombia. The structure is an applicative periphrastic construction (APC), i.e., it is a bi-verbal structure where one of the verbs is the main semantic predicate and the other one, *DAR* 'give', functions as an applicative marker. The APC has several non-canonical features: first, it is mostly specialized in the introduction of a deputative-beneficiary applied phrase, which although coded as an object, does not increase the (semantic) valence of the root. Second, the applied phrase can also be a prepositional phrase (PP); in this case, the AP does not bear the role of deputative, but that of recipient-beneficiary or possessor. Third, the presence of the applicative *DAR*, besides allowing the introduction of the AP, entails a particular semantic feature in the clause agent: its referent must be involved in the denoted event in an unexpected fashion, as a special favor to the deputative-beneficiary introduced by the AP, to the speaker, or to someone else. This type of semantic effect has not been described for applicative morphology in other languages.

1 Introduction

This paper focuses on an applicative periphrastic construction in Colombian Andean Spanish (henceforth CAS), specifically, in the variant spoken in Ipiales-

---

Sergio Ibáñez Cerda, Universidad Nacional Autónoma de México, Instituto de Investigaciones Filológicas, Circuito, Mario de La Cueva s/n, C.U., Coyoacán, Ciudad de México, México, e-mail: sergioimx@yahoo.com.mx
Alejandra Itzel Ortiz Villegas, Instituto de Educación Media Superior de la Ciudad de México, Plantel "Otilio Montaño", Academia de Lengua y Literatura, Av. Cruz Blanca, Las Flores, San Miguel Topilejo, San Miguel Topilejo, Ciudad de México, México, e-mail: alejandraitzel.ortiz@iems.edu.mx
Armando Mora-Bustos, Universidad Autónoma Metropolitana-Unidad Iztapalapa, Departamento de Filosofía, Av. San Rafael Atlixco No. 186 Col. Leyes de Reforma 1ra Secc. Del. Iztapalapa, Ciudad de México, México, e-mail: amora@xanum.uam.mx

https://doi.org/10.1515/9783110777949-005

Nariño, a city in southwestern Colombia, near the border with Ecuador.[1] Data come from two main sources: a sample of occurrences in natural discourse, i.e., in real communicative interactions of men and women in different types of formal and informal contexts, and from metalinguistic interviews with a group of informants, made with the aim of verifying issues related to the semantics and the morphosyntax of the construction.[2]

Although a similar structure in a nearby Ecuadorian variant has been already reported and described (Toscano 1953; Niño-Murcia 1992; Hurley 1992; Haboud 1998, Olbertz 2002; Bruil 2006, 2008), this is the first attempt to characterize the applicative construction in CAS. Along the lines of Creissels (2010), the structure discussed in this paper is an applicative periphrastic construction (henceforth APC); that is, a bi-verbal structure where one of the verbs is the main semantic predicate and the other functions as an applicative marker, licensing the presence of an applied phrase, as in (1a):

(1) a. *La=Runa   le=dio   haciendo   a=la=Angelita*
       ART=Runa   3SG.DAT=give.AUX.APP.3PST   make.GRD   DAT=ART=Angelita
       el=discurso   de=despedida.
       ART=speech   PREP=farewell
       'Runa made the farewell speech instead of Angelita.'

   b. *La=Runa   hizo   el=discurso   de=despedida*
       ART=Runa   make.3PST   ART=speech   PREP=farewell
       en vez de   la=Angelita.
       instead.of   ART=Angelita.
       'Runa made the farewell speech instead of Angelita.'

   c. *La=Runa   le=hizo   el=discurso   de=despedida*
       ART=Runa   3SG.DAT=make.3PST ART=speech   PREP=farewell
       a=la=Angelita.
       DAT=ART=Angelita
       'Runa made the farewell speech instead of Angelita.'

---

1 The research for this study was partially conducted under the auspices of the Dirección General de Asuntos del Personal Académico (DGAPA) of the Universidad Nacional Autónoma de México (grant PAPIIT #IN401722), whose financial support the first author gratefully acknowledges. We also thank three anonymous reviewers and the editors of this volume for helpful comments on earlier versions of this paper.

2 The data were collected in several fieldwork trips that took place during the last 5 years. The informants are around 80 speakers that belong to an extended network of family and friends in Ipiales, the main city in the area.

5 Applicative periphrastic constructions in the Colombian Spanish from The Andes — 99

In (1a), the applicative marker is the verbal form *DAR*, which means 'give' when functioning as a main predicate, as is common in other languages with applicative periphrases. The semantically bleached *DAR* simultaneously serves as an auxiliary and hosts the flectional features. It also hosts a dative clitic index, which is coreferential with the applied phrase (henceforth AP). This AP is a dative marked NP, whose referent has the deputative-beneficiary role, a semantically adjunct participant. The propositional meaning of (1a) can be alternatively expressed as in (1b) and (1c): in (1b), the deputative is introduced by means of a PP headed by *en vez de* 'instead of'; in (1c) it is also coded as a dative NP and is also cross-referred by a dative index in the verb, but the structure lacks *DAR*. We will show that (1a)-(1c) are only seemingly equivalent in terms of propositional meaning.

The APC of CAS has several non-canonical features. First, the *DAR* applicative is mostly specialized in the introduction of a deputative-beneficiary into the clause. However, this participant is not added as an "internal" argument or direct object of the main verb, which is claimed by many scholars to be a fundamental attribute of applicative constructions (e.g., Payne 1997, 2002; Bresnan and Moshi 1990; Mithun 2002; Haspelmath and Müller-Bardey 2004; Peterson 2007; Kulikov 2011; Creissels 2016, and the Introduction to this volume). Rather, the deputative is semantically related to the whole denoted event; this takes place in its entirety on his/her behalf. Although it is introduced as an object of the construction and of the applicative *DAR* form, the AP is not an argument of the verb: this does not increase its valency.

This is why the *DAR* construction can appear with two dative NPs and two dative indexes, as in (2):

(2) a. *El=Jaime*   **le$_i$=dio**   *a=la=March$_i$*
ART=Jaime   3SG.DAT=give.AUX.APP.3PST   DAT=ART=March
comprándo=le$_j$ *las=papas*   *al=patrón$_j$*.
buy.GRD=3SG.DAT   ART.PL=potatoes   DAT.ART=boss
'Jaime bought the boss the potatoes instead of March.'

b. ***A=la=March$_i$***   *el=Jaime*   **le$_i$=dio**
DAT=ART=March   ART=Jaime   3SG.DAT=give.AUX.APP.3PST
comprándo=le$_j$ *las=papas*   *al=patrón$_j$*.
sell.GRD=3SG.DAT   ART.PL=potatoes   DAT.ART=boss
'Instead of March, Jaime bought the boss the potatoes.'

In (2a), the *le* clitic attached to the applicative form cross-references the AP *a la March* and has a deputative meaning; the enclitic of the gerund verb, *comprándole* 'selling to him/her', cross-references *al patrón* and has a recipient-beneficiary interpretation. The same dative index marks two different object promotion processes: on the one hand, the recipient-beneficiary is added as a new semantic argument of the main verb and as an object through the clitic;[3] on the other hand, the deputative, although also introduced as an object by the dative clitic, is not added as a semantic argument of the main verb and does not further modify the verb's denotation and valency. It is introduced as an argument of the applicative *DAR*. This semantic and structural difference is behind the fact that in these double dative constructions, the speakers prefer the structure in (2b), with a left-dislocated deputative.

Second, the AP can also be expressed as a prepositional phrase (PP). In this case, the AP does not bear the role of deputative, but that of a recipient-beneficiary or a possessor. The prepositions that can introduce these APs are *para* and *de*, as in (3a) and (3b):

(3) a. *El=profesor   dio   escribiendo una=carta*
       ART=teacher   give.AUX.APPL.3PST   write.GRD   ART=letter
       para   los=niños.
       for   ART.PL=children
       'The teacher wrote a letter for the children.'

   b. *Mi=padrino   **le=dio**   vendando*
       1POSS=godfather   3SG. DAT=give.AUX.APPL.3PST   bandage.GRD
       *el=brazo   **del=niño**.*
       ART=arm   PREP.ART=boy
       'My godfather bandaged the boy's arm.'

(3a) and (3b) exemplified two different subtypes of oblique APCs: *DAR* clauses with an AP introduced by *para* cannot be co-referred by the dative index; the ones with an AP introduced by *de* must be cross-referenced by the clitic.

Third, the presence of the applicative *DAR*, besides allowing the introduction of an AP, entails a particular semantic value in the clause subject, semantically an agent, whose referent must be involved in the denoted event in an unexpected fashion, as a special favor to the deputative-beneficiary introduced by the AP, to

---

3 The recipient-beneficiary *al patron* is not an inherent semantic argument of the verb *comprar* 'buy'. This predicate implies that the agent, the buyer, is the one who inherently acts as the receiver of the purchased goods. So, the recipient-beneficiary is introduced as a new argument and as an object. Following scholars such as Strozer (1976), Demonte (1994) and Cuervo (2003), we only consider NPs introduced by *a* as syntactic objects when they are cross-referred by the dative index, otherwise, they are PPs. In this sense, and as proposed by Ibáñez (2001, 2004) and Cuervo (2003), the presence of a dative index indicates an object promotion.

the speaker, or to someone else. In fact, this feature is what triggers the use of the APC instead of the other seemingly alternative ways of expression – (1b) and (1c) – for the coding of the referent of the AP. Although (1b) and (1c) both have the substitutive portion of the propositional meaning, (1b) does not necessarily involve a benefit for the substituted and (1c) does not entail that the agent did the denoted action as an unexpected favor for the deputative. In fact (1b) and (1c) mean that La Runa did the farewell speech because it was part of her job or it was what was expected from her. As we will show, this semantic effect on the agent of the APC remains even in clauses where there is a beneficiary but not a substitution, as well as in clauses where the AP has another semantic role, as maleficiary, location or inalienable possessor.

The paper proceeds in the following order: in section 2 we present the formal characterization of the two syntactic subtypes of the APC: one where the AP is a dative object and one where the AP is a PP. In 3, we turn to the analysis of the semantics of the APC and compare it to those alternative structures for the expression of the referent of the AP; in section 4, we offer some final remarks.

2 Formal characterization of the APC

2.1 APC with a syntactically promoted adjunct

As mentioned in the introduction, a similar construction to the one under analysis has already been studied in the Highland Ecuadorian variety of Spanish (Toscano 1953; Albor 1975; Niño-Murcia 1992, 1995; Hurley 1992, 1995; Bustamante-López and Niño-Murcia 1995; Haboud 1998; Olbertz 2002; Bruil 2006, 2008). Nevertheless, it has mostly been described in terms of its probable origin as a calque from Quichua (Quechua), in relation to other periphrastic structures in Spanish, and in its use as a pragmatic device for the attenuation of the illocutionary force in request speech acts. Following Creissels (2010), here we analyze it as a proper applicative construction, in its uses in declarative speech acts. Its formal template is as in (4):

(4) SUBJ + CLITIC$_{DAT}$-AUX/APPLICATIVE *DAR* + MAIN PRED (GERUND) + AP$_{DAT}$/AP$_{PP}$ + (DO)

This reads as follows:
a) The subject is always preverbal in unmarked cases (not extractions or topicalization).

b) In clauses with indicative/subjunctive mood and in negative imperatives, the dative index attaches to the *DAR* applicative form as a proclitic; in affirmative imperative clauses, it appears as an enclitic.
c) The applicative *DAR* form comes fully inflected as an auxiliary.
d) The main predicate appears as a gerund.
e) The AP tends to appear adjacent to the main predicate. It is usually a dative-marked NP, but it can also be a PP. The semantic roles introduced by the AP are: deputative-beneficiary, recipient-beneficiary, plain-beneficiary, maleficiary, possessor, whole of a part-whole relation and location (source and goal).
f) If the verb is transitive, the base object (DO) tends to appear after the AP, although it can also go before it. It is unmarked when it is a lexical NP,[4] and it appears in the accusative case when pronominalized.

The applicative function of the APC can be seen in the contrast between (5a) and (5b):

(5) a. *Flojas* **le=dio** *haciendo la=cena*
 Flojas 3SG.DAT=give.AUX.APP.3PST prepare.GRD ART=dinner
 ***al=patrón**.*
 DAT.ART=boss
 'Flojas prepared the dinner instead of the boss.'

 b. *Flojas hiz-o la=cena* **en vez de**
 Flojas prepare-3PST ART=dinner instead.of
 el=patrón.
 ART=boss
 'Flojas prepared the dinner instead of the boss.'

In (5a), the AP *al patrón* codes a deputative-beneficiary. This participant is an adjunct in semantic terms; nevertheless, it is introduced into the clause as a dative object, which is cross-referred with the clitic index *le*. This contrasts with its coding as a peripheral adjunct through a prepositional phrase headed by *en vez de* 'instead of' in (5b). Therefore, (5a) implies a semantic and syntactic promotion and can be considered as a "prototypical" applicative according to some definitions.

---

4 Although when it has an animate referent it appears introduced with the *a* preposition as a Differential Object Marking (DOM), as in P*edro golpeó **a Roberto*** 'Pedro hit Roberto'.

5 Applicative periphrastic constructions in the Colombian Spanish from The Andes — 103

The introduction of a dative-marked deputative in (5a) is made possible by the presence of the verbal form *DAR* 'give', in addition to the main predicate *hacer* 'make, prepare'. *DAR* is semantically bleached and functions both as an applicative marker and as an auxiliary hosting flexional features. That *DAR* is not a semantic predicate in this type of clauses is shown by the fact that it can appear with an instance of the lexical verb *dar* 'give' as in (6):

(6) El=Martín   le=**dio**   *dando*   la=plata
    ART=Martin   3SG.DAT=give.AUX.APP.3PST   give.GRD   ART=money
    a=la=March.
    DAT=ART=March
    'Martin gave the money (to someone else) instead of March.'

We follow Creissels (2010) in considering that applicative periphrases are functionally equivalent to mono-verbal clauses with a proper morphologically affixed applicative marker. Creissels (2010: 02) defines these periphrases as two-verbal structures where one of the verbs functions as a lexical predicate (Vlex) and the other one as a verb operator (Vop), in our case *DAR*. The Vlex is the semantic and syntactic nucleus of the clause and the Vop acts as an operator that licenses the adding of an applied phrase.

For Creissels (2010), applicative periphrases constitute an intermediary stage in grammaticalization chains, either from verb to adposition-like or case-marker-like items, or from verbs to applicative verb affixes. In contexts like (7), where *DAR* appears as an infinitive form and is part of a larger periphrastic chain, it loses all its verbal features and functions only as an applicative marker.

(7) a. La=Paty   me=vien-e-a-**dar**   haciendo   la=comida.
       ART=Paty 1SG.DAT=come-3PRS-LK-give.APP   prepare.GRD   ART=dinner
       'Paty comes to prepare dinner instead of me.'

The Spanish variant under analysis belongs to a reduced group of languages, together with Mandarin Chinese (Sinitic, Li and Thompson 1981), Yongning Na (Tibeto-Burman, Lidz 2006), and Abui (Papuan, Kratochvíl 2007), where the Vop precedes the main predicate, as in (8a); the most common case in typological terms, though, is that the Vop is coded in second position inside the periphrastic complex.[5]

---

5 Here we use the term "periphrastic, verbal or predicative complex" in a pre-theoretical fashion to refer to the set-group conformed by the Vop (the applicative mark or auxiliary) and the Vlex (the gerund) plus the clitic index.

(8b) shows that this order is not possible in CAS, so in this regard, the APC follows the obligatory order of all periphrastic constructions in Spanish.

(8) a. *La=Juana* **les=dio** **haciendo**
 ART=Juana 3PL.DAT=give.AUX.APP.3PST do.GRD
 la=tarea *a=los=niños.*
 ART=homework DAT=ART.PL=kid
 'Juana did the homework instead of the kids.'

 b. **La=Juana* **haciendo** **les=dio**
 ART=Juana do.GRD 3PL.DAT=give.AUX.APP.3PST
 la tarea *a=los=niños.*
 ART=homework DAT=ART.PL=kid
 (*intended meaning: 'Juana did the homework instead of the kids.')

In the APC with a syntactically promoted adjunct, the applied phrase is an indirect or dative object. In Spanish, the dative marker on lexical NPs is *a*, which also functions as a preposition; it is obligatory, as can be seen from the contrast between (9a) and (9b):

(9) a. *El=José* *le=dio* *abriendo* ***a=la=Rosa***
 ART=José 3SG.DAT=give.AUX.APP.3PST open.GRD DAT=ART=Rosa
 la=puerta.
 ART=door
 'José opened the door instead of Rosa.'

 b. **El=José* *le=dio* *abriendo* **la=Rosa**
 ART=José 3SG.DAT=give.AUX.APP.3PST open.GRD ART=Rosa
 la=puerta.
 ART=door
 'José opened the door instead of Rosa.'

Following other scholars (Strozer 1976; Suñer and Yépez 1988; Demonte 1994, Cuervo 2003, amongst others), we consider this *a* form, when it introduces a NP that is cross-referenced by a dative clitic, as an analytic dative case marker. In the same way, when *a* heads a NP that is not doubled by the clitic, it is a preposition and the whole phrase is a PP.

Although attested in languages like German and Georgian (Haspelmath and Müller-Bardey 2004), the coding of the AP as a dative marked phrase is not common across applicative languages. In most cases, applicative constructions have an AP that is formally coded as a direct or accusative object (Payne 1997;

5 Applicative periphrastic constructions in the Colombian Spanish from The Andes — 105

Haspelmath and Müller-Bardey 2004; Kulikov 2011). In this sense, in typological terms, the APC of CAS is an atypical structure.

The AP is cross-referenced by an object index that appears attached to the applicative *DAR* unit in the form of a dative clitic. This dative index is a proclitic in indicative and subjunctive mood clauses, as in (10a), and an enclitic in imperative ones as in (10b), but it always cliticizes to the *DAR* unit: It cannot follow the main predicate, as (10c) shows:

(10) a. *La=Rosa   le=dio   vendiendo pan*
        ART=Rosa 3SG.DAT=give.AUX.APP.3PST sell.GRD   bread
        a=Doña=Lupe.
        DAT=HON=Lupe
        'Rosa sold bread instead of Doña Lupe.'

   b. *Da=**les**   haciendo   la=tarea*
       IMP.give.AUX.APP.2PRS=3PL.DAT do.GRD   ART=homework
       a=los=niños.
       DAT=ART.PL=children
       'Do the homework instead of the kids.'

   c. **Da*   haciendo=**les**   la tarea*
       IMP.give.AUX.APP.2PRS do.GRD=3PL.DAT ART=homework
       a=los=niños.
       DAT=ART.PL=children
       'Do the homework instead of the kids.'

As Olbertz (2008) posits for equivalent constructions in the Ecuadorian variety, this behavior indicates that the clitic index is an argument of the *DAR* form and not of the main predicate. She states that according to the rules of clitic climbing in periphrastic constructions in Spanish, examples like (10c) should be fully grammatical, as in this language the clitics alternatively appear on the higher or on the lower predicates of the periphrases irrespective of which one of them is licensing the arguments. However, this is not the case in examples like (10c); so, as Olbertz (2008:4–5) states, "this leads to the conclusion that the attachment of the dative clitic to the auxiliary is not a matter of clitic climbing. Rather than expressing an argument of the lexical predicate, it must somehow belong to the auxiliary, i.e., it must be the expression of a kind of "argument" of *dar*."

This is also confirmed by the fact that there can be clauses with two clitics: one attached to *DAR* and the other one adjoined to the gerund, as in (11), and also (2a) and (2b):

(11) Da=**me**   comprándo=**les**   dulces   a=**los**=**niños**.
     give=1SG.DAT   buy.GRD=3PL.DAT   Candies   DAT=ART.PL=children
     'Buy the children candies instead of me.'

In (11), there are two beneficiaries: the recipient-beneficiary *a los niños* 'to the children', cross-referenced by the index *les* attached to the main verb *comprar* 'buy', and a deputative beneficiary which is the speaker himself, referred by the first-person singular clitic *me* attached to *DAR*. As mentioned in the introduction, this is a type of construction where the dative index is used twice to mark two distinct object promotion processes yielding different results: On the one hand, *comprar* 'buy' in its inherent meaning implies a transfer from a seller to the buyer-agent, who receives the goods that he or she buys. The introduction of a new beneficiary coded as dative object, *a los niños* 'to the children' in (11), adds a new segment of meaning to the event: a transfer of the bought goods from the buyer to the beneficiary, which is the intended final recipient of the goods. As a result, *comprar* has been modified in its denotation, it has increased its valency and it is now a ditransitive predicate.[6]

On the other hand, despite also being introduced as a dative object, the deputative-beneficiary is not semantically added as part of the buying event, but is related to this event in its entirety: the buying takes place as a whole on his or her behalf. In this sense, the deputative is not introduced as a new semantic argument or internal object of the verb and does not increase the verbal valency. We claim instead, in the same vein as Olbertz (2008), that the deputative is rather introduced as an object of the applicative form *DAR* and as an object of the construction as a whole, without modifying the event denoted by the main predicate or its argument structure.

Thus, the same dative form is simultaneously used for two types of promotion processes, which yield different structural and semantic results. This analysis is similar in spirit to the one proposed by Cuervo (2003), who, following Pylkkänen (2002)'s distinction between high and low applicative forms, posits that in Spanish there are two types of dative structures: dative constructions with a high-applicative and dative constructions with a low-applicative.[7] Low

---

[6] As discussed in subsection 3.1, clauses with a dative or indirect object NP cross-referred by the dative clitic, but without *DAR*, are analyzed by Cuervo (2003) and Ibáñez (2001, 2004, 2008) as applicative constructions.

[7] Cuervo (2003) considers a large range of dative constructions as applicative. In a similar way to what it is proposed here for deputatives, Cuervo considers ethical datives as cases licensed by the presence of a high-applicative; as deputatives, they can also appear in the presence of another 'lower' dative (i), except in cases where the two datives have a third person referent, as in (ii):

applicatives introduce a participant as an object and as a new semantic argument of the verb; high applicatives add a participant as an object outside the VP (or the core), in a higher structural position, where it is semantically related to the whole denoted event. Therefore, the valency of the main predicate in the resulting construction is not increased. As Cuervo (2003: 203) puts it, "the general properties of the predicate and event structure are not altered by the presence of the (high) applicative head".[8]

The distinction between high and low applicative morphology correlates with the difference between applicative processes that imply a lexical derivation – a change in the inherent denoted event, the increase of its valency and the transitivization of the verbal base – and applicative processes that yield a new object for the construction without altering the event structure of the predicate (cf. Conti 2008: 171–172). In this same direction, Peterson (2007: 141 and onwards) recognizes the existence of a continuum that goes from applicatives with a more discourse oriented function (like topicalization), without necessarily altering the verbal valency, to those which yield a transitivization.

We propose that the use of the APC to introduce a deputative-beneficiary into the clause is a morphosyntactic operation and not a lexical derivation. Interestingly, a deputative, at least in CAS, can be applied to intransitive, mono-transitive and ditransitive verbal bases, without modifying the verb transitivity or its semantic valency. Probably, as Conti (2008: 172) suggests, this type of process is

(i) *La=profesora*   ***me$_i$=le$_j$=puso***   *diez*   ***al=niño$_j$***
     ART=teacher   1SG.DAT=3SG.DAT=give   ten   DAT.ART=kid
     en=el=examen.
     PREP=ART=exam
     'As for me$_i$, the teacher gave the kid$_j$ a rating of ten in the exam.'

(ii) **La=profesora*   ***le$_i$=puso=le$_j$***   *diez*   ***al=niño$_j$***
     ART=teacher   3SG.DAT=give=3SG.DAT   ten   DAT=ART=kid
     en=el=examen   (**a=élla$_i$*).
     PREP=ART=exam   (*DAT=3PRON)
     '(As for her$_i$), the teacher$_i$ gave the kid$_j$ a rating of ten in the exam.' (intended reading)

(iii) *El=Jaime*   ***le$_i$=dio***   *a=la=March$_i$*   *vendiéndo=le$_j$*
      ART=Jaime   3SG.DAT=give.AUX.APP.3PST   DAT=ART=March   sell.GRD=3SG.DAT
      las=papas   ***al=patrón$_j$.***
      ART.PL=potatoes   DAT.ART=boss
      'Jaime sold the potatoes to the boss$_j$ instead of La March$_i$.'

As (iii) shows, this behavior is possible for the *DAR* construction. What is more, as can also be seen in (iii), third person dative clitics can have a full expression of the cross-referred AP, behavior that is not always allowed for ethical datives, even in cases where there is just one clitic. Strikingly, Cuervo (2003) does not discuss the deputative dative constructions.

8 The content inside the parentheses was added by us.

just a way to topicalize highly prominent discursive referents. This has also been suggested by Toratani (2002) and Van Valin (2005) for the Japanese adversative passive construction.

As is common in languages with indexing on the verbal base, the dative index attached to *DAR* in the APC functions as the proper applied argument, so the coreferential NP can be elided, as in (12a), where the clitic refers to a third singular person, whose referent, a deputative, is recoverable from the immediate discursive or situational context:[9]

(12) a. *El=Danilo* **le=dio**
 ART=Danilo 3SG.DAT=give.AUX.APP.3PST
 pagando *el=dinero* *al=trabajador.*
 pay.GRD ART=money DAT=ART=employee
 'Danilo paid the money to the employee instead of someone else doing it.'

 b. *El=Danilo* **le=dio** *al=patrón*
 ART=Danilo 3SG.DAT=give.AUX.APP.3PST DAT.ART=boss
 pagando *el=dinero* *al=trabajador.*
 pay.GRD ART=money DAT=ART=employee
 'Danilo paid the money to the employee instead of the boss.'

 c. *El=Danilo* *le=dio* *al patrón*
 ART=Danilo 3SG.DAT=give.AUX.APP.3PST DAT.ART=boss
 *pagando=**le*** *el=dinero* ***al=trabajador.***
 pay.GRD=3SG.DAT ART=money DAT=ART=employee
 'Danilo paid the money to the employee instead of the boss.'

(12a) means that it was Danilo who paid the money to the employee instead of someone else unspecified but recoverable from the context, for example, the boss, which is explicitly expressed in (12b). The dative index in (12a), then, is coreferential with an elided deputative-beneficiary. However, similarly to (11), the recipient argument can be also indexed by a clitic, but in this case, the index goes attached to the main verb, as in (12c).

One last formal feature of the APC is its possibility of appearing with predicates with different transitivity values:

---

[9] First and second person indexes almost never have a co-referential AP with the form of an independent pronoun.

(13) a. *El=Martín   le=dio   bailando   a=la=Inés.*
       ART=Martin   3SG.DAT=give.AUX.APP.3PST   dance.GRD   DAT=ART=Ines
       'Martín danced instead of Inés.'

   b. *La=Rosa   le=dio   haciendo   la=tarea*
      ART=Rosa   3SG.DAT=give.AUX.APP.3PST   do.GRD   ART=homework
      al=guagua.
      DAT.ART=kid
      'Rosa did the homework instead of the kid.'

   c. *El=Fidel   le=dio   entregando   la=carta*
      ART=Fidel   3SG.DAT=give.AUX.APP.3PST   deliver.GRD   ART=letter
      al=Martín.
      DAT.ART=Martín
      'Fidel delivered the letter (to someone) instead of Martín.'

(13a) features a syntactically intransitive main semantic verb, *bailar* 'dance', (13b) a transitive one, *hacer* 'do', and (13c) a ditransitive one, *entregar* 'deliver'. As discussed before, the presence of the dative object attached to *DAR* does not alter the event semantics of these predicates.

2.2 APC with an oblique AP

In addition to the APC with an object AP, there are APCs where the AP is a non-promoted adjunct. This type is non-canonical in two ways: first, the AP is not introduced as a dative object, but as a PP; second, the semantic role of the AP is other than the deputative beneficiary. APs in this type of APCs can be headed by two different prepositions. The first one is illustrated in (14):

(14) a. *El=profesor   dio   escribiendo   una=carta*
       ART=teacher   give.AUX.APPL.3PST   write.GRD   ART=letter
       para   **los=niños.**
       for   ART.PL=children
       'The teacher wrote a letter for the children.'

    b. *La=Inés   dio   cocinando   **para***
       ART=Ines   give.AUX.APPL.3PST   cook.GRD   for
       el=patrón.
       ART=boss
       'Inés cooked for the boss.'

In (14a) and (14b) *DAR* introduces a beneficiary as a PP headed by the preposition *para*; that is, there is an oblique-peripheral adjunct despite the appearance of the applicative marker. Hence, this is an APC which does not involve an object promotion. As described in detail in section 3, this type of construction, as all that have applicative *DAR*, entails a different meaning from the one with an adjunct introduced by *para* but lacking the applicative form (i.e., *La Inés cocinó para el patrón* 'Inés cooked for the boss'): basically, that the agent does, impromptu, an action as a special favor to the beneficiary.

Importantly, this construction is used when the speaker wants to avoid the deputative reading. The AP is always interpreted as a recipient-beneficiary or as a plain beneficiary. (14a) means that the children are intended to receive the letter, but it cannot mean that the professor wrote the letter instead of them; in (14b), the boss gets a benefit from Inés's cooking (plain beneficiary reading), but he is not being substituted by her in the cooking event.

The second type of APC with an AP introduced by a preposition, is shown in (15):

(15) a. *La=Anita*   **le=dio**   *cosiendo*
ART=Anita   3SG.DAT=give.AUX.APP.3PST   sew.GRD
el=saco   **del=guagua**.
ART=sweater   GEN.ART=boy
'Anita sewed the boy's sweater.'

b. *Mi=padrino*   **le=dio**   *vendando*
1POSS=godfather   3SG.DAT=give.AUX.APP.3PST   bandage.GRD
el=brazo   **del=niño**.
ART=arm   GEN.ART=boy
'My godfather bandaged the boy's arm.'

In (15a) and (15b) the applicative *DAR* introduces an applied phrase which is formally a possessive PP headed by the preposition *de*. The Possessor referenced by the possessive PP is cross-referenced by the dative clitic index *le*. This is a type of "pseudo-possessor raising construction", where the possessor is indexed in the verbal nucleus, without its co-referential phrase being an object. This "semi-raising" process allows the registered possessor to be more identifiable and be more easily tracked in the discourse context. This type of structures has been acknowledged in the literature as "registration" constructions (see Zavala 2000, Hernández-Green 2016; cf. Payne's 2002 "nucleatives"). As is the case for the structure with *para* in (14), this one also means that the agent is involved in the action impromptu as a special favor to the possessor or someone else. This differentiates it from the seemingly alternative constructions without *DAR*, as *Mi compadre vendó el brazo del niño* 'my compadre bandaged the boy's arm' and *Anita cosió el saco del niño* 'Anita sewed the boy's sweater'.[10]

3 Functional and semantic characterization of the APC

In this section we address the semantics and functions of the APC with a syntactically promoted adjunct (see section 2.1). We assert that although the construction is most frequently used to introduce a deputative-beneficiary as an AP, the basic and constant meaning that arises from the presence of the applicative form *DAR* is that of an agent that, in an unexpected fashion, gets involved in the action as a special favor to someone else. This is typically done as a favor for a substituted agent (the deputative), but it can also be done as a substitution for another unspecified referent, which is not the beneficiary. This meaning is what distinguishes the *DAR* applicative construction from seemingly alternative non-applicative constructions available in CAS.

In fact, as we show in subsections 3.2 and 3.3, the APC can have an AP with semantic roles other than the deputative. The list of roles that the AP can have includes, besides the deputative, the other two types of beneficiaries recognized in the literature (Van Valin and LaPolla 1997; Zúñiga and Kittilä 2010), namely the recipient-beneficiary and the plain-beneficiary, as well as maleficiary, inalienable possessor and location (goal and source).

In a typological perspective and in semantic terms, the *DAR* applicative form seems to be of the specified type. It cannot introduce an AP with the range of roles that APs can have in languages like the Bantu, where, besides the beneficiary, maleficiary, instrument, location, time, purpose, and manner can all be APs (Pacchiarotti 2020). Nevertheless, in an intra-language perspective, *DAR* can be seen as an underspecified unit. Creissels (2010: 02) points out that "in most cases, the type of semantic role assigned by the Vop has a historical connection with one of the participants of the argument structure of the same verb when used in a predicate function". In the case of *DAR*, its "natural" argument is a

---

10 Although the basic semantic features of clauses with an AP formalized as a prepositional phrase are the same of the other *DAR* constructions we discuss in this work (see Section 3), their overall function remains unclear. These clauses are not frequent in our data, and more work is needed to properly account for them. For these reasons, we do not discuss them further in this work.

recipient. In Creissels' terms, neither the deputative, nor the plain-beneficiary, maleficiary[11] or location are in direct connection with the lexical meaning of the *DAR* Vop: they are rather the manifestation of an extended meaning that this unit has developed. In this sense, *DAR* is an applicative marker that has lost its predicative meaning and the connection with its former argument, the recipient, and has become a more abstract operator unit for the applying of other semantic participants. Hence, the APC with a syntactically promoted adjunct in CAS is not only a benefactive structure, as has been characterized in all previous works on the related construction in the Ecuadorian variety (Toscano 1953; Albor 1975; Niño-Murcia 1992, 1995; Hurley 1992, 1995; Bustamante-López and Niño-Murcia 1995; Haboud 1998; Olbertz 2002; Bruil 2008). It is an applicative construction which can introduce other semantic roles besides beneficiary.

In what follows, we address different types of APCs in terms of the semantic roles that the AP can have. We show that the constant meaning of the *DAR* structure regardless of the semantic role of the AP is that of an agent unexpectedly involved in the action as a favor to someone else. This is what distinguishes this construction from other only apparently alternative constructions available in CAS.

3.1 The deputative-beneficiary APC

The most common applied participant in the APC of CAS is the deputative-beneficiary. As reported by Haboud (1998) and Bruil (2008), the *DAR* construction with a deputative AP is also the most frequent in the related construction in Ecuadorian Highland Spanish. This construction has been extensively described in its pragmatic use in request speech acts (Toscano 1953; Albor 1975; Niño-Murcia 1992, 1995; Hurley 1992, 1995; Bustamante-López and Niño-Murcia 1995; Haboud 1998; Olbertz 2002; Bruil 2008), but has not been properly characterized in semantic terms. In fact, deputative constructions are seldom analyzed in the typological literature: usually, there are no reports of which of the three types of beneficiaries is the most frequent in applied clauses and functional and structural differences among beneficiary types are not addressed. For instance, in this chapter, we posit that the presence of a recipient-beneficiary in an applied clause does alter the semantics and argument structure of the main verb; the introduction of a deputative-

---

[11] In many languages there are different applicative morphemes for the introduction of malefactives and beneficiaries (Zuñiga and Kittilä 2010), which suggests that these two semantic roles do not form a natural semantic unit.

5 Applicative periphrastic constructions in the Colombian Spanish from The Andes — 113

beneficiary as a syntactic object in an applied construction does not, so they are different, and they should be treated and analyzed in terms of that difference.

As shown in (16), the *DAR* construction is not the only option for the coding of a deputative in CAS:

(16) a. *El=Danilo   compr-ó   las=papas*
       ART=Danilo   buy-3PST   ART.PL=potatoes
       en vez del   Fabio.
       instead of.ART   Fabio
       'Danilo bought the potatoes instead of Fabio.'

   b. *El=Danilo   **le=dio**   comprando*
       ART=Danilo   3SG.DAT=give.AUX.APP.3PST   buy.GRD
       al Fabio   *las=papas.*
       DAT.ART=Fabio   ART.PL=shoes
       'Danilo bought the potatoes instead of Fabio.'

   c. *El=Danilo   **le=compr-ó**   las=papas*
       ART=Danilo   3SG.DAT=buy-3PST   ART.PL=potatoes
       al=Fabio
       DAT.ART=Fabio
       'Danilo bought Fabio the potatoes / bought the potatoes instead of Fabio.'

In (16a) the beneficiary *Fabio* is coded by means of a PP introduced by *en vez de* 'instead of', whereas in the applied clause in (16b), it is coded as a dative object and is cross-referenced by the clitic index *le*. Although both are deputative constructions, they are not semantically and pragmatically equivalent. The structure with *en vez de* implies that the agent carries out the denoted action in substitution of the referent of the NP that the preposition introduces, but without any implication of a benefit for the referent of the PP. In fact, it is usually the other way round; for example, in (17) below, the substituted player, Jersson González, is removed from the team lineup, which is not a good thing, and the person who benefits is the agent (the subject), Gonzalo Martínez, who gets the opportunity to play in the (football) game.

(17)   *Maturana   anunci-ó=que   **jugar-á   Martínez***
         Maturana   say-3PST=SUB   play-3FUT   Martinez
         ***en=lugar=de*[12]   González**   *a quien   todo el mundo*
         PREP=place=PREP   Gonzalez   REL   everybody

---
[12] *En lugar de* is more or less synonymous with *en vez de*.

daba   como   fijo.
consider.3PST like   fixed
'Maturana said that Martinez will play instead of Gonzalez, who was thought by everybody as the one who was going to be the player.' (*Corpus de Referencia del Español Actual* (CREA); El colombiano, 2001).

According to most informants, (16c) means that the indirect object *al Fabio* is a recipient and not a deputative, he is the one intended as the receiver of the potatoes. In this sense, this construction is different from the one in (16b). Nevertheless, some speakers, on second thoughts, said that (16c) can also have the deputative-beneficiary interpretation. What is, then, in this case, the difference in meaning between (16b) and the deputative reading of (16c)? As reported by the informants, the applied structure with *DAR* obligatorily implies that the agent does the action as a special favor for the substituted, because that person cannot perform the action. Additionally, it is entailed that the agent gets involved in the action unexpectedly, as an answer to a sudden request by the substituted, who is benefited by the accomplishment of the denoted event. These meanings are absent in the deputative reading of (16c). Instead, (16c) in its deputative reading implies a substitution and a benefit for the substituted, but it also means that the agent was supposed to be performing that action, either because he had already planned to do it himself, as part of his obligations, or there was a previous agreement between him and the beneficiary. There is, then, no sudden involvement and neither does a special favor emerge from the given situation.

We can say, then, that *DAR* has two main functions. On the one hand it allows a syntactic promotion: the coding of an adjunct as an object. On the other hand, it triggers those special features on the agent. These two functions usually come together, but this does not need to be so. For instance, in APCs with an AP coded as a prepositional phrase (see section 2.2) there is not a syntactic promotion of an adjunct, but the semantic effect on the agent remains.

The type of clause in (16c) with a dative or indirect object NP cross-referenced by the dative clitic, but without *DAR*, has been previously analyzed, for Spanish in general, by Cuervo (2003) and Ibáñez (2001, 2004, 2008) as an applicative construction in itself. In the works of both scholars, albeit from different theoretical perspectives,[13] it is proposed that this double dative structure implies an object promotion for a beneficiary (or other semantics participants), in contrast to the

---

[13] Cuervo's proposal is done in the context of the minimalist program (Chomsky 1995). Ibáñez's proposal is presented in a functionalist approach.

construction where this participant appears coded as a PP introduced by *en vez de* or *en lugar de* 'instead of' or by *para* 'for', as in (16a) above, and (18) below:

(18)   *El=Danilo   compr-ó   las=papas   para   Fabio.*
       ART=Danilo   buy-3PST   ART.PL=potatoes   for   Fabio
       'Danilo bought the potatoes for Fabio.'

Cuervo (2003) posits that the presence of the dative clitic is the output (or the spell-out in minimalist terms) of the structural introduction of an invisible applicative head. Ibáñez (2001, 2004) proposes that the dative clitic functions simultaneously as a person index and as the applicative marker.[14]

In this context, a double dative clitic construction (double clitic and double dative NP), as in (2a), (2b), (11) and (12c), is a double applicative construction. As mentioned before, the same index form, the dative, marks to different promotion processes with different structural and semantic results: On the one hand, the presence of the dative index attached to the main predicate (the gerund) sanctions the promotion of a recipient-beneficiary which is an added argument of the main verb. On the other hand, the dative clitic adjoint to *DAR* licenses the promotion of the deputative-beneficiary which is added as a syntactic object of the whole construction, semantically related to the whole event.

The fact that, according to most of our informants, the indirect object, or applicative, construction without *DAR* in (16c) has a recipient interpretation in its first reading fits in well with the fact that the APC in CAS is specialized, in terms of frequency, in the promotion of a deputative-beneficiary.

The semantic value of the sudden involvement of the agent as a favor for someone else that is obligatorily entailed by the APC is probably linked to its high frequency of use as an attenuation expression in directive/request speech acts, where the speaker, very politely, asks his addressee to do something instead of him, as in (19):

(19) a. *Da=me   abriendo   la=puerta,   por favor*
          give.AUX.APP.3PST=1SG.DAT   open.GRD   ART=door   please
          'Please, open the door instead of me.'

---

14 Although applicative morphemes are usually distinguished from person indexes in most languages, they can have grammatical person features, as happens in Ika' (Chibchan; Frank 1990; aforementioned in Conti 2008).

b. *Da=me hablando en=la=alcaldía*
   give.AUX.APP.3PST=1SG.DAT speak.GRD PREP=ART=mayor office
   'Speak instead of me at the mayor office.'

(19a) is typically uttered in contexts where the speaker is unable to open the door by himself, because, for example, he has his hands busy with bags or something else, and his addressee is free, so he asks him, very politely, to open the door for him (the speaker) as a favor. This type of use brings about three different features: a) the sudden involvement, as a favor, of the addressee as an agent, b) the benefit for the speaker and c) extra politeness.

The pragmatic use of the APC as an attenuation expression has been the most researched for the Ecuadorian variant (Toscano 1953; Albor 1975; Niño-Murcia 1992, 1995; Hurley 1992, 1995; Bustamante-López and Niño-Murcia 1995; Haboud 1998; Olbertz 2002; Bruil 2008). The APC in CAS is very similar to the Ecuadorian ones in this pragmatic use. Basically, they are a way of softening the request.[15]

Nevertheless, several scholars (Hurley 1992, 1995; Niño-Murcia 1992; Olbertz 2002 and Bruil 2008) have already pointed out that attenuation and politeness are not obligatorily entailed by the APC. As an example, consider another very frequent use of the construction, namely the expression of an offer, as in (20):

(20) *¿Te doy planchando el pantalón?*
    2SG:IO give:1SG iron.GRD the trousers
    'Shall I iron the trousers for you?' (Bruil 2008)

In this type of clause, the speaker offers himself as the agent of the proposed action; in (20) he or she offers to iron the trousers; rather than politeness or attenuation, there is substitution and benefit, as the speaker intends to substitute his or her interlocutor in his or her benefit. More importantly, at least in its CAS version, (20) entails that it is not an obligation of the speaker to help their addressee, and that they suddenly offer their services, when noticing that the interlocutor, for whatever reason, is not able to perform the action by himself or herself.

The politeness and attenuation features are only part of the construction in request acts, and that is why, although the use of the APC in reportative/declarative

---

[15] It is not our goal here to describe the APC in terms of its illocutionary force, against other structural options, such as the plain imperatives or other indirect request constructions. We are rather focusing on the description of the semantic and syntactic characteristics of the APC as an applicative construction and the differences with other alternative options for the coding of the participants introduced by the AP.

clauses is much less frequent,¹⁶ we are basing our semantic analysis on this usage and not on the former. It is very likely that the semantic value of the sudden involvement of the agent as a favor to someone else, obligatorily entailed by the APC, comes from its pragmatic use in requests. It seems that the semantic features originating in this primary pragmatic function of the construction have been carried over to its reportative function.¹⁷

3.2 Other benefactive APCs

In this subsection, we describe the semantics of two APCs that have an AP with a semantic role other than deputative-beneficiary: the quasi-deputative APC, and the expert agent APC. We show that, as with the deputative-beneficiary (see section 3.1), the only feature that is obligatorily activated by these APCs is the fact that the agent, in a sudden way, gets involved in the action as a special favor to someone else.

3.2.1 The quasi-deputative APC

In this semantic subtype of the APC, the agent is not the original person foreseen as the doer of the action; he or she substitutes someone else intended as such, other than the beneficiary:

(21) a. *El=Jairo   le=dio   cantando   al=Alfredo*
        ART=Jairo   3SG.DAT=give.AUX.APP.3PST   sing.GRD   DAT.ART=Alfredo
        en=la=misa
        PREP=ART=mass
        'Jairo sang at mass for the benefit of Alfred instead of someone else.'
        (quasi-deputative reading)

   b. *El=Jairo   cant-ó   para   Alfredo   en=la=misa*
        ART=Jairo   sing-3PST   for   Alfredo   PREP=ART=mass
        'Jairo sang for Alfred at mass.' (plain beneficiary reading)

---

16 Bruil (2008) reports 11% of reportative clauses against 73% of requests in her data for the Ecuadorian construction; questions and offers represents another 10%, and the rest (6%) are other cases.
17 We thank Sara Pacchiarotti for pointing us to this important aspect of our work.

c. *El=Jairo   le=cant-ó   al=Alfredo*
ART=Jairo 3SG.DAT=sing-3PST DAT.ART=Alfredo
'Jairo sang for Alfred (for his ears).' (recipient reading)

In its first reading, out of context, (21a) has a deputative interpretation; it means that Jairo sang instead of Alfredo. But it can also be uttered in contexts where the speaker knew that Alfredo was in trouble, because he was expecting someone else to sing at the mass, and that person did not arrive to do it. Out of the blue, Jairo is asked to sing instead of the absentee, and, fortunately, he has agreed to do it, for the benefit of Alfredo. So, in this case the construction involves a substituted agent and a beneficiary, but these roles are not played by the same referent; therefore, it is a quasi-deputative structure. In Van Valin and LaPolla (1997)'s terms, Alfredo is a plain beneficiary. The structure does not imply politeness or an attenuation in its illocutionary force whatsoever.

In contrast, in (21b) Alfredo is also a plain beneficiary, but Jairo is not meant as a substitute for anyone; he sang because he wanted to do it from the beginning, or because he was already expected to do so. (21c), an indirect object construction, cannot have the deputative interpretation. Instead, it means that Alfredo is a recipient-beneficiary; he is intended as the sole addressee of Jairo's singing; the singing is 'for his ears only'. Complementarily, the APC in (21a) cannot have this last recipient interpretation in any context. Nor can it have the meaning of (21b). In this sense, these structures are not alternative ways to express the same propositional meaning; each one has its own semantic specifications, which are activated in a particular pragmatic niche.

3.2.2 The expert agent APC

In this semantic subtype, the speaker reports an event where the agent is not a substitute; they neither substitute for the beneficiary nor for someone else, but they willingly accept to do the denoted action as a special favor for the beneficiary:

(22) a. *La=María   le=dio   haciendo   una=ruana*
ART=Maria 3SG.DAT=give.AUX.APP.3PST make.GRD ART.IND=coat
al=Horacio
DAT.ART=Horacio
'María made Horacio a coat.'

b. *La=María   le=hizo   una=ruana   al=Horacio*
ART=Maria 3SG.DAT=make.3PST ART.IND=coat DAT.ART=Horacio
'María made Horacio a coat.'

5 Applicative periphrastic constructions in the Colombian Spanish from The Andes — 119

c. *La=María   hizo   una=ruana   para   el=Horacio*
   ART=Maria make.3PST ART.IND=coat for   ART=Horacio
   'María made a coat for Horacio.'

As reported by the informants, a clause like (22a) is uttered in a context where María is kind of an expert in making ruanas, a native type of coat; she is dedicated to that and she is very good at it (this feature gives the subtype its name). Horacio asked her to make a ruana as a special favor to him. Horacio is benefited as the recipient of the ruana, but there is no substitution involved. This clause can also have the deputative interpretation, but only in a context where Horacio is also conceptualized as an expert in making ruanas so that, under certain circumstances, he could probably have been substituted by María.

(22b) and (22c) can also have the recipient and the expert interpretations, but they lack the other feature associated with the agent: the idea that María has graciously made the ruana as a special favor, unexpectedly to all concerned. This is important, because it shows that the APC, in addition to involving an object promotion for the beneficiary, also conveys those semantic traits to the agent.

Besides a recipient-beneficiary, this semantic subtype can also appear with a plain beneficiary or a possessor as the AP, as in (23a) and (23c), respectively:

(23) a. *Diego   me=dio   haciendo=le   los=planos*
       Diego 1SG.DAT=give.AUX.APP.3PST make.GRD=3SG.DAT ART=plans
       a=la=Anita
       DAT=ART=Anita
       'Diego made Anita the plans as a favor for me.'

   b. *Diego   hizo   los=planos   para   la=Anita*
      Diego make.3PST   ART.PL=plans   for   ART=Anita
      'Diego made the plans for Anita.'

   c. *Pedro   le=dio   castrando   el=caballo*
      Pedro 3SG.DAT=give.AUX.APP.3PST castrate.GRD   ART=horse
      al=Luis
      DAT.ART=Luis
      'Pedro castrated Luis's horse.'

(23a) is a double applicative construction, where, as seen before, each instance of the dative index sanctions a different promotion process: On the one hand, *a la Anita* is cross-referenced by the third-person singular clitic *le*. Its referent is a recipient-beneficiary promoted to IO, as can be seen from the contrast with its alternative coding as a PP introduced by *para* in (23b). On the other hand, the first-person singular index *me* is introduced into the clause by the applicative form *DAR*. According to the informants, its referent, the speaker, has asked the agent, Diego, to make the plans for Anita; so, Diego has made the plans as a special favor to the speaker; in this sense, the speaker has the role of a plain-beneficiary.[18] In (23c), the dative phrase *a Luis*, is cross-referenced by the index *le*; it is the AP. In this case the semantic role is that of possessor (of the horse). Luis, as the owner, gets benefited from Pedro's actions.

In both (23a) and (23c), the agent is perceived as an expert. This reading derives from the meaning of the main predicates, which imply that the action is typically done by a professional – an architect in (23a) and a vet in (23c). In the absence of this feature, the construction would be interpreted as a deputative one. In some cases, the appropriate interpretation can only be arrived at through world knowledge, as in *María le dio haciendo un pastel a la Lupe* 'María baked a cake for Lupe', where the difference between the deputative and the expert interpretation is the knowledge that one can have about María: she either is or is not an expert in baking cakes. Context is therefore crucial in distinguishing among semantic subtypes of APC.

On the other hand, the applicative IO construction without *DAR*, – *Pedro le castró el caballo a Luis* 'Pedro castrated Luis's horse' – can also have the expert agent meaning. However, according to our informants, this construction would never be used as a report expression in a context where Pedro has graciously involved himself in the denoted action as a favor for Luis. This context is, it seems, the particular niche of the *DAR* structure. As we will show in the next section, this meaning is the only one that is constant in the APC, as there are cases where even a benefaction is not entailed.

3.3 Non-benefactive APCs

Although the beneficiary is the most common applied participant in CAS, there are APCs that have an AP with other semantic roles: maleficiary, inalienable possessor, and location-related roles.

---

18 One reviewer points out that the first-person singular index *me* can be seen as an ethical dative. The difference between this and the plain beneficiary are not clear-cut. However, the ethical meaning usually implies a more 'abstract' or indirect affectation of a participant that does not have any direct role in the reported event. In both cases, as a plain-beneficiary or as an ethical dative, the index *me* in (23a) seems to be introduced by *DAR*: it cannot be adjoint to the main predicate, e.g., **Diego dio haciéndomele los planos a la Anita* 'Diego made Anita the plans as a favor for me'. Following Cuervo (2003), ethical datives can also be considered the manifestation of a high-applicative.

5 Applicative periphrastic constructions in the Colombian Spanish from The Andes — 121

As Zúñiga and Kittilä (2010) show, there are languages that distinguish between benefactive and malefactive constructions in morphosyntactic terms, so the meanings of benefaction and malefaction do not obligatorily constitute a "semantic package". The conflation of these two semantic values in one linguistic form implies, to a certain degree, a process of semantic generalization. This is the case in languages where one single applicative morpheme covers both meanings.

The APC in CAS can also introduce maleficiaries, as is illustrated in (24):

(24) *La=March* **le=dio** *descomponiendo* **al=Jorge**
Art=March 3SG.DAT=give.AUX.APP.3PST break.GRD DAT.ART=Jorge
el=carro (*del=Martín*).
ART=car PREP.ART=Martín
'March caused Martin's car to break down to the detriment of Jorge.'

The semantic role of the bolded NP is maleficiary: The action performed by the agent is in this participant's detriment. It could mistakenly be taken to be a possessor participant, but it is not, as can be seen from the fact that an extra possessive adnominal modifier (in parentheses) can readily be added after the patient NP. Thus, the referent of the dative NP can be negatively affected without being the possessor.

In the absence of a malefactive applicative form, the "negative effect" arises from the compositional result of the meaning of the verb plus the pragmatic inferences it displays. *Descomponer* in the sense of 'to make something stop working or functioning' as in (24), activates a "negative effect" meaning in pragmatic terms.

An important aspect of the semantics of (24) is the fact that the negative effect cannot be implied as the desired effect. According to all our informants, (24) cannot mean that March voluntarily wanted to break down the car; rather, the interpretation must be that March wanted, as a favor to Jorge, to do something good, such as fixing the car, but instead, something went wrong and, as a result, the car broke down. That is, this subtype of APC still entails the feature of the involvement of the agent on the action as a favor for someone else. If this is not the case, the construction cannon be used.

According to Bruil (2008), the parallel APC in the Ecuadorian variety cannot have a maleficiary meaning. She states that her informants only accepted examples as (24) in cases where it is reported that the referent of the AP explicitly has asked the agent to do the denoted action. In this context, (24) must be interpreted as meaning that Jorge, for whatever reason, wanted the car to break down, and asked March to do it. But in this use, the construction really operates as a benefactive and not as malefactive one.

Another adjunct participant that can be applied in the APC of CAS is the inalienable possessor or the whole of a part-whole relation, as in (25):

(25) a. *El=Roberto*   **le=dio**   *rompiendo*
         ART=Roberto   3SG.DAT=give.AUX.APP.3PST   break.GRD
         el=brazo   **al=Fidel.**
         ART.arm   DAT.ART=Fidel
         'Roberto broke Fidel's arm.'
     b. *El=Mauricio*   **le=dio**   *quebrando*
         ART=Mauricio   3SG.DAT=give.AUX.APP.3PST   break.GRD
         a=la=silla   *una=pata.*
         DAT=ART=chair   ART=leg
         'Mauricio broke the leg of the chair.'

In (25a) the possessor is an animate participant, as beneficiaries and maleficiaries are by default. In (25b), on the contrary, there is an inanimate referent, *la silla* 'the chair', which includes as part of itself *la pata* 'the leg'. Although this type of clauses is not frequent, it is nevertheless important, as it shows that the APC has been extended to inanimate participants, beyond the prototypical beneficiary. This, in turn, shows that *DAR* has become a semantically underspecified applicative form.

Again, this use of the construction is only possible if the agent is meant as acting, in a sudden way, in good will and trying to do a favor to someone else, despite the bad outcomes. If this is not the case, the speakers would use the alternative indirect object construction, as in *Roberto le rompió el brazo al Fidel* 'Roberto broke Fidel's arm', which implies that Roberto did want to cause harm to Fidel.

The APC can also introduce a locative AP with change of place verbs such as *poner* 'put':

(26) a. *El=Danilo*   **le=dio**   *poniendo la=sal*
         ART=Danilo   3SG.DAT=give.AUX.APP.3PRS   put.GRD   ART=salt
         a=la=ensalada.
         DAT=ART=salad
         'Danilo put salt to the salad.'
     b. *La=señora*   *Flor* **les=dio**   *quitando*
         ART=Mrs   Flor   3PL.DAT=give.AUX.APP.3PST   take.from.GRD
         a=los=elotes *las=hojas.*
         DAT.ART.PL=corn   ART.PL=leaves
         'Mrs. Flor took the leaves off from the corn.'

In (26a) the main predicate is a change of place verb oriented to a goal; in (26b) it denotes movement from a source. Both goal and source APs (bolded) in (26a) and (26b) respectively are inanimate arguments coreferential with the dative clitic.

As all the other APCs, the locative subtype has a different meaning and a distinct context of use compared to seemingly alternative clauses where the location is coded as an oblique argument, as in (27a), and to indirect object, or applicative, constructions without *DAR*, where the location has already been promoted to a dative NP, as in (27b):

(27) a. *El=Danilo   pus-o   la=sal   en=la=ensalada.*
         ART=Jorge   put-3.PST   ART=salt   PREP=ART=salad
         'El Danilo put the salt on the salad.'

   b. *El=Danilo   le=pus-o   sal   a=la=ensalada*
      ART=Danilo   3SG.DAT=put-3PST   salt   DAT=ART=salad
      'Danilo put salt in the salad.'

In (27a), with an oblique goal, a pure locative meaning is activated: 'Danilo put the saltshaker on top of the salad inside the container where the salad is found', whereas in (27b) the interpretation is that 'Danilo has added grains of salt to the salad in order to mix the salt with the salad'. As a result, the salad is affected in a good way. (26a) also involves this affectedness of the Location, but in a clear contrast to these two other options, it also entails that 'Danilo put salt to the salad as a favor to all concerned, when it was not his obligation, and nobody expected him to do it'.

This semantic feature associated with the agent is the only constant meaning of the APC of CAS. Although this structure most frequently introduces deputative-beneficiary APs in request speech acts, neither politeness nor attenuation are inherent meanings of the construction; more surprisingly, neither a substitution nor a benefaction is necessarily implied either.

4 Conclusions

In this chapter, we have characterized the *DAR* periphrasis of CAS as a proper applicative construction. We have posited that, in terms of frequency, it is most often used to promote a deputative-beneficiary, an adjunct participant in semantic terms, to objecthood in the applied clause. The notion of the deputative is seldom described in the literature, and in particular, literature on applicative constructions rarely reports the syntactic and semantic differences between deputatives and other types of beneficiaries. In CAS, as it is probably the case in other languages, this type of participant is added as a syntactic object to all types of verb bases without altering their semantic structure and their valency; In this way, deputative applicative constructions are non-canonical. They do not imply a process of lexical derivation and they probably function as a topicalization device. We also discussed the semantic features associated to APCs introducing different semantic roles in relation to other seemingly alternative constructions for the coding of the semantic role of the applied phrase in CAS. We have shown that the APC always entails that the agent is involved in the denoted action in a sudden way, as a special favor to the speaker, the addressee or other referent in the utterance situation. As far as we know, this type of semantic effect on the agent has not been described for applicative morphology in other languages. What is more, these semantics very likely originate in the pragmatic use of the construction as an attenuation expression in directive/request speech acts. As such, this represents a new (to the best of our knowledge) diachronic route (from pragmatics to syntax with specific semantic nuances) for the development of applicative morphology. Interestingly, chapter 13, this volume reports exactly the opposite direction of change, namely, a primarily syntactic applicative construction which developed pragmatic functions in some Tibetan languages.

Abbreviations

A	agent
ACC	accusative
APP	applicative
ART	article
AUX	auxiliar
CVB	converb
DAT	dative
DEM	demonstrative
DO	direct object
FUT	future
GEN	genitive
GR	gerund
HON	honorific
IMP	imperative
IO	indirect object
LK	linker
NP	nominal phrase
O	object
P	patient

PL	plural
POSS	possessive
PP	prepositional phrases
PRED	predicate
PREP	preposition
PRON	pronoun
PRS	present
PST	past
REL	relative
SG	singular
SUBJ	subject
SUB	subordinator

References

Albor, Hugo. 1973. "Da" + gerundio, ¿un quechuismo? Y otras maneras de atenuar los imperativos. ["Da" + gerund, a Quechuismo? And other ways to mitigate the imperatives]. *Hispania* 56. 316–318.

Alsina, Alex & Sam Mchombo. 1993. Object asymmetries and the Chicheŵa applicative construction. In Sam Mchombo (ed.), *Theoretical aspects of Bantu grammar*, 17–45. Stanford: CSLI Publications.

Bresnan, Joan & Lioba Moshi. 1990. Object asymmetries in comparative Bantu syntax. *Linguistic Inquiry* 21. 147–185.

Bruil, Martine. 2006. *La construcción dar + gerundio, ¿transferencia directa o evolución?* [The construction give + gerund, direct transfer or evolution?] Leiden: Leiden University M.A. Thesis.

Bruil, Martine. 2008. Give + gerund in Ecuadorian Spanish: A calque from Quichua or a large process of contact induced change? *Leiden Working Papers in Linguistics* 5 (1). 1–23.

Bustamante López, Isabel & Mercedes Niño-Murcia. 1995. Impositive speech acts in northern Andean Spanish: A pragmatic description. *Hispania* 78. 885–897.

Chomsky, Noam. 1995. *The Minimalist Program*. Cambridge, MA.: The MIT Press.

Conti, Carmen. 2008. *Receptores y beneficiarios: estudio tipológico de la ditransitividad* [Recipients and beneficiaries: typological study of ditransitivity]. Munich: Lincom Europa.

Creissels, Denis. 2010. Benefactive applicative periphrases: a typological approach. In Fernando Zúñiga & Seppo Kittilä (eds.), *Benefactives and malefactives*, 29–70. Amsterdam: John Benjamins.

Cuervo, María Cristina. 2003. *Datives at large*. Cambridge, MA.: MIT dissertation.

Demonte, Violeta. 1994. La ditransitividad en español: léxico y sintaxis [The ditransitivity in Spanish: lexicon and syntax]. In Violeta Demonte (ed.), *Gramática del español* [Spanish Grammar], 431–470. Mexico: Colegio de México.

Gerdts, Donna B. & Kaoru Kiyosawa. 2005. Halkomelem psych applicatives. *Studies in Language* 29(2). 329–362.

Haspelmath, Martin & Thomas Müller-Bardey. 2004. Valency change. In Gert Booij, Christian Lehmann & Joachim Mugdan (ed.), *Morphology: A handbook on inflection and word formation*, 1130–1145. Berlin: De Gruyter Mouton.

Haboud, Marleen. 1998. *Quichua y castellano en los Andes ecuatorianos: Los efectos de un contacto prolongado* [Quichua and Castilian in the Ecuadorian Andes: The effects of prolonged contact]. Quito: Abya-Yala.

Hernández-Green, Néstor. 2016. Registration versus applicative constructions in Acazulco Otomi. *International Journal of American Linguistics* 82(3). 353–383.

Hurley, Joni Kay. 1992. *A cross-cultural pragmatic study of Spanish and Quichua requests strategies as influenced by language contact in Otavalo, Ecuador*. Pittsburgh: University of Pittsburgh dissertation.

Hurley, Joni Kay. 1995. Pragmatics in a language contact situation: Verb forms used in requests in Ecuadorian Spanish. *Hispanic Linguistics* 6–7. 225–264.

Ibáñez Cerda, Sergio. 2001. Functional similarities between Spanish clitic 'le' and applicatives. Paper presented at *The Workshop Voice Systems. Autonomous Queretaro University, 12–16 November*.

Ibáñez Cerda, Sergio. 2004. Introduciendo participantes en la estructura argumental: el caso del clítico *le* del español [Introducing participants in the argumental structure: the case of spanish clitic *le*]. In Víctor Sánchez (ed.), *Actas del XIII Congreso Internacional de ALFAL* [Proceedings of the XIII International Congress of ALFAL], 1125–1132. San José de Costa Rica: Costa Rica University.

Ibáñez Cerda, Sergio. 2008. El papel del clítico *le* en las construcciones de duplicación de dativo. Evidencia diacrónica [The role of the clitic le in the dative doubling constructions. Diachronic evidence]. In Concepción Company y José Moreno (eds.), *Actas del VII Congreso Internacional de Historia de la Lengua Española* [Proceedings of the VII International Congress on the History of the Spanish Language], 719–730. Madrid: Arco-Libros.

Kratochvíl, František. 2007. *A grammar of Abui: A Papuan language of Alor*. Leiden: Leiden University dissertation.

Kulikov, Leonid. 2011. Voice typology. In Jae Jung Song (ed.), *The Oxford Handbook of Linguistic Typology*, 368–398. Oxford: Oxford University Press.

Li, Charles & Sandra Thompson. 1981. *Mandarin Chinese: a functional reference grammar*. Berkeley: University of California Press.

Lidz, Liberty A. 2006. A synopsis of Yongnin Na (Mosuo). Paper presented at the *39th International Conference on Sino-Tibetan Languages and Linguistics, University of Washington, 15–17 September*.

Mithun, Marianne. 2002. Understanding and explaining applicatives. In Mary Andronis, Cristopher Ball, Heidi Elston & Sylvain Neuvel (eds.), *Proceedings of the Thirty-seventh Meeting of the Chicago Linguistic Society: Functionalism and formalism in Linguistic Theory*, 73–98. Chicago: Chicago Linguistics Society.

Niño-Murcia, Mercedes. 1992. El futuro sintético en el español norandino: Caso de mandato atenuado. *Hispania* 75(3). 705–713.

Niño-Murcia, Mercedes. 1995. The gerund in the Spanish of the North Andean Region. In Carmen Silva Corvalán (ed.), *Spanish in four continents: Studies in language contact and bilingualism*, 83–100. Washington D.C.: Georgetown University Press.

O'Herin, Brian. 2001. Abaza applicatives. *Language* 77(3). 477–493.

Olbertz, Hella. 2002. *Dar + gerundio en el español andino ecuatoriano. Sintaxis, semántica y origen* [Give + gerund in the Ecuadorian Andean Spanish. Syntax, semantics and origin]. *Círculo de Lingüística Aplicada a la Comunicación* 12 [Circle of Linguistics Applied to Communication 12]. https://webs.ucm.es/info/circulo/no12/olbertz.htm (accessed 20 May 2021).

Pacchiarotti, Sara. 2020. *Bantu applicative constructions*. Chicago: Centre for the Study of Language and Information.

Payne, Thomas Edward. 1997. *Describing morphosyntax: A guide for field linguists*. Cambridge: Cambridge University Press.

Payne, Thomas Edward. 2002. Toward a substantive typology of applicative constructions. Invited lecture at the *Third Winter Typological School*, 29 January – 6 February, Moscow, Russia.

Peterson, David. 2007. *Applicative constructions*. Oxford: Oxford University Press.

Pylkkänen, Liina. 2002. *Introducing arguments*. Cambridge, MA.: MIT dissertation.

Shibatani, Masayoshi. 1996. Applicatives and benefactives: A cognitive account. In Masayoshi Shibatani & Sandra A. Thompson (eds.), *Grammatical constructions: Their form and meaning*, 157–194. Oxford: Clarendon Press.

Strozer, Judith. 1976. *Clitics in Spanish*. Los Angeles: University of California dissertation.

Suñer, Margarita & María Yépez. 1988. Null definite objects in Quiteño. *Linguistic Inquiry* 19(3). 511–519.

Toratani, Kiyoko. 2002. *The morphosyntactic structure and logical structures of compound verbs in Japanese*. Buffalo: State University of New York dissertation.

Toscano Mateus, Humberto. 1953. *El español en el Ecuador* [Spanish in Ecuador]. (Revista de Filología Española, Anejo 61). Madrid: Consejo Superior de Investigaciones Científicas.

Van Valin, Robert & Randy LaPolla. 1997. *Syntax: Structure, meaning and function*. Cambridge: Cambridge University Press.

Van Valin, Robert D. 2005. *Exploring the syntax-semantics interface*. Cambridge: Cambridge University Press.

Van Valin, Robert D. 2013. Head-marking languages and linguistic theory. In David A. Peterson, Alan Timberlake, Balthasar Bickel & Lenore A. Grenoble (eds.), *Language typology and historical contingency: In honor of Johanna Nichols*, 91–123. Amsterdam: John Benjamins.

Zavala, Roberto. 2000. *Inversion and other topics in the grammar of Olutec (Mixean)*. Eugene: University of Oregon dissertation.

Zúñiga, Fernando & Seppo Kittilä (eds.). 2010. *Benefactives and malefactives*. Amsterdam: John Benjamins.

An Van linden
6 Spatial prefixes as applicatives in Harakmbut

Abstract: This paper focuses on valence-increasing morphology that introduces a non-Actor argument into the clause in Harakmbut (isolate, Peru). It first discusses two dedicated applicative markers which are in complementary distribution, and then homes in on a set of spatial prefixes which can also serve an applicative function. These prefixes are positionally flexible, and may simultaneously occur in distinct slots on a single verb form. Three types of uses can be distinguished for the spatial prefixes: non-syntactic, valence-neutral spatial uses, valence-increasing spatial uses and valence-increasing non-spatial uses. It is argued that these three uses can be interpreted as distinct stages on a grammaticalization pathway from spatial, lexical element to abstract, non-spatial grammatical element. The prefixes investigated turn out to occupy different places on this applicativization pathway. These spatial prefixes are a previously unreported source for applicative markers.

1 Introduction

This paper[1] investigates applicative morphology in the underdescribed language Harakmbut, more specifically the Arakmbut (Amarakaeri) dialect,[2] spoken in the

---

[1] The research reported on in this paper has been made possible by mobility grants and postdoctoral grants from the Research Foundations FWO and FNRS, as well as by research project grants from the research council of KU Leuven (GOA/12/007 & C14/18/034). It also benefitted from my research stay in Lyon from September 2020 until January 2021, funded by the Collegium de Lyon and the LabEx ASLAN at the Dynamique Du Langage lab of the University of Lyon. I thank the anonymous reviewers and the editors for their insightful comments on earlier drafts. Any errors of fact or interpretation remain my own responsibility. Finally, my sincere thanks go to the Harakmbut people, who warmly welcomed me in their communities and patiently taught me their beautiful language.
[2] I would like to point out that the speakers of this variety regard the label *Amarakaeri* as a depreciating term; it is adapted from *wa-mba-arak-a-eri* (NMLZ-VPL-kill-TRNS-AN), a verb-based nominalization meaning '(fierce) killer/murderer', which goes back to an ancient story about the

---

An Van linden, University of Liège & KU Leuven, Department of Modern Languages: Linguistics, Literature & Translation, Place Cockerill 3 - 5, Liège, Belgium, e-mail: an.vanlinden@uliege.be

https://doi.org/10.1515/9783110777949-006

south-east Peruvian Amazon (departamentos of Madre de Dios and Cusco). Harakmbut is still considered an unclassified (Amazonian) language (cf. Wise 1999: 307; WALS), although Adelaar (2000, 2007) has argued for a genetic link with the Brazilian Katukina family, which may be further linked to Macro-Jê. For more information on its genetic affiliation, internal classification, vitality and sociolinguistic context the reader is referred to Van linden (2022).

Harakmbut shows very rich applicative morphology, including dedicated applicatives, but also a set of spatial prefixes ("prefijos posicionales" in Tripp 1995: 218–219), which are sometimes found to serve applicative functions. The potential for spatial verb morphology to carry out applicative functions such as introducing an applied phrase into a main clause has been noted only recently in other language families as well (see, e.g., this volume, chapter 9 for Nilotic). In contrast to dedicated applicative morphology, spatial prefixes are not invariably valence-changing. In fact, their basic function is to specify the location/spatial configuration of participants in events. In terms of argument roles, this spatial information targets the S-argument in intransitive and the O-argument in transitive clauses. This paper will focus on three spatial prefixes: *ti*- (1), which indicates location high up, *on-~n-* (2), which signals the spatial relation of 'in', '(in)to' (Tripp 1976: 8) or 'on', and *ok-~k-* (3), which expresses 'separation' (Tripp 1995: 219).[3] While *ti*- in (1) is valence-neutral, *n*- in (2) and *k*- in (3) increase the valence of the verb.

(1) ken   on-**ti**-pok   mboerek-ta
    then   3PL.IND-SPAT:up-pass   man-ACC
    'Then they pass the man (who is high up, on a ladder).' (Pear story)

(2) o-wedn-ato   ãnĩ   bisikleta   o-**n**-kot
    3SG.IND-lie-AM:MOVE&DO   FILLER   bicycle   3SG.IND-SPAT:on-fall
    'He falls (literally: 'moves and lies down'), eh, he falls onto his bike.'
    (Pear story)

---

origin of the different ethnolinguistic groups of the Harakmbut people. They prefer to call their variety 'Arak(m)but', as distinct from the Watipaeri variety, towards whose speakers they generally entertain feelings of enmity rather than brotherhood.

3 In addition to these three, Tripp (1995: 218–219) mentions three more "positional" prefixes, viz. *taʔ-* for force against an object, rear position, or downward movement, *wa-* 'meet (someone) / find (something)' (with the action directed at another person or object), and *to-* for accompaniment. The first two prefixes, *taʔ-* and *wa-*, will be discussed in Section 4.4; the prefix *to-*, by contrast, cannot be analysed as a spatial prefix. Rather, it is a sociative causative marker (Van linden 2022). To my knowledge, *ti-*, *on-~n-*, *ok-~k-*, *taʔ-*, and *wa-* are the only spatial prefixes in the language.

(3) i-**k**-totok-me-y   eʔ-pidn   abuela-ta
    1SG-SPAT:separation-pull-REC.PST-1.IND   NPF-thorn   grandmother-ACC
    'I pulled a thorn out of grandmother('s knee).' (Fieldnotes)

In (1), *ti-* does not introduce an applied phrase, but specifies the location of the object argument (*mboerek-ta*). In (2), *n-* introduces an applied phrase to the intransitive verb root *kot* 'fall' (*bisikleta*), which is zero-marked, as is typical for inanimate object arguments of transitive verb stems. In (3), *k-* introduces the Source-location participant (viz. the person "out of whom" the 1SG A-argument pulled a thorn) as a core argument (*abuela-ta*), and thus turns a transitive root into a ditransitive stem. Note that for (2) and (3), and similar cases (see Section 4.2), the language lacks non-applicative constructions, that is, the spatial prefixes are obligatory to introduce the Goal and Source arguments respectively. Since the spatial prefixes can introduce non-Actor arguments into main clauses, as in (2) and (3), they can be analysed as applicative morphemes according to the broad definition proposed in the introduction to this volume. In (1), however, the function of the spatial prefix is non-syntactic; it characterizes the object argument in terms of location, just like verbal classifiers – also present in the language – characterize object arguments (or S-arguments in the case of intransitive verbs) in terms of shape or substance (see Rose & Van linden 2022).

Interestingly, spatial prefixes not only attach to verbs whose semantics involve motion (self-motion in (1), involuntary motion in (2), caused motion in (3)); they are also found on non-motion verbs. In some cases, their spatial meaning has been metaphorically extended or gone lost completely and their specific semantic import is more tied to the verb's lexical meaning. In such cases, the spatial prefixes are invariably valence-increasing and sometimes even syntactically optional, like *ti-* in (4b). While in the base clause in (4a) the semantic role of the person dreamt about is mapped onto a comitative adjunct (*ndoʔedn nãŋ-ere* 'with my mother'), in the applicativised clause in (4b) this participant is expressed as a core argument, i.e. the object argument signalled by the accusative case (*ndoʔedn nãŋ-ta*).

(4) a. ndoʔ-edn nãŋ-ere   i-yorok-mbedn-i
       1SG-GEN   mother-COM   1SG-dream-all.night-1.IND
       'I dreamt of my mother all night.' (elicitation)

    b. ndoʔ-edn nãŋ-ta   i-**ti**-yorok-mbedn-i
       1SG-GEN   mother-ACC   1SG-SPAT:up-dream-all.night-1.IND
       'I dreamt of my mother all night.' (elicitation)

Based on the present-day distribution of the spatial prefixes, I will set forth a diachronic hypothesis where *ti-*, *on-~n-*, and *ok-~k-* occupy different places along a grammaticalization path from spatial prefix characterizing the location/spatial configuration of S or O to non-spatial applicative, i.e. a pathway from a valence-neutral spatial use (cf. (1)) through a valence-increasing spatial use (cf. (2) and (3)) to a valence-increasing non-spatial use (cf. (4b)). In addition to these three prefixes, I will also briefly discuss two more prefixes that might be analysed similarly to *ti-*, *on-~n-*, and *ok-~k-* and can be placed on this same pathway, viz. prefixes *ta?-* and *wa-* (Section 4.4). At the same time, on some verb roots the (combinations of) spatial prefixes are no longer semantically transparent, and we thus observe lexicalization of prefix(es)-verb combinations (e.g. *e-ma-ti-on-ka* NMLZ-VPL-SPAT:up-SPAT:on-do 'hunt').

More generally, this paper contributes to the typology and diachrony of applicatives in adding a new source for applicative markers, i.e. spatial verb morphology. Importantly, the Harakmbut spatial prefixes do not originate in verbs or adpositions, both of which are well-attested diachronic sources for applicative markers (Peterson 2007: 123–141). To my knowledge, they cannot be traced back to any independent element of a particular word class. While Nordlinger (2019) and Rose (2019) recently pointed to new applicativization strategies originating in nouns, viz. noun incorporation in Murrinhpatha (non-Pama-Nyungan, Australia) and verbal classifiers in Mojeño Trinitario (Arawak, Bolivia) respectively, this paper suggests that applicative markers need not arise from free morphemes; they can also develop from verb morphology that is already in place with a basic non-applicative function. The same strategy is described for directional markers in Nilotic, see this volume, chapter 9. Interestingly, both in Nilotic and Harakmbut bound elements with spatial semantics develop into applicative markers.

The data used in this paper come from earlier work on Harakmbut, which has mainly concentrated on the Arakmbut variety (Hart 1963; Helberg 1984, 1990; Tripp 1976, 1995), as well as first-hand data collected in the field. The latter include elicited data and a collection of seven texts representing spontaneously produced language recorded in the native communities of Puerto Luz, San José del Karene and Shintuya, all with Arakmbut consultants, in the summers of 2010, 2011 and 2016. The practical orthography used in this paper is IPA-based, and different from the community spelling (see Van linden 2020: 9, note 2).

The discussion is organized as follows. Section 2 discusses the basic features of Harakmbut grammar that are needed to understand how applicatives work in the language. While Section 3 focuses on dedicated applicatives, Section 4 homes in on the three distinct uses of the spatial prefixes central to this paper, and briefly discusses two more potential candidates for the category of spatial prefix in the language. Section 5 addresses lexicalized uses of spatial prefixes. Section 6 recapitulates the major findings and elaborates on their diachronic implications.

2 Morphosyntactic-typological sketch of Harakmbut

This section discusses some basic features of Harakmbut grammar that are crucial to understand valence-changing operations. Specifically, it concentrates on verb classes in terms of transitivity, the morphological template of finite verbs, and the coding of grammatical relations, realized by both head- and dependent marking (based on Van linden 2022).

Harakmbut verbs divide into copular, intransitive, transitive and ditransitive roots[4] and require valence-changing morphology to change transitivity. For instance, the verb root *ĩrĩŋ* 'hide' is intransitive, as illustrated in (5a), and takes the transitivizer/causative suffix *-a*[5] to become a transitive stem ('hide, conceal'), cf. (5b).

(5) a. *mboerek   õ-ĩrĩŋ-me   apetpet-a*
       man   3SG.IND-hide-REC.PST   jaguar-NOM
       mbe-arak-apey-a-po
       3SG>1SG-kill-APPR-QUOT-DEP
       'The man hid lest the jaguar kill him.' (elicitation)

   b. *mboerek   õ-ĩrĩŋ-**a**-me   widn   ken   toto-ta*
       man   3SG.IND-hide-TRNS-REC.PST   stone   3/DIST   evil.spirit-ACC
       o-arak-me-niŋ
       3SG.IND-kill-REC.PST-REL
       'The man hid the stone with which he had killed the evil spirit.'
       (elicitation; Van linden 2022: 470, ex. (61))

Harakmbut also has a set of labile verb roots, such as those denoting breaking events, which can occur in syntactically transitive and intransitive constructions without dedicated valence-changing morphology depending on their (non-)volitional event semantics (see Van linden 2020: 16–17). Intransitive constructions invariably have patientive S-arguments and feature the non-volitional perfective aspect marker, while transitive constructions show the volitional perfective marker when the A-argument is acting deliberately. However, in the case of involuntary

---

[4] Or stems, if the verb lexeme derives from a non-verbal root through a verbalization process.
[5] It should be noted that this suffix does not invariably increase the valence of the verb; one of its functions on transitive verbs is also to signal a high degree of intensity of the action, e.g. on cutting events.

actions, transitive constructions feature patientive A-arguments, applicative morphology and the non-volitional perfective marker, as illustrated in (11) in Section 3.

Valence-changing morphology is found in several slots in the morphological template of finite verbs. The template is presented in Figures 1 (prefixes) and 2 (suffixes); both figures include the verb stem slot and represent optional morphology between brackets.[6] The arrows in Figure 1 indicate between which fixed slots the flexible prefixes can intervene. More details on this positional flexibility and the differences in scope entailed will be given in Sections 4 and 5.

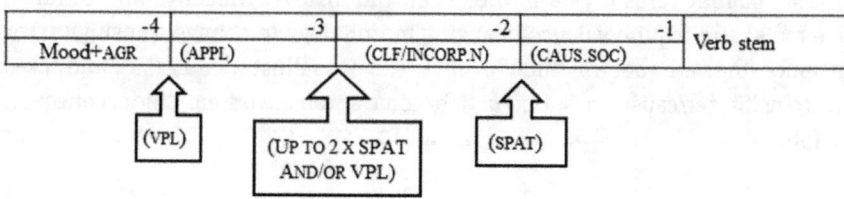

-4	-3	-2	-1	
Mood+AGR	(APPL)	(CLF/INCORP.N)	(CAUS.SOC)	Verb stem

(VPL)   (UP TO 2 X SPAT AND/OR VPL)   (SPAT)

Figure 1: The prefix string of Harakmbut finite verb forms.

Verb stem	1	2	3	4	5	6	7
	(ASP 1)	(TRNS)	(ASP 2/AM)	(AVRT)	(ASP 3)	(Tense)	Mood+AGR; MOD; EVID

Figure 2: The suffix string of Harakmbut finite verb forms (cf. Tripp 1976).

In Figure 2, only slot 2 hosts valence-changing morphology; in Figure 1, three out of four slots do so, viz. slots -3 to -1. The prefixes in slots -3 and -1 increase the valence of the verb root; noun incorporation in slot -2 is either valence-decreasing, valence-increasing or valence-neutral depending on the type of noun incorporation as distinguished by Mithun (1984) (for noun incorporation in Harakmbut, see Van linden 2022 and Rose & Van linden 2022). Interestingly, the spatial prefixes, which are focus of this paper, do not have a fixed position in the template; they are positionally flexible. The same goes for the verbal plural marker (VPL) (see Van linden 2022: 464).

Grammatical relations are coded both on finite verb forms (head marking) and on noun phrases (dependent marking). Both head and dependent marking

---

[6] Figure 1 is a revised version of the prefix string presented in Van linden (2020: 9–10), in which the two applicative morphemes discussed in Section 3 of this paper were mistakenly attributed distinct slots.

have been discussed in Van linden (2019: 461–463; 2022: 458–461, 468–469). Head marking on verb stems occurs in slots -4 and 7. On transitive stems, A-arguments are always indexed, unlike O-arguments. Specifically, the system shows hierarchical indexation: whereas third-person O-arguments are never indexed, speech act participant O-arguments (i.e. first or second person) require relational prefixes in slot -4, viz. portmanteau prefixes indexing both A and O. On the one hand, situations that involve a third person acting on another third person (i.e. non-local scenarios, cf. Zúñiga 2006) and those involving a speech act participant acting on a third person (i.e. direct scenarios) only index the A-argument with person markers that are identical to those used for S-arguments. On the other hand, situations involving a third person acting on a speech act participant (i.e. inverse scenarios) as well as situations involving one speech act participant acting on another speech act participant (i.e. local scenarios) trigger different sets of relational prefixes in slot -4. All of this means that valence changes are easiest to spot in situations involving first or second person O-arguments. Note that the participant cross-reference markers also code the verbal category of mood (cf. Van linden 2022: 457–461).

The dependent marking system on noun phrases is organized differently from the head marking system, but is no less complex. Here the complexity arises because the three argument roles (S, A and O) show differential (see Aissen 2003) or optional marking (case vs. zero exponence, see Bickel & Nichols 2007). The differential marking of O-arguments is animacy-based. Human and higher order animate O-arguments carry the accusative case marker *-ta* (e.g. *mboerek-ta* 'man' in (1)), while inanimate and lower order animate Os are zero-marked (e.g. *eʔpidn* 'thorn' in (2)). Accusative case is also marked on human indirect objects in ditransitive clauses. The differential marking of A-arguments is governed by both animacy and focus. Non-focal animate A-arguments typically go unmarked (e.g. *mboerek* 'man' in (5b)), while inanimate A-arguments are nominative-marked. Animate As that are in argument focus tend to be marked, e.g. *Lupe-a-nda* in (6), which features the focus marker *-nda* suffixed to the nominative case marker *-a*.

(6) *Lupe-a-nda   oʔ-tegŋ-me   mbiʔigŋ-tone-nda*
    Lupe-NOM-FOC 3SG.IND-cut-REC.PST fish-big-NDA[7]
    'Lupe herself cut the big fish.' (Van linden 2019: 460, ex. (5))

Animate A-arguments that are in focus within the broader discourse context also typically carry nominative case, but no focus marker (Van linden 2019: 462).

---

[7] The analysis of the suffix *-nda* on adjectival roots remains unclear (see Van linden 2022: 454).

S-marking is optional. Whether they have human referents (e.g. *mboerek* 'man' in (5a)) or inanimate ones, S-arguments are typically zero-marked. Only very rarely (and in contexts discussed by McGregor 2007, 2010) are S-arguments marked by nominative case. While the Harakmbut dependent marking system has been analysed as a nominative-accusative system in earlier work (Helberg 1984; Tripp 1995), the patterns of optional A- and S-marking described in more detail in Van linden (2019: 461–463) point to a tripartite system of alignment, in which overt marking of S is highly constrained.[8] To this should be added that external noun phrases encoding arguments are very often unexpressed, which hampers the analysis of valence changes in examples involving non-local and direct scenarios (see Sections 4.2 and 4.3).

3 Dedicated applicatives

This section concentrates on dedicated applicatives, viz. the benefactive applicative *niŋ-* (cf. Tripp 1995: 204, 217) and the semantically underspecified applicative *ta-*,[9, 10] the description of which will serve as a standard of comparison for discussing the applicative functions of spatial prefixes in Section 4. The two applicative markers are in complementary distribution in slot -3, and to a large extent meet the criteria for canonical applicatives mentioned in Peterson (2007). That is, they are morphological devices marked on the verb that "allow the coding of a thematically peripheral argument or adjunct as a core-object argument" (Peterson 2007: 1), and they are syntactically optional, i.e. the applicative constructions alternate with non-applicative constructions that have an oblique rendering of the applied phrase (Peterson 2007: 50–51). Consider the pairs in (7) to (10), which contrast non-applicative structures in the (a)-examples with their applicative counterparts in the (b)-examples.

---

8 While in Van linden (2019: 463) I mistakenly argued for an "optional ergative-accusative" alignment system, I now believe that the Harakmbut case-marking system comes closer to a tripartite system, in which O-arguments are accusative-marked, A-arguments nominative-marked, and S-arguments zero-marked.
9 An applicative prefix of the form *tV-* is one of the shared characteristics of the languages in the Guaporé-Mamoré linguistic area (Crevels & Van der Voort 2008), and further beyond in (North) western and Southern Amazonia (Crevels & Van der Voort 2020).
10 The applicative *ta-* occasionally ends in a glottal stop to demarcate a syllable boundary (cf. Van linden 2022: 443); I will nevertheless refer to it as *ta-*, while the spatial prefix *taʔ-* discussed in Section 4.4, which invariably ends in a glottal stop, will be referred to as *taʔ-*.

(7) a. *Pablo   o-matinoa   Maribel-tewapa*
       Pablo   3SG.IND-sing[11]   Maribel-BEN
       'Pablo is singing for Maribel (to cure her).' (elicitation)

   b. *Pablo   o-**niŋ**-matinoa   Maribel-ta*
       Pablo   3SG.IND-BEN.APPL-sing   Maribel-ACC
       'Pablo is singing for Maribel (to cure her).' (elicitation)

(8) a. *Yoma   oʔ-ka   wenpu   ndo-tewapa*
       Yoma   3SG.IND-make string.bag   1SG-BEN
       'Yoma is making a string bag for me.' (elicitation)

   b. *Yoma   me-**niŋ**-ka-ne   wenpu*
       Yoma   3SG>1/2SG-BEN.APPL-make-IND   string.bag
       'Yoma is making me a string bag.' (elicitation)

(9) a. *mboerek   oʔ-wadn   wettone-ere*
       man   3SG.IND-sit   woman-COM
       'The man is sitting with his wife.' (elicitation)

   b. *mboerek   o-**ta**-wadn   wettone-ta*
       man   3SG.IND-APPL-sit woman-ACC
       'The man is sitting with his wife.' (elicitation)

(10) a. *Ana   o-mba-tuk-ʔe   tareʔ   Lupe-ere*
        Ana   3SG.IND-VPL-plant-ITER   manioc   Lupe-COM
        'An is planting (a whole field of) manioc with Lupe.' (elicitation)

    b. *Ana   o-**ta**-mba-tuk-ʔe   tareʔ   Lupe-ta*
        Ana   3SG.IND-APPL-VPL-plant-ITER   manioc   Lupe-ACC
        'An is planting (a whole field of) manioc with Lupe.' (elicitation)

The pairs in (7) to (10) illustrate the syntactic optionality of the benefactive applicative as well as that of the semantically underspecified applicative when the applied phrase bears the semantic role of Comitative participant. For example, to render the meaning in (7), speakers can opt for the non-applicative construction in (7a), in which the Beneficiary of the action denoted by the verb is coded as a benefactive adjunct, or for the applicative construction in (7b), in which the verb features the benefactive applicative prefix *niŋ*- and the Beneficiary now appears

---

11 This is a lexicalized verb stem containing the spatial prefix *ti*-, as detailed in (32a) below.

as an accusative-marked direct object.[12] At the same time, the examples demonstrate the valence-changing nature of the applicative markers. The intransitive predicates in (7a) and (9a) become transitive in (7b) and (9b), while the transitive predicates in (8a) and (10a) become ditransitive in (8b) and (10b). That is, the applicatives in the (b)-examples introduce an internal argument to the argument structure of the underived verb roots; the applied phrases are marked for accusative case (cf. (7b), (9b), (10b)) or trigger a relational person prefix on the verb, as in (8b), just like direct objects and indirect objects of underived transitive and ditransitive predicates respectively (see Section 2). Semantically, the applied phrases have a thematic role that is peripheral to those dictated by the verb root, such as Beneficiary in (7b)–(8b) and Comitative in (9b)–(10b).

While *niŋ-* invariably introduces Beneficiary participants and is syntactically optional, the semantically underspecified applicative *ta-* is not restricted to introducing Comitative participants; it can also introduce Maleficiaries, Beneficiaries and Possessors. Unlike in (9) and (10), it is not straightforward to come up with non-applicative counterparts for these other thematic roles, which are to be inferred on the basis of the lexical semantics of the verb root the applicative attaches to and the event denoted by the applicative construction. In example (11), for instance, *ta-* introduces a Maleficiary and is syntactically obligatory.

(11)   mbe-***ta***-k-puk-on-ne   ilo
       3SG>1/2SG-APPL-SPAT:separation-tear-PFV.NVOL-IND   thread
       'The thread got torn on me' (Lit.: 'The thread got torn with respect to me; the thread got torn to my detriment.') (Van linden 2020: 16, ex. (12b))

Example (11) refers to a non-volitional event, viz. the breaking of the thread during sewing. In such events, the labile root *puk* is used intransitively, with a patientive subject (*ilo*) and the non-volitional perfective suffix -*on*. The applicative prefix *ta-* here introduces an object argument into the main clause which has the thematic role of Maleficiary (viz. the involuntary Agent); the 1SG participant is adversely affected by this event. The applied phrase triggers a portmanteau prefix on the verb indexing both the 3SG A-argument *ilo* and the 1SG O-argument (Van linden 2020: 16–17). Note that the spatial prefix *k-* here merely indicates that the tearing event led to two separate parts of the thread. That is, it shows a valence-neutral spatial use, as discussed in Section 4.1 below.

---

[12] The possible discourse or meaning differences between the applicative and non-applicative constructions need further research.

In example (12), *ta-* introduces a Beneficiary and is syntactically obligatory as well. The intransitive verb root *ndi* 'be asphyxiated because of barbasco' in (12) is only predicated of fish. Unlike the A-argument in (7b), which features the benefactive applicative *niŋ-*, the fish are not voluntarily engaged in the event. In (12), the applied phrase ('1/2PL'), indexed on the verb, is mapped onto the participant inferred to benefit from this involuntary event, i.e. the people who can easily collect the asphyxiated fish to eat them. The benefactive applicative *niŋ-* is not acceptable here, and thus seems to be restricted to voluntary events.

(12) ken   o-ma-ndi-me   ken=piʔ,
then   3SG.IND[13]-VPL-be.asphyxiated.by.barbasco-REC.PST   3=INDET
wakkaʔ-mon   ken
much-MIN   then
mo-**ta**-ma-ndi-me-ne
3>1/2PL-APPL-VPL-be.asphyxiated.by.barbasco-REC.PST-IND
'then they [i.e. the fish] were asphyxiated because of barbasco; somewhat many fish were asphyxiated for us [i.e. to our benefit].' (Anecdote on communal fishing activity)

In cases like (13), in turn, *ta-* introduces a Possessor as an object argument, which is indexed on the verb by a relational prefix.[14] It is also possible for the indexed Possessor to be additionally expressed by a genitive-marked free (pro)noun. Note that a possessive interpretation such as 'my thread broke' also works for (11).

(13) o-**ta**-mba-to-tiak-me-ne   e-mamboya
1<>2SG-APPL-CLF:hand;leaf-CAUS.SOC-come-REC.PST-IND   NMLZ-photograph
'I brought your photograph.' (Lit. 'I brought a photograph with respect to you.') (Fieldnotes)

While the semantically underspecified applicative *ta-* is a syntactically optional means of expressing a comitative participant, as in (9)–(10), the meanings it gives rise to in (11) to (13) do not have clear non-applicative counterparts. This means that, unlike the benefactive applicative *niŋ-*, it cannot be regarded as a canonical applicative in the sense of Peterson (2007).

---

[13] Note that plural lower animate or inanimate subjects trigger singular agreement on the verb.
[14] Only this possessive meaning of *ta-* was noted earlier (Tripp 1995: 204).

Free pronouns or noun phrases expressing the applied participant often do not occur in natural discourse, as their referents can be inferred from verb indexation if first or second person or from the preceding discourse if third person. Example (14) is a case in point for *ta-*; an example for *niŋ-* is (17) in Section 4.1.

(14) ãnĩ   pera o-***ta***-ma-nda-mbere?
 FILLER pear 3SG.IND-APPL-VPL-CLF:fruit-steal
 (Preceding context: a man is picking pears, a boy arrives on his bike and steals a basket of pears) 'Eh, he [i.e. the boy] is stealing pears from him [i.e. the pear picker].' (Pear story)

In (14), *ta-* introduces the participant from whom the boy steals the pears, i.e. the pear picker, which is not overtly expressed, as it is a discourse-given participant.[15]

If applied participants are expressed by free pronouns or noun phrases, they typically follow the pattern of differential object marking described in Section 2. However, it should be noted that in examples with *niŋ-* I have also come across third person applied participants marked for benefactive case (*-tewapa*), just like in examples with *ta-* used in possessive contexts I have found first, second and third person applied participants marked for genitive case, together with the verb indexation. These cases, which may hint at non-syntactic functions of the dedicated applicatives (see the introduction to this volume), are left for further study.

---

15 Note that the use of *ta-* in (14) is functionally equivalent to the separative applicative suffix *-apitsa* in Nanti (Arawak, Peru), which indicates "both that the applied object is the erstwhile possessor of the demoted object, and that the verbal subject is involved in depriving the possessor of the demoted object" (Michael 2012: 163–164). Comparing non-applicative (ia) with applicative (ib) below, we see that *-apitsa* introduces a 1SG object while demoting the base object *kotsiro* 'knife', which no longer triggers object marking on the verb in (ib), as opposed to (ia) (=*ro*). The applied phrase in (ib) bears the thematic role of the erstwhile possessor of the demoted object (Michael 2012: 163–164).

(i) a. *i=koshi-t-ak-i=ro*   *kotsiro*
        3MSG=steal-EPC-PFV-REAL.I=3FSG   knife
        'He stole the knife.'

    b. *i=koshi-t-**apitsa**-ak-i=na*   *kotsiro*
        3MSG=steal-EPC-APPL.SEP-PFV-REAL.I=1SG knife
        'He stole the knife from me.' (Michael 2012: 164, ex. (51))

4 Spatial prefixes as applicatives

Whereas the dedicated applicatives *niŋ-* and *ta-* discussed in Section 3 are invariably valence-increasing, spatial prefixes are not. Nor do they have a fixed slot in the morphological template of the finite verb. They can be inserted either before or after incorporated nouns in slot -2 (see Figure 1). When they occur before slot -2, there can be combinations of two contiguous spatial prefixes (see also Tripp 1995: 219), or of two prefixes each preceded by a verbal plural marker (see example (33c) in Section 5). The discussion below is organized in terms of the semantics and valence-changing behaviour of the three spatial prefixes *ti-*, *on-~n-*, and *ok-~k-*. Section 4.1 discusses the basic non-syntactic, or valence-neutral uses of the spatial prefixes: they specify the location/spatial configuration of participants in the event denoted by the verb root they attach to, but they do not introduce a core argument into the clause. Section 4.2 homes in on applicative functions of the spatial prefixes that involve spatial semantics. Section 4.3 presents cases where the spatial prefixes show valence-increasing uses as well, but their spatial meaning has been metaphorically extended or gone lost at the expense of the lexical semantics of the host verb. In Section 4.4, the discussion is widened to two more potential candidates for the category of spatial prefix.

4.1 Valence-neutral spatial uses

The three spatial prefixes studied here show valence-neutral uses and express only spatial meaning when combining with intransitive, transitive and labile verb roots that do not necessarily have a motion component in their lexical semantics. The location/spatial configuration targets the S-argument of intransitive roots or of intransitively used labile roots, as in (15), or the O-argument of transitive roots, as in (1) and (16b). Note that in (11) above, which features an intransitively used labile root with dedicated applicative marking, the spatial prefix *ok-~k-* targets the A-argument, viz. the patientive subject *ilo* 'thread'.

(15) *o-**k**-ket-on*   *pĩã*
     3SG.IND-SPAT:separation-break-PFV.NVOL arrow
     'The arrow broke into pieces.' (elicitation)

(16) a. *Lupe oʔ-tegŋ-me   mbiʔigŋ*
        Lupe 3SG.IND-cut-REC.PST fish
        'Lupe cut (into) the fish.' (Lupe made cuts in the fish, e.g. to remove the guts) (elicitation)

b. *Lupe o-**k**-tegŋ-me   mbiʔigŋ*
   Lupe   3SG.IND-SPAT:separation-cut-REC.PST   fish
   'Lupe cut the fish into pieces.' (elicitation)

Comparing (16a) with (16b), we see that the spatial prefix does not change the argument structure of the verb root it attaches to; the latter remains transitive. Together, examples (1), (11), (15) and (16) show that the prefixes serve a non-syntactic function; their basic function is semantic, viz. narrowing down the location/spatial configuration of the O-argument in the case of transitive roots and that of the S-argument in the case of intransitively used labile roots. Thus, just like verbal classifiers, spatial prefixes operate on an ergative basis in Harakmbut (see Van linden 2022: 467). In (15) and (16b), the prefix *ok-~k-* specifies the internal spatial configuration of the S and O arguments respectively. That is, it signals that the targeted entity changed from a whole entity (or an entity in one piece, whose internal parts are spatially contiguous) at the beginning of the event to an entity that is broken into pieces (which are no longer spatially contiguous) at the end of the event. The prefix *ti-* occurring on a transitive root in (1), in turn, signals that the O-argument, the man on the ladder, is high up with respect to the A-argument.

Finally, example (17) illustrates the valence-neutral spatial use of *on-~n-*. It is taken from a story in which a jaguar has killed a young girl. Her mother brings her corpse back home (having kept it safe by having thrown it into a ravine), and her kinsmen tie the corpse up on the patio as if she were seated in hopes of luring the jaguar to the village so that they can kill him (in which they succeed, see example (24b) below).

(17)   *ken-taʔ   ãrĩ-tẽ   kuru-te   on-niŋ-**on**-tuk-po,*
       DIST-LOC   FILLER-LOC   patio-LOC   3PL.IND-BEN.APPL-SPAT:on-plant-DEP
       muneyo-ta   eʔ-wadn-a-pa   on-niŋ-ka-tuy
       girl-ACC   NMLZ-sit-TRNS-manner   3PL.IND-BEN.APPL-do-REM.PST.INDIR.EVD
       'Then, eh, they planted her on the patio for him [i.e. the jaguar], as if the girl were seated (lit. 'they made the girl sit'), they did that for him [i.e. the jaguar].' (narrative)

In the first verb in (17), the spatial prefix follows the benefactive applicative *niŋ-*, whose applied phrase is left unexpressed, but can be inferred from the preceding context, namely the jaguar. The spatial prefix *on-* specifies the location of the girl (the O-argument of the transitive root *tuk* 'plant', left unexpressed) with respect to the oblique participant *kuru-te* 'patio-LOC' at the end of the event denoted by the verb; her corpse ends up on the surface of the patio whereas normally Patient participants of planting events are at least partially in the ground. Note that the prefix does not increase the valence of the transitive root *tuk* 'plant', unlike *niŋ-*, because the location *kuru-te* is expressed as an adjunct.

4.2 Valence-increasing spatial uses

We now turn to syntactic uses of the three spatial prefixes discussed in Section 4.1, more specifically to syntactic uses in which they still retain spatial semantics. This use is found on both intransitive and transitive roots, and the location/spatial configuration targets the underived S-argument of intransitive roots, i.e. the A-argument in the applicative structures in (18) to (21), and the underived O-argument of transitive roots, i.e. the base objects in (3) and (22). Examples (18) to (20) illustrate the valence-increasing use of the spatial prefixes with the intransitive verb root *kot* 'fall'. Example (18) repeats (2).

(18) o-wedn-ato   ãnĩ   bisikleta   o-**n**-kot
     3SG.IND-lie-AM:MOVE&DO FILLER   bicycle   3SG.IND-SPAT:on-fall
     'He falls (literally: 'moves and lies down'), eh, he falls onto his bike.' (Pear story)

(19) o-**k**-mba-kot-onka-me-te   yave
     3SG.IND-SPAT:separation-VPL-fall-suddenly-REC.PST-INDIR.EVD   key
     An-ta
     An-ACC
     'An's keys fell all of a sudden.' (Lit. 'The keys suddenly fell away from An.') (Fieldnotes)

(20) Pomelo-a   o-ku-**ti**-kot-ay   Joeri-ta
     grapefruit-NOM 3SG.IND-head-SPAT:up-fall-AVRT   Joeri-ACC
     'A grapefuit almost fell on Joeri's head.' (Fieldnotes)

The constructions in (18)–(20) are all transitive, with the applied phrases functioning as direct objects that are either accusative-marked or are unmarked for case, in accordance with the patterns of differential O-marking (see Section 2). In (18), the prefix *n-* introduces the applied phrase *bisikleta* 'bicycle', which expresses the Goal participant of the falling event. In (19), the prefix *k-* introduces the applied phrase *An-ta* 'An-ACC', which expresses the Source participant of the falling event. In (20), the prefix *ti-* introduces the Goal participant of the (averted) falling event, i.e. *Joeri-ta* 'Joeri-ACC'. Note that the incorporated noun *-ku* 'head' is interpreted as the relevant subpart of the Goal participant, as rendered in the translation provided (cf. Type II noun incorporation in Mithun (1984: 857–858)). Semantically, while *n-* and *ti-* both introduce Goal arguments, they differ in that *n-* is underspecified in terms of the location of the moving entity (the underived S) at the beginning of the event, while *ti-* signals that it falls from high up, viz. from a grapefruit tree. The three prefixes thus introduce a Location argument into the clause, and locate the underived S-argument (now A-argument) with respect to this applied phrase, either at the beginning or at the end of the event denoted by the verb.

This valence-increasing use of spatial prefixes with intransitive verb roots is rather frequent in the texts analysed; they typically occur on self-motion verbs like 'go (out)' or posture verbs like 'lie' (see (32d) below), but also introduce Location arguments with verbs like 'urinate'. A motion-verb example with *ok-~k-* is given in (21).

(21) *pĩã   o-**k**-mã-õrõk-on-po*
arrow   3SG.IND-SPAT:separation-VPL-go.out-PFV.NVOL-DEP
wa-tiak-ya
NMZL-come-LOC
'[Kumamin went], having gone out of the hideout leaving his arrow behind.'
(Lit. 'having gone out of the hideout away from his arrow') (narrative)

In (21), the spatial prefix introduces the applied phrase *pĩã* 'arrow', which expresses the Source participant of the leaving event. Note that the verbal plural marker precedes – and thus scopes over – the verb root rather than the applied phrase. Here, verbal plurality is interpreted in terms of dispersedness, viz. 'going out in various directions', not knowing where to go because of fear. Note also that (21) contains a Source participant coded as adjunct, viz. *watiak-ya* 'from the hideout'. However, the applied Source participant, the arrow, is far more topical in the events related than the oblique one, the hideout. That is, the spatial prefix is used here to introduce discourse-topical information as a core argument.

The valence-increasing potential of spatial prefixes on intransitive verbs has been noted by Tripp (1995: 204) – albeit for other spatial prefixes, namely *ta?-* and *wa-* (see Section 4.4). Tripp (1995: 204) claims that spatial prefixes do not have valence-increasing effects when used with transitive verbs. However, this is only partially true. That is, while spatial prefixes may be valence-neutral on transitive roots, as shown in Section 4.1, they sometimes do change the valence of a transitive root, turning it into a ditransitive stem. In these contexts, they typically express caused motion as in (3) and (22).

(22) tiaway-we õʔ-ẽ,   sowata-yo   o-**k**-mbere?   ken
    see-NEG   3SG.IND-be   silence-LOC 3SG.IND-SPAT:separation-steal 3
    'he [i.e. the pear picker] doesn't see him [i.e. the boy]; he [i.e. the boy] is stealing them [i.e. the pears] from him [i.e. the pear picker] secretly, while the pear picker is away.' (Pear story)

Just like in (3), the spatial prefix *k-* introduces a Source argument 'from him' (left unexpressed) in (22) with respect to which it locates the base object 'the pears' (also unexpressed in (22)). While in (3) the Source argument benefits from the pulling event, in (22) the Source argument is adversely affected by the stealing event, and can additionally be interpreted as a Maleficiary, similarly to the applied phrase of the dedicated applicative *ta-* in (14). The difference with *ta-* in (14) is that *k-* adds spatial information about the Maleficiary in (22), indicating that he was not physically present at the stealing event. That is, while *ta-* can be used, for instance, to introduce victims of pickpockets, *ok-~k-* cannot, as it necessarily implies a physical distance between the (base) O-argument and the applied O-argument throughout the stealing event.[16] By using the spatial prefix *ok-~k-* rather than the dedicated applicative *ta-*, Harakmbut speakers can thus convey very specific spatial information in an economical way.

A last question that needs discussing is whether the valence-increasing uses illustrated above have "alternative constructions in which the semantically peripheral entity is expressed as an oblique" (Peterson 2007: 121). They do not, at least not without losing spatial details expressed in the examples given. For instance, the intransitive root *kot* 'fall' does occur with obliques (and without spatial prefixes), but such examples express events like 'fall into a river', i.e. into a container, which have a different spatial configuration than the events in (18) to (20). The examples given here thus illustrate obligatory applicative constructions, and are hence more similar to the non-comitative uses of the dedicated applicative *ta-* than to the examples with the benefactive applicative *niŋ-*.

4.3 Valence-increasing non-spatial uses

The second valence-increasing use of the spatial prefixes discussed so far is one in which their spatial meaning has weakened to mere involvement in the event.

---

[16] Note that in the pulling event in (3) this requirement of distance only holds at the end of the event; at the beginning, the O-argument ('thorn') and the applied O-argument ('grandmother') are spatially contiguous.

It has been attested for only two of them, on-~n- and ti-. In this use, the semantic role of the participant introduced by the spatial prefixes depends much more on the lexical semantics of the verb they attach to. In some cases we can see metaphorical extension at work; in others it is more difficult to account for the shift from spatial to non-spatial meaning. Also, in this use, on-~n- and ti- typically introduce human non-Actor arguments into the clause, while the spatial valence-increasing uses do not show this animacy restriction. Examples (23) and (24) offer contrastive pairs, in which the (b)-examples come from different parts of the same story.

(23) a. *kate-apo   ken-pa   ya-mba-suhka*
what-REAS   DIST-manner   3SG.DUB-VPL-eat.crumbs
'Why are they eating crumbs like that?' (elicitation)

b. *kate-apo   ken-pa   me-**n**-mba-suhka-ne*
what-REAS   DIST-manner   3SG>1/2SG-SPAT:on-VPL-eat.crumbs-IND
'[The girl fished with barbasco, but she did not kill any fish.] "Why are they [i.e. the fish] eating crumbs to me like that [instead of being asphyxiated]?"' (narrative)

(24) a. *on-harak-uy-ate   ken-ta?   sik-yo,*
3PL.IND-kill-REM.PST-INDIR.EVD   DIST-LOC black-LOC
'Then they killed him/her/it/them at night.' (elicitation)

b. *on-**ti**-harak-uy-ate   ken-ta?   sik-yo,*
3PL.IND-SPAT:up-kill-REM.PST-INDIR.EVD   DIST-LOC black-LOC
*watimbuy-a-nda   o-**ti**-harak-po*
brother.in.law-NOM-FOC   3SG.IND-SPAT:up-kill-DEP
'Then they killed him [i.e. the jaguar] at night in her defence [i.e. the girl's defence]. Her brother-in-law himself killed him [i.e. the jaguar] in her defence.' (narrative)

Unlike in (17), in (23b) the spatial prefix on-~n- does not specify the location of an argument, nor does it introduce a Location argument into the clause, as it does in (18). Rather, it is functionally equivalent to the dedicated applicative ta- introducing a human Maleficiary, as in (11); the applied phrase is indexed on the verb by a relational prefix. The speaker, the girl referred to in (24b), is wondering why the fish are just eating the barbasco rather than getting asphyxiated by it. This situation affects her negatively, because her mother takes this as a sign from the spirits that her daughter is not respecting the social mores; she thinks her daughter is having an illicit relationship with her brother-in-law. In (23a), by contrast, the action of eating crumbs is not represented as affecting anybody. Similarly to (23b), unlike in (1), the spatial prefix *ti-* in (24b) does not convey any spatial information about an argument, neither does it introduce a Location argument and specify the moving entity's location at the beginning of the event talked about, as it happens in (20). Instead, it introduces an (unexpressed) argument, namely 'the girl' who was killed (see example (17)), with a semantically peripheral role. Specifically, it expresses that the girl's kinsmen killed the jaguar to prevent the latter from eating the girl's propped-up corpse, i.e. they killed him in her "defence". This contrasts with (24a), where the killing event is not represented as serving to protect someone. The semantic role of Maleficiary in (23b) and that of a Beneficiary in whose defence the Agent carries out an action in (24b) have no spatial semantics to them.

Non-spatial, purely valence-increasing uses of *ti-* and *on-~n-* are very frequent in naturally occurring discourse. For example, clauses introducing reported speech typically feature the verb *n-a* (SPAT:on-say) 'say to someone, tell', with the Addressee as the applied phrase. An example is given in (25), where the reported speech clause is underlined. The applied phrase is again left unexpressed, but its referent can be gathered from the preceding context: the mother is addressing her daughter. Reporting clauses with transitivized *n-a* are much more frequent than those with the intransitive root *a* 'say'.

(25) in-pa   o-**n**-a-tuy-ỹã
     PROX-manner   3SG.IND-SPAT:on-say-REM.PST.INDIR.EVD-REP.EVD
     ta?mba-yo   ya-wa-atu   o-**n**-a-po
     swidden-LOC   2SG.IMP-go-short.while 3SG.IND-SPAT:on-say-DEP
     wã-ỹẽ-ã
     NPF-mother-NOM
     'Her mother said to her like this – so they say: "Go to the swidden for a short while!", telling her.' (narrative)

Another frequently occurring verb that often takes *on-~n-* is *ka* 'do, make', which comes to mean 'do something to someone', as illustrated in (26). Example (26) is uttered by Maribel, interrupting her aunt who is telling a story. Prior to Maribel's turn in (26), her aunt told about a little boy who had special powers; he made every pond next to which he was seated dry up so that his mother and her associates could easily collect the fish (no need for nets, fishhooks, or barbasco). The people of the village were suspicious and jealous, and they killed the boy. Maribel then asks how the people did this to the little boy, that is, how they killed him.

(26) men-pa   an-**on**-ka-tuy,   tia
     which-manner   3PL.DUB-SPAT:on-do-REM.PST.INDIR.EVD   aunt
     'How did they do it to him, auntie?' (narrative)

Note that the applied phrase 'the boy' in (26) is again left unexpressed because it is discourse-given at that stage. In the turns following (26), Maribel's aunt answers by saying that they made the boy suffer from fatal diarrhoea.

For the frequent uses in (25) and (26), I invoke metaphorical extension to explain the semantic shift of the spatial prefix: the prefix on-~n- introduces an argument that is the human Goal of the actions of saying and doing respectively. That is, the concept of Goal is extended from the concrete spatial domain to the abstract domain of human cognition and interaction (cf. Givón 2009: 89).

In relation to the question of syntactic optionality of this non-spatial applicative use of spatial prefixes, it should be noted that for (23b), (24b), (25) and (26) it is hard to come up with an alternative structure that lacks the valence-increasing spatial prefixes and yet includes reference to the participant in the corresponding applied phrase. These examples thus instantiate obligatory applicative constructions. Yet, ti- proves to be syntactically optional when occurring on the intransitive root *yorok* 'dream' in (4) above, repeated here as (27).

(27) a. ndoʔ-edn   nãŋ-ere   i-yorok-mbedn-i
        1SG-GEN   mother-COM   1SG-dream-all.night-1.IND
        'I dreamt of my mother all night.' (elicitation)

    b. ndoʔ-edn   nãŋ-ta   i-**ti**-yorok-mbedn-i
        1SG-GEN   mother-ACC   1SG-SPAT:up-dream-all.night-1.IND
        'I dreamt of my mother all night.' (elicitation)

The prefix ti- does not contribute any spatial meaning to (27b); the circumstance that (27b) is semantically equivalent to (27a) suggests that the thematic role of the applied phrase is that of a comitative participant similarly to what the dedicated applicative ta- introduces in (9b) and (10b). Yet, in view of the meaning of the verb root *yorok* 'dream',[17] the thematic role of the applied argument is rather that of Stimulus. I have no insights into the semantic difference between the applicative and non-applicative variants in (27).

---

[17] Note that both (27a) and (27b) are used when the person dreamt of is still alive at the moment of dreaming. When a deceased person visits you in your dreams, the Harakmbut use the verb *tiaway* 'see' but at the same time attach the suffix -*kundak* 'deceased' to the noun coding the direct object.

If we consider the cases discussed in this section in isolation, the gloss 'SPATIAL' seems inappropriate for the prefixes studied.[18] In this valence-increasing non-spatial use, their use on specific verb roots does not seem to be semantically motivated; it is unclear why one verb root combines with *on-~n-*, another with *ti-*, and yet another with the dedicated applicative *ta-*. Unlike the verb root *kot* 'fall' in Section 4.2, the verb roots in the examples discussed in this section do not show variation in terms of the spatial prefixes they combine with. What the examples do share is that the applied argument is invariably a human participant. In terms of syntactic optionality, finally, the spatial prefixes resemble the dedicated applicative *ta-* in being obligatory for some and optional for other semantic roles.

4.4 Other spatial prefixes?

Besides *ti-*, *on-~n-*, and *ok-~k-* discussed in Sections 4.1–4.3, Tripp (1995: 218–219) mentions three additional "positional" prefixes, viz. *taʔ-*, *wa-*, and *to-* (see note 3). While there are reasons to analyse the last one as a sociative causative marker which fills slot -1 in the morphological template of the verb (Van linden 2022: 465), the prefixes *taʔ-* and *wa-* might indeed receive a similar treatment to the threesome central to this paper.

The prefix *taʔ-* formally differs from the semantically underspecified applicative *ta-* merely by a final glottal stop, and signals "force against an object, rear position, or downward movement" (Tripp 1995: 218). Examples are in (28) and (29).

(28) e-mba-**taʔ**-tegŋ-nãỹõ   õwẽỹ,   mon-ka   taʔmba
      NMLZ-VPL-SPAT:force.against-cut-COND   tree   1PL.IMP-do   swidden
      'If he fells the trees, we will make a swidden.' (elicitation)

In (28), the prefix *taʔ-* does not affect the valence of the verb root it attaches to; *tegŋ* 'cut' remains transitive. Although the event of cutting trees in (28) results in chopped up tree pieces (stumps and felled trees), speakers do not use the spatial prefix *ok-~k-* to indicate separation (see (16b)), but rather *taʔ-*, highlighting the force used to cut down a tree as well as the falling movement of the tree. The prefix *taʔ-* in (28) thus shows a valence-neutral spatial use.

---

18 Yet I have kept their spatial origin in the glosses for the sake of consistency; identical forms attaching to identical host types (verbs) and having related meanings receive a single gloss.

An example of valence-increasing spatial use can be found in Tripp's (1995: 204) grammar notes. Prefixing *taʔ-* to the intransitive root *wa* 'go' (see (30)) yields the transitive stem *taʔ-wa*, meaning 'follow, chase, track down (an enemy or prey)'.

A non-spatial use of *taʔ-* is illustrated in (29), where it combines with the spatial prefix *on-~n-* (see also Section 5). The complex verb stem *nõ-põ-ẽ* 'know; think' is transitive, with *ndigŋ* 'pain, anger, hate' serving as the direct object; together the verb and object mean 'become angry'. The prefixes *n-* and *taʔ-* together introduce just one internal argument 'at her/her mother', which is left unexpressed.

(29) õ-kỹẽ-ãtõ-põ   wa-yombu   ndigŋ
      3SG.IND-arrive-AM:MOVE&DO-DEP   NPF-daughter   anger
      õ-n-**tãʔ**-nõ-põ-ẽ-tuy
      3SG.IND-SPAT:on-SPAT:force.against-vital.centre-CLF:round-be-REM.PST.
      INDIR.EVD
      ken   o-wik-ato-po
      then   3SG.IND-cry-AM:MOVE&DO-DEP
      'When her_i daughter_j arrived, she_j got angry at her_i [i.e. her_j mother_i] and started crying.' (narrative)

In (29), the linear order of *n-taʔ-* precludes an analysis of *taʔ-* as the dedicated applicative *ta-* (ending occasionally in a glottal stop to demarcate a syllable boundary, see note 10), because spatial prefixes never occur before the dedicated applicatives in slot -3 (see Figure 1 in Section 2). In (29), we thus have a combination of two spatial prefixes which together introduce the participant against whom pain or anger is felt, but – as usual in third-person narratives – the lexical applied phrase is omitted, as it is identifiable in the discourse. Semantically, the prefixes do not convey literal spatial meaning, but the spatial meaning contributed by *taʔ-* can be understood to apply metaphorically, with the force of anger being targeted against the mother. Together with *on-~n-*, *taʔ-* thus shows a valence-increasing non-spatial use in (29).[19]

The second candidate to be discussed is *wa-*, which according to Tripp (1995: 219) means "meet someone or find something, action directed at another person

---

[19] An alternative analysis suggested by one of the editors is that the prefix *n-* has a valence-increasing non-spatial function, introducing a human metaphorical Goal argument like in (25) and (26), while *taʔ-* only adds strength to the action of feeling anger. However, the force in (29) is no physical force like in (28), but rather a metaphorical force. Hence, this alternative analysis suggests a fourth use not found for other spatial prefixes, viz. valence-neutral non-spatial uses, which is hard to fit in with the grammaticalization pathway I propose in Section 6.

or object." However, I have only found examples where *wa-* signals that the event has a human Goal argument. Its syntactic optionality is illustrated in (30). When it combines with a motion verb, the semantic import of *wa-* is spatial, conveying goal-directed movement.

(30) a. *Luis-en-mba-yo   ih-wa-y*
       Luis-GEN-place-LOC   1SG-go-1.IND
       'I go to Luis's place' (elicitation)

   b. *Luis-ta   ih-**wa**-wa-y*
       Luis-ACC   1SG-SPAT:human.goal-go-1.IND
       'I am going to visit Luis.' (elicitation)

At the same time, the pair in (30) illustrates the valence-increasing nature of *wa-*, which turns the intransitive verb root *wa* 'go' into the transitive stem 'visit'; the human applied phrase is marked for accusative case (*Luis-ta*) and functions as direct object. A similar use is exemplified in (31), where the 1SG applied Goal argument triggers a relational person prefix on the verb. The reported thought clause is underlined.

(31) <u>taka   mẽ-**wã**-õrõk-ne</u>
     Taka   3SG>1/2SG-SPAT:human.goal-go.out-IND
     <u>õ-nõ-põ-ẽ-po</u>   wa-tiak-ya
     3SG.IND-vital.centre-CLF:round-be-DEP NMZL-come-LOC
     '"A Taka person will come out to me," he thought at the hideout.' (narrative)

While in (30) *wa-* is syntactically optional, in (31) it is obligatory. This is because in (30b) the introduced Goal argument is a fixed location, i.e. Luis' house, while in (31) the introduced Goal argument is a moving entity itself, i.e. a character in a story.

Finally, there are also cases where *wa-* attaches to the intransitive root *a* 'say' and seems to be used in a metaphorical sense, but more research is needed here.

5 Lexicalized uses

Whereas in the examples analysed so far the spatial prefixes could be neatly identified in morphologically complex verb forms, in some cases complex verb stems are no longer semantically transparent, and while one might still be able to identify distinct morphemes, the overall meaning of the verb stem is no longer compositional, or too little predictable to warrant morpheme breaks. Examples of such lexicalized uses of spatial prefixes and combinations thereof are given in (32) in Table 1 in the form of dictionary entries. The nominalizer *e(ʔ)-* is used in the citation form of verbs (cf. Van linden 2019: 457). The translations come from Tripp (1995), but the morphological analyses are mine. Abbreviations used in Tables 1 and 2 are: intr = intransitive; tr = transitive; cop-intr = copular-intransitive; ditr = ditransitive.

Table 1: Lexicalized verb stems containing spatial prefixes.

(32)	Verb root	Valence of root	Lexicalized verb stem	Morphological analysis	Meaning	Valence of stem
(a)	a	intr	e-ma-**ti**-no-a (Tripp 1995: 82b)	NMLZ-VPL-SPAT:up-vital.centre-say	'to sing'	intr
(b)	ka	tr	e-ma-**ti**-**on**-ka[20] (Tripp 1995: 82b)	NMLZ-VPL-SPAT:up-SPAT:on-do	'to hunt'	tr
(c)	ka	tr	eʔ-**ti**-ka (Tripp 1995: 96a)	NMLZ-SPAT:up-do	'to kill (an insect)'	tr
(d)	wedn	intr	eʔ-**ti**-wedn (Tripp 1995: 95b)	NMLZ-SPAT:up-lie	'to be full (of a container object)'	intr
					'to brood (eggs)'	tr
(e)	ẽ	cop-intr	eʔ-**ti**-**ok**-pō-ẽ (Tripp 1995: 82b)	NMLZ-VPL-SPAT:up-SPAT:separation-CLF:round-be	'to annoy'	tr
(f)	ẽ	cop-intr	e-k-ma-**ti**-**ok**-pō-ẽ (Tripp 1995: 41b)	NMLZ-SPAT:separation-VPL-SPAT:up-SPAT:separation-CLF:round-be	'to commit adultery with so. else's wife'	tr

In (32a), (32b), (32c) and in the first meaning of (32d), the spatial prefixes do not affect the valence of the verb roots, which is identical to that of the stems. In the other examples, the prefixes do increase the valence of the roots. In relation to the semantic contribution of the prefixes, Tripp (1995: 219) also provides descriptions of combinations of spatial prefixes. The combination *ti-on-*, for instance, expresses "downward or inward movement", which contributes to the meaning

---

[20] Tripp provides the form *e-ma-ti-oŋ-ka* for 'to hunt' (1995: 82b). I believe orthographic <ŋ> represents [ŋ], which is an allophonic variant of /n/ in front of velar /k/ here.

of the stem in (32b) in a transparent way: hunting animals could be conceived of as getting or 'doing' them down. For the combination *ti-ok-*, Tripp (1995: 219) provides the paraphrase "join parts", which does not seem to be immediately relevant for the meaning of the stem in (32e). However, the meaning of (32f) can be partially related to that of (32e), with the spatial prefix *k-* locating the O-argument, viz. the victim of the adultery, at a physical distance of the A-argument, viz. the perpetrator, throughout the event.

In the set of examples in (33) in Table 2, the spatial prefixes are valence-increasing, and the meaning of the stems is overall more transparent than in the examples in (32). Hence, the examples in (33) could be called semi-lexicalized. For instance, Tripp's (1995: 219) paraphrase "join parts" works well for (33a), where the Agent brings together several pieces of clothing on their body.

Table 2: Semi-lexicalized verb stems containing spatial prefixes.

(33)	Verb root	Valence of root	Semi-lexicalized verb stem	Morphological analysis	Meaning	Valence of stem
(a)	*ot*	intr	*e-**ti**-ok-ot* (Tripp 1995: 87b)	NMLZ-SPAT:up-SPAT: separation-get.dressed	'to put on clothes on top of other clothes'	tr
(b)	*a-pak*	intr	*e-**ti**-a-pak* (Tripp 1995: 33b)	NMLZ-SPAT:up-say-VBZ	'to narrate; to tell'	tr
(c)	*a-pak*	intr	*e-ma-n-mba-**ti**-a-pak* (Tripp 1995: 80a)	NMLZ-VPL-SPAT:on-VPL-SPAT:up-say-VBZ	'to tell tidings to everyone; to inform'	ditr

Compare (33b) to (33c) for scope relations of the spatial prefixes with the verbal plural marker. Example (33c) shows that spatial prefixes can be scoped over by verbal plural markers separately; it involves the telling of a plurality of tidings or stories (*mba-ti-*) to a plurality of addressees (*ma-n-*). As is the case with dedicated applicatives (see Van linden 2022: 464), the verbal plural marker takes the immediately following element in its scope. Given this interaction with the verbal plural marker, and the fairly transparent semantic contribution of the spatial prefixes, (33c) is only semi-lexicalized in comparison with, for instance, (32a). All in all, the examples given in this section indicate that spatial prefixes are important building blocks of Harakmbut verb lexemes. Their proneness to lexicalization further corroborates their affinity to derivational morphology.

6 Conclusions and diachronic implications

This paper has focused on valence-increasing morphology that introduces a non-Actor argument into the clause in Harakmbut, more specifically in the Arakmbut/Amarakaeri variety. While the language boasts two formally and functionally distinct applicative morphemes which share the same slot in the morphological template of the verb, the benefactive applicative *niŋ-* and the semantically underspecified applicative *ta-*, there is also a set of spatial prefixes which can also serve an applicative function, and may – in the context of the present volume – be better analysed as (potentially spatial) applicatives which also have non-syntactic functions. Unlike the dedicated applicative markers, the spatial prefixes are positionally flexible, and may simultaneously occur in distinct slots on a single verb form. In this preliminary account, I focused on *ti-* 'location high up', *on-~n-* 'in', '(in)to' or 'on', and *ok-~k-* 'separation'. In their non-syntactic valence-neutral function, observed on both intransitive and transitive verb roots, these spatial prefixes contribute spatial information to the event depicted in the clause by characterizing the S or O argument in terms of location or spatial configuration. In their syntactic or valence-increasing function, observed on both intransitive and transitive verb roots, they introduce a Location argument into the clause, and specify the location of the underived S or O argument with respect to this applied phrase. Two of these prefixes also developed purely valence-increasing applicative-like uses without any additional spatial specification. In such cases, they only introduce human non-Actor arguments, such as Maleficiaries, Beneficiaries and human Goals. Building on Tripp (1995: 218–219), this paper also presented preliminary evidence in favour of the spatial prefix status of two additional prefixes, *taʔ-* for force against an object, rear position, or downward movement and *wa-* for human goals.

In keeping with Hopper's (1991) idea of layering, the present-day syntactic and semantic behaviour of the spatial prefixes suggests a diachronic scenario in which the three uses discussed in Sections 4.1 to 4.3 can be regarded as distinct stages on a single grammaticalization path, from spatial element to non-spatial applicative. That is, the prefixes are assumed to have undergone a gradual change from a lexical to a grammatical element (cf. Hopper & Traugott 1993). In the first stage, the spatial prefixes are lexical derivational morphemes, which add information about the (internal or external) spatial configuration of a participant involved in the event denoted by the verb root (S or O), without changing its valence, e.g. from 'to cut' to 'to cut into pieces'. This use is similar to that of verbal classifiers characterizing S or O arguments in terms of shape or substance (see Rose & Van linden 2022). In the second stage, they acquire the grammatical function of introducing a Location argument into the clause while still retaining their spatial semantics: they locate the underived S or O with respect to the Location applied phrases. At this stage, their spatial meaning no longer involves the internal spatial configuration of a participant; it is restricted to external spatial configuration. Speakers arguably developed this second use to meet the communicative need to locate topical participants with respect to each other, i.e. to expand the spatial resources of the language. In the last stage, the prefixes only retain their grammatical, applicative-like function. While for some verb roots, we can see metaphorical extension at work, for others we see a complete loss of spatial meaning. At the same time, we can note a specialization for introducing human non-Actor arguments. Table 3 recapitulates the findings for the spatial prefixes investigated, which allows us to place them at different stages on the grammaticalization cline.

Table 3: The present-day uses of the five spatial prefixes.

Syntax	valence-neutral	valence-increasing	
Semantics	spatial	spatial	non-spatial
ok-~k-	✓	✓	✗
ti-	✓	✓	✓
on-~n-	✓	✓	✓
taʔ-	✓	✓	(✓)
wa-	✗	✓	(✓)

From the five prefixes included in Table 3, *ok-~k-* shows the least degree of grammaticalization, as it has not been observed with non-spatial meaning so far. The prefixes *ti-* and *on-~n-* have gone further down the path, as they do show non-spatial meaning in some contexts. For the prefixes *taʔ-* and *wa-*, there are indications that they have reached this last stage as well, but I put the tick symbols for this use between brackets, awaiting further evidence.

The first two stages of the grammaticalization path described here are prone to lexicalization. As discussed in Section 5, the Harakmbut lexicon comprises a number of complex verb stems featuring spatial prefixes that are no longer semantically transparent. Occasional idiosyncratic meanings are found in both valence-neutral and valence-increasing spatial uses of the prefixes. These effects of lexicalization further testify to the affinity of the spatial prefixes with derivational morphology.

Finally, the diachrony of the spatial prefixes raises a number of questions. A first set relates to the diachronic origin of the Harakmbut spatial prefixes. Do these ultimately derive from independent elements, and if so, from which word class?

And can we accumulate evidence for positing spatial verb morphology as a new source for applicative markers, besides well-attested sources like verbs, adpositions and nouns (Peterson 2007; Rose 2019)? In this respect, the data on Nilotic valence-increasing directionals (this volume, chapter 9) and associated motion markers (Bond & Reid 2021) add to the Harakmbut scenario proposed here. A second set of questions pertain to the role of the expression of space in these recently discovered grammaticalization pathways. What makes the domain of space prone to being used for valence-increasing derivation? And if applicative markers can develop from verb morphology, what other semantic domains could they come from, apart from the spatial domain? These questions will have to await further study.

Abbreviations

1	first person
2	second person
3	person
>	'acts on'
A	transitive subject
ACC	accusative
AGR	agreement
AM	associated motion
AN	animate
APPL	applicative
APPR	apprehensive
ASP	aspect
AVRT	avertive
BEN	beneficiary/benefactive
CAUS	causative
CLF	classifier
COM	comitative
COND	conditional
DEP	dependent verb form
DIST	distal
DUB	dubitative
EPC	epenthetic consonant
EVID	evidential
F	feminine
FILLER	filler/word search
FOC	focus
GEN	genitive
IMP	imperative
INCORP.N	incorporated noun
IND	indicative

INDET	indeterminate
INDIR.EVD	indirect evidential
ITER	iterative
LOC	locative
M	masculine
MIN	minimizer
MOD	modality marker
NEG	negation
NMLZ	nominalizer
NOM	nominative
NPF	noun prefix
NVOL	non-volitional
O	transitive object
PFV	perfective
PL	plural
PROX	proximal
PST	past
QUOT	quotative
REAL.I	realis for i-class verb
REAS	reason
REC	recent
REL	relativizer
REM	remote
REP.EVD	reported evidential
S	intransitive subject
SEP	separative
SG	singular
SOC	sociative
SPAT	spatial prefix
TRNS	transitivizer
VBZ	verbalizer
VPL	verbal plural

References

Adelaar, Willem F.H. 2000. Propuesta de un nuevo vínculo genético entre dos grupos lingüísticos indígenas de la Amazonía occidental: Harakmbut y Katukina. In Luis Miranda Esquerre (ed.), *Actas del I Congreso de Lenguas Indígenas de Sudamérica, Vol. 2*, 219–236. Lima: U. Ricardo Palma.

Adelaar, Willem F.H. 2007. Ensayo de clasificación del katawixí dentro del conjunto harakmbut-katukina. In Andres Romero-Figueroa, Ana Fernández Garay, Ángel Corbera Mori (eds.), *Lenguas indígenas de América del Sur*, 159–169. Caracas: Universidad Católica Andrés Bello.

Aissen, Judith. 2003. Differential object marking: iconicity vs. economy. *Natural Language & Linguistic Theory* 21(3). 435–483.

Bickel, Balthasar & Johanna Nichols. 2007. Inflectional morphology. In Timothy Shopen (ed.), *Language typology and syntactic description, Volume III: Grammatical categories and the lexicon*, 169–240. Cambridge: Cambridge University Press.

Bond, Oliver & Reid, Tatiana. 2021. Lexical restrictions on associated motion verbs. Paper presented at the Workshop: Lexical restrictions on grammatical relations, online (University of Amsterdam), 29–30 March, 2021.

Crevels, Mily & Van der Voort, Hein. 2008. The Guaporé-Mamoré region as a linguistic area. In Pieter Muysken (ed.), *From linguistic areas to areal linguistics*, 151–179. Amsterdam: John Benjamins. https://doi.org/10.1075/slcs.90.04cre

Crevels, Mily & Hein van der Voort. 2020. Areal Diffusion of Applicatives in the Amazon. In Norval Smith, Tonjes Veenstra & Enoch Oladé Aboh (eds.), *Advances in contact linguistics: In honour of Pieter Muysken*, 180–216. Amsterdam: John Benjamins. https://doi.org/10.1075/coll.57.06cre

Givón, Talmy. 2009. *The genesis of syntactic complexity: diachrony, ontogeny, neuro-cognition and evolution*. Amsterdam: John Benjamins.

Hart, Raymond. 1963. Semantic components of shape in Amarakaeri Grammar. *Anthropological Linguistics* 5(9). 1–7.

Helberg Chávez, Heinrich A. 1984. *Skizze einer Grammatik des Amarakaeri*. Tübingen: Tübingen University dissertation.

Helberg Chávez, Heinrich A. 1990. Análisis funcional del verbo amarakaeri. In Rodolfo Cerrón Palomino & Gustavo Solís Fonseca (eds.), *Temas de lingüística amerindia*, 227–249. Lima: Concytec.

Hopper, Paul J. 1991. On some principles of grammaticization. In Elizabeth Closs Traugott & Bernd Heine (eds.), *Approaches to grammaticalization, Vol. I*, 17–36. Amsterdam: John Benjamins.

Hopper, Paul J. & Elizabeth Closs Traugott. 1993. *Grammaticalization*. Cambridge: Cambridge University Press.

Michael, Lev. 2012. Possession in Nanti. In Alexandra Aikhenvald & R.M.W. Dixon (eds.), *Possession and Ownership*, 149–166. Oxford: Oxford University Press.

McGregor, William B. 2007. Ergative marking of intransitive subjects in Warrwa. *Australian Journal of Linguistics* 27(2). 201–229. https://doi.org/10.1080/07268600701531351

McGregor, William B. 2010. Optional ergative case marking systems in a typological-semiotic perspective. *Lingua* 120(7). 1610–1636. https://doi.org/10.1016/j.lingua.2009.05.010

Mithun, Marianne. 1984. The evolution of noun incorporation. *Language* 60(4). 847–879. https://doi.org/10.1353/lan.1984.0038

Nordlinger, Rachel. 2019. From body part to applicative: Encoding 'source' in Murrinhpatha. *Linguistic Typology* 23(3). 401–433.

Peterson, David A. 2007. *Applicative constructions*. Oxford: Oxford University Press.

Rose, Françoise. 2019. From classifiers to applicatives in Mojeño Trinitario: A new source for applicative markers. *Linguistic Typology* 23(3). 435–466.

Rose, Françoise & An Van linden. 2022. The derivational use of classifiers in Western Amazonia. In Steve Pepper, Francesca Masini & Simone Mattiola (eds.), *Binominal lexemes in cross-linguistic perspective: Towards a typology of complex lexemes* [Empirical Approaches to Language Typology], 237–276. Berlin/Boston: De Gruyter Mouton https://doi.org/10.1515/9783110673494-008.

Tripp, Robert. 1976. Sustantivos verbales y frases de sustantivos verbales en Amarakaeri. In *14. Datos Etno-Lingüísticos: Colección de los archivos del ILV 50*. Lima: Instituto Lingüístico de Verano.

Tripp, Robert. 1995. *Diccionario amarakaeri-castellano*. Yarinacocha: Ministerio de Educación & Instituto Lingüístico de Verano.

Van linden, An. 2019. Nominalization in Harakmbut. In Roberto Zariquiey, Masayoshi Shibatani & David W. Fleck (eds.), *Nominalization in the languages of the Americas*, 455–490. Amsterdam: John Benjamins. https://doi.org/10.1075/tsl.124.12lin

Van linden, An. 2020. Constructional effects of indirect evidential marking in Harakmbut. *Functions of Language* 27(1). 7–28 [Special issue 'Notes from the field on perspective-indexing constructions: Irregular shifts and perspective persistence', edited by Stef Spronck, An Van linden, Caroline Gentens & María Sol Sansiñena]. https://doi.org/10.1075/fol.20004.lin

Van linden, An. 2022. Harakmbut. In Patience Epps & Lev Michael (eds.), *Amazonian languages: An international handbook. Language Isolates,* Volume 1: Aikanã to Kandozi-Shapra, 437–477. Berlin: De Gruyter Mouton. https://doi.org/10.1515/9783110419405-010

WALS- Dryer, Matthew S. & Martin Haspelmath (eds.). 2013. *The World Atlas of Language Structures Online*. Leipzig: Max Planck Institute for Evolutionary Anthropology. (Available online at http://wals.info.)

Wise, Mary R. 1999. Small language families and isolates in Peru. In R. M. W. Dixon & Alexandra Y. Aikhenvald (eds.), *The Amazonian languages*, 307–340. Cambridge: Cambridge University Press.

Zúñiga, Fernando. 2006. *Deixis and alignment: Inverse systems in indigenous languages of the Americas*. Amsterdam: John Benjamins.

Part II: **Africa**

Hannah Gibson, Lutz Marten, Maarten Mous, and Kristina Riedel

7 Valency and saliency in Bantu applicatives: A diachronic reanalysis

Abstract: This chapter examines apparent competing functions of applicatives, prepositions and locative-marked phrases in a number of Bantu languages, focussing on the interaction of these types of categories in various applicative constructions. We show that in a number of Bantu languages, prepositional constructions compete with applicatives. The interaction between the two construction types revolves around valency (the licensing of an additional object) and saliency (the encoding of pragmatic effects), two hallmarks of applicative constructions more widely. Evidence from this interaction, we propose, helps to better understand the diachronic development of applicatives. We further observe a diachronic reanalysis of the applicative marker from expressing both syntactic and pragmatic effects to a pure pragmatic marker of saliency, in the context of functionally and structurally ambiguous locative phrases.

Acknowledgements: This paper is based on a talk presented at the workshop entitled 'Neglected syntactic and non-syntactic functions of applicative morphology' which was part of the Societas Linguistica Europaea (SLE) conference in 2020. We are grateful to the audience of the talk for their comments and questions, as well as the other participants and organisers of the workshop Sara Pacchiarotti and Fernando Zúñiga. Thanks go also to Hlumela Mkabile for providing additional judgements on the isiXhosa examples and the Sesotho speakers who provided judgements reported on here. We also gratefully acknowledge the extensive feedback we received from two anonymous reviewers and the editors which served to improve the paper. Any errors naturally remain our own.

Hannah Gibson, Department of Language and Linguistics, University of Essex, Wivenhoe Park, Colchester, Essex, UK, e-mail: h.gibson@essex.ac.uk
Lutz Marten, School of Languages, Cultures and Linguistics, SOAS University of London, Thornhaugh Street, Russell Square, London, UK, e-mail: lm5@soas.ac.uk
Maarten Mous, LUCL: Institute for Linguistics, Leiden University, Reuvensplaats 3-4, Leiden, The Netherlands, e-mail: m.mous@hum.leidenuniv.nl
Kristina Riedel, Department of Linguistics and Language Practice, University of the Free State, Bloemfontein, South Africa, e-mail: riedelk@ufs.ac.za

https://doi.org/10.1515/9783110777949-007

1 Introduction

As stated in this volume's introduction, applicatives are typically defined as derivational processes which i) impact syntax; ii) introduce an object argument (in contrast with the non-derived stem); and iii) are associated with a wide range of semantic roles which are mapped onto an applied phrase. In many ways therefore, applicatives in Bantu are often regarded as typical examples of the construction. Bantu applicatives can introduce an applied phrase into the clause which would otherwise be more peripheral or not be licensed. These applied phrases can fulfil a wide range of semantic roles such as benefactive, location, instrument, substitutive and reason (see e.g. Ngonyani 1996, 1998; Marten 2011; Marten and Kula 2014). The different semantic roles are typically introduced by the same applicative morpheme, reconstructed to Proto-Bantu as *-ɪd (Meeussen 1967: 92), although there is some variation in the reflexes of *-ɪd and therefore the morphological form of the applicative found across Bantu languages. However, unlike the more typologically common pattern, applicative constructions in Bantu (and in Niger-Congo more broadly) are often obligatory (Creissels 2004, Creissels et al. 2008).

Applicative construction in Bantu have attracted considerable attention in the linguistics literature. Early descriptive work, such as that found in grammatical descriptions of Bantu languages, typically provides overviews of different uses and often notes a functional parallel between applicative constructions and propositional phrases in European languages. Ashton (1944), for example, discusses Swahili applicatives under the heading of 'the prepositional (or applied) form', although she notes that 'it is unwise to try to associate these verbs with any one English preposition' (1944: 217). Formal analyses of Bantu applicatives within theoretical linguistic frameworks have brought into focus constraints on the syntax of applicatives and the cross-linguistic variation found within Bantu. These topics are explored, for example, in several papers in Mchombo's (1993) landmark collection on comparative Bantu grammar, while Pylkkänen (2008) develops a formal, cross-linguistic analysis of applicative constructions, taking Bantu applicatives (and English dative-shift) as a starting point. In the typological literature, Peterson (2007) is a comprehensive, cross-linguistic study, while Pacchiarotti (2020) provides a fine-grained, cross-Bantu typology of applicatives.

This previous work on Bantu applicative shows that these constructions often exhibit the core features associated with applicative constructions cross-linguistically, in particular in relation to valency-change. However, an increasing amount of scholarship has shown that traditional characterisations of applicatives in Bantu as just allowing for the addition of an argument have been too simplistic. In particular, in many cases, applicative verbs in Bantu languages do not alternate systematically with non-applicative verbs, nor do they change valency, but rather applicative verbs have a pragmatic effect of marking emphasis or focus (e.g. Trithart 1983, Marten 2003, Creissels 2004, Voisin 2006, Cann and Mabugu 2007, Marten and Mous 2014, Jerro 2016, Sibanda 2016, Marten and Mous 2017, Pacchiarotti 2017, 2020).

It is the development of pragmatic functions of the applicative that we are interested in in this paper. We argue that where there are alternative strategies in a language for an applicative construction next to a preposition-like construction there is room for pragmatic functions of the applicative to come to the foreground, especially where there is no associated valency change. We look at languages where applicatives and preposition-like construction compete, as well as their differences and co-occurrence patterns. We concentrate on the pragmatic effects, rather than delving into the syntactic properties of the applicatives in these languages. As such our approach is not within the formal syntactic line of research on applicatives, nor is it focused on the typological classification of applicatives into types.

Bantu languages may have prepositions which interact with applicatives in different ways. This includes some prepositions that have come to be used in constructions in which they compete with or reinforce the applicative extension, as in (1) below. The prepositions involved can be morphologically simple (and presumably old) prepositions such as *na* 'with' in Bemba (1), as well as innovative prepositions such as *ɔ́ŋgírá* 'for' in Mbuun (2). We also see borrowed forms such as *for* from English in Sesotho (3) and *para* from Portuguese in Makhuwa, as discussed further below.[1]

(1) Bemba
Mutálé a-léé-ˈípík(-íl)-a   na   supuni
Mutale   SM1-PROG-cook(-APPL)-FV   with   9.spoon
'Mutale is cooking with a spoon.'
(Marten and Kula 2014: 21)

(2) Mbuun
ó-á-mó-dzwíllé   ɔ́ŋgírá   n-dzim
SM1-PRS.PROG-OM1-kill.APPL   for   9-money
'He kills her *for the money*.'
(Bostoen and Mundeke 2011: 192)

---

[1] We use both prefixed and unprefixed versions of the language names (e.g. Sesotho, Bemba) in accordance with the original authors' usage and the discourse surrounding language naming conventions in the area where the language is spoken.

(3) Sesotho
    a. *Ke-rek-etse*   *di-konopo*   *se-lamba*   *sa-ka*
        SM1SG-buy-APPL.PRF   10-button   7-jacket   7-POSS.1SG
        'I bought buttons for my jacket.'

    b. *Ke-rek-ile*   *di-konopo*   *for*   *se-lamba*   *sa-ka*
        SM1SG-buy-PRF   10-button   for   7-jacket   7-POSS.1SG
        'I bought buttons for my jacket.'
        (Riedel and Gibson 2021)

In the Bemba example (1), the preposition is required whereas applicative marking is optional. When both are used together, emphasis is placed on the instrument (in this case *supuni* 'spoon'). In Mbuun, applicative marking and the use of the preposition are alternative coding strategies but they can also be combined (Bostoen and Mundeke 2011: 192–193). Like in Bemba, when both are used together, emphasis is placed on the applied object (2). In Sesotho either the applicative (3a) or the preposition (3b) can be used, but not both, and (as far as we know), there is no difference in information structure associated with either structure. We will show in this paper that the interaction of applicative marking and the use of prepositions in Bantu is related to information structure on the one hand (e.g. in Bemba and Mbuun) and to providing alternative syntactic coding strategies on the other hand – as in Mbuun and Sesotho, but not in Bemba, where, with instruments at least, the use of the preposition is obligatory.

An interesting further effect has been noted in some languages for applicatives with locatives (Mabugu 2001, Marten and Mous 2014, 2017, Pacchiarotti 2020). In some languages, the applicative is optional with some semantic roles. For example, a goal applied phrase which can optionally be introduced by the applicative can appear as either an NP argument or can maintain its locative/prepositional meaning even in the applicative construction. Mabugu (2001: 119–120) notes that in Shona an applicative-marked goal, whether preposition marked (4c) or not (4b), is interpreted as having an endpoint while the adjunct PP goal (4a) is not. When the applicative is used with the locative marking (4c) this focuses the goal and that this endpoint of the action has been reached. Note here that in (4), *Muchaneta* and *Vimbai* are human proper names.

(4) Shona
    a. *Muchaneta*   *a-ka-sund-a*   *cheya*   (*ku-na*   *Vimbai*)
        1a.Muchaneta   SM1-PST-push-FV   9.chair   17-ASSO   1a.Vimbai
        'Muchaneta pushed a chair (towards Vimbai).'

b. *Muchaneta   a-ka-sund-ir-a   cheya   Vimbai*
    1a.Muchaneta   SM1-PST-kick-APPL-FV   9.chair 1a.Vimbai
    'Muchaneta pushed a chair to Vimbai.'

c. *Muchaneta   a-ka-sund-ir-a   cheya   ku-na   Vimbai*
    1a.Muchaneta   SM1-PST-kick-APPL-FV   9.chair 17-ASSO 1a.Vimbai
    'Muchaneta pushed a chair to Vimbai.'
    (Mabugu 2001: 118)

The examples show that the use of applicative marking can determine the semantic interpretation of the expression. Marten (2002) uses the Relevance-theoretic notion of "concept strengthening" (cf. Carston 2002) to characterise the semantic and pragmatic effects of applicatives.

In light of this more detailed understanding of Bantu applicatives, this paper explores the interaction between applicatives and prepositions in Bantu. The aim of the chapter is to understand how morphological applicative constructions and functionally related prepositional constructions interact and thereby to contribute to a better understanding of applicative constructions more generally. Based on evidence from different Bantu languages, we will develop an analysis of the relationship between applicatives and prepositions, as well as applicatives and locative phrases. Specifically, we are interested in how this interaction provided the context for a dissociation of syntactic valency change and the marking of pragmatic saliency, and a diachronic reanalysis of the applicative marker as saliency marker. Under this analysis, the original function of applicatives combined syntactic and pragmatic effects, and the purely pragmatic functions, without attendant change of valency, resulted from this dissociation. The development can be understood as an effect of subjectification, i.e. development of meaning towards what the speaker is talking about (Traugott 1989: 35), and more widely as one aspect of the grammaticalization of applicatives. This is the neglected function of the applicative in Bantu which the current study focuses on and which contributes to the broader aims of the volume as a whole.

The empirical discussion below will take the more familiar cases of locatives as a starting point, where the interaction of applicatives and functional prepositions is well-known. After summarising previous work, we will turn to instrument and benefactive applicatives and show that a similar interaction can be observed. This will then provide the basis for our discussion of applicatives and the relevance of the comparison with prepositional constructions for our understanding of applicatives.

Applicatives, as can be seen from the papers in this volume, have a range of different functions, and as we show here, also compete and interact with prepositional constructions in complex ways across Bantu. To help the reader differentiate between the different types of constructions, we define applicatives for Bantu languages as constructions with one or more morphological marker that is reconstructable to Proto-Bantu *-ɪd (Meeussen 1967: 92), and that have at least one of the semantic/syntactic/pragmatic functions associated with the applicative in Bantu (Trithart 1983). This is illustrated by the examples from Swahili in (5) below where the erstwhile applicative marker -e(l) has become part of a verb stem through lexicalization (5a), while in (5b), the applicative marker alternates with the non-applied form and introduces an additional participant (the person being visited).

(5) Swahili
    a. *ku-tembe-a*
       INF-walk-FV
       'to move' [non-applicative in present-day Swahili]

    b. *ku-tembel-e-a*
       INF-walk-APPL-FV
       'to visit' [applicative of -*tembea*][2]
       (Our own knowledge)

This paper compares applicative constructions with their competing or functionally related syntactic constructions in a number of Bantu languages. We focus on a relatively small number of Bantu languages mostly spoken in East and Southern Africa, for which relevant data or published descriptions are available. Based on this comparative evidence, we propose 1) an extension to the cross-linguistic, functional-diachronic paths of development of applicatives as developed in Peterson (2007: 142,152) to include a stage of "salience marking" and 2) that the particular use of applicative morphemes as saliency markers without a change in valency results diachronically from reanalysis of applicative markers from licensing arguments to encoding saliency in the context of applicative constructions with both applicative markers and prepositional complements. From this perspective it appears that the syntactic function of applicatives – the introduction of arguments – diachronically precedes their pragmatic function as marking focus or saliency, a hypothesis set forth by De Kind and Bostoen (2012). We hope that

---

[2] Note that although the appearance of the intervocalic /l/ in Swahili in these cases may make it appear as if there are two productive morphemes, this is not supported by the morphosyntax or semantics of these verbs.

this will lay the foundation for a systematic survey, employing a representative sample, to test the hypotheses argued for here in future work.

We show that the interaction of applicative marking and the use of prepositions in Bantu is related to information structure on the one hand and to providing alternative syntactic coding strategies on the other hand. We will also see examples of borrowed prepositions which are the result of language contact where it seems that semantic role encoding plays a more important role than information structure

The paper is structured as follows: Section 2 explores the interaction between prepositions and applicatives, focusing on the co-occurrence of prepositions with applicative marking (in §2.1), the interaction between locative marking and applicatives (§2.2), and prepositions which introduce specific thematic roles (§2.3), drawing on data from across the Bantu languages. Section 3 examines wider processes of change and cycles of historical development. Section 4 constitutes a summary and makes a number of concluding comments, as well as highlighting directions for future research.

2 The interaction of prepositions and applicatives

2.1 Co-occurrence of prepositions and applicative marking

Bantu languages typically have comparatively small, often poorly described, preposition inventories. As noted above, these inventories include morphologically simple forms, the results of more recent grammaticalization (e.g. from prepositional or associative phrases), and borrowings. In this section we provide a short overview of how the various types of prepositions found in different Bantu languages interact with applicatives.

Meeussen (1967: 115) reconstructs two non-predicative "index forms" – nonconcordial elements which can precede a nominal or pronominal. These are the associative *na(-) 'with, also, and' and comparative *nga(-) 'like'. For example, Bemba (6) (repeated from (1) above) and Herero (7) retain reflexes of the simple preposition *na* 'with'. Cognates of the Bemba and Herero *na* 'and, with' are widespread across Bantu. In Bemba, morphologically simple prepositions can co-occur with applicative marking in instrumental applicatives (6). In Herero, applicative marking is not required for an instrumental reading (7). Note that the construction in (7) is comprised of the preposition *na* plus the initial vowel *o-*, resulting in *no*.

(6) Bemba
   Mutálé   a-léé-ˈípík(-íl)-a   na   supuni
   Mutale   SM1-PROG-cook(-APPL)-FV   with   9.spoon
   'Mutale is cooking with a spoon.'
   (Marten and Kula 2014: 21)

(7) Herero
   Mbì-ryá   òn-yámà   n-òrútúwò
   SM1SG-eat   9-meat   with-11.spoon
   'I usually eat meat with a spoon'
   (Marten field notes, 03-08-2005, 18, 6)

For Chichewa, Trithart (1977: 16) also describes the optionality of the applicative in (8) and notes that the applicative verb form "directs more attention to the fact that an instrumental appears in the sentence but it does not alter the behaviour of the sentence."

(8) Chichewa
   Jóni   a-ná-lí-lemb(-er)-a   dzíˈná   láké   ndí   péni
   John   SM1-PST-OM5-write-APPL-FV   name   his   with pen
   'John wrote his name with a pen.'
   (Trithart 1977: 16)

Mbuun has the form *ɔ́ŋgírá* which is derived from a prepositional phrase meaning 'on the body of' (Bostoen and Mundeke 2011: 187). The preposition *ɔ́ŋgírá* and the morphological applicative are two possible ways of introducing certain semantic roles into a main clause in Mbuun. The *ɔ́ŋgírá*-construction can be used where the applicative is not grammatical. But the two strategies can also be combined, resulting in a construction in which the *ɔ́ŋgírá*-marked beneficiary or reason noun phrase is focussed, as shown in (9). Thus, while example (9a) sees the use of the preposition *ɔ́ŋgírá* 'for', (9c) and (9d) combine both the applicative derivation and the prepositional phrase and the double expression results in what Bostoen and Mundeke (2011: 192) describe as a "discursive function" which places focus on the oblique beneficiary/reason argument.

(9) Mbuun
   a. *Mo-íb   ó-á-dzúú   máám   ɔ́ŋgírá   nke?*   [preposition only]
      1-thief   SM1-PRS.PROG-kill   mother   for   what
      'Why does the thief kill mother?'

b. ó-á-mó-dzwíllé   ɔ́ŋgírá
    SM1-PRS.PROG-OM1-kill.APPL for
    n-dzim   [APPL + preposition]
    9-money
    'He kills her FOR THE MONEY'

c. Mo-íb   ó-á-dzwíllé   máám ɔ́ŋgírá
    1-thief SM1-PRS.PROG-kill.APPL mother for
    nke?   [APPL + preposition]
    what
    'WHY does the thief kill mother?
    (Bostoen and Mundeke 2011: 192)

Swahili has a number of grammaticalized prepositions: *katika* 'in, at' (< *kati*, *katikati* 'middle, centre'), *kwa* 'at' (< locative class 17 *ku-* and connective *-a*), and *mpaka* 'until, up to' (< *mpaka* 'boundary'); the latter is a preposition that is used with noun phrases and clausal complements. As a preposition, *mpaka* has spread to numerous languages in East Africa, including both Bantu and non-Bantu languages (Mous 2020). However, Swahili prepositions do not combine with applicatives. As we argue below, Swahili prepositions are rarely used alongside a productive applicative derivation (although see Section 2.3 for discussion of the use of *kwa* in Swahili applicatives alternations). There are other Bantu languages that avoid the combination of applicative derivation and the use of a preposition. The few examples that we found of *mpaka* in East-African Bantu languages in combination with an applicative contain lexicalised applicatives. In the following Rangi example, the verb *-sɛkɛra* 'sift' is a lexicalised applicative (10).

(10) Rangi
     Hapana tɔ-sɛkɛr-a   mpaka vaa-fum-irɛ   ha-ra
     NEG   take-sift.APPL-FV until   SM2.PRF-leave-PRF 16-DISTAL.DEM
     'Don't go sift until they're out of there.'
     (Dunham 2005: 181)

2.2 Locative marking and applicatives

In many Bantu languages, the applicative can co-occur with an applied object with locative marking (cf. i.a. Damman 1961, Guthrie 1962, Kähler-Meyer 1966, De Kind and Bostoen 2012, Marten and Kula 2014). Here we treat locative markers, such as the class 18 marker *mu-* in (11a, b), as a morphological category rather than as a (possibly proclitic) preposition, following how these morphemes are treated in the sources we used. This is not to imply that there are consistent systematic differences between prepositions and all morphemes labelled as locative markers in different Bantu languages. In fact, locative-marked nouns function as prepositional phrases in some Bantu languages and noun phrases in others (cf. Riedel and Marten 2012, Zeller 2017). For our cross-linguistic sample the relevant information is not always available and the difference is not central to the paper, so we follow the descriptive labels employed in our sources.

The interaction between applicatives and locative marking has been described in a number of previous studies. Here we summarise some of the findings on the combined expression of a morphological applicative and locative marking with a preposition-like function. One such case is Bemba where the use of the applicative-marked verb form in (11b) results in an emphatic reading which focuses the locative complement (see also this volume, chapter 8 for parallel data in Fwe).

(11) Bemba
    a. *N-de-ly-a*   *mu-mu-putule*
        SM1SG-PRS-eat-FV 18-3-room
        'I am eating in the room' [without term focus; as answer to: What are you doing?]

    b. *N-de-li-il-a*   *mu-mu-putule*
        SM1SG-PRS-eat-APPL-FV 18-3-room
        'I am eating in the room' [Emphatic; as answer to: Where are you eating?]
        (Marten 2003: 217)

In Bemba, the locative marker is required while the applicative marking is optional. When both are used together, emphasis is placed on the instrument (cf. (1)) or locative (cf. (11b), i.e. the applied object or applied phrase).

One other common function of locative applicatives across Bantu is as directionals where the applicative changes the verbal semantics in terms of movement towards/away from the applied object and does not add an argument; Guthrie (1967–71, Vol 1: 89) reconstructs directive as part of the meaning of applicative *-ɪd*. In Sesotho, the locative form *motseng* 'at/in/to/from the village' can appear either with a non-applicative marked verb as in (12a) or with an applicativised verb as in (12b) and the applicative verb means 'return to' rather than 'return from' (12a). This kind of meaning change is commonly associated with applicatives of directionals in Bantu.³

(12) Sesotho
    a. *Ngwana o-tla-khutl-a   mo-tseng*
       1.child   SM1-FUT-return-FV   3-village.LOC
       'The child will come back from the village.'

    b. *O-tla-khutl-el-a   mo-tseng*
       SM1-FUT-return-APPL-FV   3-village.LOC
       'S/he will go back to the village.'
       (Doke and Mofokeng 1957: 323)

Another difference in interpretation between the non-applicativised and the applicative form in Setswana results in a difference between location (running 'on the road') (13a) and direction (running 'to the road') (13b), the later with the applicativised verb form. In constructions of this type therefore the use of the applicative adds the Goal argument (13b). Expressing direction requires the applicative in these cases.

(13) Setswana
    a. *Ke-tlaa-tabog-a   ko   tseleng*
       SM1SG-FUT-run-FV   PREP   9.road.LOC
       'I will run on the road.'

    b. *Ke-tlaa-tabog-el-a   ko   tseleng*
       SM1SG-FUT-run-APPL-FV PREP   9.road.LOC
       'I will run to the road.'
       (Creissels 2004: 11)

Again, we see differences in interpretation related to marking only the locative (here with *ko* and the locative suffix on the noun) in (13a) and the double marking of both the verb with the applicative and the locative phrase (13b).

Such double expression with applicative functions is not always possible. For example, Swahili does not allow prepositions or locative marking with applicatives

---

3 Note, the applicative morpheme in Sesotho is obligatory here insofar as a directional meaning cannot obtain with a preposition in this context. See however Creissels (2004) and Pacchiarotti (2020: 130–132) for alternative analyses of these construction types.

in directional constructions. Rather, these are obligatorily marked with the applicative morpheme and appear with non-locative marked complements (14).[4]

(14) Swahili
    a. *Wa-li-po-pand-i-a*   *ile*   *mi-buyu*
        SM2-PST-REL16-climb-APPL-FV   DEM.4   4-baobab
        'When they climbed up the baobab trees...'
        (Swahili, Ashton 1944: 219)

    b. *M-toto*   *a-li-m-kimbil-i-a*   *mama*   *wake*
        1-child   SM1-PST-OM1-run-APPL-FV   1.mother   1POSS.3SG
        'The child ran off to his mother.'
        (Swahili, Ashton 1944: 219)

    c. *Waziri*   *a-li-anguk-i-a*   *chini*
        1.minister   SM1-PST-fall-APPL-FV   9.down
        'The minister fell down'
        (Abdulaziz (1996: 32) cited in Marten and Mous 2017: 9)

Nyambo exhibits a more complex interplay between prepositions and applicatives for locatives (see also this volume, chapter 8 and Pacchiarotti (2020: 124) for a discussion of this strategy more broadly). The language requires applicative marking for locative complements with certain verbs. Generally, these are verbs with no inherent locative meaning ('speak' in (15a/b) versus 'store' in (15c/d)). In (15d) the applicative broadens the scope of the locative to include the subject and hence 'while in the house'. There are other verbs which do not allow an applicative to express location ('find' in (15e/f)).

(15) Nyambo
    a. *gamb-ir-á*   *omu-nju*
        speak-APPL-FV   LOC-house
        'to speak in the house'

    b. **gamb-a*   *omu-nju*
        speak-FV   LOC-house

    c. *biik-á*   *omu-nju*
        store-FV   LOC-house
        'store (something) in the house'

---

4 Although the form *chini* ends in *ni*, it does not synchronically contain the Swahili locative suffix *-ni*.

d. *biic-ir-á*   *omu-nju*
store-APPL-FV   LOC-house
'store (something) while in the house"

e. *a-ka-mu-sang-á*   *omu-nju*
SM1-PST-OM1-find-FV   LOC-house
'he found her in the house'

f. **a-ka-mu-sanj-ir-á*   *omu-nju*
SM1-PST-OM1-find-APPL-FV   LOC-house
(Rugemalira 1993: 71–72)

In a final category of Nyambo verbs, the locative and applicative alternate (16).

(16) Nyambo
    a. *A-ka-sitamá*   *aha-ntébe*   [locative]
        SM1-PST3-sit   LOC16-9.chair
        'He sat on a chair.'

    b. *A-ka-sitam-ir-á*   *e-ntébe*   [applicative]
        SM1-PST3-sit-APPL-FV   AUG-9.chair
        'He sat on a chair.'
        (Rugemalira 2005: 95)

In (16a), there is no applicative marking on the verb, while the noun expressing the location (the chair) is locative marked. In (16b), the verb is marked for the applicative, but the location is expressed by a bare (class 9) noun phrase and is not locative marked. There is no difference in meaning between the two sentences indicated in the source, although more contextualised examples might reveal a (semantic or pragmatic) difference in interpretation.

To summarize, there is variation among Bantu languages with respect to the co-occurrence of applicative marking and locative marked or prepositional phrases. While in some languages the two patterns are in complementary distribution, e.g. in Swahili (14) and Nyambo (16), in other languages applicative marked verbs and locative-marked phrases can or must be used together, e.g in Sesotho (12b) and Setswana (13b). Different marking patterns are often associated with differences in interpretation, which also depend on the lexical meaning of the verb. In particular, the use of applicatives often integrates the locative more closely semantically in the verb meaning (e.g. the action is directed towards the location) or adds a pragmatic meaning of focus or emphasis. As we will show in the next section, these comparatively well-described effects of applicatives in locative contexts are replicated across a wide range of applicatives in non-locative contexts.

2.3 Prepositions introducing specific thematic roles

A number of Bantu languages have constructions where a preposition introduces a beneficiary, reason or other thematic role, similarly to the applicative construction. Speakers of Sesotho (cf. 3) and isiXhosa use a construction based on the borrowed English preposition *for* (17a), as well as the regular applicative verbal extension found across the Bantu languages (17b) with equivalent meanings.

(17) isiXhosa
    a. *Ndi-zo-phek-a*   *u-ku-tya*   *for*   *a-ba-ntwana*
        SM1SG-FUT-cook-FV   AUG-15-food   for   AUG-2-child
        'I will cook food for the children'

    b. *Ndi-zo-phek-el-a*   *a-ba-ntwana*   *u-ku-tya*
        SM1SG-FUT-cook-APPL-FV   AUG-2-child   AUG-15-food
        'I will cook food for the children'
        (Simango 2019: 324, glossing added)

As Riedel and Gibson (2021) show, the Sesotho construction with a borrowed preposition can be used with a wide range of verbs and different types of thematic roles but has not grammaticalized to the point where the *for*-marked noun phrase is treated as a grammatical object. In Sesotho, unlike in Mbuun or the applicative-locative combinations in Sesotho, Bemba and other languages, either the applicative (3a) or the preposition *for* (3b) can be used, but not both for the same verb/applied noun phrase (18).

(18) Sesotho
     *Ke-rek-etse   ***for***   *se-lamba*   *sa-ka*   *di-konopo*
      SM1SG-buy-APPL.PERF   for   7-jacket   7-POSS.1SG   10-button
      Int: 'I bought buttons for my jacket'
      (Riedel and Gibson 2021)

According to Machobane (1989), in Sesotho, certain intransitives do not allow benefactive applied objects (19a) but only locative applied objects (19b), as well as locative adjuncts which are not applicative marked. However, the *for*-construction can be used in such cases as the example in (19c) shows.

(19) Sesotho
    a. *Baeti   ba-fihl-etse   mo-rena
        2-visitor   SM2-arrive-APPL.PERF   1-chief
        'The visitors have arrived for the chief'
        (Machobane 1989: 60)

    b. Ba-eti   ba-fihl-etse   mo-reneng
        2-visitor   SM2-arrive-APPL.PERF   1-chief.LOC
        'The visitors have arrived at the chief's place'
        (Machobane 1989: 60)

    c. Mo-eti   o-fihl-ile   for   wena
        1-visitor   SM1-arrive-PERF   for   2SG
        'A visitor has arrived for you.'
        (Riedel and Gibson 2021)

This restriction on Sesotho beneficiaries looks similar to the restrictions on morphological applicatives with some verbs in Mbuun which also do not allow benefactive applicative constructions (20a).

(20) Mbuun
    a. *maam   o-á-témmé   m-bwá   ɔ́-ŋgáŋ
        mother   SM1-PRS.PROG-call.APPL   9-dog   1-doctor
        'Mother calls the doctor for the dog.'

    b. maam   o-á-tém   ɔ́-ŋgáŋ   ɔ́ŋgírá   m-bwa
        mother   SM1-PRS.PROG-call   1-doctor   for   9-dog
        'Mother calls the doctor for the dog.'

    c. maam   o-á-léŋŋé   m-bwá   ɔ́-ŋgáŋ
        mother   SM1-PRS.PROG-seek.APPL   9-dog   1-doctor
        'Mother seeks a doctor for (the benefit of) the dog'
        (Bostoen and Mundeke 2011: 192)

As in Sesotho, the ungrammaticality in Mbuun does not apply to the prepositional construction (20b). Example (20c) shows that the ungrammaticality of (20a) is not related to the human versus non-human status of the beneficiary, but rather to the verb root with which the applicative combines.

In some Mozambican Bantu languages, prepositions borrowed from Portuguese are found with applicative-like functions. In Cuwabo, the preposition *para* 'for' introduces a reason *wh*-word without the verb being marked with an applicative (21), seemingly similar to the Sesotho and isiXhosa borrowed prepositions.

In Makhuwa the preposition is used with the applicative but is required for the sentence to be grammatical (22), which is similar to the Mbuun pattern and the locative/preposition applicative combinations.

(21) Cuwabo
    o-ní-já   *weeká*   *pára=ni*
    SM2SG-PRS.CJ-eat   2SG.alone   for=what
    'Why do you eat on your own?'
    (Guérois 2015: 223)

(22) Makhuwa
    Saárá   *onthumenlé*   *ekolár'*   *íile*   **(para)*   *páni?*
    Sara   o-n-thum-el-ale   ekolar   ile   para   pani
    1.Sara   SM1-OM1-buy-APPL-PFV.CJ   9.necklace   9.DEM.DIST   for   1.who
    'Who did Sara buy the necklace for?'
    (Jenneke van der Wal, p.c.)

The Cuwabo example in (21) mirrors a construction with a non-borrowed preposition found in Sambaa, as shown in (23). Here the preposition *kwa* together with the question word meaning 'what' is used to form a why-question.[5]

(23) Sambaa
    Kwa   *mbwai*   *a-ku-et-e-a*   *ma-tagi?*
    PREP   what   SM1-OM2SG-bring-APPL-FV   6-egg
    'Why did s/he bring you eggs?'
    (Riedel field notes, 2006, example 00844)

Sambaa also has an applicative plus 'what' construction for forming a why-question that arguably competes with the prepositional construction in (23). This kind of construction, where the applicative together with a *wh*-word or a *wh*-clitic meaning 'what' is interpreted as a why-question, has been described for a number of Bantu languages (cf. the list of languages with this construction in Trithart 1983: 148) illustrated with the example from Sambaa in (24) and Zulu data in (25).

---

[5] Note that while the verb in (23) also contains an applicative, this applicative introduces the second person singular beneficiary here, not the reason *wh*-phrase.

(24) Sambaa
　　A-chi-kund-iy-a-i?
　　SM1-OM7-like-APPL-FV-what
　　'Why does s/he want it?'
　　(Riedel field notes 2006)

(25) Zulu
　　U-cul-el-a-ni?
　　SM2SG-sing-APPL-FV-what
　　'Why are you singing? What are you singing for?'
　　(Buell 2011: 805)

Across Bantu, this adds another example of functional overlap between morphological applicatives and prepositional constructions.

A final pattern to consider are prepositions which introduce goal arguments, and so provide a structural alternative to applicative constructions. This is the case in Swahili, where the preposition *kwa* can be used in this way, but only in lexically restricted cases. Verbs such as *-andika* 'write' allow for a goal to be added with the preposition *kwa*. This can be seen in (26a) where *kwa* is used to introduce the goal *mwenyekiti* 'chairperson'. However, it is not acceptable for the morphological applicative *-i-* in such a verb and the preposition *kwa* to co-occur. This is illustrated by the ungrammaticality of both examples (26b) and (26c). Moreover, this use of the preposition *kwa* does not extend to other verbs that can take a beneficiary but not a goal such as *-pika* 'cook', meaning that constructions such as those in (26d) are ill-formed with an intended meaning of 'I cooked for the children'.

(26) Swahili
　a. *Ni-li-andika　　　　　　barua　kwa　mw-enyekiti.*
　　　SM1SG-PST-write　　　9.letter　PREP　1-chairperson
　　　'I wrote a letter to the chairperson.'

　b. *Ni-li-andik-(*i)-a　　　　barua　kwa　mw-enyekiti.*
　　　SM1SG-PST-write-APPL-FV　9.letter　PREP　1-chairperson
　　　'I wrote a letter to the chairperson.'

　c. *Ni-li-mw-andik-i-a　　　　barua　(*kwa)　mw-enyekiti.*
　　　SM1SG-PST-OM1-write-APPL-FV　9.letter　PREP　1-chairperson
　　　'I wrote a letter to the chairperson.'[6]

---

[6] This sentence would be grammatical with the reading of 'I wrote him/her$_{i/*i}$ a letter at the chairperson$_i$'s place'.

d. #*Ni-li-pika*   *kwa*   *wa-toto.*
SM1SG-PST-cook   PREP   2-children
*'I cooked for the children'
'I cooked at the children's place'
(Swahili, Riedel 2019)

In isiXhosa, an applied noun phrase such as the beneficiary *abantwana* 'children' in (27a) can appear with locative marking as in (27b). Du Plessis and Visser (1992) describe this type of construction as having a focus-related meaning.

(27) isiXhosa
     a. *Ndi-nik-el-a*   *abantwana*
        SM1SG-give-APPL-FV   2.child
        iiswiti   [non-locative marked beneficiary]
        10.sweet
        'I hand over sweets to the children.'

     b. *Ndi-nik-el-a*   *iiswiti*
        SM1SG-give-APPL-FV   10.sweet
        e-bantwaneni   [locative-marked beneficiary]
        LOC-2.child.LOC
        'I hand over sweets to the children.'
        (Du Plessis and Visser 1992: 59, cited in Riedel 2019)

This isiXhosa construction has the same word order and also the same object-marking restrictions[7] as the Sesotho *for* and the Mbuun *ɔ́ŋgírá* constructions, discussed above. This behaviour is thus not limited to innovated prepositions. This means there is evidence for an entire category of prepositions introducing semantic roles but not (yet) showing the morphosyntactic properties of morphological applicatives in Bantu. The fact that these locative marked phrases (27) are not full arguments in isiXhosa is also noted in Andrason (2018), and in part reflects the restructuring of the locative system in Southern Bantu, where locatives no longer behave as noun phrases (Marten 2010, Creissels 2011).

In this section we have reviewed the role of applicative verb forms and prepositionally marked complements. We have taken the interaction of applicatives and locatives as a starting point, where variation with respect to both co-occurrence restrictions and interpretive effects have been well documented.

---

[7] Whether object marking is acceptable in these constructions is not mentioned in Du Plessis and Visser (1992). We thank Hlumela Mkabile for providing additional judgements.

We then showed that similar variation occurs with other thematic roles such as instrument, benefactive and theme objects. While in the case of locatives, the coding of the locative phrase is typically achieved through noun class morphology, the coding of non-locative phrases relies on the use of prepositions, and so results in complex interaction between the two construction types. In the following section, we will explore this interaction in terms of its typological and diachronic implications.

3 Valency and saliency: A reanalysis account

Considerable work has been produced over the years on the diachrony of the applicative suffix *-ɪd in Bantu (see Pacchiarotti 2020 for a recent overview) as well as cross-linguistically (Peterson 2007). We will provide a brief review of this work here, and then develop a novel account of the development of applicatives based on a reanalysis of applicatives as markers of saliency.

3.1 Previous accounts

Pacchiarotti (2020) discusses two fairly widely agreed hypotheses about the original function of Bantu applicative *-ɪd. First, applicatives, like other Bantu extensions, are likely to have a verbal origin, probably as main or auxiliary verbs following non-finite verbal complements in a head-final structure (Givón 1971, Voeltz 1977, Hyman 2007a, 2007b). Cross-linguistically, Peterson (2007) proposes that the most common etymological sources for applicatives in general are adpositions (mostly postpositions) and verbs. However, due to the paucity of adpositions in Bantu, a verbal origin seems the more likely scenario. With respect to the function of *-ɪd, two main proposals have been made, namely that the original function was the introduction of a benefactive argument (e.g. Trithart 1983), or that the original function of the applicative was related to introducing locatives, which is the analysis we will follow here (see Pacchiarotti 2020: 272–278 for arguments in favour of an original Location-related function of PB *-ɪd). Under this view, *-ɪd originally functioned to bring a locative phrase closer into the predication expressed by the verb, to direct the action expressed by the verb to a particular endpoint (e.g. Schadeberg 2003: 74), or to provide an abstract notion of space which could be filled by different expressions denoting location and, subsequently, by non-locations (Marten and Kula 2014).

However, while the relationship between valency changing and semantic and pragmatic effects brought about by applicatives discussed earlier in this paper has been noted frequently, no fully developed analysis about the diachronic relation between these different functions has been proposed. Pacchiarotti (2020) presents evidence from lexicalised reconstructed Proto-Bantu verb forms which might support an analysis set forth by Schadeberg (n.d.) in which pragmatic functions precede the syntactic functions of applicatives – e.g. first the pragmatic saliency of a locative phrase is highlighted, and this function then grammaticalizes into the syntactic introduction of an additional argument (see also Creissels 2004). This scenario is consistent with grammar ontogenesis, whereby discourse-related structures often develop into syntax (see, e.g., Givón 1979). However, the lexical evidence is somewhat inconclusive and the link between pragmatics and syntax is a widespread, but not a necessary effect.

An alternative analysis is developed by De Kind and Bostoen (2012), who, as noted above, propose that applicatives originally introduced locative arguments, and this meant that locatives could be brought into postverbal focus position, from which then pragmatic effects resulted.

3.2 A new account

Based on the interaction of applicatives and prepositions discussed in this paper, we will here propose a novel analysis of the developments of applicatives, which centrally involves a reanalaysis of applicatives in the context of (ambiguous) double marking of the applied argument. Like De Kind and Bostoen (2012) we assume that applicatives originally licensed an additional (locative) argument. This licensing was likely to be linked to semantic effects (e.g. directing the action of the verb towards a location), and probably also to pragmatic effects (by highlighting the saliency of the location for the predication). However, at this stage we do not assume that applicatives could be used solely as a marker of saliency, without underlying syntactic operation.

We also assume that locatives even at the Proto-Bantu stage were ambiguous in terms of their syntactic function, and could function as either argument or adjunct (see Riedel and Marten 2012). Furthermore, locative marking – that is, at this stage, noun class morphology – could be interpreted as more nominal-like or preposition-like. This assumption is based on the change of locatives from nominal to prepositional syntax, as noted above. This process has been observed across the Bantu-speaking area, for example in the comparative work by Grégoire (1975), by Kuperus and Mpunga wa Ilunga (1990) in Luba, by Marten (2010) and Creissels (2011) for Southern Bantu, and by Beermann and Asiimwe (forthcoming) for Runyankore-Rukiga. It is therefore likely that the process was already apparent in Proto-Bantu. As discussed above, the ambiguity of locative complements can still be seen today, and leads to differences in the coding of locative phrases in applicative constructions.

What we propose, then, is that originally applicatives licensed a locative object, and gave rise to pragmatic effects. However, locatives were in themselves ambiguous between arguments and adjuncts, and so in some contexts would not have needed syntactic licensing for use as objects. In these contexts, locatives were effectively doubly licensed, by the applicative and by the locative morphology. This had two potential effects: 1) the double licensing might have had pragmatic effects, as it was unnecessary from a syntactic point of view (akin to reduplication, e.g. intensity, emphasis, saliency) and 2) applicatives could be associated solely with pragmatic effects, as there was no need for syntactic licensing. Once applicatives were reanalysed in this way, they could be used as pure saliency markers, without any attendant change in valency. The steps in the process are summarised in Table 1.

Table 1: Stages of development from syntactic to pragmatic functions.

Stage 1	Applicative constructions may be used to license locative complements, which are not subcategorised by the verb, directing the action towards a location
	Locatives are ambiguous between argument and adjunct
	Then a (locative) applicative with a locative marked complement is an instance of double licensing, leading to heightened pragmatic effects
Stage 2	Applicative morphology is reanalysed as marking pragmatic effects, while the locative verbal complement is licensed by the locative morphology only
Stage 3	Innovative speakers can use applicative markers without change in valency – purely as a saliency marker.

The scenario developed here, tying the grammaticalization of applicatives to the ambiguity of locatives as arguments or adjuncts, explains why pragmatic focus and saliency effects are most well described for locatives. With other thematic roles, this ambiguity is less well-documented. As we have shown, this is because of the relative paucity of prepositions in Bantu languages. However, on closer investigation, similar effects can be seen once relevant prepositions are available to mark functional alternatives to applicative constructions. These prepositions include a small set of prepositions already available in Proto-Bantu, as well as more recently grammaticalized and borrowed prepositions. Since instruments and benefactive arguments marked by prepositions are not ambiguous in the way locative marked phrases are, the interaction between the two functionally equivalent construction types can actually be seen more clearly in these cases, as we have shown.

The reanalysis proposed here will have occurred once applicatives could be used without change in valency, and the change would be transmitted through the different speech communities, and possibly through diffusion – thus underlying (some of) the variation observed in Bantu languages. Of course, speakers would still be able to use applicatives in the older function, to license a change in valency. The rise of the new function does not entail the demise of the old, and either, or both, functions may disappear over time. However, according to our analysis, the use of applicatives purely as a marker of pragmatic saliency, without a syntactic change, would have required the reanalysis outlined above.

The analysis proposed here can be seen as an instance of grammaticalization. Although it does not involve a change in word category and entails reanalysis that remains within syntax, it shows a development in time to a more pragmatic function. There is a well-known tendency in language change, and in particular in semantic-pragmatic change, and that is the tendency of subjectification, first developed in Traugott (1989). According to Traugott, semantic change, especially semantic change underlying processes of grammaticalization, proceeds from more objective depictions of state of affairs, to more internal, subjective representations or valuation of the external. From this perspective, the semantic development of applicatives underlying our proposed analysis can be seen as a development from expressing external spatial relations (the directing of the action to a location) to the expression of a subjective judgement of the saliency of the location with respect to preceding discourse or context – possibly via the more metaphorical use of locations discussed in Marten and Kula (2014) – to the expression of saliency of the action as such. Viewed from this perspective, the analysis is compatible with both established mechanisms of syntactic change and of semantic processes underlying grammaticalization.

4 Summary and concluding remarks

In this paper we have shown that the interaction of applicative marking and prepositions provides a novel perspective on the variation displayed by applicative constructions in Bantu. This perspective highlights (and reinforces) the importance of two dimensions of applicatives – argument structure/transitivity/valency on the one hand and information structure/discourse/focus/saliency on the other.

The interaction between applicative marking and prepositions in Bantu provides valuable insights into a number of features of the syntax and semantics of Bantu languages. Eastern Bantu languages typically have a small inventory of prepositions – where a range of different sources/origins can be identified – and often with comparatively little lexical semantic content. Borrowed prepositions (such as those seen in Sesotho, Makhuwa and Cuwabo) can co-occur with applicatives – the former enabling the addition of arguments (changes in valency) and the latter performing a more focus/saliency-related function. Semantic relations rather than information structure are encoded by borrowed prepositions.

In the case of borrowed prepositions however, it seems that syntactic coding, rather than information structure, plays a defining role in the recruitment and integration of these elements into the target language.

More generally, we have shown that the interaction of applicatives and functionally equivalent prepositionally marked constructions helps to better understand the diachronic development of applicatives. Following an established position in the literature, we have proposed that the original function of applicatives was related to location, and involved the licensing of an additional (locative) object in the clause. However, due to the ambiguity of locative phrases as arguments and adjuncts, locative applied objects could be interpreted in some contexts as doubly licensed. This in turn, provided the context for a reanalysis of the applicative marker as a saliency marker, which could encode pragmatic effects without attendant changes in valency. We have also suggested that this analysis not only involves reanalysis, but is also compatible with Traugott's (1989) notion of subjectification in semantic change.

Abbreviations

1	class 1, etc.
1SG	first person singular, etc.,
APPL	applicative
ASSO	associative
AUG	augment
CJ	conjoint
DEM	demonstrative
DIST	distal
FUT	future
FV	final vowel
INF	infinitive
LOC	locative
NEG	negative
OM	object marker
PFV	perfective
POSS	possessive
PREP	preposition
PRF	perfect

PROG   progressive
PRON   pronoun
PRS   present
REL   relative
SM   subject marker

References

Abdulaziz, Mohamed H. 1996. *Transitivity in Swahili*. Cologne: Rüdiger Köppe Verlag.
Ashton, Ethel O. 1944. *Swahili grammar*. London: Longmans.
Andrason, Alexander. 2018. The argument-adjunct scale: Applied nominal and locative phrases in Xhosa. *Linguistic Discovery* 16(2). Doi:10.1349/PS1.1537-0852.A.478.
Beermann, Dorothee & Allen Asiimwe. Forthcoming. Locatives in Runyankore-Rukiga. In Eva-Marie Bloom-Ström, Hannah Gibson, Rozenn Guérois & Lutz Marten (eds.), *Approaches to morphosyntactic variation in Bantu*. Oxford University Press.
Bostoen, Koen and Léon Mundeke. 2011. The causative/applicative syncretism in Mbuun (Bantu B87, DRC): Semantic split or phonemic merger? *Journal of African Languages and Linguistics* 32. 179–218.
Buell, Leston Chandler. 2011. Zulu *ngani* "why": Postverbal and yet in CP. *Lingua* 121(5). 805–21. https://doi.org/10.1016/j.lingua.2010.11.004
Cann, Ronnie & Patricia Mabugu. 2007. Constructional polysemy: The applicative construction in chiShona. *Metalinguistica* 19. 221–245.
Carston, Robyn. 2002. *Thoughts and utterances: The pragmatics of explicit communication*. Oxford: Blackwell.
Creissels, Denis. 2004. Non-canonical applicatives and focalisation in Tswana. Paper presented at SWL1, Leipzig, August 2004.
Creissels, Denis. 2011. Tswana locatives and their status in the inversion construction. *Africana Linguistica* 17. 33–52.
Creissels, Denis, Gerrit J. Dimmendaal, Zygmunt Frajzyngier & Christa König. 2008. Africa as a morphosyntactic area. In Bernd Heine & Derek Nurse (eds.), *A linguistic geography of Africa*, 86–150. (Cambridge Approaches to Language Contact). Cambridge: Cambridge University Press.
Dammann, Ernst. 1961. Das Applikativum in den Bantusprachen. *Zeitschrift der Deutschen Morgenländischen Gesellschaft* 36. 160–169.
De Kind, Jasper & Koen Bostoen. 2012. The applicative in ciLubà grammar and discourse: A semantic goal analysis. *Southern African Linguistics and Applied Language Studies* 30(1). 101–124.
Du Plessis, Jacobus A. & Marianna Visser. 1992. *Xhosa Language – Syntax*. Pretoria: Via Afrika.
Givón, Talmy. 1971. On the verbal origin of the Bantu verb suffixes. *Studies in African Linguistics* 2(2). 145–63. (Revised and reprinted in Talmy Givón (ed.). 2015. *The diachrony of grammar, Vol. 1*, 117–29. Amsterdam: John Benjamins).
Grégoire, Claire. 1975. *Les locatifs en bantou*. Tervuren: Musée royal de l'Afrique centrale.

Guthrie, Malcolm. 1962. The status of radical extensions in Bantu languages. *Journal of African Languages* 1(3). 202–220.

Guthrie, Malcolm. 1967–1971. *Comparative Bantu: An Introduction to the Comparative Linguistics and Prehistory of the Bantu Languages, Vols. I–IV*. Farnborough: Gregg.

Hyman, Larry M. 2007a. Niger-Congo verb extensions: Overview and discussion. In Doris L. Payne & Jaime Peña (eds.), *Selected Proceedings of the 37th Annual Conference on African Linguistics*, 149–163. Somerville, MA: Cascadilla.

Hyman, Larry M. 2007b. Reconstructing the Proto-Bantu verbal unit: Internal evidence. In Nancy C. Kula & Lutz Marten (eds.), *Bantu in Bloomsbury: Special Issue on Bantu Linguistics*, 201–211. (*SOAS Working Papers in Linguistics*, Volume 15). London: SOAS.

Jerro, Kyle. 2016. *The syntax and semantics of applicative morphology in Bantu*. Austin: University of Texas dissertation.

Kähler-Meyer Emmi. 1966. Die örtliche Funktion der Applikativendung in Bantusprachen. In Johannes Lukas (ed.), *Neue afrikanistische Studien: Festschrift für A. Klingenheben*, 126–136. Hamburg: Deutsches Institut für Afrika-Forschung.

Katamba, Francis, 2003. Bantu nominal morphology. In Derek Nurse & Gérard Philippson (eds.), *The Bantu languages*, 103–120. London: Routledge.

Kimenyi, Alexandre. 1995. Kinyarwanda applicatives revisited. Keynote address presented at the 8th Niger-Congo Syntax-Semantics Workshop, Boston University. Available at http://www.kimenyi.com/kinyarwanda-applicatives-revisited.php

Kuperus, Julianna & A. Mpunga wa Ilunga. 1990. *Locative markers in Luba*. (Annales Sciences Humaines 130). Tervuren: Royal Museum for Central Africa.

Marten, Lutz. 2002. *At the syntax-pragmatics interface: Verbal underspecification and concept formation in dynamic syntax*. Oxford: Oxford University Press.

Marten, Lutz. 2003. The dynamics of Bantu applied verbs: an analysis at the syntax-pragmatics interface. In Kézié K. Lébikaza (ed.), *Actes du 3e Congrès Mondial de Linguistique Africaine Lomé 2000*, 207–221. Cologne: Rüdiger Köppe Verlag.

Marten, Lutz. 2010. The great siSwati locative shift. In Anne Breitbarth. Christopher Lucas, Sheila Watts & David Willis (eds.), *Continuity and change in grammar*, 249–267. Amsterdam: John Benjamins.

Marten, Lutz & Nancy C. Kula. 2014. Benefactive and substitutive applicatives in Bemba. *Journal of African Languages and Linguistics* 35(1). 1–44.

Marten, Lutz & Maarten Mous. 2014. Non-valency-changing valency-changing derivations. In Rose-Juliet Anyanwu (ed.), *Transitivity in African languages*. *Frankfurter Afrikanistische Blätter* 26. 89–105.

Marten, Lutz & Maarten Mous. 2017. Valency and expectation in Bantu applicatives. *Linguistics Vanguard* 3(1). https://doi.org/10.1515/lingvan-2016-0078

Mchombo, Sam A. (ed.). 1993. *Theoretical aspects of Bantu grammar 1*. Stanford: CLSI Publications.

Mous, Maarten 2020. Transfer of Swahili 'until' in contact with East African languages. In Norval Smith, Tonjes Veenstra & Enoch Oladé Aboh (eds.), *Advances in contact linguistics: In honour of Pieter Muysken*, 217–234. (CoLL 57). Amsterdam: John Benjamins.

Ngonyani, Deogratias S. 1996. *The morphosyntax of applicatives*. Los Angeles: University of California dissertation.

Ngonyani, Deo. 1998. Properties of applied objects in Kiswahili and Kidendeule. *Studies in African Linguistics* 27(1). 67–93.

Pacchiarotti, Sara. 2017. *Bantu applicative construction types involving *-id: Form, functions and diachrony*. Eugene: University of Oregon dissertation.

Pacchiarotti, Sara. 2020. *Bantu applicative constructions*. (Stanford Monographs in African Languages). Stanford: CSLI Publications.

Peterson, David A. 2007. *Applicative constructions*. Oxford: Oxford University Press.

Pylkkänen, Liina. 2008. *Introducing Arguments*. (Linguistic Inquiry Monographs 49). Cambridge, Ma.: MIT Press.

Riedel, Kristina. 2019. Locative alternations in isiXhosa and the argument structure of applied objects. Ms., University of the Free State.

Riedel, Kristina & Hannah Gibson. 2021. For-applicative constructions in Sesotho. Ms., University of the Free State & University of Essex.

Riedel, Kristina & Lutz Marten. 2012. Locative object marking and the argument-adjunct distinction. *Southern African Linguistics and Applied Language Studies* 30(2). 277–292.

Rugemalira, Josephat M. 1993. Runyambo verb extension and constraints on predicate structure. Berkeley: University of California dissertation.

Rugemalira, Josephat M. 2005. *A grammar of Runyambo*. Utrecht: LOT Publications.

Schadeberg, Thilo C. 2003. Derivation. In Derek Nurse & Gérard Philippson (eds.), *The Bantu languages*, 71–89. London: Routledge.

Schadeberg, Thilo C. n.d. Applicative. Ms., Leiden University.

Sibanda, Galen. 2016. The Ndebele applicative construction. In Doris Payne, Sara Pacchiarotti & Mokaya Bosire (eds.), *The Selected Proceedings of the 46th Annual Conference on African Linguistics*, 309–333. Berlin: Language Science Press.

Simango, Silvester Ron. 2019. English prepositions in IsiXhosa Spaces: Evidence from code-switching. In Raymond Hickey (ed.), *English in multilingual South Africa*, 310–328. Cambridge: Cambridge University Press. doi:10.1017/9781108340892.015.

Traugott, Elizabeth Closs. 1989. On the rise of epistemic meaning in English: an example of subjectification in semantic change. *Language* 65(1). 31–55.

Trithart, Mary Lee. 1983. *The applied suffix and transitivity: A historical study in Bantu*. Los Angeles: University of California dissertation.

Trithart, Mary Lee. 1977. *Relational Grammar and Chichewa subjectivization*. Los Angeles: University of California M.A. thesis.

Voeltz, Erhard Friedrich Karl. 1977. *Proto Niger-Congo verb extensions*. Los Angeles: University of California dissertation.

Voisin, Sylvie. 2006. Applicatif et emphase. In Daniel Lebaud, Catherine Paulin & Katja Ploog (eds.), *Constructions verbales et production de sens*, 155–170. Besançon: Presses Universitaires de Franche-Comté.

Hilde Gunnink and Sara Pacchiarotti
8 Neglected functions of the Bantu applicative in relation to Locations: new insights from Fwe (K402)

Abstract: This paper deals with two seldom described discourse functions of the reflexes of Proto-Bantu applicative *-ɪd in Fwe (K402), a Bantu language spoken in Zambia and Namibia. These functions are: (i) signaling some sort of narrow focus on an applied phrase expressing General Location, and (ii) widening the "orientation" of a locative phrase from involving the object of a transitive verb root to involving also the subject of that transitive verb root (e.g. *John saw Mary on the boat* implies only Mary is for sure on the boat; *John saw Mary-APPL on the boat* implies both John and Mary are on the boat). The Fwe data are special in that they reveal so-far unattested variations and interpretations in these two uses. With respect to (i), we show that the applicative can optionally combine with other focus-marking strategies such as cleft constructions to express completive and contrastive focus. With respect to (ii), preliminary data suggest that the applicative in Fwe can modify the scope of the Location applied phrase to include the speaker who utters a sentence instead of the grammatical subject of the utterance. To our knowledge, this possibility has not been previously attested. Finally, we conclude by showing how Fwe data bear on the diachrony of the functions of PB applicative *-ɪd.

1 Introduction

Fwe [fwe] is a Bantu language spoken in the Zambezi region of Namibia (formerly known as Caprivi strip), and in the southwestern tip of the Western province of Zambia. Within the referential classification commonly used in Bantu languages, Fwe is assigned the alphanumeric code K402 (Guthrie 1971; Maho 2009). Fwe has been classified as part of a subgroup called "Bantu Botatwe", more specifically its Western branch (Bostoen 2009; de Luna 2010). The Bantu Botatwe subgroup

---

Hilde Gunnink, Ghent University, BantUGent - UGent Centre for Bantu Studies, Blandijnberg 2, Ghent, Belgium, e-mail: hilde.gunnink@ugent.be
Sara Pacchiarotti, Ghent University, BantUGent - UGent Centre for Bantu Studies, Blandijnberg 2, Ghent, Belgium, e-mail: sara.pacchiarotti@ugent.be

https://doi.org/10.1515/9783110777949-008

itself is part of the large Eastern branch of Bantu (Grollemund et al. 2015). Previous research on Fwe is fairly limited. The data presented in this paper were collected by the first author through fieldwork between 2013 and 2017, as part of her PhD project (see also Gunnink 2022). Data were collected through elicitation as well as in the form of natural texts (narratives, songs, conversation).[1] In grammatical descriptions of present-day Bantu languages, reflexes of the polyfunctional and semantically underspecified Proto-Bantu (PB) applicative suffix *-ɪd are usually described as a purely syntactic device which introduces a variety of peripheral semantic roles.[2] Nevertheless, it is by now well known that reflexes of *-ɪd applicative suffix are not always valence-increasing and can perform a variety of semantic and discourse-related functions (see, e.g., Bentley 1887, Damman 1961, Kähler-Meyer 1966, Whiteley 1968, Guthrie 1970, Kimenyi 1980, Trithart 1983, Schaefer 1985, Harford 1993, Rugemalira 1993, Rapold 1997, Mabugu 2001, Kawasha 2003, Marten 2003, Creissels 2004, Simango 2012, Marten and Mous 2017, among others). The discourse functions of the reflexes of *-ɪd in Bantu are restricted to locative phrases. This paper provides novel data on two pragmatic functions of the applicative: (i) the use of the applicative alone and in combination with cleft constructions to place a locative marked phrase under narrow completive or replacing focus; (ii) the use of the applicative to modify the semantic scope of a locative-marked phrase in a main clause. Additionally, we show that the applicative in Fwe is often the sole morphological means to introduce a Location-related semantic role into a main clause with certain verb roots. We consider this as additional evidence for the fact that if PB *-ɪd originally introduced an applied phrase into a main clause, this phrase was most likely either a Spatial Goal or a Location.

In order to describe the functions of applicative morphology in Fwe, we make use of the five-way language-specific, root-specific distinction among Bantu applicative constructions (form and function pairings) set out in Pacchiarotti (2020). This approach departs from the assumption that reflexes of the semanti-

---

[1] We are grateful to three anonymous reviewers and Fernando Zúñiga for their stimulating comments on previous drafts of this chapter. The first author acknowledges the support of the FWO (Fonds Wetenschappelijk Onderzoek Vlaanderen) postdoctoral fellowship n° 12P8419N. The second author acknowledges the support of the FWO postdoctoral fellowship n° 12ZV721N.

[2] *-ɪd is the only applicative suffix reconstructed to PB (Meeussen 1967: 92). While innovations of PB verbal derivational morphemes such as the causative happened repeatedly in the history of Bantu languages (see Bosteen and Guérois forthcoming for a discussion), to our knowledge, no applicative morpheme has been innovated since PB. Occasionally, in some Bantu languages reflexes of other reconstructed verbal derivational suffixes can take on applicative functions, e.g., in Ruanda (JD61), the reflex of the PB causative *ic is used to introduce Instrument applied phrases into a main clause (Kimenyi 1980: 32).

cally underspecified Proto-Bantu applicative *-ɪd suffix in modern Bantu languages are syntactically valence increasing by default. The five applicative construction types are distinguished by the following criteria: (i) whether the applicative introduces an obligatorily present applied phrase; (ii) whether the applicative performs semantic and/or pragmatic functions; (iii) whether the construction is productive; (iv) whether the construction is subject to lexicalization (see Pacchiarotti 2020: 111 for a summary of structural and functional differences among the constructions). Based on these four criteria, five construction types can be distinguished. In any given Bantu language, a given verb root can/must participate in more than one construction type. In Type A, the applicative has a purely syntactic function and is the sole morphological means to introduce an applied phrase with a given semantic role in a main clause. For instance, in the eastern Bantu language Haya, the root 'fall' must undergo applicative derivation to express the General Location where the event of falling happens. This means that the applicative is the only means in this language to specify a General Location in a main clause containing the root *gw* 'fall'. Without the applicative, the sentence in (1) would mean that the person fell *into* the house from another location.

(1) Haya (JE22, Hyman and Duranti 1982: 234)
 n-ka-gw-el' *ómú-nju*
 1SG.SUBJ-PST-fall-APPL in-house
 'I fell [while I was] in the house.'

In Type B, the applicative introduces an applied phrase with a semantic role which has an alternative way of expression, e.g. as an oblique. There is usually a semantic and/or discourse difference between the construction of the root plus the oblique and the construction of the applicative, for instance, the latter is used as a device to ensure topic continuity. For instance, animate Beneficiaries in Lingala can be optionally expressed in the construction with the root as a prepositional phrase, as in (2), or by means of an applicative construction, as in (3).

(2) Lingala (C30B, Rapold 1997: 43)
 Kengo a-lámb-í *tií póna bána*
 K. 3SG.SUBJ-prepare-PFV tea PREP children
 'Kengo prepared tea for the children.'

(3) Lingala (C30B, Rapold 1997: 43)
 Kengo a-lámb-él-í *bána*
 K. 3SG.SUBJ-prepare-APPL-PFV children
 'Kengo prepared tea for the children.'

Rapold (1997: 43) argues that (2) can be used as a thetic statement to express a state of affairs or when the Beneficiary is rhematic or in assertive focus, for instance, as an answer to *For whom did he prepare tea?* On the other hand, (3) is most naturally used when the Beneficiary is a discourse topic, e.g., as the answer to a question such as *What did he prepare for the children?* Type C applicative constructions target only applied phrases with a Location-related semantic role: the applicative introduces an obligatorily present applied phrase which could be optionally present in the construction with just the root, and performs semantic or pragmatic functions on this applied phrase (or on the whole clause) which are different from those in Type B, e.g., the applicative is used to narrow-focus the Location-related applied phrase. Consider the Zimbabwean Ndebele root 'cry' in (4) which can optionally combine with a locative phrase expressing General Location without the need of applicative derivation. In (5) the root 'cry' combines with applicative derivation and the locative phrase becomes obligatory. While (4) is pragmatically a general statement, in (5) the applicative places focus on the locative constituent and the sentence is the most usual answer to the question *Where is the baby crying?* (In Zimbabwean Ndebele this *where* question also features an applicative on the main verb).

(4) Zimbabwean Ndebele (S44; Galen Sibanda p.c.)
 u-sane   lu-ya-khal-a   (pha-ndle)
 cl11-baby 11.SUBJ-TNS-cry-FV CL16-outside
 'The baby is crying (outside).'

(5) Zimbabwean Ndebele (S44; Sibanda 2016: 316)
 u-sane   lu-ø-khal-el-a   pha-ndle
 CL11-baby 11.SUBJ-TNS-cry-APPL-FV CL16-outside
 'The baby is crying *outside*.' (emphasis is our own)

Unlike in Types A, B, and C, in Type D the applicative does not introduce an applied phrase. Instead, it signals that the action/event described by the root is performed to completion, continuously, with intensity, excess, etc. This function is often available only with a restricted set of verb roots. The syntactically transitive Swahili root *pig* 'hit' in (6) must combine with two applicative suffixes in (7) to convey the idea that the action of hitting is being performed multiple times.[3] Note that in (7), the derived stem still takes only one object NP 'nail' just like in (6).

---

[3] In other Bantu languages, one, two, or up to three applicative suffixes are used to convey repetitiveness, intensity, completeness etc. depending on the phonotactic shape of the verb root.

(6) Swahili (G41–43; Mokaya Bosire, p.c.)
    Juma   a-li-pig-a   m-sumari   (u-kuta-ni)
    J.   3SG.SUBJ-PST-hit-FV   CL3-nail   CL11-wall-LOC
    'Juma hit the nail (through the wall).'

(7) Swahili (G41–43; Mokaya Bosire, p.c.)
    Juma   a-li-pig-il-i-a   m-sumari   (u-kuta-ni)
    J.   3SG.SUBJ-PST-hit-APPL-APPL-FV   CL3-nail   CL11-wall-LOC
    'Juma hit the nail repeatedly/through (the wall).'

Finally, Type E pseudo-applicative constructions are semantically noncompositional (lexicalized) applicativized stems where the applicative has lost its ability to introduce an applied phrase and perform semantic and/or pragmatic functions described for other types. To see this, consider the Tswana applicative stem *lalel* [lál-él] 'have dinner' in (9) and its corresponding root *lal* [lál] 'lie down, spend the night, sleep' in (8). Both the root and the derived applicative stem are syntactically intransitive as shown by the optionality of the prepositional phrases with which they combine. Additionally, the applicative stem *lalel* has developed a noncompositional meaning with respect to the verb root from which it is derived ('lie down, stay overnight, spend the night' > 'have dinner').[4]

(8) Tswana (S31; Creissels 1999: 148)
    Re tlaa lala mo nageng
    rì-tɬàà-lál-à   (mó nàχé-ŋ)
    1PL.SUBJ-fut-lie.down-FV   LOC CL9.bush-LOC
    'We will lie down/spend the night/sleep (in the bush).'

(9) Tswana (S31; Creissels 1999: 149)
    Re tlaa lalela ka dikgobe
    rì-tɬàà-lál-él-à   (ká dí-qʰɔ́ːbɛ̀)
    1PL.SUBJ-FUT-lie.down-APPL-FV   INS CL10-beans.and.maize
    'We will have dinner (with beans and maize).'

---

4 The pseudoapplicative *lalel* [lál-él] is the regular reflex of a PB verb stem which likely already contained an applicative morpheme at some node of PB, namely *dáadɪd 'have supper, look after, brood' according to the online database Bantu Lexical Reconstructions 3 (BLR3; Bastin et al. 2002). The verb form *dáadɪd is derived from the verb form *dáad 'lie down, sleep, spend the night'.

There are two major advantages in using this approach to Bantu applicative constructions. First, these construction types capture all the different synchronic functions of the polyfunctional applicative suffix in Fwe. Second, they bypass the need to dive into the murkiness of distinguishing between syntactic arguments and adjuncts brought about by definitions based solely on the potential valence-increasing nature of applicative morphology (see §2).

Because reflexes of the PB *-ɪd in present-day Bantu languages are semantically underspecified, the function(s) of applicative morphology on a verb root become(s) evident only when the derived verb stem occurs in a discourse context. In any given language, in order to know which applicative construction type a verb root is participating in, one needs to know minimally: (i) the argument structure of the root, that is, how many core syntactic arguments the root can take, what non-core obliques the root can freely combine with (without the need of derivational morphology), and what semantic roles these can have; and (ii) the communicative context in which the applicative construction is used, that is, why the speaker is using the applicative. While going through different Bantu applicative construction types in this paper, the reader should keep in mind that in Bantu, by definition, whenever the applicative introduces an applied phrase into a construction, this morphosyntactic element always becomes an obligatorily present constituent.[5] This paper is organized as follows. In §2, we present morphosyntactic features of Fwe essential to understanding the data presented in other sections. In §3, for the sake of completeness, we discuss applicative functions which are not the focus of this paper, namely Types B, D, and E. In §4, we show that applicative morphology is obligatory with certain verb roots to express a variety of Location-related semantic roles (Type A). In §5, we discuss two discourse-related functions of applicative morphology in relation to Locations (Type C): narrow focus (§5.1) and argument orientation (§5.2), that is, the modification of the semantic scope of a locative constituent in a main clause. Throughout this paper, we specify the language name, alphanumeric code and source only for examples from languages other than Fwe. Fwe examples that do not specify a source are from the first author's field notes. The Fwe data used in this chapter were collected for a general description of the grammar of Fwe, and not for a detailed syntactic and semantic analysis of applicative constructions. This means

---

5 An anonymous reviewer wonders whether there are really no examples in Bantu of applicatives that alter the argument structure of the verb by adding an argument that is left unexpressed, e.g., because it is given in discourse. Data from Mbuun B87 (Democratic Republic of the Congo) in Bostoen & Mundeke (2011: 191–192) suggest that in this language a Beneficiary applied phrase can indeed be realized as a zero anaphora, in which case "the involvement of the beneficiary is implicit". More research is definitely needed in this area.

that unfortunately there are gaps. More targeted data collection, informed by the present analysis of Fwe applicative constructions, would be needed to resolve these gaps and come to a better understanding of the precise workings of the applicative in Fwe.

2 Morphosyntactic features of Fwe

In this section, we discuss morphosyntactic aspects of Fwe which are immediately relevant for the discussion of applicative constructions throughout this paper. As is common in Bantu and many Niger-Congo languages, Fwe nominal morphology is characterized by the presence of a noun class system. Fwe has retained most of the noun classes reconstructed for Proto-Bantu (Meeussen 1967). Noun class membership is indicated by a noun class prefix on the head noun and agreement with the head noun is marked on adjectives, possessives, connectives, demonstratives, and verbs. The different agreement prefixes triggered on possessives by a CL3 and a CL14 noun can be seen by comparing (10) and (11).

(10) mùnzí ꜜwétù
 mu-nzí u-etú
 CL3-village AP3-1PL.POSS
 'our village'[6] (Gunnink 2022: 194)

(11) βùhárò βwétù
 βu-háro βu-etú
 CL14-life AP14-1PL.POSS
 'our life'

Classes 16, 17 and 18 are locative noun classes, each with their own semantics (see §5.1 for examples). Class 16 can be used for general locations, or for a location on top of something. Class 17 can be used for general location or direction. Class 18 can be used for a contained location, e.g. inside of something. Although

---

[6] Transcription of the Fwe data in this paper follows IPA conventions, with the following exceptions: <y> stands for [j], and <m> or <n> before an obstruent represents prenasalization. Fwe is a tone language, distinguishing high-toned and toneless moras on an underlying level. Through a number of tonal processes, these are realized as high (á), low (à), downstepped high (ꜜá), and falling (â). In each example, the first line gives the surface realization of tones, and the second line gives the underlying tonal representation.

traditionally called "locative classes", classes 16–18 also have non-locative functions in Fwe. They can express time (rather than a location in space), partitive meanings, politeness, and can be used to mark Beneficiaries or Agents (see Gunnink 2022: 143–149). Locative noun classes differ morphosyntactically from non-locative noun classes in two ways. First, locative noun class prefixes can be added to any noun already displaying an inherent noun class prefix to derive a locative meaning. In this case, the locative noun class prefix precedes the noun's primary noun class prefix. Second, dependents of a locative noun created in this way agree with the inherent noun class of the head noun and not with the locative noun class. This can be seen by comparing (10) and (12). In (10), *mu-nzi* 'village' appears with its inherent CL3 prefix *mu-*, while in (12), *mu-* is preceded by CL17 *ku-* and still triggers CL3 agreement on the following possessive.

(12) kùmùnzí ↓wétù
    ku-mu-nzí   u-etú
    CL17-CL3-village AP3-1PL.POSS
    'to our village'

Noun class prefixes and their corresponding noun phrase and verbal agreement prefixes are in Table 1, where the symbol "–" means absence of a form.

Table 1: Nominal and verbal agreement prefixes in Fwe.

Class	noun class prefix	NP agreement	Subject index	Object index[7]
1	mu-	u-/ʒu-	a-	mu-
1a	ø-	u-/ʒu-	a-	mu-
2	βa-	βa-	βa-	βá-
3	mu-	u-	u-	ú-
4	mi-	i-	i-	í-
5	ø-/ri-	ri-	ri-	rí-
6	ma-	a-	a-	á-
7	tʃi-	tʃi-	tʃi-	tʃí-
8	zi-	zi-	zi-	zí-
9	N-	i-	i-	í-
10	N-	zi-	zi-	zí-
11	ru-	ru-	ru-	rú-
12	ka-	ka-	ka-	ká-

---

7 All subject markers are toneless, whereas object markers (with the exception of first and second person singular speech act participants and classes containing human referents such as 1/1a) are high-toned. In certain tense/aspect constructions, however, the high tones of object markers are not realized. This is, among others, the case for the present tense construction.

Table 1 (continued)

Class	noun class prefix	NP agreement	Subject index	Object index
13	tu	tu-	tu-	tú-
14	βu-	βu-	βu-	βú-
15	ku-	ku-	ku-	kú-
16	ha-	ha-	ha-	—
17	ku- / kwa-[8]	ku-	ku-	—
18	mu- /mwa-	mu-	mu-	—

Fwe is a head-marking language with rich verbal morphology: grammatical relations, valence, tense, aspect, mood, deixis, polarity, and relativization can all be marked through verbal affixes, as can be seen in (13).

(13) níndàícènèsà
ní-ndi-a-í-cen-es-a
REM-1SG.SUBJ-PST-9.OBJ-become_clean-CAUS-FV
'I have cleaned it.'

Following Meeussen (1967) and Nurse (2008), the morphological slots of an inflected verb form in Fwe are in Figure 1, where TAMP stands for Tense, Aspect, Mood and Polarity.

−4	−3	−2	−1	0	+1	+2	+3
TAMP	SUBJ	TAMP	OBJ	root	derivation	final vowel	locative

Figure 1: Fwe verb template.

Fwe has only one applicative morpheme, the derivational suffix -ir (<*-ɪd), which is one of the eleven verbal derivational suffixes of Fwe. Some of these are highly productive while others are unproductive and/or lexicalized. The applicative suffix is subject to both vowel and nasal harmony. It is realized as -er when the verb stem contains a mid-vowel /e/ or /o/, see (14). When it is directly preceded by a nasal consonant, it is realized as -in or -en (depending on whether nasal harmony co-occurs with vowel harmony), see (15). Like all derivational suffixes

---

8 A slash in the noun class prefixes of CL17 and CL18 separates two allomorphs. The forms kwa- and mwa- occur only when the noun is a proper name, while ku- and mu- everywhere else.

in Fwe, the applicative suffix is toneless, surfacing with a low tone unless a high tone is assigned by tone rules or as the result of the verbal inflection.

(14) kù-fùnd-ìr-à   'to carve-APPL'
     kù-bóz-èr-à   'to bark-APPL'
     kù-ʒá:k-ìr-à   'to build-APPL'
     kù-tènd-èr-à   'to do-APPL'
     kù-hík-ìr-à   'to cook-APPL'

(15) kù-rím-ìn-à   'to farm-APPL'
     kù-ká:n-ìn-à   'to refuse-APPL'
     kù-tém-èn-à   'to chop-APPL'

Syntactically, Fwe shows a nominative-accusative alignment. Subjects are obligatorily indexed on the verb as shown in (16) and (17). Subjects typically occur preverbally.

(16) àrírà mbómùcècè
     a-rir-á   mbó-mu-cece
     3SG.SUBJ-cry-FV   ADV-CL1-baby
     'She cries like a baby.' (Gunnink 2022: 222)

(17) òmbwá àbòzá βàβàrà
     o-Ø-mbwá   a-boz-á   βa-βara
     AUG-CL1a-dog   1.SUBJ-bark-FV CL2-visitor
     'The dog barks at visitors.'

Objects in Fwe usually appear immediately after the verb, as in (18).

(18) ndìʃáká ⁺énswì
     ndi-ʃak-á   e-N-swí
     1SG.SUBJ-want-FV   AUG-CL10-fish
     'I want fish.'

An object can be indexed on the verb only if (i) the object noun phrase to which it refers appears preverbally as in (19); or (ii) the object noun phrase appears postverbally but is separated from the verb by a prosodic boundary as in (20), where this is marked by the occurrence of high tone retraction (see Gunnink 2022: 82–84 for details). Postverbal objects that are not separated from the verb by a prosodic boundary cannot combine with a verbal object marker, as shown by the ungrammaticality of (21).

(19) énswì ndìzìʃákà
 e-N-swí   ndi-zi-ʃak-á
 AUG-CL10-fish 1SG.SUBJ-10.OBJ-want-FV
 'The fish, I want them.'

(20) ndìzìʃákà énswì
 ndi-zi-ʃak-á   e-N-swí
 1SG.SUBJ-10.OBJ-want-FV AUG-CL10-fish
 'I want the fish.'

(21) *ndìzìʃáká ↓énswì
 ndi-zi-ʃak-á   e-N-swí
 1SG.SUBJ-10.OBJ-want-FV AUG-CL10-fish
 *(intended meaning: 'I want the fish.')

A third feature of objects is that they can be made the subjects of passive constructions as shown in (22)-(23). In (23), a passive verb is derived with the suffix -iw, and the CL9 object of (22) èndʒûò 'house' becomes the subject and triggers subject agreement.

(22) ndìùrìsá èndʒûò
 ndi-uris-á   e-N-dʒúo
 1SG.SUBJ-sell-FV AUG-CL9-house
 'I am selling the house.' (Gunnink 2022: 226)

(23) èndʒúò ìùrìsìwâ
 e-N-dʒúo   i-uris-iw-á
 AUG-CL9-house 9.SUBJ-sell-PASS-FV
 'The house is getting sold.' (Gunnink 2022: 227)

In sum, objects in Fwe have all the properties which are typically considered as diagnostic to claim objecthood in Bantu (Hyman et al. 1980; Hyman & Duranti 1982): immediate postverbal position, indexation on the verb, and access to passivization. This is also the case for multiple objects in ditransitive constructions (see Gunnink 2022: 291–292). On the other hand, nouns marked with a locative noun class prefix display only some of the object properties discussed so far. For historical reasons, locative marked nouns in Bantu languages often have a morphosyntactically fluctuating status in between objects and adjuncts (see Kuperus & Mpunga wa Ilunga 1990 and references therein; Creissels 2011; Pacchiarotti 2020: 66–73 for a general overview). In Fwe, locative-marked phrases usually occur in clause final position as do other adjuncts, see (24)-(25). Non-locative marked object phrases occur before the locative marked phrase. As Creissels (2003) observes for Tswana, the "basic" word order in Fwe is SVOX where X stands for an oblique(-like) constituent.

(24) ndìyá ↓kúmùnzì
    ndi-y-á   kú-mu-nzi
    1SG.SUBJ-go-FV   CL17-CL3-village
    'I go to the village.'

(25) βàkàʒá:rà màʃáʃà kúmùnzì
    βa-ka-ʒá:r-a   ma-ʃáʃa   kú-mu-nzi
    3PL.SUBJ-DIST-spread-FV   CL6-mat   CL17-CL3-village
    'They spread out mats at the village.'

Locative-marked nouns can be fronted like non-locative-marked nouns, compare with (19) above. In this case, cross-referencing on the verb through use of a locative enclitic is obligatory, as in (26), where the verb takes the class 17 clitic =ko.

(26) kùmùnzì, ndìyákò
    ku-mu-nzi   ndi-y-a=kó
    CL17-CL3-village   1SG.SUBJ-go-FV=LOC17
    'To the village, I go there.'

While objects in Fwe can be indexed through object prefixes on the verb, locatives cannot because there are no object indexes for the locative noun classes 16, 17 and 18 (see Table 1). Thus, non-locative marked nouns functioning as syntactic objects and locative-marked nouns differ in their ability to be indexed on the verb and to appear in immediate postverbal position whenever more than one postverbal constituent is present in the clause. However, passivization treats non-locative-marked object nouns and locative-marked nouns the same. This is shown in (27), where the locative-marked noun hàmùkítí 'at the party' functions as the subject of the passivized verb hàzànìwâ.

(27) hàmùkítí hàzànìwâ
      ha-mu-kití   ha-zan-iw-á
      CL16-CL3-party   16.SUBJ-dance-PASS-FV
      'Dancing may take place at the party (lit: The party is danced at).' (Gunnink 2022: 227)

Locative-marked nouns can also function as subjects in locative inversion constructions, where the locative-marked noun is indexed on the verb through subject indexes, in order to focus the postverbal, non-locative constituent (Gunnink 2022: 435–437).[9] Due to the difficulties in determining the syntactic status of locative marked phrases and given that both non-locative and locative marked phrases can be introduced by the applicative in Fwe (see §3 and §4), in the remainder of this paper we use the term APPLIED PHRASE instead of applied or applicative object, to refer to the morphosyntactic entity introduced or semantically or pragmatically manipulated by the applicative without any specification of its syntactic category or argumenthood status. We use the term LOCATIVE PHRASE as a general cover term for a phrase that has locative or temporal semantics and carries a locative noun class prefix of CL16, 17, or 18 without specifying the syntactic category to which the phrase belongs.

3 Semantic functions and lexicalized applicatives

In this section, we briefly discuss Type B, D, and E applicative constructions in Fwe. In Type B applicative constructions, the applicative morpheme introduces an obligatorily present applied phrase expressing a semantic role which *could* have been syntactically expressed as an optional oblique in a main clause construction featuring an underived verb root. Type B corresponds to what has been called in the more general literature "optional applicative constructions" (Pacchiarotti 2020: 91). Semantic roles which can be optionally introduced by applicative morphology with certain Fwe verb roots include Beneficiary, Maleficiary, Recipient,

---

[9] As suggested by an anonymous reviewer, a possible diagnostic for distinguishing the syntactic status of non-locative marked object nouns and locative-marked nouns could be their linear order with respect to an applicativized verb stem. In the case of underived verb roots, locative constituents must follow any object NP, see (16). With applicativized stems, if the applied phrase is *not* a locative marked constituent, the order of the applied phrase and the base object NP (if any) is free (see Gunnink 2022: 244). Unfortunately, we currently lack the necessary data to establish the linear order of a locative marked applied phrase with a transitive applicativized verb stem.

and Reason but not Instrument (see Trithart 1983 and Pacchiarotti 2020: 139 for a list of Bantu languages where this semantic role can be introduced by applicative morphology). Alternatively, on a root-by-root basis, these semantic roles can also be introduced as NPs marked by the locative class 17 prefix *ku-* (see Mabugu 2001: 117 and ff. for a similar alternation in Shona S11–15). An example of the alternation between the applicative and the CL17 locative prefix *ku-* to introduce a Beneficiary with the root *βerek* 'work' is in (28) and (29).[10]

(28) ndìβérékèrè   BEN: APPL
    ndi-βerék-er-e
    1SG.OBJ-work-APPL-SBJV
    'Work <u>for me</u>.' (just for today) (Gunnink 2022: 243)

(29) òβèrèké ↓*kwángù*   BEN: *ku-*
    o-βerek-é   ku-angú
    2SG.SUBJ-work-SBJV AP17-1SG.POSS
    'Work <u>for me</u>.' (permanent job)

In Type B the function of applicative derivation is not purely syntactic. Since there is an alternative way to express the given semantic role, with a given root, in a given construction, there is often a semantic or discourse related difference between the construction with the underived root and the construction with the applicative. As can be seen by comparing (28) and (29), the applicative construction implies that the job is temporary while the construction with *ku-* implies the job is permanent (see Mabugu 2001: 117 for similar semantic differences in Shona S11–15). Alternatively, in some Bantu languages, Type B constructions are used when the participant expressed by the applied phrase is a discourse topic (Trithart 1983: 181, Rapold 1997 for Lingala C30B, Kisseberth and Abasheikh 1977 for Mwiini G412). No such uses are attested for the applicative in Fwe. A limited number of verb roots in Fwe can also participate in Type D applicative constructions. In this type, the applicative morpheme does not introduce an applied phrase. Instead, applicative morphology indicates that the action described by the root is performed to completion, or that the action is performed continuously, with intensity, persistence, excess, or repetition, among other qualities. In some Bantu languages this function is achieved by using one applicative suffix, while in others two or three

---

[10] (28) and (29) also differ in that (29) is a subjunctive verb form featuring a subject index, while (28) is an imperative form which never carries a subject index. The subjunctive is used for polite orders, while the imperative for more direct orders.

applicative suffixes are required, depending on the phonotactics of the verb root. In Fwe, this function is always conveyed by two consecutive applicative suffixes, see (31).[11] The core meaning is intensity, but two applicative suffixes may also express completeness, long duration, high frequency or habitual, and repetition (see Gunnink 2022: 277–280). This construction type is shown in (31), where the syntactically transitive root *ur* 'buy' in (30) combines with two applicative suffixes to mean 'buy it all'. Note that this root takes two syntactic arguments both in (30) ('I' and 'salt') and (31) ('someone' and 'salt').

(30) *ndàùrí zwâyì*
 ndi-a-ur-í Ø-zwáyi
 1SG.SUBJ-PST-buy-NPST.PFV CL5-SALT
 'I bought salt [earlier today].' (Gunnink 2022: 325)

(31) *kùááʒ' ézwâyì kwìná àbó bànàkéːʒì kùríùìrìrà ryònʃêː*
 ku-aaʒá e-Ø-zwáyi ku-iná a-bó
 17.SUBJ-be.not AUG-CL5-salt 17.SUBJ-be.at AUG-DEM2
 ba-na-kéːʒ-i ku-rí-ur-ir-ir-a ry-onʃéː
 S3:2-PST-come-NPST.PFV INF-5.OBJ-buy-APPL-APPL-FV AP5-all
 'There is no salt, someone has come and <u>bought it all</u>.' (Gunnink 2022: 277)

Finally, some applicativized stems in Fwe can undergo lexicalization and lose their ability to introduce an applied phrase. These have been called Type E pseudoapplicative constructions (see Pacchiarotti 2020: 102 and ff.). For instance, the root *ŋor* 'write' in (32) can optionally combine with a locative phrase specifying the writing surface. When the root combines with the applicative in (33) there is no additional constituent compared to (32) and the verb stem acquires the non-compositional meaning 'copying down'.

(32) *ndìkwèsì ndìŋòrá (↓hépèpà)*
 ndi-kwesi ndi-ŋor-á (há-e-Ø-pepa)
 1SG.SUBJ-PROG 1SG.SUBJ-write-FV CL16-AUG-CL5-paper
 'I'm writing (on a piece of paper).'

---

11 Unlike in other Bantu languages (see e.g. Creissels 2004 for Tswana), in Fwe the applicative *-ir* cannot be used twice in a main clause on the same verb to introduce two distinct applied phrases.

(33) ndìkwèsì ndìŋòrèrá ↓hépèpà
      ndi-kwesi   ndi-ŋor-er-á   há-e-Ø-pepa
      1SG.SUBJ-PROG   1SG.SUBJ-write-APPL-FV   CL16-AUG-CL5-paper
      'I'm copying (it) down on a piece of paper.'

Similarly, the root *hár* 'live' in (34) means 'make one's living' when combined with the applicative in a construction such as (35).

(34) èndʒúò òmò ndí↓hárà
      e-N-dʒúo   omo   ndí-har-á
      AUG-CL9-house   DEM18   1SG.SUBJ-live-FV
      'the house where I live'

(35) èndʒúò òmò ndíhàrírà
      e-N-dʒúo   omo   ndí-har-ir-á
      AUG-CL9-house   DEM18   1SG.SUBJ-live-APPL-FV
      'the house that I depend on/where I survive'

In the Appendix we provide a list of seemingly lexicalized applicative stems which do not have a corresponding synchronic root without the applicative.

4 Syntactic functions

Several Fwe verb roots must participate in Type A applicative constructions to combine with applied phrases with certain semantic roles. In Type A, the applicative introduces an obligatorily present applied phrase which could not otherwise be expressed with that root. This means that the root itself does not "subcategorize" for a particular semantic role and the sole morphological device to express such a semantic role is applicative morphology. Within any given language, the semantic roles for which an applicative is required are a lexicalized property of individual verb roots, where by "lexicalized" in this context we mean the properties of a linguistic unit which are memorized or cognitively stored in long-term memory, such as form, meaning, argument structure, and restrictions on morphological, syntactic, and pragmatic use (Pacchiarotti 2020: 81). Type A constructions, by and large equivalent to what have been called "obligatory applicative constructions" in the literature, have a purely syntactic function: applicative derivation is the only structural means with a given verb root to express a given semantic participant. The semantic roles which can be mapped onto the applied phrase depend heavily on the lexical meaning of the verb root, the meaning of other constituents present in the clause, and on the communicative intention of the speaker (Stapleton 1903, Voeltz 1977, Schaefer 1985, Bresnan and Moshi 1990, Rugemalira 1993, Rapold 1997, Mabugu 2001, Creissels 2004 just to mention a few). In Fwe, verb roots participate in this construction type to express distinct types of Location related semantic roles. Although seldom reported and/or illustrated in grammars, it seems that in many Bantu languages, the applicative is required for certain verb roots to combine with a locative phrase expressing a variety of Location-related semantic roles in a main clause (see Trithart 1983: 150, Rugemalira 1993: 71, 2004: 287, Jerro 2016, Pacchiarotti 2020: 124–134). For instance, the Fwe root *rí* 'eat' requires the applicative in order to combine with a locative phrase expressing the Location where the event of eating takes place, e.g. 'in the house' in (36). If the root *rí* 'eat' combines with General Location in its underived form the clause is ungrammatical, see (37). Other verb roots which behave like *rí* 'eat' are *hík* 'cook', *dam* 'beat', and *ŋor* 'write'.

(36) βànákùrírràngà mwíndʒûò
βa-náku-rí-ir-ang-a   mú-e-N-dʒúo
3PL.SUBJ-HAB-eat-APPL-HAB-FV   CL18-AUG-CL9-house
'They eat in the house.'

(37) *βànákùryángà mwíndʒûò
βa-náku-rí-ang-a   mú-e-N-dʒúo
3PL.SUBJ-HAB-eat-HAB-FV   CL18-AUG-CL9-house
(*intended meaning: 'They eat in the house.')

Verb roots such as *rá:r* 'sleep' in (38), *zyá:k* 'build', and *bar* 'read', on the other hand, can combine with a locative phrase expressing Location without the need of an applicative derivation.

(38) βànákùrá:ràngà mwíndʒûò
βa-náku-rá:r-ang-a   mú-e-N-dʒúo
3PL.SUBJ-HAB-sleep-HAB-FV   CL18-AUG-CL9-house
'They sleep in the house.'

In some cases, the verb root requiring applicative derivation to express a certain Location-related semantic role may combine with a locative phrase without the need of the applicative, but in that case the semantic role of the locative phrase is not that of (General) Location. For instance, if a locative phrase occurs after the underived verb root *ŋor* 'write' in (39), it receives a patient-like interpretation, i.e.

the writing is on the surface of the table itself. It is only when ŋor 'write' combines with the applicative in (40) that the following locative phrase can be interpreted as the Location at which the event of writing takes place.

(39) ndìkwèsì ndìŋòrá ↓héntàfùrè
ndi-kwesi   ndi-ŋor-á   há-e-N-tafure
1SG.SUBJ-PROG 1SG.SUBJ-write-FV   CL16-AUG-CL9-table
'I'm writing on the table (the writing is on the surface of the table itself).'

(40) ndìkwèsì ndìŋòrèrá ↓héntàfùrè
ndi-kwesi   ndi-ŋor-er-á   há-e-N-tafure
1SG.SUBJ-PROG 1SG.SUBJ-write-APPL-FV CL16-AUG-CL9-table
'I'm writing at the table (the writing is on a piece of paper that lies on the table).'

Certain verb roots might require applicative derivation to combine with a locative phrase expressing a general Location, but not to combine with a locative phrase expressing a much more contained Location. For instance, the underived root hík 'cook' can freely combine with an optional locative phrase indicating the vessel of cooking, e.g. a pot in (41). However, in order to combine with a locative phrase indicating the general location where the cooking takes place (e.g. the kitchen, the yard, etc.), the root hík 'cook' requires an applicative derivation, as in (42).

(41) mùnú ↓mómò ndí↓híkà
munú   mó-mo   ndí-hik-á
DEM18 COP-DEM18   1SG.SUBJ-cook-FV
'In here is where I cook (referring to a pot).'

(42) mùnú ↓mómò ndí↓híkà
munú   mó-mo   ndí-hik-ir-á
DEM18 COP-DEM18   1SG.SUBJ-cook-APPL-FV
'In here is where I cook (referring to a kitchen).'

This situation is common in several other Eastern Bantu languages and is known as "participant locative" vs. "event locative" (Rugemalira 1993: 81; Creissels 2004: 13; Rugemalira 2004: 288). Depending on the language and on the verb root, the opposite might happen. For instance, in the southern Bantu language Tswana, a root like 'cook' can optionally combine with a locative phrase expressing the General Location where the cooking takes place – for example, 'in the yard' in

(43)– without the need of any applicative derivation. However, to express a vessel as the location of cooking in (44), the root 'cook' requires the applicative.[12]

    Tswana (S31; Creissels 2004: 13)
(43) *Lorato o tlaa apaya motogo (ko jarateng)*
    lòrátɔ́   ʊ́-tɬáá-àpàj-à   mʊ̀-tɔ̀χɔ́   (kó   dʒáràté-ŋ̀)
    CL1.L. 1.SUBJ-FUT-cook-FV CL3-porridge LOC CL9.yard-LOC
    'Lorato will cook the porridge (in the yard).'

    Tswana (S31; Creissels 2004: 13)
(44) *Lorato o tlaa apeela motogo mo pitseng e tona*
    lòrátɔ́   ʊ́-tɬáá-àpè-èl-à   mʊ̀-tɔ̀χɔ́   mó   pìtsé-ŋ̀
    CL1.L. 1.SUBJ-FUT-cook-APPL-FV CL3-porridge LOC CL9.pot-LOC
    é   tónà
    CL9.LNK CL9.big
    'Lorato will cook porridge in the big pot.'

Some (translational) motion verbs combine with a locative phrase without requiring the applicative derivation, but in this case, the locative phrase can only be interpreted as the source. This is the case for, for instance, the verb roots *βútuk* 'run' and *w* 'fall', as illustrated below. With these verb roots, the applicative is required to introduce an applied phrase with the semantic role of Goal or Endpoint. This is the most widely described "locative" function of the applicative in Bantu (Trithart 1983: 160). This is illustrated in (45) and (46) with the root *βútuk* 'run', and in (47) and (48) with the root *w* 'fall'.[13]

(45) *ndàβútùkì(kò)*
    ndi-a-βútuk-i=ko
    1SG.SUBJ-PST-run-NPST.PFV=LOC17
    'I ran away (from there).'

---

12 One might think that participants such as 'in the (big) pot' are semantically more like Instruments than Specific Locations. However, in Tswana, just like in Fwe, reflexes of *-ɪd can never be used to introduce Instrumental applied phrases.
13 Some authors analyze the contrast between O and by claiming that in the applicative "changes" the semantic role of Source to that of Goal. For arguments against this analysis see Pacchiarotti (2020: 130–131).

(46) ndàβútùkìrìkò
 ndi-a-βútuk-ir-i=ko
 1SG.SUBJ-PST-run-APPL-NPST.PFV=LOC17
 'I ran to there.'

(47) náwì (héndʒìngà)
 ná-w-i   há-e-N-dʒinga
 1.SUBJ.PST-fall-NPST.PFV   CL16-AUG-CL9-bicycle
 'She fell (from the bicycle).'

(48) tʃàkàwírì hétʃìpâù
 tʃi-a-ka-w-ír-i   há-e-tʃi-páu
 7.SUBJ-PST-DIST-fall-APPL-NPST.PFV   CL16-AUG-CL7-animal
 'It fell on an animal.' (Gunnink 2022: 478)

Similar to non-motion verb roots, see (38), some motion verb roots such as *end* 'go' in (49) can freely combine with a locative marked phrase expressing location without the need of applicative derivation.

(49) àʃàkàhàrá ìyé àyéndè kútʃìkórò
 a-ʃak-ahar-á   iyé   a-énd-e   kú-tʃi-koró
 1.SUBJ-want-NEUT-FV   that   1.SUBJ-go-SBJV   CL17-CL7-school
 'He needs to go to school.'

Another semantic role which can be introduced only by means of the applicative in Fwe is the Substitutive. This can be considered as a semantic extension of the obligatoriness of the applicative to introduce Locations, based on the spatial metaphor doing something in someone's *place*. In (50), the Substitutive *for him* cannot be optionally introduced by the locative CL17 prefix *ku-* as it happens with other semantic roles (see §3). (50) was produced in a conversational context where someone wants to take the belongings of a third person who is absent. The speaker refuses on behalf of this absent person.

(50) ndàmùká:nìnì
 ndi-a-mu-ká:n-in-i
 1SG.SUBJ-PST-1.OBJ-refuse-APPL-NPST.PFV
 'I've refused on his behalf.' (Gunnink 2022: 246)

5 Discourse-related functions

The following subsections discuss usages of the applicative in Fwe related to locative phrases and their pragmatic modification in discourse (for other studies targeting specifically the interaction between locative phrases and applicative derivation see Rugemalira 1993, 2004, Simango 2012, and Jerro 2016, among others). These usages are resumed in Pacchiarotti (2020: 96) under Type C applicative constructions. In these constructions, the applicative morpheme introduces an obligatorily present applied phrase which could be optionally expressed in the construction with just the root. This expansion in argument structure does not necessarily result in an increase in the syntactic valence of the root combining with the applicative. The obligatorily present applied phrase in Type C usually has a Location-related semantic role, very often General Location, indicating where the event described by the verb root takes place. In this construction type, the applied phrase usually does not appear before other constituents such as (object) NPs. Except for becoming obligatory, there seems to be no morphosyntactic change in terms of "promotion to objecthood" between the locative phrase in the construction of the root and the Location applied phrase in the construction of the applicative. Besides introducing an obligatorily present applied phrase, the applicative suffix in Type C performs semantic or pragmatic functions on the applied phrase alone or on the whole clausal construction. However, these semantic or pragmatic functions are different from those observed for Type B (see §3). The three functions that Type C applicative structures can have throughout the Bantu domain are: (i) the applicative places the locative applied phrase under some kind of narrow focus (see §5.1); (ii) the applicative widens the semantic scope of the locative applied phrase (§5.2); and (iii) the applicative indicates that the action described by the root occurs habitually at a certain location. The data on the Fwe applicative provide hitherto undescribed variations on these attested functions.

5.1 Narrow focus on Locations

The applicative in Fwe can interact with other focus marking strategies to place the locative applied phrase under narrow focus. To account for the focus marking patterns of locative phrases discussed in this section, we refer to the system of focus types of Dik et al. (1981). In this system, (narrow) completive focus refers to focus information which fills in a gap in the pragmatic knowledge of the hearer (Dik et al. 1981: 60). The clearest cases of "completive" focus are *wh-* questions. This type of focus is also known, among others, as assertive (Watters 1979) or (new) information focus (Kiss 1998; van der Wal 2016). In (narrow) "replacing" focus, on the other hand, "a specific item in the pragmatic information of the addressee is removed and replaced by another, correct item" (Dik et al. 1981: 63).

Focus marking in Bantu is known to make use of a number of strategies. For instance, many Bantu languages have a specific syntactic position for focused constituents, most commonly immediately after the verb (Gibson et al. 2017). In Fwe, however, the immediately after verb position does not correlate with the expression of focus. This can be shown using the diagnostic test of question and answer pairs, which are expected to mark focus on the question word and the element in the answer which fills in the gap of knowledge expressed by the question word. As can be seen by comparing (51) with the ungrammaticality of (52), the question word zìndʒí 'what' has to be fronted by means of a cleft construction and cannot be used immediately after the verb. The same is true for the answer containing the focused noun màβùká 'books', cf. (53) and (54).

(51) zìndʒí ꜜáùrìsâ
Ø-zi-ndʒí á-uris-á
COP-CL8-what 1.SUBJ.REL-sell-FV
'What does he sell?'

(52) *àùrìsá zìndʒî
a-uris-á Ø-zi-ndʒí
1.SUBJ-sell-FV COP-CL8-what
(*intended meaning: 'What does he sell?')

(53) màβùká ꜜáùrìsâ
ma-βuká á-uris-á
CL6-book 1.SUBJ.REL-sell-FV
'He sells books.'

(54) *àùrìsá màβúkà
a-uris-á ma-βuká
1.SUBJ-sell-FV CL6-book
(*intended meaning: 'He sells books.')

Another common focus-marking strategy in Bantu is verbal morphology known as the conjoint/disjoint alternation. The use of the disjoint verb form usually correlates with verbal focus, while the conjoint verb form is used when the focus is on the postverbal constituent (van der Wal 2017). Fwe does not make use of a conjoint/disjoint distinction in any of its verbal inflections, though it may have had a functional disjoint form in the past which has now been reanalyzed as a tense marker (Gunnink 2022: 310).

In Fwe, locative phrases can be placed under different types of narrow focus by: (i) a cleft construction; (ii) applicative morphology; (iii) a combination of a cleft construction and applicative morphology[14]. While cleft constructions are a well-recognized focus strategy in Bantu languages, likely reconstructable to Proto-Bantu (van der Wal 2018), applicative morphology is seldom acknowledged as a focus-marking strategy (but see, e.g., Trithart 1983, Creissels 2004). Unlike other focus-marking strategies in Bantu, the focalizing function of the applicative appears to be restricted to locative phrases and likely goes back to Proto-Bantu, just like cleft constructions (Pacchiarotti 2020: 279, forthcoming). We discuss each of these possibilities in turn.

Clefts are the most productive strategy for the expression of focus in Fwe. Cleft constructions in Fwe are bi-clausal, consisting of a predicated nominal element, that is, the matrix clause (Lambrecht 2001) and a relative clause which modifies the matrix clause, as can be seen in (55).

(55) [màβísí ꜜóndʒòvù]_MATRIX [ndí ꜜyáβúʃàkà]_RELATIVE
N-ma-βisí   a-o-ø-ndʒovu   ndí-yaβú-ʃak-a
COP-CL6-milk   AP6-CON-CL1a-elephant   1SG.SUBJ.REL-LOC.PL-search-FV
'It is elephant's milk that I am looking for.'

The utterance in (55) is taken from a narrative and is an answer to the elephant's question: 'What are you looking for?'. As such, it provides completive focus on the syntactic object 'elephant's milk'. Any constituent can be clefted in Fwe regardless of its syntactic status as core argument or adjunct. Besides expressing completive focus as in (55), cleft constructions can also be used to express replacing focus (i.e. information which contradicts the hearer's beliefs) as in (56) (see Gunnink 2022: 455–459 for additional examples). (56) is an instance of direct speech taken from a narrative in which a girl becomes angry at a rabbit who is weeding in her field, pulling out crops instead of weeds. The girl corrects the rabbit by explaining that it is not maize that people usually weed, but grass.

(56) [ndìsózú]_MATRIX [ꜜbárìmângà]_RELATIVE
ndi-Ø-sozú   bá-rim-áng-a
COP-CL5-grass 2.SUBJ.REL-weed-HAB-FV
'It is grass that people usually weed.' (Gunnink 2022: 456)

---

[14] Peterson (2007: 108) reports that in Wolof (Atlantic) a topicalizatin construction sometimes described as a cleft construction may co-occur with applicative constructions.

Formally, the matrix clause of a cleft construction consists of a pronoun or a lexical noun marked by a copulative prefix, glossed as COP in (55)-(56)[15]. The relative clause of a cleft construction looks just like relative clauses elsewhere in the grammar. Unlike in main clauses, in relative clauses the verb is always the first linear constituent. Relative clause verbs differ from main clause verbs in terms of tonal behavior. In most TAM constructions, the relative clause verb form has a high tone on the subject marker which the corresponding main clause form lacks, as seen by comparing the low-toned subject index *βà-* in (57) with the same high-toned subject index in (58).

(57) *βàndʒòvù βàdʒwênga*
      βa-ndʒovu   βa-dʒwéng-a
      CL2-elephant 2.SUBJ-shout-FV
      'The elephants are shouting.'

(58) *βàndʒòvù βádʒwêngà*
      βa-ndʒovu   βá-dʒwéng-a
      CL2-elephant 2.SUBJ.REL-shout-FV
      'The elephants who are shouting'

Cleft constructions can be used to place locative constituents (as well as non-locative constituents, see (56)) under narrow focus without combining with applicative morphology. This usage is shown in (59), where the predicated nominal element *hàndʒé* 'outside' is followed by a modifying relative clause whose main verb *βákèrè* 'he is' does not carry an applicative suffix.

(59) [*hàndʒé*]_{MATRIX} [*βákèrè*]_{RELATIVE} *βàkwèsì βàfwéβà mùtômbwè*
      Ø-ha-N-dʒé   βá-kere   βa-kwesi   βa-fwéβ-a
      COP-CL16-CL9-out   2.SUBJ.REL-sit.STAT 2.SUBJ-PROG   2.SUBJ-smoke-FV
      mu-tómbwe
      CL3-tobacco
      'HE IS OUTSIDE, he is smoking a cigarette.'[16]

---

15 The basic form of the copulative prefix in Fwe is a homorganic nasal, but the prefix has a number of allomorphs based on the noun class of the noun to which it is affixed. When affixed to a noun whose noun class prefix starts in a nasal consonant as in (55), the homorganic nasal prefix is not realized so that there is homophony between nouns with and without a copulative prefix.
16 In (50), the plural CL2 prefix *ba-* functions as an honorific noun class prefix. This prefix is required when the speaker wants to refer to anyone older than themselves, as well as to anyone

The utterance in (59) was given as an answer to the question: 'Where is he?', and as such is an instance of completive focus. While clefts can be used to place non-locative phrases under other types of narrow focus such as replacing (see (56)), this is not possible for locative phrases. Replacing focus on a locative phrase cannot be expressed by a cleft construction alone, as shown by the ungrammaticality of (60) which is an infelicitous answer to a question such as 'Is she getting dressed in the garden?'

(60) *mùndʒúò ázwàtà
 [N-mu-n-dʒúo]ᴍᴀᴛʀɪx [á-zwat-á]ʀᴇʟᴀᴛɪᴠᴇ
 cop-CL18-CL9-house 1.SUBJ.REL-dress-FV
 *('intended meaning: it is IN THE HOUSE she is getting dressed (and not somewhere else))'

The use of applicative morphology to express focus in Fwe is restricted to locative phrases. Only verb roots which do not require applicative derivation to optionally combine with a locative phrase expressing Location (see also Creissels 2004 for Tswana) can combine with the applicative to convey focus on the locative phrase. This is illustrated below with the root ʒá:k 'build': (61) shows that this root does not require the applicative in order to combine with a locative phrase, whereas in (62), the applicative derivation makes the locative phrase obligatory and the target of new information focus. Only (62) would be a pragmatically felicitous answer to the question 'Where do they build?'[17]

(61) βàʒá:kà (kùmbárì yórwîʒì)
 βa-ʒá:k-a   ku-N-βári   í-o-ru-íʒi
 2.SUBJ-build-FV CL17-CL9-near AP9-CON-CL11-river
 'They build (close to the river).'

(62) βàʒà:kìrá (kùmbárì yórwîʒì)
 βa-ʒa:k-ir-á   ku-N-βári   í-o-ru-íʒi
 2.SUBJ-build- APPL-FV CL17-CL9-near AP9-CON-CL11-river
 'They build CLOSE TO THE RIVER.' (answer to: 'Where do they build?')

---

who generally commands respect, such as an authority (see Gunnink 2022: 133–134). It is also used with personal names, see (58).

17 We expect sentences such as (61) and (66) further down to be appropriate answers to *What are they/is she doing?* or *What's happening (over there)?*. However, this assumption needs to be confirmed with native speakers.

Applicative morphology can also be used to place the locative phrase under replacing focus. In (63) the locative demonstrative of CL17 *ókù* 'here' is under replacing focus. Recall from (38) that the root *ra:r* 'sleep' does not require applicative derivation to combine with a locative phrase expressing General Location.

(63) *βú:kè òrà:rìré ókù*
 βú:k-e   o-ra:r-ir-é   okú
 wake-SBJV   2SG.SUBJ-sleep-APPL-SBJV   DEM17
 'Get up and sleep OVER HERE/ON THIS SIDE (said to someone who is sleeping on the other side).'

Cleft constructions and applicative morphology in Fwe can combine to express different types of narrow focus. This is illustrated with the root *βerek* 'work' in (65), which does not need an applicative to combine with a General Location locative phrase, see (64): note that in this example, the focus is on the verb, as indicated by the use of the fronted infinitive (see Gunnink 2019 for more details on this construction). In (65), the locative phrase *kwàsìòmà* is clefted and the root *βerek* 'work' in the following relative clause carries the applicative suffix *-er*. The locative phrase is the target of completive focus: (65) would be a felicitous answer to the question: 'Mr. Bonard, where does he work?'

(64) *àβàntù kùβèrèkà βákàβèrèkà mwààngòrà*
 a-βa-ntu   ku-βerek-a   βá-ka-βerek-á   mwa-angora
 AUG-CL2-people   INF-work-FV   2.SUBJ.REL-DIST-work-FV   CL18-Angola
 'The people are working in Angola.' (Gunnink 2022: 363)

(65) *βàbónádì [kwàsìòmà]*_{MATRIX} *[βáβèrèkérà]*_{RELATIVE}
 βa-bonádi   Ø-kwa-sioma   βá-βerek-er-á
 CL2-Bonard   COP-CL17-Sioma   COP-CL17-Sioma
 'Mr. Bonard, it is IN SIOMA that he works.' (Gunnink 2022: 249)

Applicative morphology and the cleft construction can also be combined to convey narrow replacing focus. This is shown with the root *zwát* 'get dressed' in (67). (66) shows that this root can freely combine with a Location in its underived form.

(66) *àkwèsì àzwátà múndʒûò*
 a-kwesi   a-zwát-a   mú-N-dʒúo
 1.SUBJ-PROG   1.SUBJ-dress-FV   CL18-CL9-house
 'She is getting dressed in the house.'

(67) ààʒá òkùzwátìrà mútʃìʃàmbìrò, mùndʒúò ázwàtîrà
     a-aʒá   o-ku-zwát-ir-a   mú-tʃi-ʃambiro
     1.SUBJ-be.not   AUG-INF-dress-APPL-FV CL18-CL7-bathroom
     [N-mu-n-dʒúo]_{MATRIX} [á-zwat-ir-á]_{RELATIVE}
     COP-CL18-CL9-house 1.SUBJ.REL-dress-APPL-FV
     'She is not getting dressed IN THE BATHROOM, IT IS IN THE HOUSE that she is getting dressed.'

The multi-clausal construction in (67) is an answer to 'Is she getting dressed in the bathroom?'. The first part of the construction is a main clause, and the applicative appears on the lexical verb of the progressive construction ààʒá òkùzwátìrà to signal that the following locative phrase is under replacing focus. The main clause is followed by a cleft construction consisting of a matrix and a relative clause. The relative verb form in the cleft construction must appear in combination with the applicative in order to express replacing focus – that is, a cleft by itself cannot be used to express this type of narrow focus, see the ungrammaticality of (60).

Table 2 summarizes the different strategies to place locative phrases under narrow focus in Fwe. Recall that *only* roots which do not require applicative morphology to combine with locative phrase in their underived form within a main clause can participate in the focus constructions in Table 2. "–" means that the speaker is not placing any constituent of the clause under narrow focus.

Table 2: Strategies for placing locative phrases under narrow focus (only for verb roots which subcategorize for Location).

	UNDERIVED ROOT	ROOT+APPL
MAIN CLAUSE	—	completive and replacing focus
CLEFT CONSTRUCTION	completive focus	completive and replacing focus

As can be seen from Table 2, there are several different combinatorial possibilities to express the same type of focus. However, when asked in elicitation, speakers consider different focus constructions to be equivalent. For instance, the following elicited examples were all considered interchangeable with (62) where the applicative conveys completive focus. In (68), the locative phrase is focused by means of a cleft construction. In (69), the locative phrase is clefted and the verb in the modifying relative clause carries the applicative. All three constructions were offered in elicitation as interchangeable answers to the question: 'Where are they building?'

(68) kùmbárì yó⁀rwízì βázâ:kà
 Ø-ku-N-βári   í-o-ru-ízi   βá-zá:k-a
 COP-CL17-CL9-near AP9-CON-CL11-river 2.SUBJ.REL-build-fv
 'IT IS CLOSE TO THE RIVER that they build.'

(69) kùmbárì yó⁀rwízì βázà:kírà
 Ø-ku-N-βári   í-o-ru-ízi   βá-za:k-ir-á
 COP-CL17-CL9-near AP9-CON-CL11-river 2.SUBJ.REL-build-APPL-FV
 'IT IS CLOSE TO THE RIVER that they build.'

Analyzing the occurrence of these constructions in natural discourse contexts might reveal differences which are obscured in elicitation. Whatever the case might be, the Fwe data presented in this section are noteworthy because they show that reflexes of PB applicative *-ɪd in modern Bantu languages can interact with other focalizing devices, in this case clefts. More research is needed in order to understand this interaction.

5.2 Argument orientation

In some Bantu languages, the presence of the applicative on a syntactically transitive verb root may change the "orientation" of a locative applied phrase expressing General Location with respect to the participants involved in the utterance. The term "orientation" or "argument orientation" originates in formal semantics (Keenan and Faltz 1985) and refers to the semantic effects of some English locative modifiers in combination with different types of predicate. To give an example, if the English sentence *John saw Mary in the park* is true, then *John saw Mary* and *Mary was in the park* are also true. However, *John was in the park* does not logically or necessarily follow as a true statement from *John saw Mary in the park* – John could have been across the street in a coffee shop when he saw Mary, and the sentence would still be true (see Keenan and Faltz 1985: 158ff). This means that the orientation of the locative modifier *in the park* in the English sentence *John saw Mary in the park* is toward the direct object NP but not necessarily toward the subject NP. In some Bantu languages, applicative morphology can apparently be used to widen the orientation of a locative phrase from involving the object of a transitive verb root to also involving the subject of that transitive verb root. Consider the following data from Shona.

Shona (S11–15; Cann and Mabugu 2007: 18)
(70) Patrick   a-ka-on-a   va-sikana   mu-gomo
     CL1a.P.   1.SUBJ-PST-see-FV   CL2-girl   CL18-CL5.mountain
     'Patrick saw the girls [while they were] on the mountain.'

Shona (S11–15; Cann and Mabugu 2007: 18)
(71) Patrick   a-ka-on-er-a   va-sikana   mu-gomo
     CL1a.P.   1.SUBJ-PST-see-appl-FV   CL2-girl   CL18-CL5.mountain
     'Patrick saw the girls [while he was] on the mountain.'

According to Cann and Mabugu (2007), in (70), where the verb root 'see' is in its underived form, the location of the object NP 'girls' must be on the mountain but the location of the subject doing the seeing is vague: he may or may not have been on the mountain when he saw the girls. On the other hand, in (71), where the verb root 'see' undergoes applicative derivation, the event of Patrick seeing the girls is true if and only if he was also on the mountain while seeing the girls (see Mabugu 2001: 127 for additional examples). This usage of the applicative, called "implicit contrast" by Trithart (1983) and "event localizer" by Kimenyi (1995), is reported by Trithart (1977) and Hyman et al. (1980) for Haya, Kimenyi (1995) for Rwanda and Rugemalira (2004: 288) for Swahili.

Whereas in other Bantu languages the applicative includes the subject of the verb in the location of the event, in Fwe the applicative can specify the location of the speaker uttering the sentence, even if they are not referenced in the utterance itself. In (72), the underived verb root *zan* 'play' can freely combine with the locative phrase 'outside', and the speaker who utters the sentence is understood as being inside while those who are playing are located outside. In (73), where the root 'play' combines with the applicative, the locative applied phrase 'outside' becomes obligatory and the only possible interpretation is that the speaker uttering the sentence is also located outside.

(72) βàkwèsì βàzánà (hándʒè)
     βa-kwesi   βa-zán-a   ha-N-dʒé
     2.SUBJ-PROG   2.SUBJ-play-FV CL16-CL9-outside
     'They are playing outside (said by someone who is inside).'

(73) βàkwèsì βàzànìná (↓hándʒè)
     βa-kwesi   βa-zan-in-á   ha-N-dʒé
     2.SUBJ-PROG   2.SUBJ-play-appl-FV CL16-CL9-outside
     'They are playing outside (said by someone who is outside).'

What is special about these Fwe data is that they show that, depending on the language, the change in the orientation of the General Location applied phrase operated by the applicative can affect not only the subject of a transitive verb (which does not necessarily need to coincide with the speaker who utters the sentence, compare Shona examples above), but also the speaker who utters a sentence describing an intransitive event in which he or she is not directly involved. So far, no data parallel to (70) and (71), where the applicative is used to specify the location of the subject argument of a transitive verb root, are attested in Fwe. As suggested by an anonymous reviewer, the use of the applicative in (73) is reminiscent of evidentiality, the grammaticalized marking of information source (see Crane et al. forthcoming for the use of aspect morphology to mark evidentiality in Fwe), or even egophoricity, the grammaticalized marking of personal knowledge or involvement.

6 Conclusions

In this chapter, we showed that the applicative in Fwe can among others: (i) function as the sole morphological means to introduce a locative phrase with the semantic role of General Location or Spatial Goal; (ii) place some kind of narrow focus on a General Location applied phrase (alone or in combination with cleft constructions); (iii) widen the semantic scope of a General Location applied phrase. Although these functions are attested throughout the Bantu domain, Fwe shows novel patterns with respect to (ii) and (iii): the applicative as a focalizing strategy can be used in combination with other focalizing strategies such as clefts, and the applicative can be used to widen the semantic scope of a General Location locative phrase to include not the grammatical subject of the clause but the speaker who utters the sentence. In §4, we illustrated the considerable root-specific variation and idiosyncrasy as to whether a verb root requires the applicative to combine with a phrase expressing Spatial Goal and other types of Location-related semantic roles such as Specific Location, General Location, etc. This fact is not epiphenomenal to Fwe but is true for many other Bantu languages (see Pacchiarotti 2020: 124–133 for an overview). On a language-specific, root-specific basis, the applicative is very often the only morphological means to introduce Spatial Goals and General Locations (see also the 40 Bantu language survey in Trithart 1983: 149, 160). The diversification and accretion of complexity found in the Location-related functions of applicative morphology across Bantu languages bears on one of its original functions. Most scholars agree that *-ɪd in PB (and possibly further back in Niger-Congo) had a valence-increasing function in that it added a participant to the argument structure of a verb root. Authors differ, however, in what the original semantic role of the applied phrase might have been. Some (e.g. Trithart 1983) argue that it was a Beneficiary, others that it was more likely a Location or a Spatial Goal (e.g. Endemann 1876, Kähler-Meyer 1966, van Eeden 1956, Schadeberg 2003, Hyman 2007). It has been recently argued (Pacchiarotti 2020: 272–278; forthcoming) that the attested directions of change in the literature on grammaticalization and semantic change suggest that PB *-ɪd initially introduced or, in Schadeberg's (2003) words, "tied" a Spatial Goal closer to a verb root, and that this use was extended to Human or Animate Goals (i.e. Beneficiaries, Recipients). Along similar lines, Mabugu (2001) and Cann and Mabugu (2007) on one hand, and De Kind and Bostoen (2012) on the other propose an underlying Spatial Goal meaning from which they derive synchronic functions of the applicative in Shona S11–15 and Luba-Kasai L31a, respectively. The degree of idiosyncracy on a root-by-root and language-by-language basis as to whether the applicative is required to introduce Locations/Spatial Goals suggests that the locative function is old(er) and had time to develop complexity and idiosyncratic behavior. The Fwe data supports this diachronic scenario in at least two ways. First, applicative morphology is the only morphological means to express Locations and Spatial Goals for roots which do not subcategorize for these semantic roles. Second, the spatial meaning of the applicative has been metaphorically extended to human referents through the Substitutive (in one's place). Possibly from there, it was then extended to the *optional* expression of Beneficiaries, Purposes and Reasons.[18]

The data discussed in this paper with parallels elsewhere in Bantu raise several questions. The first is whether the functions presented here are diachronically related to one another. For the syntax and focus functions, some scholars have proposed that the syntax function might have arisen out of the focus function since syntactic structures can be the result of the fossilization of discursive devices (Creissels 2004). Others (De Kind and Bostoen 2012) rather posit that the focus function might have developed out of the applicative's syntactic function of introducing an applied phrase: assuming that *-ɪd originally introduced Spatial Goals, the applicative effect of introducing applied phrases in immediately post-

---

18 On the other hand, an anonymous reviewer suggests that Reason/Purpose roles might have been the original roles introduced by *-ɪd in PB (see also Sibanda 2016: 327 who shows that in Zimbabwean Ndebele Reason and Location are the only semantic roles which can be introduced by the applicative across all semantic classes of verbs). While this is entirely possible, the literature on grammaticalization (Heine et al. 1993: 12, Heine and Kuteva 2002: 37) suggests that Purpose/Reason meanings often develop from Spatial Goal meanings (go to a place > go to a place *in order to* do something).

verbal focus position was extended to focalize locative phrases, which usually do not occur in this focus position. Whatever the case might be, assuming that the syntax and focus function are somewhat related, another question is whether and/or how the argument orientation function relates to these two.

Abbreviations

("x" stands for a number and parentheses indicate optionally present elements)

1	first person
3	third person
ADV	adverbializer
AP	agreement prefix
APPL	applicative
AUG	augment
CAUS	causative
CLX	noun class prefix of class x
CON	connective
COP	copula
DEM	demonstrative of class x
DIST	distal
FV	final vowel
HAB	habitual
INF	infinitive
INS	instrumental preposition
LOC	locative
LOC.PL	locative pluractional
LNK	linker
NEUT	neuter (verbal suffix)
NPST	near past
(x)OBJ	object index (of class x)
PASS	passive
PFV	perfective
PL	plural
POSS	possessive pronoun
PREP	preposition
PROG	progressive
PST	past
REL	relative form of the verb
REM	remoteness
SG	singular
STAT	stative
(x)SUBJ	subject index (of class x)
SUBJV	subjunctive

References

Bastin, Yvonne, André Coupez, Evariste Mumba & Thilo C. Schadeberg (eds.). 2002. *Reconstructions lexicales bantoues 3/Bantu lexical reconstructions 3.* Tervuren: Royal Museum for Central Africa. Online database: http://linguistics.africamuseum.be/BLR3.html

Bentley, William Holman. 1887. *Dictionary and grammar of the Kongo language, as spoken at San Salvador, the ancient capital of the old Kongo empire, West Africa. Compiled and prepared for the Baptist Mission on the Kongo River, West Africa, by the Rev. W. Holman Bentley, missionary of the Baptist Missionary Society on the Kongo.* London: Trübner.

Bostoen, Koen. 2009. Shanjo and Fwe as part of Bantu Botatwe: A diachronic phonological approach. In Akinloye Ojo & Lioba Moshi (eds.), *Selected Proceedings of the 39th Annual Conference on African Linguistics*, 110–130. Somerville, MA: Cascadilla Proceedings Project.

Bostoen, Koen & León Mundeke. 2011. The causative/applicative syncretism in Mbuun (Bantu B87, DRC): Semantic split or phonemic merger? *Journal of African Languages and Linguistics* 32. 179–218.

Bostoen, Koen & Rozenn Guérois. forthcoming. Reconstructing suffixal phrasemes in Bantu verbal derivation. In Koen Bostoen, Gilles-Maurice de Schryver, Rozenn Guérois & Sara Pacchiarotti (eds.), *Reconstructing Proto-Bantu grammar.* Berlin: Language Science Press.

Bresnan, Joan & Lioba Moshi. 1990. Object asymmetries in comparative Bantu syntax. *Linguistic Inquiry* 21(2). 147–185.

Cann, Ronnie & Patricia Mabugu. 2007. Constructional polysemy: The applicative construction in ChiShona. *Metalinguistica* 19. 221–245.

Crane, Thera Marie, Hilde Gunnink, Ponsiano Kanijo & Tim Roth. forthcoming. Aspect and evidentiality in four Bantu languages. In Marie-Astrid De Wit, Frank Brisard, Carol Madden-Lombardi, Michael Meeuwis & Adeline Patard (eds.), *Aspectual constructions beyond time.* Oxford: Oxford University Press.

Creissels, Denis. 1999. Dictionnaire tswana-français. Unpublished manuscript.

Creissels, Denis. 2003. Présentation du tswana. *Lalies: Actes des sessions de linguistique et de littérature 23.* Aussois: Éditions Rue d'Ulm.

Creissels, Denis. 2004. Non-canonical applicatives and focalization in Tswana. Paper presented at Syntax of the World's Languages, Leipzig, Available at: http://email.eva.mpg.de/~cschmidt/SWL1/handouts/Creissels.pdf.

Creissels, Denis. 2011. Tswana locatives and their status in the inversion construction. *Africana Linguistica* 17. 33–52.

Damman, Ernst. 1961. Das Applikativum in den Bantusprachen. *Zeitschrift der Deutschen Morgenländischen Gesellschaft* 111(1). 160–169.

De Kind, Jasper & Koen Bostoen. 2012. The applicative in Cilubà grammar and discourse: A semantic goal analysis. *Southern African Linguistics and Applied Language Studies* 30(1). 101–124.

de Luna, Kathryn. 2010. Classifying Botatwe: M60 languages and the settlement chronology of south central Africa. *Africana Linguistica* 16. 65–96.

Dik, Simon, Maria E. Hoffman, Jan R. de Jong, Sie Ing Djiang, Harry Stroomer & Lourens de Vries. 1981. On the typology of focus phenomena. In Teun Hoekstra, Harry van der Hulst & Michael Moortgat (eds.), *Perspectives on functional grammar*, 41–74. Dordrecht: Foris.

Endemann, Karl. 1876. *Versuch einer Grammatik des Sotho.* Berlin: W. Hertz.

Gibson, Hannah, Andriana Koumbarou, Lutz Marten & Jenneke van der Wal. 2017. Locating the Bantu conjoint/disjoint alternation in a typology of focus marking. In Jenneke van der Wal & Larry M. Hyman (eds.), *The conjoint/disjoint alternation in Bantu*, 61–99. Berlin: De Gruyter Mouton.
Gunnink, Hilde. 2022. *A Grammar of Fwe*. Berlin: Language Science Press.
Gunnink, Hilde. 2019. The fronted-infinitive construction in Fwe. *Africana Linguistica* 25. 65–88.
Guthrie, Malcolm. 1967–1971. *Comparative Bantu: An introduction to the comparative linguistics and prehistory of the Bantu languages, Vols. I–IV*. Farnborough: Gregg.
Guthrie, Malcolm. 1970. The status of radical extensions in Bantu languages. In Malcolm Guthrie (ed.), *Collected papers on Bantu linguistics*, 92–110. Farnborough: Gregg International Publishers Limited. (Originally published in 1962 in *Journal of African Languages* 1(3). 202–220).
Harford, Carolyn. 1993. The applicative in Chishona and lexical mapping theory. In Sam A. Mchombo (ed.), *Theoretical aspects of Bantu grammar*, 93–112. Stanford: CSLI Publications.
Heine, Bernd, Tom Güldemann, Christa Kilian-Hatz, Donald A. Lessau, Heinz Roberg, Mathias Schladt & Thomas Stolz. 1993. *Conceptual shift: A lexicon of grammaticalization processes in African languages*. (Afrikanistische Arbeitspapiere 34/35). Cologne: Institut für Afrikanistik.
Heine, Bernd & Tania Kuteva. 2002. *World lexicon of grammaticalization*. Cambridge: Cambridge University Press.
Hyman, Larry M. & Alessandro Duranti. 1982. On the object relation in Bantu. In Paul Hopper & Sandra Thompson (eds.), *Studies in transitivity*, 217–239. New York: Academic Press.
Hyman, Larry M., Alessandro Duranti & Malillo Morolong. 1980. Towards a typology of the direct object in Bantu. In Louis Bouquiaux (ed.), *L'expansion Bantoue: Actes de Colloque International de CNRS Viviers (France): 4–16 avril 1977, vol. 2, theme 3 (Problèmes spécifiques de grammaire comparée du bantou : Innovations dans le système grammatical : Dérivation, formes verbales, système des classes nominales)*, 563–582. Paris: SELAF.
Hyman, Larry M. 2007. Niger-Congo verb extensions: Overview and discussion. In Doris L. Payne & Jaime Peña (eds.), *Selected Proceedings of the 37th Annual Conference on African Linguistics*, 149–163. Somerville, Ma.: Cascadilla Press.
Jerro, Kyle J. 2016. *The syntax and semantics of applicative morphology in Bantu*. Austin: University of Texas dissertation.
Kähler-Meyer, Emmi. 1966. Die örtliche Funktion der Applikativendung in Bantusprachen. In J. Lukas (ed.), *Neue afrikanistische Studien: Festschrift für A. Klingenheben*, 126–136. Hamburg: Deutsches Institut für Afrika-Forschung.
Kawasha, Boniface Kaumba. 2003. *Lunda grammar: A morphosyntactic and semantic analysis*. Eugene: University of Oregon dissertation.
Keenan, Edward L. & Leonard M. Faltz. 1985. *Boolean semantics for natural language*. Dordrecht: D. Reidel.
Kimenyi, Alexandre. 1980. *A relational grammar of Kinyarwanda*. (University of California publications in linguistics 91). Berkeley: University of California Press.
Kimenyi, Alexandre. 1995. Kinyarwanda applicatives revisited. Keynote address at the 8th Niger-Congo Syntax-Semantics Workshop, Boston University. www.kimenyi.com/kinyar-wanda-applicatives-revisited.php
Kiss, Katalin É. Identificational focus versus information focus. *Language* 74(2). 245–273.

Kisseberth, Charles W. & Mohammad Imam Abasheikh. 1977. The object relation in Chi-Mwi:ni, a Bantu language. In Peter Cole & Jerrold M. Sadock (eds.), *Syntax and Semantics 8: Grammatical relations*, 179–218. New York: Academic Press.

Kuperus, J. & A. Mpunga wa Ilunga. 1990. *Locative markers in Luba*. Tervuren: Musée Royal de l'Afrique Centrale.

Lambrecht, Knud. 2001. A framework for the analysis of cleft constructions. *Linguistics* 39(3). 463–516.

Mabugu, Patricia Ruramisai. 2001. *Polysemy and the applicative verb construction in Chishona*. Edinburgh: University of Edinburgh dissertation.

Marten, Lutz. 2003. The dynamics of Bantu applied verbs: An analysis at the syntax-pragmatics interface. In Kézié. K. Lébikaza (ed.), *Actes du 3e Congrès Mondial de Linguistique Africaine Lomé 2000*, 207–221. Cologne: Rüdiger Köppe Verlag.

Marten, Lutz & Maarten Mous. 2017. Valency and expectation in Bantu applicatives. *Linguistics Vanguard* 3(1). 1–15.

Maho, Jouni Filip. 2009. NUGL Online: The online version of the New Updated Guthrie List, a referential classification of the Bantu languages. http://goto.glocalnet.net/mahopapers/nuglonline.pdf

Meeussen, Achilles Emile. 1967. Bantu grammatical reconstructions. *Africana Linguistica* 3. 79–121.

Nurse, Derek. 2008. *Tense and aspect in Bantu*. Oxford: Oxford University Press.

Pacchiarotti, Sara. 2020. *Bantu applicative constructions*. (Stanford Monographs in African Languages). Stanford: CSLI Publications.

Pacchiarotti, Sara. forthcoming. On the reconstructable main clause functions of Proto-Bantu applicative *-ɪd. In Koen Bostoen, Gilles-Maurice De Schryver, Rozenn Guérois & Sara Pacchiarotti (eds.), *Reconstructing Proto-Bantu grammar*. Berlin: Language Science Press.

Peterson, David A. *Applicative constructions*. (Oxford Studies in Typology and Linguistic Theory). Oxford: Oxford University Press.

Rapold, Christian. 1997. *The applicative construction in Lingala*. Leiden: Rijksuniversiteit Leiden M.A. thesis.

Rugemalira, Josephat M. 1993. *Runyambo verb extensions and constraints on predicate structure*. Berkeley: University of California dissertation.

Rugemalira, Josephat M. 2004. Locative arguments in Bantu. In Akinbiyi Akinlabi & Oluseye Adesola (eds.), *Proceedings of the 4th World Congress of African Linguistics New Brunswick 2003*, 285–295. Cologne: Rüdiger Köppe.

Schaefer, Ronald P. 1985. Motion in Tswana and its characteristic lexicalization. *Studies in African Linguistics* 16. 57–87.

Schadeberg, Thilo C. 2003a. Derivation. In Derek Nurse & Gérard Philippson (eds.), *The Bantu languages*, 71–89. (Routledge Language Family Series 4). London: Routledge.

Sibanda, Galen. 2016. The Ndebele applicative construction. In Doris L. Payne, Sara Pacchiarotti & Mokaya Bosire (eds.), *Diversity in African languages: Selected papers from the 46th Annual Conference on African Linguistics*, 309–333. (Contemporary African Linguistics 1). Berlin: Language Science Press.

Simango, Silvester Ron. 2012. The semantics of locative clitics and locative applicatives in ciCewa. In Bruce Connell & Nicholas Rolle (eds.), *Selected Proceedings of the 41st Annual Conference on African Linguistics*, 141–149. Somerville, Ma.: Cascadilla Proceedings Project.

Stapleton, Walter Henry. 1903. *Comparative handbook of Congo languages: Being a comparative grammar of the eight principal languages spoken along the banks of the Congo river from the west coast of Africa to Stanley Falls, and of Swahili, the "lingua franca" of the country stretching thence to the east coast, with a comparative vocabulary giving 800 selected words from these languages, with their English equivalents, followed by appendices on six other dialects*. Bolobo, Congo Independent State: Hannah Wade Printing Press of the Baptist Missionary Society.

Trithart, Mary Lee. 1977. Locatives. In Ernest Rugwa Byarushengo, Alessandro Duranti & Larry M. Hyman (eds.), *Haya grammatical structure*, 89–98. (Southern California Occasional Papers in Linguistics 6). Los Angeles: Linguistics Department, University of Southern California.

Trithart, Mary Lee. 1983. *The applied suffix and transitivity: A historical study in Bantu*. Los Angeles: University of California at Los Angeles dissertation.

van der Wal, Jenneke. 2016. Diagnosing focus. *Studies in Language* 40(2). 259–301.

van der Wal, Jenneke. 2017. What is the conjoint/disjoint alternation? Parameters of cross-linguistic variation. In Jenneke van der Wal & Larry M. Hyman (eds.), *The conjoint/disjoint alternation in Bantu*, 14–60. Berlin/Boston: De Gruyter Mouton.

van der Wal, Jenneke. 2018. Bantu focus (re)constructions. Paper presented at Reconstructing Proto-Bantu Grammar, Ghent, 19–23 November 2018.

van Eeden, Bernardus Izak Christiaan. 1956. *Zoeloe-Grammatika*. Stellenbosch: Die Universiteitsuitgewers en Boekhandelaars.

Voeltz, Erhard Friedrich Karl. 1977. *Proto Niger-Congo verb extensions*. Los Angeles: University of California dissertation.

Whiteley, Wilfred Howell. 1968. *Some problems of transitivity in Swahili*. London: School of Oriental and African Studies (sole agents: Luzac & Co. Ltd.).

8 Appendix

Fwe lexicalized applicative stem	Fwe underived root
kù-àrìrà 'to follow (in order of birth)'	
kù-àzyàrìrà 'to wish (onto s.o.)'	*kù-àzyàrà* 'to plan'
kù-círìrà ~ kú-cìrìrà 'to follow'	
kù-fútàtìrà to stand with one's back to s.o.; to quit a job	
kù-fúzìrà to blow on a fire to get it going	
kù-fúzìrìrà to blow on a fire	
kù-fwáfwàtìrà to get crushed	
kù-gángìrà to freeze	
kù-gáyìrà to fence in	*kù-gàyà* to sew
kù-kácìkìrà to be interrupted	
kù-kákàtìrà to become stuck	

(Continued)

Fwe lexicalized applicative stem	Fwe underived root
kù-kúmbìrà to beg	
kù-kúrìrà to infect, be infectious	
kù-rárìrà to eat dinner	
kù-rárìrà to sleep close to a sick person	
kù-rítàbìrìrà to ignore advice	
kù-shírìrà to desire	
kù-shwátìrà to whip	
kù-sùbìrà to be red	
kù-zùbìrìrà to put the first flour into a pot of boiling water to make porridge	kù-zùbùrà take food from a boiling pot
kù-zyàmbìrà to gather	
kù-ᵍ/ákàmìnà to sit with arms and legs extended (to catch fish; to warm oneself by the fire)	
kù-zùmìnà to believe, agree, accept a marriage proposal	
kù-shúmìnìnà to be engaged	
kù-shúmìnà to tie	cf. kù-shûmà to bite
kù-rísùngàmìnà to look down	
kú-mìnìnà to sink	cf. kú-mìnà to set (of the sun)
kù-mànìnà to disappear	cf. kù-mànà to finish
kù-hímìnìnà to sink, go down	
kù-dèbèrà to be not taut	
kù-dékèshèrà to move the shoulders in a dancing movement	kù-dékètà to move the shoulders up and down in a dancing movement
kù-hòmpwèrà to hammer	
kù-nyérèrà to hang from, dangle	
kù-ròbèrà to capsize; to eat fast	
kù-shèndèkèrà to joke, mock	cf?. kù-shèndèkà to put into a leaning position
kù-sòsèrà 'to poke (a fire)'	
kù-tèrèrà 'to be soft, slippery'	
kù-tòmbwèrà 'to weed'	
kù-zèrà ~ kù-zérèrà to hang, dangle	
kù-tèngènà to carry on the head	

Doris L. Payne
9 The applicative(-like) function of Nilotic directionals: Introducing THEMES

Abstract: Nilotic languages have so-called dative applicatives covering applied BENEFACTIVE/MALEFACTIVE, GOAL-REACHED, and other closely-related semantic concepts, and some have a second INSTRUMENTAL applicative which may be extended to LOCATION, MANNER, COMITATIVE, etc. In addition, nearly all Nilotic languages have itive and ventive directionals. With most verb stems the directionals indicate orientation relative to a point of reference, associated motion, or aspectual concepts. These functions would not place the directionals in the domain of applicatives as usually defined. However, when they occur on roots with <ACTOR SOURCE/GOAL> argument frames, the directionals can change the semantic role of the non-Actor object argument of an otherwise transitive root. In particular, they can derive an <ACTOR THEME> frame, where the applied THEME undergoes movement. If the base SOURCE or GOAL occurs in the derived clause, it must be in an oblique phrase. This function corresponds to that of an applicative because it introduces a non-Actor semantic argument into a main clause as a primary or direct object, which the verb would otherwise not allow. This is a "redirective" applicative function in the sense of Kiyosawa (2006) because the transitivity of the stem is not changed though the semantic role frame is changed. The cognitive basis for the argument manipulation finds a ready explanation if the directionals come from movement verbs or at least associated motion functions of the directionals.

Acknowledgements: I am grateful to Leonard Ole-Kotikash, A. Keswe Mapena, Sarah Tukuoo, Stephen Muntet, Loatha Lesilale, Peter Ndetio, Lazaro Ole-Melubo, Neema, and many others for assistance with the Maa data. I am also grateful to two anonymous reviewers and Sara Pacchiarotti for generous comments which have helped improve this study, though perhaps not entirely to the reviewers' satisfaction. Funding for the Maa research was partially provided by NSF grant SBR-9616482 and Fulbright Foundation fellowships.

Doris L. Payne, University of Oregon & SIL International, Department of Linguistics, Eugene, Oregon, USA, e-mail: dlpayne@uoregon.edu

1 Introduction

This paper argues that itive and ventive directionals in the Nilotic family (Nilo-Saharan phylum) have a kind of "redirective" applicative function, even though the semantic role they add is THEME rather than what is typically thought of as peripheral, such as BENEFICIARY, INSTRUMENT, SOURCE, GOAL, POSSESSOR, REASON, MANNER, or some other non-THEME (and non-AGENT) role (see the introduction to this volume). The affiliation of Nilotic directionals to applicative devices becomes even more compelling when we see that they have a further, perhaps incipient, extension in at least one branch of Nilotic to adding COMITATIVE and BENEFICIARY roles as core arguments, albeit in particular situations. I suggest that one component in the development of applicative functions rides on an associated motion function of the directionals. The paper thus adds to our understanding of pathways via which applicative morphemes can develop.[1]

The Nilotic family divides into three branches (Köhler 1955). Itive and ventive directionals occur in all three. Languages displaying this verbal morphology include but are not limited to: Western Nilotic (WN) Agar Dinka (Andersen 1992–1994, 2012), Mabaan (Andersen 1999), Anywa (Reh 1996), Shilluk (Remijsen et al. 2016, Remijsen & Ayoker 2020); Southern Nilotic (SN) Nandi (Creider & Creider 1989, Creider 2002), Cherang'any and Kony (Mietzner 2016), Kupsapiny (Kawachi 2011), Tugen (Jerono 2019), Asimjeeg Datooga (Griscom 2019), Barbayiiga and Gisamjanga Datooga (Bruckhaus 2021); and Eastern Nilotic (EN) Bari (Spagnolo 1933), varieties of Maa (Tucker & Mpaayei 1955), Turkana (Dimmendaal 1983), Toposa (Schroeder 1999), Ateso (Barasa 2017), and Lopit (Moodie 2019, Moodie & Billington 2020). Given the diversity of alignment systems and object properties across the family, and depth of available grammatical descriptions, this paper will highlight one language from each branch of the family but other languages will be mentioned in passing.

Before looking at the directionals, we first note that languages in all three Nilotic branches have one or more rather classic applicatives which can increase valence and result in applied object phrases that express so-called "peripheral" semantic roles. The most widespread of these is usually called dative (Dimmendaal 2009), which expresses BENEFICIARY, MALEFACTIVE, GOAL-REACHED and some other closely-related semantic concepts. Some languages have an additional

---

[1] I use small capitals for semantic roles like INSTRUMENT, BENEFACTIVE, etc., while terms in plain type like instrument, dative, itive, and ventive refer to specific morphemes or verb derivations. In examples, I sometimes regularize authors' original glossing for uniformity, notably using ventive (VEN) and itive (ITV) where a grammar source may have used centripetal, centrifugal, or some other synonymous term.

instrumental applicative, which may be extended beyond the role of INSTRUMENT to express LOCATION, MANNER, and some other notions.[2] The primary focus of this paper, however, is not on these fairly classic applicatives, but on the applicative(-like) functions of itive and ventive directionals.

In contrast to dative, instrumental, and sometimes other applicatives, the directionals can introduce a moved or moving THEME (Gruber 1965) into the clause as the grammatical object, in place of the semantic argument that the simple root or stem would otherwise have as object. If expressed, the erstwhile object argument of the base root/stem can only be in an oblique phrase. This phenomenon occurs with a particular class of transitive verb roots. The example set in (1) gives a first illustration.

(1) Maa (EN)[3]
    a. *Á-púrr   ol=dúka*
       1SG-rob MSG=shop
       'I (will) rob the shop.'

    b. *N-é-purr-óo   ɔl=áyíóní   il=mósorr*
       CN1-3-rob-ITV MSG=boy.NOM MPL=eggs
       'The boy stole/will steal eggs.'

    c. *Á-púrr-ú   ɛnk=alámu tɔ l=dúkâ.*
       1SG-rob-VEN FSG=pen OBL MSG=shop.NOM
       'I will steal a pen from the market.'

In (1a), the transitive root *purr* 'rob' entails a scene in which something is '(re-) moved from' someone or something. *Oldúka* 'shop' is not a prototype THEME as it is not even fictively moving nor is it predicated as being 'in a location'. Hence, 'shop' is a SOURCE. With the verb form in (1a), 'shop' could not be in an oblique phrase.[4] If *il=mósorr* 'eggs' were substituted for *ol=dúka* in (1a), the clause could only anomalously mean #'I am stealing [something] from the eggs'. The same

---

[2] The cognate affix to the dative is called 'terminative' in SN studies. In some languages, the dative is obligatory for expressing at least BENEFACTIVE/MALEFACTIVE. In those languages which have it, the instrumental applicative is a syntactically optional strategy for expressing INSTRUMENT and other relevant roles.
[3] All Maa examples are from my field notes. If from a text, a text and line code is given. In most Maa examples, any English tense translation is possible, depending on context.
[4] With verbs of other types, a SOURCE could occur in an oblique phrase in Maa; I have not found this for GOALS.

lexeme *purr* occurs in (1b-c), but now with the directionals. Now the syntactic object expresses the item moved. Thus, the directionals have derived a syntactically relevant <ACTOR THEME> frame from a root with a basic transitive <ACTOR SOURCE> frame. In (1c), note that 'shop' is now in an oblique phrase.

The paper is organized as follows. Section 2 introduces Nilotic verbal typology so that the directional categories can be appreciated even when not easily parsable. It also briefly comments on the various functions of Nilotic directionals. Importantly for the current paper, these functions include that of an 'associated translational motion' event, which is distinct from the situation expressed by the lexical verb root (Koch 1984, Guillaume 2016). Section 3 discusses the argument-manipulation effects of the directionals, and then takes a typological look at how the Nilotic system compares to some other applicative(-like) systems discussed in the literature. Section 4 explores the rise of the Nilotic applicative-like function out of an associated motion function, and some further applicative-related extensions of the directionals. Section 5 concludes the paper.

2 Nilotic verbs and directional morphemes

In SN languages, verbs are fairly agglutinative, with prefixes, suffixes, tonal and vowel-harmony based morphological alternations. Inflection is both prefixal and suffixal, while derivation is primarily suffixal including all applicative and directional forms; the well-established 'ambulative' necessarily co-occurs with a directional (Rottland 1982; Creider & Creider 1989; Zwarts 2004; Kawachi 2011; Meitzner 2016; Griscom 2019; among others). EN verbs have agglutinative characteristics but with co-occurrence restrictions among sometimes discontinuous morphemes, tonal morphology, and some difficult-to-parse morpheme complexes (Tucker & Mpaayei 1955; Dimmendaal 1983; Payne 2015; Barasa 2017; Karani 2018; Moodie & Billington 2020; among others). Inflectional morphology is mostly though not exclusively prefixal, while derivational morphology is mostly though not exclusively suffixal. WN verb templates are phonologically shorter than SN and EN ones due to highly fusional morphology. Derivation as well as some inflection may involve stem-internal changes in vowel length, voice quality, consonant voicing, nasalization, and tone (Andersen 1992–1994, 1999; Reh 1996; Reid 2010; Remijsen, Miller-Naudé and Gilley 2016; among others).

2.1 Alignment and classic applicatives

Nilotic languages vary in their alignment systems, involving case, argument indexation, and constituent order. There is not room here to elaborate on all issues that pertain to identifying grammatical object status, but as background for discussing the effect of directionals, I illustrate some relevant issues from a few languages and simultaneously present several classic applicatives found in each branch.

Some WN languages have some constructions with ergative-absolutive case features, but others do not. Agar Dinka (Andersen 1992–1994; 2012) is not described as having ergativity, but has two dominant clause constructions. One has verb-initial structure (see (21) below), and one has a pre-verb Topic position.[5] In the Topic construction, morphological patterns on the finite verb or auxiliary reflect whether the preverbal Topic is the grammatical "Subject" versus "Non-subject". Pronominal subjects are indexed on the finite verb/auxiliary if the preverbal Topic is a grammatical object, as in (2).

(2) Agar Dinka (WN; Andersen 1992–1994: 22)
 a. wḛŋ   ạ̀-cụ̀uk   mḭ̀ḭt
   cow   D-PF.1PL   pull.NF
   'We have pulled the cow.'

 b. wḛŋ   ạ̀-cậak   mḭ̀ḭt
   cow   D-PF.2PL   pull.NF
   'You (plural) have pulled the cow.'

 c. wḛŋ   ạ̀-cị̀ik   mḭ̀ḭt
   cow   D-PF.3PL   pull.NF
   'They have pulled the cow.'

In contrast to the preceding, subject marking does not occur on the finite verb/auxiliary in (3a) because the subject is preverbal and not pronominal. Subject marking also does not occur on the verb in (3b) because, even though the object is in Topic position, the postverbal subject is a lexical phrase. Postverbal objects occur in an "absolutive" case form, which for most nouns is distinct from nominative, allative, and essive/ablative case forms.[6]

---

[5] Andersen uses the term *Topic* as a strictly a structural designation for the preverbal phrase, and not for a discourse-related notion.
[6] Andersen's term *absolutive* should not be interpreted in the sense of an ergative-absolutive system, but as the default, unmarked case form.

(3) Agar Dinka (Andersen 1992–1994: 13)

a. *d̪ɔ̤̀ɔ̤k à̰-mḭ̀it wḛ́ŋ nè̤ juiê̤en*
boy D-pull cow PREP rope
'The boy is pulling the cow with the rope.'

b. *wḛ́ŋ à̰-mḭ́it d̪ɔ̤̀ɔ̤k nè̤ juiê̤en*
cow D-pull.NTS boy PREP rope
'The boy is pulling the cow with the rope.'

If the Topic is what Andersen calls a circumstantial rather than subject or object, then a pronominal subject will occur in a free genitive form after the verb, and is not marked on the verb. Thus in (4), though the subjects are pronominal, they are expressed as genitive case free pronouns because the Topic is not a grammatical object (despite loss of the preposition; compare the treatment of 'rope' in (3) and (4)).

(4) Agar Dinka (Andersen 1992–1994: 31)

a. *juiê̤en à̰-mḭ́it ɣó̰ok wḛ́ŋ*
rope D-pull.NTS 1PL:GEN cow
'We are pulling the cow with the rope.'

b. *juiê̤en à̰-mḭ́it jḛ́en wḛ́ŋ*
rope D-pull.NTS 3SG:GEN cow
'He is pulling the cow with the rope.'

WN languages have obligatory benefactive applicative derivations (Andersen 1992–1994; Reh 1996; Remjisen et al. 2016): the applied form is sometimes the only way to express a BENEFICIARY role. The contrast between (5a) and (5b) demonstrates this for Agar Dinka. Most WN languages do not, to my knowledge, have instrumental applicatives.

(5) Agar Dinka (Andersen 1992–1994: 9)

a. *d̪ɔ̤̀ɔ̤k à̰-mḭ̀it wḛ́ŋ*
boy D-pull cow
'The boy is pulling the cow.'

b. *d̪ɔ̤̀ɔ̤k à̰-mî̤it wḛ́ŋ mò̰c*
boy D-pull.BEN cow man
'The boy is pulling the cow for the man.'

Most EN and SN languages have verb-initial syntax, though Bari (EN) and Asimjeeg (SN) have dominant subject–verb–object orders. Most languages in both branches

9 The applicative(-like) function of Nilotic directionals: Introducing THEMES — **233**

have marked-nominative case systems (König 2008) for lexical NPs and free pronouns, and nominative-accusative alignment in most other parts of their grammars. Verbal indexation systems can differ by language and by construction.

We will survey alignment and object properties in the EN language Maa. In Maa, verbs precede nominal and adpositional phrases as the unmarked norm, but order of NPs is somewhat flexible. Each noun and most nominal modifiers have two tonal case melodies. The case used for grammatical objects is the distributionally unmarked form, being used in citation, for fronted arguments regardless of grammatical relation, possessors, after the associative preposition, and in some other environments. Nominative tone melodies are restricted to postverbal subjects, after the general oblique preposition, and by some speakers for nouns after one clause-initial conjunction. Subjects and 1SG and 2SG objects are indexed in (sometimes portmanteau) verb prefixes, as in (6). A single 'inverse' form *kɪ*- marks 3rd person acting on 2SG (3>2SG) and 2SG acting on 1SG (2SG>1SG) (Payne, Hamaya & Jacobs 1994). Third person (and most plural objects) are not indexed on the verb, but may be indicated by a full NP as in (6b), a free pronoun, or a definite-null.

(6) Maa
    a. *Áa-yá   ɔl=páyian*
        3>1SG-take   MSG=man.NOM
        'The man will take (marry) me.' (said by a woman)

    b. *é-yá   ɪl=mʊ́rrân   in=kíshú*
        3-take MPL=warriors.NOM FPL=COWS
        'The warriors will take (e.g. steal) cows.'

Maa has a few underived ditransitive verb roots. If a RECIPIENT is 1SG or 2SG, it is indexed on the verb as the primary object, as in (7). If the primary object were 3rd person in (7), the verb prefix would be a short *á-*, which marks only 1SG subject.

(7) Maa
    ɛn=kíɔ̄ɔk áá-íshɔ́
    FSG=ear 1SG>2SG-give
    '(It is) the ear I give to you.' (olgol.026)

Dative and instrumental applicatives can create ditransitive stems from transitive roots, though with an already-transitive verb, the dative sometimes just indicates that a goal is reached or very nearly so; and it can sometimes just indicate greater intensity. In (8a), the dative applicative adds a RECIPIENT object to the transitive root *ya* 'take'. The RECIPIENT is 2SG so it is marked on the verb, just like the non-applied 2SG object in (7).[7] Example (8b) illustrates the BENEFICIARY sense of the dative. Neither the human 3rd person BENEFICIARY-object nor the 3rd person THEME-object is overtly marked on the verb. The contrasts in (9) illustrate the 'greater intensity' and 'GOAL-reached' uses of the dative, as well as BENEFICIARY. Note that (9a) shows *sʊj* 'follow' is a transitive root; (9b) demonstrates that an unmarked geographic GOAL 'mountain' can be added without an applicative; (9c) shows a greater intensity effect of the dative; and (9d) shows its BENEFICIARY and GOAL-reached readings (as well as intensity).

(8) Maa
    a. *k=áá-y-ákī*   *én=adúóó*   *tóki*   *ní-kí-tiááka*
       CN2-1SG>2SG-take-DAT   FSG=relevant   thing   REL.F-INV-tell.PF
       'I will bring you the thing that you told me.'

    b. *n-é-duŋ-okin-í*   *ɔl=payián*   *enkíook*   *ɔ́l=mʊ́rráni*
       CN1-3-cut-DAT-IMPS   MSG=elder   ear   of.MSG=warrior
       'The ear of a warrior was cut for the elder.' (emutata.024)

(9) Maa
    a. *m-í-ntóki*   *taá*   *a-sʊ́j*   *iyíóók*
       NEG-2-do.again   EMPH   INF.SG-follow   1PL
       'Do not again follow us.' (iloikop1.128)

    b. *áa-sʊ́j*   *ol=dóinyó*
       3>1SG-follow   MSG=mountain
       'S/he will follow me to the mountain.'

    c. *áa-sʊj-akí*   *ol=dóinyó*
       3>1SG-follow-DAT   MSG=mountain
       'S/he will track me (all over the place, through whatever routes I might take) to the mountain.

---

[7] One might use the term GOAL in a macro-role sense to include RECIPIENT and BENEFACTIVE/MALEFACTIVE, but what is most significant to the grammar of Maa is whether the GOAL is human. Maa *ya* 'take' can have the sense of 'take to' where an inanimate GOAL like 'river', 'village', 'salt-lick', etc. can be added without requiring the dative applicative (though one can optionally occur with a concomitant implication that the goal is specifically reached). If the GOAL is human (whether more precisely RECIPIENT or BENEFACTIVE/MALEFACTIVE), the dative applicative must occur. Furthermore, RECIPIENT and BENEFACTIVE/MALEFACTIVE participants cannot be expressed in oblique phrases.

d. áa-sʊj-akí   ɛn=kítéŋ
   3>1SG-follow-DAT   FSG=cow
   i. 'S/he will follow the cow for me.' (e.g. It is lost and I'm unable to go after it.)
   ii. 'S/he will pursue me all the way to the cow.' (e.g. I'm running to find safety behind a cow but s/he will follow me all the way there.)

The INSTRUMENT role in Maa can be conveyed via an oblique phrase, as in (10); or by the instrumental applicative which increases valence, as in (11).

(10) Maa
ɛ-gírái   áa-dam   ɔl=púrríshói   ɪ=sɛdérī   tɔɔ́
3-PROG-IMPS   INF.PL-slap   MSG=thief   FPL=cheeks   OBL.PL
nk=aík
FPL=hands.NOM
'The thief is being slapped (on) the cheeks with the hands.'

(11) Maa
n-ɛ-taá   duó   ɪnk=áík   e-dol-íé
CN1-3-be.PF   relevant   FPL=hands   3-see-INST
'It is with the hands she sees it.' (referring to a blind person) (enkong'u.109)

With the ditransitive root *pɪk* 'put', shown in (12a), adding the instrumental or dative applicative yields a stem with a syntactic valence of four, as in (12b-c). All objects (INSTRUMENT, THEME, GOAL, BENEFICIARY, etc.) occur in their absolute case form with no oblique preposition. Though there is a tendency for an applied object to occur immediately after the verb and before other objects (or to be fronted if contrasted), this is not syntactically required.[8]

(12) Maa
a. én-chɔm   én-tɪ-pɪk   en=teré   ɛ=makát
   IMP.PL-go.SBJV IMP.PL-SBJV-put   FSG=trough   FSG=salt
   'Go put salt in the trough.'

---

[8] In a corpus study of ditransitives (Payne, 2022), 100% of animate applied dative NPs were immediately after the verb, while 83% of animate applied instrument objects were. For the underived ditransitives *pɪk* 'put' and *ɪshɔ* 'give', 94–96% of animate NP objects were immediately postverbal.

b. á-pík-ie   en=kikómpe   ɛnk=áré   e=motí
   1SG-put-INST   FSG=cup   FSG=water   FSG=pot
   'I will use the cup to put water into the pot.'

c. ɛ-pɪk-ákɪ   en=kitók   en=kijíko   en=kikómpe
   3-put-DAT   FSG=woman   FSG=spoon   FSG=cup
   'S/he will put the spoon in the cup for the woman.'

In terms of object alignment, singular speech act participants outrank any 3rd persons, regardless of semantic role and animacy/humanness and regardless of base versus applied status. Thus, the Maa indexation system does not exactly conform to either a direct/indirect object nor to a primary/secondary object system in the sense of Dryer (1986), but is instead more sensitive to person. I present two examples to illustrate. In (13) with the verb *isis* 'praise', the base object of the relativized verb is the 2nd person who is praised. The instrumental applicative *-iek* occurs on the relativized verb, creating a double-object verb with 'power' as its second object ('power' is also the base object of *ata* 'have'). 'Praise' carries the 'inverse' prefix, which marks either 3>2SG or 2SG>1SG; here it indexes 2SG. The verb does not carry the prefix *e-*, which would be expected if the verb were indexing the applied 3rd person instrument object 'power' (here, a semantic REASON) via a definite null form. This shows that the applied 3rd person object does not displace the base 2nd person object in terms of verb indexation.

(13) Maa
      í-áta   ŋolón   ɛnk=áí   papâ   ní-k-ísís-íék-i
      2-have   power   FSG=God   father   REL.F-INV-praise-INST-IMPS
      'You have power, father God, that you are praised for.' (Camus2.180)

Example (14) combines the dative and instrumental applicatives on the transitive root 'cut'. The dative (BENEFICIARY) applied participant is 1SG, which is indexed on the verb via the inverse prefix. Both the base THEME and the applied INSTRUMENT are 3rd person. Neither is overtly expressed in (14).

(14) Maa
      kí-dúŋ-ókín-yie   táatá
      INV-cut-DAT-INST   now
      'You will cut it for me using it now.'

If the applied instrumental phrase is human, it is interpreted as a causee.[9] Since the INSTRUMENT/CAUSEE is 1SG in (15), it is indexed as object in the verb – unlike the applied instrument object in (14).

(15) Maa
 áa-iger-ie
 3>1SG-inscribe-INST
 'He will make me write/brand/tattoo (something).'

We now turn to SN languages, which divide into Kalenjin and Datooga sub-branches, and first briefly elaborate on Nandi (Kalenjin). Nandi has unmarked verb-initial clause structure, but subject and object can occur in any order (Creider 2002: 171). Nouns display a marked nominative case system (Creider & Creider 1989: 41–43). Pronominal subjects are indexed by verb prefixes, 1st and 2nd person objects by verb suffixes, and 3rd person objects are not indexed on the verb (Creider & Creider 1989: 97).

There is a dative applicative *-ci* (often called 'terminal' in SN studies), covering BENEFICIARY, ADDRESSEE, GOAL, etc., as in (16). Creider & Creider comment that the only means Nandi has to indicate a 3rd person BENEFICIARY is by this applicative (whether this is true also for 1st and 2nd person BENEFICIARY is unclear).

(16) Nandi (SN; Creider & Creider 1989: 126)
 kí:-sô:man-cì   kípe:t   la:kwé:t   pû:kú:t
 PST-read-DAT   Kibet   child   book
 'Kibet read the child the book.'

Nandi also has an instrumental applicative *-e*, which covers INSTRUMENT as in (17), various LOCATIVE notions, and other meanings (Creider 2002 uses the term 'peripheral' for the applicative). These notions may be expressed either as applied objects or in oblique prepositional phrases, as in (17b).

(17) Nandi (Creider & Creider 1989: 126–127)
 a. *kyâ:-pat-e: ímpáré:t   mókó:mpé:t*
    PST.1SG-dig-INST field   hoe
    'I cultivated the field with a hoe.'

---

9 This is particularly apparent with what are called Class 2 verbs, which have no other morphological causative besides the instrumental.

b. *kyâ:-pat-í:*   *ímpáré:t* *e:ng* *mókó:mpé:t*
   PST.1SG-dig-INST field   with hoe
   'I cultivated the field with a hoe.'

Like Nandi, the SN language Cherang'any has the instrumental applicative *-ɛ(ɛ)* and the dative applicative *-ci(ni)*, each able to communicate a range of semantic roles (Mietzner 2016: 129–135). Cherang'any indexes subject by verb prefixes (though 3rd person is sometimes zero), and 1st and 2nd person "direct" object by suffixes. 1st and 2nd person "indirect" (BENEFICIARY) objects are marked by a suffix complex involving the ventive directional plus the object indexation suffix, while 3rd person "indirect" objects are expressed simply by the dative applicative (Mietzner 2016: 106–111). Mietzner (2009) surveys applicative morphology with spatial meaning in various additional (especially Kalenjin) Nilotic languages, along with directional morphemes.

For Asimjeeg Datooga, Griscom (2019: 125–127, 235) describes three (non-directional) applicatives. The 'terminal' applicative *-s(V:n) ~ -s(a) ~ s(i)* expresses GOAL, BENEFICIARY, and some LOCATIONS for 3rd persons; this is likely cognate with the dative applicative in EN if not WN (Reh 1996; Dimmendaal 2009). Griscom refers to an 'oblique' applicative *-an* which can express TIME and other notions, which is not mentioned as an applicative in the Kalenjin sub-branch. Griscom's 'locative' applicative *-e:(w) ~ -ɛ:(w)* can express 3rd person LOCATION, MANNER, and ACCOMPANIMENT, and is presumably cognate with the 'instrument' applicative in Kalenjin languages. Additionally, the ventive directional (discussed below) functions as a BENEFACTIVE/RECIPIENT applicative for 1st and 2nd persons.

2.2 Itive and ventive directionals: Non-applicative functions

We now briefly introduce the non-applicative functions of the directionals, as background for their applicative-like functions (Section 3). Depending on the root they occur with and contextual factors, the itive and ventive directionals can indicate orientation relative to a point of reference (typically the speaker); but they need not add an additional motion event beyond any motion meaning lexicalized in the verb root. Examples (18)–(19) illustrate this for an EN and a SN language.[10]

---

[10] The Proto-Nilotic ventive may have had a high vowel plus nasal. The Proto-EN and Proto-SN itive likely had a coronal consonant plus low vowel. The Proto-WN itive possibly had a breathy vowel and final-consonant allomorphs. Payne (2021: 704) summarizes various reconstructions.

(18) Ateso (EN; Barasa 2017: 161)
   a. kɔ́-lɔ̀m-ʊ̀   ò-tógò
      IMP-enter-VEN LOC-house.LOC
      '(please) enter the house' [Speaker is inside the house]

   b. kɔ́-lɔ̀m-à   ò-tógò
      IMP-enter-ITV LOC-house.LOC
      '(please) enter the house' [Speaker is outside the house and indicates visitor should enter first]

(19) Asimjeeg Datooga (SN)
   a. Ø-ruŋ-ní
      2.SG-tell-VEN
      'Tell (me).' (Griscom 2019: 224)

   b. g-à-fúf   à: g-à-mútʃ   á: g-á-bug-dà
      AFF-3-relax   CONJ AFF-3-sun.rise CONJ AFF-3-return-ITV
      'She relaxes and the next day returns (there).' (Griscom (2019: 227)

Though the directionals themselves do not always express (an additional) translational motion separate from the lexical root event, this is in fact one of their functions. That is, the directionals can express directed associated motion (Koch 1984, Guillaume 2016), whether physical or fictive. The associated motion may apply to intransitive or transitive subjects of the base lexeme, as in (20) and (21) respectively, and/or to an object participant, as in (22) (see Payne 2021 for details). In (20) and (21), the AGENT of the lexical verb is also the moving participant, while in (22) the moving participant is not the one doing the seeing.

(20) Anywa (WN; Reh 1996: 254, 257)
   làáJ- / láaJ-   láaɲɲ-   láaJJ-[11]
   urinate   urinate.VEN.M   urinate.ITV.M
   'urinate'   'come and urinate here' 'go and urinate there'

(21) Agar Dinka (Andersen 2012: 162–163)
   a. à̱=rà̱ak   wḛ́ŋ
      D=milk   COW.ABS
      'He is milking a cow.'

---

[11] In Reh (1996), J represents a palatal stop which is underspecified for voicing.

b. *à̱=rè̱ɛk   wɛ́ŋ*
     D=milk.VEN   COW.ABS
     'He is milking a cow in order to bring milk.'

  c. *à̱=rè̱ɛk   wɛ́ŋ*
     D=milk.ITV   COW.ABS
     'He is milking a cow and taking the milk to somebody.'

(22) Bari (EN; Spagnolo 1933: 147; parsing and glossing mine)
  a. *nan   a-mɛt-undya   Wani*
     1SG   1SG-see-VEN   Wani
     'I watched Wani coming.'

  b. *nan   a-mɛt-ara'   Wani*
     1SG   1SG-see-ITV   Wani
     'I watched Wani go away.'

Across SN, associated motion can be expressed only by the directionals in combination with a historical ambulative morpheme; the ambulative cannot occur without a directional, but a directional can occur in non-associated-motion functions without the ambulative.

(23) Cherang'any (SN; Meitzner 2016: 139)
  a. *tíl-ʎʎtí   sùùswék*
     cut-AMB.ITV   grass
     'S/he cuts the grass while going.'

  b. *tíl-ʎʎnu   sùùswék*
     cut-AMB.VEN   grass
     'S/he cuts the grass while coming.'

The directionals can have various aspectual meaning extensions (inchoative, distributive, pluractional, etc.; see Payne 2021 for an overview). As one example, in (24b) the itive correlates with, if not imparts, a distributive meaning relative to (24a).[12] Note that the object is the space or container searched, both with and without the directional.

---

[12] Payne (2013: 270–274) discusses frequency of the itive relative to plurality of actions and participants.

(24) Maa
    a. *á-yét*   *e=motí*
        1SG-search.by.feel   FSG=pot
        'I will search the pot' (e.g. with a stick in order to remove something from the pot)

    b. *é-yét-áa*   *ɪl=beniá*
        3-search.by.feel-ITV   MPL=bags
        'S/he will search the bags' (e.g. like a pickpocket or because something is lost)

In EN Ateso and Turkana, the directionals have extended into evidentiality, as they indicate the speaker can attest that something happened towards or away from her/him (Barasa 2017: 161). The directionals are also lexicalized into some verbs. With rare exception, the directionals do not change syntactic valence.

3 Itive and ventive with <AGENT SOURCE/GOAL> transitive verbs

None of the functions introduced in the preceding section would place the Nilotic directionals in the domain of applicatives as often defined (Peterson 2007; Pacchiarotti 2020: 35–56). However, with a certain class of transitive verb roots, the directionals can change the semantic role of the grammatical object but without changing syntactic valence. This corresponds to what Kinkade (1980) and Kiyosawa (2006) call a "redirective" function, and to an applicative according to the definition used in this volume: any derivational morphology occurring on a verb root/stem that has amongst its functions the introduction of a non-ACTOR semantic argument into a main clause. In the case of Maa directionals, this non-ACTOR is a THEME realized syntactically as a core grammatical object which would otherwise not be allowed as a core syntactic argument.

3.1 Demonstrating the phenomenon across the family

The argument-manipulation function arises with verbs such as 'rob (from)', 'sweep (from)', 'weed (from)', 'wring/squeeze (from)', 'throw (at)', 'hit by throwing at', 'spear (into something)', 'search a space by feeling', etc.[13] What is notable about these verbs is that in their simple root form, the clause cannot express a THEME but only what I call a GOAL or SOURCE (see (1a)). Once a directional is added, the derived argument frame has a THEME as the grammatical object, and the GOAL/SOURCE can no longer be expressed as a core argument (though it can be expressed in an optional oblique phrase).

The phenomenon was introduced in (1) above, but we now consider it in more depth. First, the Maa (EN) root *naŋ* 'hit by throwing at' occurs in (25); this is a continuous excerpt from a magical story in which houses and many other typically inanimate items are animated. In (25c), the subject is a 3rd person anaphoric participant, and the definite null object of the transitive verb *naŋ* is the anaphoric GOAL 'house', mentioned in (25a) and (25b). What actually hits the house is not expressed nor anaphorically understood. The 'house' is clearly not the item which is thrown.[14]

(25) Maa
    a. *n-é-jo   á-nyík-ákɪ   ɛnk=áŋ*
       CN1-3-try INF.SG.SBJV-approach-DAT FSG=home
       'He (a warrior) tried to approach to the home'

    b. *n-é-íŋat-áa*
       CN1-3-withdraw-ITV
       'and it (the house) withdrew'

    c. *n-é-naŋ*
       CN1-3-throw.at
       'He (the warrior) hit it (the house, by throwing).' (enamuke2.0049)

In contrast to (25c), in (26) the itive occurs on the same root *naŋ*. Now the object is the THEME, which undergoes movement, and not the GOAL to which the child is thrown. The itive in (26) does not impart distributivity or pluractionality, as only one instance of throwing one child is intended.

---

[13] The directionals do not have this effect with verbs like 'go', 'come' which can have a geographic ('river', 'mountain') or spatial ('there', 'home') GOAL expressed as an unmarked NP. Whether such verbs should be considered a type of (potentially extended) intransitive as opposed to transitive is not clear. A SOURCE with such verbs must occur in an oblique phrase in Maa. In Agar Dinka, GOAL and SOURCE NPs with 'go' and 'leave' occur in locative, allative, or ablative/essive case forms (Andersen 2012).

[14] The verb *a-nyík* 'to approach, meet, be close to' in (25a) is transitive in its simple form. The effect of the dative here is to indicate that the house is reached (or very nearly so), i.e. GOAL-reached.

(26) Maa
í-wa   taá   ɛnâ   kɛráí   shɔ́mɔ   tá-naŋ-á-í
2-take.SBJV EMPH this.F child go.SBJV IMP.SG-throw.at-ITV-SBJV
'Take this child and go throw it (the child) away' (kitejine.040)

The base argument frame of verb roots with which directionals have this effect requires discussion. In their simple form, these roots allow expression of only two arguments. In this paper, a participant conceived of as undergoing (abstract or concrete) translational motion has been identified as a THEME.[15] The non-ACTOR syntactic argument of the relevant roots is not a THEME, but is either a SOURCE from which, or a GOAL to which, an implicit (non-expressable) THEME could be moved. The verbs in question might be considered "surface contact" verbs with an ACTOR and where the "most patient-like" participant (the P in Comrie 1978) is touched on its surface or interior to some degree but the verb does not express a change of location or substantive change of state of the "contacted" P.

One might be tempted to group 'shop' in (1), 'animal' in (30) and 'cloth' in (31a) below, together with the non-ACTORs of verbs like 'burn' and break' – putting them all into a broad "PATIENT" category due to the possibility that a person can be emotionally or otherwise affected by being robbed, a cloth can be completely wrung out, etc. Or one might be tempted to group the non-ACTORs of 'burn' and 'break' into a broad "THEME" category together with translationally moving participants in that the non-ACTOR has metaphorically "gone" to a new state (Dowty 1991: 572). These lumping approaches to what "PATIENT" and/or "THEME" might mean do not account for the nature of the semantic changes effected by the directionals with the Nilotic verbs discussed in this section and in (1). Thus, I distinguish the non-ACTOR objects 'shop' in (1), 'animal' in (30), 'cloth' (31a), etc. as SOURCE or GOAL depending on the verb, while THEME refers more narrowly to a (concretely or figuratively) moving or moved participant.

Example (27a) might initially suggest that a more general notion of LOCATION is perhaps pertinent to the verb set in question, rather than specifically SOURCE (or GOAL). However, when the directionals are added, as in (27b–c), it shows that the concept of SOURCE is indeed part of the base argument frame in (27a), as the notion of something being 'removed from' a bag (not just moved around in or inserted into) results.

---

15 The THEME role also includes a participant in a state or location (Gruber 1965). Even this broader THEME category differs from the much broader use of the term THEME found in Dowty (1991) and Kiyosawa (2006).

(27) Maa
    a. *á-yét-íta*   *ɔl=béné*
        1SG-search.by.feel-PROG   MSG=bag/pocket
        'I am searching inside the bag.'

    b. *á-yét-ʊ*   *ɪn=kírí*   *tɛ*   *móti*
        1SG-search.by.feel-VEN   FPL=meats   OBL   pot
        'I will remove the meats (out) from the pot.'

    c. *k=é-yét-áa*   *i=ropiyani*
        CN2=3-search.by.feel-ITV   FPL=money
        'S/he picks pockets.' (lit. 'S/he removes money [from things]')

When a directional occurs on a verb of this class, the SOURCE or GOAL of the base argument frame may be simply absent from the clause, or occasionally is expressed as an oblique, as in (1b) above. But another – infrequent – strategy at least in Maa is to employ a directional along with the instrumental applicative, in a kind of "double applicative" derived verb. This is seen in (28). Here the itive derives an <ACTOR THEME> frame, with 'bags' as the THEME object. The instrumental applicative then allows (re-)addition of the SOURCE as a core argument, which here is the 1SG participant. Recall that the instrumental applicative allows a range of interpretations including some locative notions (though not GOAL, as the dative applicative covers the GOAL semantic space).

(28) Maa
     áa-purr-or-ié   *ɔl=mʊrraní*   *im=beniá*
     3>1SG-rob-ITV-INST   MSG=warrior.NOM   FPL=bags
     'The warrior will steal the bags from me.'

In other EN languages, directionals likely have similar effects with similar verbs. Though information in available grammars is scarce, the following from Lopit is suggestive. In (29), the root *idoŋ* with no directional is glossed as 'throw at' and *múnú* 'snake' is the GOAL, not the item thrown. But in various tables throughout Moodie (2019), *idoŋ* is glossed just as 'throw' including when it carries the itive.

(29) Lopit (EN; Moodie 2019: 276)
     è-ŋà-dúm-ú   *íŋé*   *mórwó*   *x-o-îdóŋ*   *múnú*
     3-PFV-take-VEN   3SG.NOM   stone.ABS   SEQ-3-PFV.throw.at   snake.ABS
     'He took a stone and threw it at the snake'

Pragmatically, the extent to which the non-ACTOR argument of a basic <ACTOR SOURCE/GOAL> verb is interpreted as undergoing a change-of-state is rather contextually or situationally dependent. Consider the examples in (30) from Agar Dinka. Recall that Agar Dinka marks a pronominal subject by a verb inflection if the pre-verbal Topic is the grammatical object. In (30), all verbs carry subject inflection, thus all equally treating the pre-verb words as grammatical objects. In (30a) with the simple verb form, the preverbal object is the entity which receives the spear in its body. In (30b–c) with the directional verb forms, the preverbal object is the spear which undergoes movement. One might opine that the animal is PATIENT in (30a), not GOAL, because the animal must be affected by the spearing. But the animal is clearly an intended endpoint (GOAL) of the spearing trajectory and this verb behaves like other <AGENT SOURCE/GOAL> verbs surveyed in this section relative to the effect of the directionals. Importantly, note that the examples in (30) differ from (4) above with circumstantial-Topics, where the pronominal subjects are free pronouns in the genitive case.

(30) Agar Dinka (Andersen 1992–1994: 31)
    a.   *lâj*   *à-tèer*
         animal   D-spear:3SG
         'He is spearing an animal'

    b.   *tòŋ*   *à-téer*
         spear   D-spear:ITV:3SG
         'He is throwing a spear thither'

    c.   *tòŋ*   *à-tèer*
         spear   D-spear:VEN:3SG
         'He is throwing a spear hither'

The examples in (31) have subject-verb-object order and hence no marking of subject on the verb. But the example set nevertheless shows the argument-manipulation effects of the itive and ventive derivations. In (31a), *ɲiàc* 'squeeze, wring' carries no directional, and 'cloth' (the item squeezed) is the object. Though one might argue that the cloth is affected, it really does not undergo a substantive change in state. The itive occurs on 'squeeze' in (31b), and the ventive occurs in (31c). With these derived stems, the object must be the THEME that undergoes movement out of the cloth. Regardless of the specific directional, the now-implicit item that is "squeezed" must be the SOURCE from which the water flows; the different directionals show the differing directions of the flow.

(31) Agar Dinka (Andersen 1992–1994: 10)
    a. ti̭ik   a̱-ṋia̠c   a̠la̠a̱t
       woman D-squeeze cloth
       'The woman is wringing the cloth.'

    b. ti̭ik   a̱-ṋiɛ́ɛc   pî̭iw
       woman D-squeeze:ITV water
       'The woman is squeezing out water thither.'

    c. ti̭ik   a̱-ṋiɛ̠ec   pî̭iw
       woman D-squeeze:VEN water
       'The woman is squeezing out water hither.'

The following shows similar facts with an <ACTOR GOAL> root.

(32) Agar Dinka (Andersen 1992–1994: 10)
    a. dɔ̠̂ɔk a̱-bo̠k   dí̠t
       boy D-throw bird
       'The boy is throwing at the bird'

    b. dɔ̠̂ɔk a̱-bó̠ok   doo̠ot
       boy D-throw:ITV stone
       'The boy is throwing a stone thither.'

    c. dɔ̠̂ɔk a̱-bo̠ok   doo̠ot
       boy D-throw:VEN stone
       'The boy is throwing a stone hither.'

The examples in (33) show the same argument-manipulation effect with an <AGENT SOURCE> root in Mabaan, another WN language.

(33) Mabaan (WN; Andersen 1999: 109)
    a. ʔέkkèn ʔʌ̄n   wiiêj-έ
       3PL house sweep-PST.3PL.3
       'They swept the house'

    b. ʔέkkèn ɉ̂ik-én   wiiêc-έ
       3PL rubbish-PL sweep:ITV-PST.3PL.3
       'They swept the rubbish (into something)'

    c. ʔέkkèn ɉ̂ik-én   wêɛw-w-έ
       3PL rubbish-PL sweep-VEN-PST.3PL.3
       'They swept the rubbish hither'

Analogously to the preceding EN and WN examples, in (34a) from SN Nandi, *sè:sé:t* 'dog' is the GOAL object of the throwing action and does not undergo movement; it is implicit that something is thrown, but this is not expressed. In (34b) with the itive, *koytà* 'stone' is the THEME object that undergoes movement.

(34) Nandi (Creider 2002: 184)
    a. *ke:-wi:r*   *sè:sé:t*
       INF-throw.at   dog
       'to throw at the dog'

    b. *ke:-wi:r-tá*   *koytà*
       INF-throw.at-ITV stone
       'to throw the stone thither'

It is not clear how robust or productive the redirection is of the object from SOURCE/GOAL to THEME in the Datooga branch of SN, but Stefan Bruckhaus (personal communication) reports that in Barbayiiga/Gisamjanga Datooga, the root *jagwad* 'rob, steal from' has a default SOURCE as the grammatical direct object, while the ventive derivation *jagwad-un* is glossed as 'steal something and bring'. This suggests that the ventive both yields associated motion and redirects the direct object from SOURCE to THEME.[16] Section 4 will further elaborate on applicative effects of the directionals within SN.

In sum, if one function of applicatives is to manipulate the semantic role of the grammatical object (if the base verb is already transitive; cf. Kiyosawa 2006, Pacchiarotti 2020: 35), then in this respect the Nilotic directionals share a significant function of applicatives. What is unusual relative to typical definitions of applicatives, however, is that the directionals bring in a THEME argument as the applied object in place of the core SOURCE/GOAL. We will explore this further in the next section.

3.2 Accounting for the applicative-like function of Nilotic directionals: Typology and theory

We now address the directional function demonstrated in Section 3.1 relative to what Kiyosawa (2006; following Kinkade 1980) calls "redirective applicatives",

---

[16] Bruckhaus notes that the itive derivation is not possible with *jagwad*. Conceivably this is due to semantic pre-emption if the root already has some implicit idea of movement away from a source.

the "profiling" of participants (Goldberg 1995), and to what Lehmann & Verhoeven (2006) call "extraversion".

In discussing Salishan languages, Kiyosawa (2006: 4, 144–149) defines redirective applicatives as those that apply to a transitive base and "redirect" the semantics of the direct object "from the theme to a semantically oblique nominal" (p. 144), without affecting syntactic valence.[17] The new applied object may be a "dative" (i.e., the GOAL or target of an action), BENEFICIARY, POSSESSOR, or SOURCE.

Kiyosawa notes that Salishan languages generally allow only two syntactic arguments in a clause. The Salishan verbs on which redirective applicatives operate are syntactically transitive both before and after the applicative is added, and include a wide range of transitive verb types. But in contrast to the syntax, Kiyosawa states that the redirective applicatives allow for an "increase in the semantic valence of the verb" (p. 145) as they create situations that may semantically involve three participants. For example, in Central Salishan languages, three unmarked core nominals are not allowed in a clause, and even semantically ditransitive verbs like 'give' will carry a redirective applicative; the RECIPIENT is the default syntactic object, and the THEME is in an oblique phrase.[18]

The interaction of the Nilotic directionals with <ACTOR SOURCE/GOAL> verbs discussed in this paper is like the Salishan "redirective applicative" situation in that the relevant roots/stems are transitive both before and after adding the directional/applicative, and the effect of the directional/applicative is to change the semantic role of the grammatical object. But Nilotic and Salishan differ in that the Nilotic phenomenon redirects the grammatical object to a THEME, while the Salishan one redirects the grammatical object to a GOAL, BENEFICIARY, POSSESSOR, or SOURCE. The latter are the sorts of roles classically expected to be newly mapped to object by applicatives. But I would put forward that if the basic role frame of a verb is <ACTOR SOURCE> or <ACTOR GOAL>, then for such a verb a THEME role might well be peripheral.

One might well opine that it is impossible to have a SOURCE or GOAL in the frame of a verb without also having a THEME in the scene; but this does not resolve what is syntactically core versus peripheral for a given root. For an analogy to the problem, consider the English verb *cut*. I contend that it is difficult for an ACTOR

---

[17] Comrie (1985: 314) uses the term "valency-rearrangement" for changes in the semantic role of transitive verbs. I eschew the term "valency-rearrangement" for the Nilotic phenomenon because the verb root/stem is syntactically transitive both with and without the directional. Thus, there is no "rearrangement" of syntactic valence – only of what is mapped to the transitive object.

[18] Kiyosawa (2006: 1) defines "theme" as the combination of the "patient of transitive verbs and also the object [i.e., item – DP] being transferred in a ditransitive". This is a broader definition of THEME than the one used in this paper.

to 'cut' an item (the P) without the involvement of an INSTRUMENT. In *Johann cut the bread, Samantha cut the cloth*, or *I cut my finger* an instrument is part of the CUT "frame" in the script or scenario sense of Fillmore (1982) – even if it is not spelled out as to whether the INSTRUMENT is a knife, a pair of scissors, or broken glass. But despite the CUT-scenario evoking (or priming) an INSTRUMENT, it does not necessarily follow that the English verb *cut* is lexicalized as having INSTRUMENT as part of its core syntactic argument frame. That is, there is potentially a difference between what participant types are scene-evoked versus what are lexically subcategorized as part of the core argument frame of the underived verb root. The latter interacts with the morphosyntactic clause construction(s) in which that underived or basic verb form can be used.

A second model for thinking about what is going on with these Nilotic verbs and directionals draws on the concept of what is merely within a verb's argument (or possibly script) frame versus what is "profiled" in that frame (Langacker 1987, Goldberg 1995). I agree that it is impossible for a SOURCE/GOAL to conceptually exist without a THEME: the very notion of SOURCE means that something moves or emanates from it, and the very notion of GOAL means that something moves to or approaches it (literally or metaphorically). We might, then, suggest that the relevant Nilotic verbs have <ACTOR **THEME SOURCE/GOAL**> elements in their frame, but that the bolded elements are what are cognitively profiled for these verbs; the difference in what is profiled is also part of what is lexicalized. For example, English *rob* and *steal* both have ACTOR, THEME, and SOURCE elements in their frames, but *rob* profiles the ACTOR/thief and the person or establishment (from which something is taken), while *steal* profiles the ACTOR/thief and item taken (from someone or somewhere).

While not discussed in terms of profiling, Lehmann & Verhoeven's (2006) analysis of Yucatec Mayan "extraversion" is conceptually somewhat similar. In Yucatec Maya, Lehmann & Verhoeven contend that some active syntactically intransitive roots have an implicit THEME or PATIENT, in addition to an AGENT. The relevant verbs express such concepts as 'write, sweep, weed, shell, borrow/lend, haul water, pull on a rope, dissolve, make tortilla, stir' and many others. For example, a PATIENT would be intrinsic to the intransitive verb 'make tortilla'; a THEME would be intrinsic to the intransitive verb 'pull on a rope', etc.[19] They further assert that since this implicit participant is a THEME or PATIENT, it is perforce a "central participant" inherent to the scene or event.

---

19 They suggest these verbs may derive historically from nominal roots, which perhaps accounts for their intransitivity. They also analyze some Oceanic languages as allowing extraversion with intransitive verbs.

Lehmann & Verhoeven's analysis is motivated by a transitivizing morpheme -*t* which can be added to various syntactically intransitive roots and which, in the majority of cases, adds a THEME or PATIENT.[20] They suggest that this THEME/PATIENT is in fact implicit but has now been exteriorized. The extraversion objects have properties of full objects (in contrast to cognate objects of verbs like 'dream (a dream)', 'cough (a cough)' in some languages, which lack all the properties of full grammatical objects). Furthermore, -*t* is said to also be able to exteriorize STIMULUS, PATH, GOAL, SOURCE, PLACE, BENEFICIARY, ADDRESSEE, and RECIPIENT, but in many fewer cases than THEME and PATIENT. More specifically, Lehmann & Verhoeven allow that implicit roles with (presumably all intransitive) verb types might include:

- STIMULUS with experiential verbs
- ADDRESSEE or THEME with communication verbs
- PLACE, GOAL or SOURCE with position and motion verbs

An example set illustrating extraversion is in (35). Note that the exteriorized phrase cannot be expressed in an adjoined (oblique) phrase.

(35) Yucatec Maya (Lehmann & Verhoeven 2006: 471)

a. *láahk'iin   táan   u   che'h*
    all.day   PROG   SUBJ.3   laugh
    'he laughs the whole day.'

b. *t-in   che'h-t-ah   in   wíits'in*
    PFV-SUBJ.1SG   laugh-TRR-CMPL   POSS.1SG   younger.sibling
    'I laughed at/derided my younger sibling.'

c. **h   che'h-nah-en   ti'   in   wíits'in*
    PFV   laugh-CMPL-ABS.1SG   LOC   POSS.1SG   younger.sibling
    intended: 'I laughed at/about my younger sibling'

The Yucatec Maya -*t* can behave as a classic applicative with "prototypically" peripheral participants (LOCATIVES, ADDRESSEES, participants toward which action is directed such as 'laugh/cry/complain/growl about or at'). In Lehmann & Verhoeven's analysis, what differentiates true applicatives from extraversion is that the former are propositionally completely synonymous with clauses that contain the peripheral participant in an oblique phrase. Extraversion, in their analysis, does

---

[20] The transitivizing -*t* can also be added to various other root types, but always yields a transitive stem.

not involve an alternation with a supposedly peripheral participant in an oblique phrase. An example set illustrating what they consider the applicative use of *-t* is in (36).

(36) Yucatec Maya (Lehmann & Verhoeven 2006: 471)
 a. *táan u bin bàab (ich le ha'-o')*
    PROG SUBJ.3 go swim in DEF water-DIST
    'he is going to swim (in the water)'
 b. *táan u bin u bàab-t le ha'-o'*
    PROG SUBJ.3 go SUBJ.3 swim-TRR(SBJV) DEF water-DIST
    'he is going to swim in the water'

Lehmann & Verhoeven restrict extraversion to intransitive bases, while they state that applicatives can apply to either intransitive or transitive bases. Though they allow that *either* ADDRESSEE or THEME might be implicit with communication verbs, they curiously do not consider that THEME could also be an implicitly lexicalized participant of a syntactically transitive verb root. To more or less extend the extraversion analysis to the Nilotic case, one would need to add something like the following to the inventory of verbs with implicit roles.
 – GOAL/SOURCE or THEME with 'removal' and 'caused-motion' (transitive) verbs

How the idea of an implicit role in Lehmann & Verhoeven's (2006) sense might be like a contained but non-profiled role in Goldberg's (1995) sense merits further investigation.

4 Origins and further development of applicative uses of the directionals

Whether the Nilotic directionals come historically from verbs has not been determined.[21] However, verbal sources would not be surprising (also for the SN ambulative) given their associated motion function; and if so, the cognitive basis for their argument manipulation function would find a ready explanation.

As noted in Section 2.3, literal associated motion necessarily involves the notion of a participant moving through space (translational motion). By definition,

---

21 Heine & Claudi (1986: 71) suggest the ventive derives from a Proto-EN verb **buon* (SG) /**puon-tu* (PL) meaning 'come'. This is speculative and cognates of the EN ventive clearly occur in SN.

such a participant is a THEME (Gruber 1965, Jackendoff 1972: 39). This is seen with the itive and ventive in (22) above: by itself, the Bari root *mɛt* 'watch' does not imply movement of either of its two participants, but the directional stem entails that the grammatical object *Wani* moves away or towards the point of reference.

Examples like (22) do not show the redirective applicative function of the directional, but only directed associated motion. However, since translational motion entails a moving THEME, both the associated motion and introduction of a THEME make sense if the directionals come from old translational motion roots. When a translational motion morpheme (whether a verb root or an associated motion derivation) is combined with an <AGENT SOURCE/GOAL> verb root – which at most has an implicit but not profiled THEME – the result is that a moving-THEME is then profiled to the extent that it becomes part of the core argument frame of the verb.

What is not directly explained by this scenario is why the Nilotic derived directional stems should remain transitive instead of becoming ditransitive, given that some Maa verb roots allow up to three arguments (see (12)). However, the directionals are not generally transitivizing morphemes. For instance, the Anywa verbs in (20) are intransitive both before and after adding a directional. Thus, we may suggest that the directionals semantically profile THEME+direction, but are not primarily syntactic valence manipulating devices.

Another bit of mystery is why SN languages (unlike EN and WN) require a specifically 'ambulative' morpheme, in addition to but historically parsable from the directionals, for associated motion. The answer might be hinted at by what we find in EN Maa, where corpus study shows that though the directionals certainly can add associated motion to a clause, this is not synchronically their most frequent function (Payne 2021). Conceivably the loss of a 'translational motion' feature from the directionals might have extended further in SN, to the point that when communication of 'translational motion' was desired, it had to be reinforced by an additional explicit 'ambulative' morpheme. Regardless, the directionals have kept their [+THEME-profiling] feature with a particular class of transitive roots in languages like Nandi, even if the [+MOTION] feature has faded.

In some SN languages, the directionals have extended to broader applicative-related functions, though detailed information remains somewhat limited and there are interesting person-related restrictions.

First, in some SN languages, the directionals have developed a transitivizing function on at least some occasions. For Asimjeeg Datooga, Griscom (2019) finds that the itive *-d(a) ~ -d(i)* and ventive *-n(i) ~ -u(n)* sometimes add new participants to a clause. In Tugen (Kalenjin sub-branch), Jerono (2019: 131) finds that the ventive turns intransitive *week* 'return' into transitive 'return something'.

The SN directionals are also developing toward adding so-called "peripheral" roles to the clause. In Asimjeeg Datooga, the ventive has BENEFICIARY effects but just with 1SG and 2SG applied objects. Consider the commercial transaction verb *ʃa* in (37). In (37a), the verb lacks a directional and has a 1SG subject and 3SG object. There is no explicit directionality or associated motion, and the sense is 'buy'. In (37b) the itive directional is added, and the effect is that the action proceeds away from the 1st person deictic center, hence the translation of 'sell'. In (37c), the ventive occurs with the effect that 'buying' is interpreted as for the benefit of the 1SG participant. The person-sensitive nature of this benefactive extension is interesting but quite straightforward, as something 'coming' toward speech act participants may be evaluated to being to their benefit (or, I surmise, possibly their detriment in some circumstances). Note that the BENEFACTEE (or GOAL) in (37c) is treated as the primary object, being indexed by an object suffix on the verb.

(37) Asimjeeg Datooga (Griscom 2019: 225–226)
    a. *g-ì-dà-ʃà*   *déː-d* ...
       AFF-FUT-1SG-buy   COW-SS.SG
       'I will buy a cow ...'

    b. *q-àː-ʃà-d*   *dájéːg*   *íːjèɲ*
       AFF-1SG-buy-ITV   kid/lamb:PS.PL:SS.PL   two
       'I sold two baby goats.'

    c. *g-éː-ʃà-n-àːn*   *háŋ-d*
       AFF-IMPS-buy-VEN-1SG   shawl-SS.SG
       'I was bought a shawl.'

In contrast to 1st and 2nd person, 3rd person BENEFICIARIES are expressed by cognates of the pan-Nilotic dative applicative. This is found in Datooga varieties (Griscom 2019: 222–223; Bruckhaus 2021; both of whom use the term "terminative"), and in Kalenjin varieties (Creider & Creider 1989: 99, who use the term "indirect object" for Nandi).

In SN, the itive directional has extended to expressing applied-INSTRUMENT and applied-COMITATIVE phrases. Griscom (2019: 226) finds that in Asimjeeg Datooga, the itive allows expression of a 3rd person INSTRUMENT, as in (38).

(38) Asimjeeg Datooga (Griscom 2019: 226)
    m-à-nd-án   *gísír-dʒ-àn-d*   *m-ɛɛː-bár-dà*
    NEG-3-COP-OBL   hoe-PS.SG-PS.SG-SS.SG   NEG-IMPS-hit-ITV
    'There weren't any hoes, they weren't used to farm.' (lit. they weren't hit with)

In Nandi, the itive has extended to also express COMITATIVE meaning while also increasing valence. In (39a), there is no directional but the transitive root *nam* 'grasp, hold' has a (possibly moving) THEME. In (39b), *nam* occurs with the itive, and the clause is now ditransitive. 'Pot' would be the base THEME, while according to Creider 'cloth' is a COMITATIVE argument licensed by the itive.

(39) Nandi (Creider 2002: 182)
    a. *nam   la:kwé:t*
       grasp   child
       'Catch the child!'

    b. *nam-té   sapúryé:t inkoryê:t*
       grasp-ITV:COM pot   cloth
       'Hold the pot together with a cloth!' (so it doesn't burn you)

Though one might debate whether 'cloth' in (39) is COMITATIVE versus INSTRUMENT, the following are quite convincing about extension to a COMITATIVE sense because 'clothes' are not really a means of carrying out the action of sleeping, but rather just a concomitant of the person sleeping, and vegetables are a concomitant of bread.

(40) Nandi (Creider 2002: 183)
    ke:-ru-ta   ínkoráî:k
    INF-sleep-ITV:COM clothes
    'to sleep with clothes on'

(41) Nandi (Creider & Creider 1989: 127)
    á-ám-ta-e   kímyé:t   íngkwê:k
    1SG-eat-ITV-IPFV bread   vegetables
    'I'll eat bread with vegetables.'

The COMITATIVE extension conceivably developed from conceptualizing a THEME as 'moving along with' other participant(s) in the event, and then further to simply being 'with' them as a possible [+MOTION] meaning component was dropped from the directional.

To summarize, the BENEFICIARY, INSTRUMENT and COMITATIVE extensions of the directionals in SN start to look more like the semantic profile of classic applicatives typologically. An item moved (THEME) in an (erstwhile) movement co-event is used to carry out the lexical event, and hence becomes an INSTRUMENT; or it simply goes along with or is together with other participants and hence becomes a COMITATIVE. An item moved toward the deictic center is interpreted as being for the benefit of the participant at the deictic center, and hence becomes a BENEFICIARY. Further, at least some instances of SN directionals have taken on valence-increasing functions, as both the base and applied objects can co-occur in the clause with neither in an oblique form.

5 Conclusions

A comprehensive typology of any phenomenon should address the boundaries and the prototype of the posited phenomenon, even if these cannot be sharply defined given normal processes of human cognition at play in language change. One criterion usually put forward for identifying applicatives is that they introduce peripheral semantic roles as applied phrases, such as BENEFICIARY, INSTRUMENT, LOCATION, POSSESSOR, REASON, MANNER. If one proposes a semantic map for the applicative domain, derivations that add a THEME as applied object would not be part of the prototype of the category– if on the map at all – given typical (but I suggest not sufficiently examined) suppositions about what is peripheral to the argument frame of a particular verb. Lehmann and Verhoeven (2006) suggest that the Yucatec Mayan "extraversion" construction is not an applicative because it introduces a THEME, and not a semantically peripheral participant which can be synonymously expressed in an oblique phrase. This begs the question of what "semantically peripheral" means. Lehmann and Verhoeven suggest that a central participant is inherent in the concept of the predicate, such that if it is subtracted from the predicate meaning, the same predicate concept no longer obtains. It is important to note, however, that Lehmann & Verhoven (2006: 488) emphasize that "In purely structural terms and disregarding paraphrase relationships, extraversion and applicative formation are the same thing. We have repeatedly emphasized that the distinction we are making is gradual."[22]

The construction explored in this paper differs from Lehmann & Verhoeven (2006)'s extraversive in that they identify an extraversive as applying solely to active syntactically intransitive roots, with a range of possible semantic roles for the implicit participant including but not limited to THEME. The Nilotic verb roots discussed here raise the question of why this sort of thing should be *a priori*

---

[22] Lehmann & Verhoeven (2006: 488) say that applicative formation "is a syntactic process marked on the verb" while extraversion is "a lexical process with syntactic consequences". I find this to be quite a theory-bound distinction, especially given how even classic applicatives can become highly lexicalized into certain stems (see also Chapter 6 of Pacchiarotti 2020).

limited to intransitives, and also raise the issue of differences in what is lexically profiled. I have suggested that the relevant Nilotic verbs have an <ACTOR SOURCE/GOAL> frame in terms of what is profiled. Though a THEME is not profiled as part of their basic lexical meaning, it is certainly latent or implicit in the event scenario, given that SOURCE/GOAL cannot exist without the notion of a THEME. For instance, the Maa root *purr* 'rob' profiles an actor and a deprived participant, and not an item taken from the deprived participant; but to understand that someone is deprived, there must also be the implication that something is taken from or denied to them.

I have suggested that development of the applicative(-like) function of Nilotic directionals may have crucially ridden on their associated motion function. What looks somewhat like "extraversion" in Nilotic seems to be an epiphenomenal result of what associated motion is primarily about: a participant moving through space, which by definition is THEME. When THEME is implicit but perhaps not profiled in the lexical meaning of a verb, an associated-motion directional has the effect of profiling it at the expense of a SOURCE/GOAL which is also part of the verb's meaning. The applicative(-like) function of Nilotic directionals appears to apply only to a subset of transitive roots in EN and WN branches, yielding transitive stems with THEME-objects. But in SN languages this may be broadening towards more traditional notions of what classic applicatives do.

Abbreviations

ABS	absolutive/unmarked case form
AFF	affirmative
AMB	ambulative
BEN	benefactive
CMPL	completive
CN	connective
COM	comitative
CONJ	conjunction
COP	copula
D	declarative
DAT	dative
DEF	definite
DIST	distal
EMPH	emphatic
EN	Eastern Nilotic
F	feminine
FPL	feminine plural
FSG	feminine singular

FUT	future
GEN	genitive
IMP	imperative
IMPS	impersonal
INF	infinitive
INST	instrument
INV	inverse
IPFV	imperfective
ITV	itive
ITV.M	monovalent itive
LOC	locative
M	masculine
MPL	masculine plural
MSG	masculine singular
NEG	negative
NF	non-finite
NOM	nominative
NTS	non-topical subject
OBL	oblique
PF	perfect
PFV	perfective
PL	plural
POSS	possessive
PREP	preposition
PROG	progressive
PS	primary suffix
PST	past
REL	relativizer/relative clause
SBJV	subjunctive
SEQ	sequential
SG	singular
SN	Southern Nilotic
SS	secondary suffix
SUBJ	subject
TRR	transitivizer
VEN	ventive
VEN.M	monovalent ventive
WN	Western Nilotic

References

Andersen, Torben. 1992–1994. Morphological stratification in Dinka: On the alternations of voice quality, vowel length and tone in the morphology of transitive verbal roots in a monosyllabic language. *Studies in African Linguistics* 23(1). 1–63.

Andersen, Torben. 1999. Vowel quality alternation in Mabaan and its Western Nilotic history. *Journal of African Languages and Linguistics* 20. 97–120.

Andersen, Torben. 2012. Spatial roles and verbal directionality in Dinka. *Journal of African Languages and Linguistics* 33. 143–179. DOI 10.1515/jall-2012-0007.

Barasa, David. 2017. *Ateso grammar*. Munich: Lincom.

Bruckhaus, Stefan. 2021. *Lexico-grammar of motion in Barbayiiga and Gisamjanga (Datooga)*. Hamburg: University of Hamburg dissertation.

Comrie, Bernard. 1978. Ergativity. In Winfred Lehmann (ed.), *Syntactic typology: Studies in the phenomenology of language*, 329–394. Austin: University of Texas Press.

Comrie, Bernard. 1985. Causative verb formation and other verb-deriving morphology. In Timothy Shopen (ed.), *Language typology and syntactic description, Vol. III: Grammatical categories and the lexicon*, 309–348. Cambridge: Cambridge University Press.

Creider, Chet. 2002. The semantics of participant types in derived verbs in Nandi. *Revue québécoise de linguistique* 31. 171–190.

Creider, Chet & Jane Tapsubei Creider. 1989. *A grammar of Nandi*. Hamburg: Helmut Buske Verlag.

Dimmendaal, Gerrit. 1983. *The Turkana language*. Dordrecht: Foris.

Dimmendaal, Gerrit. 2009. Datives in Nilotic in a typological perspective. *Afrikanistik Aegyptologie Online*. https://www.afrikanistik-aegyptologie-online.de/archiv/2009/2355. urn:nbn:de:0009-10-23558.

Dowty, David. 1991. Thematic proto-roles and argument selection. *Language* 67(3). 547–619.

Dryer, Matthew. 1986. Primary objects, secondary objects, and antidative. *Language* 62(4). 808–845.

Fillmore, Charles. 1982. Frame semantics. In Linguistics Society of Korea (eds.), *Linguistics in the morning calm*, 111–137. Seoul: Hanshin.

Goldberg, Adele. 1995. *Constructions: A construction grammar approach to argument structure*. Chicago: University of Chicago Press.

Griscom, Richard. 2019. *Topics in Asimjeeg Datooga verbal morphosyntax*. Eugene: University of Oregon dissertation.

Gruber, Jeffrey. 1965. *Studies in lexical relations*. Cambridge, Ma.: MIT dissertation.

Guillaume, Antoine. 2016. Associated motion in South America: Typological and areal perspectives. *Linguistic Typology* 20(1). 81–177.

Heine, Bernd & Ulrike Claudi. 1986. *On the rise of grammatical categories: Some examples from Maa*. Berlin: Dietrich Reimer.

Jackendoff, Ray. 1972. *Semantic interpretation in Generative Grammar*. Cambridge, Ma.: MIT Press.

Jerono, Prisca 2019. Typology of motion events in Tugen. *Lodz Papers in Pragmatics* 15. 123–139. DOI: 10.1515/lpp-2019-000.

Karani, Michael. 2018. *Syntactic categories and the verb-argument complex in Parakuyo Maasai*. Stellenbosch: Stellenbosch University dissertation. http://hdl.handle.net/10019.1/103451

Kawachi, Kazuhiro. 2011. Meanings of the spatial deictic verb suffixes in Kupsapiny, the Southern Nilotic language of the Sebei region of Uganda. In Osamu Hieda (ed.), *Descriptive studies of Nilotic languages*, 65–107. (Studies in Nilotic Linguistics 3). Tokyo: Research Institute for Languages and Cultures of Asia and Africa.

Kinkade, M. Dale. 1980. Columbian Salish -xí, -ɬ, -túɬ. *International Journal of American Linguistics* 46. 33–36.

Kiyosawa, Kaoru. 2006. *Applicatives in Salish languages*. Vancouver: Simon Fraser University dissertation.
Koch, Harold. 1984. The category of "associated motion" in Kaytej. *Language in Central Australia* 1. 23–34.
Köhler, Oswin. 1955. *Geschichte der Erforschung der nilotischen Sprachen. Afrika und Übersee, Beiheft 28*. Berlin: D. Reimer.
König, Christa. 2008. *Case in Africa*. Oxford: Oxford University Press.
Langacker, Ronald. 1987. *Foundations of Cognitive Grammar*. Stanford: Stanford University Press.
Lehmann, Christian & Elisabeth Verhoeven. 2006. Extraversive transitivization in Yucatec Maya and the nature of the applicative. In Leonid Kulikov, Andrej Malchukov & Peter de Swart (ed.), *Case, valency and transitivity*, 465–493. Amsterdam: JohnBenjamins.
Mietzner, Angelika. 2009. *Raumliche Orientierung in nilotischen Sprachen*. Cologne: Rüdiger Köppe.
Mietzner, Angelika. 2016. *Cherang'any, a Kalenjin language of Kenya*. Cologne: Rüdiger Köppe.
Moodie, Jonathan. 2019. *A grammar of the Lopit language*. Melbourne: University of Melbourne dissertation.
Moodie, Jonathan and Rosey Billington. 2020. *A grammar of Lopit: An Eastern Nilotic language of South Sudan*. Leiden: Brill.
Pacchiarotti, Sara. 2020. *Bantu applicative constructions*. (Stanford Monographs in African Languages). Stanford: CSLI.
Payne, Doris L. 2013. The challenge of Maa 'away'. In Tim Thornes, Erik Andvik, Gwendolyn Hyslop & Joana Jansen (eds.), *Functional-historical approaches to explanation: In honor of Scott DeLancey*, 259–282. Amsterdam: John Benjamins.
Payne, Doris L. 2015. Perspectives on Nilotic verb composition: Why can't we agree on the Maa verb? In Angelika Mietzner & Anne Storch (eds.), *Nilo-Saharan – Models and Descriptions*, 211–229. Cologne: Rudiger Köppe.
Payne, Doris L. 2021. The extension of "associated motion" to aspect and argument structure in Nilotic languages. In Antoine Guillaume & Harold Koch (eds.), *Associated motion*, 695–746. Berlin: De Gruyter Mouton.
Payne, Doris L. 2022. Proximal to distal: Information flow and order in Maa. Word Order Variation: Semitic, Turkic and Indo-European Languages in Contact (*Studia Typologica 31*), Edited by: Hiwa Asadpour and Thomas Jügel, 15–38. Berlin: de Gruyter Mouton.
Payne, Doris L., Mitsuyo Hamaya & Peter Jacobs. 1994. Active, inverse, and passive in Maasai. In Talmy Givón (ed.), *Voice in Discourse*, 283–315. Amsterdam: John Benjamins.
Peterson, David. 2007. *Applicative constructions*. Oxford: Oxford University Press.
Reh, Mechthild. 1996. *Anywa language*. Köln: Rüdiger Köppe.
Reid, Tatiana. 2010. *Aspects of phonetics, phonology and morphophonology of Thok Reel*. Edinburgh: University of Edinburgh dissertation.
Remijsen, Bert & Otto Gwado Ayoker. 2020. Forms and functions of the associated-motion derivations of Shilluk transitive verbs. In Bert Remijsen & Otto Gwado Ayoker, *A grammar of Shilluk*, Chapter 3, 1–59. (Language Documentation & Conservation, Special Publication 14.) University of Hawaii. http://hdl.handle.net/10125/24779
Remijsen, Bert, Cynthia Miller-Naudé & Leoma Gilley. 2016. The morphology of Shilluk transitive verbs. *Journal of African Languages and Linguistics* 37. 201–245.
Rottland, Franz. 1982. *Die südnilotischen Sprachen: Beschreibung, Vergleichung und Rekonstruktion*. (Kölner Beiträge zur Afrikanistik 7). Berlin: Dietrich Reimer.

Schroeder, Martin. 1999. *Dictionary, Toposa-English, English-Toposa*. (Bilingual Dictionaries of Sudan 2, Summer Institute of Linguistics – Sudan). Nairobi: SIL International.

Spagnolo, Lorenzo M. 1933. *Bari grammar*. Verona: Missioni africane.

Tucker, Archibald N. & John T. O. Mpaayei. 1955. *Maasai grammar – with vocabulary*. London: Longman, Green.

Zwarts, Joos. 2004. *The phonology of Endo*. (LINCOM Studies in African Linguistics 59). Munich: Lincom.

Part III: **Asia (including the Middle East)**

Shuan Osman Karim and Ali Salehi
10 An applicative analysis of Soranî "absolute prepositions"

Abstract: Soranî (Central Kurdish) possesses a set of formatives of (pro)nominal and adpositional origin that combine with a verbal stem to introduce an additional pronominal indexed argument. Based on the definition used in this volume, these formatives fit neatly under the umbrella of applicative markers. However, they have only recently been described as such (Karim and Salehi 2020). Instead, traditional grammars have labeled these formatives "absolute prepositions," a term that acknowledges their sometimes adpositional origin and their phonological similarity to synchronic adpositions. This study outlines the distribution of Soranî applicatives, their integration into the alignment system, and the formal differences between adpositional phrases and applicative constructions. Additionally, we provide a diachronic account of Soranî applicative markers. We show that they are likely just the latest stage in a grammaticalization cycle which took place several times in the history of Soranî.

1 Introduction

Although only recently described as such (e.g., Karim and Salehi 2020), Soranî[1] possesses a rich system of applicative markers. In this study[2], we show how morphemes

---

[1] The term Soranî is often used interchangeably with Central Kurdish. However, we use the term Soranî in a narrow sense to refer to the Central Kurdish variety of Suleymanî (Iraq) and Bane (Iran). All Kurdish examples are given in the native orthography. Examples from other modern languages are written in the script employed in the source text. Examples from Ancient languages are given in the transliteration system that is typically used in the literature. These are the symbols employed in this chapter that differ from IPA: Kurdish: <e> = /ə/, <r> = /ɾ/, <ê> = /e/, <i> = /ɪ/, <î> = /i/, <ř> = /r/, <y> = /j/, <u> = /ʊ/, <û> = /u/, <ş> = /ʃ/, <j> = /ʒ/, <ḥ> = /ħ/, <'> = /ʔ/, <ç> = /t͡ʃ/; Avestan: <š> = /ʃ/, <å> = /ɔ/, <uu> = /w/.
[2] We would like to thank three anonymous reviewers that helped us refine our argument as well as the editors Sara Pacchiarotti and Fernando Zúñiga for their guidance integrating our ideas into the broader themes of this volume.

Shuan Osman Karim, The Ohio State University, Department of Linguistics, Oxley Hall 1712 Neil Avenue, Columbus, Ohio, USA. Email: karim.56@osu.edu
Ali Salehi, University at Buffalo, Department of Linguistics, 609 Baldy Hall, North Campus, Buffalo, New York, USA. Email: asalehi@buffalo.edu

https://doi.org/10.1515/9783110777949-010

known as "absolute prepositions" in traditional Soranî grammars (e.g., Thackston 2004, MacKenzie 1961) are better described as applicative markers. The basic facts of Soranî applicatives have been known to scholars for quite some time. In an early account of Soranî adpositions, Edmonds (1955) describes a set of adpositions that are non-compounds and can only host a pronominal affix or be indexed on the verb. Likewise, Haig (2008: 277–310) provides an indepth description of these formatives and gives the first hints of the analysis we present here. He suggests that one possible analysis is that they can be analyzed as "emergent 'particle verb[s]'" which bring in an additional object, something akin to Indo-European preverbs (see section 5).

There have been several studies focusing on Soranî absolute prepositions (Samvelian 2007, Mohammadirad 2020, Edmonds 1955, Salehi 2018). Of particular interest is the way they combine with pronominal arguments. In this sense, there has been a great deal of disagreement. For instance, Thackston (2004) describes them as prepositions with preposed pronominal prepositional complements, a label that is only applicable in restricted contexts. Samvelian (2007) classifies Soranî "(absolute) prepositions" along two lines: (1) the affixal realization of the complement, e.g., affixal versus non-affixal (i.e., cliticized) and (2) the complement's local versus non-local realization, e.g., whether or not it is adjacent to the preposition (applicative) in linear constituent order. The main theoretical benefit of Samvelian's (2007), linearization approach, adapted from Crysmann (2003) based on Kathol (2000), is "that the relationship between word-level signs and the word order domain object they contribute need not to be isomorphic and that word-level signs can contribute more than one domain object into syntax" (Samvelian 2007: 246). This analysis conflicts with our underlying assumption that both absolute prepositions (i.e., applicatives) and their complements are inherently morphological.

In section 2 of this chapter, we provide an outline of Soranî alignment and argument indexing. In section 3, we present Soranî applicatives in the context of the definition of applicatives proposed in the introduction to this volume and discuss formal arguments in favor of an applicative analysis of Soranî absolute prepositions. In section 4, we outline the historical development of two types of applicatives in Soranî: one originating in simplex adpositions, which have merged with third-person singular pronouns, and one originating in complex adpositions consisting of an adpositional and a nominal element. Because Soranî applicatives have developed diachronically from (pro)nominal-adposition combinations, there are nearly as many distinct applicative morphemes as there are adpositions. These formatives specify the semantic role of the applied argument. Soranî applicatives can be valence increasing or valence neutral, the unifying thread being that they have amongst their functions "the introduction of a non-Actor semantic argument into a main clause" (see the introduction to this volume). They are valence-increasing when they replace adjunct phrases and valence-neutral when they replace mandatory arguments syntactically realized as adpositional phrases.

In section 5, we show how Soranî has gone through many cycles of applicative recruitment from Proto-Indo-European through its Old and Middle Iranian ancestors. We claim that there were at least five historical stages of applicative recruitment in Soranî. The first three resulted in the creation of preverbs in Sorani. These are: (1) the recruitment(s) that led to the system of preverbs in Old Iranian/PIE, (2) the recruitment before the Middle Iranian period that resulted in the preverbs *heł* and *wer*, which were nominals in Old Iranian, and (3) the recruitment that resulted in preverbs like *ser*, which were nominals in Middle Iranian. The last two stages led to the development of so-called absolute prepositions into synchronic applicatives. These are: (4) the recruitment that brought pronominal prepositional phrases into the verbal structure (e.g., *pê, tê, lê,* and *=ê*), and (5) the recruitment that brought nominal prepositional phrases into the verbal structure (e.g., *legeł, le ser,* and *=e ser*). Additionally, we show how in some cases, Soranî applicative markers have univerbated with simplex verbal stems deriving new lexemes. This lexicalization fits into known diachronic tendencies of applicative markers. Formatives from stages one through three only serve in this capacity. However, formatives from the most recent stage (5) never serve to derive new lexemes, formatives from stage (4) sometimes combine with simplex verbal stems to derive new lexemes (e.g., *lêdan* 'to hit' < *lê* [ABL.APPL] + *dan* 'to give') alongside their productive use as applicatives.

Examples in the current study are sourced from studies of Central Kurdish (e.g., MacKenzie 1961, Thackston 2004, Edmonds 1955) and broader studies of Iranian (e.g., Mohammadirad 2020). Examples without a reference correspond to hypothetical forms created by the current authors and confirmed by native speakers from Bane (Iran) and Suleymanî (Iraq).

2 An overview of Soranî grammar

The discussion of applicatives in Soranî is intrinsically related to the way that verbal arguments are indexed. There are three sets of morphemes traditionally described as agreement markers: a set of clitic person markers (CPMs), which are etymologically oblique clitics, and two sets of affix person markers (APMs), which are etymologically verbal affixes or, in the past tense, the copula. In this study, we largely eschew this etymologically oriented terminology and focus on the function of the indexes instead. A summary of these indexes and the arguments they can index is provided in Table 1.

Table 1: Argument indexing in Soranî.

APM$_1$ PRS:[3] S/A PST: —		CPM PRS: O/O$_{APPL.INTR}$/O$_{APPL.TR}$ PST: A/O$_{APPL.INTR}$		APM$_2$ PRS: — PST: S/O/O$_{APPL.TR}$	
SG	PL	SG	PL	SG	PL
1 –im	–în	=(i)m	=man	–im	–în
2 –î(t)	–(i)n	=(i)t	=tan	–î(t)	–(i)n
3 –ê(t)/a(t)[4]	–(i)n	=î	=yan	–Ø	–(i)n

Here, we use the abbreviations S for the single argument of an intransitive verb, A for the agent of a transitive verb, O for the patient of a transitive verb (Dixon 1994), and O$_{APPL}$[5] for applied object. The first set of person markers in Table 1 (APM$_1$) are present-tense verbal suffixes used to index S and A arguments. The second set of person markers (CPM) are used in the present tense to index O and in the past tense to index A. The third set of person markers (APM$_2$) are past-tense verbal suffixes used to index S and O. In clauses where the base verb is transitive, O$_{APPL}$ is indexed with the same person markers as O (CPMs in the present tense and APM$_2$s in the past tense). However, in intransitive clauses, where the alignment is not tense-sensitive, O$_{APPL}$ is indexed with CPMs regardless of tense. The distribution of these formatives can be described as a tense-based split-ergative alignment. In other words, in the present tense, there is a nominative-accusative pattern where the formatives used to index A and S (APM$_1$) are the same, and a different set of formatives indexes O and O$_{APPL}$ (CPM). In contrast, in the past tense there is an ergative-absolutive pattern where the formatives used to index S, O and O$_{APPL}$ (APM$_2$) are the same, and a different set of formatives indexes A (CPM).

In the present tense, both S and A are indexed using the same set of verbal affixes (APM$_1$). Compare (1) and (2). In (1), the APM$_1$ third-person singular verbal affix -*ê* indexes S, *baldareke* 'the bird'.

---

3 In Soranî, the present-tense stem is also used for expressions of the future. For this reason, non-past would be a more accurate label. However, we continue the tradition found in the Iranianist literature of marking these as present tense (PRS).
4 The two third-person singular APM$_1$ suffixes -*ê(t)* and -*a(t)* are lexically specified allomorphs; they represent two different conjugation classes.
5 Here we use O$_{APPL}$ for applied object in contrast to Mohammadirad's (2020) use of R for complement of an absolute preposition (i.e., applicative). Note that Mohammadirad (2020) uses R regardless of the precise semantic role assigned to the applied object.

(1) bałdar-eke e-fř-**ê**
    bird-DEF.SG IPFV-fly.PRS-3SG.S
    'The bird flies'

Likewise, in (2), the APM₁ third-person singular verbal affix -*a* references A, *ew pyawe* 'that man'.

(2) ew   pyaw=e   nan-eke   e-xw-**a**
    DIST.DEM man=DEM bread-DEF.SG IPFV-eat.PRS-3SG.A
    'That man is eating the bread'.

In contrast, in the past tense, A and S are indexed differently. S is indexed by verbal affixes (APM₂), and A is indexed by markers that are affixed to the first verbal argument or morpheme (CPM). Compare (3) and (4). In (3), the third-person plural verbal affix -*n* indexes S, *bałdarekan* 'the birds'.

(3) bałdar-ek-an fř**ř-n**
    bird-DEF-PL fly.PST-3PL.S
    'The birds flew'.

In contrast, in (4), the third-person singular marker =*î* indexing A, occurs on the conominal *ew pyawe* 'that man'. Note that this morpheme is affixed to the O argument in this sentence.

(4) ew   pyaw=e   nan-eke=**î**   xward
    DIST.DEM man=DEM bread-DEF.SG=3SG.A eat.PST
    'That man ate the bread'.

The split alignment pattern of Soranî is also evident in the way that O is indexed. Note that in the previous transitive examples (2) and (4), there is an overt patient *naneke* 'the bread', which is not indexed in the verbal morphology. In the absence of an overt object NP, O must be indexed in the verbal morphology. The indexes used for O are tense-sensitive. Compare (5) and (6). In (5), the third-person plural =*yan* (CPM), indexes an anaphorically retrievable O 'them' in the present tense. Note that this morpheme is affixed to the first verbal morpheme in the absence of another verbal argument.

(5) e=**yan**-xw-a
    IPFV=3PL.O-eat.PRS-3SG.A
    'S/he is eating them'.

In contrast, in the past tense in (6), it is the third-person plural verbal suffix -*in* (APM₂) that indexes the anaphorically retrievable O, 'them'.

(6) xward-**in**=î[6]
 eat.PST-3PL.**O**=3SG.A
 'S/he ate them'.

Examples (1) through (6) show that A and S are indexed by the same set of affixes in the present tense (APM₁), while there is a separate set that indexes O (CPM), yielding nominative-accusative alignment. In the past tense, the same set of affixes indexes S and O (APM₂), while a separate set indexes A (CPM), yielding ergative-absolutive alignment.

Another feature of Soranî grammar that affects the alignment pattern is the wide range of complex predicates including light-verb constructions and verbs with preverbs. In Soranî light-verb constructions, it is the light verb stem that determines the formatives that index S, A, O, and O$_{APPL}$. For instance, the verb *kirdin* 'to do' (syntactically transitive) and *bûn* 'to be(come)' (syntactically intransitive) used in light verb constructions dictate the pattern of argument indexation, while the nominal complement in the construction supplies the semantics. For instance, the light-verb construction PYASE KIRDIN 'to walk (lit. do a walk)' is semantically intransitive. However, S is indexed by the marker expected for A. Compare (7), where the first-person singular CPM =*im*, used for A arguments, marks S in the past tense light-verb construction, and (8), where the first-person singular APM₂ -*im*, used for S arguments, marks S in the past-tense construction of a syntactically intransitive verb such as *řoyştin* 'to go, leave'; light-verb constructions with the verb *kirdin* are conjugated like transitive verbs because the light verb *kirdin* 'to do' is transitive.

(7) *pyase*=**m** *e-kird*
 walk=1SG.**A** IPFV-LV.PST
 'I was walking'.

(8) *e-řoyşt-**im***
 IPFV-go.PST-1SG.**S**
 'I was going'.

---

[6] The third person-singular marker =î is unique among past-tense A markers as it comes after the morpheme indexing O.

The preverb-verb constructions behave similarly. A verb stem is accompanied by a relational element inducing a semantic derivation. The argument indexing strategy is dictated by the verb stem. For instance, the verb *girtin* 'to hold' combines with the preverb *wer* 'away' becoming *wergirtin* 'to take'. Compare (9) and (11). In (9), the verb *girtin* has a core argument structure VP: NP V. A is indexed with the first-person singular CPM =*im*, and O is indexed with the third-person plural APM$_2$ -*in*.

(9) *girt=im-in*
     hold.PST=1SG.A-3PL.O
     'I held them'.

In (10), the verb *wergirtin* has a core argument structure VP: NP PP V. A and O are indexed just as they were in (9), while the core argument with the semantic role of source is a prepositional phrase. In (11), the core argument encoding the source is pronominal. In this case, the pronominal core argument is indexed by the same type of marker used to index O, an APM$_2$ index for 2SG.O -*î*, and is assigned the role of source by the ablative-applicative marker *lê*-.

(10) *le   jin-eke   wer=im-girt-in*
     from   woman-DEF-SG   PV=1SG.A-take.PST-3PL.O
     'I took them from the woman'.

(11) *lê=m-wer-girt-in-î*
     ABL.APPL=1SG.A-PV-hold.PST-3PL.O-2SG.O$_{APPL}$
     'I took them from you'.

Similarly, the verb *kewtin* 'to fall' combines with the preverb *ser* 'up, head' becoming *serkewtin* 'to climb'. In (12), the verb *kewtin* has a core argument structure VP: V, i.e., is syntactically intransitive. S is indexed with the first-person singular APM$_2$ -*im*.

(12) *kewt-im*
     fall.PST-1SG.S
     'I fell'.

In (13), the verb *serkewtin* 'to climb' is semantically transitive and has a core argument structure VP: PP V. However, the verbal argument indexing is dictated by the syntactically intransitive stem *kewtin* 'to fall'; the derived verb *serkewtin* 'to climb' indexes an S (and not A) argument just like in (12) by means of the APM$_2$ -*im*.

(13) le   şax-eke=a   ser-kewt-im
     on   mountain-DEF.SG=on   PV-climb.PST-1SG.S
     'I climbed the mountain'

In (14), the PP argument is pronominal. As in (11), it is referenced by a CPM index for 3SG.O$_{APPL}$ =î, and is assigned the role of location by the ablative-applicative marker tê-.

(14) tê=î-ser-kewt-im
     LOC.APPL=3SG.O$_{APPL}$-PV-fall.PST-1SG.S
     'I climbed it (i.e., a mountain)'

In Soranî, adjuncts are introduced by means of adpositional phrases (See Table 2 in Section 3). The Soranî adpositional system consists of prepositions which can combine with postpositions to form circumpositions. We define prepositions and circumpositions as simplex adpositions because they consist of only adpositional elements, e.g., ta 'until', le . . .=ewe 'from', etc. We define complex adpositions as adpositions that consist of both an adpositional element(s) and a nominal element, e.g., legeł. . .(=a) 'with (comitative, lit. le geł 'in flock of')', -e ser . . . 'on to (lit. to the head of)'. Simplex adpositional phrases consist of a simplex adposition and an overt NP, e.g., le mał=ewe 'from home' (15a). Complex adpositional phrases may take an overt nominal complement in addition to the one that forms the complex adposition, e.g., legeł ew pyawe 'with that man'. However, they may also take a pronominal affix phonologically identical to the CPMs (see Table 1), e.g., legeł-î 'with him/her'. Note that Soranî adpositional phrases, whether simplex or complex, can freely occur in any order before or after the verb, cf. (15b)–(15d).

(15) a. le   mał=ewe   ne-hat-in   legeł-î
        from   house=from   NEG-come.PST-3PL.S with-3SG
     b. ległî le małewe nehatin
     c. le małewe legełî nehatin
     d. legełî nehatin le małewe
        'They didn't come from home with him' (a: MacKenzie 1961 2: 12)

3 The case for applicatives in Soranî

In the introduction to this volume, applicatives are defined as "any derivational morphology occurring on a verb root/stem that has amongst its functions the introduction of a non-Actor semantic argument into a main clause. This non-Actor is usually mapped onto an applied phrase. The latter term, coined by Denis Creissels, refers to any morphosyntactic entity introduced and/or semantically/ pragmatically manipulated by the applicative without any specifications about its syntactic category, argument status, and/or semantic role". This definition includes several points constituting essential properties of applicatives: (1) applicatives are derivational morphology; (2) applicatives tend to develop functions in addition to "the introduction of a non-Actor semantic argument into a main clause;" (3) applicatives manipulate applied phrases. Note that this definition does not specify the form the applied phrase must take. Applied phrases in the world's languages can take the form of NPs, prepositional or oblique-marked phrases, clauses with a non-finite verb, morphologically indexed arguments, or even zero anaphora. Soranî applicatives satisfy these points in line with what is observed in other languages that possess applicative morphology.

What we call applicatives in this chapter are known in the literature on Soranî as absolute prepositions (MacKenzie 1961). Soranî applicatives fall into two categories based on their formation. The first category consists of applicatives that differ from their simplex prepositional counterparts systematically. If the preposition starts in a voiced stop, the stop is devoiced, and the vowel /e/ is replaced by /ê/. The applicative morphemes *lê-, tê-,* and *pê-* can be derived in this way from the simplex prepositions *le,* *de,[7] and *be.* These forms can be understood diachronically as a contraction between simplex prepositions *le,* *de, and *be* and the third-person singular (feminine) oblique pronoun *(e)wê* now defunct in Central Kurdish (see section 4). The second category contains applicative forms originating in complex adpositions. These are identical in form, whether functioning as prepositions, as in *legeł em dêwe* 'with this demon' (16) and *legełî* (15) 'with him' or as an applicative, as in *zoranit legeł girtim* 'you wresteled with me' (17).

---

[7] The preposition *de* exists in other Central Kurdish varieties. However, it is missing in Soranî, where its prepositional functions have been assumed by *le.* Traces of *de remain as part of the applicative markers *tê* (< *de) and *tya* (< *deda).

(16) ew   sê   kuř=e   ne-bê   legeł   em
     DIST.DEM three   boy=DEM   NEG-be.PRS.3SG:S   with   PROX.DEM
     dêw=e   kes=î
     demon=DEM person=3SG:O_APPL
     lê-ne-ma-w-e
     LOC.APPL-NEG-remain.PST-PRF-3SG:S
     'there was nobody left in it but those three brothers with this demon'.
     (MacKenzie 1961 2: 18)

(17) hewt   řoj   zoran=it   legeł-girt-im
     seven   day   wrestle=2SG:A   COM.APPL-LV.PST-1SG.O_APPL
     'You wrestled with me for seven days'. (MacKenzie 1961 2: 24)

Soranî applicative markers are verbal derivational morphemes that introduce a non-Actor semantic argument into a main clause. The applied phrase (O_{APPL}), the entity introduced and/or semantically/pragmatically manipulated by the applicative, is indexed in the same way as O. Importantly, Soranî applicatives are only obligatorily used to introduce pronominal objects (i.e., not lexical NPs). In transitive clauses, applied objects are indexed differently depending on tense, just like O arguments, see Section 2. In the present tense, O_{APPL} is indexed by the person marker (CPM) also used to index O, which attaches to the first verbal argument or morpheme. In (18), the light-verb stem *eka* indexes A. The ablative applicative prefix *lê-* attaches to the verb and introduces a third-person plural applied object *=yan*, which is cliticized to the nominal complement of the light verb *eka*. The ablative applicative introduces a pronominal O_{APPL} with the semantic role of Source.

(18) su'al=**yan**   lê-e-k-a
     ask.LV=3PL.**O**_APPL   ABL.APPL-IPFV-ask.LV.PRS-3SG.A
     'he asks them (lit. he does a question from them)' (MacKenzie 1961 2: 8)

In the past tense, the APM_2 used to index O are also used to index O_{APPL}. In (19), the third-person singular CPM *=î* indexes A. Just as in the present tense counterpart (18), the applicative marker *lê-* attaches to the verb and introduces a source the applied object. However, unlike (18), the applied object is represented by the third person plural APM_2 *-in* attached to the light-verb stem *kirdin*, not the third person plural CPM *=yan*.

(19) su'al=î   lê-kird-**in**
     ask.LV=3SG.A   ABL.APPL-ask.LV.PST-3PL.**O**_APPL
     'he asked them (lit. he did a question from them)' (MacKenzie 1961 2: 8)

In intransitive clauses, O_APPL is always indexed with the markers used to index present-tense Os (CPM). There is no tense sensitivity. In (20) and (21), the applicative marker *lê-* introduces an applied object, indexed by the third person singular CPM =*î* to the first verbal argument.

(20) *jin-êk=î*
woman-IND=3SG.O_APPL
lê-e-hat-Ø-e der
ABL.APPL-IPFV-come.PST-3SG.S-outward
'A woman was coming out from it'. (Edmonds 1955: 498)

(21) *jin-êk=î*
woman-IND=3SG.O_APPL
lê-yêt-e der
ABL.APPL-IPFV.come.PRS.3SG.S-outward
'A woman is coming out from it'. (adapted from (20))

There are nearly as many applicative markers in Soranî as there are adpositions. In principle, new ones could be added to the system as new nominal elements are recruited as adpositions. For this reason, an exhaustive list is not possible. The most common applicatives along with their synchronic adpositional sources are in Table 2. Note that the majority of applicative markers are prefixes, while -*ê* and -*e ser* are verbal suffixes. This difference is a result of the original position of the argument or adjunct from which they developed (see section 4). Additionally, all the complex prepositions in Table 2 have corresponding applicative forms. However, the simplex prepositions in the top portion of the table do not always correspond to applicative markers and vice versa. For instance, the simplex prepositions *ta* 'until', *bê* 'without', and *wekû* 'like' never combine with the element /ê/ to form an applicative marker (see section 4 for a diachronic explanation). Conversely, the malefactive applicative marker *lê-* does not correspond to any synchronically attested adposition; it is the only way to express a malefactive in Soranî.

Soranî applicatives are derivational in the sense that they create a slot for an object which is not part of the argument structure of the root. Additionally, the applicatives are verbal morphemes, a feature that has not been recognized in the relevant literature. The applicative construction in Soranî is a way of introducing a non-Actor semantic argument into a main clause only when it is pronominal. Overt nominal non-Actor arguments are only expressed via adpositional phrases with roots/stems that do not undergo applicative derivation. Unlike preverbs (see section 2 and 5), Soranî applicative affixes are productive, i.e., they can combine with any verb without restrictions.

For verbs with an underlying phrase structure VP: V, the derived form is structured VP: PRN V, where PRN stands for pronoun. One interpretation is that valence has increased by one. Note that the applied object must be morphologically indexed, represented here as PRN and in the examples as O_{APPL}. For instance, a syntactically intransitive verb such as *çûn* 'to go' takes only an S argument and can optionally combine with an adjunct adpositional phrase like *=e Kurdistan* 'to Kurdistan' to signify the goal as in (22).

Table 2: Adpositions, corresponding applicative markers and their meanings.

Simplex adpositions	Gloss	Applicative	Gloss
be ...	'to'	–ê	DAT.APPL
be ...	'by (experiencer)'	pê–	EXP.APPL
be ... =a	'out of'	pya–	ELA.APPL
be ... =ewe	'by (instrument)'	pêwe–	INS.APPL
le ...	'from'	lê–	ABL.APPL
—	—	lê–	MAL.APPL
le ...	'on'	tê–	LOC.APPL
le ... =a	'on'	tya–	LOC.APPL
le ... =ewe	'from'	lêwe–	ABL.APPL
–e ...	'to'	–ê	ALL.APPL
ta ...	'until'	—	—
bê ...	'without'	—	—
wekû ...	'like'	—	—
Complex adpositions			
be des ...	'to (by hand)'	be des–	DAT.APPL
bo[8] ...	'for'	bo–	BEN.APPL
le des ...	'from (by hand)'	le des–	ABL.APPL
legeł ... =a	'with'	legeł–	COM.APPL
–e ser ...	'on to'	–e ser	SUPL.APPL
le ser– ...	'on top of'	le ser	SUPE.APPL

---

8 Note that *bo* was described as a simple[x] preposition by Edmonds (1955). If this is correct, this would appear to be an exception to the rule that absolute preposition require a nominal element. However, it has been suggested that *bo* is actually a contraction of *be ew* 'with that', perhaps a ellipsed form of 'with this reason' (Karim 2020). This suggestion is ultimately based on its use as the interogative 'why' and similar strategies in other Iranian languages; e.g., New Persian: be īn sabab 'for this reason'.

(22) çû-n=e   Kurdistan
    go.PST-3PL.S=TO   Kurdistan
    'They went to Kurdistan'.

The same verb can appear in a construction with the applicative *tê-*, and the location must be expressed as a pronominal object, i.e., *=î* in (23). Note that once the root combines with *tê-* the applied object *=î* cannot be omitted, i.e., *têçûn* is unacceptable.[9] However, the presence of the applicative does not change the argument structure of the verb; it simply adds an indexed argument.

(23) *tê=î-çû-n*
    LOC.APPL=3SG.O$_{APPL}$-go.PST-3PL.S
    'They went there (on it)'.

For verbs with an underlying phrase structure VP: NP V, the derived form is structured VP: NP PRN V, i.e., valence increased by one. Note that the applied object must be morphologically indexed unlike the patient, which is only optionally indexed. For example, a syntactically transitive verb such as *xwêndin* 'to read/study' takes A and O arguments and can combine with an optional adjunct adpositional phrase as in (24).

(24) *ktêb-ek-an=im   legeł   minał-ek-an=a   xwênd*
    book-DEF-PL=1SG.A   with   child-DEF-PL=with read.PST
    'I read the books with the children'.

The same verb can appear in a construction with the comitative applicative *legeł-*, and the concomitant is no longer expressed as an adpositional phrase but indexed as a pronominal object, i.e., *-in* in (25).

(25) *ktêb-ek-an=im   legeł-xwênd-in*
    book-DEF-PL=1SG.A   COM.APPL-read.PST-3PL.O$_{APPL}$
    'I read the books with them'.

In Soranî, an anaphorically retrievable patient must always be indexed in the absence of an overt NP. The sentence in (24) is adapted in (26); here the patient

---

9 The unacceptability of *têçun* was hypothesized by us and confirmed by a native speaker from Bane. The form *têçûn* is easily mistaken for the correct *tê=î-çûn* due to the difficulty native speakers have distinguishing certain vowels and vowel-glide combinations, e.g., *ê*, *êî* (= *êy*), and *eî* (=*ey*) as well as *o*, *ow*, and *ew*.

ktêbekan 'the books' is replaced by the morphological index *-in* 'them'. Note that the A index *=im* attaches to the first verbal argument or morpheme, which is the verb stem *xwênd*, and not the first linear constituent which is a non-core adpositional phrase *legeł minałekana*.

(26) legeł minał-ek-an=a   xwênd=im-in
     with child-DEF-PL=with   read.PST=1SG.A-3PL.O
     'I read them with the children'.

When the same verb occurs in a construction with the comitative applicative *legeł-*, both the patient and the concomitant can be indexed as pronominal objects, i.e., *-in* and *-in* in (27). Note that *=im* attaches to the first verbal argument or morpheme, which in this case is the comitative applicative marker *legeł-*.

(27) legeł=im-xwênd-in-in
     COM.APPL=1SG.A-read.PST-3PL.O-3PL.O$_{APPL}$
     'I read them with them'.

The linear order of indexation after the root is O followed by O$_{APPL}$. This is unclear in (27), where both O and O$_{APPL}$ are third-person plural. (28) shows that the second object index *-im* is the one introduced by the applicative *legeł-* assigning it the commitative role.

(28) legeł=yan-xwênd-in-im
     COM.APPL=3PL.A-read.PST-3PL.O -1SG.O$_{APPL}$
     'They read them with me'.

In Soranî, semantically ditransitive verbs have the underlying phrase structure VP: NP PP V. In these constructions, the adpositional phrases (PP) are core verbal arguments. For a ditransitive verb with the structure VP: NP PP V, the derived form is structured VP: NP PRN V, i.e., valence neutral. For example, a ditransitive verb like *dan* 'to give' has A and O arguments, as well as a mandatory prepositional phrase headed by *be* marking the Recipient (R) as in (29).

(29) kitêb-ek-an=im   be   mamosta-k-an   da
     book-DEF-PL=1SG.A   to   teacher-DEF-PL give.PST
     'I gave the books to the teachers'.

The same verb can occur in a construction with the dative applicative *-ê*, and R is no longer expressed as an adpositional phrase but indexed as a pronominal object, i.e., -(i)n in (30). Note that the verb *dan* 'to give' is ditransitive; the sentence *kitêbêkim da 'I gave a book' is infelicitous because it lacks an R argument.

(30) kitêb-ek-an=im   da-n-ê
     book-DEF-PL=1SG.A give.PST-3PL.O$_{APPL}$-DAT.APPL
     'I gave them the books'.

When an anaphorically retrievable O is indexed in the absence of an overt NP, the A index may occur on the core prepositional argument. In (31), the first-person singular A marker =im attaches to the adpositional phrase encoding the recipient *be mamostakan* 'to the teachers'. The verb cross-references the third-person plural O by means of the suffix -(i)n.

(31) be mamosta-k-an=im   da-n
     to teacher-DEF-PL=1SG.A give.PST-3PL.O
     'I gave them to the teachers'.

When the same verb occurs in a construction with the dative applicative, both the patient and the recipient might be indexed as pronominal objects. In (32), the agent marker =(i)m attaches to the first verbal morpheme, the stem in this case, and -in and -in index O and O$_{APPL}$ respectively.

(32) da=m-in-in-ê
     give.PST=1SG.A-3PL.O-3PL.O$_{APPL}$-DAT.APPL
     'I gave them to them'.

We now turn to formal evidence distinguishing the so-called absolute prepositions (applicatives in our view) from other synchronic adpositions in Soranî. Past works on what we call applicatives in Soranî and other related varieties (Samvelian 2007, Edmonds 1955, Öpengin 2016, MacKenzie 1999 etc.) are couched in the foundational assumption that these formatives are actually prepositions albeit with complements that are often displaced. Their status as verbal morphemes is therefore an integral part of the analysis proposed here. In section 2, we showed the mobility of adpositional phrases. Despite their phonological similarity due to etymological reasons, applicatives are not mobile like the adpositions they derive from. Adpositional phrases may occur initially before an object NP, medially after an object NP, and finally after the verb phrase, see (15). In contrast, applicative markers are in a fixed position and only other bound verbal morphemes may intervene between the applicative and the stem, e.g., (APPL-)(PV-)(NEG-)(TAM-)STEM.

The examples in (33) show that an adjunct adpositional phrase with either a enclitic pronominal complement, *legełit* 'with you', or an overt nominal complement, *legeł kiçeke* 'with the girl' can be placed anywhere in the sentence except immediately before the verb, cf. the ungrammaticality of (33d).

(33) a. *fîlm-êk=im   legeł   =it/kiç-eke   temaşa   kird*
       movie-INDF=1SG.A   with   =2SG/girl-DEF.SG watch   LV.PST

   b. *fîlm-êk=im   temaşa   kird   legeł   =it/kiç-eke*
      movie-INDF=1SG.A   watch   LV.PST   with   =2SG/girl-DEF.SG

   c. *legeł =it/kiç-eke   fîlm-êk=im   temaşa   kird*
      with =2SG/girl-DEF.SG   movie-INDF=1SG.A   watch   LV.PST

   d. ** fîlm-êk=im   temaşa   legeł   =it/kiç-eke   kird*
      movie-INDF=1SG.A   watch   with   =2SG/girl-DEF.SG LV.PST
      'I watched a movie with you/the girl'.

This is in sharp contrast with the bound applicative marker *legeł-*, which occurs as a prefix on the verb form. The examples in (34b)–(34c) show that unlike the preposition from which it derives (33), the applicative *legeł-* is a morphologically bound form with a fixed slot within the verb template which cannot occur in any other position within the clause.

(34) a. *fîlm-êk=im   temaşa   legeł-kird-î*
       movie-INDF=1SG.A   watch   COM.APPL-LV.PST-2SG.O$_{APPL}$

   b. **fîlm-êk=im   temaşa   kird-î   legeł*
      movie-INDF=1SG.A   watch   LV.PST-2SG.O$_{APPL}$ COM.APPL

   c. **legeł   fîlm-êk=im   temaşa   kird-î*
      COM.APPL   movie-INDF=1SG.A   watch   LV.PST-2SG.O$_{APPL}$
      '(* intended: I watched a movie with you'.)[10]

Likewise, in the present tense, where O$_{APPL}$ is encoded on the first verbal argument or morpheme, the applicative must be in the same fixed position as in past tense clauses, compare with (34). The examples in (35) provide additional evi-

---

[10] For (34b) and (34c), there are no possible felicitous interpretations.

dence that the applicative *leɫeł-* is a morphologically bound form with a fixed slot within the verb template. Only in preverbal position can the applicative introduce the second-person singular applied object *=it*.

(35) a. *fîlm-êk=it temaşa leɫeł-e-ke-m*
movie-INDF=2SG.O_APPL watch COM.APPL-LV.PRS-1SG.A

b. **fîlm-êk=it temaşa e-ke-m leɫeł*
movie-INDF=2SG.O_APPL watch LV.PRS-1SG.A COM.APPL

c. **leɫeł fîlm-êk=it temaşa e-ke-m*
COM.APPL movie-INDF=2SG. watch LV.PRS-1SG.A
'I will watch a movie with you'.

An additional piece of evidence that separates applicative morphemes from adpositions is that the lexical stress of the verb falls on the applicative marker in affirmative clauses just as described by Thackston (2004: 3) for preverbs. This phenomenon is not observed with adpositions: when combined with adpositonal phrases in a main clause, the verb maintains its own lexical stress.

An applied phrase in Soranî can only be pronominal. Although there are aspects of the system that are unique, parallels in other languages suggest this is but an idiosyncratic variation of what is common among applicative systems, particularly those that have developed from adpositional constructions. There are languages in which the applied object is encoded as an NP (or a prepositional phrase). In (36) from Nadëb (Nadahupan), a language without argument indexing, the applied object is the full syntactic (NP) argument *bxaah* 'tree', and the applicative marker *ya* encodes the superessive relationship of the applied object.

Nadëb (Weir 1987: 300, glosses adjusted)
(36) *bxaah kalapéé ya-sooh*
tree child SUPE-be.sitting
'The child is sitting on the tree'.
(Lit., 'The child is on-sitting the tree'.)

There are languages in which the applied object is indexed only morphologically with some applicative markers. In the Bantu language Bukusu, there are several different types of applicative markers. (37) shows one of the locative applicatives *=xo*. Unlike the Nadëb example, the applicative *=xo* only allows the morphological indexing of the applied object in bound pronominal form, see *-n* [1SG. O_APPL] in (37). See (38), where the applied object *lukaratasi* 'the paper' is infelicitously expressed syntactically by the applicative *=xo*.

Bukusu (Peterson 2007: 12, glosses adjusted)
(37) *a-xu-n-der-a=xo*
3SG.A-2SG.O-1SG.O_APPL-bring-IND=APPL
'He brought you to me'.

Bukusu (Peterson 2007: 14, glosses adjusted)
(38) *n-a-mwaat-a=xo lu-karatasi sii-tabu
1SG.A-TAM-toss-IND=APPL CL11-paper CL7-book
'I tossed the book on the paper'.

Additionally, there are languages where both syntactic and morphological applied phrases are possible. The Bantu *-ɪd applicative, which has -*il* as a reflex in Bukusu, is just such a marker. (39) shows the applied object encoded as a (syntactic) NP *omuxasi* 'woman', while (40) shows the applied object indexed morphologically with the third-person singular human object index *mu-* [CL1].

Bukusu (Peterson 2007: 7, glosses adjusted)
(39) *wanjala a-a-kul-il-a omu-xasi sii-tabu*
Wanjala CL3.A-PST-buy-APPL-IND CL1-woman CL7-book
'Wanjala bought the book for the woman'.

Bukusu (Peterson 2007: 8, glosses adjusted)
(40) *wanjala a-mu-kul-il-a sii-tabu*
Wanjala 3SG.A-CL1.O_APPL-buy-APPL-IND CL7-book
Bukusu: 'Wanjala bought her the book'.

Based on the argumentation we developed, one would think that Soranî patterns with languages like Bukusu in its usage of applicative =*xo* which can only introduce pronominal constituents. However, readers should know that in Kurdish studies, Soranî clitic applied objects (i.e. those occurring in the present tense) are traditionally considered syntactic entities, while affixed applied objects (i.e. those occurring in the past tense) are considered morphological entities. This family-specific debate is largely irrelevant for the purposes of this chapter and this volume more generally. The definition of applicative morphology following the introduction to this volume does not specify the morphosyntactic nature of the entity introduced by the applicative. This is an area where there appears to be variability among the applicative systems observed in the world's languages.

  We conclude with the observation that as expected for verbal derivational morphology, some Soranî applicative-verb combinations have lexicalized. These derived forms can have a non-compositional meaning which is hardly relatable to that of their simplex counterparts, e.g., *geyştin* 'to arrive' [VP: V] ~ *pêgeyştin* 'to ripen' [VP: V]. They can have a non-compositional meaning while preserving a valence-increasing function, e.g., *birîn* 'to cut' [VP: NP V] ~ *lêbirîn* 'to deduct (X from Y)' [VP: NP NP V]. There are also cases where the lexicalized applicative stem shows a paradoxical decrease in valence compared to their simplex counterparts, e.g., *dan* 'to give' [VP: NP PP V] ~ *lêdan* 'to hit' [VP: NP V].

4 The development of applicatives out of prepositional phrases

In this section, we offer evidence for the source and diachronic trajectory of Soranî applicatives based on synchronic data from the closely related Kurmancî (Northern Kurdish) language. Soranî and Kurmancî diverge from each other in many ways. Their divergence is due to individual innovations in both languages. Both Soranî and Kurmancî feature a tense-based split ergative alignment with slightly different features. Soranî features tense-based split ergative alignment only in the verbal argument indexing, while nominals are not case-marked synchronically. In contrast, Kurmancî has two cases, direct (DIR) and oblique (OBL).[11] It uses the direct case to mark all S arguments regardless of tense, past-tense objects (O), and present-tense agents (A). It uses the oblique case to mark present-tense objects, past tense agents, and nominal complements of prepositions.

(Pro)nominal complements of Kurmancî prepositions appear in the oblique case.[12] In (41), the preposition *li* 'to' combines with the third-person singular oblique-marked NP *kurê xwe* 'his son' to form the phrase *li kurê xwe* 'to/at his son'.

Kurmancî (Thackston 2002: 28)
(41) *Wî   li   kur-ê   xwe   di-nêrî*
     he.3SG.M.OBL to   boy-EZ.M.SG   self IPFV-look.PST
     'He looked at his son'.

---

11 We describe Kurmancî as a split ergative (i.e., S = A ≠ O in the present tense and S = O ≠ A) language based on the standard variety. It should be noted that some varieties have developed other marking systems (e.g., transitive/double-oblique alignment: A = O ≠S).

12 Oblique case is a term used in the Iranianist literature to refer to the marked case form in the bicasual nominal systems common in Iranian languages. These forms are most often the reflexes of the Old Iranian genitive case but sometimes reflect Old Iranian accusative (following Korn 2016). The term oblique is used here primarily to contrast with direct case and does not necessarily imply the type of marking of non-core syntactic arguments.

When the pronominal complement of a preposition is third-person singular, the form of the simplex prepositional phrase is contracted. For instance, *lê* 'to her' in (42) is a contraction of *li* 'to' and *wê* 'her'.

Kurmancî (Thackston 2002: 22)
(42) te   l-ê   ve-gerand
     2SG.OBL   to-3SG.OBL   PV-reply.PST.3SG
     'You replied to him/her'.

The contracted forms feature two additional idiosyncrasies with respect to full forms such as the one in (41): (1) the onset stops in the prepositions *bi* and *di* are devoiced in the contracted form; and (2) the gender distinction is lost. The simple prepositions *li, ji, bi,* and *di* become the forms *lê, jê, pê,* and *tê* when contracted with third-person singular masculine and feminine oblique pronouns *wî* or *wê* respectively. Despite the loss of case and gender marking on nominals, these contracted forms featuring the oblique-case marked pronouns still survive as applicative markers in Soranî.

It is clear from Kurmancî how the phonological shapes of the applicatives developed in Soranî because Kurmancî has crucially preserved the third-person singular oblique pronouns *wî* and *wê* now absent from Soranî. Soranî possesses simplex prepositional forms such as *le*, cognate with Kurmancî *li* in (41) and contracted forms like *lê* in (42). For instance, in (43), the preposition *le* is used to form the prepositional phrase *le pyaweke* 'from the man' just as in Kurmancî.

Soranî
(43) pirsyar   le   pyaw-eke   e-ke-m
     ask   from   man-DEF.SG   IPFV-LV.PRS-1SG.A
     'I will ask the man (lit. from the man)'

However, the Soranî form *lê* cannot be parsed in the same way as Kurmancî *lê* in (42). Instead it requires the presence of an additional morpheme indexing O_{APPL} to be well formed as in (44).

Soranî
(44) pirsyar=**î**   lê-e-ke-m
     ask=3SG.**O**$_{APPL}$ ABL.APPL-IPFV-LV.PRS-1SG.A
     'I will ask him a question'.

The Kurmancî contracted prepositional forms carry both the case relations assigned by the prepositions and the third-person singular pronominal. In contrast, the Soranî forms carry only the role assigned to the applied phrase. The pronominal is, instead, indexed in the verbal morphology. There is an idiosyncrasy of the verbal morphology in New Iranian languages that was the bridging context for this change.

In Soranî, past-tense transitive verbs can take a direct object expressed as an overt NP or can index their direct object pronominally on the verb itself. This pronominal construction is formed with the past-tense verb stem and person markers. Unlike all other person-number combinations, third-person singular objects have no overt morphological marker, e.g., *dît-im* [see.pst-1sg.O] 'saw me', *dît-î* [see.PST-2SG.O] 'saw you(sg)', *dî-Ø* [see.PST-3SG.O] 'saw him', etc.

This leaves the meaning of *dî* ambiguous; it could be parsed as *dî-Ø* [see.PST-3SG.O] or alternatively as *dî* [see.PST]. The latter would require a syntactic direct object to precede the verb form because Soranî does not allow zero anaphora.

Soranî, along with most varieties of Central Kurdish, has lost case marking on both nominals and pronominals. In older stages, Soranî had oblique pronouns that would have been used as the complements of prepositions. Just like Kurmancî, the oblique pronouns had contracted forms in the third-person singular that would have been parsed as [PREP-3SG.OBL] as in (45).

Soranî
(45) *ktêb=im*   **l-ê*[13]   *wer-girt*
       book=1SG.A   from-3SG   PV-hold.PST
       'I took the book from him'.

Once the third-person singular oblique pronouns *wî* and *wê* were lost in Soranî, *lê* was no longer synchronically segmentable into preposition plus a pronoun as it is in Kurmancî. However, the bare verb stem could alternatively be parsed as [STEM. PST] as in (45) or [STEM.PST.3SG.O] as in (46). (45) and (46) are formally identical. The only difference is the parsing of the verb form.

Soranî
(46) *ktêb=im*   *lê-wer-girt-Ø*
       book=1SG.A   ABL.APPL-PV-hold.PST-3SG.O$_{APPL}$
       'I took the book from him'.

---

[13] The asterisk marks a reconstruction based on the Kurmancî way of parsing the morphemes, which is synchronically impossible in Soranî.

Note that the use of Ø here to represent the pronominal index is an expositional tool. The form *girt* is ambiguous. It could always be interpreted as a verb with a 3SG indexed object, e.g., *girt* [hold.PST.3SG.O] or a verb that requires an object argument to be well formed, i.e., *girt-Ø* [hold.PST]. The extension of the O indexation pattern in (46) to the non-zero exponents of the APM$_2$ paradigm in the past tense (see Table 1) suggests that the unmarked verb has been reinterpreted as indexing an implicit third-person singular argument. The Kurmancî equivalent cannot be used to index adpositional complements or any other oblique-marked nominals. See (47) where the verb indexes the second person singular object, and the applicative marker indicates how to interpret the applicative object's semantics.

Soranî
(47) ktêb=im   lê-wer-girt-î
     book=1SG   ABL.APPL-PV-hold.PST-2SG.O$_{APPL}$
     'I took the book from you'.

It is a coincidence that the third-person singular pronouns would contract with prepositions yielding fused forms and that Iranian verbs were zero-marked in the third-person singular. This coincidence provided the bridging context by which the prepositional complement was integrated into the verbal morphology. Similarly, other languages have also incorporated whole adpositional phrases into the verbal morphology to form applicatives (e.g., Navajo, see Mithun 2001 section 4).

The ambiguity that made third-person singular the bridging context for argument indexing on the verb is only present in the past-tense transitive constructions. However, Soranî applicatives occur in all tense-aspect-mood combinations on transitive and intransitive verbs. Past-tense transitive clauses provided the bridging context for oblique arguments to be incorporated into the verbal morphology. Then, this pattern must have extended by analogy into all tense-transitivity combinations.

While the majority of applicatives occur as verbal prefixes (see, the case of *le-* illustrated above), there is a small set of applicatives that are verbal suffixes. This set includes the dative applicative *-ê* and the superessive applicative *-e ser*. These applicatives evolved in the same way as their prefix counterparts, i.e. through a third person zero as a bridging context, but from a different historical source. The difference in their placement is a result of their semantics and another idiosyncrasy of Iranian languages. All the members of this applicative set indicate motion towards a goal or recipient. In Iranian languages, including Kurmancî, NP or PP arguments expressing goal or recipient are often postverbal. This is exemplified in (48), where the New Persian verb *dādæn* has a direct object *ye ketabī* 'a book' in preverbal position and a recipient *be zæne* 'to the woman' in postverbal position, and (49), where the Kurmancî verb *dan* has an oblique direct object *pirtûkekê* 'a book' in preverbal position and an oblique recipient *jinê* 'the woman' in postverbal position.

New Persian
(48) ye   ketāb-ī   mī-d-æm   be   zæn-e
     IND   book-IND   IPFV-give.PRS-1SG.A to   woman-DEF.SG
     'I will give the woman a book'.

Kurmancî
(49) ez   pirtûk-ek-ê   di-di-m   jin-ê
     1SG.DIR   book-IND-F.SG.OBL   IPFV-give.PRS-1SG.A   woman-SG.F.OBL
     'I am giving the woman a book'.

The Kurmancî ditransitive verb *dan* 'to give' has a structure VP: NP V NP. Both arguments are in the oblique case. When the recipient is a third-person singular oblique pronoun *wî* or *wê*, it occurs as =*ê* encliticized to the verb as in (50). Note the loss gender distinction when =*ê is* encliticized to the verb just as it happens when in a contracted form in combination with prepositions.

Kurmancî
(50) ez   pirtûk-ek-ê   di-di-m=ê
     1SG.DIR   book-IND-3SG.OBL   IPFV-give.PRS-1SG.A=3SG.OBL
     'I am giving him/her a book'.

The form =*ê* is identical to the dative applicative -*ê* in Soranî which introduces an indexed R. Its occurrence as a verbal suffix is reflective of the word order in Kurmancî clauses with a lexical Goal/Recipient phrase.

As shown in (51), Soranî uses a CPM in the present tense to index R. The Soranî sentence in (51), structurally and functionally equivalent to the Kurmancî clause in (50), has too many arguments assuming the reconstructed meaning of the applicative =*ê* as a third-person singular oblique pronoun following Kurmancî.

(51) *ktêb-êk=î   e-de-m=ê
     book-INDF=3SG.OBL   IPFV-give.PRS-1SG.A=3SG.OBL
     'I am giving her a book her'

However, (51) is felicitous parsing =*î* as [3SG.O$_{APPL}$] and =*ê* as [DAT.APPL]. Thus, the applicative suffix -*ê* is different from the other applicatives introduced thus far in that it originated in a pronoun not a contraction of a preposition plus a pronoun.

In the early history of Soranî, a construction like the Kurmancî one in (50) would have been possible. The third-person singular oblique pronouns *wî* and *wê* contracted with the verb *dan* 'to give;' *da=ê* would have been parsed as [give.PST=3SG.OBL] as in (52).

Soranî
(52)   ktêb-êk=im   da=*ê
       book-IND=1SG.A   give.PST=3SG.OBL
       'I gave him/her a book'.

Once the third-person singular oblique pronouns *wî* and *wê* were lost in Soranî, *=ê* was no longer synchronically understood as a pronoun as it is synchronically in Kurmancî. However, the form *da* is ambiguous. It could always be interpreted as a verb with an indexed object (represented as either *da-Ø* [give.PST-3SG.O]) or a verb that requires an object argument to be well formed. (52) and (53) are formally identical. The only difference is the parsing of the verb form. Just like with the other applicatives, zero-marking of the third-person singular in the past tense served as the ambiguous context that allowed the oblique pronominal *=ê* to become the dative applicative *-ê*.

Soranî
(53)   ktêb-êk=im   da-Ø-ê
       book-IND=1SG.A   give.PST-3SG.O$_{APPL}$-DAT.APPL
       'I gave him/her a book'.

The applicative suffix *-ê* was integrated into the applicative system by the same process that integrated the prepositive applicative markers (e.g., *lê-*, *tê-*, and *pê-*). The only difference was the original syntactic placement of the formatives. Additionally, there are postpositive complex applicative markers, like *-e ser* [-SUPL. APPL], which consist of the preposition *=e* 'to' encliticised to the verb and the nominal element *ser* 'head'. According to Mahmoudveysi *et al.* (2012), the preposition *=e* is likely a sandhi variant of *be* 'to.' If Mahmoudveysi *et al.*'s (2012) theory is taken to be correct, the complex preposition *=e ser* 'onto' should be understood as the preposition *be ser* 'onto' in postverbal position. The postpositive complex applicative markers, like *-e ser*, were integrated into the verbal system in the same way as other complex adpositions albeit with a different original syntactic placement (see discussion of applicatives from complex adpositions below).

We now turn to the diachronic development which might have given rise to the set of applicatives originating in complex adpositions (see Table 2). They bear primary verbal stress when used as applicatives. In the case of applicatives derived from complex prepositions (i.e., prepositions consisting of a preposition and a noun), the pronominal complement of the preposition could always take the form of an enclitic pronominal, e.g., *legeł=it* 'with you'. The likely path by which complex adpositions were integrated into the applicative system was through an ambiguous context different from the one that integrated the simplex adpositions with their pronominal complements. Our hypothesis is that this ambiguous context was the present-tense intransitive construction. With intransitive verbs regardless of tense, a PP consisting of a complex adposition with an enclitic complement (54) in clause-initial position, and an applicative with its applied object (55) are nearly identical. (54) must be understood as a PP *legełit* 'with you' followed by the verb e-ç-im 'I go'. As such, each gets its own lexical stress. However, (55) is a single word that carries a single prosodic stress.

(54) *legeł=it*   e-ç-im
    with=2SG   IPFV-go.PRS-1SG.S
    'I'll go with you'.

(55) *legeł=it-e-c-im*
    COM.APPL=2SG-IPFV-go.PRS-1SG.S
    'I'll go with you'.

To corroborate this hypothesis, one would of course need to provide evidence that at a certain stage in the history of Sorani, complex prepositional phrases were frequently placed at the beginning of the sentence. Whatever the case might be, one might legitimately argue that once a form like *lê* was recruited as an applicative prefix, it could be the analogical exemplar for other prepositions or prepositional phrases (e.g., *legeł, le ser*, etc.) to become applicative prefixes, albeit from different sources and pathways. However, we must assume that adpositions were not inducted into the applicative system by analogy alone because not all of them have been recruited as applicative markers. For instance, *bê* 'without' and *ta* 'until' cannot be used as "absolute prepositions" or applicatives in our terms (Mohammadirad 2020: 74). *Bê* and *ta* belong to a larger group of prepositions that do not have applicative counterparts. However, these prepositions do not carry the etymological third-person singular oblique pronoun –*ê* or a nominal element like *geł*, or *ser*.[14] We propose that these are essential prerequisites for the integration of the applicative into the verbal morphology.

---

14 Note the striking similarity between *bê* and the applicatives *pê-*, *lê-*, and *tê-*. If this were analogy alone, one might reasonably expect *bê* to be inducted into the applicative system. However, it

5 The spiral of applicative recruitment

The Soranî applicatives discussed in sections 3 and 4 represent the most recent of recurring layers applicative recruitment. From Indo-European origins through Old and Middle Iranian to Soranî (Central Kurdish) as we know it, there have been as many as five separate cycles where adpositions were recruited to become applicatives. There were a series of adpositions and adverbials in Proto-Indo-European that were still separate words in the oldest attested Anatolian and Indo-Iranian languages. "[W]hen used to modify the content of verbs, [they] are called preverbs" (Fortson 2004: 71). When of adpositional origin, they went from being syntactic constituents, to verbal prefixes that added an additional non-Actor argument to a verb phrase (following Gaedicke 1880: 91).[15] In the old (Indo-)Iranian period, many preverbs could still function as adpositions governing an oblique noun.

In what we call stage 1, the (Indo-)Iranian branch of the Indo-European language family (including Soranî) inherited a series of preverbs. These formatives have long been known for their derivational effects e.g., Avestan:[16] GAM 'to go' ~ APAGAM 'to go away' (Cheung 2007: 98) as well as their transitivizing properties, i.e., as applicatives (Kulikov 2012: 725). For instance, the Avestan verb STĀ 'to stand' is intransitive. In (56), *hištaiti* 'he stands' has but one argument, which is the subject *srīrō* 'beautiful (one)' referring to Tištriya, the star Sirius.

Avestan (Yt.8.59[17])
(56) srīrō   hištaiti   rāmanivå
      beautiful.NOM.SG.M   stand.3SG.PRS.IND   joy-spreading.NOM.SG.M
      'He, beautiful and joy-spreading, stands'.

---

remains a simplex preposition without an applicative counterpart. Similarly, if bê had originally contained an oblique pronoun like *pê*, *tê*, and *lê*, we would expect the initial stop to be devoiced.
15 Kulikov (2012) ultimately concluded that these "verbal prefixes belong to the very periphery of the Vedic valency-changing markers" based on two facts: (1) most if not all preverbs in early Vedic, which show an increase in valence, also contribute some semantic content, and (2) preverbs have a "weak transitivizing force" Vedic is thought to preserve an early stage of what becomes "complete transitivization" (and univerbation) "in many other ancient Indo-European languages" (Kulikov 2012: 739).
16 Avestan is the oldest extant member of the Iranian branch of the Indo-Iranian languages. Examples from Avestan are employed here as an imperfect exemplar of what Soranî might have looked like in the Old Iranian period, although Avestan is not a direct ancestor of Soranî. The oldest attested Soranî only dates back to 1762 (Sheyholislami 2021: 637).
17 All examples from the Avesta have been taken from Avesta.org and are given in standard notation, e.g., the collection (Yt. = Yashts, Vd. = Videvdad). the hymn number, and the verse number.

When the verb STĀ combines with the preverb *auua* 'down', the result is a verb meaning to touch. AUUA-STĀ is transitive as exemplified by the direct object in the accusative case *nasāum* 'corpse' see (57).

Avestan (Vd.8.33)
(57) nasāum   auua   hištāt
     corpse.ACC PV   stand.PRF.3SG
     'S/he has touched a corpse'.

Some Old Iranian preverbs were derivational and valence changing and also functioned as adpositions taking complements in oblique cases; e.g., *ā* +ACC 'towards', +LOC 'around', *upa* 'into', +LOC 'in', etc. (de Vaan and García 2014: 77). It is impossible to say for sure what path adpositions took on their way to becoming preverbs because this change happened before the oldest extant texts. However, the diachronic development of adpositions into preverbs proposed for languages such as Rama (Chibchan, Craig and Hale 1988) and Nadëb (Nadahupan, Weir 1987) works for the predecessor of Old Indo-Iranian. For instance, a hypothetical sentence such as (58) carries an adjunct adpositional phrase marking the recipient *ā Yimam* 'to Yima'.

Proto-Iranian (hypothetical)
(58) yānam   ā   Yimam   barati
     gift.ACC.SG.N to 1SG.ACC bring.3SG.PRS.IND
     'He brings a gift to me'.

When subject to zero anaphora, the adpositional phrase appeared as a stranded adposition, in this case *ā*, see (59).[18]

Proto-Iranian (hypothetical)
(59) yānam   ā   barati
     gift.ACC.SG.N to bring.3SG.PRS.IND
     'He carries a gift to (him)'.

---

18 There is evidence for verbs with preverbs in Old Iranian occurring without an overt argument, which must be gleaned from context, e.g., *paiti-auua-jasa* 'come down to (us)' (Yt.5.85; translation by Skjærvø 2003). Here, the preverb *awa* 'down' changes the meaning of the verb *jasa* 'go[2SG.IMP]' to 'go/come down'. The preverb *paiti* 'to' is expected to introduce the anaphorically retrievable goal argument 'us' which is omitted from the sentence.

The stranded adposition then univerbated with the verbal stem creating a newly derived lexeme with an anaphoracally retrievable object, e.g., *ābarati* 'he brings to (him)'. Note that this form, the etymological source of Kurdish *hawirdin* 'to bring', was still separable into verb and preverb in Avestan.

Many of the Old Iranian preverbs still exist in Soranî (and other Iranian daughter languages). They can be divided into two groups: (1) preverbs that have univerbated with the associated stem and are no longer separable. These forms are not synchronically understood as preverbs (e.g., *ha* (cf. Av. *ā* 'toward'): *hatin* 'to come' (< OIr. (H2[19])ĀGAM), *hawirdin* 'to bring' (< OIr. (H₂)ĀBAR); *westan* 'to stop' (< OIr. AWASTĀ); (2) preverbs that have maintained their separability. They are synchronically preverbs in Soranî just as they were in Old Iranian; e.g., *řa-bînîn* 'to expect' (< *řa* 'forth' + *bînîn* 'to see' (cf. Av. *fra* 'forth').

By the Middle Iranian period, these preverbs were no longer productive applicative markers. It was in this period that the core inventory of prepositions and the third-person singular oblique pronominals univerbated to form applicatives (described in section 4); these new applicatives may have been created in part because those originating in preverbs could no longer be used productively. The recruitment of these applicatives can be described as a spiral because there is evidence that as new material is recruited to form new adpositions, they are then recruited as new applicative markers. These layers are demonstrated in (60), where newer applicatives and preverbs (i.e., older applicatives) form a stack of multiple recruitment cycles. The superessive applicative *le ser* attaches to the verb *hełwestan* 'to stand up'. This verb has two preverbal elements: *we-* that was already a preverb in Old Iranian and *heł-* that was recruited as a preverb between Old and Middle Iranian.

Soranî
(60) *le ser=î-heł-we-sta-n*
SUPE.APPL=3SG.O$_{APPL}$-PV-PV-stand.PST-3PL.S
'They stood up on it'.

As shown in (60) with *heł-*, there was in fact another round of recruitment between Old and Middle Iranian. In the Iranian daughter languages, the inherited adpositions and preverbs solidified their functions either as preverbs or adpositions. As old adpositions grammaticalized as preverbs, new adpositions were

---

19 The Hs in these reconstructed forms refer to Proto-Indo-European so-called "laryngeal" consonants. Their precise phonetic value is unknown. Kümmel (2014) suggests that *H$_1$ corresponds to [h], *H$_2$ to [X], and *H$_3$ to [G].

recruited from the nominal system. These forms could be used adpositionally in Old Iranian albeit with persistent aspects of their nominal origin, e.g., their complements were in the genitive case. For example, the nominal *pasca* 'behind (portion)' (cf. Soranî: *paş* 'behind'), could be used adpositionally in Avestan with the genitival complement *hū* 'sun[gen]' to form the phrase *pasca hū* 'after the sun' (Yt.V.94). Additionally, there were several new prepositions of denominal origin extant in Middle Iranian languages that were still nouns in Old Iranian e.g., Av.: *ərəzu* – 'right, straight (< PIE *reĝ 'right', Pokorny 1959: 2474), and the Soranî reflex *heł* 'PV (up)' (Hasandust 2011: 111). These forms represent the second recruitment of (stage 2) preverbs. The Middle Persian cognate *ul* 'up' was in use both as a preverb (cf. *ēstēd* 'he stands' (Jügel 2016: 9) ~ *ul ēstēd* 'he dwells') and as part of a complex preposition (e.g., *ul ō* 'up to' in *ul ō wahištaw̄* 'up to paradise' Boyce 1975 y.8.1). Although these preverbs are not synchronically applicatives in Soranî, we tentatively assume, following Kulikov (2012), a stage when they were applicative based on the their weak valence increasing effect in the Middle Iranian period based on the Middle Persian data.

In Soranî, the word *ser* 'head, up' has replaced the adpositional functions of *heł*, and it can also occur as a preverb (cf. *serkewtin* 'to climb' ~ *kewtin* 'to fall'). The three uses as noun 'head', a complex preposition, and a preverb, compared to *heł*'s use only as a preverb, illustrate multiple waves of recruitment. Both *heł* and *ser* have the meaning 'up'. Using the Middle Persian data as an exemplar for what Soranî might have been like in the Middle Iranian period, *heł* was likely used both adpositionally and as a preverb. As *heł* lexicalized with particular verbs, new material was recruited for the adpositional function (i.e., *ser*). Once *ser* took on the adpositional functions, it then became a productive preverb in Soranî.

This line of reasoning is reminiscent of Kuryłowicz's fourth law of analogy: "Quand à la suite d'une transformation morphologique une forme subit la differenciation, la forme nouvelle correspond à sa fonction primaire (de fondation), la forme ancienne est reservee pour la fonction secondaire (fondèe)." [When as a consequence of a morphological change, a form undergoes differentiation, the new form takes over its primary ('basic') function, the old form remains only in secondary ('derived') function] (Kuryłowicz (1947: 30) translation by Hock (1991)). This is exemplified by the Soranî twin complex verbs *hełkewtin* and *serkewtin*. They both could be translated based on their etyma as 'to up-fall'. However, in Soranî, *hełkewtin*, representing the older layer of recruitment, has the restricted (lexicalized) meaning 'to happen by chance;' this meaning is not synchronically derivable from its constituent parts. In contrast, *serkewtin* has the more transparent meaning 'to climb', see (13) and (14), as well as a few derived (metaphorical) meanings 'to elevate, advance, etc'. Essentially *ser* has replaced *heł* in conveying the transparent meaning 'up(ward)'. This transparency in comparison with *heł* leads us to consider preverbs like *ser* to be a third stage (stage 3).

Additionally, *serkewtin* maintains the valence increasing property of a preverb in Soranî. The simplex verb *kewtin* 'fall' (61) can always occur with an optional adjunct phrase like *le ser şaxekeya* 'on the mountain' (62).

(61) befir   kewt
     snow   fall.PST.3SG
     'Snow fell'

(62) befir   [le ser şax-eke=ya]   kewt
     snow   on   mountain-DEF.SG=on   fall.PST.3SG
     'Snow fell on the mountain'

However, *serkewtin* must occur with a locative argument marking the thing that is climbed (*ew serkewt) as shown in (63). This valence increasing function can be understood as an example of persistence (following Hopper 1991), that is, the tendency of formatives to retain elements of their etymon. In other words, *ser* marks a semantic derivation forming a new lexeme from a simplex verbal stem. The new derived verb has higher valence than its simplex counterpart, although *ser* cannot be synchronically understood to be an applicative marker because it is not productive.

(63) ew   be ser   şax-eke=ya   ser-kewt
     (s)he   onto   mountain-DEF.SG=on   up-fall.PST.3SG
     '(S)he climbed up the mountain'

The more restricted and less transparent function of *heł* in Soranî points to its older age as a preverb compared to *ser*. This, coupled with the retention of the earlier nominal and adpositional functions of *ser* beside the innovative function as a preverb, leads to the conclusion that there were at least five different stages when applicatives were recruited from before PIE up to Soranî, and some of these then lexicalized as preverbs. These are: stage(s) (1) that led to the system of preverbs inherited into the attested ancient Indo-European languages; stage (2) before the Middle Iranian period when nominals like Av. ərəz- 'right, upward' (> So. *heł* MP. *ul*) were recruited as adpositions and then as applicative ultimate lexicalizing as preverbs; stage (3) when prepositions were recruited along with their third-person singular pronominal complements as applicatives; stage before the New Iranian period when a new set of nominals (e.g., So. *ser*) were recruited as adpositions and then as preverbs which ultimately lexicalized; and stage (5) that recruited prepositions along with nominal complements as applicatives. Note that Only stages (3) and (5) are synchronically applicatives in Soranî, and the only difference among stages (1), (2), and (4) is their time depth relative to each other. These stages are summarized in Table 3.

Table 3: Stages of applicative recruitment.

#	Stage	Formative	example
1	OIr. PVs	So.: *ha* (cf. Av.: *ā* 'to')	*hatin* 'to come'
2	OIr. > MIr. PVs	So.: *heł* (cf. Av..: *ərəz-*)	*hełbijardin* 'to elect'
3	MIr. APPLs	So.: *pê*	*pêhatin* 'come by(INS)'
4	MIr. > NIr. PVs	So.: *ser* (cf. Av.: *sara* 'head')	*serkewtin* 'to climb'
5	NIr. APPL	So.: *legeł*	*legeł hatin* 'come with(COM)'

Note that the relative chronology presented here is primarily based on data from other extant Iranian languages. In Middle Persian, stage (2) has already taken place, and in some texts, there are examples of simplex prepositions with third-person singular complements existing alongside indexed or overt nominals. These formatives, termed "placeholder constructions" by Jügel (2016), differ from Soranî applicatives according to the nature of the argument they introduce but have the same etyma. For this reason, we have tentatively ordered stages (2) and (3) before (4) and (5), where (5) is attested only in Soranî. However, this ordering is contingent on the Soranî developments coinciding with cognate constructions in Middle Persian. Based on the Soranî-internal facts alone, stage (3) cannot be crucially ordered with respect to stage (2). The fact that there are no stage (5) applicatives that have lexicalized with certain verbs, while many stage (3) applicatives have, points to (3) predating (5).

6 Conclusions

Soranî applicative markers have most often been called absolute prepositions following MacKenzie's (1961) original terminology. This and other epithets have missed that these formatives have developed from the same material and carry a subset of the range of functions of applicatives in the world's languages. In this chapter, we showed that the label applicative accurately describes these formatives. The original term absolute preposition reflects the prepositional source of these formatives but crucially misses aspects of their morphosyntax.

Features of Soranî applicatives include: (1) there is more than one formally and functionally distinct applicative morpheme in the language. Applicative affixes are semantically specified, i.e., each can introduce a specific, close set of semantic roles.

(2) With the exception of malefactive, the set of semantic roles expressible by applicative constructions is a proper subset of the semantic roles expressible by prepositional phrases. All semantic roles except equative, privative, and limitative, expressed by the prepositions *wekû, bê* and *ta* respectively, have corresponding applicative markers.

(3) These applicative constructions are mandatory when the referent is anaphorically retrievable (i.e. a pronoun) but not topicalized or contrastive.

(4) The applied phrase introduced by the applicative is always indexed morphologically. In this sense, applied phrases always behave like pronominal objects. However, the adpositional phrases that they replace can be either core arguments realized as adpositional phrases or adjuncts.

(5) The combination of applicative marker and verb has lexicalized in some instances. These new lexemes have developed derived meanings with or without the corresponding valence increase.

(6) Unlike preverbs, applicative affixes in Soranî are synchronically productive.

From Proto-Indo-European through its Old and Middle Iranian ancestors, Soranî has gone through many cycles of applicative recruitment. Based on comparative historical evidence, we claimed that there were at least five historical stages of applicative recruitment: (i) the recruitment(s) that led to the system of preverbs in Old Iranian/PIE; (ii) the recruitment before the Middle Iranian period that resulted in the preverbs *heł* and *wer*, which were nominals in Old Iranian; (iii) the recruitment that resulted in the preverbs like *ser*, which were nominals in Middle Iranian; (iv) the recruitment that brought pronominal prepositional phrases into the verbal structure (e.g., *pê-, tê-, lê-,* and *-ê*); and (v) the recruitment that brought nominal prepositional phrases into the verbal structure (e.g., *leget, le ser,* and *-e ser*).[20] As for why some preverbs have such longevity while others are fully absorbed by the verbs that they complement, there are a variety of likely factors. Following Bybee (2002), frequency of occurrence with and without the verbal stems with which they pair may play a role. Essentially, as the adpositions leave the adpositional system and become used exclusively with verbs, they become verbal morphemes. If the prefix only occurs with a few verbs, and the

---

[20] See Karim (2020) for a more complete explanation of all the forms of the absolute prepositions. Of particular interest are the forms =ê, which originated in a pronoun alone (i.e., without a preposition, see section 4), and bo, which originates in a complex preposition. However, its constituent parts are not transparent like other absolute prepositions in its class (< be ew).

combined forms are more common than the verbs alone, they may be reanalyzed as morphologically simplex. This certainly is the case of *hatin* 'to come' from Old Iranian ĀGAM 'idem'. Soranî has no reflex of the simplex counterpart GAM 'to go'. Additionally, following Elsner *et al.* (2020), the phonological shape of the morphemes could affect whether or not sound changes render the prefix-verbal-stem combinations imparsable (fusional).

There have been many studies focusing on Soranî absolute prepositions (Samvelian 2007, Mohammadirad 2020, Edmonds 1955, Salehi 2018). The present study represents the first attempt to place these formatives under the umbrella of applicative markers. Soranî shows how throughout history applicatives can develop from multiple sources. Perhaps the most unique characteristic of Soranî applicatives is that the applied object has been integrated into the tense-sensitive argument indexing observed for Os. Additionally, applicatives have lexicalized as they univerbate with verb stems losing the original applicative functions. At the point when their productive functions are lost, they cease to be applicative markers synchronically. This process has proven to be cyclical throughout the history of the language.

Abbreviations

1	first person
2	second person
3	third person
ABL	ablative
ACC	accusative
ALL	allative
APM_1	present-tense affix person marker
APM_2	past-tense affix person marker
APPL	applicative
Av	Avestan
BEN	benefactive
CL	Bantu noun class
COM	comitative
CPM	clitic person marker
DAT	dative
DEF	definite
DEM	demonstrative
DIR	direct case
DIST	distal
ELA	elative
EXP	experiencer

EZ	ezafe;[22]
FV	final vowel
GEN	genitive
IMP	imperative
IND	indicative
INDF	indefinite
INS	instrumental
IPFV	imperfective
LOC	locative
LV	light-verb stem
M	masculine
MAL	malefactive
MIr	Middle Iranian
N	neutral gender
NEG	negative
NIr	New Iranian
NOM	nominative
NP	noun phrase
O	direct object
O$_{APPL}$	applied object
OBL	oblique case
OIr	Old Iranian
PIE	Proto-Indo-European
PL	plural
PP	adpositional (prepositional) phrase
PRF	perfect
PRH	prohibitive
PRN	pronominal index
PROX	proximal
PRS	present tense
PST	past tense
PV	preverb
S	single argument of an intransitive verb
SG	singular
So.	Soranî
SUPE	superessive
SUPL	superlative
TAM	tense, aspect, mood
Vd	Videvdad (section of the Avesta)
VP	verb phrase
Yt	Yasht (section of the Avesta)

References

Boyce, Mary. 1975. *A reader in Manichaean : Middle-Persian and Parthian*. Leiden: Brill. Bybee, Joan. 2002. Word frequency and context of use in the lexical diffusion of phoneti-cally conditioned sound change. *Language Variation and Change* 14(3). 261–290.
Cheung, Johnny. 2007. *Etymological dictionary of the Iranian verb*. Leiden: Brill.
Craig, Colette & Ken Hale. 1988. Relational Preverbs in Some Languages of the Americas: Typological and Historical Perspectives. *Language* 64(2). 312–344.
Crysmann, Berthold. 2003. Clitics and coordination in linear structure. In Birgit Gerlach & Janet Grijzenhout (eds.), *Clitics in phonology, morphology and syntax*, 121–59. Amsterdam: Benjamins.
Dixon, R. M. W. 1994. *Ergativity*. Cambridge: Cambridge University Press.
Edmonds, C. J. 1955. Prepositions and Personal Affixes in Southern Kurdish. *Bulletin of the School of Oriental and African Studies* 17(3). 490–502.
Elsner, Micha, Martha Booker Jonson, Stephanie Antetomaso, & Andrea D. Sims. 2020. Stop the Morphological Cycle, I Want to Get Off: Modeling the Development of Fusion. In *Proceedings of the society for computation in linguistics (scil) vol. 3, article 40*.
Fortson, Benjamin W. 2004. *Indo-European Language and Culture: An Introduction*. Hoboken, NJ: Wiley-Blackwell.
Gaedicke, Carl. 1880. *Der Accusativ im Veda*. Breslau: Koebner.
Haig, Geoffrey. 2008. *Alignment change in Iranian languages : a construction grammar approach*. New York: Mouton de Gruyter.
Hasandust, Muhammad. 2011. *Farhang-i tatbiqi-mawzu'i-i zubanha u guvishha-i irani-i naw*. Tehran: Nashar Asar.
Hock, Hans Henrich. 1991. *Principles of Historical Linguistics*. Berlin / New York: Mouton de Gruyter. 727.
Hopper, Paul J. 1991. On some principles of grammaticization. In Elizabeth Closs Traugott & Bernd Heine (eds.), *Approaches to grammaticalization, vol. i*, 17–36. Amsterdam: John Benjamins.
Jügel, Thomas. 2016. Enclitic Pronouns in Middle Persian and the Placeholder Construction. In Mahmoud Jaafari Dehaghi (ed.), *Quatery journal of language and inscription 1/1 [1396 h..], dedicated to professor Mansour Shaki*, 41–63. Tehran: Language and Inscription.
Karim, Shuan Osman. 2020. *From phrases to formatives: the diachrony of Soranî (Central Kurdish) applicative markers*. Columbus, OH: (in review).
Karim, Shuan Osman and Ali Salehi. 2020. *Soranî Valence Changing Affixes: Teetering on the boundary between morphology and syntax. Presented at the 94th Annual Meeting of the Linguistic Society of America*. New Orleans, LA.
Kathol, Andreas. 2000. *Linear syntax*. Oxford: Oxford University Press.
Korn, Agnes. 2016. *Western Iranian Pronominal Clitics*. Universitet, Uppsala dissertation. 159–171.
Kulikov, Leonid. 2012. Vedic preverbs as markers of valency-changing derivations. *Studies in Language* 36(4). 721–746. https://doi.org/10.1075/sl.36.4.01kul.
Kümmel, Martin Joachim. 2014. The development of laryngeals in Indo-Iranian. In *The sound of indo-european*. Opava.
Kuryłowicz, Jerzy. 1947. La nature des procés dits Analogiques. *Acta Linguistica* 5. 17–34.
MacKenzie, David N. 1961. *Kurdish Dialect Studies*. London: Oxford University Press.

MacKenzie, David N. 1999. The 'Indirect affectee' in Pahlavi (1964). In Carlo G Cereti and Ludwig Paul (eds.), *Iranica diversa i*, 3–6. Roma: Istituto italiano per l'Africa e l'Oriente.
Mahmoudveysi, Parvin., Denise. Bailey, Ludwig. Paul, & Geoffrey. Haig. 2012. *The Gorani Language of Gawraju, a village of West Iran: texts, grammar, and lexicon*. Wiesbaden: Reichert. 276.
Mithun, Marianne. 2001. Understanding and explaining applicatives. In Mary Andronis, Christopher Ball, Heidi Elston, & Sylvain Neuvel (eds.), *Proceedings of the thirty-seventh meeting of the Chicago Linguistic Society: functionalism and formalism in linguistic theory*, 73–97. Chicago: Chicago Linguistics Society.
Mohammadirad, Masoud. 2020. *Pronominal clitics in Western Iranian languages: Description, mapping, and typological implications*. Université Sorbonne Nouvelle Paris 3 dissertation. https://tel.archives-ouvertes.fr/tel-02988008/document.
Öpengin, Ergin. 2016. *The Mukri variety of Central Kurdish : grammar, texts, and lexicon*. Wiesbadn: Reichert Verlag.
Peterson, David A. 2007. *Applicative constructions*. Oxford; New York: Oxford University Press.
Pokorny, Julius. 1959. *Indogermanisches etymologisches Wörterbuch*. Bern: Francke. Salehi, Ali. 2018. *Constraints on Izfa in Sorani Kurdish*. Univerity of Kentucky MA thesis. https://doi.org/10.13023/etd.2018.351.
Samvelian, Pollet. 2007. A Lexical Account of Sorani Kurdish Prepositions. In Stefan Müller (ed.), *Proceedings of the 14th international conference on head-driven phrase structure grammar*, 235–249. Stanford: CSLI Publications.
Sheyholislami, Jaffer. 2021. The History and Development of Literary Central Kurdish. In Hamit Bozarslan (ed.), *The Cambridge history of the kurds*, 633–662. Cambridge: Cambridge University Press.
Skjærvø, Prods Oktor. 2003. *An Introduction to Young Avestan*. Boston: Harvard University.
Thackston, Wheeler M. 2002. *Kurmanji Kurdish: A reference grammar with selected readings*. Boston: Harvard University.
Thackston, Wheeler M. 2004. *Sorani Kurdish: A reference grammar with selective readings*. Cambridge, Mass.: Harvard University.
de Vaan, Michiel & Javier Martínez García. 2014. *Introduction to avestan*. (Brill Introductions to Indo-European Languages). Leiden: Brill.
Weir, E M H. 1987. 'Footprints of Yesterday's Syntax: Diachronic Development of Certain Verb Prefixes in an OSV Language (Nadëb)'. *Lingua* 68. 291–316.

Yankee Modi and Mark W. Post

11 Applicatives in Macro-Tani languages (Trans-Himalayan, Eastern Himalaya): Forms, functions and historical origins

Abstract: This chapter discusses applicative constructions in Macro-Tani, a small group of Trans-Himalayan languages spoken in northeastern India and Tibet. We first present a background discussion of Macro-Tani grammatical relations and predicate structures. We then outline some basic properties of Macro-Tani applicatives, focusing more closely on less-commonly identified applicative properties. We find that: (a) there is no "promotional" relationship between base and applied phrases in Macro-Tani languages; Macro-Tani applicatives do not function to "promote" an oblique to core argument status, but instead add an argument which in most cases could not otherwise be expressed in the clause at all. (b) While Macro-Tani applicatives principally add grammatical (indirect) Objects, some applicatives add oblique phrases such as Goals and Instruments. (c) Macro-Tani applicatives form an unusually large class (at least dozens), and include semantically rich and typologically rare functions such as "Territive" (addition of an object that is "shocked" as a result of the predicate) and "Eruditive" (an object that is "educated" or "shown how" by means of the predicate). (d) Macro-Tani applicatives are closely aligned to Macro-Tani causatives, and could be argued to constitute a single formal and functional class. The chapter closes with our reconstruction of the origin of Macro-Tani applicatives via morphologization of an earlier serial verb construction.

Yankee Modi, University of Sydney, Department of Linguistics, A18 Manning Road, Sydney, Australia, e-mail: yankee.modi@sydney.edu.au
Mark W. Post, University of Sydney, Department of Linguistics, A18 Manning Road, Sydney, Australia, e-mail: mark.post@sydney.edu.au

1 Introduction

This chapter[1] discusses applicative constructions in Macro-Tani, a small group of Trans-Himalayan[2] languages spoken in northeastern India and Tibet. Section 2 first presents some background information regarding Macro-Tani grammars, focusing on predicate and clause/argument structures. Section 3 is the main section of the paper, and discusses the forms and functions of Macro-Tani applicatives. Like other chapters in this volume, special emphasis will be placed on features of Macro-Tani applicatives which seem less well-reflected in the literature on applicatives more generally; these will include (a) the lack of a "promotional" relationship between base and applied phrases, (b) the existence of some applicatives which appear to add obliques either in alternation with or instead of objects, (c) the very large number of semantically rich applicatives that occur in Macro-Tani languages, and (d) the close categorical resemblance of Macro-Tani applicatives to other valence-interacting derivations, especially causatives. Section 4 will seek to explain some of these special features in relation to the historical origins of Macro-Tani applicatives, while section 5 will conclude our presentation with some remarks concerning the contribution of Macro-Tani languages to applicative typology.

---

1 The alphabetically listed authors have contributed equally to this chapter. Both authors acknowledge helpful discussions with the editors, as well as with Peter Arkadiev, Chris Donlay, Guillaume Jacques, Pavel Ozerov, and two anonymous reviewers, while taking full responsibility for the contents. This work was supported by a University of Sydney SOAR Fellowship to the second named author, for which both authors are grateful.

2 "Trans-Himalayan" refers to the language family that, for the past several decades, has most often been labelled "Sino-Tibetan". The label "Sino-Tibetan" has the disadvantages of (a) implying a primary bifurcation between "Sinitic" and "Tibeto-Burman" macro-phyla, which is a theory that remains controversial, and (b) assigning prominence to "major" (written and state-sanctioned) languages or subgroups at the expense of most languages in the family, which are traditionally oral languages spoken by small populations. "Trans-Himalayan" is a neutral geographic label on the model of "Trans-New Guinea", and its substitution for "Sino-Tibetan" can thus be compared to replacement of "Hamito-Semitic" with "Afro-Asiatic". Further discussion may be found in van Driem (2014) and Blench and Post (2014); for a dissenting opinion, see LaPolla (2016a).

2 Preliminaries

2.1 Macro-Tani languages

"Macro-Tani" names a group of around 8–12 Trans-Himalayan languages spoken by perhaps around one million people, primarily in the northeastern Indian states of Arunachal Pradesh and Assam, and in much smaller numbers in Tibet. The term "Macro-Tani" is relatively new, and refers to our inclusion of the Milang language together with more mainstream Tani languages in this chapter. Although Milang seems not to descend directly from the most recent common ancestor of all Tani languages proper (Post and Modi 2011), Milang and Tani grammars are extremely similar – a consequence both of their probable genealogical relatedness at a deeper level, and of a long period of subsequent language contact – and so can be profitably discussed in a shared context. Unless otherwise noted, all general statements made in this chapter may be assumed to hold true of all Macro-Tani languages thus defined, to the extent that we have been able to determine.

2.2 Macro-Tani grammars 1: Predicate structure

Like most other languages with applicatives, Macro-Tani languages are morphologically synthetic and agglutinating, with an expansive predicate structure. Macro-Tani predicates contain an obligatory root; final (non-embedded, non-chained) predicates are also terminated by at least one and as many as three tense-aspect-mood inflections. Between the root and inflection is an optional derivational position, which is one of the most interesting and productive aspects of Macro-Tani grammars. Predicate derivations handle a very large number of functions relating to manner, result, aktionsart, (associated) motion and direction, modality and valence interaction (enhanced specification, rearrangement and/ or change), and may be stacked in sets of as many as five or six (Figure 1). The applicative morphemes we will discuss in this chapter all fall within this macro-category of predicate derivations (1).

[[VRoot(-**PDer**)]PStem-PInfl]Pred

Figure 1: Basic structure of a Macro-Tani predicate.

(1) bɨ   tatɨk=əm   gok-**ta-kɨ-ram-hɨ**-to=pə.
    3SG   frog=DEF.ACC   [call-**INCP-TENT-FRUS-SAUT**-PFV]=DUB
    NP.SBJ   NP.OBJ   [VROOT-**PDER**-PINFL]_PRED=PARTICLES

'He must have **tried but failed to** call the frog.' (Upper Minyong; Eastern Tani, Arunachal Pradesh) [attested utterance adapted for presentation in this chapter][3]

2.3 Macro-Tani grammars 2: Clause/argument structure

Macro-Tani clause syntax is predicate-final, and shows accusative relational alignment with differential object marking. Clauses headed by a simple (non-derived) predicate may be atransitive, intransitive, (mono)transitive, or ditransitive, having zero, one, two or three core arguments, respectively. Subject (S/A) is a robustly coded grammatical relation in Macro-Tani languages, and is distinguished in most languages by an absence of overt relational marking (2)–(3), a dedicated subject nominalizer, cross-clause co-reference restrictions, and person-sensitive inflections such as egophoric TAM markers (cf. Post 2011: 262).

(2) ŋo   yup-to.
    1SG   sleep-PFV
    SBJ   PRED
    'I slept.' (Lower Adi; Eastern Tani, Arunachal Pradesh and Assam)

(3) ŋo   apin   do-to.
    1SG   cooked.rice   eat-PFV
    SBJ   OBJ   PRED
    'I ate (cooked rice ~ my meal).' (Lower Adi)

---

[3] All illustrative examples in this chapter are from the authors' field data, publications (where noted), or native speaker knowledge of the first named author (Lower Adi data only, which thus form the majority of all constructed examples in this chapter). Data have been orthographically regularized for sake of presentation, largely following IPA but with the exceptions that y = [j], č = [tɕ], and ǰ = [dʑ]. Certain alternations have been orthographically regularized, e.g. s = [s] in some languages but [ɕ] in others. Lexical tones are represented only in those Macro-Tani languages whose tone systems have been fully described and analysed; in Galo, superscripted numerals represent underlying tone categories, e.g. um^2- 'grunt'.

Grammatical objects are typically unmarked for relationality when generic (3) or indefinite (4). Generic objects additionally take no referential marking, almost always immediately precede the predicate, and further tend to form a prosodic unit together with the predicate (3). Accordingly, there is at least some basis for considering generic objects to be both grammatically and phonologically integrated within a Macro-Tani predicate ("incorporated", in some sense of the idea). Indefinite objects form no such prosodic unit with the predicate, have greater syntactic freedom,[4] and must be considered as forming an independent, relationally unmarked noun phrase (4).

(4) ŋo   əkum   ko   kaa-to.
     1SG   house   INDF   see-PFV
     SBJ   OBJ   PRED
     'I saw a house.' (Lower Adi)

Definite objects take a variety of markers, depending on both grammatical and semantic/pragmatic factors. Most object pronouns (including demonstratives) obligatorily take an accusative suffix reflecting Proto-(Macro-)Tani *-m. Definite common nominal-headed noun phrases typically take an enclitic əm, which reflects an earlier definite article + accusative composition P(M)T *ʰə-m;[5] in Milang, these forms occur as (u)m. Noun phrases headed by human or human-like proper names, as well as those headed by nominals referring to non-human high animates or otherwise discourse-prominent entities, typically take a non-agentive postposition whose form differs from language to language; in most Eastern Tani languages, the non-agentive postposition mə seems relatable to the accusative marker (5). In the Western Tani language Galo, non-agentive ne² seems to reflect a distinct etymon.

(5) ŋo   no-m /   əkum=əm /   aabu=mə   kaa-to.
     1SG   2SG-ACC /   house=DEF.ACC /   father=NAGT   see-PFV
     SBJ   OBJ   PRED
     'I saw you / the house / Father.' (Lower Adi)

Clauses in Macro-Tani languages may contain multiple grammatical objects, marked according to the principles outlined above. Although preferred order

---

[4] For example, in the order of subject and indefinite object noun phrases could be inverted, with a pragmatic difference but with no difference in meaning. Inversion of subject and generic object is not generally possible (examples omitted in the interest of space).
[5] In some languages, such as Galo (Western Tani, Arunachal Pradesh), third person pronouns pattern with common nouns in this respect.

seems to be [A R T PRED] – possibly reflecting principles of animacy and/or discourse prominence – semantic roles are disambiguated pragmatically in the cases of full (definite or indefinite) noun phrases, and other orders are also possible (6).

(6) ŋo   no-m   do-nam   ko   bi-ye.
    1SG   2SG-ACC   eat-NMLZ.OBJ   INDF   give-IRR
    A/SBJ   R/OBJ   T/OBJ   PRED
    'I'll give you something to eat.' (Lower Adi)

R and T arguments are thus alike in terms of relational marking and ordering conventions. Similarly, object nominalizer -*nam* 'NMLZ.OBJ' – which references the single O argument of Lower Adi *do-* 'eat' in (6) above – can reference either the R or T arguments of a ditransitive verb such as Lower Adi *bi-* 'give' (7).

(7) ŋo-k   si-m   bi-**nam**
    1SG-GEN PRX-ACC   give-**NMLZ.OBJ**
    (a) '**the (person) to whom** I gave <u>this (thing)</u>' (-*nam* references R) or
    (b) '**what** I gave to <u>this (person)</u>' (-*nam* references T) (Lower Adi)

R and T arguments differ, however, in their capacities to stand as a generic argument and form a single grammatical and prosodic unit with the predicate ("accessibility to incorporation", in one possible analysis): although T arguments can do so, R arguments cannot. There is accordingly at least some basis for describing ditransitive T arguments as "direct objects (OBJ.D)", and R arguments as "indirect objects (OBJ.I)" (8)–(9) – despite that such a distinction would appear neutralized in most constructions.

(8) ŋo   əki=əm   do-nam   bi-ye.
    1SG   dog=DEF.ACC   eat-NMLZ.OBJ   give-IRR
    A/SBJ   R/OBJ.I   T/OBJ.D   PRED
    'I'll feed the dog [I'll give the dog food].' (Lower Adi)

(9) */?ŋo   do-nam=əm   əki   bi-ye.
    1SG   eat-NMLZ.OBJ=DEF.ACC   dog   give-IRR
    (*intended meaning: 'I'll give the food to a(ny) dog.'; ?'I'll give dog to the food.') (Lower Adi)

The acceptability of (6) and (8) notwithstanding, it is rare for more than one or at most two core argument noun phrases to be overtly represented in a Macro-Tani clause in natural discourse. As in most languages of East/Southeast Asia, arguments which are highly predictable within a discourse tend to be omitted (10).

(10) *bi-ye.*
 give-IRR
 '(Someone) will give (something to someone).' (Lower Adi)

Finally, Goal noun phrases have some unique properties in Macro-Tani languages, being neither precisely grammatical objects nor adjuncts (hence, "obliques"). Goals tend to occur predicate-adjacent like a generic object nominal (11), yet they tend to lack other object properties such as capacity to be marked in the accusative or non-agentive when definite. They are also referenced by a locative nominalizer (usually *-ko*, as in Galo *in¹-ko²* 'place of going ~ place that (somebody) went to'), rather than by an object nominalizer. This patterning is relevant to our discussion of certain applicative morphemes in section 3.

(11) bɨ   iskul   gi-duŋ.
 3SG   school go-IPFV
 SBJ   OBL   PRED
 'He's going to school.' (Lower Adi)

3 Applicatives in Macro-Tani languages: Forms and functions

3.1 Basic applicative forms and functions

As discussed in section 2.2, Macro-Tani morphemes with applicative functions occur to the right of a root, in the derivational area of predicate structure. Their core function is to *add a semantic participant* to the event structure that a Macro-Tani predicate projects – in most though perhaps not all cases, a non-Actor (we will discuss some possible cases in which Macro-Tani applicatives may add Actors in section 3.5). In Table 1 from Lower Adi, note that the derived (applicativized) predicate stem obligatorily entails reference to some usually non-Actor participant, in addition to the A and O arguments for which the root is lexically specified.

Table 1: Base and applicativized stems in Lower Adi (selection).

Type	Base	Appl	Meaning
Benefactive/ Malefactive		do-**bi**	'(someone) eat (something) **for/against (someone)**'
Instrumental		do-**na**	'(someone) eat (something) **with/using (something)**'
Comitative	do- 'eat (something)'	do-**bo**	'(someone) **co**-eat (something) **with (someone); bring or lead (someone)** in one's eating (of something)'
Comparative		do-**yaŋ**	'(someone) eat (something) **more than (someone)**'
Prioritive		do-**poŋ**	'(someone) eat (something) **before (someone)**'
Expugnative		do-**kum**	'(someone,) by eating (something), **cause (someone) to be defeated**'
...		...	...

The bolded "applied participants" in Table 1 are understood as logically present in the event structure whether or not they are overtly expressed in the clause syntax (in keeping with the overall character of the language as regards the overt syntactic expression of logical arguments; see section 2.3). In example (12) from Tangam, note that the applied object *ŋoru* '1.PL' is only overtly expressed in the first of two coordinated clauses, but is just as clearly understood in the second, in which it is omitted.

(12) *ŋorumme paasa geaabikumaape, aha dadaabikumaape. ella.*
ŋoru=me paasa ge-aŋ-**bi**-ku-ma(ŋ)-pe aha
1.PL=NAGT firewood carry/wear-INWARD-BEN-COMPL-NEG-SBRD.MAN sago
dat-aŋ-**bi**-ku-ma(ŋ)-pe en-la.
remove.skin.from.plant-INWARD-BEN-COMPL-NEG-SBRD.MAN say-NF
'"You're not bringing **us** firewood; you're not getting **(us)** sago," they say.'
(Tangam; pre-Western-Tani, Arunachal Pradesh) (Post 2017: 59)

Macro-Tani applicatives can occur without apparent restriction in clauses of any base transitivity type, including atransitives, intransitives, monotransitives, and ditransitives (cf. section 2.3). Examples of applicativized transitive clauses appear widely in this chapter; here, we further present examples of applicativized atransitive, intransitive and ditransitive clauses (13)–(15).

(13) waah! silo **ŋolu-m** gai-ruu=pə dooɲi-**bi**-duŋ!
     EXCL today **1.PL-ACC** good-INTS=AVZR shine.sun-**BEN**-IPFV
     'Wah! The sun is shining so nicely **for us** today!' ~ 'Today it's so nicely sunny **for us**!' (Lower Adi)

(14) sa, **yaalek mə** ib-**bo**-la.
     CONC **NAME NAGT** sleep-**COMIT/BEN**-HORT.POL
     'Go ahead, **take/put Yalek to** bed (to sleep).' (Lower Adi)

(15) yaalek kə **ŋolu-m** rooŋ bi-**bo**-nam=ə
     NAME GEN **1.PL-ACC** colour give-**COMIT/BEN**-NMLZ:OBJ=DEF
     kampu=ə!
     pretty=COP.MIR
     'The picture Yalek made **for us** [in the course of our shared experience of painting, e.g.] is so pretty!' (Lower Adi)[6]

3.2 Grammatical status of applied phrases

As examples (12)–(15) have also illustrated, Macro-Tani applicatives most often license a grammatical *(indirect) object*.[7] For example, in (12) above, note that the Tangam lexical root *ge-* 'carry/wear' is monotransitive, and normally takes only a single (direct) object. Benefactive applicative *-bi* licenses the second object and assigns it the semantic role of Beneficiary or Maleficiary (according to context; Beneficiary in example (12)). In the following examples from Milang, (16) illustrates a canonical monotransitive clause based on *tu-* 'eat'; (17) shows that *samus* 'spoon' cannot occur as a second object in such a clause, while (18) shows that the same phrase is licensed by the Instrumental applicative *-na* (cf. Modi 2017: 423–424).

---

[6] Lower Adi Comitative *-bo* has a somewhat Benefactive "feel" in this example. The distinction between the Lower Adi Comitative and the true Lower Adi Benefactive *-bi* is one in which, in the case of the Comitative, both the Agent and the applied argument are understood as co-participants in the event, with the applied argument typically understood as benefiting in some way from the Agent's direction of the activity. In a true Benefactive, the Agent carries out an action "on behalf of" the applied argument. This distinction is very difficult to represent using succinct English translations; some further discussion will be found in section 3.5.
[7] By "license" is here meant "enable an expression to appear in clause syntax which would otherwise be disallowed."

(16) ŋa   adu=um   tu-tu.
      1SG   rice.cooked=DEF.ACC eat-PFV
      'I ate the rice.' (Milang, Macro-Tani; Arunachal Pradesh)

(17) *ŋa   **samus=um**   adu=um   tu-tu.
      1SG   **spoon=DEF.ACC** rice.cooked=DEF.ACC eat-PFV

(18) ŋa   **samus=um**   adu=um   tu-**na**-tu.
      1SG   **spoon=DEF.ACC** rice.cooked=DEF.ACC eat-**INSTR**-PFV
      '**I used the spoon** to eat the rice **with** ~ I ate the rice **with the spoon**.' (Milang)

Evidence for the "indirect" as opposed to "direct" object status of applied phrases in Macro-Tani languages consists primarily in their incapacity to immediately precede the predicate as a generic, unmarked nominal ("access to incorporation"; see section 2.3). In the following examples, also from Milang, (19) contrasts with (16) above to show that a lexically-specified Patient object can immediately precede the predicate with generic reference. (20) contrasts with (18) above to show that applied objects can occur in any order relative to the predicate and the lexically-specified object – crucially, including in predicate-adjacent position – when they are marked as referential. (21) and (22) then show that while the lexically-specified object can immediately precede the predicate with generic reference, the same is *not* true of the applied object, which *must* be overtly marked for referentiality in this position.

(19) ŋa   adu   tu-tu.
      1SG   rice.cooked   eat-PFV
      'I ate rice ~ I ate food ~ I had my meal.' (Milang)

(20) ŋa   adu=um   **samus=um**   tu-**na**-tu.
      1SG   rice.cooked=DEF.ACC **spoon=DEF.ACC**   eat-**INSTR**-PFV
      I ate the rice **with/using the spoon**.' (Milang)

(21) ŋa   **samus=um**   adu   tu-**na**-tu.
      1SG   **spoon=DEF.ACC** rice.cooked   eat-**INSTR**-PFV
      '**I used the spoon** to eat rice (on/with).' (Milang)

(22) *^{/?}ŋa adu=um   **samus** tu-**na**-tu.
      1SG   rice.cooked=DEF.ACC **spoon** eat-**INSTR**-PFV
      (*intended meaning, 'I used a(ny) spoon to eat the rice with.'[8] (Milang)

Also consider example (23) from Lower Adi: in this example, *ami* 'person' occurs inside an externally headed relative clause, whose head is its logical Patient (grammatical object of *laa-* 'take'). Here, *ami* 'person' can only be interpreted as an Agent (grammatical subject of *laa-* 'take'); in order for *ami* 'person' to be interpretable as an applied object, it would need to be definite and case-marked. Note that in (23), the logical applied object *ŋo-m* '1SG-ACC' is omitted; if overt, it must precede the (non-referential) subject *ami* 'person'.[9]

(23) ami   laa-bi-nam   əki=ə   dug-ɲok-kai
      person take-BEN-NMLZ:OBJ   dog=DEF   run-LOST.RESULT-PF
      [RELC   N=REF]$_{NP.SUB}$ PRED
      'The dog that someone gave (me) ran away.'
      * 'The dog that was given to someone ran away.' (Lower Adi)

So far, we have only considered the licensing by Macro-Tani applicatives of grammatical objects. Although objects are certainly the most frequent type of applied phrase, they may not be the only type. For example, a frequent "Inseritive" directional (and/or associated motion) applicative reflecting Proto-Tani *-*lik* is found widely among Tani languages; its primary function is to add a (Locative-marked) Goal oblique noun phrase "into" which an action is directed. In (24), we see that the base predicate headed by *dəm-* 'beat' can optionally take a Locative-marked Location adjunct, but cannot accommodate a Locative-marked Goal argument (25). However, a Goal argument is licensed by the Inseritive applicative in (26). Note that despite their both being marked by a Locative, these two phrase types are grammatically distinct, and the Locative adjunct can continue to occur in the applicativized clause (27).[10]

---

[8] The odd-seeming reading ?'I used the rice to eat spoons with' could be understood if *adu* 'cooked rice' were somehow interpretable as an Instrument/applied object. The point here is that *samus* 'spoon' is *not* interpretable as an Instrument/applied object if it is unmarked and predicate-adjacent.

[9] This of course assumes that *ami* 'person' occurs verb-adjacent with generic reference. If *ami* 'person' were marked for referentiality, either argument could appear in either position.

[10] Further discussion of the question of "promotion" will be found in the following section. Note that in (24)–(27) we have substituted 'dog' for 'nail' for semantic reasons.

(24) ŋo (əkum lo) əkiəm dəmto.
      ŋo   **(əkum lo)**   əkii=əm   dəm-to
      1SG   **house LOC**   dog=DEF.ACC   beat-PFV
      'I beat the dog **((while located) in the house)**.' (Lower Adi)

(25) ŋo kiliəm (*giaalo) dəmto.
      ŋo   kilii=əm   **(giaŋ=lo)**   dəm-to
      1SG   nail=DEF.ACC   **pillar=LOC** beat-PFV
      'I hit the nail **(*into the pillar)**.' (Lower Adi)

(26) ŋo kiliəm giaalo dəmlɨkto.
      ŋo   kilii=əm   **giaŋ=lo**   dəm-**lɨk**-to
      1SG   nail=DEF.ACC   **pillar=LOC** beat-**INSR**-PFV
      'I hit the nail **into the pillar**.' (Lower Adi)

(27) ŋo əkum lo kiliəm giaalo dəmlɨkto.
      ŋo   **əkum lo**   kilii=əm   **giaŋ=lo**   dəm-**lɨk**-to
      1SG   **house LOC**   nail=DEF.ACC   **pillar=LOC** beat-**INSR**-PFV
      'I hit the nail **into the pillar (while located) in the house**.' (Lower Adi)

The Inseritive applicative operates differently on predicates (such as those headed by motion verbs) that are already specified for a Goal argument. In such cases, -*lɨk* 'INSR' functions to add an *object* argument which is understood as being "inserted" into the Goal (28)–(29).

(28) ŋo (*koo də-m) iskul gɨ-to.
      1SG   kid   ANAP-ACC   school go-PFV
      'I went to school.' (Lower Adi)

(29) ŋo **koo də-m** iskul gɨ-**lɨk**-to.
      1SG   **kid**   **ANAP-ACC**   school go-**INSR**-PFV
      'I walked **the kid** to school.' (Lower Adi)

In a few cases, an applied noun phrase can appear to take either object or adjunct-like marking. In the Lower Adi examples (30)–(32), note first that a Mediative-marked Instrument noun phrase can occur as an optional adjunct to a monotransitive clause (30). (31) and (32) then show that the same Instrument noun phrase can be referenced by the Instrumental applicative -*na*, marked *either* as a Mediative noun phrase (like the adjunct in (30)) *or* as a Definite accusative object. In both (31) and (32) – unlike in (30) – the Instrument is understood whether overt or not, due to the presence of the applicative. The difference between Mediative and Definite accusative marking in (31)–(32) is semantico-pragmatic: (31) might be uttered in a case where instrumentality was in focus, as in answer to the question "did you eat the rice with a fork?", while (32) might be uttered in a case where the spoon was a focal referent (as in answer to the question "what did you do with the spoon?"). However, Definite accusative marking as in (32) relies on the presence of the applicative; in its absence, (32) would be unacceptable (cf. the identically-structured Milang example in (17)).

(30) ŋo **(samus ki)** apin=əm do-to.
 1SG **spoon MED** rice=DEF.ACC eat-PFV
 'I ate the rice **(with a spoon)**.' (Lower Adi)

(31) ŋo **(samus ki)** apin=əm do-**na**-to.
 1SG **spoon MED** rice=DEF.ACC eat-**INSTR**-PFV
 I **used (a spoon) to** eat the rice **(with)**.' (Lower Adi)

(32) ŋo **(samus=əm)** apin=əm do-**na**-to.
 1SG **spoon=DEF.ACC** rice=DEF.ACC eat-**INSTR**-PFV
 'I **used (the spoon) to** eat the rice.' (Lower Adi)

Thus, the question might again arise as to whether a sentence such as (32) should constitute a case of "promotion", of the adjunct noun phrase in (30) to object status. The acceptability of sentences such as (31) suggests that this is probably *not* the case; rather, the Instrumental applicative simply functions to add a *semantic* argument, which for this particular clause type can be marked either as an object or as an adjunct depending on the pragmatics of focus (see also this volume, chapters 3, 7, and 8).

Applicatives can similarly interact with semantically-compatible non-object noun phrases when the applied object is absent from the clause. Such cases would seem to be attributable to pragmatic inference rather than to grammatical relationship. For example, from the Lower Adi base clause in (33), (34) illustrates addition of an applied Maleficiary object; (35) then shows that an object-embedded genitive phrase is preferentially interpreted as referring to the same (applied) referent. However, (36) shows that if there is an overt applied object, this "default" interpretation is no longer available. This indicates that the embedded genitive phrase is in fact not an applied phrase.

(33) əki=ə   adin=əm   do-duŋ.
     dog=DEF   meat=DEF.ACC   eat-IPFV
     'The dog is eating meat.' (Lower Adi)

(34) əki=ə   **ŋo-m**   adin=əm   do-**bi**-duŋ.
     dog=DEF   **1SG-ACC**   meat=DEF.ACC   eat-**BEN**-IPFV
     'The dog is eating the meat **against/negatively affecting me**.' (Lower Adi)

(35) əki=ə   ŋo-k   adin=əm   do-**bi**-duŋ.
     dog=DEF   1SG-GEN   meat=DEF.ACC   eat-**BEN**-IPFV
     'The dog is eating my meat **against/negatively affecting (me)**.' (Lower Adi)

(36) əki=ə   **no-m**   ŋo-k   adin=əm   do-**bi**-duŋ.
     dog=DEF   **2SG-ACC**   1SG-GEN   meat=DEF.ACC   eat-**BEN**-IPFV
     'The dog is eating **my** meat **against/negatively affecting you**.' (Lower Adi)

Similarly, we find that a dative-marked noun phrase is interpretable as being at least semantically (if not grammatically) associated with the Benefactive applicative derivation in a sentence such as (37). However, such an interpretation again relies on the absence of an overt second object in the clause syntax: (38) shows that addition of such an overt second object forces a reading in which the second object is referenced by the applicative. If a non-co-referential dative noun phrase continues to occur in the clause syntax, it must then be interpreted as an adjunct.

(37) **ŋolu-k**   **ləgaa=pə**   asi=əm   koo kidar=ə   ǰoo-**bi**-duŋ.
     1.PL-GEN **reason=DAT** water=DEF.ACC kid group=DEF   heft-**BEN**-IPFV
     'The kids are hefting water **to/for us**.' (Lower Adi)

(38) ŋolu-k   ləgaa=pə   **bulu-m**   asi=əm   koo kidar=ə
     1.PL-GEN   reason=DAT   **3.PL-ACC**   water=DEF.ACC kid group=DEF
     ǰoo-**bi**-duŋ.
     heft-**BEN**-IPFV
     'The kids are hefting water **to/for them** to benefit us/on our behalf.'
     (Lower Adi)

3.3 The derivational nature of applicatives

As is discussed in this volume's introduction, many standard definitions of applicative morphemes focus on a putative derivational relationship between a base clause – in which a given lexically un-specified noun phrase is expressed as an adjunct – and an applied clause in which "the same argument" is "promoted" to object. For example, Peterson, writing in the *Oxford Bibliography of Linguistics*, defines applicatives as "constructions [that] allow languages to express **what otherwise would be expressed as an oblique participant** as a core object participant" (Peterson 2019; our emphasis).[11] A few definitions of applicatives focus on their capacity to expand clause argument structure through introduction of a new object argument, and do not necessarily consider a relationship to a base oblique as criterial; however, such definitions tend nonetheless to acknowledge that such a relationship may exist (Polinsky 2013, Zúñiga and Kittilä 2019: 53).

We argue that, as far as Macro-Tani languages are concerned, there is no relationship whatsoever between applied (core) arguments and any oblique or adjunct noun phrases that may or may not appear in the base clause. Our claim is that Macro-Tani applicatives function solely to add a participant to a base clause, in most cases when such a participant could not have otherwise been understood to have been present at all. It is possible in Macro-Tani languages to create base/applicativized clause pairs in which applied participants at least appear to bear the same semantic role as do base obliques or adjuncts (39)–(40) (cf. also (30)–(32)). However, we consider such similarities to be purely fortuitous: a closer examination reveals that while base obliques/adjuncts and applied phrases may refer to the same participant, they do so in semantically quite different ways. For example, in the base clause of (39) below, the bolded adjunct noun phrase presents a more elaborated construal of the beneficiary, who is placed at a distance from the event. In the applicativized clause of (39), the applied object is construed as closer to the core to the event.

(39) **ŋolu-k ləgaa=pə** asi=əm koo kɨdar=ə ǰoo-duŋ.
   1.PL-GEN reason=DAT water=DEF.ACC kid group=DEF heft-IPFV
   'The kids are hefting the water **to/for us**.' ~ 'The kids are hefting the water **on our behalf**.' (Lower Adi)

(40) **ŋolu-m** asi=əm koo kɨdar=ə ǰoo-**bi**-duŋ.
   1.PL-ACC water=DEF.ACC kid group=DEF heft-**BEN**-IPFV
   'The kids are hefting the water **to/for us**.' ~ 'The kids are hefting **us** the water.' (Lower Adi)

---

[11] Also see Peterson (2007: 1).

In other cases, it is simply not possible to paraphrase an applicativized clause by adding an oblique or adjunct noun phrase to the base clause. Consider the below set of clauses, which illustrate use of a Lower Adi Adfective applicative.[12] Example (41) demonstrates that an object cannot be present in the intransitive base clause. (42) illustrates addition of an applied object via the Adfective applicative. As far as we have been able to ascertain, there is no way of expressing the given meaning via a paraphrased base clause, neither in Lower Adi nor in any Macro-Tani language with which we are familiar. Examples (43)–(46) present the full set of available oblique or adjunct noun phrase types in Lower Adi, formed via the full set of available postpositions: Locative, Dative, Ablative and Mediative, respectively. None yields the semantic interpretation achieved through use of an Adfective applicative.

(41) koo   də   (*əki=əm)   ɲil-duŋ.
     child ANAP dog=DEF.ACC laugh-IPFV
     'The kid is laughing (*the dog).' (Lower Adi)

(42) koo   də   əki=əm   ɲil-**kaa**-duŋ.
     child ANAP dog=DEF.ACC laugh-**ADF**-IPFV
     'The kid is laughing **at the dog**.' (Lower Adi)

(43) koo   də   əki=lo   ɲil-duŋ.
     child ANAP dog=LOC   laugh-IPFV
     'The kid is laughing **in (i.e., while inside) the/a dog**.' (Lower Adi)

(44) koo   də   əki=pə   ɲil-duŋ.
     child ANAP dog=DAT   laugh-IPFV
     'The kid is laughing **like/as a dog**.' (Lower Adi)

(45) koo   də   əki=lok   ɲil-duŋ.
     child ANAP dog=ABL   laugh-IPFV
     'The kid is laughing **with/using the/a dog**.' (Lower Adi)

(46) koo   də   əki=kɨ   ɲil-duŋ.
     child ANAP dog=MED   laugh-IPFV
     'The kid is laughing **by means of the/a dog**.' (Lower Adi)

---

12 The Macro-Tani Adfective applicative (Proto-Tani *-*kaŋ*) adds an Experiencer object which is construed as being affected by an action directed at or upon them.

Since we do not see how it would be possible to derive the applied argument of an applicativized clause from a base clause that cannot be demonstrated to exist, we therefore conclude that there can be no derivational relationship between applied objects and base clause obliques in Macro-Tani languages. Instead, we observe that Macro-Tani languages tend to have "obligatory applicatives" (Creissels 2010), which function in most if not all cases to add a semantic participant to a clause in which it would otherwise not be permitted to occur.

3.4 Applicative subtypes and properties

Other than the Adfective and Inseritive applicatives described in section 3.3, we have so far considered only a handful of the most frequently occurring types of applicative in Macro-Tani languages (also cf. Table 1 above). These most frequently occurring Macro-Tani applicatives, such as Benefactive (40), Comitative (14) and Instrumental (18), are also those which we find among the most frequently attested applicatives cross-linguistically (Polinsky 2013).

Yet there is in fact a much larger number of derivational morphemes with applicative functionality in Macro-Tani languages – so many, in fact, that it is not currently possible to give a full inventory for any single Macro-Tani language; certainly, the number would be at least a few dozens for all languages with which we are familiar. This is a general characteristic of the predicate derivational macro-class in which Macro-Tani applicatives are found: as discussed in Post (2010), Macro-Tani predicate derivations are so numerous – more than 350 members in all well-described Macro-Tani languages – that they could potentially be argued to constitute an open class. With such a large and potentially open class, there is certain to be a great deal of semantic richness and diversity among Macro-Tani applicatives, and that is indeed what we find. Here we can give only a few characteristic examples.

In (47) from the Western Tani language Galo, the "Territive" applicative *-lom^2* adds an accusative-marked object to an intransitive clause headed by *um^2-* 'grunt', representing an Experiencer who is 'shocked' or 'frightened' as a result of the grunting. As discussed in section 2.2, Result is one of the general categories into which Macro-Tani predicate derivations are observed to fall. Derivations such as *-lom^2* can therefore be thought of as having both Result and Applicative functionality – in addition to the more particularized meaning of 'shock' pertaining to the applied Experiencer.

(47) arúm kán bə̀, homén ə́ ŋunnə̀m rɨgîi lò umlôm dagèe.
arum¹ kanə¹ bə² homen¹=ə¹ **ŋunu²=əm²** rɨgii² lo¹
evening dark DAT tiger=DEF **1.PL=DEF.ACC** field.boundary LOC
um²-**lom²**-dak²=ee¹
grunt-**TERR**-COS=ANT.VIS
'Late in the evening, a tiger at the field's edge **frightened us** with its roar.'
(lit. ~ 'roar-**shocked us**') (Galo; Western Tani, Arunachal Pradesh)

(48) presents an "Imitative" applicative derivation drawn from the Manner subclass of predicate derivations. This morpheme functions to introduce an object referencing an entity whose manner the subject is construed as "imitating" in its performance of the given action.

(48) koo si **ŋo-m** gɨ-**yul**-duŋ !
child PRX **1SG-ACC** go-**IMIT**-IPFV
'This kid is **imitating me** in his (manner of) walking!' (Lower Adi)

(49) illustrates use of a Lower Adi "Eruditive" applicative with both Manner and Result entailments. It introduces an object who, through the subject's activity, is "taught" to perform that same type of activity. In this clause, the object of "teaching" is syntactically omitted, however it is logically entailed and could be present with accusative marking.

(49) abìŋ=ə dəmpə geem keli-**nom**-ma
elder.brother=VOC ANAP.SIMIL game play-**ERUD**-PROH
'Hey Elder Brother, don't (through your video game-playing) thus/like that **teach (him) to** play (video) games!' (Lower Adi)

In this section, we have only introduced a small number of the many applicatives that appear to be available in Macro-Tani languages. Although we judge our discussion and examples are likely to be representative of the types of applicative morphemes and applicative properties that would be found through a wider survey of applicatives in Macro-Tani languages, we also note that this larger survey remains to be conducted. The challenge here is that while morphemes with applicative functionality certainly occur with ample frequency in our database of natural and narrative discourse, they often occur with few or no overt syntactic arguments in the clauses as spoken. A full survey of Macro-Tani applicatives would therefore test the properties of each candidate applicative more systematically, through extended elicitation.

3.5 Relationships of applicatives to other valence-interacting derivations

As was briefly mentioned in section 2.2, Macro-Tani applicatives can be considered to fall within a functional class of valence-interacting predicate derivations. Within this class, applicative morphemes are seen to form the overwhelming majority. Very few valence-reducing derivations have been attested in Macro-Tani languages; in some languages, such as Lower Adi, a passive-like marker whose form is usually *-ko* reduces valence, while in others, such as Galo, it seems not to. A middle-like morpheme whose form is usually *-si* or *-hi* patterns with reflexives and reciprocals in most Macro-Tani languages, but quite unusually functions to highlight subject autonomy rather than reducing valence as is more common among middle markers cross-linguistically (Post and Modi 2022). Other morphemes such as plural and dual Collectives interact with subject or object persons by forcing a plural or dual interpretation, but do not affect predicate valence *per se*.[13]

The construction which is both structurally and functionally most closely aligned with applicatives in Macro-Tani languages is the Causative. Macro-Tani Causatives are marked by a predicate derivation whose form is typically *-mo*, and which reflects a Proto-Tani verb **mo* 'make' (still available as a lexical root *mo-* in most modern languages). Causative *-mo* functions to increase clause valency by one, and additionally functions to modify the default semantic roles of predicate arguments in the following way: the clause subject (A of the causativized clause) must be understood as a volitional, non-acting Causer, while a referenced clause object (DO or IO of a causativized transitive or ditransitive clause) must be understood as a less volitional Actor. Accordingly, there is a clear basis for developing a more or less traditional analysis of Macro-Tani Causatives, one in which *-mo* has the two related functions of "adding" a volitional Causer to the clause – expressed as subject – and of "demoting" the base clause subject/Agent to (indirect) object status (50)–(51) (cf. Shibatani 2006, Song 2018, Zúñiga and Kittilä 2019, among others).

(50) **bi**   gaari   ko   rə-to
     3SG   vehicle   INDF   buy-PFV
     A   O   PRED
     '**He** bought a car.' (Lower Adi base clause)

---

[13] See e.g. Post (2007: 545) for plural and dual Collectives in Galo.

(51) ŋo   bɨ-m   gaari   ko   rə-**mo**-to
      1SG   3SG-ACC   vehicle INDF   buy-**CAUS**-PFV
      A   IO   DO   PRED
      '**I made/let/had him** buy a car.' (Lower Adi causativized clause)

Looking beyond -mo, however, we also find other predicate derivations with basically causative functionality, yet whose semantic entailments are somewhat richer. In some cases, such constructions might be viewed as blurring the line between "causative" and "applicative" constructions. For example, (52) illustrates an Assistive derivation, which functions to (a) increase valence, and also to (b) indicate that the subject "helps" a referenced object to bring about the mentioned event. The nature of the "help" provided is potentially ambiguous, or context-dependent; for example, the subject may or may not contribute funds to the purchase of a vehicle – and thus participate more or less as an Actor of the predicate – however, the animate object is clearly understood as the principal Actor, i.e. the principal purchaser and resulting owner of the vehicle. Thus there is at least some basis for analysing the Assistive derivation as a type of causative – beginning with the base clause in (50), -*gul* would have the functions of adding a Causer (or "Helper") realised as subject, and of demoting the principal Actor to O. Yet -*gul* is unlike a prototypical causative in that the causativized A can still be read as an Actor.

(52) ŋo   bɨ-m   gaari   ko   rə-**gul**-to
      1SG   3SG-ACC   vehicle INDF   buy-**ASST**-PFV
      '**I helped him** buy a car.' (Lower Adi)

Also consider example (53), which illustrates a Lower Adi Comitative-Benefactive derivation. The Comitative-Benefactive, which has primarily been attested in Eastern Tani languages such as Lower Adi, has a core sense of A "leading" or "guiding" O in the predicated event. Yet while A is always understood as relatively more volitional and enabling, and O as less volitional and benefiting, different portrayals of agency can modulate this relationship in potentially significant ways. For example, A can be understood as accompanying O and somehow facilitating a purchase – perhaps by driving O to a shop, or helping to fill out a form; in this reading, -*bo* could be read as having a basically causative function, in which A is "added" and O represents the "demotion" of erstwhile A (53a). Yet A can also be understood as a leading co-participant in the activity – basically, a comitative (applicative)-like reading (53b). In fact, A can also be understood as the sole Agent, while O is understood as a non-acting Beneficiary; according to this reading, -*bo* would look more like a Benefactive applicative (53c).

(53) ŋo **bi-m** gaari ko rə-**bo**-to
1SG 3SG-ACC vehicle INDF buy-**COMIT/BEN**-PFV
(a) '**I took him to** buy a car.' (A facilitates, O buys) *or*
(b) 'I went car-buying **with him**.' (A leads, both A and O buy) *or*
(c) 'I bought **him** a car.' (A buys, O receives/benefits) (Lower Adi)

Thus the question naturally arises as to whether Eastern Tani *-bo* is better analysed as a "causative" or as an "applicative" morpheme. Along the lines of the "causative" analysis, *-bo* could be understood as "adding a more volitional A and demoting base A to less volitional O" (closer to 53a). Alternatively, an "applicative" analysis could represent *-bo* as "adding a less volitional Beneficiary O" (closer to 53c).

The seeming flexibility of this analysis thus raises a further question as to whether a categorical "causative vs. applicative" dichotomy is in fact well-motivated in terms of the internal organization of Macro-Tani grammars. Indeed, we would argue that there is an at least equally strong argument for subsuming Causatives (perhaps as a sub-category) within the much larger and already highly diverse category of Macro-Tani applicative derivations. First, we note that Macro-Tani Causative and applicative morphemes occupy the same derivational slot within a predicate stem. Second, we note that Causative and applicative morphemes both function to add a semantic participant to the clause. Third, we note that there is at least one morpheme – Eastern Tani *-bo* – which seems to be polysemous among Causative, Comitative and Benefactive readings.

We do observe one major difference between Causative and applicative morphemes (or readings) in Macro-Tani languages, which is that the subject of a clause causativized with *-mo* 'CAUS' must be understood as a *non-Agent* of the predicate – which is different from what we find in most if not all strictly applicative morphemes that we have discussed (in which the semantic roles of base clause subjects remain unaffected). Yet it does not necessarily follow from this that Macro-Tani "causatives" must be understood as "adding an A" to a base clause, while simultaneously "demoting erstwhile A to O". An alternative analysis would view Macro-Tani "causatives" as fundamentally applicative: as "adding an O" at the same time as they "change the semantic role of A". Thus, either (54) or (55) could be understood as representing the base clause of (56), depending on whether a (traditional) causative or (non-traditional) applicative analysis was preferred. If the analysis that we are proposing is accepted – in which Macro-Tani "causatives" are understood fundamentally as a sub-type of applicative construction – then polysemous constructions such as (53) would have a simpler interpretation involving within-category rather than cross-category polysemy.[14]

(54) **bɨ** gaari ko rə-to
 3SG vehicle INDF buy-PFV
 A O PRED
 'He bought a car.' (Lower Adi base clause A, "Causative" analysis)

(55) **ŋo** gaari ko rə-to
 1SG vehicle INDF buy-PFV
 A O PRED
 'I bought a car.' (Lower Adi base clause B, "Applicative" analysis)

(56) ŋo bɨ-m gaari ko rə-mo-to
 1SG 3SG-ACC vehicle INDF buy-CAUS-PFV
 ADDED DEMOTED   "Causative analysis"
 ALTERED ADDED   "Applicative analysis"
 'I made/let/had him buy a car.' (Lower Adi increased transitivity clause)

We are aware that our proposed analysis of Macro-Tani "causative applicatives" is at variance with received typologies of both applicative and causative constructions cross-linguistically (again see Shibatani 2006, Song 2018, Zúñiga and Kittilä 2019, among others).[15] Yet we can see no language-particular reason not to prefer it. In choosing to adopt this analysis, we are thus heeding the advice of LaPolla (2016b) to "stick to the facts of the languages", and to avoid imposing categories derived from the study of other languages onto newly-described languages whose categories might be at variance with them. We take this advice to also extend to the analysis of categorical interrelationships, when undertaken on a language-particular basis.

---

14 This analysis would also commit us to proposing that applicatives, while they might prototypically function to add a non-Actor participant, could also function to add Actors. For our own part – and particularly given the flexibility around construals of Actor-hood that we have observed among applied non-subject arguments in Macro-Tani languages – we would be comfortable with such a commitment.

15 Here we can note that one parameter of distinction between "causatives" and "applicatives" is the putative relationship between applied objects and obliques within the base clause in the case of applicatives, which is not applicable in the case of causatives (e.g. Song 2018: 391). As we hope to have showed in section 3.3 of this chapter, this criterion is foreign to the analysis of Macro-Tani languages, at least.

4 Diachronic origin of Macro-Tani applicatives

In section 2.2 and elsewhere, we discussed the fact that Macro-Tani applicatives exist within a larger macro-category of predicate derivations. They accordingly appear to share a common diachronic origin with other predicate derivations, which we will argue to have begun with earlier serial verb constructions. Our analysis thus complements that of Peterson (2007: 130), who also identified a potential source of applicatives in serial verb constructions; it is, however, somewhat more general, in applying over the entire macro-class of predicate derivations of which Macro-Tani applicatives form a functional subclass – rather than being peculiar to Macro-Tani applicatives *per se*.

As discussed by Post (2010, 2015), many if not most modern-day Macro-Tani predicate derivations are either homophonous with and semantically relatable to lexical verb roots, or can be reconstructed to earlier lexical verb roots; for example, Macro-Tani Inseritive applicative *-lik* 'INSR' is clearly relatable to a lexical verb root *lik-* 'insert' which continues to occur in many (though not all) Macro-Tani languages, and Macro-Tani Benefactive applicative *-bi* is clearly relatable to a verb root *bi-* 'give'. Although predicate derivations in all Macro-Tani languages with which we are familiar occur as morphologically bound formatives within a grammatical predicate word (cf. Figure 1), it is plausible to hypothesize that an earlier state of the languages might have existed in which those same morphemes occurred as post-head serialized verbs. We therefore suggest that the grammaticalization pathway for morphemes with applicative functionality in Macro-Tani languages is, in the initial instance, via clause union through verb serialisation (57)–(59). This would have been followed by morphologization of the serialized predicate as schematized in Figure 2 (60).

(57) *ŋo *ən *rjə.
 1SG go be
 'I will go.' (pre-Proto-Tani simple clause 1)

(58) *ŋo *no-m ***bo*** *rjə.
 1SG 2SG-ACC **invite** be
 'I will invite you.' (pre-Proto-Tani simple clause 2)

(59) *ŋo *no-m *ən ***bo*** *rjə.
 1SG 2SG-ACC go **invite** be
 'I will bring you.' (lit. 'I will go, inviting you.') (pre-Proto-Tani clause union through verb serialization)

(60) ŋo   no-m   ən-**bo**-jə
     1SG   2SG-ACC   go-**COMIT**-IRR
     'I will bring you.' (modern-day Lower Adi applicativized clause)

[*V1 *V2 *V3] > [VROOT-PDER-PINFL]

Figure 2: Diachronic development of predicate derivations from earlier serialized verbs in Macro-Tani languages.

Verb-final and serializing Trans-Himalayan languages found to the east and southeast of the Macro-Tani area display constructions that are notably similar to our reconstructed pre-Proto(-Macro)-Tani syntax. For example, and although the author does not seem to directly address the capacity of serialized verbs such as *ma̱* 'show-how' and/or *pî* 'give' to add overt syntactic arguments (nor how they might be marked), free translations from Matisoff's pioneering (1969) study of verb serialization in Lahu – a Lolo-Burmese language of the Loloish Lahoid group found well to the east of the Macro-Tani area – nonetheless suggest that such constructions are indeed likely to have the functional status of applicatives (61)–(62).

(61) cì   g̱ɔ̂   tô?   **ma̱**   pî   cɔ̂.
     teeth   pull   out   **show-how**   BEN   ought
     '(They) ought to **show (them) how** to pull out teeth.' (Matisoff 1969: 104, translation slightly adjusted)

(62) g̱a   qɔ̂?   chî   tɔ̂?   **pî**
     must   again lift   out   BEN
     'must lift it out again **for (someone)**' (Matisoff 1969: 117)

In Donlay's (2019) description of Khatso, another Lolo-Burmese language of the Loloish Kazhouish group, we find a clear explication of the argument structure of such constructions. In Khatso, an overt applied object sits between an initial subject and a predicate-adjacent object in the clause syntax (63). Similar constructions, often involving a cognate marker seemingly reflecting a Proto-Trans-Himalayan verb along the lines of *bi* 'give', may also be found in more westerly languages such as Tamang, Camling and Belhare (LaPolla 2017: 52).

(63) i^{33} **ŋa^{33}**   tho^{33} vʁ^{323} **kuɨ^{31}**   wa^{323}
     3.SG   **1SG**   clothes   buy   **give**   PFV
     'She bought clothes **for me**.'

Closer to the Macro-Tani area, Peng and Chappell (2011) describe a benefactive applicative construction in Jingpho (Sal > Jingphoic) which appears to have the precise character of our reconstructed pre-Proto(-Macro)-Tani syntax (64). Note again the syntactic position of the applied object, and that it takes accusative marking in preference to the lexically-projected object – as we have also seen in Macro-Tani.

(64) ngai³³ **ma³¹koʔ⁵⁵** hpeʔ⁵⁵ u³¹   sat³¹ ya³³   sa³³ngai³³·
       1.SG   **NAME**   ACC   chicken kill   **give** 1SG.SBJ.PFV
       'I killed the chicken **for/instead of Ma Ko**.' (Peng and Chappell 2011: 139, glossing regularized by the present authors for consistency within this chapter)

Although the above examples deal exclusively with benefactive applicative constructions – seemingly, the most widely-attested type in Trans-Himalayan languages, as well as more generally among the languages of the world – similar examples including a wider range of applicatives can be found in Kuki-Chin languages such as Hakha Lai and Daai Chin. The morphological status of Kuki-Chin predicate formatives may be represented quite differently from description to description; for example, the Kuki-Chin Relinquitive applicative *ta(ak)* – which seems to be in some way relatable to Proto-Kuki-Chin **taaŋ* 'remain' (Van Bik 2009: 102) – appears in Peterson's description of Hakha Lai as a fully grammaticalized morphological suffix (65), and in So-Hartmann's description of Daai Chin as what could in principle be understood as a post-head serialized verb (66). In the latter case, note in particular that the applicative *taak* occurs in the (shorter) "B Stem" form – a general feature of verbal stems in Daai Chin as in many Kuki-Chin languages. Whatever the synchronic descriptive facts for a given Kuki-Chin language, then, it seems clear that the origin of this and other Kuki-Chin post-head applicatives is in some sort of serial verb construction.

(65) tsewmaŋ=niʔ   door=ʔaʔ   ʔa-ka-kal-**taak**.
      tsewmang=ERG   market=ALL/LOC   3SG.SBJ-1SG.OBJ-go₂-**RELINQ**
      'Tsewmang went to the market, **leaving** me **behind**.'
      (Peterson 2007: 132)

(66) Ling=noh   lou: nah   phyoh   **ta**=kti.
      Ling=ERG   field   IO.AGR:1SG   weed.A.STEM   **APPL:RELINQ.B.STEM**=NFUT
      'Ling weeded the field **without waiting for** me.' (So-Hartmann 2009: 199)

Since the precise genealogical relationships between Macro-Tani, Jingphoic, Kuki-Chin and Lolo-Burmese languages within Trans-Himalayan has not yet been clarified, we are not currently able to demonstrate that the morphosyntax of Loloish and Jingphoic or Kuki-Chin applicative serial verbs must necessarily be conservative in relation to that of Macro-Tani predicate structures. In addition, our understanding of these languages' (or their ancestors') serial verb constructions does not obviously lead us to the conclusion that they could plausibly have given rise to the great richness and variety of applicative morphemes that we observe in Macro-Tani languages today. We must therefore also keep in mind the possibility that the derivational slot in Macro-Tani predicate structure, once established, might have served as an attractor for morphologization of additional verb roots, enabling expansion of Macro-Tani applicative classes into the exceptionally large sets that we find today. These being topics beyond the scope of our present enquiry, we nonetheless consider that the above examples at least confirm that our reconstruction in Figure 2 is well enough supported by the modern-day syntax of Trans-Himalayan languages to merit further investigation as a potential avenue for the grammaticalization of applicative constructions in Macro-Tani languages.

5 Conclusion

In this chapter we have outlined a basic description of applicatives in Macro-Tani languages. We have found that Macro-Tani applicatives occur as derivational formatives to a grammatical predicate word, and function to add a semantic participant to a clause. Our finding is thus largely consistent with the definition of applicatives proposed in the introduction to this volume ("any derivational morphology occurring on a verb root/stem that has amongst its functions the introduction of a non-Actor semantic argument into a main clause"). However, if our analysis in section 3.5 of Macro-Tani Causatives as a subtype of Applicative is accepted, this definition would need to be amended to omit "non-Actor".

Macro-Tani applied phrases are typically instantiated as grammatical objects, however at least some Macro-Tani applicatives introduce oblique arguments, and others permit the applied phrase to be marked as either an object or an oblique (according to information structure). While this is not a commonly reported property of applicatives cross-linguistically, it is common in other language families, e.g. Bantu (Pacchiarotti 2020), suggesting that it may be a more common property of applicatives than is sometimes noted.

In clear contrast with much of the typological literature on applicatives, we find no evidence for a derivational relationship in Macro-Tani languages between applied objects and base obliques. This means that applicative constructions in Macro-Tani languages are the sole morphological means to express a given semantic role in a main clause.

We have identified only a few of the very large number of morphemes with applicative functionality that appear to exist in all known Tani languages, and we have further suggested that Macro-Tani Causatives should be properly subsumed within the larger applicative category, to which they are formally and functionally almost identical (in Macro-Tani languages if not indeed more widely among East and Southeast Asian languages). Finally, we have advanced a hypothetical account of the diachronic development of Macro-Tani applicatives out of earlier serial verb constructions in a verb-final language. Further research on valence change in verb-final serializing languages of the Trans-Himalayan area, and in particular those to the immediate east and southeast of the Macro-Tani-speaking area, may yield information that could help to further assess this hypothesis' plausibility.

Abbreviations

A	transitive more agentive argument
ABL	ablative
ACC	accusative
ADF	adfective
ALL	allative
ANAP	anaphoric
ANT	anterior
APPL	applicative
ASST	assistive
AVZR	adverbializer
BEN	benefactive
CAUS	causative
COMPL	completive
COMIT	comitative
CONC	concessive
COS	change of state
DAT	dative
DEF	definite
DO	direct object
DUB	dubitative
ERG	ergative
ERUD	eruditive
EXCL	exclamative
FRUS	frustrative
GEN	genitive

HORT	hortative
IMIT	imitative
INCP	incipient
INDF	indefinite
INSR	inseritive
INSTR	instrumental
INTS	intensifier
IO	indirect object
IO.AGR	indirect object agreement
IPFV	imperfective
IRR	irrealis
LOC	locative
MAN	manner
MED	mediative
NAGT	non-agentive
NEG	negative
NF	non-final
NFUT	non-future
NP	noun phrase
NMLZ	nominalizer
O	transitive less agentive argument
OBJ	object
OBL	oblique
PDER	predicate derivation
PF	perfect
PFV	perfective
PINFL	predicate inflection
PL	plural
P(M)T	Proto-(Macro-)Tani
POL	polite
PRED	predicate
PROH	prohibitive
PRX	proximate
PSTEM	predicate stem
R	ditransitive indirectly-affected argument
RELINQ	relinquitive
S	intransitive single argument
SAUT	subject autonomy
SBRD	subordinator
SG	singular
SIMIL	similitive
SBJ	subject
T	ditransitive directly-affected argument
TENT	tentative
TERR	territive

v	verb
voc	vocative
vis	visual
vroot	verb root

References

Blench, Roger & Mark W. Post. 2014. Re-thinking Sino-Tibetan phylogeny from the perspective of North East Indian languages. In Nathan Hill & Tom Owen-Smith (eds.), *Trans-Himalayan linguistics: Historical and descriptive linguistics of the Himalayan area*, 71–104. Berlin/Boston: De Gruyter Mouton.

Creissels, Denis. 2010. Benefactive Applicative Periphrases. In Fernando Zúñiga & Seppo Kittilä (eds.), *Benefactives and malefactives: Typological perspectives and case studies*, 29–70. Amsterdam: John Benjamins.

Donlay, Chris. 2019. *A Grammar of Khatso*. Berlin/Boston: De Gruyter Mouton.

LaPolla, Randy J. 2016a. Once again on methodology and argumentation in linguistics: Problems with the arguments for recasting Sino-Tibetan as "Trans-Himalayan". *Linguistics of the Tibeto-Burman Area* 39(2). 282–297.

LaPolla, Randy J. 2016b. On categorization: Stick to the facts of the languages. *Linguistic Typology* 20(2). 365–375.

LaPolla, Randy J. 2017. Overview of Sino-Tibetan morphosyntax. In Graham Thurgood & Randy J. LaPolla (eds.), *The Sino-Tibetan languages*, 40–69. London: Routledge.

Matisoff, James A. 1969. Verb concatenation in Lahu: The syntax and semantics of 'simple' juxtaposition. *Acta Linguistica Hafniensia* 12(2). 69–120.

Modi, Yankee. 2017. *A grammar of Milang*. Bern: University of Bern dissertation.

Pacchiarotti, Sara. 2020. *Bantu applicative constructions*. (Stanford Monographs in African Languages). Stanford: CSLI Publications.

Peng, Guozhen & Hilary Chappell. 2011. Ya33 'give' as a valency increaser in Jinghpo nuclear serialization: From benefactive to malefactive. *Studies in Language* 35(1). 128–167.

Peterson, David A. 2007. *Applicative constructions*. Oxford: Oxford University Press.

Peterson, David A. 2019. Applicatives. In Mark Aronoff (ed.), *Oxford bibliography of linguistics*. Oxford: Oxford University Press. doi: 10.1093/OBO/9780199772810-0227

Polinsky, Maria. 2013. Applicative Constructions. In Matthew S. Dryer & Martin Haspelmath (eds.), *The World Atlas of Language Structures Online*. Leipzig: Max Planck Institute for Evolutionary Anthropology. http://wals.info/chapter/109, Accessed on 2022-03-31.

Post, Mark W. 2007. *A grammar of Galo*. Melbourne: LaTrobe University dissertation.

Post, Mark W. 2010. Predicate derivations in the Tani languages: Root, suffix, both or neither? In Stephen Morey & Mark Post (eds.), *North East Indian linguistics, Volume 2*, 175–197. New Delhi: Cambridge University Press India.

Post, Mark W. 2011. Nominalization and nominalization-based constructions in Galo. In Foong Ha Yap, Karen Grunow-Hårsta & Janick Wrona (eds.), *Nominalization in Asian languages: Diachronic and typological perspectives*, 255–287. Amsterdam: John Benjamins.

Post, Mark W. 2015. Morphosyntactic reconstruction in an areal-historical context: A pre-historical relationship between North East India and Mainland Southeast Asia? In Nick J. Enfield & Bernard Comrie (eds.), *Languages of Mainland Southeast Asia: The state of the art*, 205–261. Berlin/Boston: De Gruyter Mouton.

Post, Mark W. 2017. *The Tangam language: Grammar, lexicon and texts*. Leiden: Brill.

Post, Mark W. & Yankee Modi. 2022. Subject autonomy marking in Macro-Tani and the typology of middle voice. *Linguistics* 60(1). 215–238.

Post, Mark W. & Yankee Modi. 2011. Language contact and the genetic position of Milang (Eastern Himalaya). *Anthropological Linguistics* 53(3). 215–258.

Shibatani, Masayoshi. 2006. On the conceptual framework for voice phenomena. *Linguistics* 44(2). 217–269.

So-Hartmann, Helga. 2009. *A descriptive grammar of Daai Chin*. (STEDT Monograph Series Volume 7). Berkeley: University of California.

Song, Jae Jung. 2018. *Linguistic Typology*. Oxford: Oxford University Press.

van Driem, George. 2014. Trans-Himalayan. In Nathan W. Hill & Thomas Owen-Smith (eds.), *Trans-Himalayan linguistics: Historical and descriptive linguistics of the Himalayan area*, 11–40. Berlin/Boston: De Gruyter Mouton.

Zúñiga, Fernando & Seppo Kittilä. 2019. *Grammatical voice*. Cambridge: Cambridge University Press.

Thomas E. Payne and Voltaire Q. Oyzon

12 Canonical and Non-canonical applicatives in Waray

Abstract: This chapter deals with applicative constructions in Waray, an Austronesian language spoken in Samar, Northern and Eastern Leyte, and parts of Biliran islands in the Eastern Visayas region of the Philippines. The existence of applicative constructions in Philippine languages is controversial. One view sees reflexes of the Proto-Austronesian affixes *-an and *Si- (Wolff 1973, Blust 2002) as components of simulfixal "voice" markers. The other view, represented in this chapter, is that the reflexes of these affixes in Waray are insightfully analyzed as markers of applicative constructions. First we show that Waray verb morphology includes three productive affixes, -an, -i and i- (reflexes of Proto-Austronesian voice affixes), which qualify as markers of applicative constructions according to the characteristics outlined in the introduction to this volume. Next, we show that between them, these affixes participate in five additional constructions that lack one or more of the definitional characteristics of "canonical" applicatives. We name these additional constructions "non-canonical" applicatives. We argue that each of the non-canonical constructions is a logical extension of a canonical applicative construction. Our conclusion is that the overarching semantic function of the canonical and non-canonical applicative constructions in Waray is to mitigate transitivity. The applicative 1 forms, -an and -i, mitigate transitivity by reducing or diffusing the affectedness of the undergoer, while the applicative 2 form, i-, mitigates transitivity by reducing the sovereign control of the actor.

Epigraph
... there is such a thing as a basic plan, a certain cut, to each language. This type or plan or structural "genius" of the language is something much more fundamental, much more pervasive, than any single feature of it that we can mention, nor can we gain an adequate idea of its nature by a mere recital of the sundry facts that make up the grammar of the language.
Edward Sapir (1921: 120)

Thomas E. Payne, University of Oregon & SIL International, Department of Linguistics, Eugene, Oregon, USA, e-mail: tpayne@uoregon.edu
Voltaire Q. Oyzon, College of Arts and Sciences, Leyte Normal University, Tacloban City, Philippines, e-mail: v.oyzon@lnu.edu.ph

https://doi.org/10.1515/9783110777949-012

1 Introduction

Waray is the mother tongue and language of wider communication for most inhabitants of Samar, Northern and Eastern Leyte, and parts of Biliran islands in the Eastern Visayas region of the Philippines.[1] With over three million speakers, it is the sixth most widely spoken language in the country. This paper is part of a larger project to document the grammar of Waray for purposes of L1 Based Multilingual Education (L1B-MLE) under the auspices of Leyte Normal University and the Commission on Higher Education (CHED). It is based on a large corpus of spoken and written data (3NS Corpora project 2021), as well as extensive input from teachers, students, and intellectual leaders throughout the Waray speaking region. Unless otherwise specified, examples appearing in this paper are from the variety of Waray spoken in Northern Leyte.[2]

The existence of applicative constructions in Western Austronesian languages south of the Philippines is widely accepted (see Blust 2002 and other studies in Wouk and Ross 2002, this volume, chapter 14 and references cited therein). For the most part, this literature follows arguments summarized in Kaufman (2017) that applicatives in the languages of Malaysia and Indonesia are reflexes of Proto-Austronesian (PAN) voice affixes, as proposed by Wolff (1973). As Austronesian speakers migrated south from the island of Taiwan through the Philippines to other areas of insular Southeast Asia, their voice systems were simplified and reconfigured into the applicative morphology that is now a feature of the Austronesian languages of Malaysia, Indonesia, Brunei, and Papua New Guinea. In most languages of the Philippines, however, the reflexes of the Proto-Austrone-

---

[1] We would like to thank many Waray speakers from various regions who participated in long and intense discussions of the data appearing in this paper, including especially Amado Arjay Babon, Firie Jill Ramos, John Tan, Danika Astilla-Magoncia, Kenneth Alvin Cinco, Ryan Destura, Angeles R. Lopez, Genevieve Chua, Carol Ann Araneta and many others who willingly participated on social media, and students in MTB-MLE 101 at Leyte Normal University from 2015 to the present. We would also like to thank Dr. Ricardo Nolasco and Dr. Doris Payne for many discussions that influenced the analysis presented in this paper, and the editors and anonymous reviewers of the present volume for very helpful input. Of course, any and all errors are our own. We also acknowledge and appreciate the support of Leyte Normal University, SIL Philippines, the Pike Center for Integrative Scholarship, the US Fulbright Foundation, and the Fulbright Commission in the Philippines.

[2] Although Tacloban City is the capital of the Waray speaking region, there is no specific variety of Waray that can be considered the "Tacloban variety." Rather, because of urbanization, the language as used in Tacloban tends to mix features of all regional varieties. For this reason, the baseline for this study is the much more uniform variety of Waray spoken in Barugo, a medium sized municipality on the northern coast of Leyte Island. Variations from this standard are noted when they affect the presentation in this paper.

sian voice affixes *-an and *Si- are still components of a rare or unique "Philippine type" voice system, rather than applicatives (Himmelman 1991; Foley 2008; Kaufman 2009, 2017; Chen 2017, among others).

In this paper, we will first show that the affixes -an and i- (from PAN *-an and *Si-) in Waray are reasonably analyzed as markers of prototypical applicative constructions, given the properties outlined in the introduction to this volume. This approach to clause structure in Philippine languages is not new with us – similar proposals have been made in several works beginning notably with Bell (1979), and more recently by Aldridge (2004, 2012), based on formal theoretical arguments. Others, working in more general typological frameworks have come to similar conclusions (e.g., Payne 1982; Mithun 1994, 2002, 2019; Brainard 1994; Liao 2004; Reid and Liao 2004; Peterson 2007: 160–162; Polinsky 2013).

Second, we will show that applicative morphology in Waray has at least five extended, "non-canonical" functions (section 4). We conclude in section 5 that the canonical and non-canonical functions of these applicative forms are united by an overarching semantic function of "mitigated transitivity".

2 Background assumptions and definitions

The applicative analysis presented in this paper rests on the observation that the basic grammatical relations in Waray are absolutive and ergative rather than subject and object. This perspective has been debated extensively in previous literature (some of which is cited above). Full argumentation for and against the ergative analysis of Philippine languages lies outside the scope of the present paper. Suffice to say that it is controversial, but highly reasonable. The following basic Waray examples are illustrative of the perspective taken in this paper:

(1) a. *Tumawà hiya.*
    t<um>awà   hiya
    <INTR.R>smile 3SG.ABS
    'S/he smiled.'[3]

---

[3] In this paper, the first line in Waray examples is the official Waray orthography, as described in Nolasco, Oyzon and Ramos (2012; 2017 revision currently under consideration by the Department of Education). The second line provides morphological analyses helpful for the point illustrated by the example, following the Leipzig formatting conventions (https://www.eva.mpg.de/lingua/pdf/Glossing-Rules.pdf). The third line gives the morpheme-by-morpheme glosses. Finally, the last line gives a free English translation.

b. *Tumawà an batà.*
t<um>awà an batà
<INTR.R>smile ABS child
'The child smiled.'

c. *Hinilot níya an batà.*
h<in>ilot níya an batà
<TR.R>massage 3SG.ERG ABS child
'S/he massaged the child.'

d. *Hinilot hiya han batà.*
h<in>ilot hiya han batà
<TR.R>massage 3SG.ABS ERG child
'The child massaged her/him.'

Examples (1a) and b are intransitive clauses in which the only argument is expressed by the 3rd person singular absolutive case pronoun *hiya* in (1a) and the full noun phrase *an batà* in (1b). These same forms are used in the grammatically transitive clauses (1c) and (1d) expressing the patients. Distinct ergative case forms *níya* '3SG.ERG' and *han batà* 'the.ERG child' express the agents of transitive clauses. This pattern is consistent throughout the language. Central to this perspective is that the verbal infixes *<um>* and *<in>* (as well as their counterparts in other modalities) are morphological markers of intransitive vs. transitive constructions respectively (see Table 1 below).

In the current official orthography, syllable prominence (either word stress, vowel length, or both) is not indicated when it is predictable. When it is unpredictable given the context, an acute accent indicates syllable prominence. Briefly, if the final syllable is prominent, no accent is needed. If there is a "heavy" syllable (CVC, or CV:) anywhere in the word other than the last syllable, the prominence predictably moves to the left, and so is not indicated. All other prominent syllables in indigenous Waray words are indicated with an acute accent. In Spanish and English loan words, stress is not indicated at all. Syllable prominence alone may distinguish lexical items. In addition, many grammatical categories are expressed or accompanied by changes in syllable prominence patterns. The glottal stop is indicated in one of four ways: 1) Sequences of vowel graphemes always involve an intervening glottal stop, e.g., *tiil* [ti'ʔil], 'foot', *bao* [ba'ʔo] 'tortoise'; 2) Following a consonant, the glottal stop is indicated with a hyphen, e.g. *mag-áanak* [mag'ʔaʔanak] 'will give birth'; 3) At the end of a word in a prominent syllable, it is indicated with a circumflex over the final vowel, e.g., *kitâ* [ki'taʔ] 'to see'; 4) At the end of a word in a non-prominent syllable, it is indicated with a grave accent over the final vowel, e.g., *sikò* ['si:koʔ] 'elbow'. In such cases the penultimate syllable is predictably prominent. Unfortunately, most published material in Waray does not employ diacritics at all.

Secondly, we recognize a distinction between semantic transitivity and grammatical transitivity. Semantic transitivity is a property of situations in real, imagined, or abstract worlds, as conceptualized and presented by speakers involved in communicative acts. As is common in semantic domains, semantic transitivity is continuously variable. Hopper and Thompson (1980: 253) describe semantic transitivity as "a matter of carrying over or transferring an action from one participant to another." They then describe ten "components" that contribute to the degree of transitivity in any given situation. Particular languages include grammatical constructions (or "morphosyntax") that are sensitive to one or more of these components. Since the human mind is not capable of dealing comfortably with infinite variability, grammatical structures tend to "discretize," or make distinct categories out of infinitely variable semantic spaces such as transitivity.

Grammatical transitivity, then, involves syntactic and/or morphological structures that function in the domain of semantic transitivity. For example, the presence of a referential expression referring to an actor of a situation may be one syntactic manifestation of higher transitivity, while the absence or indefiniteness of an actor would be an indication of lower transitivity. This is because activity can't "carry over" or "transfer" from one participant to another if there is no actor or identified starting point of the activity. Aspect is another possible grammatical expression of transitivity. Perfective aspect may be a morphological indicator of higher transitivity than imperfective aspect, since action that is ongoing or incomplete has not (yet) "transferred" or "carried over." There are many other possible grammatical structures that address the functional domain of semantic transitivity.

Semantic transitivity of situations evoked by verbal roots and grammatical transitivity of the constructions in which those roots appear need not coincide in a one to one relationship. For example, the concept evoked by an English verb like *dance* may be considered low in semantic transitivity because it does not inherently involve action carrying over from one participant to another. However, this verb may be used in a grammatically transitive construction if it suits the communicative needs of the speaker, as in *She danced me into a corner*, or *We danced the tango*. Similarly, the concept evoked by the verb *eat* is high in semantic transitivity because it necessarily involves an eater and an eaten thing. However, in context a clause like *Philipp already ate* makes no reference to an eaten thing, and so is grammatically intransitive. The manipulation of grammatical transitivity is an important function that allows speakers to present different perspectives on the scenes they wish to communicate (see, e.g., the literature on Frame Semantics, beginning with Fillmore 1977, and finding its most recent expression in the extensive literature on Construction Grammar, such as Goldberg 2019 and references cited therein).

Part of our analysis of Waray is that inflectional verb morphology divides transitivity into two values – Transitive and Intransitive.[4] The higher a situation is in semantic transitivity (from the perspective of a speaker), the more likely it is to receive Transitive inflection (see the description of the inflectional system in Table 1 below). Conversely, situations very low in semantic transitivity are likely to receive Intransitive inflection.

Finally, we propose that verb morphology in Waray consists of two groups of morphological categories,[5] which we term inflectional and stem-forming groups (Payne and Oyzon 2020). Again, this perspective is not new with us. Several authors, notably Wolff (1972) on Cebuano, have used the term "inflection" to describe essentially the same group of affixes we are calling inflectional in this paper. Also, we follow DeGuzman (1978) in using the term "stem-forming" for verb morphology not designated as inflectional. We consciously avoid the term "derivational" for the stem-forming group because 1) this term is used in different ways in different theoretical traditions and some question its validity altogether (see. e.g., D. L. Payne 1985; van Marle 1996; Bauer 2003: 105–107), and 2) the prototype evoked by the term "derivational" does not fit the stem-forming group very well. In particular, many stem-forming formatives (or "stem formatives") in Waray are much more common and regular than derivational formatives in a more isolating language like English. Nevertheless, whatever terminology one prefers, the two groups of morphological categories are quite easily distinguished, the main difference being that the inflectional categories are paradigmatic, whereas the stem-forming categories are not (see below).

The set of verbal inflections, according to our current analysis, is given in Table 1. We consider this to be a paradigm because one and only one of these formatives is required to complete a verbal predicate and integrate it into discourse. Furthermore, inflections express exactly two dimensions of meaning in a well-defined array – transitivity and modality. Because of the requirement that one inflection be present to complete a verbal predicate, the absence of an overt

---

[4] We capitalize the terms "Transitive" and "Intransitive" when referring to the inflectional categories of Waray verbs, or argument structure frames in Waray. We do not capitalize them when referring to semantic transitivity.
[5] In this paper we use the term "morphological category" (or just "category") to refer to dimensions of meaning expressed morphologically, e.g. transitivity, modality, aspect, etc. A "morphological value" (or just "value") is a particular member of a morphological category, e.g., transitive, irrealis, perfective, etc. We use the term "exponent" to mean a particular expression of a morphological value, e.g., exponents of the irrealis value include *ma-*, *-on*, and zero.

formative is meaningful. In other words, a "zero" is not just the lack of inflection, but is a meaningful member of the inflectional set. We present this table simply as background to the major claims of the current paper, which involve stem-forming morphology, specifically applicatives.

Table 1: The inflectional paradigm of Waray verb morphology.

Modality ↓	Transitivity →	Transitive	Intransitive
Realis	Controlled	<in>	<ín> / <um>[6]
	Happenstantial/Neutral[7]	na-	na-
Irrealis	Prospective	-on / -Ø	ti-
	Controlled		ma-
	Happenstantial/Neutral	ma-	
	Subjunctive	-a	-Ø

Note that the happenstantial inflections may occur in grammatically Transitive (ergative and absolutive arguments) or Intransitive (absolutive only) argument frames depending on the context. This seems understandable to us since accidental situations with two participants are qualitatively less transitive than similar

---

6 In most varieties of modern spoken Waray, the <um> infix is the only exponent of this confluence of values. In Eastern Samar, sometimes <ín> (long vowel) is used. Historically, both <in> (short i) and <um> appeared together, *kinumáon. This form shortened to kinmaon (which is also still heard in some areas). This form further shortened to <ín>, with the extra length on the vowel compensating for the truncated /m/. Such compensatory lengthening occurs in other contexts as well, as discussed in Payne and Oyzon (in prep.).

Wolff (1970) speaking of Cebuano, described the <um> verbal infix as expressing "general time." "Controlled" mood in Waray can be understood as general time in the sense that the event is expressed as usually, normally, or effortlessly happening. However, this form contrasts with neutral and happenstantial moods, rather than with other values in an aspectual dimension. All realis moods may occur in perfective, imperfective, present or past contexts depending on other contextual or constructional features, such as the second-position aspectual enclitics *pa* 'CONTINUING' and *na* 'COMPLETED'. Therefore, we conclude that modality, rather than aspect or tense, is a major dimension of the paradigm. Any temporal effects that arise from the inflectional categories are collateral.

7 The happenstantial meaning of the *na-* and *ma-* prefixes is neutralized when they combine with incomplete *á-* or deliberate *g-* stem-forming prefixes. Also, when used with transitive, volitional stems, the happenstantial categories are commonly interpreted as abilitative, e.g. *Nakúha ko an tinapay* 'I was able to get the bread.' We consider this to be a logical consequence of happenstantial semantics applied to volitional concepts: An action may be volitional, but the ability to perform the same action is non-volitional. For this reason, abilities have more in common with non-volitional rather than volitional activities.

events controlled volitionally by an active initiator (Hopper and Thompson's 1980 component E – volitional events are higher in transitivity than non-volitional events). For example, I might find something on purpose if I am searching for it, or I might accidentally come across something I wasn't necessarily searching for. Both situations are semantically transitive to a certain extent because they do involve activity "carrying over" from a starting point, me, to an endpoint, the thing found. However, happenstantial situations are relatively less transitive than those in which the starting point initiates and controls the action purposely. Waray reflects this semantic feature by neutralizing grammatical transitivity in verb morphology for all happenstantial (uncontrolled, accidental) situations. This is one way in which Waray speakers have developed, unconsciously, over time, grammatical resources that allow them to manipulate the scenes they express according to the degree to which activity carries over from a distinct, conscious actor to a definite, individuated undergoer.

Stem formatives are distinct from the inflectional forms displayed in Table 1 in that they are non-paradigmatic. By this we mean 1) stem formatives are "optional" – none are required to complete a verbal predicate, 2) they do not express a single well-defined array of meanings, and 3) they may be "stacked", i.e., several may be involved in the formation of a stem. For this reason "zero" does not itself represent a value in the stem-forming system, but rather is just the absence of any overtly expressed value. One may think of stem formatives as conspiring with the root to create very specific and nuanced discourse "scenes". Once a scene is set, one inflection is required to complete that scene, and integrate it into a coherent predication.

Oyzon and Payne (in preparation) identify sixteen distinct stem formatives in Waray, including the applicatives, *-an/-i* and *i-*. Briefly, our arguments for calling the applicatives stem-forming rather than inflectional are:
1. They each occur in realis or irrealis contexts, therefore they do not express modality, as do all inflectional forms.
2. They each co-occur with clearly inflectional forms. As mentioned above, one and only one inflection may occur in a verbal predicate.

The differences between inflectional and stem-forming morphology are summarized in Table 2.

In our view, the existence of these two distinct groups of formatives is what gives rise to a view of Philippine verb morphology that involves simulfixal voice marking. The simulfixes in question (e.g., <in> . . . -an, na- . . . -an, i- . . . <in> and others) are more insightfully viewed as combinations of an inflectional marker of transitivity+modality, and a stem-forming applicative marker. Such combinations contribute significantly to the "genius" of Philippine type languages. We

Table 2: Contrasting characteristics of inflectional and stem-forming verbal morphology.

Inflectional formatives	Stem Formatives
Obligatory to complete a verbal predicate. Therefore "zero" is a potentially meaningful member of the set.	Optional. Therefore "zero" is simply the absence of overt stem formatives.
One and only one may occur in a verbal predicate.	Several may occur in the formation of a single stem.
Express exactly two dimensions of meaning in a well-defined array: transitivity and modality.	Constitute logically unrelated dimensions of meaning, including aspect (incompletive, iterative, imperfective), actional type (distributive, attenuative, associative, pluraction, indirection), valence (causative, applicative, reciprocal), modality (deliberate, abilitative), among others.

contend that the "voice system" of Waray is the result of the interaction between the dimension of transitivity in the inflectional paradigm and applicative markers in the stem-forming group (following Payne and Oyzon 2020):

(2) Inflectional values   Stem-forming values   Common voice designations
    Intransitive   + no applicative   = Actor Voice
    Transitive   + no applicative   = Patient/Undergoer Voice
    Transitive   + applicative 1 (-an, -i)   = Locative/Recipient Voice
    Transitive   + applicative 2 (i-) =   = Conveyance/Benefactive/
                                                         Instrumental Voice

We believe that this way of looking at clause structure in a Philippine language is more consistent with what is known about the typological characteristics of languages in general than the "focus" (Schachter and Otanes 1972) or "voice" (e.g., Foley 2008) approaches. While Philippine languages are indeed unique and special in many ways, there is no need to posit a typologically rare or unique "Philippine type" voice system.

3 Canonical applicatives in Waray

In this section we describe what we consider to be the canonical usages of the applicative suffixes -*an* and -*i*, and the prefix *i*- in Waray. These usages are canonical mainly because they correspond to the usages commonly considered definitional for applicative constructions in other parts of the world. In addition to their canonical usages, each of the affixes has "non-canonical", yet still recognizably applicative usages. In the case of *-an/-i*, 'applicative 1', the canonical usages are the most frequent and most productive. In the case of the prefix *i-*, 'applicative 2', however, one non-canonical usage, though limited to certain verb classes, appears to be more common in discourse than the canonical usages (see section 4.5). All of the non-canonical usages of the applicative forms lack one or more of the characteristics considered definitional for applicative constructions. These extended usages will be discussed in section 4.

Pacchiarotti and Zúñiga in the introduction to this volume mention four identifying properties of applicative morphology. All of these properties (paraphrased and amplified here for our purposes) are relevant to the canonical applicative constructions in Waray. Some of them do not hold for one or more of the non-canonical usages:

1. Lexicon: The applicative construction (AC) is an optional variant of a base construction (BC) to express a given state of affairs. We understand this to mean that applicative morphology creates lexical items (stems) that express the same general state of affairs as a non-applicative counterpart. All Waray applicative forms are stem-formatives as described in section 2. That is to say, they are distinct from the inflectional forms (see Table 1 and related discussion) and can be thought of as creating lexical stems. "Obligatory applicatives" (section 4.1) are not optional – the only transitive form of the verb is based on an applicative stem. "Adversative applicatives" and "evaluative applicatives (sections 4.4 and 4.5) involve constructional meanings that do not hold for the corresponding base constructions, and so describe different states of affairs.

2. Morphology: The predicate in an AC is overtly derived from the predicate of the BC. We understand this to mean that the AC involves overt morphological marking. This is true of all applicative constructions in Waray, with the exception of one situation in which an instrumental applicative construction may be unmarked. This is discussed in section 3.2.

3. Syntax: The AC may have a higher syntactic valency than the BC. In the case of a monovalent BC, the corresponding AC will be divalent. An "applied phrase" (AppP) corresponds to an optional adjunct in the BC which becomes an absolutive in the AC. In the case of a divalent (transitive) BC, the corresponding AC in some languages will either be trivalent, or the AppP will displace the affected participant in the BC, resulting in a divalent AC. All applicative constructions in Waray are grammatically Transitive (as discussed in section 2). All the canonical usages of the applicative affixes in Waray represent an increase in valence when compared to an intransitive base construction. "Partitive applicatives" (section 4.3) and "registration

applicatives" section (4.5) relate only to Transitive base constructions, and do not affect the argument structure of the clause in any way.
4. Semantics: The AppP is a non-agentive participant. This property distinguishes applicative constructions from causatives. This is true of all the usages of applicative morphology in Waray.

While the notion of "canonical applicative" may or may not be a viable concept universally, we are comfortable identifying constructions with all of these characteristics in Waray as canonical. One reason for this is that both applicatives are very productive and common in these usages. For activities involving transfer of an item from a source to a destination (if inanimate) or recipient (if animate), the applicative 1 formatives (*-an* and *-i*) consistently present a destination/recipient or source of the item transferred as the absolutive of the clause. For verbs describing other physical activities, applicative 1 formatives present the location of the activity as the absolutive (see Mithun 2002; 2019 for similar observations regarding applicative constructions in Kapampangan and Hiligaynon respectively). The applicative 2 prefix *i-* is also very common and productive, occurring freely on Austronesian as well as borrowed Spanish and English roots whenever responsibility for the activity is presented as distributed between a primary actor and a co-actant.[8] This co-actant can be understood as a beneficiary, an associate, or an instrument.

3.1 *-an/-i* 'applicative 1': Location, destination, recipient, source

The applicative 1 value is evinced by two forms: *-i* in subjunctive mood, and *-an* in indicative (non-subjunctive) mood.[9] The applied phrase in an applicative 1 construction may be the location of the activity, or a destination, recipient or source

---

[8] In this paper we use the term "co-actant" to refer to a participant that acts with, influences, motivates or facilitates the action of the primary controller of an activity. This semantic characterization implies an asymmetric relationship between the primary controller and the co-actant. The primary controller accomplishes, and bears primary responsibility for the activity, but the co-actant participates in the initiation of the activity in some way. Traditional semantic roles included under the cover notion of co-actant for Waray include beneficiary (because the beneficiary motivates the activity, consciously or not), associate, and instrument.
[9] What we are calling "subjunctive" is sometimes referred to as "dependent" mood (see, e.g., Wolff 1973). In Waray it is used in certain negatives, certain dependent clauses, questions, and imperatives. We currently prefer the term "subjunctive", but it is not to be equated with subjunctive mood in any European language.

of a moving object, depending on the semantic class of the root. In all these usages, the referent of the applied phrase may be expressed in an oblique role in a corresponding non-applicative base construction (BC). Example (3a) is an Intransitive construct with a locative element optionally expressed in an oblique phrase preceded by the general locative preposition *ha*. Example (3b) is an applicative construct (AC) describing a similar state of affairs in which the location is now expressed as an absolutive rather than an oblique nominal. Correspondingly, the verb in (3b) is inflected as Transitive with the infix <*in*>. In the following examples, the inflectional and applicative formatives are bolded, as are the absolutive arguments, in both Waray and in the English free translations:

(3) BC: a. ***Nagsayaw* hi Lillia** *(ha entablado).*
na-g-sayaw hi Lillia (ha entablado)
INTR.NEU.R-DEL-dance ABS.PERS Lillia LOC stage
'**Lillia** danced (on stage).'

AC: b. *Ginsayawan ni Lillia **ini nga entablado** han daraga pa hiya.*
g<in>-sayaw-an ni Lillia ini nga entablado
DEL<TR.R>-dance-APPL1 ERG.PERS Lillia DEM.ABS LK stage
han daraga pa hiya
GEN.DEF girl INCMPL 3SG.ABS
'Lillia danced **on this stage** when she was young.' (Wolff and Wolff 1967).

The root for both of these examples is *sayaw* 'dance'. This can be identified as an inherently intransitive root for two reasons: 1) Semantically it describes a situation that requires only one participant – someone who dances; 2) Grammatically, this root must take valence increasing stem-forming affixation in order to be used in a transitive frame. The three possible valence increasing affixes are the causative *pa-*, as in example (4), an applicative 1 suffix as in (3b), and the applicative 2 prefix (ex. [12b] further below).

(4) *Ginpasayaw ni Nánay **hi Lillia** ha entablado.*
g<in>-pa-sayaw ni Nánay hi Lillia ha
DEL<TR.R>-CAUS-dance ERG.PERS Mom ABS.PERS Lillia LOC
entablado
stage
'Mom let/had/made **Lillia** dance on stage.'

The prefix *pa-* in example (4) increases the valence of the root *sayaw* by adding a causal agent, to form an inherently transitive stem *-pasayaw* 'cause/let dance'. Because this stem depicts a deliberate action that requires special effort, the deliberate mood marker *g-* also appears, yielding the stem *-gpasayaw*.[10]

Verbal clauses with more than one absolutive argument do not occur in Waray. Therefore the valence of the clause is not strictly-speaking increased when an applicative is added to an inherently transitive root or stem such as *-gpasayaw* in (4). Rather, the grammatical relations of the arguments are rearranged to bring the location into the absolutive role, while the patient or causee is displaced to an oblique role. As in (3b), the applicative suffix "points to" the location as the absolutive argument. The causee then must be expressed in an oblique role. The result is the Transitive clause illustrated in (5).

(5) *Gi**npasayaw**an ni Nánay kan Lillia **ini nga entablado**.*
g<in>-pa-sayaw-an   ni   Nánay   kan   Lillia
DEL<TR.R>-CAUS-dance-APPL1   ERG.PERS   Mom   LOC.PERS   Lillia
ini   nga   entablado
DEM.ABS   LK   stage
'Mom let/had/made Lillia dance **on this stage**.'

The Tagalog equivalents of constructs such as (3b) and (5) are what Schachter and Otanes (1972) described as "location focus." The function of such constructs is to call special attention to a location. There is something notable about the location of the activity, and the speaker is commenting on that.

Applicative 1 morphology may also occur with stems that express transfer or removal, in which case the destination/recipient or source becomes the absolutive. For example, the verb in (6a) is the bare root *hátag* 'to give', which may be considered semantically trivalent because the scene it evokes involves three participants: An agent (or giver), a theme (the item transferred) and a recipient. With no valence-related stem forming affixes, *hátag* selects the agent as the ergative argument and the theme as the absolutive (6a). The recipient appears in an oblique role. Example (6b) is based on the applicative stem *-hatágan* 'to give to'.

---

10 Our analysis of this *g-* as a stem-forming prefix indicating deliberate mood is controversial. There are other ways of looking at the verb morphology (see, e.g., Mithun 2019 on Hiligaynon, a language closely related to Waray), though full argumentation for and against this detail lies beyond the scope of this paper. Suffice to say that this particular part of our analysis does not affect the central claims of the present paper.

(6) BC: a. *Ginhatag han batà **an regalo** kan Tátay.*
g<in>-hátag   han batà an   regalo kan   Tátay
DEL<TR.R>-give ERG child ABS gift   LOC.PERS Dad
'The child gave **the gift** to Dad.'

AC: b. *Ginhatag**an** han batà **hi Tátay** hin regalo.*
g<in>-hátag-an   han batà hi   Tátay hin
DEL<TR.R>-give-APPL1   ERG child ABS.PERS Dad   GEN.INDEF[11]
regalo
gift
'The child gave **Dad** a gift.'

The applicative *-an* tells the hearer that the absolutive is the recipient of the gift. Again, because Waray does not allow two absolutives in the same verbal clause, the theme in (6b) must appear in an oblique role. The case-marked determiner *hin*, 'GENITIVE.INDEFINITE', is employed for indefinite displaced absolutives.

In subjunctive mood, applicative 1 is evinced by the suffix *-i*. This is also completely regular and predictable. Example (7a) illustrates the affirmative irrealis form of an applicative 1 construct, whereas (7b) illustrates the negative equivalent, which requires the subjunctive mood. In every instance where *-an* appears in a declarative, affirmative clause, *-i* will appear in the corresponding subjunctive. This includes imperatives, as illustrated further below (see example 30b):

(7) a. *Dádad-**an** ni Lóla **hi Maria** hin kendi.*
0-dá~dara-an   ni   Lóla   hi   Maria
TR.IR-INCOMP-bring-APPL1   ERG.PERS grandmother ABS.PERS Maria
hin   kendi
GEN.INDEF candy
'Grandma will bring **Maria** candy.'

b. *Waray pa dad-**i** ni Lóla **hi Maria** hin kendi.*
waray pa   Ø-dara-i   ni   Lóla
NEG   INCOMPL TR.IR-bring-APPL1.SBJV ERG.PERS grandmother
hi   Maria hin   kendi
ABS.PERS Maria GEN.INDEF candy
'Grandma has not yet brought **Maria** candy.'

---

11 The terms "definite" and "indefinite" are convenient labels for certain grammatically expressed pragmatic statuses in Waray. They are similar to, but not to be equated with definite and indefinite as expressed in English. This concept is discussed in some depth in Oyzon and Payne (in prep.).

Verbs of removal, such as *kuhà* 'to get', *kawat* 'to steal' and *hukas* 'to strip/detach', in the applicative 1 construction select the source as the applied phrase. These usages may be considered canonical because they are related to corresponding base constructs in which the source may be expressed as an oblique:

(8) BC: a. **Nag*kuhà **hiya** hin kwarta (tikang) kan Tátay.*
  na-g-kuhà hiya hin kwarta (tikang)
  INTR.NEU.R-DEL-get 3SG.ABS GEN.INDEF money from
  kan Tátay
  LOC.PERS Dad
  'S/**he** got money from Dad.'

  BC: b. *G*in*kuhà níya **an kwarta** (tikang) kan Tátay.*
  g<in>-kuhà níya an kwarta (tikang) kan Tátay
  DEL<TR.R>-get 3SG.ERG ABS money from LOC.PERS Dad
  'S/he got **the money** from Dad.'

  AC: c. *G*in*kuha**an** níya **hi Tátay** hin kwarta.*
  g<in>-kuhà-an níya hi Tátay hin kwarta
  DEL<TR.R>-get-APPL1 3SG.ERG ABS.PERS Dad GEN.INDEF money
  'S/he got money **from Dad**.'

When a beneficiary of a verb of removal is expressed in the absolutive case, the applicative 2 construction may be used (see section 3.2). Thus, there is no possibility of construing example (8c) as 'S/he got money for Dad'.

Like example (8c), examples (9) and (10) from conversations illustrate the canonical applicative 1 construction with verbs of removal expressing the source as the absolutive. Constituents in parentheses in the free translations are understood from the context in Waray:

(9) *G*in*kawat**an kami** kagab-i.*
  g<in>-kawat-an kami kagab-i
  DEL<TR.R>-steal-APPL1 1EXCL.ABS last.night
  '(Someone) stole (something) **from us** last night.'

(10) *H*in*ukas**an** hin ranggo **an pulis**.*
  <in>hukas-an hin ranggo an pulis
  <TR.R>strip-APPL1 GEN.INDEF rank ABS police.officer
  '**The police officer** was stripped of her/his rank.'

3.2 *i-* 'Applicative 2': Benefactive, associative, instrumental

In the applicative 2 construction, responsibility for the completion of an activity is distributed between a primary actor and a beneficiary, associate or instrument. We think of this feature as involving a reduction in "sovereignty" of the actor. In other words, the situation is presented as not solely and completely driven by the will and control of the ergative-marked actor, but is shared with another person or instrument, which we name the "co-actant." In the canonical situation, the co-actant is explicitly mentioned in the absolutive case. In the non-canonical situation, the argument structure of the base does not change, and the co-actant is usually not explicitly mentioned. This characterization will be elaborated in the discussion of registration applicatives in section 4.5.

In the Eastern Samar variety of Waray, the usages of the applicative 2 prefix *i-* overlap with those of *-an/-i*, as described in section 3.1. In this section we describe the canonical uses of *i-* in Northern Leyte. The difference between the canonical benefactive, associative and instrumental usages depends on the semantic class of the host verb and the animacy of the arguments.

In its most frequent and productive canonical usage, the prefix *i-* identifies the absolutive as a beneficiary. This usage is evoked for inherently transitive situations which do not mention an instrument. Consider the examples in (11):

(11) BC: a. **Naglutò ako** *(para kan Nánay).*
na-g-lutò ako (para kan Nánay)
INTR.NEU.R-DEL-cook 1SG.ABS for LOC.PERS Mom
'I cooked (for Mom).'

BC: b. **Ginlutò ko an isdâ** *(para kan Nánay).*
g<in>-lutò ko an isdâ (para kan Nánay)
DEL<TR.R>-cook 1SG.ERG ABS fish for LOC.PERS Mom
'I cooked **the fish** (for Mom).'

AC: c. **Iginlutò ko hi Nánay hin isdâ.**
i-g<in>-lutò ko hi Nánay hin isdâ
APPL2-DEL<TR.R>-cook 1SG.ERG ABS.PERS Mom GEN.INDEF fish
'I cooked **Mom** fish.'

The root *lutò* 'cook' may be considered semantically transitive because it portrays a scene in which there are two participants – someone who cooks and something that gets cooked. In Waray, all semantically transitive verbs may occur with no mention of the endpoint of the activity, in which case the agent is the only argument of the verb and the verb is inflected as Intransitive, as in example (11a) (and earlier in 8a). Example (11a) simply describes the activity of cooking. Hearers know that something got cooked because of the semantics of the root, but the identity of the cooked item or items is not relevant to the speaker's message. Example (11b) illustrates the same root in a transitive frame. In this example the item cooked is a central participant, and is expressed in the absolutive case. In both (11a) and (11b) a beneficiary may be expressed in an oblique role. Example (11c) may be considered the applicative 2 version of either (11a) or (11b). The prefix *i-* on the verb indicates that the action is carried out not simply for the benefit of the actor, but there is another person motivating (consciously or not) the situation. That other person is mentioned as the absolutive of the clause. The patient, *isdâ* 'fish', if present, appears in the genitive case. If the patient is not present, ambiguity may result, which we discuss in section 4.5.

The second canonical usage of the applicative 2 prefix is to bring an associate into the core argument structure of the clause as an absolutive. This usage is evoked for certain inherently intransitive situations that do not involve instruments.

(12) BC: a. **Nagsayaw kami ni Nánay**
na-g-sayaw   kami   ni   Nánay
INTR.NEU.R-DEL-dance 1EXCL.ABS GEN.PERS   Mom
'I danced with Mom/We danced, Mom and I.'[12]

AC: b. **Iginsayaw ko hi Nánay.**
i-g<in>-sayaw   ko   hi   Nánay
APPL2-DEL<TR.R>-dance   1SG.ERG ABS   Mom
'I danced with **Mom**.'

The root *sayaw*, 'to dance' is inherently intransitive, as discussed earlier in section 3.1. There are several ways in Waray of expressing the idea that two or more people act together. One of those ways is illustrated in (12a). In this example, the speaker is the primary actor, and *ni Nanay* 'of Mom' is the associate, expressed in the genitive case. This may be considered a base construct for (12b) in which the verb takes the applicative 2 prefix, and is inflected as Transitive. The argument structure selects the primary actor in the ergative case (*ko*), and the associate as absolutive. One possible inference from (12b) is that *Nanay* did not know how to dance, and so simply followed the steps of the primary actor.

---

12 Since the speaker and Nánay are presented as dancing together, the 1st person plural exclusive pronoun must be used here. The singular *ako* would result in ungrammaticality. The meaning, however, is clear that the speaker alone danced with Nánay, hence the English translation with a first person singular subject is appropriate.

It is also possible to construe the construction in (12b) as a benefactive applicative, e.g. 'I danced for Mom (to entertain her, or as her replacement)'. However, such interpretations require significantly more context than does the associative interpretation. For this particular verb, and others that describe cooperative activity, the associative meaning is much more salient.

Example (13) illustrates an associative usage of the applicative 2 construction from the corpus.

(13) *Sumiring **iton nga kuan**, tawo na, baga íya na **iginkákahimangraw**.*
s\<um\>iring   iton   nga kuan   tawo   na
\<INTR.R\>speak DEM.ABS   LK whatever   person   CMPL
baga íya   na   i-g\<in\>-ká~ka-himangraw
seem 3SG.ERG CMPL   APPL2-DEL\<TR.R\>-INCMPL~VBZ-conversation
'**This kuan** spoke, (it's) now a person, (and) he seems now to be conversing (**with it**).'

The text from which (13) is extracted is about a dog that was transformed into a man, and became able to speak. In this three-clause sequence, the absolutive is the same in all three clauses. The speaker uses the word *kuan* meaning roughly 'thingamajig' or 'whatever you call it', because they weren't sure at first whether to call the referent a person or a dog. Conversing, like dancing together, is an inherently cooperative activity, so the associative meaning of the applicative 2 construction is the only possibility in this context. In other words, the last clause cannot be understood as "he was conversing for it."

The third canonical usage of the applicative 2 prefix is to bring an instrument into the core argument structure of the clause as an absolutive. Consider the examples in (14) and (15):

(14) BC: a. *Buaka han martilyo **an alkansiya**.*
buak-a   han   martilyo   an   alkansiya
break-TR.SBJV GEN.DEF   hammer   ABS   piggybank
'Break open **the piggybank** with a hammer.'

AC: b. *Ibúbuak **ini nga martilyo** hit' alkansiya.*
Ø-i-bú~buak   ini   nga   martilyo   hito
TR.IR-APPL2-INCMPL~break   DEM.ABS   LK   hammer   DEM.OBL
alkansiya
piggybank
'Break open this piggy-bank with **this hammer**.' (Wolff and Wolff 1967).

Example (15) illustrates the instrumental use of the applicative 2 prefix from the corpus:

(16) *Igpápasahi ko **ini nga sinsilyo**.*
 Ø-i-g-pá~pasahi   ko   ini   nga sinsilyo
 TR.IR-APPL2-DEL-INCMPL~pay.fare 1SG.ERG DEM.ABS LK coins
 'I will pay the fare with **these coins**.'

Again, an instrument can be understood as sharing part of the responsibility for a situation; the actor together with the instrument accomplishes the act. Since beneficiaries and associate actors are (normally) animate, and instruments are (normally) inanimate, there is little to no possibility of ambiguity between instrumental and benefactive/associative meanings. The meaning of the predicate plus the nature of the arguments makes it clear that the absolutives in examples (14b) and (15) are presented as instruments.

Applicative constructions in which transitive activity is "redirected" to a non-patient argument are common in other language families. For example, Kiyosawa and Gerdts (2010:117) name this type of construction in Salish languages as "redirective" applicatives. Comrie (1985: 313–314) also discusses similar constructions in German and Russian as "valency rearrangement" constructions.

There is a tendency for the *i-* prefix to be dropped in instrumental applicatives. This may be considered the beginning of an "unmarked" applicative construction. For example, consider the following (from a conversation):

(16) *Ginhugas ko **an túbig ha balde**.*
 g<in>-hugas   ko   an   túbig ha balde
 DEL<TR.R>-wash 1SG.ERG ABS water LOC bucket
 'I used **the water in the bucket** to wash (something).'

In example (16), the absolutive is obviously the instrument rather than the patient of washing, even though there is no *i-* prefix on the verb. This clause cannot be construed as a non-applicative because the root *hugas* involves washing something solid (like dishes, hands) using water. Water is an implicit instrument for this root, and cannot possibly be the patient (see section 4.1 for a discussion of this root). Therefore it would be somewhat redundant to include the *i-* prefix. Speakers are aware of this tendency to drop the *i-* in an instrumental construction for verbs such as *hugas* that involve an implicit instrument, and agree there is no difference in meaning whether the *i-* is included or not. This may be considered a kind of unmarked "extraversive" construction in which an implicit argument is made explicit via an applicative-like construction (see section 4.1). However, we prefer to consider this as simply a case of conversational dropping of the prefix because of redundancy.

3.3 Arguments against the applicative analysis of -*an* and *i*-

In this section we will briefly address one of the major critiques of the applicative analysis of -*an* and *i*- for other Philippine languages. Kaufman (2009: 188–189) argues against the applicative analysis of Proto-Austronesian *-*an* and *Si*- (reflexes -*an* and *i*- in Tagalog and in Waray) on four grounds, as follows:

> First, we do not expect that an applicative affix (i.e., PAN *-*an*, *Si*-) would replace a transitive voice affix (i.e., *-*en*), but this clearly appears to have been the situation from the beginning in Austronesian. Second, the two putative applicatives cannot create new objects, but are rather restricted to creating new subjects. As noted by Ross [2009] (this volume, fn. 4) and argued for by Aldridge (2004), it may be possible that applicatives in ergative languages behave differently in promoting applicative objects directly to subject/absolutive. Nonetheless, it is odd for there to be a ban on applicatives co-occurring with the actor voice/antipassive, as this is seen to occur in other robustly ergative languages. Third, the two putative applicatives cannot cooccur with each other, a common possibility afforded to applicatives cross-linguistically. Finally, it is not clear that reflexes of *-*an* and *Si*- can be considered any more valency-increasing than reflexes of *-*en*.

Each of these arguments is challenged by the view, discussed in section 2, that "actor voice" affixes indicate grammatical intransitivity, and the "undergoer voice" affixes indicate grammatical transitivity. First, if *-*en* reflects grammatical transitivity, it is not at all surprising that an applicative affix might be complementary with it (would "replace" it in Kaufman's terminology), rather than co-occur with it. In our proposal, -*on* in Waray (reflex of PAN *-*en*) is an inflectional suffix marking transitive, irrealis verbs (see Table 1). As such, -*on* indicates that the absolutive argument has the semantic role, usually patient, which is expected for the non-applicative host stem, whereas the applicative -*an* indicates that the absolutive has a different semantic role (locative, recipient, destination or source). Since verbal predicates may not have two absolutives in Waray, it is understandable that -*on* and an applicative would not co-occur. Second, the argument that *-*an* and *Si*- create new subjects rests on the premise that subject and object are the basic grammatical relations. If one takes the view that the arguments licensed ("created" in Kaufman's terminology) by *-*an* and *Si*- are absolutives, this objection evaporates (as conceded by Kaufman in his references in the above quote to Ross 2009, and Aldridge 2004). Furthermore, as argued by Mithun (2002) and much of the typological literature on valence, applicative constructions provide a resource for bringing a particularly salient participant into the direct object or absolutive role. Antipassive constructions, on the other hand, downplay an absolutive, placing it in a less salient syntactic position. From this point of view, we might wonder why speakers would ever need to combine the two. If antipassive and applicative may co-occur in some languages, it may indicate that the two construction types have different functional profiles than they do in Philippine languages. From the point of view of Waray, at least, it makes sense that applicative constructions always cooccur with transitive or ambitransitive verb inflections – they always involve activity that "carries over" (Hopper and Thompson 1980) from a specific starting point to a distinct and salient endpoint. Third, Kaufman mentions cross-linguistic evidence that multiple applicatives may occur in the same clause. While there are languages that allow two applicative markers in the same clause, this phenomenon is relatively rare (see, e.g., the study of multiple applicatives in Samkoe 1994, and Polinsky 2013). And again, since Waray does not allow two absolutives in a verbal clause, it is understandable why two applicatives, both of which involve absolutive applied phrases, would not co-occur. Finally, the applicative analysis does not entail that reflexes of *-an and *Si- are "more valence increasing" than reflexes of *-en. As shown above (examples [6b], [7a, b] and [11c]), and well documented in many distinct language families, applicative constructions do not necessarily increase numerical valence (see Peterson 2007; Polinsky 2013; Kiyosawa and Gerdts 2010, and several studies in the present volume).

4 Non-canonical applicatives

In section 3 we described the canonical uses of the applicative affixes, -an, -i and i-. As with most or all applicative formatives identified in other language families, there are also several "non-canonical" or extended usages of the Waray applicative affixes. In this section we describe five such usages. These are non-canonical in that they lack one or more of the definitional properties mentioned in section 3 and in the introduction to this volume. Some of these usages also involve specialized meanings (adversative, evaluative, partitive), and none are as productive and regular as the canonical usages. We name these non-canonical usages "obligatory applicatives" (section 4.1), "adversative applicatives" (section 4.2), "partitive applicatives" (section 4.3), "evaluative applicatives" (section 4.4), and "registration applicatives" (section 4.5).

4.1 Obligatory applicatives ("extraversive" constructions)

One common feature of applicative formatives according to Peterson (2007: 160–162) is that they are often lexicalized with certain roots. In Waray, several verbs require an applicative affix in order to "externalize", or make explicit, a semantic role that is implicit in the verb root in some way. This usage can be considered an extension of the canonical locative usage of the applicative 1 construction insofar as a location is implicit for any event involving physical activity. For example, events of dancing, playing, eating, drinking, etc. all must occur in a place, though the place is not particularly central to their core meanings. For such concepts in Waray, the location may always be expressed as an oblique constituent preceded by a general oblique preposition *ha* (*kan* for personal names). Alternatively, the canonical applicative 1 construction can be employed to bring that location into the core case frame of the clause as an absolutive (see examples (3b) and (5) above). However, some verbs evoke scenes that more strongly involve a semantic role that is not explicitly present in the core argument structure of the bare root. Lehmann and Verhoeven (2006) describe a class of intransitive verbs in Yucatec Maya for which a theme or patient is implicit, and which must be transitivized to make that participant explicit. For example, the verb *húuy* 'to stir' in Yucatec Maya implies a liquid patient as in (17a). In order to make that patient explicit, a transitivizer -*t* is required, (17b):

(17) BC: a. h   *húuy-nah-en*[13]
          PFV   stir-CMPL-ABS.1.SG
          'I stirred (sth.).'

     AC: b. *Húuy-t*   *le*   *sa'-o'*   *bik*   *táak'-ak!*
          stir-TRR(IMP) DEF atole-D2 PROHIB stick\DEAG-DEP
          'Stir the atole lest it sticks!'

The -*t* in example (17b) is the same form that occurs in prototypical applicative clauses in Yucatec Maya. However, Lehmann and Verhoeven distinguish constructs such as (17b) from applicatives because the liquid undergoer may not be expressed as an oblique in the base construction. Rather, the -*t* "externalizes" an undergoer that is implicit in the root itself. In the words of Lehmann and Verhoeven (2006: 1), "extraversive constructions provide an intransitive base with an undergoer slot."

---

[13] Glosses in the Yucatec Maya examples have been regularized. Lehmann and Verhoeven's analysis is not affected by this regularization.

There is a large class of inherently intransitive verbs in Waray that function in precisely this way. However, rather than considering these to represent a distinct extraversive construction, we prefer to treat these simply as a non-canonical usage of the applicative 1 form. Verbs that belong to this class in Waray include the roots *hugas* 'to wash (something solid using liquid)', *laba* 'to launder (clothes)', *harok* 'to kiss (someone)', *tilaw* 'to taste (food)', and *tutdo* 'to teach (someone)', along with many others. For example, *laba* 'to launder' (from Spanish *lavar*) implies clothes as a patient (ex. 18).

(18) BC: **Naglálaba ako.**
    na-g-lá~laba   ako
    INTR.NEU.R-DEL-INCMPL~launder   1SG.ABS
    'I'm laundering (clothes).' (Idiomatically in English: 'I'm doing the laundry.')

The bare root of this verb is inherently intransitive because, like *sayaw* 'to dance' mentioned earlier, it may not occur in a transitive frame without valence increasing morphology, either the causative prefix *pa-* or an applicative. Example (19) illustrates the ungrammaticality of this verb in a transitive form without an applicative marker:

(19) *Ginlálaba ko **an bado**.
    g<in>-lá~laba   ko   an   bado
    DEL<TR.R>-INCMPL~launder   1SG.ERG ABS   dress
    (intended meaning 'I am laundering **the dress**'.)

Although laundering is a physical activity that occurs in a location, the applicative 1 construction for this verb, and other members of its class, does not bring the location into the absolute role. Rather, the applicative 1 suffix "extraverts" (makes explicit) the implicit undergoer, as in (20):

(20) AC: **Ginlabhan ko an bado ni Nánay.**
    g<in>-laba-an   ko   an   bado   ni   Nánay
    DEL<TR.R>-launder-APPL1   1SG.ERG ABS   dress GEN.PERS   Mom
    'I laundered **mom's dress**.'

What such roots have in common semantically is that they all describe activities in which the affected participant is only slightly, superficially or invisibly affected by the activity. Not all concepts of this sort belong to this class, but all concepts in this grammatically defined class do exhibit this semantic characteristic. For another example, the root *hugas* 'wash (something solid using liquid)' must take the applicative *-an* (or *-i* in the subjunctive) when occurring in a transitive frame:

(21) a. *Ginhugasan ko na **an mga pinggan**.*
  g<in>-hugas-an   ko   na   an   mga   pinggan
  DEL<TR.R>-wash-APPL1 1SG.ERG CMPL ABS PL dish
  'I already washed **the dishes**.'

  b. *Hugási **ini nga pinggan**!* *Hugása* ...
  hugas-i   ini   nga   pinggan   *hugas-a
  wash-APPL1.SBJV DEM.ABS LK dish wash-TR.SBJV
  'Wash **these dishes**!'

The following is an example of *harukan/hadkan* (the difference is dialectal or idiolectal) 'to kiss' from the corpus. This verb always implies a human or anthropomorphized patient. In this example, a body part of the human patient is the absolutive:

(22) ... *ug akon hadkan **an imo rapadápa*** ...
  ... ug   akon   Ø-harok-an   an   imo   rapadápa
  and 1SG.ERG TR.IR-kiss-APPL1 ABS your sole.of.foot
  '... and I kiss **the sole of your foot**.'

This verb belongs to the same class as *hugas, laba*, and the others mentioned above because it does not occur in a transitive frame without a causative or applicative affix, as shown by the ungrammaticality of the realis (*g<in>-harok* 'DEL<TR.R>-kiss') and irrealis (*harok-on* 'kiss-TR.IR') transitive forms without applicative marking.

4.2 Adversative applicatives

For certain roots, the applicative 1 suffix *-an* plus happenstantial mood gives rise to an adversative construction. In this construction, the applied phrase refers to someone who is adversely affected by the activity. The adversative applicative construction is non-canonical because a) it is infrequent, occurring only with a limited class of verb roots, and b) the adversative meaning is very construction-specific – in the base construction obliques are not necessarily understood as being adversely affected. Roots that may enter into this construction are all those for which the only argument in the intransitive form is an undergoer, such as *matay* 'to die', *sunog* 'to burn (as a building)', *warâ* 'disappear', *sara* 'to close', *túnaw* 'to melt', *anod* 'drift off,' etc. Similar examples of applicatives functioning as malefactives have been documented in Salish languages (Kiyosawa and Gerdts 2010: 147–184), and Mapudungun (Zúñiga 2010: 203–218):[14]

(23) BC: a. ***Na**matay **an báboy** (ha amon)*.
　　　　　na-matay　　an　　báboy　(ha　　amon)
　　　　　R.HAP-die　ABS　pig　　　LOC　1EXC.OBL
　　　　　'**The pig** died (at our place).'

　　　AC: b. ***Na**matáy**an** kami han báboy*.
　　　　　na-matay-an　　　kami　　　han　　　　báboy
　　　　　R.HAP-die-APPL1　1EXCL.ABS　GEN.DEF　pig
　　　　　'The pig died on **us**.'

(24) BC: a. ***Na**sunog **an balay**.*
　　　　　na-sunog　　　　　　an　　balay
　　　　　R.HAP-burn.down　　ABS　house
　　　　　'**The house** burned down.'

　　　AC: b. ***Na**sunóg**an** hira han balay*.
　　　　　na-sunog-an　　　　hira　　　han　　　balay
　　　　　R.HAP-burn-APPL1　3PL.ABS　GEN.DEF　house
　　　　　'**Their** house burned down.' (or 'The house burned down on **them**', understood to be their house.)

(25) BC: a. ***Na**warâ **an kwarta** (ha akon)*.
　　　　　na-warâ　　　　　　an　　kwarta　(ha　　akon)
　　　　　R.HAP-disappear　　ABS　money　　LOC　1SG.GEN
　　　　　'**The money** disappeared (at my place).'

---

14 In Mapudungun, there is a special applicative marker, *-ñma*, used in malefactive constructions. In Waray, the applicative 1 formation, plus happenstantial mood inflection results in a construction that is completely analogous to malefactives with *-ñma* in Mapudungun. However, we prefer the term "adversative" to "malefactive" because there is no "malice" involved in the meaning of this construction, i.e., the adversity is not intentional. In fact, the verb is overtly marked as happenstantial, indicting that there is no intentionality involved. The consequences are disadvantageous for the absolutive participant, but not maliciously so.

AC: b. **Nawad-an ako** hin kwarta.
na-warâ-an ako hin kwarta
R.HAP-disappear-APPL1 1SG.ABS GEN.INDEF money
'I lost some money.' (or 'Money disappeared on **me**.')

(26) BC: a. **Nasara an purtahan**.
na-sara an purtahan
R.HAP-close ABS door
'**The door** closed.'

AC: b. **Nasadhan kami** han purtahan.
na-sara-an kami han purtahan
R.HAP-close-APPL1 1EXC.ABS GEN.DEF door
'The door closed on **us**.'

While (23a) and (25a) may be considered the syntactic base constructs for (23b) and (25b) respectively, the semantics of the applicative constructs is quite different. The optional oblique participants in (23a) and (25a) simply describe the locations of the respective events, and may only incidentally be understood as being adversely affected by the situation – pigs dying and money disappearing are bound to affect someone adversely, but oblique participants in such clauses are not necessarily the adversely affected participant. However, in the corresponding applicative clauses, the applied phrase must be an adversely affected participant.

This is an infrequent construction in Waray that only applies to adverse situations. There are no examples in the corpus of this construction used to express beneficial situations, and such examples cannot easily be composed out of context. The examples in (26) illustrate a root that does not necessarily describe an adverse situation (the closing of a door is not an inherently bad thing), but in the applicative construction, the implication is that this event was somehow disadvantageous for *kami* '1EXC.ABS'. Therefore, the adversative meaning arises from the construction as a whole, and not from any of its individual components.

As mentioned in section 2, the happenstantial inflectional prefixes *na-* and *ma-* are "ambitransitive," i.e., they may occur in intransitive or transitive frames depending on the verb class and the context. Adversative applicatives (as well as evaluative applicatives described in section 4.4) depict a scene in which a stimulus affects a distinct participant in the absolutive case. However, the effect is not intentional, and does not involve a visible, concrete change in state. Therefore, such clauses are somewhat transitive, but are very low on the transitivity scale. The stimulus is presented as the thing that dies, disappears, closes, etc., taking one of the genitive prenominal determiners *han* or *hin*. This stimulus cannot simply be omitted, so it is not strictly speaking an oblique. However, neither can it be ergative. While *han* is the determiner for common nouns in the ergative role, ergative pronouns (27a) or the personal noun ergative determiner *ni* (27b) may not be used in this construction:

(27) a. ***Namatáyan níya an íya asáwa**.
 na-matay-an   níya   an   íya   asáwa
 R.HAP-die-APPL1 3SG.ERG ABS 3SG.GEN spouse
 (intended meaning: 'S/he died on **her/his spouse**.')

 b. ***Namatáyan ni Pedro an íya asáwa**.
 na-matay-an   ni   Pedro   an   íya   asáwa
 R.HAP-die-APPL1 ERG.PERS Pedro ABS 3SG.GEN spouse
 (intended meaning: 'Pedro died on **his spouse**.')

The genitive determiners *han/hin* express displaced absolutives in several other constructions (including causatives and applicatives of Transitive constructions, as illustrated in examples [6b] and [7b] above); therefore we consider the stimulus in the adversative construction to be displaced from its grammatical role as absolutive in the corresponding intransitive construction. However, because of the lack of an ergative actor, and the ambitransitive verbal inflection, this construction and the evaluative construction described in section 4.4 are the least transitive applicative constructions described in this paper.

For some roots, there may be no external stimulus expressed. In such cases, the stimulus is implicit in the root itself, i.e., there is no intransitive base construction. For example:

(28) **Nabahaan hira.**
 na-baha-an   hira
 R.HAP-flood-APPL1 3SG.ABS
 'They were flooded.'

The root *baha* 'flood' (from Spanish *baja* 'under, lower') implicitly involves water, and in the adversative construction, the water is normally not expressed. This construction may be considered morphologically as well as syntactically intransitive, since the predicate includes the ambitransitive happenstantial inflection, and there is no external controller expressed.

Adversative (along with evaluative applicatives discussed in section 4.4) represent the non-canonical usages of applicative morphology that most strongly deviate from the canonical usages, since they are only slightly transitive. Nevertheless, we would like to consider these to be reasonable extensions of the canonical applicative 1 construction for reasons discussed in section 5.

4.3 Partitive applicatives

For roots describing acquiring, receiving or disposing of something, an applicative 1 construction may express a partitive meaning. This usage is non-canonical because the argument structure of the clause remains the same as in the base construction. The absolutive argument in the AC has the same semantic role in the activity as the absolutive argument in the corresponding BC, but with a partitive meaning. For example:

(29) BC: a. *Ginkuhà ko **an tinápay**.*
g<in>-kuhà   ko   an   tinápay
DEL<TR.R>-get 1SG.ERG ABS   bread
'I got **the bread**.'

AC: b. *Ginkuhaan ko **an tinápay**.*
g<in>-kuhà-an   ko   an   tinápay
DEL<TR.R>-get-APPL1 1SG.ERG ABS   bread
'I got **(some of) the bread**.'

(30) BC: a. *Inma **ito**!*
inom-a   ito
drink-TR.SBJV DEM.ABS
'Drink (all of) **that!**'

AC: b. *Inmi **ito**!*
inom-i   ito
drink-APPL1.SBJV DEM.ABS
'Drink (some of) **that!**'

Note that the absolutive participant in a partitive applicative is the same as in the corresponding non-applicative construction. Waray speakers also have the sense that the partitive patient is presented as the location for the activity, though there is no corresponding base construction in which the patient is expressed as a locative oblique. We are reminded of English expressions like "she painted on the wall", in which the oblique can be understood as a partitive patient (the wall is only partly affected), as well as the location of the painting event. Note also that the absolutive in a partitive applicative is still understood as definite and specific, and the verb is still inflected as grammatically Transitive (i.e., this is not an antipassive clause). The applicative 1 marker on the verb simply indicates that the affected participant is less than completely affected.

In the canonical applicative 1 construction (section 3.1), the applied phrase is sometimes understood to be more highly affected than the same participant would be in a corresponding non-applicative (see, e.g., example [5]). However, in all such canonical examples, the applicative construction "promotes" an oblique argument to a direct argument status. The Waray partitive applicative construction does not involve promotion (i.e. an alternative argument structure) at all. In fact, one could say it pragmatically "demotes" an argument by assigning it to a role ("applied absolutive") that is usually reserved for locatives, recipients or other typically peripheral semantic roles.

4.4 Evaluative applicatives

Perhaps the most striking non-canonical usage of applicative morphology in Waray is what have been called "evaluative" clauses (Ricardo Nolasco, p.c., speaking of Tagalog). Evaluative clauses are non-canonical because a) they are infrequent, occurring only with a limited class of roots, and b) there is no non-applicative base in which the evaluator is expressed in an oblique phrase. In other words, the evaluative meaning is construction-specific. The evaluative construction can be represented as follows:

(31) INFL-ATTRIBUTE-APPL1   ABS-EVALUATOR   LOC/GEN-STIMULUS

The three obligatory parts of this construction are: 1) a verb consisting of a stem formed from a root describing an attribute, plus the applicative 1 suffix -*an*. This stem is usually inflected in happenstantial mood; 2) an evaluator in the absolutive case, and 3) a stimulus in a locative or genitive oblique case. The stimulus is the participant that the evaluator considers to exhibit the attribute mentioned in the predicate. Normally in evaluative applicatives, human stimuli occur following the locative preposition *ha* (*kan* for personal names), and non-human stimuli follow the definite ergative/genitive determiner *han*. For example:

(32) **Nahúsáyan si Pedro** ha íya.
      ATTRIBUTE   EVALUATOR   STIMULUS
      na-hú~húsay-an   si   Pedro   ha   íya
      R.HAP-INCMPL~beauty-APPL1   ABS.PERS Pedro   LOC   3SG
      '**Pedro** considers him/her beautiful.' (or: 'S/he is beautiful to Pedro.')

(33) **Maráraútan hiya** han lingkuran.
      ma-rá~raút-an   hiya   han   lingkuran
      IR.HAP-INCMPL~ugly-APPL1   3SG.ABS GEN.DEF chair
      '**S/he** will find the chair ugly.' (or: 'The chair will be ugly to him/her.')

(34) **Nadádakóan hiya** han baraydan.
      na-dá~dakô-an   hiya   han   baraydan
      R.HAP-INCMPL~big-APPL1   3SG.ABS GEN.DEF bill
      '**S/he** considers the bill too expensive (big).' (or: 'The bill is too big to him/her.')

Note that in these examples, the stimulus is expressed in a locative (32), or genitive (33), (34) case. As in adversative applicatives (section 4.2), the stimulus in an evaluative applicative cannot be ergative, as evidenced by the fact that an ergative pronoun is not possible. Compare (32) to (35):

(35) *__Nahúsáyan níya si Pedro__
      na-hú~húsay-an   níya   si   Pedro
      R.HAP-INCMPL~beautiful-APPL1 3SG.ERG ABS.PERS Pedro
      (intended meaning: '**Pedro** considers her/him beautiful.')

As with adversative applicatives, these evaluative constructs are somewhat transitive because they involve a starting point (the stimulus) and an endpoint (the evaluator) in the absolutive case. A possible functional motivation for the non-ergative expression of the stimulus is that this participant is not agentive. It is the locus, or starting point of the property described by the root, but does not actively control the situation. According to Jacques (2013), a similar usage of applicative morphology, termed "estimative" or "tropative", is found in Japhug Rgyalrong, a Trans-Himalayan language spoken in China.

4.5 Registration applicatives

The applicative 2 prefix may be used in a non-canonical way to evoke the presence of a beneficiary or other co-actant in a scene without presenting that participant in the absolutive case. This usage is similar to "registration" constructions in Acazulco Otomí as described in Hernández-Green (2016). In Acazulco Otomí, an applicative marker may indicate the presence of an oblique marked peripheral participant in the clause. In other words, the applicative marker simply "registers" the presence of the oblique participant, without licensing it as a core argument of the clause. In Waray registration applicatives, the registered peripheral participant is usually not expressed at all, though it may be expressed in an oblique role, as in (36).

(36) *Iginlutò ko **an isdâ** (para kan Nánay).*
    i-g<in>-lutò   ko   an   isdâ (para kan   Nánay)
    APPL2-DEL<TR.R>-cook 1SG.ERG ABS fish for   LOC.PERS Mom
    'I cooked **the fish** (for Mom).'

In this construction, a co-actant is implied, but may or may not be overtly expressed.[15] Without the optional expression of a beneficiary (*para kan Nanay*), this construct means 'I cooked the fish under the influence of someone else' perhaps a beneficiary, an associate, or a possessor of the fish, i.e., 'I cooked someone else's fish.' Without the applicative 2 prefix, *ginlutò ko an isdâ* simply means 'I cooked the fish,' implying the event is instigated by and under the sovereign control of the actor. The applicative 2 prefix simply "registers" the presence of a co-actant in the scene described by the clause.

Wolff (1973: 79) describes a similar usage of **Si-* in Proto Austronesian as a "conveyance" construction, because the absolutive is presented as being conveyed away from the actor. This interpretation may be applied to Waray examples such as (36) in the sense that the cooked item may be thought of as moving away from the person cooking, i.e., 'I cooked the fish (and gave it to someone).' Informal text counts reveal that indeed the registration applicative construction in Waray is very common with clauses in which the absolutive is a semantic theme (in the sense of Gruber 1965: 47–59) that is transferred, attached, uttered, or demonstrated to a registered co-actant. However, this does not seem to be an

---

15 It is worth noting that speakers consider it redundant, though fully grammatical, to use the applicative 2 prefix together with oblique expression of the beneficiary in this out-of-context example. However, this construction does naturally occur with overt expression of the co-actant in an oblique role, as illustrated in examples (42) and (43) below.

absolute requirement; for example, (41) and (45) below illustrate this usage in situations where the absolutive is not a theme.

Because there is a canonical benefactive applicative use of *i-* (described in section 3.2 above), sometimes ambiguity between the canonical and non-canonical usages may technically result.[16] For example:

(37) **Iginlutò ko hi Nánay.**
i-g<in>-lutò   ko   hi   Nánay
APPL2-DEL<TR.R>-cook 1SG.ERG ABS.PERS Mom
'I cooked **for Mom**' (canonical benefactive applicative); or 'I cooked **Mom** for someone' (registration applicative).

The ambiguity of this clause is resolved if the item cooked is expressed in the genitive case, as in (38). This is a canonical applicative 2 construction that can only be understood as indicated:

(38) **Iginlutò ko hi Nánay hin isdâ.**
i-g<in>-lutò   ko   hi   Nánay hin   isdâ
APPL2-DEL<TR.R>-cook 1SG.ERG ABS.PERS Mom   GEN.INDEF fish
'I cooked fish **for Mom**.'

It is significant that, though registration applicatives do not affect the argument structure of the clause, they are nevertheless strictly impossible in a grammatically Intransitive construction (39):

(39)   **Inagsayaw ako.*
i-na-g-sayaw   ako
APPL2-INTR.NEU.R-DEL-dance   1SG.ABS
(intended meaning: 'I danced for/with someone.')

This fact provides corroborative evidence that *i-* in its registration usage is still a kind of applicative, rather than a distinct homophonous morpheme. Applicative morphology creates stems that are grammatically transitive, and therefore occur with verb inflections from the Transitive set (see example [12b] above).

---

[16] Though of course in context, such ambiguity is pragmatically impossible. This reminds us of technically ambiguous English expressions like *Would you like me to make you a sandwich?*, to which a clever addressee might jokingly reply *But I don't want to be a sandwich!*.

The co-actant in a registration applicative construction may be understood as a beneficiary, as in (35) and (36), an associate, or some other external force. The generalization seems to be that the primary actor acts with or under the influence of someone or something else. Example (40) is from a folk story in which the protagonist, Doña Fidelina, is bound by the cultural value of returning something to its owner:

(40) **Igin**hatag **an sudlay** ni Donya Fidelina didto ha panganuron.
 i-g<in>-hátag   an   sudlay ni   Donya   Fidelina
 APPL2-DEL<TR.R>-give ABS   comb   ERG.PERS Doña   Fidelina
 didto   ha   panganuron
 there   LOC   cloud
 'Doña Fidelina had to give **the comb** to the cloud.'

In this example, the external force is not mentioned in the clause, but is registered by the presence of the *i-* applicative marker. Recall that *hátag*, 'to give', is a verb of transfer for which the transferred item, the theme, is the normal, non-applicative absolutive participant (as in example [6a] above). Therefore, in this construction *i-* does not adjust the argument structure, but simply expresses the idea that there is another force present in the background that can be understood as a co-actant of the activity expressed. This is captured roughly in the English free translation with the deontic modal auxiliary *had to*. Example (40) is fully grammatical without the *i-*, with no further changes to the verb or arguments, but would then constitute a more ordinary description of something Doña Fidelina did on her own. Examples such as (40) may be understood as semantic usages of an applicative morpheme, with no syntactic effects.

It turns out that most of the examples of the *i-* prefix in spontaneous discourse appear to be this registration usage. It is most common in clauses involving transfer, attachment, utterance or demonstration. Occasionally the co-actant is mentioned in an oblique phrase (as in [42] and [43] below), but more often it is left implicit. The following is a selection of examples from the corpus of the *i-* prefix registering a non-absolutive participant. We've categorized these examples according to the semantic role of the co-actant in the context of the text in which the example occurs. In each of these examples, the co-actant is underscored in the English free translations, and in Waray when overt.

Co-actant is a beneficiary:

(41) *Ikinasubô ko **an íya kamatay**.*
 i-k<in>a-subô   ko   an   íya   kamatay
 APPL2-<TR.R>VBLZR-grief 1SG.ERG ABS 3SG.GEN death
 'I grieved (for him) **his death**.'[17]

(42) *Ha akon ihinátag **an bayad** para kan Intoy.*
 ha   akon   i-h<in>átag   an   bayad para kan   Intoy
 LOC 1SG.GEN APPL2-<TR.R>give ABS pay for LOC.PERS Intoy
 '**The pay** for Intoy was given to me.'

(43) *Samtang ako nag-íisplikar hiunong hadto,*
 samtang   ako   na-g-í~isplikar   hiunong hadto
 while   1EXC.ABS INTR.NEU.R-DEL-INCMPL~explain about   DEM.OBL
 'While I was explaining about that,

 *iginpakità ko gihap ha anak **an ak' nahibaróan** . . .*
 i-g<in>-pa-kitâ   ko   gihap ha   anak   an
 APPL2-DEL<TR.R>-CAUS-see 1SG.ERG also   LOC offspring ABS
 akon   na-hibaru-an
 1SG.GEN HAP.R-learn-APPL1
 'I also demonstrated to the son/daughter what **I have learned** . . .

(44) *Isinugba ni Tátay **an bangus nga isdâ**.*
 i-s<in>ugba   ni   Tátay   an   bangus nga isdâ
 APPL2-<TR.R>roast ERG.PERS Dad   ABS milkfish LK fish
 'Dad grilled **the milkfish** (for us).'

(45) *Iginkákasubô namon **an pagpasabot** nga hi X tumalikod na ha kadayunan . . .*
 i-g<in>-ká~ka-subô   namon   an   pag-pa-sabot   nga
 APPL2-DEL<TR.R>-INCMPL~VBZ-grief 1EXC.ERG ABS INF-CAUSE-agree LK
 hi   X   t<um>alikod   na   ha   kadayunan . . .
 ABS.PERS (name) <INTR.R>turn.away CMPL LOC world
 'We regret **to inform** (you) that X has abandoned (turned away from) the world.' (formal, euphemistic expression announcing a death).

---

17 It is actually unclear or ambiguous in this example whether the co-actant is the deceased person, or the external cultural value of grieving someone's death. The semantic contribution of *i-* is simply that there is a co-actant. The first interpretation given by native speakers upon reading the example in context is that the deceased person is the cause/beneficiary of grieving, but this is not a necessary assertion of this construction.

In example (41), the beneficiary happens to be expressed as a possessor of the absolutive argument. In (42), the beneficiary is expressed in an oblique phrase, *para kan Intoy*, within the absolutive noun phrase headed by *bayad* 'pay', and in (43) it is expressed in an oblique phrase. In examples (44) and (45), the beneficiary is not expressed at all in the clause, but is only understood from the context, as indicated in parentheses in the English free translations.

Co-actant is an external force or motivation:

(46) *Diin nimo **iginhigot an im' tudo?***
 diin nimo i-g\<in\>-higot an imo tudo
 where 2SG.ERG APPL2-DEL\<TR.R\>-tie ABS 2SG.GEN bull
 'Where did you tie **your bull**?'

In example (46), *ginhigot* without the *i-* prefix is grammatical, with no change in basic meaning. However, the use of *i-* indicates that there was a previous request to tie the bull in another place, and the questioner is checking on the hearer's compliance with the request, i.e. "Where did you tie your bull (as you were told earlier)?"

(47) *Maganansya pa kita kun **igbaligya ta.***
 ma-ganansya pa kita kun Ø-i-g-baligya ta
 HAP.IR-gain/profit INCMPL 1INC.ABS if TR.IR-APPL2-DEL-sell 1INC.ERG
 'We can still profit if we sell **(it)**.'

In (47), the absolutive is understood from the context, and the external force in this instance is pressure from the fact that a television set is not functioning, and so the primary actors can only gain from it by selling it. A more idiomatic English translation may be "We need to sell it so we can profit from it".

5 Mitigated transitivity as a unifying semantic function for applicative constructions in Waray

We have shown in the previous sections that the applicative formatives *-an/-i* and *i-* in Waray are multifunctional. In this section we try to articulate our intuitive sense of the semantic/functional commonality among all the usages of these forms in verbal predicates, thus justifying the decision to describe them all as applicatives, with the non-canonical usages being reasonable extensions of the canonical applicative functions.[18]

Transitivity is a multi-faceted functional domain, with morphological, syntactic, semantic and discourse pragmatic consequences in many, if not all languages of the world. The very pervasiveness of transitivity in human languages makes it challenging to isolate individual functional bases for the structural phenomena that participate in its expression. In fact, numerous studies have shown not only that transitivity is a scale rather than a bi- or tripartite distinction, but also that the scale itself is multidimensional (see, e.g., the components of transitivity identified in Hopper and Thompson 1980, and elaborated in several subsequent studies, notably Kemmer 1993; Næss 2007; and LaPolla, Kratochvíl and Coupe 2011).

We have argued elsewhere (Oyzon and Payne in prep.; Payne and Oyzon 2020) that the semantic basis for the structural category of absolutive in Waray is its status as the "most affected participant" in the scene expressed by the predicate. There are also pragmatic correlates to this status, such as the absolutive tends to be definite, specific, referential, topical and individuated (see similar observations in Mithun 2002, 2019, and Hemmings 2021 for other Philippine languages). The applied phrase in an applicative construction in Waray has all the structural and discourse pragmatic characteristics common to absolutives in the language. The difference between applied absolutives and other absolutives, we suggest, is primarily semantic. Namely, applied absolutives, while still qualifying as "the most affected participant in the clause" are presented as being in some sense indirectly, invisibly or "obliquely" affected by the activity described by the verb. For the canonical applicatives, the absolutive may be a location, destination, recipient or source (applicative 1), or it may be a beneficiary, associate or instrument (applicative 2). For the most part, applied absolutives do not undergo a physical change in state, other than becoming clean for verbs involving washing. For the non-canonical applicatives, the applied absolutives are superficially or invisibly affected patients (obligatory applicatives), partially affected patients (partitive

---

18 Note that we are not discussing the usages of *i-* and *-an* as nominalizers, e.g., *sayawan* 'dancing place,' *ipurúlod* 'thing for cutting wood,' etc. We analyze these and many others as formed with the applicative morphemes plus nominalization as a distinct process often involving a shift in stress (as described in Oyzon and Payne, in prep.). However, arguments for and against such analyses lie outside the scope of the present paper. It may be worth noting that applicative morphology is often employed in nominalizations in other language families (see, e.g., Peterson 1997, and Pacchiarotti 2020). In fact Starosta, Pawley and Reid (1982) argued that nominalization is the historical source of the voice system in Proto Austronesian. This perspective, though broadly accepted, has been debated without clear resolution in much subsequent work, see, e.g. Ross (2002), Kaufman (2009), (2017), and references cited therein.

applicatives), or psychologically affected experiencers (adversative and evaluative applicatives). In the case of registration applicatives, the pragmatic or semantic status of the absolutive is not adjusted at all by the presence of the applicative form. Rather, the situation is presented as being under the shared control of the ergative actor and some other instigating force or participant that is not necessarily explicitly mentioned. Thus for registration applicatives the transitivity is mitigated by dispersing the responsibility of the actor, rather than adjusting the pragmatic or semantic status of an applied phrase.

Here we summarize the usages of the constructions involving applicative morphology identified in this paper, along with the semantic status of the arguments:

1. Canonical applicatives (section 3)	Applicative 1 (-an/-i): Ergative is a sovereign actor. Absolutive is a location, destination, recipient or source of the activity.
	Applicative 2 (i-): Ergative shares responsibility for the activity with a co-actant. Absolutive is a co-actant (beneficiary, associate or instrument).
2. Obligatory applicative verbs (section 4.1)	("Extraversive" constructions): Applicative 1: Ergative is a sovereign actor. Absolutive is superficially (wash, kiss), or invisibly (teach, answer) affected by the activity.
3. Adversative applicatives: (section 4.2)	Applicative 1: No ergative controller expressed. The stimulus is something that undergoes a happenstantial change in state. Absolutive is emotionally or indirectly affected in an adverse way by the situation.
4. Partitive applicatives: (section 4.3)	Applicative 1: Ergative is a sovereign actor. Absolutive is partially affected by the activity.
5. Evaluative applicatives: (section 4.4)	Applicative 1: No ergative controller. The stimulus is something that may exhibit a property. Absolutive deems the property to hold of the stimulus.
6. Registration applicatives: (section 4.5)	Applicative 2: Ergative shares responsibility for the situation with a beneficiary, associate, or external force. Absolutive is a patient or theme (a transferred, attached, uttered, or demonstrated item).

The clause structure of Waray is highly sensitive to semantic transitivity. We have argued elsewhere (Payne and Oyzon 2020) that transitivity and modality are major categories in the inflectional paradigm of verbal predicates. There are many components of semantic transitivity – ten of which are proposed in Hopper and Thompson (1980). Affectedness of the undergoer is the component that the applicative 1 construction most directly addresses. Sovereignty of the actor is the component that the applicative 2 construction most directly addresses. Other areas of the grammar of Waray address other components of transitivity, with a certain degree of semantic crossover from one system to the next.[19] Part of the "genius" of Waray, and probably most languages of the Philippines, is to provide finely nuanced and clear grammatical expression of control and effect.

6 Conclusion

We have shown that there are two grammatically distinct applicative forms in Waray. These we have named "applicative 1", represented by the suffixes -*an* and -*i*, and "applicative 2" represented by the prefix *i*-. Both of these forms have productive valence related applicative functions, which we have termed their "canonical" functions (section 3). In addition, like many or all applicative constructions in the world's languages, both applicatives in Waray have multiple extended, or "non-canonical" usages. These usages are non-canonical, first because they are less productive than the canonical usages, and second because they lack one or more of the properties associated with prototypical applicatives as identified in other language families and mentioned in the introduction to this volume. Finally, certain non-canonical applicative constructions tend to express construction-specific semantics (adversative, evaluative, partitive) not predictable from the propositional meaning of the verb and its arguments alone. We have documented five such non-canonical usages, and provided a characterization of a unified semantic function of the applicative forms as involving "mitigated transitivity". All canonical and non-canonical usages involve mitigated transitivity, either indirect, invisible, superficial, partial, or experiential affect on the endpoint of the transitive situation, or distributed control or responsibility on the part of the starting point.

The non-canonical functions of applicative morphology in Waray represent several of the neglected functions of applicatives noticed in other language families, some of which are mentioned in the introduction to this volume. In particular, the obligatory applicatives (section 4.1) introduce central, rather than peripheral participants as absolutives, as has been observed in Yucatec Maya (Lehman and Verhoeven 2006) and other languages (Peterson 2007). The adversative applicatives (section 4.2) introduce an adversely affected participant, as has been observed in Salish languages (Kiyosawa and Gerdts 2010) and in Mapu-

---

19 For example, there is no transitive/intransitive distinction in the happenstantial moods. Happenstantial mood directly expresses reduction in control on the part of the starting point. Therefore it is not surprising that the grammatical transitive/intransitive distinction is neutralized in precisely this situation. See Table 1.

dungun (Zúñiga 2010). Registration applicatives (section 4.5) register the presence of a co-actant in a scene expressed by the predication without requiring it to be presented in the absolutive case. Similar constructions have been observed in Acazulco Otomí (Hernández–Green 2016). Partitive applicatives (section 4.3), and evaluative applicatives (section 4.4) may be considered applicative constructions with specialized semantic consequences, and both are common in Philippine languages. Certain diminutive/attenuative usages of applicative morphology, which may be considered similar to the partitive usages in Philippine languages, have been documented by Sharman (1963) in Bemba and certain other Bantu languages. A function similar to Waray evaluative functions of applicative morphology has been documented by Jacques (2013) for Japhug Rgyalrong, a Trans-Himalayan language spoken in China. Jacques relates these to "tropative" constructions in Arabic, Turkish, and other languages.

Finally, we have shown that the "voice system" of Waray can be described in terms that are well-understood from other language families of the world, namely morphologically expressed transitivity and applicative marking. We hope that this way of looking at the morphosyntax of Waray will be helpful to linguists and others who are struggling to appreciate and articulate the genius of Philippine type languages.

Abbreviations

1	first person
2	second person
3	third person
ABS	absolutive case
APPL1	applicative 1 (Locative, destination/recipient, source applicative, -an/-i)
APPL2	applicative 2 (Benefactive, instrumental applicative, i-)
COMP	complementizer
CMPL	completive
CAUS	causative
D2	distal deixis
DEAG	deagentive
DEF	definite
DEL	deliberate mood
DEM	demonstrative
DEP	dependent
DIST	distributive
ERG	ergative case
GEN	genitive case
HAP	happenstantial mood,

IMP	imperative
INCMPL	incompletive aspect
INDEF	indefinite
INF	infinitive
INTR	intransitive
IR	irrealis
IT	iterative
LK	linker
LOC	locative
NEG	negative
NEU	neutral (with respect to happenstantial vs. controlled moods)
OBL	oblique
PAN	proto Austronesian
PERS	personal name
PL	plural
PROHIB	prohibitive
PFV	perfective
R	realis
SG	singular
TR	transitive
TRR	transitivizer
VBZ	verbalizer

References

3NS Corpora project. (https://corporaproject.org/). National Network of Normal Schools, Philippines. (Accessed 31 August 2021).
Aldridge, Edith C. 2004. *Ergativity and word order in Austronesian languages*. Ithaca, New York: Cornell University dissertation.
Aldridge, Edith C. 2012. Antipassive and ergativity in Tagalog. *Lingua* 122(3). 192–203.
Bauer, Laurie. 2003. *Introducing linguistic morphology*. 2nd edition. Washington D.C.: Georgetown University Press.
Bell, Sarah. 1979. *Cebuano subjects in two frameworks*. Bloomington: Indiana University Linguistics Club.
Blust, Robert A. 2002. Notes on the history of 'focus' in Austronesian languages. In Fay Wouk & Malcolm Ross (eds.), *The history and typology of Western Austronesian voice systems*, 63–79. (Pacific Linguistics). Canberra: Research School of Pacific and Asian Studies, the Australian National University.
Brainard, Sherri. 1994. *Voice and ergativity in Karao*. Eugene: University of Oregon dissertation. https://doi.org/10.1075/tsl.28.17bra.
Sharman, John Campton. 1963. *Morphology, morphophonology and meaning in the single-word verb-forms in Bemba*. Pretoria: University of South Africa dissertation.
Chen, Victoria. 2017. *A reexamination of the Philippine-type voice system and its implication for Austronesian primary-level subgroupings*. Manoa: University of Hawai'i dissertation.

Comrie, Bernard. 1985. Causative verb formation and other verb-deriving morphology. In Timothy Shopen (ed.), *Language typology and syntactic description, Vol. III: Grammatical categories and the lexicon*, 309–348. Cambridge University Press.

DeGuzman, Videa P. 1978. *Syntactic derivation of Tagalog verbs*. (Oceanic Linguistics Special Publications 16). Honolulu: The University of Hawai'i Press. Stable URL: http://www.jstor.org/stable/20006688

Fillmore, Charles J. 1977. The case for case reopened. In Peter Cole & Jerrold M. Sadock (eds.), *Syntax and Semantics 8: Grammatical relations*, 59–81. New York: Academic Press.

Foley, William A. 2008. The place of Philippine languages in a typology of voice systems. In Peter K. Austin & Simon Musgrave (eds.), *Voice and grammatical relations in Austronesian languages*, 22–44. Stanford: CSLI Publications.

Gruber, Jeffrey. 1965. *Studies in lexical relations*. Cambridge, Ma.: MIT dissertation. https://dspace.mit.edu/handle/1721.1/13010 (Accessed, September 28, 2021).

Goldberg, Adele E. 2019. *Explain me this: Creativity, competition and the partial productivity of constructions*. Princeton: Princeton University Press.

Hernández-Green, Nestor. 2016. Registration versus applicative constructions in Acazulco Otomi. *International Journal of American Linguistics* 82(3). 353–383.

Hemmings, Charlotte. 2021. When an antipassive isn't an antipassive anymore: The actor-voice construction in Kelabit. In Katarzyna Janic & Alena Witzlack-Makarevich (eds.), *Antipassive: Typology, diachrony, and related constructions*, 579–620. (Typological Studies in Language 130). Amsterdam: John Benjamins.

Himmelman, Nikolas P. 1991. *The Philippine challenge to universal grammar*. (Arbeitspapier Nr. 15, Neue Folge). Institut für Sprachwissenschaft, Universität zu Köln.

Hopper, Paul, & Sandra A. Thompson. 1980. Transitivity in grammar and discourse. *Language* 56(2). 251–299.

Jacques, Guillaume. 2013. Applicative and tropative derivations in Japhug Rgyalrong. *Linguistics of the Tibeto-Burman Area* 36(2). 1–13.

Kaufman, Daniel. 2009. Austronesian typology and the nominalist hypothesis. In Alexander Adelaar & Andrew Pawley (eds.), *Austronesian historical linguistics and culture history: a festschrift for Robert Blust*, 187–215. (Pacific Linguistics). Canberra, School of Pacific and Asian Studies, the Australian National University.

Kaufman, Daniel. 2017. Lexical category and alignment in Austronesian. In Jessica Coon, Diane Massam & Lisa Demena Travis (eds.), *The Oxford handbook of ergativity*, 589–630. Oxford University Press.

Kemmer, Suzanne. 1993. *The middle voice*. (Typological Studies in Language 23). Amsterdam: John Benjamins.

Kiyosawa, Kaoru & Donna B. Gerdts. 2010. Benefactive and malefactive uses of Salish applicatives. In Fernando Zúñiga & Seppo Kittilä (eds.), *Benefactives and malefactives: Typological perspectives and case studies*, 147–184. (Typological Studies in Language 92). Amsterdam: John Benjamins.

LaPolla, Randy J., František Kratochvíl, & Alexander Coupe. 2011. On transitivity. In František Kratochvíl, Alexander R. Coupe & Randy J. LaPolla (eds.), *Studies in transitivity: Insights from language documentation*. Studies in Language special issue 35(3). 469–491. Amsterdam: John Benjamins.

Liao, Hsiu-chuan. 2004. *Transitivity and ergativity in Formosan and Philippine languages*. Manoa: University of Hawai'i dissertation.

Lehmann, Christian & Elisabeth Verhoeven. 2006. Extraversive transitivization in Yucatec Maya and the nature of the applicative. In Leonid Kulikov, Andrej Malchukov & Peter de Swart (eds.), *Case, valency and transitivity*, 465–493. (Studies in Language Companion Series 77). Amsterdam: John Benjamins.

Marle, Jaap van. 1996. The unity of morphology: On the interwovenness of the derivational and inflectional dimension of the word. In Geert Booij & Jaap van Marle (eds.), *Yearbook of Morphology 1995*, 67–82. Dordrecht: Springer.

Mithun, Marianne. 1994. The implications of ergativity for a Philippine voice system. In Barbara Fox & Paul Hopper (eds.), *Voice: Its form and function*, 247–277. (Typological Studies in language 27). Amsterdam: John Benjamins.

Mithun, Marianne. 2002. Understanding and explaining applicatives. In Mary Andronis, Christopher Ball, Heidi Elston & Sylvain Neuvel (eds.), *Proceedings of the Thirty-seventh Meeting of the Chicago Linguistic Society: Functionalism and formalism in Linguistic Theory*, 73–98. Chicago: Chicago Linguistic Society.

Mithun, Marianne. 2019. Grammatical relations in Hiligaynon. In Alena Witzlack-Makarevich & Balthasar Bickel (eds.), *Argument selectors. A new perspective on grammatical relations*, 131–184. Amsterdam: John Benjamins.

Næss, Åshild. 2007. *Prototypical transitivity*. (Typological Studies in Language 72). Amsterdam: John Benjamins.

Nolasco, Ricardo M., Voltaire Q. Oyzon & Firie Jill T. Ramos. 2012. *An Bag–o nga ortograpiya han winaray*. Tacloban City: Leyte Normal University Press.

Pacchiarotti, Sara. 2020. *Bantu applicative constructions*. (Stanford Monographs in African Languages). Chicago: University of Chicago Press.

Payne, Doris L. 1985. Inflection versus derivation: is there a difference? In Scott DeLancey & Russell S. Tomlin (eds.), *Proceedings of the First Annual Pacific Linguistics Conference*, 247–260. Eugene: University of Oregon Department of Linguistics.

Payne, Thomas E. 1982. Role and reference related subject properties and ergativity in Yup'ik Eskimo and Tagalog. *Studies in Language* 6(1). 75–106.

Payne, Thomas E. & Voltaire Q. Oyzon. 2020. Transitivity, modality and voice in Waray. *Philippine Journal of Linguistics* 51. 1–29.

Payne, Thomas E. & Voltaire Q. Oyzon. In preparation, *Pagsantop han Winaray: Understanding Waray grammar*.

Peterson, David A. 1997. The evolution of applicative constructions and Proto-Austronesian morphosyntax. In Matthew Juge & Jeri Moxley (eds.), *Proceedings of the twenty-third annual meeting of the Berkeley Linguistics Society: General session and parasession on pragmatics and grammatical structure*, 278–289. Berkeley: Berkeley Linguistics Society.

Peterson, David A. 2007. *Applicative constructions*. (Oxford Studies in Typology and Linguistic Theory). New York: Oxford University Press.

Polinsky, Maria. 2013. Applicative constructions. In Matthew S. Dryer & Martin Haspelmath (eds.), *The world atlas of language structures online*. Leipzig: Max Institute for Evolutionary Anthropology. (http://wals.info/chapter/109, Accessed on 2019-01-26.)

Reid, Lawrence A. & Hsiu-chuan Liao. 2004. A brief syntactic typology of Philippine languages. *Language and Linguistics* 5(2). 433–490.

Ross, Malcolm. 2002. The history and transitivity of Western Austronesian voice and voice-marking. In Fay Wouk & Malcolm Ross (eds.), *The history and typology of Western Austronesian voice systems*, 17–62. (Pacific Linguistics). Canberra: Research School of Pacific and Asian Studies, the Australian National University.

Ross, Malcolm. 2009. Proto Austronesian verbal morphology: A reappraisal. In Alexander Adelaar & Andrew Pawley (eds.), *Austronesian historical linguistics and culture history: A festschrift for Robert Blust*, 295–326. Canberra: Pacific Linguistics.

Samkoe, Lori M. 1994. *Mapping multiple applicatives*. Vancouver: Simon Fraser University M.A. thesis.

Sapir, Edward. 1921. *Language: An introduction to the study of speech*. New York: Harcourt Brace.

Schachter, Paul & Fe Otanes. 1972. *Tagalog reference grammar*. University of California Press.

Starosta, Stanley, Andrew K. Pawley & Lawrence A. Reid. 1982. The evolution of focus in Austronesian. In Amran Halim, Lois Carington & Stephen A. Wurm (eds.), *Papers from the third international conference on Austronesian linguistics 1: Tracking the travellers*, 145–170. Canberra: Pacific Linguistics.

Wolff, John U. 1970. The classification of Cebuano verbs. *Philippine Journal of Linguistics* 1(1). 74–91.

Wolff, John U. 1972. *A dictionary of Cebuano Visayan*. 2 vols. Data paper number 87. Ithaca, N.Y.: Cornell University Southeast Asia Program.

Wolff, John U. 1973. Verbal inflection in Proto-Austronesian. In Andrew Gonzalez (ed.), *Parangal kay Cecilio Lopez*, 71–91. Manila: Linguistic Society of the Philippines.

Wolff, John & Ada Wolff. 1967. *Beginning Waray-Waray*. 4 vols. Ithaca, N.Y.: Cornell University Southeast Asia Program.

Wouk, Fay & Malcolm Ross (eds.), 2002. *The history and typology of Western Austronesian voice systems*. (Pacific Linguistics). Canberra: Research School of Pacific and Asian Studies, the Australian National University.

Zúñiga, Fernando. 2010. Benefactive and malefactive applicativization in Mapudungun. In Fernando Zúñiga & Seppo Kittilä (eds.), *Benefactives and malefactives: Typological perspectives and case studies,* 203–218. (Typological Studies in Language 92), Amsterdam: John Benjamins.

Camille Simon
13 The sociative/benefactive applicative construction and the introduction of attitude holders in Tibetan

Abstract: Several Tibetic languages feature a cognate sociative/benefactive applicative construction which grammaticalised from a root related to the idea of 'association' or 'help'. The applicative nature of this construction is rarely recognized in the relevant literature. The majority of authors focus on the most common use of this construction – in the imperative mood – and consequently depict it as a "polite imperative" form. This chapter describes the basic, valency-related functions of the sociative/benefactive applicative construction and its semantic characteristics, as well as its derived, pragmatic uses. From a diachronic perspective, I show how the sociative/benefactive applicative construction developed pragmatic functions through its conventionalised use in polite commands and complaints. I argue that the sociative/benefactive applicative construction evolved into a means to introduce an Attitude Holder (i.e. a participant related to the described event through a pragmatic role, usually in the form of a specific attitude toward the event) rather than a Beneficiary.

1 Introduction

Cognate applicative constructions with an identical etymological origin can be found in several Tibetic languages. In this chapter, I refer to this construction as the Sociative/Benefactive Applicative construction (henceforth SBA construction), since it combines both benefactive and sociative (Shibatani and Pardeshi

---

Acknowledgements: I would like to thank, first and above all, all the Tibetan people who accepted to answer my questions and to be recorded. No research would have been possible without their patient help and collaboration. I also thank the editors of this volume and the anonymous reviewers for their comments and questions that allowed to improve this chapter – all the remaining mistakes are mine.

Camille Simon, Université de Picardie Jules Verne, Centre d'Etudes des Relations et Contacts Linguistiques et Littéraires, 10 rue des Français Libres, Amiens adjunct member of Langues et Civilisations à Traditions Orales (LACITO), CNRS, 7 rue Guy Môquet, Villejuif, France, e-mail: camille.simon2@gmail.com

2001: 122) semantic features. The SBA construction is grammaticalised from a root related to the idea of 'association' or 'help', but its applicative function is rarely mentioned in the relevant literature. If ever evoked, this construction is typically described with reference to the etymological meaning of the morphemes that compose it, and translated as a construction meaning 'to help' or 'to accompany' someone doing something. A majority of authors focus on the most common use of this construction – in the imperative mood – and consequently depict it as a "polite imperative" form (Kretschmar 1986: 72; Schwieger 1989: 39; Tournadre and Sangda Dorje 2009 [1998]: 211; Haller 2000: 54, 94; Hoshi 2003: 35–36).

This chapter presents data from various Tibetic languages including Classical Tibetan. This language family is introduced in section 2. Section 3 describes the basic, valency-related functions and the semantic characteristics of the SBA construction. Section 4 details the derived, pragmatic uses of the SBA construction and shows how it is used as a means to introduce an Attitude Holder (a participant related to the described event through a pragmatic role, usually in the form of a specific attitude toward the event) rather than a Beneficiary. Finally, in section 5, I argue that the pragmatic role of Attitude Holder derives, historically, from the original Beneficiary role of the applied phrase: the pragmatic uses of the sociative/benefactive applicative construction evolved out of its syntactic function. This chapter shows how a SBA construction may develop pragmatic functions through conventionalised use in polite commands and complaints.

2 The Tibetic languages

The Tibetic languages form a "well-defined family of languages derived from Old Tibetan [. . .] (7th–9th century)" (Tournadre 2014: 108), sharing Classical Tibetan (attested since the 11th century) as their written language. They are spoken all over the Tibetan plateau: Tournadre and Suzuki (2021: 366–367) list 76 Tibetic languages or groups of dialects spoken in Tibet proper and outside Tibet, in India, Bhutan, Nepal and Pakistan. These authors further organize these groups of dialects into eight "major sections", labelled after their location on the Tibetan plateau: South-Eastern, Eastern, North-Eastern, Central, Southern, South-Western, Western and North-Western. This classification is "essentially based on a genetic approach, but it also includes the notion of mutual intelligibility as well as geographical parameters, migration and language contact factors" (Tournadre and Suzuki 2021: 368). The applicative construction examined in this chapter is attested in the

Central, North-Eastern and South-Eastern Tibetic languages but seems to be absent in the North-Western, Western, Southern and South-Western Tibetic languages.[1]

The modern Tibetic languages considered in this chapter are mostly located in Tibet: Lhasa, Shigatse and on both sides of the Nepalese border (Tö Pastoralists) for Central Tibetic languages; Nangchen and Derge in the Kham region for South-Eastern Tibetic; and various Amdo-Tibetan varieties for North-Eastern Tibetic. The approximate geographic location of these languages is shown with red dots on Map 1.[2] I also consider common Tibetan, the central Tibetan variety spoken among the Tibetan diaspora in India, Europe, Northern America and Australia. Amdo-, Lhasa- and common Tibetan data come from the corpus collected by the author during fieldwork sessions in Tibet and Paris, France. The place of recording, as well as the broader context (elicitation or discourse on a specific topic) are systematically provided for each example. Other data are cited from the literature, with an adaptation of the glossing conventions. Examples from spoken Tibetic varieties are transcribed phonologically according to their respective phonological system, whereas examples of written, Classical Tibetan are transliterated.

In terms of morphosyntax, the Tibetic languages are verb-final and show an ergative alignment strongly influenced by semantic and pragmatic factors (Tournadre 1996: 75–79, Zeisler 2004: 254–258, Zeisler 2007, Simon 2012, 2016 413–468). For example, in Lhasa Tibetan, the single argument S of monovalent verbs is usually marked as an absolutive (i.e. zero-morpheme), but might display differential case marking. Agent-like S may receive either absolutive or ergative marking, while Patient or Recipient-like S can either be marked as absolutive or dative (Simon 2012: 47, 52). The choice between absolutive and a morphologically marked case depends on pragmatic factors. The extent to which semantic and pragmatic factors play a role in the definition of valency categories may vary in different Tibetic languages, but they remain important factors to explain valency categories and case marking in these languages.

---

[1] No data is available for the Western Tibetic varieties. For North-Western Tibetic, Zemp (2018) does not mention this construction in his detailed grammar of Purik Tibetan. In Ladakhi, Zeisler (2019: 330) mentions a specific construction with the verb 'to give' used to introduce a Beneficiary or a Maleficiary. A similar applicative form, with another verb stem meaning 'to give' is also attested in the Southern Tibetic language Dzongkha, spoken in Bhutan (Tournadre and Suzuki 2021: 261). Such constructions grammaticalised from the verb 'to give' will not be discussed in this chapter.
[2] Amdo-Tibetan varieties are arbitrarily located in the Rebkong area, although, being a group of several varieties, they are spoken on a wider area compared to the other languages.

Map 1: Location of the Tibetic languages analysed in this chapter.[3]

Two additional features of Tibetic languages are that no argument is indexed on the verb phrase and zero-anaphora may concern any argument of the verb. Thus, a minimal utterance may consist of a verb phrase with a Tense-Aspect-Mood-Evidentiality/Epistemicity (TAME/E) marker only, without any argument explicitely mentioned (Tournadre 1996: 99), as in (1).

(1) North-eastern Tibetic, Amdo, Hualong (The Pear Story, F64 2014)[4]
ཁྱིན་བཏང་ཐལ།
^{F}ʃən-taŋ-tʰa
give.PST-PFV-PFV.SENS
'[The boy] gave [him the hat].'

---

3 This map is based on:https://upload.wikimedia.org/wikipedia/commons/7/7d/Tibetan_Autonomous_Areas_Map.png. No machine-readable author provided. Ufudu~commonswiki assumed (based on copyright claims)., CC BY-SA 3.0 <http://creativecommons.org/licenses/by-sa/3.0/>, via Wikimedia Commons.
4 Linguistic examples are presented as follows: the first line indicate the Tibetic variety. For examples from the author's corpora, information is given in this order: Tibetic subgroup and region, local variety and/or place of recording followed by, in brackets, the type of document or the main topic of the conversation, gender and age of the speaker, e.g., F(emale) 64 in (1), and year of recording. The second line renders the Tibetan (etymological) spelling; the third line gives the phonological transcription (examples from the literature are given with the phonolog-

Speech acts participants, which are always topical, must be realized through zero-anaphora in Tibetan unless they are focused or introduce a new discourse topic. Thus, natural language data usually present one or more arguments realized as zero-anaphora. The full argument structure governed by a verb phrase can mainly be seen in specifically elicited sentences. This generalised zero-anaphora tendency makes it difficult to test a number of syntactic parameters. Crucially, the distinction between core and peripheral arguments is often problematic. This is especially true for the dative-marked arguments, which may realise various semantic roles such as Recipient, Beneficiary, Goal, Location, Ceptor[5] and partially affected Patient. The question of the distinction between core and peripheral arguments in Lhasa Tibetan is discussed in detail in Simon (2012) and Tournadre (2009, 2010). Following this discussion, I consider that core arguments are defined by the combination of two properties: a) they are marked by case markers (as opposed to postpositions); and b) their formal omission in an utterance triggers a zero-anaphora to reconstruct the identity of the missing argument (whereas non-core arguments, if omitted, do not trigger a zero-anaphora). For instance, in example (1) if the linguistic or extra-linguistic context is not clear enough to reconstruct the Agent, Patient and Recipient's identities, the hearer automatically asks about their identity, but such enquiry is not observed for other participants. Thus, this zero-anaphora test indicates that a given argument is part of the semantic valency of the verb phrase. The zero-anaphora test obviously has little empirical value since it relies on the linguistic intuition of native speakers. However, in the absence of a better test, this is the criterion used in this chapter to distinguish between core and peripheral arguments in the Tibetic languages.

---

ical transcription provided by the authors and, in the case of Classical Tibetan, a transliteration is provided instead of a phonological transcription); the fourth line is the morpheme-by-morpheme gloss; and the fifth line is the free translation. Examples from German or French sources are followed by a second free translation in English. Finally, the last line indicates the source of examples cited from the literature. Some Tibetan languages have lexical tones whereas other do not. In varieties with tonal distinctions, tones are indicated by diacritic signs and accents. Arguments not overtly expressed in Tibetan are noted in square brackets in the free translation. The glosses of quoted examples and corpora excerpts have been added or adapted and harmonized throughout the chapter. The Tibetan spelling (following an etymological principle) has been added wherever it was absent but the phonological transcription remains the original author's transcription.

5 The term Ceptor refers to the first argument of predicative possession and 'get' verbs, which corresponds to the subject in the English translation (Tournadre 2009b, unpublished manuscript).

3 The Sociative/Benefactive Applicative (SBA) construction

3.1 Etymology and morphology of the applicative construction

The SBA construction studied in this chapter[6] can be found in several of the Tibetic languages belonging to Central, North-Eastern and South-Eastern Tibetic languages. It consists of a compounding process: the bound root <rogs> (or an allomorph), whose meaning is related to the ideas of 'association' or 'help', follows the main verb, in order to form a compound noun. This compound noun formed by the lexical verb and <rogs> is then re-verbalised by a semantically bleached light verb. The resulting verb phrase is followed by a TAME/E marker or a non-finite marker. Hence, the construction can be schematised as follows:

(2) Main Verb-རོགས་ <rogs> + LIGHT VERB-TAME/E ~ NON.FIN

The construction is illustrated in example (3), where it introduces a dative-marked applied phrase:

(3) Central Tibetic, Common Tibetan, India, Dharamsala (Picture description, M25 2015)

པོ་གསར་   དེ་   རྨོ་ལགས་་ལ་   ཡི་གེ་   དེ་   ཀློག་རོགས་
pʰōsa: tʰe   mō:la-**la**   jige   tʰe   lō²-**ro**²
young.man DEM   grandmother.HON-**DAT**   letter   DEM   read.aloud-**APPL**
བྱེད་ ་ཀྱི་ཡོད་པ་འདྲ།
ʧʰe-gijøpaḍa
LIGHTV-IPFV.EPIST.SENS

'This young man seems to be reading aloud this document for the old woman.'

Etymologically, <rogs> is a bound root present in several verbs and nouns conveying the idea of association, relationship and help. Dictionaries (Padma Rdorje 2005 [1979]; Hill 2010; Bielmeier et al. 2018) list lexemes such as <'grog(s)> 'to associate with, to bind', <sgrog> 'to sew, to bind, to tie', <drags> 'to bind', <sbrag(s)> 'to

---

[6] Other applicative construction, grammaticalised from other sources such as the verb 'to give' exist in some Tibetic languages, but are not considered here.

put together' and the nouns <rogs.pa> 'companion, helper', <grogs.po> 'friend', <drogs.pa> 'bundle, pack'. In all of these lexemes the root *rVg(s) can be retraced.

Whether Main Verb-<rogs> is a V-N→N or a V-V→N compound is unclear, since both types of compound nouns (i.e., V-N and V-V) are widely attested in Tibetic. The derivation pattern of this applicative construction, is, however, highly productive in the Tibetic languages to derive, among others, aspectual and modal meanings of the main verb. The Appendix provides a list of derivations following the structure schematised in (2) in different Tibetic languages, where the second root of the compound can either be of nominal or verbal origin. In Lhasa Tibetan, the fact that the verb followed by ro^{γ} <rogs> results in a compound noun is made clear by the fact that only the first syllable of the compound carries a tone: ro^{γ} <rogs> is toneless, as are all non-first syllables of nouns in this language.[7] In Amdo-Tibetan varieties, *rok* <rogs> is also productively used as a nominalizer to derive co-Agent nouns, as in (4).

(4) North-eastern Tibetic, Amdo, Hualong (Picture description, M25 2012)
བུ་མོ་ཞིག་གིས་   ཨེཨེ་   ཕལ་ཆེར་   ཁོའི་   ཟ་ས་   ཟ་རོགས་
wəmo-sək-kə   eee   hatɕʰer   kʰə   sama   sa-**rok**
girl-INDF-ERG   HES   probably   3SG.GEN   food   eat-**NMLZ.COAG**
མ་ཡོང་བ་
ma-joŋ-wa
NEG-come-NMLZ

'A girl, ehm, probably the **person with whom** she eats hasn't come and...'

In Shigatse Tibetan, the same morpheme derives nouns from verbs meaning 'the one who helps V' (Haller 2004: 54). In other Tibetic languages it seems to be lexicalised, and limited to a few lexemes, such as <dga' rogs> 'lover' (from the verb <dga'> 'to love'). These pieces of evidence paired with the presence of a light verb in all the varieties considered here, necessary to use the construction as a predicate, confirm the nominal nature of the Main Verb-<rogs>compound in (2).

The phonological form of the root <rogs> varies in the different Tibetic languages. Similarly, languages may vary in the number of allomorphs they display. Variation is also observed in the light verb used to to re-verbalise the construction: different Tibetic languages may use different light verbs (e.g. <byed> with differ-

---

[7] Other morphophonological criteria may be used in the other Tibetic varieties having this construction, but the systematic comparison of the morphophonological properties of compound nouns would go beyond the aims of this chapter.

ent phonological realisations is used in most Tibetic languages, whereas another, etymologically distinct light verb, <bgyid>, is used in the imperative in Derge and Nangchen Tibetan). All these light verbs are semantically bleached and can be translated as 'to do'. They may also vary according to register, i.e. honorific (abbreviated as HON) vs. non-honorific. Table 1 summarises the variants found in the examples throughout this chapter. In this table, the symbol ~ indicates free or phonologically conditioned allomorphs, whereas "or" indicates a lexical alternation.

Table 1: Morphophonological form of the applicative construction in the seven Tibetic languages discussed.

Language	Applicative morpheme	Light verb 'to do' (present tense stem)
Classical Tibetan	<rogs> ~ <grogs>	<byed> or <mdzod> (HON)
Lhasa / Common (Central) Tibetan	/ro²/	/tʃʰe̠/ or /nāng/ (HON)
Shigatse (Central) Tibetan	/ròa/	/tɕhe̠:/ or /nā̃/ (HON)
Tö pastoralists' (Central) Tibetan	/rok/	/tʃi̠:/
Amdo (North-eastern) Tibetan	/rok/ ~ /tok/	/je/
Kham, Derge (South-eastern) Tibetan	/ro²/ ~ /rō:/	/ɕe̠:/ (or /tɕi:/ in imperative)
Kham, Nangchen (South-eastern) Tibetan	/rɔ'/	/we'/ ~ /sˆe⁸/ (or /tʃˆi:/ in imperative)

While the construction schematised in (2) is attested in several Tibetic languages, including Classical Tibetan, it is usually not identified as an applicative construction in descriptive grammars of Tibetic languages but described with reference to the etymological meaning 'to help'. For instance, in her dictionary, Hoshi (2003: 50) translates the construction as "'to V together' ~ 'to help someone V'" Similarly, Häsler (1999: 212) mentions: "In declarative sentences, [this construction] expresses that the agent helped somebody to perform the action described by the main verb."

In most grammars, the SBA construction is described as a "polite imperative" form (Kretschmar 1986: 72, Causemann 1989: 109–110, Schwieger 1989: 39, Goldstein 1991: 177–178, Beyer 1992: 365–366, Tournadre 1996: 259, Haller 2000: 94). The possibility of using this construction in declarative contexts is often not even mentioned. Even though this applicative construction might be more common with

---

8 The circumflex accent is part of Causeman's system of phonological transcription: It indicates a breathy voice. (Causeman 1989: 28).

the imperative than with other TAME/E markers,⁹ Section 3.2 shows that it may occur with any TAME/E marker in different Tibetic languages and varieties, such as imperfective, as in (3), (6b), (8) and (11c), perfective, as in (7b), (9a), (9b), (10), (12) and (15), future or optative, as in (14), as well as non-finite verb forms, as in (5) and (16).

3.2 Semantics and morphosyntax of the applicative construction

Semantically, the applied phrase introduced by the SBA construction is usually a Beneficiary marked in dative, as in (3), but it may also be a co-Agent, as shown with the example from Classical Tibetan in (5):

(5) Classical Tibetan (Poem attributed to Tshangsdbyangs Rgyamtsho, 6ᵗʰ Dalai-lama, 1683–1706)¹⁰

ཞག་   གསུམ་   ཉལ་རོགས་   བྱས་པས།།
zhag   gsum   nyal-**rogs**   **byas**-pas
day   three   lie.down-APPL   LIGHTV.PST-CONV

(The aspiration of the young man from Kongpo is like that of a bee trapped in a web)
'[I/he] **slept** three nights **with** [you/her], and [I/he] remembered the ideal of pure Dharma.'

In this example, the agent of the verb 'to sleep' is co-referent with 'the young man from Kongpo', and correspond to the author of the poem (the 6ᵗʰ Dalai-lama was born in the Kongpo region). The presence of a co-Agent, translated by '[you]', is brought about by the applicative construction. Both arguments are expressed as zero-anaphora and their translation as first and second persons respectively, rather than third persons, is a stylistic choice.

In the modern Tibetic languages, the applied phrase most often has the semantic role of a Beneficiary (*stricto sensu*, i.e. not a Maleficiary) rather than a co-Agent, and is realised as a dative-marked argument, as shown in (6) and (7).

---

9 A statistical survey would be needed to confirm this intuition. Given the relatively low frequency of the construction altogether, such a survey would require a large corpus in the different Tibetic languages, which was not available for this research.
10 In this example, as well as in example (19), I provide for context the translation of the full four-verse poem before the free translation.

(6) North-eastern Tibetic, Amdo, Xining (Picture description, F27 2017)
   a. ཁྱི་   དེས་   སྒམ་ཆུང་ཞིག་གི་   སྒོ་   ཕྱེ་གི་ཡོད་གི
      $tc^h\partial$ ti $^hgamt\!f^hoŋ$-sək-kə ^hgo $^F\!fe$-kokə
      big.dog   DEM.ERG   cupboard-INDF-GEN   door   open-IPFV.SENS
      'This big dog opens a cupboard.'

   b. ཁྱི་   དེས་   མི་ཞིག་ལ་   སྒམ་ཆུང་ཞིག་གི་   སྒོ་
      $tc^h\partial$ ti $^mɲə$-sək-**a** $^hgamt\!f^hoŋ$-sək-kə ^hgo
      big.dog   DEM.ERG   person-INDF-**DAT**   cupboard-GEN   door
      ཕྱེ་རོགས་   བྱེད་གི་ཡོད་གི
      $^F\!fe$-**rok**   **je**-kokə
      open-APPL   LIGHTV-IPFV.SENS
      'This big dog opens a cupboard **for someone**.'
      (Picture description, F27 2017)

(7) Central Tibetic, Common Tibetan, Paris (Elicited, M40 2020)
   a. སྟོད་ཐུང་   འདི་   རྙེད་བྱུང་
      tōtuŋ   di   ɲē-tʃuŋ
      shirt   DEM   find-PFV.EGO.CENTR.UNCONTR
      '[I] found this shirt.'

   b. Central Tibetic, Lhasa (Elicited, M36 2010)
      ངའི་   ཨ་ལྕག་ལ་   སྟོད་ཐུང་   འདི་   རྙེད་རོགས་
      ŋɛ: ātʃa-**laja**   tōtuŋ   di   ɲē-**ro**ˀ
      1SG.GEN   elder.sister-**DAT**   shirt   DEM   find-APPL
      བྱས་པ་ཡིན
      tʃʰɛ-pajin
      LIGHTV-PFV.EGO.CONTR
      '[I] found this shirt **for my sister**.'

In the different Tibetic languages considered here, the applied phrase is never marked as an absolutive – like a Patient – but as a dative – like a Recipient or a Beneficiary. This type of case-marking is consistent with the fact that Tibetic languages tend to follow a semantic alignment, or at least, that case marking is heavily influenced by semantic and pragmatic factors (Zeisler 2007 for Ladakhi, Simon 2011: 34–85 for Lhasa Tibetan): any argument that has semantic features of a Recipient or a Beneficiary is marked in dative. Thus, for instance, in Lhasa-Tibetan, first argument of 'get' verbs such as 'to find' or to 'to earn, to obtain' are marked in dative (Tournadre and Sangda Dorje 2009: 130). In sum, this construction is valency increasing and introduces a dative-marked applied phrase with the semantic features of a Beneficiary.

The SBA construction may occur with mono- and bivalent lexical verbs selecting different types of argument frames. Examples (6b) and (7b) illustrate its use with bivalent verbs, while (5) and (8) illustrate its use with monovalent lexical verbs:

(8) North-eastern Tibetic, Amdo, Xining (Elicited, F26 2014)

ཨ་མ་གིས་	སྒྲོལ་མ་སྐྱབས་ན་	འགྲོ་རོགས་	བྱེད་ གི་ཡོད་གི
ama-gə	ʰɖomaʳtɕap-a	ᴺdʐo-**rok**	**je-kokə**
mother-ERG	D.-DAT	go-APPL	LIGHTV-IPFV.SENS

'The mother walks for/with ʰDomaʳtɕap.'
(ʰDomaʳtɕap is a small child, currently learning how to walk and her mother walks a few steps to train him.)

Whereas the SBA construction combines freely with mono- and bivalent lexical verbs, its use with trivalent verbs is uncommon: it could only be found in elicitation, and even then, speakers show hesitations about how to build such sentences. Only one interviewed speaker could produce constructions involving the SBA construction and a trivalent lexical verb in a relatively straightforward way, see (9a) and (9b). In (9a), the original Recipient and the Beneficiary applied phrase appear in the dative; in (9b) the original Recipient retains dative marking while the applied phrase is marked with the postposition *tʃʰētu* 'for'.[11]

(9) Central Tibetic, Lhasa (Elicited, F28 2010)

a.

ཁོང་གིས་	བཀྲ་ཤིས་ ལ་	གནས་ཚུལ་	འདི་	མི་	ཚང་མར་
kʰōŋ-gi	ṭāʃi-**la**	nētsü:	di	mi	tsʰāŋma:
3SG.HON-ERG	Tashi-**DAT**	information	DEM	person	all.DAT

འགྲེལ་བཤད་	བརྒྱབ་ རོགས་	བྱས་ པ་རེད།			
ɖe:ʃɛ	ɟap-**ro**²	tʃʰɛ-pare			
explanation	LIGHTV-**APPL**	LIGHTV-PFV.FACT			

'He explained this news to everybody on behalf / for the benefit of Tashi.'

---

11 As discussed below, this postposition has a formal or literary connotation and is not normally used in spontaneous speech. Its occurrence in (9b) indicates that the elicited sentence is probably not very natural.

b. ཨ་མ་ལགས་ཀྱིས་ བྷོལ་དཀར་ལ་ བཀྲ་ཤིས་ཀྱི་ ཅེད་དུ་ བྱེ་རིལ་ དེ་
   āma-la-gi   dø:ka:-la   ṭāʃi-gi   tʃʰētu   tʃʰeri: tʰe
   mother-H-ERG Dölkar-DAT   Tashi-GEN for   sweet   DEM
   སྤྱད་རོགས་   བྱས་པ་རེད།
   ṭē-ro²   tʃʰɛ-pare
   give-APPL   LIGHTV-PFV.FACT
   'The mother gave this sweet to Dölkar on behalf /for the benefit of Tashi.'

Thus, the SBA construction appears to be rarely, if ever, used with trivalent verbs whose verb frame already selects a dative-marked Recipient. Notably, no such restriction seems to occur with trivalent verbs selecting a comitative-marked third argument: (10) is considered much more acceptable than (9a) or (9b).

(10) Central Tibetic, Lhasa
   ཚེ་རིང་གིས་   པ་སངས་ལ་   བཀྲ་ཤིས་དང་ རྩོད་པ་   བརྒྱབ་རོགས་
   tsʰēriŋ-gi   pāsaŋ-la   ṭāʃi-taŋ   tsōpa   jap-ro²
   T-ERG   P-DAT   T-COM   argument LIGHTV-APPL
   བྱས་པ་རེད།
   tʃʰɛ-pare
   LIGHTV-PFV.FACT
   'Tsering had an argument with Tashi on behalf of Pasang.'
   (Elicited, F28 2010)

The SBA construction described in this section is obligatory: while semantic roles such as Instrument and Location do not require any additional morphology to combine with the verb phrase in a main clause, the SBA construction is required with all mono- and bivalent verbs which do not subcategorize for a Beneficiary or a Recipient, i.e. it is obligatory with all verbs except those of 'giving' and 'saying' (cf. (9a) and (9b)). A Beneficiary may be alternatively expressed by the postposition 'for' which governs a noun in genitive or in absolutive case. However, in the two Tibetic languages (Amdo and Lhasa/Common Tibetan) for which first hand data could be elicited, this usage is considered very formal. The postposition 'for', tʃʰela in Amdo Tibetan and tʃʰētu in Lhasa/Common Tibetan does not occur in everyday speech and only appears in elicited utterances produced by literate speakers. Examples in (11) illustrate the introduction of a Beneficiary into a clause governed by the bivalent verb 'to wash' (11a). The Beneficiary can be expressed as a dative-marked applied phrase when the verb carries the applicative derivation (11c), or by the postposition tʃʰela in the construction of the root (11d), with a strong formal and literary connotation. (11b) shows that the verb 'to wash' in its underived form cannot combine with a dative-marked phrase with the semantic role of Beneficiary.

(11) North-eastern Tibetic, Amdo, Xining (Picture description and elicitation, F27 2017)

a. ཚེ་རིང་སྐྱིད་གིས་ ཧྲམ་ འཁྲུད་གི་ཡོད་གི
   tsʰeraŋʳtɕi-kə   tʰərma   ᴺtɕʰə-kokə
   T.-ERG   chopstick   wash.PR/FUT-IPFV.SENS
   'Tserangkyi is washing the dishes.'

b. * ཚེ་རིང་སྐྱིད་གིས་ ཨ་ཡེ་ཞིག་ན་ ཧྲམ་
   tsʰeraŋʳtɕi-kə   aje-sək-**a**   tʰərma
   T.-ERG   grandmother-INDF-**DAT**   chopstick
   འཁྲུད་གི་ཡོད་གི
   ᴺtɕʰə -kokə
   wash.PR/FUT-IPFV.SENS
   Intended meaning: 'Tserangkyi is washing the dishes for an old woman.'

c. ཚེ་རིང་སྐྱིད་གིས་ ཨ་ཡེ་ཞིག་ན་ ཧྲམ་ འཁྲུད་རོགས་
   tsʰeraŋʳtɕi-kə   aje-sək-**a**   tʰərma   ᴺtɕʰə-**rok**
   T.-ERG   grandmother-INDF-**DAT**   chopstick   wash-**APPL**
   བྱེད་གི་ཡོད་གི
   je-kokə
   LIGHTV.PR/FUT-IPFV.SENS
   'Tserangkyi is washing the dishes **for an old woman**.'

d. # ཚེ་རིང་སྐྱིད་གིས་ ཨ་ཡེ་ཞིག་གི་ ཆེད་ན་ ཧྲམ་
   tsʰeraŋʳtɕi-kə   aje-sək-kə   **tɕʰel-a**   tʰərma
   T.-ERG   grandmother-INDF-GEN   **for-DAT**   chopstick
   འཁྲུད་གི་ཡོད་གི
   ᴺtɕʰə-kokə
   wash.PR/FUT-IPFV.SENS
   # 'Tserangkyi is washing the dishes **for an old woman**.'

On the semantic level, a verb phrase containing the SBA construction necessarily implies the presence of a Beneficiary, overtly mentioned or referred to by a zero-anaphora (Simon 2016: 587–600). Hence, like any other argument, the applied phrase can be omitted by the speaker, as in (12) and (13). In this case, its identity must be reconstructed by the hearer. Notably, Haller (2000) explicitly mentions a zero-anaphora first person Beneficiary in the free translation of (13).

(12) Central Tibetic, Lhasa (Movie comment, M25 2010)[12]
ཁོང་གིས་ བྲིས་རོགས་ བྱས་སོང་ང་།
kʰōŋ-gi *tʰi̱-ro⁷* *tʃʰɛ-soŋ-ŋa:*
3SG-ERG write-**APPL** **LIGHTV**.PST-PFV.SENS-PHAT
'He wrote [the punishment] **for [the pupil]**, right?'
(Simon 2011: 206)

(13) Central Tibetic, Shigatse[13]

ཐོབ་	སྤྲིན་ཆར་	ཕག་ཕག	སྐྱོན་རོགས་	གནང་
thoa	*tsĩtɕa:*	*phakpa:*	*cø̃-roa*	*nã*
hammer	thundershower	fall.REDUP[14]	LIGHTV-**APPL**	LIGHTV.HON

ཡང་ མི་དགོས་ལགས།
jã *mu-kœ-la*
even NEG-need-H

'[Sie] brauchen nicht **[für mich]** zu hämmern, [wie] der Gewitterschauer herniederprasselt.'
'[You] don't need to hammer **[for me]** [like] the thundershower falls,

སྐམ་པ་	གློག་དམར་	རྒྱག་རྒྱག	འཐེན་རོགས་	གནང་
kampa	*loama:*	*cakca:*	*thẽ-roa*	*nã*
pliers	lightnings	hit.REDUP	draw-**APPL**	LIGHV.HON

ཡང་ མི་དགོས་ལགས།
jã *mu-kœ-la*
even NEG-need-H

'[Sie] brauchen die Zange nicht **[für mich]** zu ziehen, wie die roten Blitze zucken.'
'[You] don't need to draw the pliers **[for me]** [like] lightnings strike.'
(Haller 2000: 144)

---

12 This example is a spontaneous comment uttered by a speaker while watching a movie in which a child has been punished and must stay in detention until he has finished copying lines. However, he is so slow that finally the supervisor decides to write the punishment himself, for the child's benefit.
13 This example comes from a song included in a narrative. For this reason, Haller did not indicate the tones in his transcription, although Shigatse Tibetan belongs to the tonal Tibetic languages.
14 Haller does not indicate the function of the verb reduplication in Shigatse Tibetan. In this example, it could correspond to an intensification of the meaning and/or an adverbial derivation. Not having more precise information, I gloss it as "reduplication".

Examples (14) and (15) show parallel constructions in two Tibetan languages of Kham. In both examples, the Beneficiary applied phrase is not realised by a dative-marked overt NP but can be reconstructed from context: in (14) it is co-referent with the Patient of the verb 'to escort', and in (15), it is co-referent with the Possessor of the 'hand' and the Patient of the verb 'to lead'.

(14) South-eastern Tibetic, Kham, Nangchen

tˆa	tšu	ñin-län	tsäik	tši-**rɔ'**	**we'**
DISC	2SG	day-way	INDEF	escort-**APPL**	**LIGHTV**.PR/FUT

'Ich werde dich einen Tagesweg (weit) bringen!'
'Well, [I] shall escort you (for the distance of) one day!'
(Causeman 1989: 260)

(15) South-eastern Tibetic, Kham, Derge

ŋɛ:	kʰȳ:	la:pā-ki	ndʑy:-le	tsʰē-**rō:**	**ɕe:-zĩ:**	jĩ:
1SG.ERG	his	hand-INSTR	grasp-CONV	lead-**APPL**	**LIGHTV**-PFV	be

'I took [him] by the hand and led [him] for [his benefit].'[15]
(Häsler 1999: 212)

In both (14) and (15), the identity of the Beneficiary applied phrase is reconstructed through zero-anaphora (see Introduction). Such a reconstruction indicates that the newly introduced Beneficiary participant is a core argument of the verb phrase (and not an adjunct), directly governed by the verb phrase, and semantically bound to it. Thus, even when the applied phrase is not overtly realised, this construction is actually valency-increasing.

While the applied phrase introduced by the SBA construction is usually a Beneficiary, it may also have co-Agentive features. In (8), the applied phrase (the little girl learning to walk) has both semantic features of a Beneficiary and a co-Agent. Similarly, (16) shows an instance of a Beneficiary/Co-Agent applied phrase in Amdo Tibetan. In this utterance, the applied phrase '[my] mother' does not appear in the dative case as would be expected. Rather, it is marked with *ɲampe* 'with, together', a postposition governing a noun in genitive case.

---

15 Here, Häsler's translation is adapted to render the morphosyntactic structure more accurately. The original translation reads: 'I took him by the hand led him.'

(16) North-eastern Tibetic, Amdo, Rebkong (Childhood, F38 2017)

ཨ་མ་གི་   མཉམ་པེ་   ཟོག་   དེ་   བཞོ་རོགས་   བྱས།
ama-kə   *ɲampe*   sok   te   ᶠʐo-**rok**   ji
mother-GEN **with** bovine DEM milk-APPL   LIGHTV.PST

'(When I was a child,) I used to milk the cows with [and] for [my] mother, and then...'

The speaker explains that, being the only child of her single mother and having very poor living conditions, she did not go school and performed different tasks at home. Considering that in the traditional gender division of work in Tibetan milking is a women's task, the mother responsible for the subsistence of the household in (16) is the Beneficiary of the speaker's action. A dative-marked applied phrase would have implied that the action was performed by the daughter only for the benefit of the mother, whereas the use of the postposition *ɲampe* 'with, together' stresses the fact that both the mother and the daughter are Agents, while allowing a possible simultaneous benefactive reading. Thus, this example is somehow ambiguous regarding the semantic features of the applied phrase: co-Agent only or both co-Agent and Beneficiary.

Contrary to dative-marked Beneficiaries, co-Agents marked by a postposition can be freely added into a clause, without the need of any additional morphology on the verb phrase, as illustrated in (17):

(17) North-eastern Tibetic, Amdo, Sokdzong (Childhood, F29 2017)[16]

འདི་   རོགས་བ་   མཉམ་གི་   རྒྱབ་   སོང་།
ᴺdə   **rokwa**   ᵐɲamkə   ʰdza: sʰoŋ
DEM   **friend** **with** behind.DAT go.PST

'[I] used to graze these [calves] **with friends**, and...'

In sum, in the Tibetic languages displaying a SBA construction featuring <rogs>, this construction is obligatory to introduce a Beneficiary applied phrase with mono- and bi- and trivalent verbs which do not subcategorize for a Beneficiary or a Recipient. This applied phrase usually appears in the dative case. Occasionally, the Beneficiary applied phrase may have co-agentive features and be realized syntactically as a comitative postpositional phrase. This type of coding emphasises the co-Agentive semantic features of the Beneficiary. Given this characterisation,

---

[16] In this example, ᵐɲamkə is a dialectal variant of *ɲampe*, and the verb 'to graze' literally means 'to go behind [the cattle]'.

the SBA construction falls into the broad definition of applicative morphology proposed in the Introduction to this volume.

4 The applicative construction introducing attitude holders

The applicative construction described in section 3 appears to be frequently used in imperative utterances, to express polite commands. At least in Common Tibetan, it is also typically used in negative utterances to express complaints. As mentioned in section 3.1, the literature on Tibetic languages that display this construction usually misses its basic sociative/benefactive applicative function described in section 3.2 and defines it as a "polite imperative" form. In this section, I argue that identifying a basic applicative function of the SBA construction allows to account for its use in polite commands and complaints. Such conventionalised uses can, in fact, be explained by a shift in the function of the applied phrase: from the semantic role of Beneficiary to the pragmatic function of Attitude Holder.

4.1 Polite commands and complaints

The SBA construction commonly occurs in the imperative mood, to express polite commands.[17] Such a use can be traced back to Classical Tibetan:

(18) Classical Tibetan (Life of Milarepa)
སྣམ་བུ་   འདི་ལ་   སྨད་གཡོགས་ཤིག་ཀྱང་   འཚེམ་དྲོགས་
snambu   *'di-la*   *smadg.yogs-shig-kyang*   *'tshem-**drogs***
serge   DEM-DAT   lower.garment-INDF-also   sew-**APPL**
མཛོད་ཅིག
mdzod-cig
LIGHTV.HON.IMP-IMP
'**Please**, also sew a lower garment in this [piece of] serge.'
(Ruspa'i Rgyancan, 1488)

---

17 The same overlap between applicative-benefactive and polite command functions is found in Meiteilon, a Tibeto-Burman language spoken in North-eastern India (Betholia 2005). The applicative construction in Meiteilon is etymologically unrelated to the Tibetic applicative construction. Thanks to an anonymous reviewer who brought this data to my attention.

(19) Classical Tibetan (Poem attributed to Tshangsdbyangs Rgyamtsho, 6th Dalai-lama, 1683–1706)

བྱ་རེ་ སྨྲ་མཁན་ ནེ་ཙོ། ཁ་རོག་ བཞུགས་རོགས་
*byade sma-mkhan   netso   kharog   bzhugs-**rogs***
bird   speak-NMLZ.AG parrot silent   stay.H-APPL

མཛོད་དང་།།
mdzod-dang
LIGHTV.HON.IMP-IMP

'Speaking bird, parrot, **please** stay silent!
(I/Someone need(s) to translate the song of Sister Nightinghale in the willow grove.)'

In (18), the verb <'tshem> 'to sew' takes an ergative-marked Agent, and an absolutive Patient (Padma Rdorje 2005: 621). The verb <bzhugs> 'to stay' (HON) in (19) gouverns an agentive S argument coded as absolutive (Padma Rdorje 2005: 684). Both examples show that the SBA construction is not used to introduce an explicit Beneficiary argument. In (18) and (19), the broader context does not allow to identify such a Beneficiary easily. The sentence in (18) is pronounced by the sister of the Tibetan mystic Milarepa, when she begs him to cover his naked and emaciated body, because she is ashamed of his behaviour. Thus, Milarepa is invited to sew for himself something to wear, but also for the benefit of his sister, i.e. to alleviate her shame. In (19), the Beneficiary, presumably the speaker himself, can be recovered as the one who needs to translate the nightingale's song.

Several modern Central and South-eastern Tibetic languages show the same use of the SBA construction in the imperative, without an explicit Beneficiary argument. Examples (20) to (24) illustrate a use parallel to (18) and (19) in different Tibetic languages: with a monovalent verb gouverning an agentive S argument in (20), bivalent verbs gouverning an Agent and a Patient in (21) and (22), and with trivalent verbs gouverning Agent, Patient and Beneficiary in (23) and (24).

(20) Central Tibetic, Shigatse

ངའི་ ནང་ལ་ ཕྱུགས་ཙམ་ ཕེབས་རོགས་ གནང་།
*ŋiẹ   naŋ-la   chūktsa   phè-**ròa***   *nā̃*
1SG.GEN inside/home-DAT briefly   come.HON-APPL   LIGHTV.HON

'Kommen Sie **bitte** schnell zu mir nachhause!'
'**Please** come briefly to my house!'
(Haller 2000: 126)

(21) South-Eastern Tibetic, Kham, Derge
ཆོད་   ཆུ་   ཁྱེར་རོགས་   གྱིས།
tɕʰō: tɕʰɤ̄   kʰɤ̄-ro²   tɕi:
2SG   water carry-APPL LIGHTV.IMP
'**Please**, carry some water!'
(Häsler 1999: 220)

(22) Central Tibetic, Tö, Drongpa pastoralists
འདི་   ཆེད་   བཞག་རོགས་   གྱིས།
ni̠   chē: šā̠:¹⁸-rok   tši̠:
DEM you.HON put-APPL   LIGHTV.IMP
'Nimm du diesen [Rosenkranz] **bitte** an dich!'
'**Please** take this [rosary]!'
(Kretschmar 1986: 72, 278–279)

(23) South-eastern Tibetic, Kham, Nangchen
རྟ་དྲེལ་   བདུན་   འདི་   གཏད་རོགས་   གྱིས།
taḍi   däin   ndɨ   te-rɔ'   tšʼi:
horse-mule seven   DEM   give-APPL   LIGHTV.IMP
'**Bitte**, gib die sieben Pferde und Maultiere zurück!'
'**Please**, give the seven horses and mules back!'
(Causemann 1989: 110)

(24) Central Tibetic, Lhasa
ཐུག་ཅེར་   ང་ར་   བསྟན་རོགས་   གནང་།
tʃʰākkje: ŋa: tēn-ro²   nāŋ
passport 1SG.DAT show-APPL   LIGHTV.HON
'Montrez-moi votre passeport, **s'il vous plait**.'
'**Please** show me your passport.'
(Tournadre and Sangda Dorje 2009: 164–165)

In the literature, these "imperative forms" are usually depicted as being polite, indirect or honorific. For instance, in the Central Tibetic variety that she describes, Kretschmar (1986: 71–72) indicates that this form is used to express "polite commands". Similarly, for Nangchen Tibetan, Causeman (1989: 109) notes: "Ein Verbalnomen, gebildet mit *rɔ'* 'Hilfe' und verbalisiert mit *tšʼi:* (Imp) bildet eine

---

18 Kretschmar (1989: 501) indicates that this verb means 'setzen, platzieren' / 'to put, to place', but translates it as 'nehmen' / 'to take' in this utterance.

Imperativform, die ebenfalls einen leicht höflichen Charakter hat." [A deverbal noun built with *rɔ'* 'help' and verbalised with *tšîː* (Imp) builds an imperative form that also has a light polite character] (my own translation). Tournadre and Sangda Dorje (2009: 168) only mention the construction as an imperative form, with the honorific light verb *nāng* 'to do': "Ce suffixe [*ro²nang*] peut être adjoint à n'importe quel verbe volitif, de préférence honorifique, pour formuler une demande ou un ordre poli." [This suffix [*ro²nang*] may be attached to any volitional verb, preferably a honorific one, to formulate a request or a polite command.] (my own translation). Finally, Haller (2000: 94) indicates that this form, among the other imperative markers, "hat einen stärker bittenden Charakter" [has a more pleading character] (my own translation). This honorific or indirect value of the imperative form featuring the SBA construction could explain the lack of this use in North-Eastern Tibetic languages, since honorific forms are severely restricted in these languages.

Before discussing the morphosyntactic differences between the use of the SBA construction in imperative vs. other tense-aspects, the way these imperative uses relate to the applicative benefactive syntactic nature of the construction must be highlighted. In (18)–(24), the speaker herself can be reconstructed as the Beneficiary of each event. Hence, the utterances above could be translated as: (18) 'Please, *do me a favour and* sew also a lower garment in this [piece of] serge.'; (20) 'Please come briefly to my house *and I will be pleased*!'; (21) 'Please, carry some water *for me*!' etc. Even if these instances could, at first sight, be analysed as an applicative construction in which the Beneficiary is realised through zero-anaphora, see (12) and (13), in section 4.2, I show that (18)–(24) have some morphosyntactic specificities which distinguish them from the constructions in (12) and (13).

The same can be said about a second use of the SBA construction, namely, in complaints expressed through imperfective negative utterances. This use is attested at least in Common Tibetan and is especially common when parents complain about their children's behaviour:[19]

(25) Central Tibetic, Common Tibetan, Paris (Elicited, M38 2018)
   ཕུ་གུ་   འདི་   ཉལ་རོགས་   བྱེད་ཀྱི་མི་འདུག
   pūgu   *di*   *ɲɛː-ro²*   *tʰɛ-gimindu²*
   child   DEM   lie.down-APPL   LIGHTV-IPFV.NEG.SENS
   'This child won't go to bed.'

---

[19] I have not been able to find a similar use in the data consulted for other Tibetic languages. However, given the very specific context in which it mostly occurs, this might well be due to the limitations of accessible data.

(26) Central Tibetic, Common Tibetan
དོན་གྲུབ་ཀྱིས་   དབྱིན་སྐད་   བཀའ་རོགས་   བྱས་མ་སོང་།
*tʰøndup-ki   ĩnkɛʔ   jap-**ro**ʔ   **tʃʰɛʔ**-ma-soŋ*
T.-ERG   English   LIGHTV-**APPL**   **LIGHTV**-NEG-PFV.SENS
'Dondup did not speak English.'
(Dagar Namgyal Nyima 2008: 30)

In these case too, one could hypothesize that the Beneficiary of the event corresponds to the speaker herself. Thus, (25) could be paraphrased as 'This child doesn't sleep *[even for me / even to please me / although I wish him/her to do so]*' and (26) as 'Dondup did not speak English [even though it would have been useful for me/us.]'.[20] Dagar Namgyal Nyima (2008: 30) proposes the following context to explain his example : 'Dondup did not speak English *(when others expected him to speak)*' (emphasis added).[21] Whether in (26) the Beneficiary could be a third person (i.e. a participant external to the speech act) is doubtful. We will see in section 4.2 that this entity must correspond, in fact, to a first person.

The two uses illustrated in (18)–(26) look like standard applicative constructions in which the Beneficiary argument is omitted for pragmatic reasons. However, we will see that from a morphosyntactic point of view, (18)–(26) are not strictly equivalent to the applicative constructions discussed in section 3.2. For this reason, I propose that the noun phrase newly introduced by the SBA construction can have two distinct roles: a Beneficiary in declarative contexts and an Attitude Holder in polite commands and complaints.

---

20 Two anonymous reviewers suggested that in (25) and (26), the speaker is, semantically speaking, a Maleficiary rather than a Beneficiary, but it is not the case. In fact in Tibetan, the negation marker may appear in two slots: (a) prefixed to the main verb if the negation has scope over this verb only, or, more commonly (b) as part of the TAME/E suffix if it has the scope over the whole verb phrase comprising the main verb and the applicative derivation, as it happens in (25) and (26). Interpreting (25) and (26) as cases where the SBA construction introduces a Maleficiary applied phrase would be correct if the negative marker was prefixed to the main verb, and had scope over the main verb 'to sleep' only: 'The child [doesn't sleep], and this event is detrimental to me' rather than 'The child doesn't perform the action of [sleeping for me]'.
21 It should be noted that Dagar Namgyal Nyima's book is not a grammar proper, but a collection of sentences classified by key-words that often represent specific use patterns. Hence, although it is undoubtedly a precious resource as a corpus of utterances, it contains no grammatical analysis and the translations and contexts offered are not always exact.

4.2 Morphosyntactic specificities of the applicative construction used in orders and complaints

Contrary to the standard SBA construction described in Section 3.2, the Beneficiary recovered in polite commands and complaints can never be overtly mentioned as a noun phrase. Its presence is implied by the presence of the applicative construction but is always realised as a zero-anaphora. (27a) repeats (12), where the Beneficiary 'the pupil' is realised as zero-anaphora. (27b) shows that this Beneficiary applied phrase can be optionally expressed as a dative NP in the utterance. By contrast (28) shows that the introduction of a dative NP in a construction such as (25) is not possible. Moreover, it must be emphasized that the reconstructed applied phrase in commands and complaints always corresponds to the speaker, and therefore, a first person, while in the applicative derivations described in Section 3, the applied phrase can also be a second or a third person.

(27) Central Tibetic, Lhasa (Movie comment and elicitation, M25 2010)
  a. ཁོང་གིས་ བྲིས་རོགས་ བྱས་སོང་ངཱ།
     $k^h\bar{o}\eta$-gi t^hi-**ro**ʔ $tf^h\varepsilon$-soŋ-ŋa:
     3SG-ERG write-**APPL** LIGHTV.PST-PFV.SENS-PHAT
     'He (i.e. the supervisor) wrote [the punishment] for [the pupil], right?'
     (Simon 2011: 206)

  b. ཁོང་གིས་ སློབ་ཕྲུག་ལ་ བྲིས་རོགས་ བྱས་སོང་ངཱ།
     $k^h\bar{o}\eta$-gi $lopt\underline{u}$ʔ-**la** t^hi-**ro**ʔ $tf^h\varepsilon$-soŋ-ŋa:
     3SG-ERG pupil-**DAT** write-**APPL** LIGHTV.PST-PFV.SENS-PHAT
     'He wrote [the punishment] for the pupil, right?'

(28) Central Tibetic, Common Tibetan, Paris (Elicited, M38 2018)
     *ཕུ་གུ་ འདི་ ང་ལ་ ཉལ་རོགས་ བྱེད་ཀྱི་མི་འདུག
     *$p\bar{u}gu$ di $\eta\underline{a}$-**la** $\eta\varepsilon$:-**ro**ʔ $tf^h\underline{e}$-kimindu?
     child DEM 1SG-**DAT** lie.down-APPL LIGHTV.PR/FUT-IPFV.NEG.SENS
     Intended meaning: 'This child doesn't want to sleep [even] for me / as a favour to me.'

Similarly in (29) the introduction of a dative NP is considered ungrammatical by native speakers.[22]

---

[22] Example (24) seems to contradict the fact that the introduction of a dative NP is ungrammatical in such sentences. However, the dative marked first person pronoun in (24) can be an-

(29) Central Tibetic, Common Tibetan, Paris (Elicited, M41 2021)
* ད་   ཁྱེད་རང་   ང་ལ་   ལྷོད་ལྷོད་   བཞུགས་རོགས་   གནང་།
  tʰa̱   cʰēraŋ   ŋa̱-la   lhōlø̄ʔ   ʃu-roʔ   nāŋ
  now   2SG   1SG-DAT relax   stay.HON-APPL   LIGHTV.HON
  Intended meaning: 'Do me a favour and stay relaxed!'

Although the grammars of Tibetic languages include numerous examples of the SBA construction used in polite commands, it has not been possible to find a single occurrence of an overtly mentioned Beneficiary in this context.

Note, however, that in specific contexts, benefactive readings with an overt first or third person Beneficiary are also possible in the imperative mood, as illustrated in (30):

(30) Central Tibetic, Common Tibetan, Paris (Elicited, M41 2021)
  a. དེ་རིང་   འགྲོ་ཐུབ་ས་མ་རེད།   བྱས་ཙང་   ང་ལ་   འགྱུར་བ་
     tʰe̱riŋ   do̱-tʰūp-samare   ʨʰe̱tsaŋ   ŋa̱-la   ɟurwa
     today   go-can-EPIST.NEG.FUT   so   1SG-DAT change
     བཏང་རོགས་   གནང་།
     tāŋ-roʔ   nāŋ
     LIGHTV-APPL   LIGHTV.HON
     'Today I probably won't be able to come. So, please change [it] **for me**!'

  b. དེ་རིང་   འགྲོ་ཐུབ་ས་མ་རེད།   བྱས་ཙང་   ཁོང་ལ་   འགྱུར་བ་
     tʰe̱riŋ   do̱-tʰūp-samare   ʨʰe̱tsaŋ   kʰōŋ-la   ɟurwa
     today   go-can-EPIST.NEG.FUT   so   3SG-DAT change
     བཏང་རོགས་   གནང་།
     tāŋ-roʔ   nāŋ
     LIGHTV-APPL   LIGHTV.HON
     'Today s/he probably won't be able to come. So, please change it **for him/her**!'

Besides the impossibility of overtly expressing a Beneficiary applied phrase in commands and complaints, SBA constructions used in these communicative contexts show no restrictions on the valency of the main verb with which they combine. This contrasts sharply with the fact that outside of commands and complaints, applicative derivation with trivalent main verbs gouverning a dative

---

alysed as the original Recipient argument of the lexical verb 'to show' rather than the applied phrase.

marked Beneficiary is highly unusual in natural speech (see Section 3.2). The absence of restrictions on the valence of the main verb in polite commands was shown in (24) with the trivalent verb 'to show', where the Beneficiary of the main verb is co-referent with the Beneficiary of the applicative construction (i.e. the speaker herself). Similarly in (31), the verb 'to help, to give help' is trivalent in its underived form, governing an Agent (the helper), a Patient ('help') and a Recipient. In this example, the third person explicitly mentioned Recipient is distinct from the applied phrase, which is an unexpressed first person.

(31) Central Tibetic, Common Tibetan, Paris (Elicited, M41 2021)
བྱས་ན་ གྲོགས་པོ་ རང་གིས་ ཁོ་རང་ལ་ རོགས་པ་ བྱེད་རོགས་
tʰɛna tʰokpo raŋ-gi kʰoraŋ-la rokpa tʃʰɛ-ro^ʔ
then friend 2SG-ERG 3SG-DAT help LIGHTV-APPL
བྱོས་ཨཱ།
tʃʰi-a:
LIGHTV.IMP-IMP
'Then, friend, please you (as opposed to me or someone else) help him **for [me]**!'

In sum, the SBA construction in polite commands and complaints shows two morphosyntactic differences with respect to its use outside of these pragmatic contexts: the impossibility to make explicit the supposed Beneficiary applied phrase introduced by the applicative and the possibility for the applicative to combine with any verb regardless of its valency at the root level. These differences can be analysed as a shift in function of the newly introduced argument, from the semantic role of a Beneficiary, to the pragmatic role of an Attitude Holder. In this pragmatic function, the applicative construction is no longer valency-increasing since the Attitude Holder is not part of the argument structure of the main verb on the morphosyntactic or semantic level.

4.3 From beneficiary to attitude holder

Attitude Holders (Bosse, Bruening and Yamada 2012) are defined as non-selected arguments, i.e. they have a pragmatic relation – a specific attitude – to the event rather than being morphosyntactically or semantically bound to it. In polite commands and complaints, the applied phrase represents an entity who is somehow affected by whether the event occurs or not and therefore, this entity has a positive attitude toward the realisation of this event (i.e. wishes that the event occurs, or regrets that the event is not occurring). Thus, in these two uses the SBA construction introduces an Attitude Holder, rather than a Beneficiary proper. In the Tibetic languages studied here, whereas proper Beneficiaries may refer to any (animate) entity – whether speech act participant or not – Attitude Holders always refer to the speaker herself.[23] Such a restriction regarding the entities that can be assigned this pragmatic role is common. As Bosse, Bruening and Yamada (2012: 1196) observe, "Attitude holders, like affected experiencers, have to be sentient. However, this may be attributed to the fact that they are limited to (groups including) the speaker and the hearer." In the Tibetic language, Attitude holders are further restricted to the speaker only.

To understand how an applicative construction might have developed this pragmatic function, I hypothesize that the role of the newly introduced participant evolved from the semantic role of Beneficiary, marked in dative, to the pragmatic role of Attitude Holder, through the role of Affected Experiencer, that is, an entity somehow positively or negatively affected by the realisation of the event. The hypothesis of an intermediate Affected Experiencer stage cannot be demonstrated with morphosyntactic data, but seems semantically plausible, insofar as it represents a likely bridge between a Beneficiary proper and an Attitude Holder: the entity holds a specific attitude toward the event in question because it is somehow affected by it (non-)realisation. Thus, the role of Affected Experiencer establishes a link between the roles of Beneficiary and Attitude Holder of the applied phrase. Table 2 summarises this hypothesised pragmaticisation path.

Table 2: Pragmaticisation path of the applicative construction in polite commands and complaints.

		Applied phrase	Commands	Complaints
①	Beneficiary ↓	overtly expressed dative-marked NP or pronoun, 1st, 2nd or 3rd person or zero anaphora	'Do it **for me/sb**.'	'S/he doesn't do it [even] **for me/sb**.'
②	Affected Experiencer ↓		'Do it, **[and] it would please me**.'	'S/he doesn't do it, [so] **I'm displeased**.'
③	Attitude Holder	zero anaphora, can only refer to the speaker	'**I wish** you do it.'	'**I regret** s/he doesn't do it.'

---

23 Bergqvist and Knuchel (2017) show that Attitude Holders can be related to egophoricity and epistemic stance. More research is needed to explore the possible relations between these domains (grammaticalised in a particularly complex way in the Tibetic languages) and the use of the applicative construction in commands.

This evolution of the applicative construction in Tibetan results in a function comparable to that of the forms labelled "ethical dative" in languages such as German, as in (32):

(32) German
    *Du   sollst **mir**   nicht wieder fernsehen*
    you   shall **me.DAT** not   again   watch.television
    'You shall not watch TV again (and I want this to come true).'
    (Bosse, Bruening and Yamada 2012: 1196)

The originality of the Tibetic languages, compared to languages with ethical dative, lies in the fact that the presence of an Attitude Holder is indicated in an indirect way, through the use of an applicative construction. This applicative construction implies the existence of such a pragmatic role, attributed to the speaker, but this role cannot be expressed by an overt applied phrase. In fact, the Attitude Holder can only be the main speech-act participant, the speaker herself (hence, a first person), in polite commands and complaints. Speech act participants are necessarily identified, and, unless they are focused or correspond to a new topic, they must be realized through zero-anaphora in Tibetan. The fact that Attitude Holders are never overtly realized is thus consistent with this general principle.

Like the German example in (32), the first person in the Tibetic examples is not a participant to the event described by the verb phrase. Therefore, it cannot be described as a speaker-benefactive form proper and the applicative construction is no longer valency-increasing. Thus, synchronically, polite commands and complaints expressed with the V-<rogs> + LIGHTV construction in the Tibetic languages can be analysed either as a typologically non-prototypical applicative constructions or as a diachronic evolution toward pragmaticisation, in polite commands and complaints, of the originally valence-increasing syntactic function of the SBA construction.

Finally, in some Tibetic languages, the SBA construction has further grammaticalised into an imperative morpheme, as shown in (33a). The construction is reduced to the morpheme <rogs> rok (without a light verb), which commutes with other imperative markers, for instance, the morpheme -lä in (33b).

(33) Central Tibetic, Tö, Drongpa pastoralists
    a. བུ་མོ་ ང་ལ་ སྟེར་རོགས།
        phön *ŋa-la* *tē:-**rok***
        girl   1SG-DAT give-**IMP**
        'Gib mir das Mädchen bitte!'
        'Please give me the girl.'
        (Kretschmar 1986: 72)

b. ད་   བང་མཛོད་   ནང་ལ་   གསེར་   བཏོན་ལས།
   tā   phaṅtsö̂   naṅ-la   sēr   tö̂n-**lä**
   now treasury inside-LOC gold   bring.out-**IMP**
   'Nun holt Gold aus der Schatzkammer heraus!'
   'Now, bring out gold from the treasury!'
   (Kretschmar 1986: 71)

5 Conclusions

The analysis of the V-<*rogs*> + LIGHTV construction in Central and Eastern Tibetic languages as a SBA construction allows to find a unified concept underlying its different uses. From a functional perspective, the applicative function of introducing an otherwise unexpressable dative-marked Beneficiary applied phrase with certain lexical verbs is the primary, original function of this construction. Like any other argument in the Tibetic languages, this applied phrase can be omitted (i.e. realised as a zero-anaphora), and this omission is especially common if the applied phrase refers to a (non-focused) speech-act participant. The Attitude Holder function likely arose when the applicative construction started to be used to express a Beneficiary coreferential with the speaker of the utterance, typically in the contexts of requests and complaints. Whether there was a stage in which a (focused) Attitude Holder could be optionally expressed as a dative-marked first person pronoun needs to be further researched. Whatever the case might be, once the construction gained discourse usage and became purely pragmatic, the dative-marked phrase could no longer be expressed (for an exactly opposite direction of change in the Colombian Spanish of the Andes, i.e., the syntacticisation of an applicative construction originating as a face-preserving strategy in commands, see this volume, chapter 5).

Thus, an originally prototypical sociative/benefactive applicative function is posited in this chapter as the basic function of this construction. Its secondary, more periperhal use in polite commands and complaints was accounted for by positing the "pragmaticisation" of the erstwhile Beneficiary semantic role of the applied phrase. However, synchronically, the original syntax-related function seems to be relatively rare in the Tibetic languages compared to the pragmatic use. This suggests that the function of introducing an Attitude Holder can no longer be considered peripheral. Although the V-<*rogs*> + LIGHTV construction is a morphosyntactically obligatory applicative, it is rarely mentioned in grammars and mainly appears in targeted elicited data. This might be due to a preference on the part of the speakers for expressing benefactive meaning through bi-clausal strategies, rather than through the applicative derivation. Moreover, the lack of substantial corpora and the fact that grammatical voices (with the exception of causatives) are rarely thoroughly treated in grammars of Tibetic languages could also explain this seeming scarcity of the SBA construction with its original sociative/benefactive argument-adding function. Whatever the case might be, such a pragmaticisation is ancient: already in Classical Tibetan, the Tibetan SBA construction appears to be more commonly used with a derived, pragmatic function than with its original semantic-syntactic function. For instance, in *The Life of Milarepa* (Ruspa'i Rgyancan, 1488, 117 folios), there are seven occurrences of the V-*rogs* ~ *grogs* + LIGHTV construction: six of these appear in polite requests, whereas only one introduces a Beneficiary applied phrase. A quantitative corpus study could shed new light on the frequency and distribution of the pragmatic and syntactic functions of the V-<*rogs*> + LIGHTV SBA construction in the Tibetic languages.

Abbreviations

1	first person
2	second person
3	third person
AG	Agent
APPL	applicative
COAG	co-Agent
COM	comitative
CONTR	controllable
CONV	converb
DAT	dative-directive
LOC	locative
DEM	demonstrative
DISC	discourse particle
EGO.CENTR	ego-centripetal
EPIST	epistemic
ERG	ergative
FACT	factual
HON	honorific
HES	hesitation
IMP	imperative
INDF	indefinite
INSTR	instrumental
IPFV	imperfective
LIGHTV	light verb
N	noun

NEG	negative
NMLZ	nominalizer
PFV	perfective
PHAT	phatic
PR	present
FUT	future
PST	past
REDUP	reduplication
SENS	sensory
SG	singular
GEN	genitive
UNCONTR	uncontrollable
V	verb

References

Bergqvist, Henrik & Dominique Knuchel. 2017. Complexity in egophoric marking: From agents to attitude holders In Seppo Kittilä & Henrik Bergqvist (eds.), *Person and knowledge: from participant role to epistemic marking*. 359–377. Special Issue of Open Linguistics 3.

Betholia, Chandam. 2005. Politeness and power: An Analysis of Meiteilon suffixes. *Linguistics of the Tibeto-Burman Area* 28(1). 71–87.

Beyer, Stephan V. 1992. *The Classical Tibetan language*. Albany: State University of New York Press.

Bielmeier, Roland, Katrin Häsler, Chungda Haller, Felix Haller, Veronika Hein, Brigitte Huber, Marianne Volkart, Thomas Preiswerk, Tsering, Ngawang, Manuel Widmer & Marius Zemp. 2018. *Comparative Dictionary of Tibetan Dialects (CDTD) vol. 2: Verbs*. Berlin/Boston: De Gruyter Mouton.

Bosse, Solveig, Benjamin Bruening & Masahiro Yamada. 2012. Affected experiencers. *Natural Language & Linguistic Theory* 30 (4). 1185–1230.

Causemann, Margret. 1989. *Dialekt und Erzählungen der Nangchenpas*. Bonn: VGH Wissenschaftsverlag.

Dagar Namgyal Nyima / Brag dkar Rnam rgyal Nyi ma. 2008. *Colloquial and Literary Tibetan: Practical usage*. Berlin: Self-published.

Goldstein, Melvyn C. 1991. *Essentials of Modern Literary Tibetan, a reading course and reference grammar*. Berkeley: University of California Press.

Haller, Felix. 2000. *Dialekt und Erzählungen von Shigatse*. Bonn: VGH Wissenschaftsverlag.

Häsler, Katrin. 1999. *A grammar of the Tibetan Dege* སྡེ་དགེ་ *(sde dge) dialect*. Bern: University of Bern dissertation.

Hill, Nathan W. 2010. *A lexicon of Tibetan verb stems as reported by the grammatical tradition*. Munich: Bayerische Akademie der Wissenschaften.

Hoshi, Izumi. 2003. *A verb dictionary of the Modern Spoken Tibetan of Lhasa, Tibetan-Japanese*. Tokyo: Research Institute for the Languages and Cultures of Asia and Africa, Tokyo University of Foreign Studies.

Kretschmar, Monika. 1986. *Erzählungen und Dialekt der Drokpas aus Südwest-Tibet*. Bonn: VGH Wissenschaftsverlag.

པདྨ་རྡོ་རྗེ། Padma Rdorje (ed.). 2005 [1979]. དག་ཡིག་གསར་བསྒྲིགས། *Dag yig gsar bsgrigs*. [New orthographic dictionary]. Xining: Qinghai's People's Publishing House.

རུས་པའི་རྒྱན་ཅན། Ruspa'i Rgyancan *alias* གཙང་སྨྱོན་ཧེ་རུ་ཀ Gtsangsmyon Heruka. 1488. རྣལ་འབྱོར་གྱི་དབང་ཕྱུག་དམ་པ་རྗེ་བཙུན་མི་ལ་རས་པའི་རྣམ་ཐར། *Rnal 'byor gyi dbang phyugs chen po mi la ras pa'i rnam thar*. [The Life of Milarepa, the Great and Powerful Among the Yogins]. Electronic text: Otani University, Kyoto, Japan. [2006] 2008. Original Text: block print edition, 117 folios, kept in The Library of Otani University (Zogai no.11854).

Schwieger, Peter. 1989. *Tibetisches Erzählgut aus Brag-g.yab, Texte mit Übersetzungen, grammatischem Abriß und Glossar*. Bonn: VGH Wissenschaftsverlag.

Shibatani, Masayoshi & Prashant Pardeshi. 2001. The causative continuum. In Masayoshi Sibatani (ed.), *The grammar of causation and interpersonal manipulation*, 85–126. Amsterdam: John Benjamins.

Simon, Camille. 2011. *Dérivation causative en tibétain (Lhasa)*. Aix-en-Provence: Aix-Marseille Université M.A. thesis.

Simon, Camille. 2012. Valence sémantique et diathèses en tibétain (Lhasa). *Lidil 46*. 127–151. https://doi.org/10.4000/lidil.3248

Simon, Camille. 2016. *Morphosyntaxe et sémantique grammaticale du salar et du tibétain de l'Amdo : Analyse d'un contact de langues*. Paris: Université Paris 3 Sorbonne Nouvelle, dissertation. https://tel.archives-ouvertes.fr/tel-01542960

Tournadre, Nicolas. 1996. *L'ergativité en tibétain, approche morphosyntaxique de la langue parlée*. Louvain: Peeters.

Tournadre, Nicolas & Sangda Dorje. 2009 [1998]. *Manuel de tibétain standard, langue et civilisation*. Paris: L'Asiathèque.

Tournadre, Nicolas. 2009. Core grammatical roles in Tibetan, with special reference to their syntactic behaviour in subordinate clauses. Unpublished manuscript presented in Tübingen University, January 2009.

Tournadre, Nicolas. 2010. The classical Tibetan cases and their transcategoriality. From sacred grammar to modern linguistics. *Himalayan Linguistics* (9)2. 87–125.

Tournadre, Nicolas. 2014. The Tibetic languages and their classification. In Thomas Owen-Smith & Nathan Hill (eds.), *Trans-Himalayan linguistics, historical and descriptive linguistics of the Himalayan area*, 105–130. Berlin: De Gruyter Mouton.

Tournadre, Nicolas & Hiroyuki Suzuki. To appear in 2021. *The Tibetic languages, an introduction to the family of languages derived from Old Tibetan*. Villejuif: Lacito Publications (CNRS).

ཚངས་དབྱངས་རྒྱ་མཚོ། [Tshangsdbyangs rgyamtsho, 6th Dalai-lama]. Date unknown. མགུར་གླུ *mgur glu* [songs]. https://bo.wikipedia.org/wiki/ཚངས་དབྱངས་རྒྱ་མཚོའི་མགུར་གླུ།

Zeisler, Bettina. 2004. *Relative tense and aspectual values in Tibetan languages: A comparative study*. Berlin: Mouton de Gruyter.

Zeisler, Bettina. 2007. Sentence patterns and pattern variation in Ladakhi: a field report. In Roland Bielmeier & Felix Haller (eds.), *Linguistics of the Himalayas and beyond*, 399–425. Berlin: Mouton de Gruyter.

Zeisler, Bettina. 2019. Ambiguous verb sequences in Ladakhi (a Tibetic language spoken in Ladakh, India, formerly part of the state Jammu and Kashmir). In Éva Á. Csató, Lars Johanson & Birsel Karakoç, (eds.), *Ambiguous verb sequences in Transeurasian languages and beyond*, 313–340. Wiesbaden: Harrassowitz.

Zemp, Marius. 2018. *Grammar of Purik Tibetan*. Leiden: Brill.

Appendix

This appendix provides a non-exhaustive list of V-N or V-V nominal compounds + light verb constructions in different Tibetic language, in order to show that the morphological pattern of the applicative construction described in the chapter is a highly productive derivation pattern in this language family (See Table 3).

Table 3: Survey of the V-N / V-V compounds + Light Verb constructions in Tibetic languages (Simon 2016: 545).

Dialect		Compounding form (translitteration and etymological meaning)	Light Verb	Meaning
Lhasa, Amdo:	V+	*grabs* གྲབས་ ('vicinity'?)	*byed pa* བྱེད་པ	To be about + V, To almost V
Dhingri:	V+	*lakha* ལཁ་ 'surface'	*byed pa* བྱེད་པ	To be about + V
Amdo:	V+	*la zig* ལ་ཟིག 'surface'	*byed pa* བྱེད་པ	To almost + V
Lhasa:	V+	*tsam* ཙམ་ ('a bit')	*byed pa* བྱེད་པ	To V a bit, To V quickly
Lhasa:	V+	*tshul* ཚུལ་ ('manner') *khul* ཁུལ་ ('manner'?) *khag* ཁག་ ('section'?) *mdog* མདོག་ ('colour, appearance')	*byed pa* བྱེད་པ	To pretend + V
Amdo, Dhingri:	V+	*kha* ཁ་ ('face, surface')	*byed pa* བྱེད་པ	To pretend + V
Nangchen:	V+	/ta/ (?)	/wä/	To do like + V
Lhasa:	V+	*res* རེས་ ('turn' or 'each + ERG')	*brgyab pa* བརྒྱབ་པ *rtse ba* རྩེ་བ	Reciprocal voice
Amdo:	V+	*res* རེས་ ('turn' or 'each + ERG')	*rgyag pa* རྒྱག་པ *byed pa* བྱེད་པ	Reciprocal voice
Drongpa past.:	V+	*skyor* སྐྱོར་ 'to repeat'	*byed pa* བྱེད་པ	To V again
Drongpa past.:	V+	/ñe/ (?) or *re* རེ་ 'hope'	*byed pa* བྱེད་པ	To hope + V
Lhasa:	V+	*rtsis* རྩིས་ ('to count')	*byed pa* བྱེད་པ	To intend + V
Drongpa past.:	V+	/tɕü/ (?)	*byed pa* བྱེད་པ	To intend + V
Drongpa past.:	V+	'*dod* འདོད་ 'to desire'	*byed pa* བྱེད་པ	Want V
Nangchen:	V+	/tɕi/ (?)	/wä/	Want V (immediately)
Drongpa past.:	V+	/cāŋ/ (?)	*byed pa* བྱེད་པ	To V immediately
Drongpa past.:	V+	/rōk/ (?)	*byed pa* བྱེད་པ	Can V
Drongpa past.:	V+	/lāk/ (?)	*byed pa* བྱེད་པ	To start + V
Lhasa:	V+	*yag* ཡག (NMLZ irrealis)	*byed pa* བྱེད་པ	To decide + V
Amdo:	V+	*rgyu-bo* རྒྱུ་བོ་ (NMLZ irrealis-DF)	*byed pa* བྱེད་པ	To decide + V
Lhasa:	V+	*par* པར་ (NMLZ realis + DAT)	*byed pa* བྱེད་པ	To try + V

Christina L. Truong and Bradley McDonnell
14 Neglected functions of western Indonesian applicatives

Abstract: Many of the Austronesian languages of western Indonesia make use of applicative morphology that licenses a core argument with a peripheral semantic role, such as a location, beneficiary, goal, or instrument. However, the same morphology that forms these prototypical applicative constructions is consistently polyfunctional across the languages of western Indonesia. A number of these functions fall outside of what is often considered prototypical of applicatives, resulting in a diversity of syntactic, semantic, and even pragmatic effects. In this chapter, we describe the diversity of functions of applicative suffixes in nine western Indonesian languages that are geographically dispersed across the region and represent different subgroups, highlighting "neglected" functions that are often not discussed in the literature on applicatives. In doing so, we show that there is considerable overlap between forms, functions, and morphosyntactic properties across these languages, but despite these similarities, variation among and within applicative constructions in these languages presents a complex synchronic and diachronic picture.

1 Introduction

Many western Indonesian languages make use of a small number of verbal suffixes that license a semantic argument in the clause, such as a location, beneficiary, goal, among others[1]. Some constructions formed with these affixes exhibit features consistent with definitions of prototypical applicatives common in the literature, such

---

[1] We are would like to recognize three individuals who shared their expertise on some of the languages in this paper: Khairunnisa for Sasak, Dewi Setiani for Sundanese, and Hendi Feriza for Besemah. Additionally, we are grateful to the editors, Sara Pacchiarotti and Fernando Zúñiga as well as Kamil Deen, Sander Adelaar, and two anonymous reviewers for comments on an earlier version of this paper. Finally, the second author would also like to thank the Ministry of Research and Technology in Indonesia for permission to conduct research on Besemah and the Language and Culture Center at Atma Jaya Catholic University of Indonesia for sponsoring this research.

Christina L. Truong, Bradley McDonnell, University of Hawai'i at Mānoa,
Department of Linguistics, 1890 East-West Road, Moore 569, Honolulu, Hawai'i, USA.
Emails: cltruong@hawaii.edu, mcdonn@hawaii.edu

https://doi.org/10.1515/9783110777949-014

as the coding of this applied phrase (AppP) as a core argument, the stipulation that the AppP should be mapped to a "peripheral" semantic role and an increase in syntactic valency over the corresponding non-applicative construction (see the introduction to this volume). However, the verbal affixes which form applicative constructions in these languages are consistently polyfunctional. In this paper, we describe the diversity of functions of applicative affixes in nine western Indonesian languages. In doing so, we emphasize functions of these which are seldom described in the literature, especially in descriptions of applicatives, i.e. what the editors of this volume are referring to as "neglected" functions. The goals of this paper are 1) to contribute to a fuller understanding of applicative morphology, by drawing attention to functions which have been largely overlooked, and 2) to present patterns in the properties, functions, and forms of such morphology. In doing so, we aim to shed light on the usage and development of applicatives in one group of related languages which are rich in applicative morphology. We show that while there is considerable overlap between funtions, forms, and morphosyntactic properties of these constructions across languages of western Indonesia, variation among them presents a puzzling and complex synchronic and diachronic picture.

For this paper, we use a sample of nine languages that are geographically dispersed throughout western Indonesia (and eastern Malaysia), represent different subgroups within Malayo-Polynesian, and include understudied languages. The languages in the sample, presented with their Glottocode and ISO-639-3 codes for identification, are as follows: Karo Batak (bata1293, btx), Besemah (cent2053, pse), Salako (kend1254, knx), Indonesian (indo1316, ind), Sundanese (sund1252, sun), Sasak (sasa1249, sas), Pendau (pend1242, ums), Balantak (bala1315, blz), and Tukang Besi (North) (tuka1249, bhq). These languages were selected based on geographic spread and several factors of convenience, including authors' previous experience with the language and robust descriptions of applicative morphemes. One noticeable absence is Javanese, which is described in chapter 15, this volume. We use the term *western Indonesian* to refer to languages in the Malayo-Polynesian branch of the Austronesian family that include applicative morphology that is clearly separate from voice marking. To determine the functions of applicative morphology presented in this paper, and whether a language in the sample has a given function, we primarily rely on the following grammatical descriptions: Woollams (1996) for Karo Batak, McDonnell (2016, in prep) for Besemah, Adelaar (2005) for Salako, Sneddon et al. (2010) for Indonesian, Hanafi (1997) for Sundanese, Khairunnisa & McDonnell (in prep) for Sasak, Quick (2007) for Pendau, van den Berg & Busenitz (2012) for Balantak, and Donohue (1999) for Tukang Besi. Dictionaries, corpora, journal articles, and original data are also used when available and are cited accordingly. We follow the orthographic conventions of the original sources with the following exceptions: 1) morpheme breaks are added for clarity, 2) where the first stem consonant is opaque due to morphophonemic processes, the underlying segment is included in parentheses, as in *non-(t)uju* in Example (1a), 3) we adopt a common glossing convention across sources (see Section 2 for more on grammatical terms and glosses).

The paper is organized as follows. In Section 2, we lay out preliminaries including a brief typological overview of the syntax of basic transitive clauses in the languages in the sample. In Section 3, we describe applicative functions of the morphology in question, that is, constructions in which an applied phrase (AppP) with a "peripheral" semantic role is licensed in the clause. We describe both prototypical and unexpected syntactic properties of these applicative constructions (ACs), especially cases in which valency does not increase with respect to the base construction (BC). Following this, we describe non-applicative functions of applicative morphology in the sample. Section 4 includes functions which can be characterized as syntactic, i.e. those which change the syntactic structure or category of the base, and Section 5 describes those which affect the semantic meaning of the verb or its use in discourse, without any difference in syntactic structure. In Section 6, we present cross-linguistic patterns observed in the sample, in particular, where there is a recurrent relationship between form and function. In Section 7, we summarize the contributions of our findings to the understanding of applicatives in these languages.

2 Preliminaries

Typologically, western Indonesian languages are mildly agglutinative. Three languages in the sample—Tukang Besi, Pendau, and Balantak, which are all located on or near the island of Sulawesi—have a limited system of prenominal clitics that mark case on noun phrases. The others show little to no case marking on nominals; core arguments are generally unmarked in these languages, and obliques are generally marked with a preposition or case marker. All of the languages in the sample make use of more than one set of pronominal forms, and the distinction between these sets is used to some extent in marking grammatical relations.

Western Austronesian languages, of which Western Indonesian languages are a subset, are perhaps most well-known for their typologically marked voice systems, commonly referred to as symmetrical voice (see Himmelmann 2005, Riesberg 2014, Chen & McDonnell 2019). While analyses of these voice systems vary and each language evinces different properties of such systems, they can all be characterized by the presence of multiple transitive constructions, none of which is clearly derived from the other. In this chapter we utilize the macro-role labels A, for the most agent-like argument of a transitive clause, and P, for the patient-like argument of a transitive clause (Comrie 1989). Western Indonesian languages typically distinguish two transitive voices: an A-Voice (AV), in which the A argument is the privileged syntactic argument, and a P-Voice (PV), in which the P argument is the privileged syntactic argument. Although there is considerable variation in terminology, the privileged syntactic argument is most commonly referred to as the subject in descriptions of these languages (see e.g. Riesberg 2014). A distinguishing feature of these voice systems is the treatment of what we will call the "non-subject (core) argument": P in AV constructions and A in PV constructions. Unlike languages with an active/passive or ergative/anti-passive alternation that demote A and P, respectively, symmetrical voice alternations are generally non-demoting. Therefore, both AV and PV contain two core arguments: a subject and a non-subject argument[2].

An example of this sort of system is given in (1) from Pendau (Quick 2007)[3]. In Pendau transitive clauses with unmarked word order, the subject occurs in the preverbal position while the non-subject occurs post-verbally, and voice is indicated by a verbal prefix, as in (1). In the AV construction in (1a), the subject is an A argument *si=ama='u* 'my father', while the non-subject is a P argument *si=ina='u* 'my mother'. In the PV construction in (1b), the subject is the P argument *si=amu'u* 'my father' while the non-subject is the A argument *ni=ina='u* 'my mother'. While there is a difference in case marking between Pendau non-subject P, as in (1a), and non-subject A, as in (1b), neither *si=* nor *ni=* are used for obliques or adjuncts[4]. Non-subject arguments in AV and PV constructions show the same restrictions on word order and the same evidence of tight constituency with the verb (e.g. with floating adverbials or serial verbs) (Quick 2008). On the other hand, subjects of AV and PV clauses show privileged access to syntactic operations (e.g. relativization, quantifier float, equi-NP deletion) and share a unique distribution in clausal word order, distinct from non-subject arguments (Quick 2007: 127–132).

(1) Pendau, alternation between AV and PV
    a. *Si=ama='u*   *non-(t)uju*   *si=ina='u*
       PN=father=1SG.GEN   AV.RLS-send   PN=mother=1SG.GEN
       [Subject A]   [Verb in AV]   [Non-subject P]
       'My father sent my mother.'

---

[2] The core/oblique distinction for non-subject arguments has been the topic of much discussion (see Chen & McDonnell 2019 for a current summary).
[3] Quick (2007) uses the term "primary transitive voice" for the construction in Pendau that is equivalent to AV, and "inverse voice" for the construction that is equivalent to PV. The PV construction has functional and distributional differences with inverse voice and passive voice in other languages.
[4] Case markers only appear on personal nouns in Pendau.

b. *Si=ama='u   ni-tuju   ni=ina='u*
   PN=father=1SG.GEN   PV.RLS-send   PN.GEN=mother=1SG.GEN
   [Subject P]   [Verb in PV]   [Non-subject A]
   'My mother sent my father.'   (Quick 2007: 124)

Because the non-subject P in AV and the non-subject A in PV share syntactic properties, "object" is not a useful category in the languages considered in this paper, as Musgrave (2001), Arka (2003), Riesberg (2014) and others have pointed out. Thus, to describe arguments in symmetrical voice languages, we instead follow conventions used among Indonesianists by employing the terms "subject" and "non-subject" alongside macro-roles A and P. Throughout the paper, we have used a common glossing conventions for voice and other grammatical categories across sources but otherwise retain orthographic conventions from source publications.

For all of the languages in our sample, applicative morphemes represent an affix or series of affixes which is distinct from voice, and which can be combined with all available voices (see Himmelmann & Riesberg 2013 on distinguishing voice and applicative alternations in symmetrical voice systems, and chapter 12, this volume, for a different view).

In applicative constructions, the addition of an applicative morpheme licenses a non-A argument, which is mapped onto an applied phrase (AppP). Because voice and applicatives are separate categories in western Indonesian languages, and both can co-occur on the verb, the AppP may be realized as a non-subject argument in AV or a subject in PV. Consider the Pendau examples in (2), formed on the root *oli* 'buy', which is lexically transitive. In (2a), the verbal root has an AV prefix *mong-* and applicative suffix *-a'*, which in this case licenses an additional beneficiary AppP *io* '3SG'. The resulting construction is ditransitive with two postverbal non-subject core arguments. When the same verbal root and applicative suffix occur with a PV prefix *ro-* in (2b), the beneficiary AppP *a'u* '1SG' is the subject P argument in preverbal position.

(2) Pendau, benefactive applicative construction
   a. Beneficiary AppP as non-subject in AV
      A'u   mong-oli-a'   io   vea.
      1SG   AV.IRR-buy-APPL   3SG   rice.
      'I will buy **him** rice.'

b. Beneficiary AppP as subject in PV
   Ma-ala   **a'u** ro-oli-a'   miu   kaeng salana?
   IRR-may 1SG   PV.IRR-buy-APPL 2SG.HON/2PL cloth pants
   'Can you (sg. hon.) buy **me** cloth pants?'

For the sake of simplicity, in this paper we show applicative constructions in AV with the AppP as a non-subject argument whenever possible. However, applicative constructions in PV with the AppP as subject are just as common in these languages. Also common is the nonrealization of verbal arguments, including AppPs, when their identity is recoverable from the discourse or communicative context. For clarity, we use examples with overt AppPs, but most grammatical descriptions contain many examples where the AppP is not realized.

3 Applicative functions

In this section, we describe applicative constructions (ACs) as characterized above in western Indonesian languages. In our sample, ACs are formed with one of a small number of verbal suffixes. In most languages of the sample, there are two formally distinct applicative suffixes, but only one (i.e. Sasak) or up to three (i.e., Balantak, Tukang Besi) are possible.

Table 1 below presents a general overview of applicative suffixes in the sample languages. Each row represents a language, and these are ordered by the number of distinct applicative forms from top to bottom. Suffix forms and the semantic roles of the AppPs that they license are listed across the row. Placement of forms in columns shows that the applicative suffixes represent three general shapes, i.e. *-an, -i,* and *-aken* (labelled as Groups 1–3 in the table, respectively), though there are some differences in form due to diachronic change[5,6]. AppPs in these languages commonly map to the semantic roles of goal (also called recipient or directional in some descrip-

---

5 Quick (2007: 282) considers Pendau *-a'* to be cognate with our Group 3, reflecting *-akən. This *-a'* almost certainly is not cognate with Group 1 suffixes reflecting *-an or *-ən because Pendau glottal stop is a reflex of earlier *k, not *-n. Pendau has a separate suffix *-ong* that appears to be a reflex of *-an. This *-ong* forms locative nominalizations, among other functions.

6 Note that Salako *-AN*, which is a member of Group 1, shows irregular morphophonemic alternations and has several allomorphs. Following Adelaar (2005), we use capital letters to represent this suffix in general discussion, and orthographic transcription to represent the allomorph occurring with a particular stem, e.g. *nunà* 'tries to follow' + *-AN* → *nunà-ʔàtn* 'follows behind s.o.' (pronounced [nũn5ʔ5ⁱn]).

tions) (GOAL), location (LOC), beneficiary (BEN), and instrument (INS), and less commonly, comitative (COM), source (SRC), reason (REAS), and purpose (PURP). In a good number of cases, the AppP can also map to certain other types of non-agentive participants, which we label theme (THM) in Table 1. Theme here is a general role label for non-agentive participants in events of certain semantic classes, including the entity which changes location in a caused-motion event, the content of an act of speech or cognition, and the stimulus of a perception or emotion event (see van Valin 1990, Jackendoff 1976). Some applicative suffixes in the languages of the sample show semantic specification in the role of the argument which they license, e.g. Tukang Besi -*ngkene*, which only licenses comitatives, and Balantak -*ii*, which only licenses beneficiaries. However, a few of the suffixes are more semantically general, e.g. Balantak -*kon* and Tukang Besi -*ako*, which license AppPs with a wide variety of roles, and in certain languages there is some semantic overlap between suffixes, e.g. both Sundanese -*an* and -*keun* license content AppPs with verbs of speech.

Table 1: Western Indonesian applicative affixes.

Language	#	Group 1		Group 2		Group 3		Other	
Sasak	1	-*an*	THM, BEN, GOAL, LOC	–	–	–	–	–	–
Besemah	2	–	–	-*i*	GOAL, LOC	-*ka*	THM, BEN, INS	–	–
Karo Batak	2	–	–	-*i*	GOAL, LOC	-*ken*	THM, INS	–	–
Indonesian	2	–	–	-*i*	GOAL, LOC	-*kan*	THM, BEN, INS	–	–
Pendau	2	–	–	-*i*	GOAL, LOC	-*a'*	THM, BEN, INS	–	–
Salako	2	-*AN*	THM, BEN	-*iʔ*	GOAL, LOC	–	–	–	–
Sundanese	2	-*an*	THM, BEN, GOAL, LOC	–	–	-*keun*	THM, BEN, INS,	–	–
Balantak	3	–	–	-*i*	GOAL	-*kon*	THM, BEN, INS, GOAL, COM, REAS, PURP	-*ii*	BEN
Tukang Besi	3	–	–	-*VCi*	GOAL, LOC	-*ako*	THM, BEN, INS, REAS, PURP	-*ngkene*	COM

An example of an AC using one of the suffixes in Table 1 and a non-applicative BC with a similar meaning is given in (3). In BCs, parallel semantic arguments may optionally be expressed with a prepositional phrase or subordinate clause in all languages in the sample. An example of the former is seen in the BC in (3a), where the beneficiary is realized with the prepositional phrase *untuk Eric* 'for Eric'. In the BC, the beneficiary is an optional argument; prepositional phrases like *untuk Eric* may be freely omitted.

(3) Standard Indonesian, benefactive applicative
    a. *Saya mem-(p)anggang roti*   ***untuk Eric***.
       1SG   AV-bake   bread for   E.
      'I baked bread ***for Eric***.' (BC)

    b. *Saya mem-(p)anggang-**kan** Eric roti.*
       1SG   AV-bake-APPL   E.   bread
      'I baked ***Eric*** bread.' (AC)   (Cole & Son 2004: 341)

In fact, in discourse, the non-affixed "base" forms of many verbs are most commonly used without any mention of optional semantic arguments. Beneficiaries, instruments, reasons and the such are frequently expressed in discourse in a separate clause. An example from Balantak is shown below in (4). Here (4a) is a non-applicative construction with reason and (resulting) event expressed in separate parallel clauses, while (4b) is an AC where the reason is expressed as an AppP that is realized as the complement of the main verb bearing the applicative affix *-kon*.

(4) Balantak, reason applicative
    a. *Yaku' ning-inum   wala'on   men   ma-rere,   pa-nggeo.*
       1SG   AV.IRR-drink boiled.water REL   INTR.IRR-dirty INTR.GER-sick
      'I drank dirty water, and so I got sick.'
                                                            (van den Berg & Busenitz 2012: 83)

    b. *Na-barang-**kon**   k<um>aan biai'.*
       INTR.RLS-sick-APPL INTR-eat   many
      'He is sick because he ate (too) much.'
                                                           (van den Berg & Busenitz 2012: 240)

Some additional examples of ACs with common semantic roles for AppP are given below. Example (5) shows an instrumental applicative in Tukang Besi. In (5b), the instrument, *kolikoli* 'canoe' is the AppP. It appears in object position and is case marked as a core argument. Example (6) shows a locative applicative construction in Karo Batak. In (6b), the location *amak é* 'that mat' is the AppP and appears as a postverbal subject P. Finally, example (7) shows a goal applicative construction in Besemah. In (7b), the goal, *kabah* 'you (sg.)' is the AppP, and appears as a postverbal non-subject P[7].

(5) Tukang Besi, instrumental applicative
    a. *Oho, no-wila.*
       Yes, 3.RLS-go
       'Yes, he's going.' (BC)   (Donohue 1999: 155)

    b. *No-wila-**ako** te kolikoli.*
       3.RLS-go-APPL CORE canoe
       'He went by means of a canoe.' (AC)   (Donohue 1999: 235)

(6) Karo Batak, locative applicative
    a. *Amin kundul i das amak é.*
       A. AV.sit LOC top mat DEM
       'Amin is sitting on that mat.' (BC)

    b. *I-kundul-**i** Amin amak é.*
       PV-sit-APPL A. mat DEM
       'Amin is sitting on that mat.' (AC)   (Woollams 1996: 293–294)

(7) Besemah, goal applicative
    a. *endung Erda n-(t)anye ngaghi aku.*
       mother E. AV-ask with 1SG
       'Erda's mom asked me.' (BC)

    b. *endung Erda n-(t)anye-**ghi** aku.*
       mother E. AV-ask-APPL 1SG
       'Erda's mother asked me.' (AC)
          (Based upon naturally occurring examples in McDonnell 2016: 98)

Additionally, with certain bases the suffixes function to license an argument which is a theme, content, or stimulus participant. Example (8) shows an alternation in Besemah in which the unsuffixed verb *injik* 'love' is used in an intransitive construction and the suffixed verb *ng-injik-ka* is used in a transitive construction with a stimulus as P.

---

[7] As seen in this example, the Besemah suffix -*i* surfaces as -*ghi* after a central vowel.

(8) Besemah, transitive from intransitive verb base
    a. *Bapang=(ny)e   tu   injik   nga   anak=(ny)e.*
        father=3   DEM   love   with   child=3
        'The father loves his child.'

    b. *Bapang=(ny)e   tu   ng-injik-**ka**   anak=(ny)e.*
        father=3   DEM   AV-love-APPL child=3
        'The father loves his child.'   (McDonnell in prep)

Such constructions are found with intransitive verbal bases for at least one applicative suffix in eight of nine languages in the sample (all except Pendau). In two additional cases, applicative suffixes (i.e. Salako *-AN*, Tukang Besi *-ako*) license theme AppPs when added to certain transitive or ditransitive bases. The use of an applicative suffix with an intransitive base appears to be particularly common with verbs denoting perception, speech, and emotion, as in the Karo Batak examples below in example (9).

(9) Karo Batak, transitive from intransitive verb base
    a. *begi*   'to hear'
        *begi-**ken*** 'to listen to'

    b. *nge-rana*   'to talk'
        *rana-**ken*** 'to talk about, discuss'

    c. *tangis*   'to cry'
        *tangis-**i*** 'to cry over, mourn'   (Woollams 1996: 56–58)

There is broad agreement in the literature that ACs of the type presented thus far in this section, and the suffixes with which they are formed, constitute applicatives (Donohue 2001, Cole & Son 2004, Peterson 2007, Kroeger 2007, Polinsky 2013). These constructions exhibit characteristics often included in definitions of applicatives: the AppP is assigned a peripheral semantic role (neither agent nor patient) and it appears to be a core argument of the verb, i.e. it is not marked by a preposition nor an oblique case marker associated with non-core arguments. In constructions of this type, western Indonesian ACs appear to differ little from "prototypical" ACs. This notwithstanding, many western Indonesian applicative constructions exhibit unexpected and non-prototypical syntactic behavior.

Specifically, many western Indonesian ACs do not exhibit increased valency relative to the BC. Two examples are given below. Example (10) is a locative applicative from Sundanese. In the BC in (10a), the patient (that which is planted, i.e. 'banana trees') is realized as the postverbal P argument and the location is expressed in a prepositional phrase headed by the locative preposition *di*. In the corresponding AC in (10b), the location is now mapped to the postverbal P argument, and the patient is "demoted" to oblique, being marked with the preposition *ku* 'by'.

(10) Sundanese, valency-preserving locative applicative
    a. *Asep m-(p)elak tangkal cau di kebun.*
        A. AV-plant tree banana LOC field
        'Asep planted banana trees in a field.' (BC)

    b. *Asep m-(p)elak-**an** kebun kosong **ku tangkal cau**.*
        A. AV-plant-APPL field empty by tree banana
        'Asep planted an empty field with banana trees.' (AC)
                                                (Truong fieldnotes)

Example (11) is an instrumental applicative from Balantak. In (11a), the non-applicative verb *mom-bobok* 'hit, strike' takes a patient (that which is hit, i.e. 'the fingers of thieves') mapped to P as the unmarked, first postverbal argument. An example of the applicative form of the verb is shown in (11b), where *mom-bobok-kon* takes an instrument (that which is used to hit, i.e. 'his hand') as the postverbal P argument, and the semantic patient (that which receives the hitting action, i.e. 'table') is marked as an oblique with the locative marker *na*.

(11) Balantak, valency-preserving instrumental applicative
    a. *Pulisi malia' mom-bobok rangkum-na mian men ma-mangan.*
        police often AV.IRR-hit finger-3SG person REL INTR.IRR-steal
        'Police often strike the fingers of thieves.' (BC)

    b. *Ia mom-bobok-**kon** lima-na **na meja**.*
        3SG AV.IRR-hit-APPL hand-3SG LOC table
        'He hit (with) his hand on the table.' (AC)
                                          (van den Berg & Busenitz 2012: 102)

Both (10b) and (11b) are valency-preserving rather than valency-increasing ACs. While it is not clear that instances of valency-preserving ACs are exhaustively reported in existing grammatical descriptions of western Indonesian languages, they are not uncommon in the languages of our sample. We found examples of such constructions in Besemah, Karo Batak, Sundanese, Indonesian, Pendau, and Balantak[8]. The AppP in such constructions most commonly has the semantic role of instrument, goal, or location.

It is possible that variable effect with respect to syntactic valency is under-reported in the literature for western Indonesian applicative suffixes. This is especially the case because some constructions show variation in the syntactic realization of the AppP. For instance, the Indonesian suffixed verb *beli-kan* 'buy-APPL' is often presented as an example of a valency-increasing benefactive applicative, as in Kroeger (2007), where this construction is exemplified with the alternation shown in (12). In the prototypical AC in (12b), the beneficiary is the first non-subject P argument in a ditransitive construction. Thus the use of *mem-beli-kan* in (12b) is valency-increasing over the BC in (12a), i.e. ditransitive compared to monotransitive.

(12) Standard Indonesian, valency-increasing benefactive applicative
 a. *John mem-beli buku itu untuk Mary.*
    J.   AV-buy book that for   M.
    'John bought that book for Mary.' (BC)

 b. *John mem-beli-**kan** Mary buku itu.*
    J.   AV-buy-APPL   M.   book that
    'John bought Mary that book.' (AC)   (Kroeger 2007: 229)

However, examination of Indonesian corpus resources (see Goldhahn, Eckart & Quasthoff 2012) shows that there is a second construction formed with *beli-kan*, as exemplified in (13a) and (13b)[9]. In this construction, the applicative suffix still functions to introduce a beneficiary to the argument structure. Note that *beli-kan* cannot be used unless a beneficiary participates in the event. However, the beneficiary AppP is realized with oblique marking. In both (13a) and (13b) the

---

8 Similar constructions have also been called "remapping" (Zúñiga & Kittilä 2019: 57) or "valency-rearranging" (Comrie 1985: 319) applicatives in the literature. Valency-preserving ACs in western Indonesian languages appear similar to redirective applicatives in Salishan (see chapter 9, this volume). However, unlike Salishan languages, which do not allow ditransitive syntactic clauses at all, these western Indonesian languages allow ditransitive syntactic structures with some ACs but not others.

9 In example (13) morpheme breaks were added to highlight the syntax of ACs with *mem-beli-kan*, but omitted outside of the relevant clauses.

verb *beli-kan* appears to be monotransitive with the patient as the first and only non-subject P argument, while the beneficiary is marked with a preposition, e.g. *untuk* 'for' or *kepada* 'to'. To date, corpora are not available for most western Indonesian languages, and the extent of variation for valency and syntactic realization of AppPs across all types of ACs is not yet clearly known. However, it appears that non-valency-increasing ACs, while relatively neglected in discussions, are not negligible in actual language use.

(13) Standard Indonesian, valency-preserving benefactive applicative
    a. *Sebelum pulang, Vino pun mem-beli-**kan** es krim **untuk Kasih**.*
       before return V. also AV-buy-APPL ice cream for K.
       'Before leaving, Vino also bought ice cream ***for Kasih**.'

    b. *[…] para pemilik kenderaan… pasti berfikir dua kali*
       group owner vehicle certainly think two time
       *mem-beli-**kan** mobil **kepada anak dan istri=nya** jika*
       AV-buy-APPL car to child and wife=3 if
       tidak ingin mendapat tagihan atas penggunaan jalan yang
       NEG want get bill on use road REL
       kelewat batas.
       exceed limit
       '… vehicle owners… would certainly think twice before buying a car ***for their children and wives*** if they do not want to receive bills for excessive road use.' (Indonesian Newscrawl [Leipzig] 2012)

Valency may even decrease relative to the base form when a verb bears the applicative suffix. This occurs in Sasak and Besemah, where a number of verbs are ditransitive in the unaffixed form but become monotransitive when the verb takes an applicative suffix. An example from Sasak is shown below in (14). In the BC in (14a), the verb takes three core arguments. The theme (i.e. that which is asked about, *amplop* 'envelope') appears in the preverbal subject P position since this verb is PV. The agent argument (i.e. the asker) is expressed as an enclitic A argument, *=ne*, on the verb. It is in a non-subject A position, and constitutes a core argument. The goal (i.e. one whom is asked, *aku* '1SG') is realized as a postverbal non-subject P argument, again a core argument position. In contrast, in (14b), where the verb bears the applicative suffix *-an*, the goal argument *aku* '1SG' is oblique and marked with the locative preposition *léq*. Thus the AC here has lower valency by one than the BC. The patient and agent in the AC remain in the same core argument positions as in the BC.

(14) Sasak, valency-reducing construction
   a. *Amplop   ketuan=ne   aku.*
      envelope PV.ask=3   1SG
      'He asked me about the envelope.' (ditransitive)

   b. *Amplop   ketuan-**an**=ne   **léq**   **aku**.*
      envelope PV.ask-APPL=3   LOC   1SG
      'He asked me about the envelope.' (monotransitive)

      (Khairunnisa & McDonnell in prep)

Apart from valency preservation or reduction, ACs in the sample languages display other unexpected syntactic characteristics. While some definitions of applicatives hold that the AppP in an AC is (by definition or prototype) a core argument of the clause, with particular constructions in the sample languages this is not necessarily upheld, even when the AppP appears in a core argument position or with core argument case marking. For example, Donohue (1999) describes extensively the syntactic behavior of AppPs in Tukang Besi, and shows that some AppPs do not have access to all syntactic operations that core arguments in BCs normally have, such as relativization and dropping of nominal arguments for pronominal cross-referencing on the verb. This topic is in need of further study, as many grammatical descriptions do not address syntactic properties of AppPs.

In this section, we have shown that the group of applicative suffixes in our sample languages can function to form prototypical ACs, in which a non-A argument is licensed and mapped to an AppP. The semantic roles which this AppP can take are many and varied. In a given language, there are typically two to three such suffixes, with some semantic specification of the roles licensed by each. However, increased valency does not seem to be definitional or characteristic of these constructions. Valency may increase, be preserved, or decrease in ACs in these languages. It is also unclear whether all AppPs which appear in core argument position have identical syntactic properties as core arguments in BCs. These properties call into question whether increased valency and inclusion of the AppP as a core argument are truly central to the definition of applicatives. In the following sections, we turn to non-applicative functions of these same suffixes that may further illuminate their nature and development.

4 Non-applicative syntactic functions

In this section, we present non-applicative syntactic functions of applicative suffixes in the languages of the sample. Here, non-applicative functions means constructions formed on suffixed stems in which no non-A argument is licensed and mapped to an AppP in the clause. By syntactic we mean that the form bearing the suffix has a different syntactic distribution and/or licenses a different syntactic structure than the non-suffixed form of the same lexical item. Functions in this category include formation of causative constructions, derivation of transitive verbs from non-verbal bases, and formation of comparative degree constructions.

4.1 Forming causative constructions

We define a causative construction as one in which an A argument is introduced with the semantic role of causer, the entity which instigates the action or event (Dixon 2000). As such, causative functions are extremely prevalent for applicative morphemes in these languages. In eight of the nine languages in our sample, one or more of the applicative affixes function to form causative constructions. Such constructions in the sample languages are predominantly formed on stative verbs (Sun. *beureum* 'red' → *nga-beureum-an* 'to make red'), inchoatives, (Ind. *patah* 'broken', *mem-(p)atah-kan* 'to break s.t.'), dynamic intransitive verbs (e.g. Ind. *mandi* 'bathe' → *me-mandi-kan* 'bathe s.o.'), and motion verbs (Pendau *no-l<um>olon* 'swim' → *no-l<um>olon-a'* 'made to swim', i.e. 'take swimming'). Table 2 shows the distribution of the causative function for applicative morphemes in the sample languages. Note that Tukang Besi is exceptional within the sample because no causative function is reported for any of its applicative morphemes. For two affixes, Indonesian *-i* and Salako *-i?*, the causative function is not highly productive, but does occur with a small number of stems (e.g. Ind. *dalam* 'deep' → *men-dalam-i* 'to deepen'; Salako *baik* 'good' → *m-(b)aik-i?* 'to improve').

Table 2: Causative functions of applicative affixes.

Language	Causative function	No causative function
Besemah	-i, -ka	–
Karo Batak	-i, -ken	–
Salako	-AN, -i?	–
Indonesian	-i, -kan	–
Sundanese	-an, -keun	–
Sasak	-an	–
Pendau	-a'	-i
Balantak	-i, -kon	-ii
Tukang Besi	–	-VCi, -ako, -ngkene

Example (15) below from Sasak shows a causative construction formed with the applicative suffix -*an*. The BC has a single argument in the preverbal subject position. The addition of the applicative affix to the verb in the AC results in the introduction of an A-argument, *pilòt*, who instigates and controls the action—in this case, flying—that appears in the preverbal subject A position. It is the P argument, *pesawat* 'plane', now appearing in the postverbal non-subject P position, which directly engages in the flying action.

(15) Sasak, causative with intransitive verb base
    a. *Pesawat nó kèlèp.*
        plane DET fly
        'The plane flew.'

    b. *Pilòt nó kèlèp-**an** pesawat.*
        pilot DET fly-CAUS/APPL plane
        'The pilot flew the plane.' (Khairunnisa & McDonnell in prep)

A range of causative verbs in Salako formed with the *-AN* suffix are shown below in (16). The affixed verbs (in which *-AN* is realized as allomorph *-àtn* or *-ʔàtn*) are transitive, and take an A argument with the semantic role of causer and a P argument that is the entity that directly participates in the state or event indicated by the verb.

(16) Salako, causative function
    a. *koat*   'be strong' (stative)
       *ŋ-(k)oat-**àtn***   'to strengthen s.t.'
    b. *ba-komoʔ*   'to come together' (dynamic intransitive)
       *ŋ-(k)omoʔ-**àtn*** 'to collect s.t.'
    c. *adà*   'there is' (dynamic intransitive)
       *ŋ-adà-ʔ**àtn***   'to bring about s.t.' (Adelaar 2005: 45)

Cross-linguistically, it appears to be very common for causative and applicative constructions to be marked alike (see Zúñiga & Kittilä 2019: 234–237 and chapter 11, this volume).

With respect to verbs formed from stative bases with applicative affixes, such as (16a), some authors distinguish between constructions which indicate action to impart the quality to the patient, e.g. 'to make red' and action to increase the degree of the quality 'to make more red'[10,11]. Verbs with meanings like 'to make redder', which can be called comparative causative verbs, show some semantic similarities to comparative constructions discussed in Section 4.3 and the greater intensity function discussed in Section 5. The formation of causative verbs from intransitive verbal bases, e.g. from statives, inchoatives, and dynamic intransitive verbs is an example of the use of applicative affixes to derive transitive verbs. There are two other functions of applicative morphemes in the languages of the sample which likewise result in the derivation of a transitive verb from a non-transitive base: the formation of applicatives in which a theme, stimulus, or content AppP is licensed (discussed in 3 above) and the category-changing function, which we turn to next.

4.2 Category-changing function

Applicative affixes in western Indonesian languages commonly function to derive (non-causative) transitive verbs from non-verbal bases of various types. Bases found in this construction generally cannot operate as a verbal predicate without the addition of the applicative affix (or some separate verbalizing morphology). Nominal bases are the most frequently verbalized by applicative suffixes, though almost any lexical category, including numerals, adverbials, prepositions, and compounded phrases, among others, are also possible stems in such constructions.

The category-changing function is found for at least one applicative suffix in every language in the sample except Pendau. Example (17) shows derived verbs in Indonesian with bases that are non-verbal (typically) in their unaffixed forms. We do not consider these to be causative constructions because there is no base verbal construction and thus, it cannot be strictly said that an A argument is introduced syntactically to a BC. For this same reason also, we consider this to be a non-applicative function.

---

10 Here we consider both types to be causative as both constructions show inclusion of an instigating causer A argument and a P argument that directly participates in the state.
11 For Indonesian, many verb forms consisting of an adjectival verbal base + -*i* affix are not analyzed as causative because the verb does not entail that the action results in the P argument entering the state described by the verb. Thus *mem-(p)anas-i* entails application of heat, not that the P argument enters the state described by *panas* 'hot' (see Sneddon et al. 2010: 91).

(17) Indonesian, derived transitive verbs
    a. *kandang*   'cage, pen (noun)'
        *meng-(k)andang-**kan***   'to put s.t. in a cage; to house s.t.; to render s.t. useless'
    b. *kulit*   'skin (noun)'
        *meng-(k)ulit-**i***   'to remove the skin or cover of s.t.'
    b. *mesti*   'must (auxiliary); certainly (adverb)'
        *me-mesti-**kan***   'to require s.t., to determine s.t.'
    d. *satu*   'one (numeral)'
        *meny-(s)atu-**kan***   'to make s.t. one, unite'
    d. *karena*   'because (subordinating conjunction, preposition)'
        *di-karena-**kan***   'to be caused by s.t.'
    e. *pindah tangan*   'change hands (phrase)'
        *mem-(p)indah+tangan-**kan***   'to transfer the ownership of s.t. to s.o.'
                                                      (Pusat Bahasa Indonesia 2007)

It appears that some applicative suffixes in Bantu also serve to form denominal verbs (Trithart 1983, see also chapter 3, this volume for one such example in Shiwiar, a Chicham language of Ecuador).

4.3 Forming comparative degree constructions

In addition to the causative and category-changing functions, in Sundanese and Sasak, we also see applicative suffixes used to form comparative degree constructions. A Sundanese example is shown in (18) below, where the addition of the *-an* suffix to the stative verb *sedih* 'sad' results in a comparative construction meaning 'more sad'. This appears to be the typical, unmarked comparative construction in the language. When a particular lexical item takes *-an* to form the causative verb—some intransitive bases take the other applicative suffix *-keun* instead—the comparative and causative forms may be identical. For example, *gedé-an* may be a comparative form meaning 'bigger' or an imperative verb meaning 'Make it bigger!' (Hardjadibrata 1985: 149).

(18) Sundanese, comparative degree function
     *Sedih-**an**   abi   batan   alo=na.*
     sad-COMP   1SG   than   nephew=3.POSS
     'I am more sad than his/her niece/nephew.'   (Truong fieldnotes)

In grammatical descriptions, authors differ in how they categorize particular examples of the non-applicative syntactic functions which we have been presented in this section. Some subsume the causative function and the category-changing function under one label. Some divide derivational functions according to whether the derived verb has a causative meaning or a directional meaning. Others divide them according to the category of the base, regardless of the semantic roles of the arguments of the resulting derived verb. In this paper, we have defined these functions according to syntactic criteria applied consistently across languages. In doing so, we see substantial overlap in function across languages in the sample, even though descriptors used in the literature for each vary from source to source.

5 Semantic and discourse functions

In this section, we present semantic and discourse functions of the applicative suffixes in western Indonesian languages. By this we mean that the suffixed form has a different semantic meaning or pragmatic usage than the non-suffixed form, but affixed and non-affixed forms occur in the same syntactic structures. These functions include marking aspect and intensity, changes in semantic transitivity, and lexicalized differences in scope or meaning of the verb.

5.1 Aspect and intensity

An applicative affix frequently has aspectual effects in our sample, especially those related to repetition of an event. The event described by the clause may be iterative (i.e. repeated in some period of time), habitual (i.e. characteristic), or pluractional (i.e. performed by multiple actors and/or on multiple patients). In our sample, aspectual functions are found in Karo Batak (-*i*), Besemah (-*i*), Salako (-*iʔ*), Indonesian (-*i*), Sundanese (-*an*) and Sasak (-*an*). A summary of aspectual functions in our sample is given in Table 3. In Balantak, the aspectual function is not productive, but is reported as an idiosyncratic meaning for -*i* with one verb, *mom-bombok-i* 'to hit repeatedly' cf. *mom-bobok* 'to hit'. Example (19) shows an alternation between simple aspect and repeated aspect marked by -*an* in Sundanese. The Karo Batak examples in (20) below show some aspectual functions of -*i* when suffixed to various bases, and example (21) shows the aspectual function when used in a clause.

Table 3: Aspectual functions of applicative suffixes.

Language	Aspect?	Form	Functions
Besemah	✓	-i	ITER, HAB, PLUR
Karo Batak	✓	-i	ITER, HAB, PLUR
Salako	✓	-iʔ	PLUR
Indonesian	✓	-i	ITER, PLUR
Sundanese	✓	-an	ITER, HAB
Sasak	✓	-an	ITER
Pendau	✗	–	–
Balantak	✗	–	–
Tukang Besi	✗	–	–

(19) Sundanese, aspectual functions
    a. *Asep meuli baju.*
       A.   buy   clothing
       'Asep buys clothing.'
    b. *Asep meuli-**an** baju.*
       Asep buy-ITER clothing
       'Asep repeatedly buys clothing.' (iterative/habitual)

(Truong fieldnotes)

(20) Karo Batak, aspectual functions
    a. *pekpek*   'hit'
       pekpek-i 'to hit repeatedly' (iterative)
    b. *pelawes* 'to send away'
       pelawes-i 'to send (many) away' (pluractional)
    c. *nangko*   'to steal'
       nangko-i 'to steal all the time' (habitual)   (Woollams 1996: 50–51)

(21) Karo Batak, aspectual functions
    Nge-rana-i kam lalap, la bo ku-begi-ken pe.
    AV-talk-ITER 2 always NEG EMPH 1SG=hear-APPL EMPH
    'You're always chattering away, I never listen to what you say.'

(Woollams 1996: 51)

For similar aspectual functions conveyed by applicative morphology in Javanese see chapter 15, this volume. The aspectual functions of applicative morphology described here appear to be common in other language families such as Bantu (see Pacchiarotti 2020: 159).

Applicative suffixes are also used to indicate greater intensity of event or action. This function is reported for two languages in the sample. It is found with Indonesian -*i*, which is described as indicating "intensity and thoroughness" (Sneddon et al. 2010: 99). It is also found in Tukang Besi, where some forms bearing the -*VCi* suffix are said to denote "forceful application" (Donohue 1999: 99). Examples of these are given in (22) and (23) below, respectively. In such examples, the affixed form denotes a special intensive quality that is absent in the more neutral, non-affixed form. In both of these languages, instances of the greater intensity function appear to be associated with particular lexical bases rather than broadly productive. It is noteworthy that this function is similar semantically to the comparative constructions (e.g. 'is bigger (than)') and comparative causative verbs formed on statives (e.g. 'to make bigger') discussed in Section 4.3 above.

(22) Indonesian, greater intensity function
    a. *mem-(p)egang*   'hold'
       *mem-(p)egang-**i*** 'grip, hold tightly'
    b. *me-lihat*   'see'
       *me-lihat-**i***   'scrutinize, look at intently' (Sneddon et al. 2010: 99)

(23) Tukang Besi, greater intensity function
    a. *pepe*   'slap'
       *pepe-**ki*** 'slap forcefully'
    b. *busu*   'punch'
       *busu-**ki*** 'punch with forward fist'
    c. *tapa*   'inform'
       *tapa-**ki*** 'reprimand'   (Donohue 1999: 77)

We observe that there is some variation in whether languages have intensive effects or iterative effects or both. Tukang Besi -*VCi* indicates intensity but not iterativity as in (23a) meaning 'slap forcefully' while iterativity but not intensity holds for Besemah -*i* (e.g. *gucuh* 'punch' > *gucuh-i* 'punch repeatedly'). In Indonesian, whether the suffix -*i* takes an intensive meaning (e.g. *me-lihat* 'see' > *me-lihat-i* 'scrunitize') or iterative meaning (e.g. *meng-gigit* 'bite' > *meng-gigit-i* 'bite repeatedly') appears to be lexically determined. However, in all three of these languages, compatibility of the functions with bases is clearly influenced by verbal semantics and both iterative and intensive meanings tend to be used with verbal bases indicating application of physical or metaphorical force. However, in languages like Karo Batak, Sasak, and Sundanese, which allow a habitual meaning for applicative affixes there is no such restriction of compatible verbal bases to those indicating force.

5.2 Changes in semantic transitivity

In a number of other constructions, the presence of the applicative affix has no effect on the syntactic structure of the clause, but instead indicates some pragmatic contrast. This occurs in at least one language of the sample, where the applicative suffix can be described as indicating an increase in semantic transitivity (see Kittilä 2010).

One example where there is an increase in semantic transitivity is found in Besemah, where the *-ka* applicative suffix is used to show a greater degree of affectedness of the P argument. In example (24a), the unsuffixed form of the verb indicates that the coffee beans were merely moved around while remaining in the same general location (i.e., they were moved around to ensure that the coffee beans dried evenly on all sides), while in (24b) the verb suffixed with *-ka* indicates that the beans were transported from one location to another[12].

(24) Besemah, indicating greater degree of affectedness
    a. *Aku tadi ng-alih kawe.*
       1SG earlier AV-move coffee
       'I moved the coffee beans around (e.g. in the yard with a rake).'

    b. *Aku tadi ng-alih-**ka** kawe.*
       1SG earlier AV-move-APPL coffee
       'I moved the coffee beans (e.g. from the house to the yard).'

                                                (McDonnell in Prep)

Besemah *-ka* is used in some constructions to mark highly individuated P arguments, another property of discourse/semantic transitivity. This is illustrated below in (25b) with the verb *tanam* 'plant'. In (25a), the P is less individuated, as the focus is on the location where the planting occurred, and accordingly no verbal suffix is used. In (25b), the P is highly individuated, as a specific number with a classifier is mentioned, and the verb is suffixed with *-ka*.

---

12 Quick (2007: 294) writes that the *-i* suffix in Pendau, which forms locative and goal applicatives, in some cases "increases semantic transitivity but there is no increase in valency". However, he gives only a handful of examples, and from these it is not clear how semantic transitivity is defined and that affixed forms clearly show an increase relative to the base clause.

(25) Besemah, indicating highly individuated P
   a. *nyelah anu   anye di   bawah kawe-ghan   tu=lah,*
      right   umm   but   LOC   below coffee-NMLZ that=EMPH
      kudai n-(t)anam   cuklat
      first AV-plant   cocoa
      'that's it umm, but underneath the coffee plants, (he) first planted cocoa'

   b. *ade   se-ratus   batang, mangke lum   di-tanam-**ka**   gale*
      exist one-hundred   tree   so   not.yet PV-plant-APPL   all
      'there's one hundred plants, (but) they haven't all been planted'
      (McDonnell in prep)

Besides functions where the semantic or pragmatic effects are clear, it bears mention that in some languages and with particular stems, the applicative suffixes have been described as causing neither a clear semantic nor syntactic effect. An example from Indonesian is given in below, where each clause has the same translation whether or not the suffix *-kan* is used on the verb. While this use of applicative morphology is described in the literature as causing no change in meaning, it is not clear whether other subtle semantic or pragmatic factors may motivate the use of the suffix. The extent to which discourse/pragmatic factors are present in applicative constructions in western Indonesia is not yet known as very few studies have looked into these constructions in natural discourse. This is especially needed to better understand how and why speakers use an applicative suffix that apparently has "no effect".

(26) Standard Indonesian, use of *-kan* with "no effect"
   a. *Paman meng-(k)irim(-**kan**) uang   kepada saya tiap   bulan.*
      uncle AV-send-APPL   money   to   1SG   every   month
      'Uncle sends some money to me every month'

   b. *Dia   men-(t)anam(-**kan**) padi itu   di sawah=nya.*
      3SG   AV-plant-APPL   rice that   in rice.field=3SG
      'He planted the rice in his field.'   (Kroeger 2007: 245)

5.3 Lexicalized changes in meaning

Finally, with some stems, the addition of an applicative suffix derives a verb that differs in scope or meaning, often in unpredictable ways. Some examples of such lexicalized semantic changes are given below in (27) from Balantak. This behavior is characteristic for western Indonesian applicative stems. Similar examples are found in Salako for the suffix *-AN* (Adelaar 2005: 45–46). In Indonesian, verbs derived with both -*kan* and -*i* suffixes may have unpredictable meanings. Quick (2007: 302) writes about the -*i* affix in Pendau, "Many of the various occurrences on verbs are idiosyncratic and do not have a directional (or 'locative') applicative function at all." Lexicalization of applicatives appear to be a fairly common phenomenon cross-linguistically (see Peterson 2007: 50).

(27)　Balantak, lexicalized suffixed stems
　　　a.　*mang-ator*　　'to accompany'
　　　　　mang-ator-i　'to discard'
　　　b.　*mom-bolos*　　'to borrow'
　　　　　mom-bolos-i　'to replace'
　　　c.　*mim-bibit*　　'to carry in the hand'
　　　　　mim-bibit-i　'to attach/make a carrying strap/rope on s.t.'
　　　　　　　　　　　　　　　　　(van den Berg & Busenitz 2012: 105)

6 Diachrony and cross-linguistic patterns

One important factor in understanding ACs and their neglected functions is their diachronic development. However, the historical development(s) of these suffixes are complex and not well understood, often involving different layers of historical development and language contact. Thus, it is difficult to provide a full account of how "neglected" and other functions developed. Despite these gaps, there are some noteworthy developments that shed light on ACs in western Indonesian languages. In this section, we first discuss two apparent pathways for the historical development of applicative suffix forms. Then, we show how the various functions correlate with one another, by identifying three main clusters of functions. We conclude with a discussion of how these clusters of functions map onto to different forms.

While there are many outstanding questions, it is generally agreed that applicative suffixes developed from one of two sources in the languages of western Indonesia (see Ross 2002). The first source is from earlier voice (or what is sometimes referred to as focus) suffixes that are reconstructed as *-ən and *-an. Of these, *-ən is typically described as the Patient Voice marker, while *-an is reconstructed as the form of the Locative Voice marker in Proto-Austronesian (see Blust 2013: 394–396 for discussion of these suffixes in Proto Austronesian). Based on their disparate functions and sound changes, it is not clear whether Sundanese and Sasak -*an* come from the Patient Voice *-ən, the Locative Voice *-an suffix, or represent a merger of the two. The same can be said for Salako -*AN* (Adelaar p.c.).

The second source of applicative morphology in these languages is more common crosslinguistically. Prepositions, including a locative preposition *i and the preposition *akən, appear to have been grammaticalized as verbal suffixes, giving rise to applicatives. These may have replaced earlier voice suffixes as languages of western Indonesia lost features of the Philippine-type voice system. Adelaar (2011), for example, shows how applicative suffixes -aké and -akən in Standard Javanese developed from erstwhile prepositions, replacing an earlier form of the PV suffix *-ən, which is still present in the Tengger Javanese variety. This pattern of replacement likely happened elsewhere in the region, although it is still unclear exactly how it occurred and the extent to which language contact played a role in the process.

If we revisit the forms and functions summarized in Table 1 from Section 3, we can make the following three observations based on these diachronic pathways:

- Group 1 suffixes represent those that come from voice suffixes. With forms -an or -AN, these originate from an earlier Locative Voice suffix, Patient Voice suffix, or even a merger of the two. This may help to explain the diversity of functions found in this group, but leaves open several questions about their history.
- Group 2 suffixes—most often expressed as -i—revolve around goal and locative functions, and their development out of a locative preposition is relatively straightforward. However, as we will see below, the development or co-occurrence of aspectual (i.e., iterative, habitual, pluractional) effects and functions of Group 2 suffixes needs further exploration.
- Group 3 suffixes—with such forms as -kan, -kon, or -ako—also have a prepositional source but with more disparate functions. The most common of these are instrumental and benefactive, which to our minds have little in common and it is thus difficult to see a clear grammaticalization pathway.

Having established the diachronic sources of these suffixes, we now show how functions of these cluster together as observed synchronically. In order to better understand these complex patterns, in Figure 1, we visually represent the functions presented in this paper as a network map.[13]

---

[13] The data visualization in Figure 1 was produced using R 3.5.2 (R Core Team 2018) and the igraph package 1.2.5 for network visualization and analysis (Csardi & Nepusz 2006).

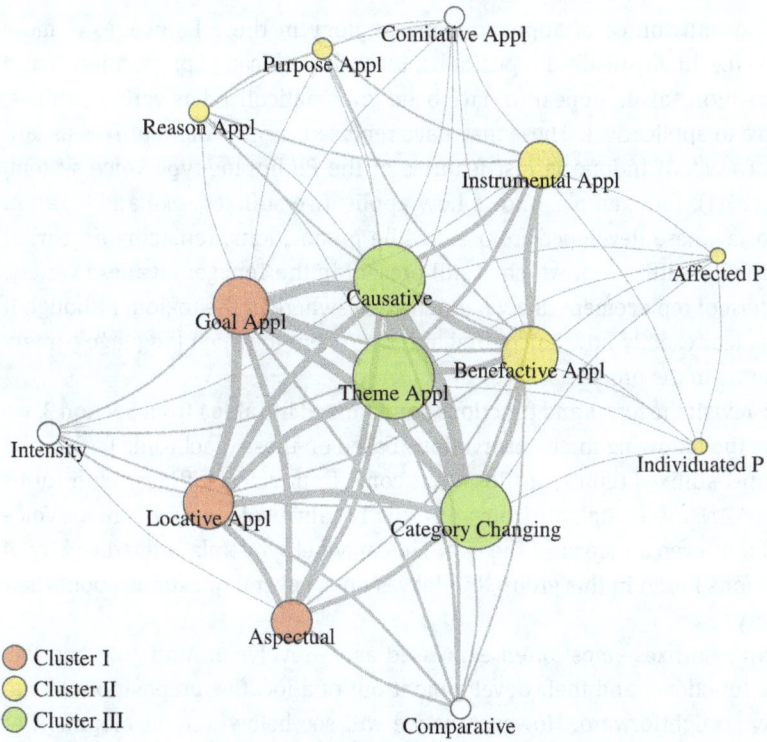

Figure 1: Function network for applicative suffixes in western Indonesian languages.

Each function identified in this paper is represented as a node in the diagram. Node size is proportional to the number of languages in the sample in which the function occurs (i.e., the more frequent the function the larger the node). When two functions co-occur with the same suffix, this is represented as a link between nodes. The thickness of these lines (i.e., link weight) is proportionate to the number of applicative suffixes in the languages of the sample that express both functions. Node color shows clusters of functions with strong tendency to co-occur.[14] Nodes with no fill color do not belong clearly to any one cluster. For example, the comparative function, which only occurs with two suffixes in the sample, correlates with both Cluster I and Cluster II. Below, we discuss each cluster in turn, highlighting how each correlates with different forms.

---

[14] For each unique pair of functions in a cluster, the function with the smaller number of total forms in the data was found to co-occur with the second function on 80–100% of those forms.

First, there is a strong association between aspectual functions and goal and locative applicatives, which is represented in Figure 1 as Cluster I. All six of the aspect-marking suffixes in the sample demonstrate this association. Four of these are Group 2 suffixes: Karo Batak -*i*, Besemah -*i*, Salako -*iʔ*, and Indonesian -*i*. In Indonesian and Besemah, these additionally indicate greater intensity. Two Group 1 suffixes also show the association between aspect, locative applicatives, and goal applicatives: Sasak -*an* and Sundanese -*an*. It is noteworthy that Cluster I functions converge on shared forms from both Groups 1 and 2 even though these have different diachronic sources. While it is still unclear why these aspectual effects are associated with the locative/goal applicatives in western Indonesian languages, it has been observed in other language families that valency-related morphology, including causative and applicative morphemes, often develop aspectual and related functions (e.g. intensity) over time (Hyman 2014, 2017). Also, several typological studies (see Wood 2007, Mattiola 2019) have shown a connection between intensity, iterativity, and pluractionality more generally.

Second, there is a tendency for benefactive and instrumental applicative functions to be expressed by the same suffix. This is represented in Figure 1 as Cluster II. Instrumental applicative functions are found in seven languages of the sample, all with Group 3 suffixes. In six of the seven cases the same suffix performs benefactive applicative functions: Besemah -*ka*, Sundanese -*keun*, Indonesian -*kan*, Pendau -*a'*, Balantak -*ako*, and Tukang Besi -*kon*. Balantak, however, appears to be diverging from this pattern. The benefactive applicative function of -*kon* is reported to be rare, while an exclusively benefactive applicative suffix -*ii* has emerged[15]. We also observe that some less common applicative functions, i.e. the licensing of reason and purpose AppPs, and pragmatic functions, i.e. the marking of a more affected or individuated P argument in Besemah are associated with the instrumental and benefactive functions.

Third, the causative function is extremely prevalent in the sample. The causative function and others associated with it are represented in Figure 1 as Cluster III. The causative function is found in eight of nine languages in the sample, and with 14 of the 19 total applicative suffixes. This prevalence may not be surprising; morphology that serves both applicative and causative functions are widely reported cross-linguistically (see Peterson 2007: 133–136 and Shibatani & Pardeshi 2002: 116–121).

In the sample, we see a strong tendency for causative-forming suffixes to also perform the the category-changing function and theme-licensing applicative

---

15 Van den Berg & Busenitz (2012: 109) suggest that it originates from the goal (directional) applicative suffix -*i* plus the prenominal marker for pronouns and personal names, *i=*.

function. The suffixes on which Cluster III functions co-occur are broadly distributed and cut across Groups 1, 2, and 3.

Historically, Proto-Austronesian had *pa- as a general causative morpheme with verbal bases (Blust 2003). In some languages of western Indonesia, this prefix remains productive as a causative. In others, it is no longer productive and only present in a small number of fossilized forms. In languages where reflexes of *pa- are no longer productive, it appears that applicative suffixes now represent the primary means to form causative constructions. For example, Besemah causative constructions are always formed with one of its two applicative suffixes, while *pa-* is non-productive. On the other end of the spectrum, applicative suffixes do not form causatives at all in Tukang Besi, but the causative prefix *pa-* is extremely productive and "can occur on any verb base, transitive or intransitive" (Donohue 1999: 204). Other languages fall somewhere in between. In Karo Batak, the applicative *-ken* serves a causative function on a limited number of intransitive predicates, but is less productive than the causative prefix *pe-*.

7 Conclusion

In this paper, we have shown that western Indonesian applicative morphology is not limited in function to the formation of prototypical applicative constructions. Crucial to the understanding of these morphemes are their other functions, which are seldom-discussed or "neglected" from our perspective, in the literature. By describing the neglected functions of these affixes carefully and including understudied languages in our sample, we aim to facilitate inclusion of these in cross-linguistic typologies of applicatives. Some implications of our findings are as follows.

First, our study highlights variation in the syntactic structure of applicative constructions, particularly with respect to syntactic valency. We see such variation both language-internally and across related languages. Interestingly, benefactive ACs appear to be more consistently valency-increasing, while instrumental ACs are predominantly valency-preserving in some languages but valency-increasing in others. These patterns call for a more nuanced understanding of the role of valency as a prototypical characteristic of applicatives, especially in languages where ditransitive constructions are not prohibited.

Second, we identify clusters of functions in western Indonesian languages that pattern together on a shared form. While some associations shown in the clusters have been discussed in the literature on applicatives, such as the tendency for causative and applicative functions to be expressed by the same affix, others have received far less attention. For example, locative/goal applicatives in these languages are strongly associated with iterative, habitual, and pluractional aspect marking, and to a lesser extent, intensive action. It is unclear how cross-linguistically common it is for locative and goal applicatives specifically to show this association. Another example is functions that increase semantic transitivity, including the marking of more affected or individuated P arguments. Although it might be expected that applicative morphology increases semantic transitivity, it is to our knowledge surprisingly not discussed in the literature.

Finally, we show that polyfunctionality is characteristic for applicative morphemes in these languages. Aside from Tukang Besi, in most of these languages, the non-applicative functions are highly productive and may in fact be more frequent than the applicative functions in discourse. In particular, the cluster of functions associated with causative meanings is broadly distributed across applicative forms in the sample. Causative-applicative syncretism and the fact that these suffixes may have been involved in historical mergers or replacement of older voice morphology are both key factors to understanding the high degree of polyfunctionality observed for these suffixes today.

As a whole, this study shows that while there is considerable overlap between functions, forms, and morphosyntactic properties of ACs across western Indonesian languages, variation among and within these languages also presents a puzzling and complex synchronic and diachronic picture. Further study of both the applicative and non-applicative functions of these suffixes, especially in natural discursive contexts is needed, particularly because the apparent pragmatic functions are still rarely described, and consequently, are not well understood. Such studies may reveal new patterns of variation and use and are needed to further illuminate this picture.

References

Adelaar, K. Alexander. 2005. *Salako or Badameá: Sketch grammar, text and lexicon of a Kanayatn dialect in West Borneo*. (Frankfurter Forschungen zu Südostasien, Bd. 2). Wiesbaden: Harrassowitz.
Adelaar, K. Alexander. 2011. Javanese *-aké* and *-akan*: A short history. *Oceanic Linguistics* 50(2). 338–350.
Blust, Robert. 2003. Three notes on early Austronesian morphology. *Oceanic Linguistics* 42(2). 438–478. https://doi.org/10.2307/3623246.
Blust, Robert. 2013. *The Austronesian languages*. Revised edn. (Pacific Linguistics A-PL 008). Canberra: Australian National University.
Chen, Victoria & Bradley McDonnell. 2019. Western Austronesian voice. *Annual Review of Linguistics* 5(1). 173–195. https://doi.org/10.1146/annurev-linguistics-011718-011731.

Cole, Peter & Min-Jeong Son. 2004. The argument structure of verbs with the suffix -*kan* in Indonesian. *Oceanic Linguistics* 43(2). 339–364. https://doi.org/10.1353/ol.2005.0003.

Comrie, Bernard. 1985. Causative verb formation and other verb-deriving morphology. In Timothy Shopen (ed.), *Language Typology and Syntactic Description*. Vol. 3, 309–348. Cambridge: Cambridge University Press.

Comrie, Bernard. 1989. *Language universals and linguistic typology: Syntax and morphology*. 2nd edn. Chicago: University of Chicago Press.

Csardi, Gabor & Tamas Nepusz. 2006. The igraph software package for complex network research. *InterJournal of Complex Systems* CX.18(1695).

Dixon, R. M. W. 2000. A typology of causatives: Form, syntax and meaning. In R. M. W. Dixon & Alexandra Y. Aikhenvald (eds.), *Changing valency: Case studies in transitivity*, 30–83. Cambridge University Press. https://doi.org/10.1017/CBO9780511627750.003.

Donohue, Mark. 1999. *A grammar of Tukang Besi* (Mouton Grammar Library 20). Hawthorne, NY: Mouton de Gruyter.

Donohue, Mark. 2001. Coding choices in argument structure: Austronesian applicatives in texts. *Studies in Language* 25(2). 217–254. https://doi.org/10.1075/sl.25.2.03don.

Goldhahn, Dirk, Thomas Eckart & Uwe Quasthoff. 2012. Building large monolingual dictionaries at the Leipzig Corpora Collection: From 100 to 200 languages. In *Proceedings of the 8th International Language Resources and Evaluation (LREC'12)*, 759–765. Istanbul: European Language Resources Association (ELRA).

Hanafi, Nurachman. 1997. *A typological study of Sundanese*. Bundoora, VIC: La Trobe University PhD Dissertation.

Hardjadibrata, R. R. 1985. *Sundanese: A syntactical analysis* (Pacific Linguistics D-65). Canberra: Australia National University.

Himmelmann, Nikolaus P. 2005. The Austronesian languages of Asia and Madagascar: Typological characteristics. In K. Alexander Adelaar & Nikolaus P. Himmelmann (eds.), *The Austronesian languages of Asia and Madagascar*. 110–181. New York: Routledge.

Himmelmann, Nikolaus P. & Sonja Riesberg. 2013. Symmetrical voice and applicative alternations: Evidence from Totoli. *Oceanic Linguistics* 52(2). 396–422. https://doi.org/10.1353/ol.2013.0021.

Hyman, Larry M. 2014. Reconstructing the Niger-Congo verb extension paradigm: What's cognate, copied or renewed? In Martine Robbeets & Walter Bisang (eds.), *Paradigm change: In the Transeurasian languages and beyond* (Studies in Language Companion Series 161), 103–126. Amsterdam: John Benjamins Publishing Company. https://doi.org/10.1075/slcs.161.10hym.

Hyman, Larry M. 2017. Common Bantoid verb extensions. In John R. Watters (ed.), *East Benue-Congo: Nouns, pronouns, and verbs* (Niger-Congo Comparative Studies 1), 173–198. Berlin: Language Science Press. https://doi.org/10.5281/ZENODO.1314327.

Khairunnisa & Bradley McDonnell. in prep. Ampenan Sasak –*an*.

Kittilä, Seppo. 2010. Transitivity typology. In Jae Jung Song (ed.), *The Oxford handbook of linguistic typology*, 346–367. Oxford: Oxford University Press.

Kroeger, Paul. 2007. Morphosyntactic vs. morphosemantic functions of Indonesian –*kan*. In Annie Zaenen, Jane Simpson, Tracy Holloway King, Jane Grimshaw, Joan Maling & Christopher D. Manning (eds.), *Architectures, rules, and preferences: Variations on themes of Joan Bresnan*, 229–251. Stanford, CA: CSLI Publications.

Mattiola, Simone. 2019. *Typology of pluractional constructions in the languages of the world* (Typological Studies in Language 125). Amsterdam ; Philadelphia: John Benjamins. https://doi.org/10.1075/tsl.125.

McDonnell, Bradley. in prep. Causative/applicative syncretism: The Besemah *–ka*.

McDonnell, Bradley. 2016. *Symmetrical voice constructions in Besemah: A usage-based approach*. Santa Barbara, CA: University of California, Santa Barbara PhD dissertation.

Pacchiarotti, Sara. 2020. *Bantu applicative constructions* (Standard Monographs in African Languages). Stanford, CA: CSLI Publications.

Peterson, David A. 2007. *Applicative constructions*. Oxford; New York: Oxford University Press.

Polinsky, Maria. 2013. Applicative constructions. In Matthew Dryer & Martin Haspelmath (eds.), *The World Atlas of Language Structures Online*. Leipzig: Max Planck Institute for Evolutionary Anthropology. https://wals.info/chapter/109 (24 February, 2021).

Pusat Bahasa Indonesia. 2007. *Kamus besar Bahasa Indonesia*. 3rd. Jakarta: Balai Pustaka Pub.

Quick, Phil. 2007. *A grammar of the Pendau language of central Sulawesi, Indonesia* (Pacific Linguistics 590). Canberra: Pacific Linguistics, Research School of Pacific and Asian Studies, Australian National University.

Quick, Phil. 2008. Is there a VP in Pendau? *Studies in Philippine Languages and Cultures* 19. 67–83.

R Core Team. 2018. *R: A language and environment for statistical computing*. R Foundation for Statistical Computing. Vienna, Austria. https://www.R-project.org/ (29 October, 2021).

Riesberg, Sonja. 2014. *Symmetrical voice and linking in western Austronesian languages* (Pacific Linguistics 646). Berlin: De Gruyter Mouton.

Ross, Malcolm. 2002. The history of western Austronesian voice and voice-marking. In Fay Wouk & Malcolm Ross (eds.), *The history and typology of western Austronesian voice systems*, 17–62. Canberra: Pacific Linguistics.

Shibatani, Masayoshi & Prashant Pardeshi. 2002. The causative continuum. In Masayoshi Shibatani (ed.), *The grammar of causation and interpersonal manipulation* (Typological Studies in Language 48), 85–126. Amsterdam: John Benjamins.

Sneddon, J. N., Alexander Adelaar, Dwi Noverini Djenar & Michael C. Ewing. 2010. *Indonesian reference grammar*. 2nd ed. Crows Nest, NSW: Allen & Unwin.

Trithart, Mary Lee. 1983. *The applied suffix and transitivity: A historical study in Bantu*. University of California at Los Angeles dissertation.

van den Berg, René & Robert L. Busenitz. 2012. *A grammar of Balantak, a language of Eastern Sulawesi* (SIL E-Books 40). SIL. https://www.sil.org/resources/publications/entry/49492 (29 October, 2021).

Wood, Esther. 2007. *The semantic typology of pluractionality*. Berkeley, CA: University of California, Berkeley PhD Dissertation.

Woollams, Geoff. 1996. *A grammar of Karo Batak, Sumatra* (Pacific Linguistics. Series C, 130). Canberra: Australian National University.

Zúñiga, Fernando & Seppo Kittilä. 2019. *Grammatical voice* (Cambridge Textbooks in Linguistics). Cambridge ; New York: Cambridge University Press.

Abbreviations

1	first person
2	second person
3	third person
A	most agent-like argument of transitive clause
AC	applicative constructive
APPL	applicative
AppP	applicative phrase
AV	voice in which A is the privileged syntactic argument
BC	base construction
BEN	beneficiary role
CAUS	causative
COM	comitative role
COMP	comparative
CORE	core argument
DEM	demonstrative
EMPH	emphatic
GEN	genitive
GOAL	goal role
HAB	habitual
HON	honorific
INS	instrument role
INTR	intransitive
IRR	irrealis
ITER	iterative
LOC	locative, location role
NEG	negative
NMLZ	nominalizer
P	patient-like argument of transitive clause
PFV	perfective
PL	plural
PLUR	pluractional
PN	personal name marker
PURP	purpose role
PV	voice in which P is the privileged syntactic argument
QUOT	quotative
REAS	reason role
REL	relativizer
RLS	realis
SG	singular
THM	theme role

Jozina Vander Klok and Bethwyn Evans

15 The evolution of non-syntactic functions of applicatives: -*i* suffixation in Javanese and neighboring languages

Abstract: Javanese, like many other Austronesian languages, has two applicative suffixes which introduce a non-actor argument as the applied phrase in the main clause. This chapter focuses on the locative applicative -*i*, which introduces an applied phrase with the semantic role of location, goal or recipient. Javanese -*i* also has a number of non-applicative functions. It has the additional syntactic function of deriving causatives by introducing an actor participant, as well as a range of non-syntactic functions, which include encoding a pluractional meaning or indicating intensity of the event or specificity of the applied phrase. This chapter describes these uses of -*i* suffixation in Javanese and other languages of the Western Indonesian subgroup. Comparison of locative applicative morphology across a small sample of Western Indonesian languages suggests that the non-syntactic functions of -*i* suffixation developed from its applicative use through the conventionalization of meanings of higher transitivity typically associated with applicative structures.

Acknowledgements: We would like to thank our Javanese language consultants in Paciran, East Java: Deti Salamah, Fina Ahsanah, Ulum Bahrul, Junaidi & Vida; and in Semarang, Central Java: Dwi Vicky Leksono, Devia Rizka Athaariqa, and Nina Setyaningsih. Thank you also to Universitas Dian Nuswantoro in Semarang for providing classroom space. Thank you to the editors Sara Pacchiarotti and Fernando Zúñiga, two anonymous reviewers, as well as Brad McDonnell and Christina Truong for detailed and helpful comments on previous versions of this chapter. Special thanks to Sara Pacchiarotti and Fernando Zúñiga for organizing the SLE 2020 workshop that led to this volume. We also gratefully acknowledge the funding from the Research Council of Norway (RCN) for the project 'Where does grammar come from? The cognitive basis of transitivity and grammatical relations', which supported the fieldwork and research.

Jozina Vander Klok, Humboldt-Universität zu Berlin, Unter den Linden 6, Berlin, Germany, e-mail: jozina.vander.klok@hu-berlin.de
Bethwyn Evans, Linguistics, School of Culture, History and Language, College of Asia and the Pacific, The Australian National University, Canberra, Australia, e-mail: bethwyn.evans@anu.edu.au

https://doi.org/10.1515/9783110777949-015

1 Introduction

This chapter describes the morphosyntactic functions of two applicative morphemes, the locative *-i* and the benefactive *-(a)ke/-no* in Javanese (Western Malayo-Polynesian; Austronesian; ISO: jav), and further investigates *-i* verbal suffixation with a focus on its non-syntactic functions. The most well-described use of *-i* is its syntactic function as an applicative, introducing a non-actor (location, recipient or goal) semantic argument into the main clause as an applied phrase (e.g., Nurhayani 2014), following typical definitions of applicative morphology (e.g., Alsina and Mchombo 1990; Bresnan and Moshi 1993; Payne 1997; Peterson 2007). The suffix can also derive a causative, introducing an actor semantic argument (Robson 2002; Hemmings 2013), showing causative-applicative syncretism. In addition to these syntactic functions, *-i* suffixation can also have a semantic function of adding an iterative or distributive meaning (Sumarlam 2004; Ewing 2005; Hemmings 2013). Other non-syntactic, less well-described functions of *-i* include intensity, specificity of the applied phrase, as well as lexicalized meanings (cf. Sudaryanto 1991; Robson 2002).

The first goal of this chapter is to show that these non-syntactic functions are an integral property of the *-i* applicative construction in Javanese, arising across different predicates. We also argue that the semantic function of iterative or distributive is best described as pluractional and is limited to transitive predicates that do not introduce a locative-type thematic role. This Austronesian language thus adds to the cross-linguistic literature on the so-called "non-prototypical" functions of applicative constructions.

Our second goal is to address the evolution of these non-syntactic functions of applicatives in Javanese by comparing the form and functions of Javanese *-i* to parallel morphemes in the neighboring languages of Indonesia, namely Indonesian, Balinese, Madurese, Sundanese, and Sasak. We have selected these languages from the Western Indonesian subgroup within Austronesian (Smith 2017) not as a way of attempting to reconstruct a broader history of change in the functions of *-i, but in order to explore the likely motivations of change in Javanese (and beyond) through the synchronic uses of locative applicatives. We show that the non-syntactic functions likely arose through semantic extension from an original locative applicative function (see Section 4). We thereby extend Peterson's (2007) pathways of evolution of applicative functions beyond topic persistence.

This chapter is organized as follows. In Section 2, we describe the morphosyntactic properties of the two applicative constructions in Javanese. The rest of this chapter focuses on the semantic functions of *-i* suffixation, which have not been subject to dedicated study before. In Section 3 we illustrate the non-syntactic properties of *-i* in Javanese before considering the likely development of these functions in Section 4. Section 5 presents the conclusions.

The data presented in this chapter are drawn from the literature as well as our own fieldwork on Javanese. The source and dialectal variety are indicated for each example given the high lexical and morphophonological variation. "Standard Javanese" refers to the variety spoken in and around the courtly cities of Yogyakarta and Surakarta (aka Solo). Despite considerable grammatical variation, as far as we are aware, all Javanese varieties have two applicative morphemes, and in all varieties the -*i* morpheme displays the semantic functions discussed in this chapter. Thus, we take our analysis in Section 4 to apply to the Javanese language as a whole.

2 Syntactic properties of two applicative constructions in Javanese

Before turning to the applicative constructions, we first introduce the three grammatical voices of Javanese: Actor Voice (AV), Patient Voice (PV), and passive, as demonstrated in (1) (see also Sudaryanto 1991; Robson 2002; Ogloblin 2005). As also shown in (1), neutral word order is SVO (Subject-Verb-Object). In terms of verbal morphology, AV is signalled by a homorganic nasal prefix on the verb, PV by a bare verb, and the passive by the *di-* verbal prefix.[1] These voices generally indicate different semantic roles of the subject; with AV, the subject is the actor, while with PV or the passive, the subject is the patient/theme. In Javanese, PV and the passive differ from each other in the person of the agent: PV is restricted to 1st and 2nd person agents, as illustrated by the 1st person proclitic in (1b), while the passive is restricted to 3rd person agents, illustrated by the pronoun *dhe'e* in (1c).

Surabayan Javanese (Krausse 2017: 50–51)[2]
(1) a. *Aku wes **n**-delok kon*   ACTOR VOICE (AV)
       1SG already **AV**-see 2SG
       'I have seen you already.'

---

1 While AV is generally encoded by a homorganic nasal prefix, and so marked with a hyphen (e.g., *n-delok* 'AV-see'), with some predicates it is realized through alternation of the initial segments of the root (aka nasal substitution), in which case the AV gloss is separated from the meaning of the verb root by a period (e.g. *mangan* 'AV.eat' versus *pangan* 'eat'). There is also a set of lexically-determined verbs which in AV occur as the unmarked stem, such as *tuku* 'to buy'. These verbs, however, do occur with the nasal prefix when used with the applicative suffixes (see Robson 2002; Sofwan 2010).
2 We have adapted or added glosses to examples from other sources to ensure consistency across the chapter. Primary changes were to Actor Voice as AV or -*i* suffixation as APPL.

b. Kon   wes   tak=delok   PATIENT VOICE (PV)
   2SG   already   1SG=**PV**.see
   'You've been seen by me.'

c. Aku   wes   **di**-delok   (ambek dhe'e)   PASSIVE
   1SG   already   **PASS**-see   by   3
   'I've been seen by him.'

Javanese *i* and *-(a)ke/-no* are derivational morphemes that occur on a verb stem and introduce a non-actor semantic argument which is mapped to an applied phrase.[3] As such, they are captured by the definition of applicative morphology in the introduction to this volume. These optional suffixes interact both with grammatical voice and transitivity, while they differ with respect to which semantic roles they introduce. Examples (2)-(3) illustrate applicative constructions and their non-applicative counterparts in AV; in both cases, the applicative construction in AV requires that the predicate has both the AV nasal prefix and applicative morphology, and the applied phrase is syntactically mapped as a direct object (cf. Sofwan 2010; Nurhayani 2014). In (2b), the verb form *ng-lungguh-i* 'sit upon' has both affixes (AV nasal prefix and *-i*), and the location *dipan iku* 'the bed' is a direct object. This construction contrasts with the example in (2a), where *dipan iku* 'the bed' is introduced as an adjunct with a preposition to the intransitive predicate *lungguh* 'to sit' which has neither AV morphology nor the *-i* suffix.[4]

A similar contrast is shown in (3) for the *-(a)ke/-no* applicative suffix. In the applicative construction in (3b), the predicate *jupuk* 'to take' requires both the AV nasal prefix and *-ake* suffixation, and the applied phrase (the beneficiary *Petrus*) is syntactically mapped as a direct object, occurring immediately after the predicate. In (3a), the transitive predicate *jupuk* 'to take' only takes the AV nasal prefix, and the beneficiary *Petrus* must be introduced with the preposition *kanggo* 'for' as an adjunct.

---

3 Concerning their phonological form, the *-i* applicative suffix is constant in form across all Javanese varieties, where an epenthetic [n] follows a verb stem that ends in a vowel (e.g., *daya* 'energy' + *-i* → *ndayani* 'to give energy to') (cf. Uhlenbeck 1978; Ewing 2005). This epenthesis is also found with the nominal definite suffix *-e*; e.g., *raja* 'king' + *-e* → *rajane* 'the king'. The *-ake* or *-ke* form is typically used in Central Javanese varieties (including Standard Javanese, as spoken in Yogyakarta and Surakarta/Solo), while *-no* is commonly used in East Javanese varieties. See also Adelaar (2011) for further discussion of the applicative forms across dialects, and their different historical sources.

4 Note that this intransitive predicate (*lungguh* 'sit') does not have or require the AV nasal prefix; see Robson (2002) for different classes of intransitives, some of which take voice morphology.

Standard Javanese (Sofwan 2010: 49, 58)
(2) a. *Dheweke lungguh ing dipan iku.*
    3SG   sit   on bed   DEF
    'S/he sat on the bed.'

   b. *Dheweke ng-lungguh-i dipan iku.*
      3SG   AV-sit-APPL bed   DEF
      'S/he sat on the bed.'

(3) a. *Jana n-jupuk buku kanggo Petrus.*
       Jana AV-take book for   Petrus
       'Jana took a book for Petrus.'

   b. *Jana n-jupuk-ake Petrus buku.*
      Jana AV-take-APPL Petrus book
      'Jana took a book for Petrus.'

These examples demonstrate that applicativization introduces a direct object, requires AV morphology, and is syntactically optional in Javanese with both *-i* or *-(a)ke/-no* with intransitive and transitive stems; below we show that applicative morphology is obligatory to introduce certain semantic roles with ditransitive and causative stems.

In PV and passive voice, the applied phrase can be promoted to subject position, as shown in (4) with the passive construction (see Davies 1993 and Sofwan 2010 for arguments that the preverbal position is the subject). This property allows semantic roles other than theme/patient (cf. (1b) and (1c)) to be in subject position, such as the locative *dipan iku* 'the bed' in (4a) or the beneficiary *Petrus* in (4b). Without the combination of the applicative construction plus PV or passive voice, these 'peripheral' semantic roles can never be subjects.

Standard Javanese (Sofwan 2010: 50, 59)
(4) a. *Dipan iku di-lungguh-i dheweke.*
       bed DEF PASS-sit-APPL 3SG
       'The bed was sat on by her/him.'

   b. *Petrus di-jupuk-ake buku dening Jana.*
      Petrus PASS-take-APPL book by   Jana
      'The book was taken for Petrus by Jana.'

In other words, the difference between the applicative and non-applicative construction has consequences for syntactic accessibility: the applied phrase in the applicative construction can be passivized (showing it is a core argument), while the adjunct cannot be passivized in the non-applicative construction (see e.g., Suhandono 1994; Nurhayani 2014). Thus, while the Javanese applicative construction is generally syntactically optional, it is an important strategy to allow different semantic roles to be direct objects in AV and subjects in PV or passive. Applicative and non-applicative constructions also differ functionally. Applied phrases are highly discourse prominent and often elided (Ewing 2005; cf. Sato 2015), although this latter function has not been well studied.

The Javanese applicative construction also interacts with transitivity. The generalization, not described before, is that in Javanese, applicative morphology is obligatory with ditransitive predicates to introduce one of their internal arguments as well as to express the causative function (see below). Elsewhere, applicative morphology is optional: the peripheral semantic argument can be expressed as an adjunct prepositional phrase in a non-applicative construction, as shown in (2)-(3) with intransitive and transitive predicates.

Concerning ditransitive predicates, examples (5)-(6) illustrate that applicative morphology is required, and the choice of applicative determines which internal argument occurs as the postverbal direct object. Consider the ditransitive verb stem *meneh* 'give'. In (5), the recipient *aku* 'me' is the applied object with *-i*, while the theme *gawean kuwi* 'that job' is the applied object with *-ake*. This complementary distribution follows the type of semantic roles that each of these applicative suffixes introduce, as discussed below with examples (11)-(12). It is ungrammatical for ditransitive predicates of this type to occur without these suffixes, as shown in (6).

Standard Javanese (Nurhayani 2014: 88; elicited (6a))
(5) a. Dheweke meneh-i aku gawean kuwi.
 3SG AV.give-APPL 1SG job that
 'He gave me that job.'

  b. Dheweke meneh-ake gawean kuwi marang aku.
 3SG AV.give-APPL job that to 1SG
 'He gave that job to me.'

(6) a. * Dheweke meneh aku gawean kuwi.
 3SG AV.give 1SG job that

  b. * Dheweke meneh gawean kuwi marang aku.
 3SG AV.give job that to 1SG

That only the applied phrase is the direct object in these examples is shown with passivization: only the direct object can be promoted to subject. Example (7) demonstrates that with -ake suffixation, only the theme *gawean kuwi* 'that job' can be passivized based on the AV counterpart in (5b). However, with -i suffixation in (8), only the recipient *Zahra* can be passivized with this same predicate based on a different AV sentence in (8a).

Standard Javanese (Nurhayani 2014: 88)
(7) a. *Gawean kuwi di-weneh-ake   dheweke marang aku.*
       job   that PASS-give-APPL 3SG   to   1SG
       'The job was given to me by him.'

   b. * *Aku di-weneh-ake   dheweke gawean kuwi.*
         1SG PASS-give-APPL 3SG   job   that
         ('I was given that job by him.')

Standard Javanese (Sofwan 2010: 65)
(8) a. *Ali meneh-i   Zahra dolanan iku.*
       Ali AV.give-APPL Zahra toy   DEF
       'Ali gave the toy to Zahra.'

   b. *Zahra di-weneh-i   Ali dolanan iku.*
       Zahra PASS-give-APPL Ali toy   DEF
       'Zahra was given the toy by Ali.'

   c. * *Dolanan iku di-weneh-i   Ali Zahra.*
         toy   DEF PASS-give-APPL Ali Zahra
         ('The toy was given by Ali to Zahra.')

Other predicates of this type beyond *menehake – menehi* 'give' as identified by Sofwan (2010: 67) are *nawakake – nawani* 'offer'; *ngirimake – ngirimi* 'send'; *masrahake – masrahi* 'entrust'; *nakokake – nakoni* 'ask'; *nyritakake – nyritani* 'tell (a story)'; *nuduhake – nuduhi* 'show'; *nyilihake – nyilihi* 'lend'; *nyuguhake – nyuguhi* 'serve'. In each case, the applicative morphology is required and in complementary distribution, where -i introduces a recipient/goal while -ake introduces a theme. Further, both internal arguments are required to be present (see Sofwan 2010: 66).

We identify these predicate types in Javanese as ditransitive, following Sofwan (2010), since both internal arguments are obligatorily overt. In this case, the applicative morphology serves to encode the semantic role of one of the internal arguments as the applied object. This seems to be the case for the majority of ditransitive verbs in Javanese, as only very few predicates (*mulang* 'teach'; *nyumbang* 'contribute') allow the recipient as direct object without -i suffixation (Sofwan 2010: 66–67). However, note that none of these predicates allow for the theme to be a direct object without -ake suffixation.

With transitive verb stems, an interesting feature of Javanese applicatives is that the applied phrase is not always syntactically mapped as a direct object. Specifically, in applicative constructions with transitive verb stems that function to increase valency (to a semantically trivalent construction), the applied phrase can be a direct object NP (noun phrase), or can remain a prepositional phrase (PP) like in non-applicative constructions, as in (9)-(10) (see also Sofwan 2010; Vander Klok to appear). In (9b-c), the transitive verb stem *nules* 'write' takes the *-i* suffix, and the recipient *Zumaroh* as the applied phrase can be a NP direct object or a PP introduced by *neng* 'to'. In (10), the verb stem *njupuk* 'take' takes the *-ake* suffix, and the beneficiary applied phrase *Aminah* can also either be a direct object or a PP, introduced by *kanggo* 'for'. The morphosyntactic difference between an NP and PP applied phrase correlates with a difference in postverbal word order: as an NP direct object, it occurs immediately post-verbally, while as a PP complement, it occurs following the base object.

Paciran Javanese (elicited, Vander Klok to appear)
(9) a. *Wanan nules surat.*
    Wanan AV.write letter
    'Wanan wrote a letter.'

 b. *Wanan nules-i* **Zumaroh** *surat.*
    Wanan AV.write-APPL Zumaroh letter
    'Wanan wrote a letter to Zumaroh.'

 c. *Wanan nules-i surat* **neng Zumaroh**.
    Wanan AV.write-APPL letter to Zumaroh
    'Wanan wrote a letter to Zumaroh.'

Standard Javanese (Sofwan 2010: 58)
(10) a. *Ali n-jupuk-ake* **Aminah** *buku.*
     Ali AV-take-APPL Aminah book
     'Ali took a book for Aminah.'

 b. *Ali n-jupuk-ake buku* **kanggo Aminah**.
    Ali AV-take-APPL book for Aminah
    'Ali took a book for Aminah.'

Vander Klok (to appear) argues that the applied phrase, whether realized as an NP or PP, is an argument of the predicate in applicative constructions, but an adjunct (as a PP) in non-applicative constructions. Further, this morphosyntactic alternation in Javanese allows for greater syntactic accessibility: the non-applied phrase is then accessible for passivization from the construction where it occurs as the postverbal direct object (such as *surat* 'letter' in (9c) or *buku* 'book' in (10b)). The possible semantic and pragmatic differences between these structures require further investigation.[5]

Thus far, we have looked at how the two applicative morphemes behave in remarkably similar ways syntactically in Javanese. However, *i* and *-(a)ke/-no* are distinguished functionally by the semantic roles they introduce. The applicative *-i* can introduce a location, goal or recipient, as in (11); while *-ake/-no* a beneficiary, displaced theme, or theme, as in (12) (see also Suhandono 1994; Ewing 2005; Ogloblin 2005; Nurhayani 2014; Vander Klok to appear).[6]

Standard Javanese (Nurhayani 2014: 44–45, 75)
(11) a. *Aku nuthuk-**i** tembok nganggo palu.* [location]
       1   AV.hit-APPL wall   with   hammer
       'I hit the wall with a hammer.'

   b. *Aku nguncal-**i** Ani duit.* [goal/recipient]
      1   AV.throw-APPL Ani money
      'I threw the money to Ani.'

(12) a. *Aku n-jahit-**ake** ibu-ku rok.* [beneficiary]
       1   AV-sew-APPL mother-my skirt
       'I sewed mother a skirt.'

   b. *Aku m-balang-**ake** watu neng uwit kuwi.* [displaced theme]
      1   AV-throw-APPL stone to   tree that
      'I hit the tree with a stone.'

   c. *Ibu-ku nyerita-**kake** dongeng marang adhi-ku.* [theme]
      mother-my AV.tell-APPL fairy.tale to   yg.sibling-my
      'My mother told a story to my younger brother.'

---

5 Although co-occurring with a prepositional applied phrase is not considered a "prototypical" feature of applicative morphology, this combination is reported more widely in Austronesian, see, e.g., this volume, chapter 14 as well as Chung (1976: 55) and Musgrave (2001: 156) for Indonesian, and also in some Indigenous Australian languages (Austin 2005) and in Abaza (Northwest Caucasian; O'Herin 2001).
6 In recent work on the Indonesian applicative suffix *-kan*, Kroeger (2007) argues that it does not in fact introduce instruments, but instead a "displaced theme", i.e., a theme that is moved or transferred. We follow this analysis for Javanese, while previous work refers to instruments (e.g., Sofwan 2010; Nurhayani 2014). Regarding the *-i* suffix, Nurhayani (2014: 45) argues that it only introduces a goal semantic role.

The specific semantic role of the applied argument with each applicative morpheme is governed by the lexical semantics of the verb. That is, with some verbs each applicative morpheme is associated with a specific semantic role, while with other verbs the same applicative suffix can be associated different semantic roles (see Suhandono 1994: 57). This is illustrated with the verb stem *nulis* 'to write' plus the *-i* suffix in (13): the applied phrase can be a location or a recipient/goal. However, the recipient *Ani* in (13b) cannot be interpreted as a beneficiary semantic role; in this case, the *-(a)ke/no* suffix is required.

Paciran Javanese (elicited)
(13) a. *Waliq* **nulis-i** *tembok* huruf A.   [✓ location]
         Waliq AV.write-APPL wall   letter A.
         'Waliq wrote the letter A on the wall.'

     b. *Waliq* **nulis-i** *Ani* surat.   [✓ goal/recipient / # beneficiary]
         Waliq AV.write-APPL Ani letter
         'Waliq wrote Ani a letter.'

We also predict that *-i* cannot introduce the semantic roles associated with *(a)ke/no* (beneficiary, displaced theme, or theme); and vice versa, that *-(a)ke/-no* cannot introduce the semantic roles associated with *-i* (location, recipient, or goal). This prediction is borne out in (14), where an attempt is made for *-i* to introduce a theme or beneficiary and *-ke* to introduce a goal or recipient. Both attempts are infelicitous (indicated by #).

Semarang Javanese (elicited)
(14) a. # *Tomo* **nulis-i** *aksara jawa kanggo Singgih*.
           Tomo AV.write-APPL script jawa for   Singgih
                                                  [# theme or beneficiary]
           (Intended for: 'Tomo wrote Javanese script for Singgih.')

     b. *Deli* **nulis-ke** *Siti surat*.   [✓ beneficiary]
         Deli AV.write-APPL Siti letter
         'Deli wrote a letter for Siti.'
         (# 'Deli wrote a letter to Siti.')   [# goal/recipient]

Thus, the data in (11)-(14) support that each applicative morpheme can introduce a set of different semantic roles, and that their sets do not overlap. In other words, the two applicative morphemes are in complementary distribution in terms of their semantic roles (cf. Nurhayani 2014).

Lastly, morphology of the same form as the applicative suffixes in Javanese can also derive a causative verb stem, primarily with intransitive verbal stems (either unaccusative or unergative), as shown in (15)-(16) (Suhandono 1994; Hemmings 2013; Nurhayani 2014). For this function, applicative morphology is obligatory and both suffixes introduce an actor semantic role. Hemmings (2013) argues that the causative function is a case of polysemy with the applicative function.

Standard Javanese (Suhandono 1994: 63)
(15) a. *Asu-ne mati.*
dog-DEF die
'The dog died.'

b. *Bambang mate-**ni** asu-ne.*
Bambang AV.die-APPL dog-DEF
'Bambang killed the dog.'

(16) a. *Bayi-ne turu.*
baby-DEF sleep
'The baby slept.'

b. *Bu Marta nuru-**ake** bayi-ne.*
Mrs. Marta AV.sleep-APPL baby-DEF
'Mrs. Marta made the baby sleep/put the baby to bed.'

In sum, in Javanese there are two formally and functionally distinct applicative morphemes, *-i* and *-(a)ke/-no*. They are functionally distinguished in terms of which semantic roles they introduce, with *-i* introducing a location, recipient or goal, while *-(a)ke/-no* introduces a beneficiary, displaced theme, or theme (Suhandono 1994; Nurhayani 2014). Both suffixes can also introduce an actor semantic role in their causative function, showing causative-applicative syncretism, which is argued to be a case of polysemy (Hemmings 2013; see also this volume, chapter 14 for this syncretism in other languages of western Indonesia). Applicative morphology is obligatory with ditransitive predicates and to derive a causative but is otherwise syntactically optional (cf. Sofwan 2010; Nurhayani 2014). While in applicative constructions the applied phrase is a core argument and highly discourse prominent, in non-applicative constructions, the same semantic roles are introduced by prepositions as adjuncts and are less discourse prominent (Ewing 2005). Further, the applied phrase can also be a prepositional phrase, and thus an oblique, in the applicative construction with transitive verb stems (Vander Klok to appear). This is an underdescribed feature that is found with applicative constructions in Austronesian and elsewhere (cf. this volume, chapter 14), the functions of which remain unclear.

3 Non-syntactic properties of -*i* suffixation in Javanese

There are also several less well-described non-syntactic functions of -*i* suffixation in Javanese: pluractionality (section 3.1), intensity (section 3.2), and specificity of the applied phrase (section 3.3). As is typical for verbal derivational morphology, applicativized stems with -*i* and -*(a)ke/-no* also have lexicalized meanings (section 3.4). Our discussion focuses on the -*i* suffix given the wide variety of semantic functions it has in Javanese, in contrast to the -*(a)ke/-no* suffix which does not seem to have such a variety of non-syntactic functions beyond lexicalized meanings.

3.1 Pluractionality

A less well-described function of -*i* in Javanese is its aspectual function with (syntactically and semantically) transitive predicates, which we argue is pluractionality.[7] That is, with many transitive predicates, -*i* is valency-preserving: there is no additional argument that is introduced by the verb stem carrying -*i*. Rather, -*i* with these predicates adds a meaning previously described either as iterativity (Uhlenbeck 1978; Sumarlam 2004) or distributive (Ewing 2005).

We show that the pluractional interpretation is obligatory with certain transitive predicates where the -*i* suffix does not introduce an applied phrase, but may be inferred when -*i* does introduce an applied phrase. Moreover, a pluractional interpretation is not obligatory with syntactically intransitive predicates or semantically ditransitive predicates in Javanese, but may be inferred, as we describe below.

For instance, Sumarlam (2004: 70) describes the hitting event in (17a) as punctual, but as 'iterative' when *ngantem* 'hit' combines with the -*i* suffix in

---

[7] Javanese has two other ways to express plurality of the agent, patient, or event. First, the auxiliary *padha* denotes the plurality of the agent in AV constructions, while in passive *di-* constructions, it can denote the plurality of either the agent or the patient (Hayward 1998; Ogloblin 2001). Second, reduplication (full or partial) can express iterative/multiplicative meanings (Robson 2002).

(17b).[8] Sumarlam (2004: 73–74) also reports that it is not possible to modify *ngantemi* 'to hit (many times)' with the adverbial *sepisan* 'once', as in (17c), whereas adverbials such as *ping telu* 'three times' are grammatical. Another example of this aspectual function of *-i* is given in (18) with the transitive verb stem *nggupuk* 'beat'. Other transitive predicates for which *-i* is reported to add an iterative meaning are: *njiwiti* 'to pinch (many times)', *mbalangi* 'to throw (many times)', *ndugangi* 'to kick (many times)' (Sumarlam 2004: 76, 139); *njupuki* 'to take s.th. (repeatedly)', *methiki* 'to pick (many things)' (Wedhawati et al. 2006: 133).

Standard Javanese (Sumarlam 2004: 70, 74)
(17) a. *Tono* **ng-antem** *Toni.*
Tono AV-hit Toni
'Tono hit Toni.'

b. *Tono* **ng-antem-i** *Toni.*
Tono AV-hit-APPL Toni
'Tono hit Toni multiple times.'

c. *Tono **ng-antem-i** *Toni. sepisan*
Tono AV-hit-APPL Toni one.time
(Intended meaning: 'Tono hit Toni once.')

Malang Javanese (Hemmings 2013: 171)
(18) a. *Ibu-ku* **ng-gupuk** *kasur* *ng-anggó sapu.*
mother-1SG.POSS AV-hit mattress AV-use broom
'My mother hit the mattress with the broom (once).'

b. *Ibu-ku* **ng-gupuk-i** *kasur* *ng-anggó sapu.*
mother-1SG.POSS AV-hit-APPL mattress AV-use broom
'My mother beat the mattress using the broom (many times).'

As Robson (2002: 49) describes, this use of *-i* conveys "...plurality, either of the subject or the object, or repetition or intensity of the action of the verb" (see also Ewing 2005: 45). For example, in (19), a single cat repeats the action of eating over time. This sentence can denote either iteration of eating one object (i.e. one big fish) or eating multiple objects (i.e. eating many different fish). Thus *-i* can denote different types of event plurality (see also Hemmings 2013: 171). A further example where the meaning denoted is the plurality of the object is given in (20b): with *-i*

---

[8] The original Indonesian free translations in (17) are *Tono memukul Toni* and *Tono memukuli Toni*.

suffixation, the noun phrase *cah cilik* 'small child' must be interpreted as more than one.

Standard Javanese (Sofwan 2010: 46)
(19) *Kucing iku **mangan-i** iwak.*
  cat DEF AV.eat-APPL fish
  'The cat ate fish again and again.'

Paciran Javanese (elicitation)
(20) a. *Fina n-dulang bayi.*
   Fina AV-feed baby
   'Fina fed a baby.'

   b. *Fina n-dulang-i cah cilik.*
   Fina AV-feed-APPL child small
   'Fina fed small children.'

Given these different possible interpretations, we adopt the current term "pluractional" (introduced by Newman 1980), which indicates plurality in the verbal domain and refers to "...a multiplicity of actions, whether involving multiple participants, times or locations" (van Geenhoven 2004: 153). This term best describes the above range of interpretations noted in Robson (2002) and Ewing (2005).

Since this function is proposed to be part of the semantics of -*i* suffixation with certain transitive verb stems, one question that arises is whether other predicate types would also have this same interpretation with -*i*. That is, does pluractionality occur with transitive predicates with which -*i* also has a valency-increasing effect? Examples (17)–(20) show that with these transitive predicates -*i* only adds pluractionality. However, pluractionality is also a possible reading with predicates where the -*i* suffix is valency-increasing. In (21), for instance, -*i* introduces a recipient applied phrase (*Ani*) to the transitive verb stem *nulis* 'write' (cf. (9a-b)). It also can be interpreted as pluractional with -*i*, as indicated by the speaker's comment that the writing is repeated every day.

Semarang Javanese (elicited)
(21) *Waliq **nulis-i** Ani surat.*
  Waliq AV.write-APPL Ani letter
  'Waliq wrote Ani letters.' Speaker comment: *mben dino* 'every day'

Yet with such predicates pluractionality is only an inferred meaning and is not present in all contexts. In (22), the derived applicative stem *nulis-i* can felicitously combine with the adverbial *sepisan* 'one.time'. Thus, the pluractional interpretation of *-i* in contexts where it adds an applied phrase to a verb stem is possible but not required (see also (9b-c)).

Paciran Javanese (elicited)
(22) Wanan **nules-i** Zumaroh surat sepisan.
 Wanan AV.write-APPL Zumaroh letter one.time
 'Wanan wrote Zumaroh a letter once.'

To summarize, the *-i* suffix encodes pluractionality with predicates that do not require *-i* in order to be used transitively (i.e., where *-i* is valency-preserving). When *-i* has a valency-increasing function (applicative or causative) or is required in the case of morphosyntactically-derived ditransitive verbs, we suggest that pluractionality can be inferred but is not an obligatory part of the semantics of the derived verb. Other verb stems which take the *-i* suffix to introduce a recipient/goal/location and allow for a pluractional reading are: *nyilihi* 'borrow (many things); lend', *nyinaoni* 'learn (many things); cause [someone] to study/learn', *nganggoni* 'try on (many articles of clothing); have on clothing', *ngedhuni* 'take (many things) off from something; unload (a train, etc.)'.[9]

3.2 Intensity and/or affectedness of the applied phrase

Another non-syntactic function of the *-i* applicative suffix is described in the literature as "intensity" (Robson 2002: 49). As illustrated in (23), both the (a) and (b) examples have the same syntactic structure. The suffix *-i* adds intensity to the meaning of the verb stem as indicated by the different free translations (Hemmings 2013: 171).

Malang Javanese (Hemmings 2013: 171)
(23) a. *Charlotte ng-rusak lawang.*
 Charlotte AV-break door
 'Charlotte broke the door.'

 b. *Charlotte **ng-rusak-i** lawang.*
 Charlotte AV-break-APPL door
 'Charlotte destroyed the door.'

---
9 These verbs were extracted from Horne (1961: 177–183) and checked with Semarang Javanese speakers in 2019.

We consider completeness of the event or affectedness of the applied phrase to be part of the intensity function. These readings are brought out in the free translation with *all* in (24)-(25). This meaning is not conveyed by the definite marker nor by reduplication in Javanese.

Standard Javanese (Horne 1961: 184)
(24) *Gedhang-e* **di-pangan-i** *bocah~bocah.*
 banana-DEF PASS-eat-APPL child~RDP
 'The children ate up all the bananas.'

Cirebon Javanese (Ewing 2005: 46)
(25) Context: 'I had done all the reporting there right, ...
 Njaluk-i *surat-~surat.*
 AV.ask-APPL document~RDP
 '(I)'d asked for all the documents.'

This function is less well-described for Javanese in comparison to the pluractional function. It does not seem to be specific to a particular class of verbs and may overlap with some of the lexicalized meanings of -*i* suffixation.

3.3 Specificity of the object and/or applied argument

Sudaryanto (1991: 62) reports that the base object of the verb root *nulis* 'write' must be generic, while the object with -*i* suffixation must be specific, as shown in (26). Note that in (26) -*i* does not increase the syntactic valency of *nulis* 'write', unlike other instances where -*i* adds a locative or a recipient applied phrase; see e.g., (21).

Standard Javanese (Sudaryanto 1991: 61–62)
(26) a. *Slamet nulis* { *buku anyar* / **buku-ku sing anyar* }
 Slamet AV.write book new / book-my REL new
 'Slamet wrote a new book / *my new book.'

 b. *Slamet nulis-i* { *buku-ku sing anyar* / *buku anyar }
 Slamet AV.write-APPL book-my REL new / book new
 nganggo tulis-an warna~warna
 for write-NMLZ color~RDP
 'Slamet wrote {my new book / *a new book} with different colored writing.'

It is not clear how widespread this function is, as other sources do not show the contrast that Sudaryanto (1991) reports for (26). In support of the "specificity" function of applicative *-i*, however, Robson (2002: 47) does note that "some verbs with suffix *-i* mean to be something or do something in a more specific relation to the object in contrast with the form without *-i*" and illustrates this with the predicates in (27). Further research is necessary to understand if these predicates (and others) require the applied phrase to be specific, as suggested by Sudaryanto, or if this meaning is optional.

(27) Standard Javanese (Robson 2002: 48)

padha	'(to be the) same'	*madhani*	'to equal, match'
duwé	'to have'	*nduweni*	'to have, get possession of (s.t. in particular)'
golèk	'to look for'	*nggolèki*	'to seek out (one thing)'
nemu	'to find'	*nemoni*	'to go and see (one person)'
wèwèh	'to give things away'	*mènèhi*	'to give (one particular thing)'

3.4 Lexicalized meanings with *-i* suffixation in Javanese

Finally, a number of stems with the *-i* suffix have developed lexicalized meanings in Javanese; some examples are given in (28). In some cases, these could also be understood as indicating 'intensity', such as *nyekeli* 'to hold fast' from the verb stem *nyekel* 'to take in the hand' (cf. Robson 2002: 49).

(28) Standard Javanese (Robson 2002: 48–49; Horne 1961: 183)

nyekel	'to take in the hand'	*nyekel-i*	'to hold fast'
nangis	'to cry'	*nangisi*	'to cry over; to take one's troubles to'
mlaku	'walk'	*ngelakoni*	'undergo or endure [punishment, procedure, treatment, etc.]'
metu	'go out, leave'	*metoni, ngetoni*	'play a part or role'
takon	'ask'	*nakoni*	'question s.o.'

With other examples given in (29), the predicate with *-i* suffixation can have both a transparent locative applicative interpretation as well as a lexically-specific interpretation.

(29) Standard Javanese

rasa	'feel; taste'	ngerasani	'feel hurt by or have complaints about s.o.; gossip' (Horne 1961:181)
nonton	'look at, watch'	nontoni	'look at or watch s.t.; inspect a girl as a prospective bride' (Horne 1961:182)
lara	'sick, ill, painful'	ngelarani	'hurt or give pain to s.o.; have childbirth pains' (Horne 1961:180)
ndandan	'get/be dressed'	ndandani	'dress s.o.; repair or fix s.t.' (Horne 1961:178)
ngapal	'know by heart'	ngapali	'learn [many things] by heart; recognize' (Horne 1961:177)
rungu	'to hear'	ngrungoni	'to have s.o. hear s.t.; communicate s.t. to s.o.' (Robson & Wibisono 2002)

3.5 Summary of non-syntactic functions of -*i* suffixation in Javanese

Section 3 has illustrated that -*i* suffixation in Javanese can have several non-syntactic functions which have been less well-described in the literature than its transitivizing functions. We have argued that iteration or distributivity, one of the most commonly noted semantic functions of -*i* in the Javanese literature, is best described as pluractionality. With this function, -*i* can convey multiplicity of events (iteration), locations (distributive), or participants (cf. van Geenhoven 2004: 153, Veselinova 2008). Other functions of -*i* identified in the literature on Javanese are specificity of the applied phrase, intensity of the event (or affectedness of the applied phrase), and lexicalized meanings. These non-syntactic functions do not seem to be restricted to a specific class of verbs as the coded meaning of pluractionality is with many transitive stems. In some instances, the lexicalized meanings have developed from the intensity function. We turn now to considering possible connections between syntactic and non-syntactic functions of -*i*.

4 Evolution of non-syntactic functions of -*i* suffixation

Javanese is not unusual among Austronesian languages in having more than one verbal affix with an applicative function (see Table 1). The non-syntactic functions of Javanese -*i* are also found with applicative affixes in other Austronesian languages, and we argue that these reflect semantic extensions of the valence-increasing applicative use.

4.1 Origins and development of applicative -i

Table 1 shows that the Javanese applicative suffixes -i and -(a)ke have cognates with parallel syntactic functions across the Austronesian language family. Each of these languages has two formally and functionally distinct verbal suffixes which can have an applicative function. Suffixes cognate with Javanese -i tend to introduce locative or goal participants, while those historically connected with Javanese -ake license instrument and/or beneficiary roles.[10]

Table 1: Applicative suffixes cognate with Javanese -i and -ake across Austronesian.[11]

Language	locative applicative	benefactive applicative
Javanese	-i	-ake
Karo Batak	-i	-ken
Balantak	-i	-kon
Tukang Besi	-((V)C)i	-ako
Wolio	-i	-aka
Buru	-i	-k
Motu	-i	-lai
Longgu	-(C)i	-(C)aʔini
Wayan Fijian	-(C)i	-(C)akini

---

10 In Oceanic Austronesian languages, like Motu, Longgu and Wayan Fijian, the so-called benefactive applicative typically does not introduce a beneficiary participant; rather, the applied argument tends to be an instrument, concomitant or cause (see Pawley 1973; Evans 2003: chapter 5).

11 The languages listed here are representative of Austronesian languages outside of Taiwan and the Philippines. Karo Batak is a Western Malayo-Polynesian language spoken in Sumatra (Woollams 1996), while Balantak (van den Berg & Busenitz 2012), Tukang Besi (Donohue 1999) and Wolio (Anceaux 1988) are Western Malayo-Polynesian languages spoken in Sulawesi. Note that Balantak additionally has -ii as a specialized benefactive applicative with transitive stems, which has developed from the applicative -i and the personal article i (van den Berg & Busenitz 2012: 109). Similarly Tukang Besi has a third applicative suffix -ngkene, which introduces a comitative participant (Donohue 1999: 225). Buru is a Central-Malayo-Polynesian language of Maluku in eastern Indonesia. In Buru, the -i suffix encodes that the event of the verb has a specific locative goal, but this locative argument occurs in a prepositional phrase (Grimes 1991: 112). Motu, Longgu and Wayan Fijian are Oceanic Austronesian languages spoken in Papua New Guinea, Solomon Islands and Fiji, respectively (Yam 2020; Hill 2011; Pawley & Sayaba 2018). Note that in a number of languages these suffixes may occur with an initial lexically-determined consonant represented here by C.

The development of applicative constructions in Austronesian languages has been argued to be part of a broad trajectory of change in clausal organization (see Starosta, Pawley and Reid 1982; Kikusawa 2012). Proto-Austronesian is typically reconstructed with a symmetrical voice system such that different voice alternations – marked by verbal affixes – signal that the syntactically-privileged argument has a particular semantic role (e.g. Wolff 1973; Ross 2002, 2009). The voice alternations are symmetrical in the sense that they encode a change in argument realization but do not promote or demote core arguments. Austronesian languages of Taiwan and the Philippines have retained systems of symmetrical voice, while Oceanic-Austronesian languages, spoken in the Pacific, typically lack any voice alternations but display valence-altering verbal morphology, including applicative affixes. Javanese, like many Austronesian languages of Indonesia, shows both inherited symmetrical voice alternations, as well as innovative asymmetrical voice alternations (i.e. a passive) and valence-altering applicative affixes (see Section 2).[12] The presence of applicatives mostly in Austronesian languages spoken outside of Taiwan and the Philippines, as well as the formal similarity between voice-marking morphology and certain applicative affixes, provides evidence that the origins and development of the applicative constructions are part of this history of change in clausal organization and verbal morphology within Austronesian.

The applicative suffixes cognate with Javanese -*ake* are generally considered to be historically connected with a form *(a)kən, which cannot be reconstructed for Proto-Austronesian but is widespread in Austronesian languages outside of Taiwan and the Philippines. Its use as an applicative suffix that introduces instrument and beneficiary object arguments is taken to reflect grammaticalization from a preposition with the same function (see e.g. Ross 2002: 55–56, Kikusawa 2012: 430, 435–436). However, fine-grained studies of the history of prepositional and applicative reflexes of *akən in groups of closely related Austronesian languages point to more complex histories without linear pathways of continuity and change. For example, Naitoro (2018) reconstructs patterns of grammaticalization *and* degrammaticalization in the histories of *akən forms in the Southeast Solomonic group of Oceanic. Similarly, Adelaar (2011) demonstrates that the applicative suffixes reflecting *akən in Javanese dialects are post-Proto-Javanese

---

[12] While useful, this characterization of the clausal organization of Austronesian languages in terms of three types – a Philippine-type, an Indonesian-type and an Oceanic-type – is an over-simplification which does not attempt to account for the considerable differences between the grammars within and across these groupings. For more detailed discussion of voice systems in western Austronesian languages, see, for example, Wouk & Ross (2002), Arka & Ross (2005), and Riesberg (2014).

developments and likely part of areal changes given the presence of suffixes with similar forms and functions in other Austronesian languages of Java and Sumatra.

By contrast, the origin of the -*i* applicative lies in the Proto-Austronesian symmetrical voice system. That is, *-i is reconstructed as a marker of Locative Voice for Proto-Austronesian meaning that it encoded a locational participant as the syntactically-privileged argument (see Ross 2002, 2009; Kikusawa 2012).[13] Applicative reflexes of Proto-Austronesian *-i have retained this function of promoting a locative participant. In Proto-Austronesian, *-i is reconstructed within the voice paradigm for non-indicative moods (e.g. imperative, hortative), and another suffix *-an denoted Locative Voice in indicative mood (Ross 2002: 33). While in most languages the locative applicative reflects *-i, reflexes of *-an are also found with this function.

Table 2 illustrates that although the same functional distinction between locative and benefactive applicative suffixes is found in Javanese and neighbouring Western Indonesian languages, the histories of the forms across and within languages are not straightforward. That is, as expected from the discussion above, the applicative suffixes in (a) introduce beneficiary, instrument, stimulus and/or theme roles, while those in (b) introduce locative, goal/recipient and source roles. The Balinese examples in (30) and (31) demonstrate how these two suffixes introduce a direct object with contrastive semantic roles parallel to the Javanese applicatives illustrated in (2) and (3). However, the forms of the affixes do not always reflect *akən and *-i. In Sundanese, for example, the locative applicative suffix is a reflex of *-an, while in Madurese the two allomorphs of the locative applicative, -*e* and -*an*, reflect the diachronic conflation of *-i and *-an. In Madurese, the locative applicative suffix is -*an* when followed by the irrealis suffix *a*, but is realized as -*e* elsewhere. Thus, the locative applicative form of the verb *kerem* 'to send' is *kerem-an-a* [send-APPL-IRR] 'to send to' when marked as irrealis and *ngerem-e* [send-APPL] 'to send to' in other contexts (Davis 2010: 106). The same is true of Javanese, where the default form of the locative applicative suffix is -*i*, but it is realized as -*an* in a range of grammatical contexts, including with passives formed with *ka-* or -*in-*, adversative passives formed with *ke-*, and with verbs in the subjunctive mood (see Robson 2002; Conners 2008).[14]

---

13 The exact nature of Proto-Austronesian clausal syntax is beyond the scope of this chapter, but note that there are different proposals for Proto-Austronesian and the likely developments that explain the clausal organization and verbal morphology of contemporary Austronesian languages. While Ross (2002, 2009) reconstructs a symmetrical voice system for Proto-Austronesian, Kikusawa (2012) reconstructs Proto-Austronesian with a set of three basic clause structures – intransitive, extended intransitive and transitive.
14 See also this volume, chapter 12 for an analysis of *-i and *-an reflexes as markers of applicative constructions in the Philippine language Waray. We will not explore here the question of why

Table 2: Applicative morphemes in Javanese and neighbouring Western Indonesian languages.[15]

	Javanese	Indonesian/Malay	Sundanese	Madurese	Balinese	Eastern Sasak	Central Sasak
(a)	-ake/-ke/ -no/-nang	-kan	-keun	-aghi	-ang	-ang	-angk, -am, -an[16]
(b)	-i/-an	-i/-an	-an[17]	-e/-an	-in	-in	—

Balinese (Arka 2003: 63, 197)

(30) a. *Ia meli-**ang** Nyoman nasi.*
   3 AV.buy-APPL Nyoman rice
   '(S)he bought Nyoman rice.'

   b. *Ia meli nasi.*
   3 AV.buy rice
   '(S)he bought rice.'

(31) a. *Tiang nyelep-**in** gua-ne.*
   I AV.go.into-APPL cave-DEF
   'I entered the cave.'

   b. *Tiang ma-celep ka gua-ne.*
   I MID-go.into to cave-DEF
   'I went into the cave.'

---

applicative reflexes of *-i are more widely attested than those of *-an or the detailed historical development of these suffixes and the pathways of change that have resulted in the different contexts in which reflexes of *-i and *-an are used.

15 The languages in Table 2 are those from the Western Indonesian grouping within Malayo-Polynesian (see Smith 2017) that are spoken in the same region as Javanese. Sundanese and Madurese are spoken in western and eastern Java, respectively, while Balinese and Sasak are spoken on the islands of Bali and Lombok to the east of Java. Data are from Wedhawati et al. (2006) and fieldnotes for Javanese; Sneddon et al. (2010) for Indonesian; Hanafi (2001) and Kurniawan (2013) for Sundanese; Davies (2010) for Madurese; Arka (2003, 2014) for Balinese; and Austin (2000, 2001) and Asikin-Garmager (2017) for Sasak varieties.

16 In the Méno-Mené dialect of Sasak, the benefactive applicative inflects for the person and number of the applied object: -angk 'APPL.1SG', -at ~ -ant 'APPL.1PL', -am 'APPL.2', and -an 'APPL.3' (Austin 2000: 23). Note that -an in Central Sasak can also have a valency-reducing function (see this volume, chapter 14, section 3).

17 We have found only one predicate with the suffix -i glossed as APPL in Kurniawan (2013), namely *ningal-i* '[AV.see-APPL]'. It is not clear to us if this is a fossilized form or if other predicates can also have -i suffixation (besides -an) in Sundanese.

Regardless of the complex histories of their forms, the applicative suffix -*i* is argued to have developed from the Proto-Austronesian Locative Voice marker *-i, and we take this to be the starting point for considering the development of the non-syntactic functions of Javanese -*i*. While Javanese has retained a distinction between AV and PV, it no longer has the additional symmetrical voice categories, such as locative voice, that can be reconstructed for Proto-Austronesian.

4.2 Development of non-syntactic functions of -*i*

In many Austronesian languages, just as in Javanese, the locative applicative suffixes have other syntactic and non-syntactic functions, as shown in Table 3 across neighbouring Western Indonesian languages. Chapter 14 of this volume also illustrates this polyfunctionality of applicative suffixes based on a sample of nine languages of western Indonesia. Often these additional functions are not the focus of descriptive or formal sources.

Table 3: Functions of locative applicative suffixes.[18]

	Javanese	Indonesian	Sundanese	Madurese	Balinese	E. Sasak
Syntactic functions						
locative applicative	✓	✓	✓	✓	✓	✓
causative	✓	✓	✓	✓	✓	
Non-syntactic functions						
verbal derivation[19]	✓	✓			✓	✓
iterative action	✓	✓		✓ (-*an*)	✓	
plurality of O	✓					
durative action	✓			✓		
intensity of action	✓	✓				✓
affectedness of O	✓	✓			✓	
specific O	✓				✓	
lexicalized meanings	✓	✓				

---

18 In addition to the sources listed above relating to Table 2, the information presented in this table relies on Natarina (2018) and Barber (1977) for Balinese; Ashriany (2008), Jordan (1998), Koch (1998) and Wouk (1999) for Sasak; Ewing (2005), Robson (2002), Sudaryanto (1991), Sumarlam (2004), and Uhlenbeck (1978) for Javanese; Arka et al. (2009) and Willemsen (2017) for Indonesian; Truong (2019) for Sundanese; and Davies (2005) for Madurese. Where there is no checkmark, this indicates that this function is not discussed in the literature we consulted.
19 In Javanese, Indonesian, Balinese and Eastern Sasak, the locative applicative can be used to derive a transitive verb from a non-verbal root. It seems likely that this use of the applicative is an extension of its use to derive transitive verbs from intransitive verbs.

The apparent polysemy of applicative and causative uses of locative applicatives is widespread among Austronesian languages, illustrated in Table 3 by its presence in all of the languages except Eastern Sasak (see also this volume, chapter 14; Evans 2003). Example (32a) illustrates the causative use of the locative applicative *-in* in contrast with the non-causative form of the predicate in (32b) in Balinese.

Balinese (Arka 2003: 187)
(32) a. **Nyoman** *nyuun-in* ia banten.
Nyoman AV.carry.on.head-CAUS 3 offerings
'Nyoman made her carry offerings on her head.'

b. *Ia nyuun banten.*
3 AV.carry.on.head offerings
'She carried offerings (on her head).'

As described in Section 3.1, in Javanese the locative applicative *-i* also has a pluractional function denoting that the action is repeated more than once and/or is carried out by or directed towards multiple participants. As shown in Table 3, this use of the locative applicative also occurs in Madurese, Indonesian, Balinese and Sundanese. Sneddon et al. (2010) and Davies (2010) describe this function of *-i* in some detail for Indonesian and Madurese, respectively. Davies (2010: 106, 264) describes *-e* as denoting a "durative" or "iterated" meaning, as shown in (33a) with the verb *mokole* 'to hit repeatedly' in contrast to *mokol* 'to hit' in (33b). In Indonesian the "repetitive" function of *-i* also indicates that an action happens more than once either repeatedly towards one object participant, as in (34a) in contrast to (34b), or separately with different object participants, as in (35a) in contrast to (35b). In Indonesian this interpretation of *-i* is only possible with simple transitive verbs which do not require the *-i* or *-kan* suffixes to be used transitively (Sneddon et al. 2010: 100), similar to the verb class restriction found in Javanese.

Madurese (Davies 2010: 264)
(33) a. *Ali ban Hasan mokol-e maleng.*
Ali and Hasan AV.hit-DUR thief
'Ali and Hasan repeatedly hit the thief.'

b. *Ali ban Hasan mokol maleng.*
Ali and Hasan AV.hit thief
'Ali and Hasan hit the thief.'

Indonesian (Sneddon et al. 2010: 99)

(34) a. *Dia mencium-i pacar-nya.*
 3 AV.kiss-ITER girl/boyfriend-3.POSS
 'He kissed his girlfriend repeatedly/a number of times.'

 b. *Dia mencium pacar-nya.*
 3 AV.kiss girl/boyfriend-3.POSS
 'He kissed his girlfriend.'

(35) a. *Mereka menebang-i pohon di sekitar rumah-nya.*
 3PL AV.cut.down-ITER tree LOC around house-3.POSS
 'They chopped the trees down around their house.'

 b. *Mereka menebang pohon di depan rumah-nya.*
 3PL AV.cut.down tree LOC front house-3.POSS
 'They chopped down the tree in front of their house.'

For Balinese and Sundanese, we have less evidence of this use of the locative applicative. However, Natarina (2018: 24) comments in a footnote that the Balinese suffix *-in* also has an iterative function, as illustrated in (36). Kurniawan's (2013) study of complementation in Sundanese includes several examples where *-an* is glossed as iterative and denotes events that appear to have a sense of repeated action, as illustrated in (37). However, it is not clear from the examples alone whether an iterative reading is an obligatory part of the meaning of these verb forms with *-an*.

Balinese (Natarina 2018: 24, 22)

(36) a. *I Nyamprut nyagur-in panak-né ibi.*
 DET Nyamprut AV.hit-ITER child-POSS yesterday
 'Nyamprut hit his child (repeatedly) yesterday.'

 b. *Cang nawang cai lakar nyagur I Bayu.*
 1 AV.know 2 FUT AV.hit DET Bayu
 'I know that you will hit Bayu.'

Sundanese (Kurniawan 2013: 227, 24)

(37) a. *Amung apal-eun pisan yén Handi osok nyitak-an*
 Amung know-3 very COMP Handi always AV.print-ITER
 duit palsu
 money fake
 'Amung knew well that Handi always printed forged bills.'

b. *Masarakat keur n-ar-éang-**an** kapal nu ragrag téa.*
   community PROG AV-PL-seek-ITER plane REL fall PART
   'The people are searching for the falling plane.'

Also as in Javanese, in Eastern Sasak and Indonesian, the locative applicative can encode a sense of intensity of the action denoted by the predicate. Ashriany (2008: 87–88, 101–104) describes the *-in* suffix in Sasak as encoding that the action is carried out with force or coercion. For example, in (38a), the presence of *-in* indicates that the *tabanas* 'national savings'[20] were taken by force and that the mother did not want to give it up, while without *-in* in (38b) the notion of force is not implied.

Eastern Sasak (Ashriany 2008: 88)[21]
(38) a. *beit-**in**-ku inaq tabanas-ne.*
       take-APPL-1SG mother *tabanas*-3SG.POSS
       'I took mother's *tabanas* with force.'

   b. *beit-ku inaq tabanas-ne.*
      take-1SG mother *tabanas*-3SG.POSS
      'I took mother's *tabanas*.'

Ashriany (2008: 103) describes the use of *-in* in (39) as indicating that the speaker arrives suddenly and without the knowledge of the person being visited. In contrast to *lalo* 'to go', *lalo-in* also has the locative applicative function of introducing a goal participant.

Eastern Sasak (Ashriany 2008: 103)[22]
(39)   *jemaq-ku lalo-**in** iye.*
       tomorrow-1SG come-APPL 3SG
       'Tomorrow I'll go to him.'

The examples in (40) show similar uses of Indonesian *-i*. In (40a) *-i* adds a sense of intensity to the action of holding, while in (40b) *-i* introduces the goal participant *saya* '1SG' and expresses a meaning of intensity (see Sneddon et al. 2010;

---

20 Possibly from Indonesian *Tabungan nasional (Tabanas)* 'national savings'.
21 The original Indonesian translations of these Eastern Sasak sentences are *Kuambil tabanas ibu dengan paksa* and *Aku ambil tabanas ibu* for (38) and (38), respectively.
22 The original Indonesian translation for (39) is *Besok aku datangi dia*.

Arka et al. 2009). This highlights the overlap of functions of the locative applicative in a single use, just as in Javanese.

Indonesian (Arka et al. 2009: 88)
(40) a. Ia memegang-**i** pencuri itu.
      3 AV.hold-APPL thief   that
      'S/he was holding the thief tightly.'

   b. Ia melempar-**i** saya dengan batu.
      3 AV.throw-APPL 1SG with   stone
      'S/he pelted me with stones.'

   c. Ia melempar batu ke saya.
      3 AV.throw   stone to 1SG
      'S/he threw stones at me.

As described in Section 3.2, in Javanese -*i* can also express greater affectedness or specificity of the object argument, and this function is also found in Balinese and Indonesian. In Balinese, for example, one of the semantic constraints on the locative applicative is that it is only used with specific locations and when "the promoted Locative can be construed as being 'affected' by the event" (Arka 2003: 196). This explains why certain kinds of locatives can be promoted with -*in*, while for others the construction is infelicitous. This is illustrated in (41b) where it is possible for *piring* 'plate', the specific location that has direct contact with the rice, to be introduced as an object argument with -*in*. However, the same structure with the more general location of *paon* 'kitchen' is problematic, which, as Arka (2003: 196) notes, reflects "the difficulty in imagining (in real life) how a kitchen full of rice could be achieved". Example (41a), in contrast, shows that both these locatives can be expressed as the object of the preposition *di*.

Balinese (Arka 2003: 196)
(41) a. Ia ngejang nasi di piring-ne   / di paon-ne.
      3 AV.put   rice at plate-3.POSS   at kitchen-3.POSS
      'S/he put rice in his plate / in the kitchen.'

   b. Ia nyang-**in**   piring-e   / # paon-ne   nasi.
      3 AV.put-APPL plate-DEF   kitchen-3.POSS rice
      'S/he put rice in his plate / in the kitchen.'

Finally, just as in Javanese in (28)–(29) above, in Indonesian there are a number of lexicalized verb stems carrying the -*i* suffix, as shown in (42).

Indonesian (Sneddon et al. 2010: 96–97)

(42)   *mendapat*   'get'   *mendapat-i*   'find'
       menunggu   'wait (for)'   *menunggu-i*   'watch over'
       mengena   'know'   *mengenal-i*   'recognise, identify'
       mengajar   'teach'   *mengajar-i*   'teach, train, coach'
       mengurus   'arrange, organise'   *mengurus-i*   'look after'

These non-applicative functions of the locative applicative suffixes in Javanese and neighbouring Western Indonesian languages are not so unexpected within the context of the Austronesian language family or more broadly. For example, causative-applicative polysemy is not infrequent cross-linguistically (see Croft 1991; Peterson 2007: chapter 3; van Geysel forthcoming; Zúñiga and Kittilä 2019), and reflexes of *-i and *akən across Austronesian often have both applicative and causative functions (see this volume, chapter 14; Evans 2003; Naitoro 2018).[23] The non-syntactic functions of the locative applicative described here are also found with applicative suffixes in both other Austronesian languages of western Indonesia (see this volume, chapter 14) and in Oceanic Austronesian languages (see Evans 2003; Naitoro 2018). Several of these functions, notably intensity, iterativity, and completeness, are also found beyond Austronesian. For example, Michaelis & Ruppenhofer (2000) describe similar functions of the German applicative *be-*, and Pacchiarotti (2020: 3–4; 100–102) describes these non-syntactic uses for a specific applicative construction in Bantu languages. Willemsen (2017: 21–22) presents a small sample of languages with locative applicatives that also have intensive and iterative uses. These are mostly Bantu languages and Austronesian and non-Austronesian languages of Indonesia, but also include a single language of South America and Australia, respectively.

That applicative morphology with the non-syntactic functions set out in Table 3 is not so uncommon cross-linguistically indicates that such polyfunctionality of the locative applicative in Western Indonesian languages does not necessarily reflect shared inheritance. Rather, we argue that these uses of locative applicatives reflect independent parallel developments and so shed light on general pathways of morphosyntactic change. While there has been considerable discussion of the origins and development of applicative morphology, both cross-linguistically and for particular languages (see, for example, Mithun 2002, Helmbrecht 2008, Peterson 2007), there is less analysis of tendencies of change

---

[23] See also this volume, chapter 11 for a description of causative-applicative polysemy in Macro-Tani, a group of Trans-Himalayan languages spoken in northeastern India and Tibet.

from applicative markers, including potential diachronic explanations for the non-syntactic functions that have – or originally had – an applicative function. Peterson (2007: chapter 5) proposes that a common development of applicatives is to become markers of topicality or oblique relativization, which may in turn become nominalizing structures. He argues that such changes are facilitated by a typical discourse function of applicative constructions, namely to "indicate high topicality status for a particular semantically peripheral participant" (Peterson 2007: 84); a non-syntactic function of applicative structures that Donohue (2001) illustrates for the Austronesian language Tukang Besi.[24] Pacchiarotti (2020: 280), following Hyman (2018), argues that non-syntactic uses of reflexes of the Bantu applicative *ɪd, such as completeness, intensity or repetition of the action, developed from an original valence-related function and in some languages replaced the syntactic function entirely.

This same direction of change – from syntactic to non-syntactic functions – best explains the history of -*i* suffixation in Javanese. The direct evidence for this direction of change is that while -*i* suffixation in contemporary Javanese displays the range of functions described above, in Old Javanese it functioned solely as a locative applicative (Nurhayani 2014: 72–73). We argue that this direction of change represents another general pathway of change originating in applicative constructions, and that it is motivated by semantic characteristics of transitivity.

While applicative constructions display language-specific syntactic characteristics (see Section 2), they often also imply meanings that are associated with the notion of transitivity. Lazard (2015: 115) suggests that there is a general consensus on the semantic components of transitivity:

> A typical transitive sentence expresses a real, compact and complete action, volitionally performed by a human agent on a well-defined and well-individuated patient that is actually affected by it.

This definition of transitivity from a semantic perspective builds on Hopper and Thompson's (1980) analysis of transitivity in terms of the ten parameters in (43), and which we argue underpin the development of non-syntactic functions of -*i* suffixation.

---

24 Peterson (1997, 2007: 160–167) suggests that the applicative uses of affixes that have been reconstructed for Proto-Austronesian as encoding locative and instrumental Undergoer voice may reflect their original function, and that these forms became relativizers and then nominalizers in some contemporary languages, and so present further support for this pathway of change from applicative structures.

(43) Hopper & Thompson's parameters of transitivity (Hopper & Thompson 1980: 252)

		High	Low
A.	Participants	2 or more participants, A and O	1 participant
B.	Kinesis	action	non-action
C.	Aspect	telic	atelic
D.	Punctuality	punctual	non-punctual
E.	Volitionality	volitional	non-volitional
F.	Affirmation	affirmative	negative
G.	Mode	realis	irrealis
H.	Agency	A high in potency	A low in potency
I.	Affectedness of O	O totally affected	O not affected
J.	Individuation of O	O highly individuated	O non-individuated

As described for Javanese and neighboring languages, the syntactic and non-syntactic functions of the applicative suffixes are not mutually exclusive and the use of locative applicative morphology with a syntactic function may also imply other meanings, which we argue relate to the semantic components of transitivity. For example, Balinese -*in*, as illustrated in (41), is only used to promote a locative participant to object position if that participant is interpreted as being affected by the event. In Indonesian, there are cases where -*i* introduces a goal or locative participant as the applied object, as well as adding a meaning of intensity or iteration of the event, as shown in (40b) with *melempar-i-* 'to pelt s.o. (with s.t.)'. This meaning of intensity also implies that the participant is more fully affected by the event than if it were described by the non-applicative structure in (40c). That is, we argue that the meanings of intensity and iteration associated with applicative morphology in the languages surveyed here imply that the action described is more effectively transferred to the object participant, which is more fully affected by it (see Hopper and Thompson 1980: 252–253).

Meanings associated with higher transitivity that are inferred from the presence of applicative morphology have become conventionalized as part of the coded or obligatory meaning of the structure. This has led to some uses of the -*i* suffix where it only denotes affectedness of the object participant, intensity or iteration of the action denoted by the event, or the volition or agency of the subject participant. For example, the difference between Javanese *ng-rusak* 'to break s.t.' and *ng-rusak-i* 'to destroy s.t.' lies in the intensity with which the action is undertaken and the affectedness of the object participant, while with *ngantem-i* 'to hit multiple times' -*i* indicates iteration of the action and implies greater of affectedness of the object participant. In contrast, Sasak *beit* 'to take' versus *beit-in* 'to take with force' differ in the degree of agency of the subject participant. As described in

Section 3.1, the iterative meaning of -*i* suffixation in Javanese is best analysed as part of a broader function of pluractionality, and so not only expresses repeated action, but also plurality of the subject and/or object participants. This seems likely to reflect a further extension of the iterative meaning of -*i*, which in some contexts can imply plurality of participants, cf. examples (19)–(21).

Peterson (2007) and Helmbrecht (2008) demonstrate the cross-linguistic tendency for verb-applicative combinations to become lexicalized through an "increase in the semantic idiosyncrasies" of the verb-applicative stem (Peterson 2007: 169). Pacchiarotti (2020: 4, 102–110, 208–210) describes pseudoapplicatives in Bantu languages as verbs stems that include fossilized applicative morphology. She illustrates how in Tswana these lexicalised applicative forms tend to be the result of certain kinds of semantic change, such as narrowing or specialization and metaphorical abstraction. Like Helmbrecht (2008), Pacchiarotti (2020) describes these original verb-applicative combinations as no longer semantically compositional. In some of the Siouan languages discussed by Helmbrecht (2008), such lexicalization along with the concomitant loss of paradigmatic pairs of derived and underived forms has led to the "loss and decay" of applicatives.

The lexicalization of verb-applicative word forms in Javanese and Indonesian appear to reflect semantic specialization, which is often related to the non-syntactic functions of applicative morphology and the inferred and/or coded meanings that relate to higher transitivity. For example, Javanese *ngapal-i* 'to learn many things by heart; to recognize', in contrast to *ngapal* 'to know by heart', implies both increased agency of the subject participant, indicated by the gloss 'to learn' rather than simply 'to know', as well as plurality of the object participant. This is similar for Indonesian *mengajar-i* 'to teach, train, coach', where the additional glosses in contrast to *mengajar* 'to teach', imply increased involvement and agency of the subject participant – the teacher. While Indonesian *menunggu-i* 'to watch over' implies greater transfer of the action to and affectedness of the object participant than *menunggu* 'to wait for' (Sneddon et al. 2010: 96–97). However, these lexicalized verb-*i* combinations tend not to be fossilized; typically, there are pairs of verb forms with and without -*i* with clear differences in meaning. The overlap between the meanings of some of these lexicalized verb forms with -*i* and the non-syntactic functions of -*i* also means that not all of the lexicalized forms can be considered to be semantically non-compositional.

In sum, we argue that the non-syntactic functions of -*i* suffixation in Javanese and the other languages have developed via an expected pathway of semantic change, namely that contextual or inferred meanings have been reanalysed as the coded or obligatory meaning of verb-applicative combinations (cf. Traugott and Dasher 2005). Meanings associated with higher transitivity can be shown to be part of the meanings of locative applicatives, and to have become the coded and sole meaning of verb-*i* forms, and a productive function of -*i* suffixation with certain classes of verbs.

In this chapter, we have only considered the locative applicative, and not the benefactive applicative, which is also present in most of the languages described here. Willemsen (2017) and Michaelis and Ruppenhofer (2000) each argue that intensive and iterative meanings of applicative morphology derive specifically from locative applicatives, but in different ways. That is, Willemsen (2017) proposes that cognitive processes relating to event structure explain the cross-linguistic connection between locative applicatives and the meanings of intensity and iteration, while Michaelis and Ruppenhofer (2000) suggest that the meanings of intensity and iteration can be explained as part of an associated network of functions of the German locative applicative *be-* linked by metaphorical extensions and semantic inference. While connections between the non-syntactic functions of applicatives and the locative function of -*i* suffixation warrant further investigation within Austronesian, it is not just locative applicatives but also benefactive applicatives that can have these non-syntactic functions. Among languages of western Indonesia, Balinese -*ang* may indicate 'to do often/intensively' (Barber 1977: 162) or specificity of the applied object (Natarina 2020), Besemah -*ka* can indicate that the patient argument is highly affected or highly individuated (this volume, chapter 14), and Madurese -*aghi* may express specificity of the applied object (Davies 2013). In Oceanic Austronesian languages, reflexes of *akən in several Southeast Solomonic and Fijian languages have both an applicative function and denote iterative and intensive meanings (see Naitoro 2018: 164–165, Dixon 1988: 215–216). Thus, further investigation of the non-syntactic functions of applicatives in Austronesian languages should encompass both the locative and benefactive applicative suffixes.

5 Conclusion

Javanese, like many Austronesian languages, has two applicative suffixes which differ in the semantic roles they introduce as the applied object argument. In Javanese -*i* is a locative applicative marker, while -*(a)ke/-no* is a benefactive applicative marker (Suhandono 1994; Ewing 2005; Nurhayani 2014). The origins and development of applicative morphology in Austronesian languages originates in clausal reorganization from an original symmetrical voice system to the systems of many Oceanic Austronesian languages, which lack voice distinctions but display a range of valency-altering derivations.

Our main interest was to take a closer look at the non-syntactic functions of the locative applicative in Javanese and neighbouring Western Indonesian languages in order to gain insights into the pathways of semantic change that applicative morphology can undergo. The non-syntactic functions of applicative morphology in Javanese, and many of the neighboring languages, include pluractionality, intensity of action, specificity and/or affectedness of the O argument, as well as lexicalized verb-applicative combinations. Our analysis of these less well-described functions of locative applicatives highlights the importance of describing the syntactic *and* semantic uses of applicative constructions, including their contextual or inferred meanings, since these can be argued to shape the non-syntactic uses of applicative morphology. We concluded that for Javanese and neighboring Western Indonesian languages, where deriving a transitive construction is a typical function of applicative morphology, it is the conventionalization of inferred meanings associated with the semantic components of transitivity that have motivated the development of the non-syntactic functions of locative applicatives. We argued that the shared non-syntactic functions of locative applicatives do not reflect a single change, but rather parallel independent changes, and so present a pathway of change *from* applicative morphology that may be relevant cross-linguistically.

Abbreviations

1	first person
2	second person
3	third person
APPL	applicative
AV	Actor Voice
CAUS	causative
COMP	complementizer
DEF	definite
DET	determiner
DUR	durative
FUT	future
ITER	iterative
LOC	locative
MID	middle
NMLZ	nominalizer
PART	particle
PASS	passive
PL	plural
POSS	possessive

PROG	progressive
PV	Patient Voice
RDP	reduplication
REL	relative
SG	singular
s.o.	someone
s.t.	something
yg	younger

References

Adelaar, Alexander. 2011. Javanese -*aké* and -*akən*: A short history. *Oceanic Linguistics* 50(2). 338–350.

Alsina, Alex & Sam A. Mchombo. 1990. The syntax of applicatives in Chichewa: Problems for a theta theoretic asymmetry. *Natural Language & Linguistic Theory* 8(4). 493–506.

Anceaux, J. C. 1988. *The Wolio language: Outline of grammatical description and texts*. Dordrecht: Foris.

Arka, I Wayan. 2003. *Balinese morphosyntax: A lexical-functional approach*. Canberra: Pacific Linguistics.

Arka, I Wayan. 2014. Locative-related roles and the argument-adjunct distinction in Balinese. *Linguistic Discovery* 12(2). 56–84.

Arka, I Wayan, Mary Dalrymple, Meladel Mistica, Suriel Mofu, Avery Andrews, and Jane Simpson. 2009. A linguistic and morphosyntactic computational analysis for the applicative -*i* in Indonesian. In Miriam Butt & Tracy Holloway King (eds.), *Proceedings of the LFG09 Conference*, 85–105. Stanford: CSLI Publications.

Arka, I Wayan & Malcolm Ross (eds.). 2005. *The many faces of Austronesian voice systems: some new empirical studies*. Canberra: Pacific Linguistics.

Ashriany, Ratna Yulida. 2008. *Sistem verba Bahasa Sasak Dilaek Bayan dari dasar verba dan nomina*. [The verbal system from basic verbs and nouns in the Bayan dialect of Sasak]. Sukarta, Indonesia: Universitas Sebelas Maret M.A. thesis.

Asikin-Garmager, Eli. 2017. *Sasak Voice*. Iowa City, Iowa: University of Iowa dissertation.

Austin, Peter K. 2000. Verbs, voice and valence in Sasak. In Peter K. Austin (ed.), *Working Papers in Sasak, Vol. 2*, 5–24. Melbourne: University of Melbourne.

Austin, Peter K. 2001. Verbs, valence and voice in Balinese, Sasak, and Sumbawan. *La Trobe Papers in Linguistics* 11(3). 47–71.

Austin, Peter K. 2005. Causative and applicative constructions in Australian Aboriginal Languages. In Kazuto Matsumura & Tooru Hayasi (eds.), *The dative and related phenomena*, 165–225. Tokyo: Hitsuji Shobo.

Barber, Charles Clyde. 1977. *A grammar of the Balinese language*. Aberdeen: University of Aberdeen.

Bresnan, Joan & Lioba Moshi. 1993. Object asymmetries in comparative Bantu syntax. In Sam Mchombo (ed.), *Theoretical aspects of Bantu grammar*, 47–92. Stanford: CSLI Publications.

Conners, Thomas J. 2008. *Tengger Javanese*. New Haven / Boston: Yale University dissertation.

Croft, William. 1991. *Syntactic categories and grammatical relations*. Chicago: University of Chicago Press.

Chung, Sandra. 1976. An object-creating rule in Bahasa Indonesia. *Linguistic Inquiry* 7(1). 41–87.

Davies, William D. 1993. Javanese subjects and topics and psych verbs. *Linguistics* 31(2). 239–278.

Davies, William D. 2005. The richness of Madurese voice, In I Wayan Arka & Malcolm Ross (eds.), *The many faces of Austronesian voice systems: Some new empirical studies*, 193–216. Canberra: Pacific Linguistics.

Davies, William D. 2010. *A reference grammar of Madurese*. Berlin: De Gruyter Mouton.

Davies, William D. 2013. Could you be a little more specific? Ruminations on a Madurese applicative suffix. The University of Iowa. Ms.

Dixon, R. M. W. 1988. *A grammar of Boumaa Fijian*. Chicago: The University of Chicago Press.

Donohue, Mark. 1999. *A grammar of Tukang Besi*. Berlin: Mouton de Gruyter.

Donohue, Mark. 2001. Coding choices in argument structure: Austronesian applicatives in texts. *Studies in Language* 25(2). 217–254.

Ewing, Michael C. 2005. *Grammar and inference in conversation: Identifying clause structure in spoken Javanese*. Amsterdam: John Benjamins.

Evans, Bethwyn. 2003. *A study of valency-changing devices in Proto Oceanic*. Canberra: Pacific Linguistics.

Grimes, Charles E. 1991. *The Buru language of Eastern Indonesia*. Canberra: The Australian National University dissertation.

Hanafi, Nurachman. 2001. A description of basic clause structure in Sundanese. In Peter Austin, Barry Blake & Margaret Florey (eds.), Explorations in valency in Austronesian languages. *La Trobe Working Papers in Linguistics* 11(5). 121–142. Melbourne: La Trobe University.

Helmbrecht, Johannes. 2008. Decay and loss of applicatives in Siouan languages: A grammaticalization perspective. In Walter Bisang & Hans H. Hock (eds.), *Studies on grammaticalization*, 135–156. Berlin: Mouton de Gruyter.

Hemmings, Charlotte. 2013. Causatives and applicatives: The case for polysemy in Javanese. *SOAS Working Papers in Linguistics* 16. 166–194.

Hill, Deborah. 2011. *Longgu grammar*. Munich: Lincom Europa.

Hopper, Paul J. & Sandra A. Thompson. 1980. Transitivity in grammar and discourse. *Language* 56(2). 251–299.

Horne, Elinor C. 1961. *Beginning Javanese*. New Haven: Yale University Press.

Hyman, Larry M. 2018. Common Bantoid verb extensions. In John R. Watters (ed.), *East Benue-Congo: Nouns, pronouns, and verbs*, 173–198. Berlin: Language Science Press.

Jordan, Mary Ellen. 1998. Morpho-semantic processes. In Peter K. Austin (ed.), *Working Papers in Sasak, Vol. 1*, 147–159. Melbourne: University of Melbourne.

Kikusawa, Ritsuko. 2012. On the development of applicative constructions in Austronesian languages. *Bulletin of the National Museum of Ethnology* 36(4). 413–455.

Koch, Emma. 1998. Causative verbs and causative constructions. In Peter K. Austin (ed.), *Working Papers in Sasak, Vol. 1*, 161–180. Melbourne: University of Melbourne.

Kroeger, Paul. 2007. Morphosyntactic vs. morphosemantic functions of Indonesian -*kan*. In Annie Zaenen, Jane Simpson, Tracy Holloway King, Jane Grimshaw, Joan Maling & Chris Manning (eds.), *Architectures, rules, and preferences: Variations on themes of Joan Bresnan*, 229–251. Stanford, CA: CSLI Publications.

Kurniawan, Eri. 2013. *Sundanese complementation*. Iowa City, Iowa: University of Iowa dissertation.

Lazard, Gilbert. 2015. Two possible universals: The Major Biactant Construction; the twofold notion of subject. *Linguistic Typology* 19(1). 111–130.

Michaelis, Laura A. & Josef Ruppenhofer. 2000. Valence creation and the German applicative: The inherent semantics of linking patterns. *Journal of Semantics* 17(4). 335–395.

Mithun, Marianne. 2002. Understanding and explaining applicatives. In Mary Andronis, Cristopher Ball, Heidi Elston & Sylvain Neuvel (eds.), *Proceedings of the 37th Meeting of the Chicago Linguistic Society: Functionalism and formalism in Linguistic Theory*, 73–98. Chicago: Chicago Linguistic Society.

Musgrave, Simon. 2001. *Non-subject arguments in Indonesian*. Melbourne: University of Melbourne dissertation.

Naitoro, Katerina. 2018. *Morphs in search of meaning: Southeast Solomonic transitive morphology in diachronic perspective*. Canberra: The Australian National University dissertation.

Natarina, Ari. 2018. *Complementation in Balinese: Typological, syntactic, and cognitive perspectives*. Iowa City, Iowa: University of Iowa dissertation.

Natarina, Ari, 2020. Specificity and the Balinese morpheme *-ang*. In Thomas J. Conners & Jozina Vander Klok (eds.), *Selected papers of the Seventh International Symposium on the Languages of Java* (ISLOJ 7). *NUSA* 69, 3–26. DOI: https://doi.org/10.15026/95699.

Newman, Paul. 1980. *The classification of Chadic within Afroasiatic*. Leiden: Leiden University Press.

Nurhayani, Ika. 2014. *A unified account of the syntax of valence in Javanese*. New York: Cornell University dissertation.

O'Herin, Brian. 2001. Abaza applicatives. *Language* 77(3). 477–493.

Ogloblin, Alexander K. 2001. Imperative sentences in Javanese. In Victor S. Xrakovskij (ed.), *Typology of imperative constructions*, 221–242. Munich: Lincom Europa.

Ogloblin, Alexander K. 2005. Javanese. In K. Alexander Adelaar & Nikolaus Himmelmann (eds), *The Austronesian languages of Asia and Madagascar*, 590–624. London: Routledge.

Pacchiarotti, Sara. 2020. *Bantu applicative constructions*. (Stanford Monographs in African Languages). Stanford: CSLI Publications.

Pawley, Andrew. 1973. Some problems in Proto-Oceanic grammar. *Oceanic Linguistics* 12(1–2). 103–188.

Pawley, Andrew & Timoci Sayaba. 2018. Words of Waya. A dictionary of the Wayan dialect of the Western Fijian language. Canberra: The Australian National University. Ms.

Payne, Thomas E. 1997. *Describing morphosyntax: A guide for field linguists*. Cambridge: Cambridge University Press.

Peterson, David A. 1997. The evolution of applicative constructions and Proto-Austronesian morphosyntax. *Berkeley Linguistics Society* 23. 278–289.

Peterson, David A. 2007. *Applicative constructions*. Oxford: Oxford University Press.

Riesberg, Sonja. 2014. *Symmetrical voice and linking in western Austronesian languages*. Berlin: De Gruyter Mouton.

Robson, Stuart. 2002. *A Javanese grammar for students*. 2nd edition. Glen Waverly, Clayton: Monash University Press.

Robson, Stuart & Singgih Wibisono. 2002. *Javanese-English dictionary*. North Clarendon: Tuttle Publishing.

Ross, Malcolm D. 2002. The history and transitivity of western Austronesian voice and voice-marking. In Fay Wouk & Malcolm D. Ross (eds.), *The history and typology of western Austronesian voice systems*, 17–62. Canberra: Pacific Linguistics.

Ross, Malcolm D. 2009. Proto Austronesian verbal morphology: A reappraisal. In Alexander Adelaar & Andrew Pawley (eds.), *Austronesian historical linguistics and culture history: A festschrift for Robert Blust*, 295–326. Canberra: Pacific Linguistics.

Sato, Yosuke. 2015. Argument ellipsis in Javanese and voice agreement. *Studia Linguistica* 69. 58–85.

Smith, Alexander D. 2017. The Western Malayo-Polynesian problem. *Oceanic Linguistics* 56(2). 435–489.

Sneddon, James N. with Alexander Adelaar, Dwi N. Djenar & Michael C. Ewing. 2010. *Indonesian Reference Grammar*. 2nd edition. London/New York: Routledge.

Sofwan, Ahmad. 2010. Applicative constructions in Javanese. *Language Circle Journal of Language and Literature* 5(1). 1–26.

Starosta, Stanley, Andrew K. Pawley & Lawrence A. Reid. 1982. The evolution of focus in Austronesian. In Amran Halim, Lois Carrington & S. A. Wurm (eds.), *Papers from the Third International Conference on Austronesian Linguistics, Vol 2: Tracking the travellers*, 145–170. Canberra: Pacific Linguistics.

Sudaryanto. 1991. *Tata Bahasa baku Bahasa Jawa*. [Standard Javanese grammar]. Yogyakarta: Duta Wacana University Press.

Suhandono. 1994. *Grammatical relations in Javanese*. Canberra: The Australian National University M.A. thesis.

Sumarlam. 2004. *Aspektualitas Bahasa Jawa*. [Javanese aspect]. Surakarta: Pustaka Cakra Surakarta.

Traugott, Elizabeth C. & Richard B. Dasher. 2005. *Regularity in semantic change*. Cambridge: Cambridge University Press.

Truong, Christina. 2019. Sundanese benefactives. University of Hawai'i. Ms.

Uhlenbeck, E.M. 1978. *Studies in Javanese morphology*. (KITLV Translation Series 19). The Hague: Nijhoff.

Vander Klok, Jozina. To appear. Post-verbal word order alternation in Javanese applicatives. In Åshild Næss, Bethwyn Evans & Jozina Vander Klok (eds.), *Prominence in Austronesian*.

Van den Berg, René & Robert I. Busenitz. 2012. *A grammar of Balantak: A language of Eastern Sulawesi*. Edited by Hein Steinhauer. (Vol. 40, SIL eBook). SIL International. https://www.sil.org/resources/publications/entry/49492.

Van Geenhoven, Veerle. 2004. For-adverbials, frequentative aspect and pluractionality. *Natural Language Semantics* 12. 135–190.

Van Geysel, Jens E. L. forthcoming. A cognitive-typological perspective on the origins of causative-applicative polysemy. In Bethwyn Evans, Kristina Gallego & Luisa Miceli (eds.), *Historical Linguistics 2019*. Amsterdam: John Benjamins.

Veselinova, Ljuba N. 2008. Verbal number and suppletion. In Martin Haspelmath, Matthew S. Dryer, David Gil & Bernard Comrie (eds.), *The World Atlas of Language Structures Online*, Chapter 80. Munich: Max Planck Digital Library. http://wals.info/feature/80.

Wedhawati, Nurlina, Wiwin Erni Siti, Setiyanto, Edi, Marsono, Sukesti, Restu & Baryadi, I. Praptomo. 2006. *Tata Bahasa Jawa Mutakhir*. [Contemporary Javanese Grammar]. Yogyakarta: Penerbit Kanisius.

Willemsen, Jeroen. 2017. Predicative augmentation applicatives. *Linguistica Online* 19. 1–22.

Wolff, John. 1973. Verbal inflection in Proto Austronesian. In Andrew Gonzalez (ed.), *Parangal kay Cecilio Lopez*, 71–91. Quezon City: Linguistic Society of the Philippines.

Woollams, Geoff. 1996. *A grammar of Karo Batak, Sumatra*. Canberra: Pacific Linguistics.
Wouk, Fay. 1999. Sasak is different: A discourse perspective on voice. *Oceanic Linguistics* 38(1). 91–114.
Wouk, Fay & Malcolm Ross (eds). 2002. *The history and typology of western Austronesian voice systems*. Canberra: Pacific Linguistics.
Yam, Stephanie. 2020. *Engagement and information structure in interaction: The intersubjective meaning of two discourse markers in Motu*. Canberra: The Australian National University BA Honours thesis.
Zúñiga, Fernando & Seppo Kittilä. 2019. *Grammatical voice*. Cambridge: Cambridge University Press.

Subject index

absolute prepositions 10, 271
affectedness 7, 365, 397, 426, 451–452, 463, 466
applicative
– adfective 314
– adversative 352–356
– associative 344–346
– comparative 422–423
– D- 5
– eruditive 316
– evaluative 357–358
– imitative 316
– inseritive 309–310
– P- 5
– partitive 356–357
– redirective 2, 241–248, 347
– relinquitive 323
– sociative, see Co-Agent
– territive 315–316
– X- 5
applied phrase 3–6
argument orientation 216–218
aspectual functions 202–203, 423–424, 431, 438, 448–451, 459–461, 466–467
associated motion 239–240, 251–252
atransitive clauses 306
attenuation 12, 101, 115–116, 118, 123
attitude holder 393, 396–397
Austronesian voice 337, 407–409, 428–429, 439–441, 456–457

causative-applicative isomorphism 6, 317–320, 419–421, 431–432, 438, 447, 459–460, 464
cleft constructions 211–216
co-actant 339, 359, 361

dative marking 311–312
definiteness 364, 426
diachronic sources of applicative morphology 10–11, 61, 132, 251–252, 281–293, 321–324, 428–429
differential object marking 56–57, 135, 140, 304

directional morphology 76, 79, 82
ditransitive clauses 442–446

ethical dative 398
event locative 206–207
extraversion 5, 249–251, 350

focus 163, 166–168, 181–185, 209–216, 310–311

grammaticalization 154–155, 263, 265, 288, 290, 294

happenstantial mood 335–336, 352–355, 357, 365–366
hierarchical indexation 135

indirective alignment 85
intensity 425–426, 431, 437, 449, 451–452, 459, 462–463, 466

lexicalization 151–153, 201–204, 427–428, 453–454, 459, 467
location highlighting 63–66

mediative marking 310–311
metaphorical extension 148
– mitigated transitivity 363–366
nominalization 86–90, 94

obligatoriness 3–4, 58, 91, 138–139, 164, 204–208, 232, 315, 350, 365, 384, 441–442
optionality 131, 137, 139, 145, 148, 166, 170, 201–202, 310, 340, 411–412, 440–441

participant locative 206–207
periphrastic applicative construction 97–98
pluractionality 437, 448–451, 459–461, 467
politeness 116, 118, 123, 389–393, 397–398
pragmaticization 396–397, 399–400
prepositions 165–166, 169–171, 176–177, 183, 185
promotion 43, 47, 311–314, 427

https://doi.org/10.1515/9783110777949-016

registration 13, 359–363
relativization 87–90, 94

semantic roles
– Addressee 237
– Beneficiary 23, 39–40, 44, 47, 76–79, 84–85, 88, 90–92, 101, 106, 110–114, 117–120, 122, 232, 234, 236–238, 253, 344–345, 411, 437, 445–447, 455–458
– Causee 237
– Co-agent (sociative) 379, 381, 387–388
– Comitative 253–254, 411
– Deputative 31, 99–100, 102, 106–108, 111–112, 114–115, 117–118, 123
– Experiencer 5, 59, 314–316, 365, 397,
– Expert Agent 117–118, 120
– Goal 208, 235, 237, 241–249, 251–252, 256, 305, 309–310, 411
– Instrument 76–81, 89, 235–238, 253, 258, 347, 411
– Location 76, 78, 82, 87–88, 90, 112, 123, 205, 237–238, 411, 437, 445–447, 455, 457–458
– Maleficiary 23–24, 31, 34, 48, 101–102, 111–112, 120–121, 138
– Patient 351–352, 356
– Possessor 23, 41–42, 44, 47–48, 100, 102, 110–111, 119–122, 138
– Recipient 31, 36–37, 44, 106, 108, 112, 114–115, 118–119, 233–234, 238
– Source 229, 241–249
– Substitutive 208
– Theme 5, 229, 241–249, 252, 411
semantic (under)specification 6, 138, 194, 204–205, 274, 306, 315–316, 365, 411
semantic transitivity 426–427, 437, 465–466
spatial morphology 76, 79, 82, 130, 141, 173–174, 238–247
specificity 364, 452–453, 463, 468

topic continuity 8, 43–46, 86, 93–94, 107–108, 144, 155, 364

valence (increase) 4–5, 24, 27–28, 164, 181, 183, 228, 235, 241, 248, 252, 254–255, 274–275, 288, 294, 333, 415–418
valence-neutral applicative constructions 164–165, 202–203, 264–265, 276, 296, 415–416
valence-decreasing applicative constructions 281, 417–418
verbalization 66–68, 357–358, 421–422

zero-anaphora 376–377, 387, 394–395

Language index

Ainu (unclassified, Japan) 2
Andean Spanish (Indo-European) 97
Avestan (Indo-European) 288–289

Barbareño Chumash (Chumashan) 73–96
Bemba (Niger-Congo) 165–166, 170, 172
Blackfoot (Algonquian) 3
Bukusu (Niger-Congo) 280

Cahita (Uto-Aztecan) 29
Chewa (Niger-Congo) 170
Cuwabo (Niger-Congo) 178

Fwe (Niger-Congo) 189

German (Indo-European) 7
Guarijío (Uto-Aztecan) 27

Harakmbut (isolate, Peru) 129–130
Herero (Niger-Congo) 170

Javanese (Austronesian)
Jingphoic languages (Trans-Himalayan) 323

Katukina (Katukinan) 130
K'iche' (Mayan) 9
Kuki-Chin languages (Trans-Himalayan) 323
Kurmancî (Indo-European) 281–282, 285

Lolo-Burmese languages
 (Trans-Himalayan) 322

Macro-Tani languages (Trans-Himalayan) 301
Makhuwa (Niger-Congo) 178
Mayo (Uto-Aztecan) 27
Mbuun (Niger Congo) 165, 170–171, 177

Nadëb (Nadahupan) 279
Navajo (Athabaskan) 284
New Persian (Indo-European) 285
Nilotic languages (Nilo-Saharan) 228
Nyambo (Niger Congo) 174–175

Rama (Chibchan) 289
Rangi (Niger-Congo) 171

Sambaa (Niger-Congo) 178–179
Seereer (Niger-Congo) 5
Shiwiar (Chicham) 52
Shona (Niger-Congo) 166–167, 217
Šmuwič, see Barbareño Chumash
Soranî (Indo-European) 265–270, 272–279, 282–284, 286–287, 290, 292
Sotho (Niger-Congo) 166, 172–173, 176–177
Swahili (Niger-Congo) 168, 171, 174, 179–180

Tarahumara (Uto-Aztecan) 27
Tibetic languages (Trans-Himalayan) 376
Trans-Himalayan languages 300, 322–324
Tswana (Niger-Congo) 173, 207

Waray (Austronesian) 329–367
Western Indonesian languages
 (Austronesian) 411, 458

Xhosa (Niger-Congo) 176, 180

Yaqui (Uto-Aztecan) 21

Zulu (Niger-Congo) 179